E–Collaborative Knowledge Construction:
Learning from Computer–Supported and Virtual Environments

Bernhard Ertl
Universität der Bundeswehr München, Germany

INFORMATION SCIENCE REFERENCE

Hershey · New York

Director of Editorial Content:	Kristin Klinger
Director of Book Publications:	Julia Mosemann
Development Editor:	Beth Ardner
Publishing Assistant:	Kurt Smith
Typesetter:	Callie Klinger
Quality control:	Jamie Snavely
Cover Design:	Lisa Tosheff
Printed at:	Yurchak Printing Inc.

Published in the United States of America by
Information Science Reference (an imprint of IGI Global)
701 E. Chocolate Avenue
Hershey PA 17033
Tel: 717-533-8845
Fax: 717-533-8661
E-mail: cust@igi-global.com
Web site: http://www.igi-global.com/reference

Library of Congress Cataloging-in-Publication Data

E-collaborative knowledge construction : learning from computer-supported and virtual environments / Bernhard Ertl, editor.
     p. cm.
  Includes bibliographical references and index.
  Summary: "This book presents best practice environments to implement e-collaborative knowledge construction, providing psychological and technical background information about issues present in such scenarios and presents methods to improve online learning environments"--Provided by publisher.
  ISBN 978-1-61520-729-9 (hardcover) -- ISBN 978-1-61520-730-5 (ebook) 1. Education--Computer network resources. 2. Web-based instruction--Design. 3. Computer-assisted instruction I. Ertl, Bernhard, 1973-
  LB1044.87.E1183 2010
  371.33'44678--dc22
                                           2009042991

British Cataloguing in Publication Data
A Cataloguing in Publication record for this book is available from the British Library.

Table of Contents

Section 1
Environments for E-Collaborative Knowledge Construction

Douglas Clark, Vanderbilt University, USA
Victor Sampson, Florida State University, USA
Karsten Stegmann, University of Munich, Germany
Miika Marttunen, University of Jyväskylä, Finland
Ingo Kollar, University of Munich, Germany
Jeroen Janssen, Utrecht University, The Netherlands
Armin Weinberger, University of Twente, The Netherlands
Muhsin Menekse, Arizona State University, USA
Gijsbert Erkens, Utrecht University, The Netherlands
Leena Laurinen, University of Jyväskylä, Finland

Marco Bettoni, Swiss Distant University of Applied Sciences, Switzerland

Michael Oehl, Leuphana University of Lüneburg, Germany
Hans-Rüdiger Pfister, Leuphana University of Lüneburg, Germany

Section 2
Approaches in the Context of E-Collaborative Knowledge Construction

Section 3
Support Measures

Detailed Table of Contents

Section 1
Environments for E-Collaborative Knowledge Construction

The book starts with a section about environments to illustrate scenarios in the context of e-collaborative knowledge construction. Chapters of this section give an impression of what is meant by e-collaborative knowledge construction and show implementations. They focus on different goals ranging from empowering learners with 21st century skills to setting up a sustainable learning community. Thereby, authors give insights into issues that came up during planning, implementing and running these environments and provide lessons learned. The chapters discuss good practices for the design, the implementation and the application of environments for e-collaborative knowledge construction.

Chapter 1
Douglas Clark, Vanderbilt University, USA
Victor Sampson, Florida State University, USA
Karsten Stegmann, University of Munich, Germany
Miika Marttunen, University of Jyväskylä, Finland
Ingo Kollar, University of Munich, Germany
Jeroen Janssen, Utrecht University, The Netherlands
Armin Weinberger, University of Twente, The Netherlands
Muhsin Menekse, Arizona State University, USA
Gijsbert Erkens, Utrecht University, The Netherlands
Leena Laurinen, University of Jyväskylä, Finland

Clark, Sampson, Stegmann, Marttunen, Kollar, Janssen, Weinberger Menekse, Erkens, and *Laurinen* show how working in e-collaborative environments can facilitate learners to develop 21st century skills. By using this term, they refer to the concepts of adaptability, complex communication skills, non-routine problem-solving skills, self-management/self-development, and systems thinking. The chapter describes four different environments for e-collaborative knowledge construction, namely WISE Seeded Discussions, CASSIS, VCRI, and DREW and analyzes to which extent each environment supports the development of these skills.

Bettoni takes a community approach to e-collaborative knowledge construction. He describes how to apply the principle of communities of practice to the design and implementation of a community of research. His chapter gives insights into the design and implementation process of a community and into the activities which occurred within this community. By that, the author derives good practices and suggestions for the design, implementation and maintenance of communities.

Oehl and *Pfister* focus on applying chat for e-collaborative knowledge construction. Besides the pure chat communication, the authors also provide a shared application for enabling knowledge construction. They discuss shortcomings of chat-based scenarios and present the approach of learning protocols to facilitate it. These learning protocols provide collaboration partners means for referencing chat contributions and to classify them according to their intention. The chapter discusses which particular aspects can be facilitated by learning protocols and provides aspects which should be considered when setting up scenarios with chat communication.

Section 2
Approaches in the Context of E-Collaborative Knowledge Construction

E-collaborative knowledge construction can be seen from different approaches, such as distributed cognitive processing, conceptual change, help-seeking, and expertise development. Each of them has a particular focus to build environments for the collaboration partners. All of them refer to cognitive processes and interactions that are taking place during e-collaborative knowledge construction and the assessment of its outcomes and they illustrate the process character of e-collaborative knowledge construction. This section will elaborate these approaches and their impact for e-collaborative knowledge construction.

The chapter of *Tscholl* and *Dowell* focuses distributed cognitive processing and describes an approach for studying processes of e-collaborative knowledge construction. It illustrates this approach by examples from discourse analysis and presents evidence for a significant overlap between critical argumentation and knowledge construction. The authors provide a refined definition of co-construction that comprises of an interrelation between interaction and co-construction. The chapter concludes with implications on the analysis and evaluation of knowledge co-construction in different environments.

Harteis elaborates how e-collaborative knowledge construction is related with the development of professional expertise. He distinguishes different types of knowledge and shows how they develop individually and during collaboration. The chapter describes how information and communication technologies can facilitate these knowledge construction processes, including a discussion about challenges for e-collaborative knowledge construction.

Schworm and *Heckner* focus on the concept of help seeking that relates to an asymmetric knowledge distribution setting. Starting from the issue of interactions in academic help seeking they summarize general aspects of collaboration in settings with asymmetric expertise. They shift their attention to peculiarities of computer-based help seeking in human-human interactions as well as in human-computer scenarios. Thereby, they identify typical weaknesses of current help systems and show how far social web can have an impact for the design of future help systems.

Liu and *Hmelo-Silver* elaborate scientific conceptual change during collaborative knowledge construction in their chapter. They present a model for collaborative scientific conceptual change (CSCC) and describe a study that was analyzed according to this model. Their analyses identified several processes of e-collaborative knowledge construction which are related to the outcomes of the collaborative setting. This enabled them to exemplify how conceptual change takes place during collaboration.

Chapter 8

*Dominique M.A. Sluijsmans, HAN University & Open University of the Netherlands,
    The Netherlands*
Jan-Willem Strijbos, Leiden University, The Netherlands

Sluijsmans and *Stribos* focus on the outcomes of e-collaborative knowledge construction, which is often some kind of group product that was created jointly by all members of the group. Research has shown that there are often differences in the individual contributions of each group member to the group outcome, which could result in inequalities and injustice for assessment. While Hu and Gollin took the approach of text-comparison in their chapter, Sluijsmans and Strijbos focus on peer-assessment to overcome this issue. Peer-assessment facilitates instructors to evaluate the individuals' contributions to a group's outcome according to mutual estimations of the learning partners. The authors present different methods for peer-assessment and discuss their advantages and disadvantages.

Section 3
Support Measures

The different settings and technologies are the key to understand how e-collaborative knowledge construction takes place and offers starting point for the design of environments for e-collaborative knowledge construction as well as for the support of collaboration partners in these environments. Support approaches focus on instructional interventions which are applied during the process of e-collaborative knowledge construction. They help learners to work more effectively on their knowledge construction. Chapters in this section focus on particular mechanisms of the described support method (scripting, trainings, and tutoring) in the context of an environment for ECKC. They allow readers to transfer the presented support methods to other environments to provide further facilitation there.

Chapter 9

Dejana Diziol, University of Freiburg, Germany
Nikol Rummel, University of Freiburg, Germany

Diziol and *Rummel* present a descriptive framework that provides dimensions for the support of collaborative e-learning. This framework allows classifying different types of support for e-collaborative knowledge construction by focussing important dimensions for support: the level of support, the domain, the mode, the timing, and the adaptivity. They exemplify their framework by the description of an adaptive domain-related assistance for a Cognitive Tutor Algebra.

Häkkinen, Arvaja, Hämäläinen, and *Pöysa* focus on the particular support method of scripting in the context of a collaborative web-based university course. They highlight the issue of different styles of script support, present a review of theoretical and empirical analyses and provide results of a design-based study which implemented three different styles of scripting. Based on this, they are able to present main applications for scripting and introduce the approach of flexible pedagogical scripts.

Pächter, Kreisler, and *Maier* raise the issue how far processes and results of e-collaborative knowledge construction in videoconferencing settings may differ from face to face. They provide evidence by the presentation of an empirical study which shows that results do not differ significantly even if there are differences in the processes. Based on these results, the authors present a study about support by trainings for facilitating collaboration in videoconferencing which enable collaboration partners to reach better collaborative outcomes.

Kopp, Germ, and *Mandl* focus on the method of tutoring for providing support for e-collaborative knowledge construction. They elaborate the issue that tutors need more than just content-specific skills if they want to set beneficial conditions for learning. They further analyze which particular skills are necessary for a tutor to facilitate learning processes in e-collaborative scenarios. Their contribution is substantiated by the description of two virtual courses, one course which dealt with e-tutoring as subject matter and another course in which these tutoring strategies were applied.

Section 4
Outlook

The outlook section puts e-collaborative knowledge construction in a broader context and discusses critically educational and organisational perspectives. Chapters in this section describe possible developments of e-collaborative knowledge construction in the future and driving and hindering forces.

Stevens provides in his chapter an educational perspective on the future development of e-collaborative knowledge construction. He focuses on the issue of rural education, which is characterized by small school sizes and often also by a decreasing number of students per school. Based on the exemplary situation of Newfoundland, he shows how e-collaborative knowledge construction can be applied in a school setting and how it can help schools, particularly in rural areas, to maintain their educational mission although to their small student numbers.

Moreland, Swanenburg, Flagg, and *Fetterman* take an organisational perspective on e-collaborative knowledge construction. They deal with the issue of transactive memory, which describes meta-knowledge about the skills of collaboration partners. They show prerequisites for the development of transactive memory and raise the issue, how far e-collaboration can support the development of transactive memory. Their conclusions show an ambivalent view on the role of technology for supporting e-collaborative knowledge construction.

Foreword

From the early days of theorizing on knowledge building, much emphasis has been put on the creation of *new* knowledge through collaborative idea refinement rather than on learning things that are already known. The basic idea has been that learners should develop skills of contributing to the generation of new knowledge in interaction with other members of a knowledge community or a network. Until recently, the technology to support these processes was not highly developed and especially not very widespread. Currently, dynamic research fields like Technology-Enhanced Learning (TEL) and Computer-Supported Collaborative Learning (CSCL) are exploring the potentials of forums, wikis, and other forms of social software to support collaborative knowledge construction processes and outcomes in a systematic way. Although some researchers and educational practitioners consider these new software types as ideal technologies for collaborative knowledge building, research on computer-supported (collaborative) learning does not warrant optimism with respect to effects of new technologies on learning. The field has seen the rise and fall of many hopes with respect to how new technologies might revolutionize learning and instruction. Rather than addressing the direct effects of technologies on learning, it seems more promising to investigate how technologies can support and change educational practices. The idea of technology enhancement should thus not only be seen in connecting distant learners with social software, but also in offering or giving access to challenging learning contexts and in support for structuring and orchestrating processes of collaborating and learning for both distant and co-present collaborators.

A focus in e-collaborative knowledge construction is on knowledge generated in technology-enhanced social interaction, rather than on information structures to be transmitted into the learners' heads with the help of technology. This does not imply that knowledge construction can be reasonably considered as being completely independent of the cognitive systems of the participating individuals. It does imply, however, that collaborative knowledge construction processes exceed individual cognitive systems. A multitude of approaches from different perspectives seems thus necessary to appropriately cover the complexity of the phenomenon. Such a multitude of approaches typically is accompanied by conceptual and methodological heterogeneity. This heterogeneity, in turn, can hamper the accumulation of scientific knowledge on the phenomenon. The present book is thus a very important and timely contribution to bring together the most important approaches to technology-enhanced collaborative knowledge construction from different disciplines and perspectives. It is a great state-of-the-art resource for researchers who want to improve our understanding of how knowledge is generated and shaped through social interaction in groups and networks and what role technology can play to support the cognitive and social processes involved. Although I am aware of the fact that scientific understanding of a phenomenon and educational innovations can be quite different things, I strongly believe that this research has a high potential to contribute to a more participatory culture of learning in our schools and universities.

Frank Fischer
Ludwig-Maximilians University of Munich, Germany

Frank Fischer *earned his Doctorate in Psychology in 1997, and his Habilitation (professorial dissertation) in Psychology and Education in 2002, both from the University of Munich. He served as an Assistant Professor for Applied Cognitive Psychology and Media Psychology at the University of Tuebingen held a professorship for Instructional Psychology at the University of Erfurt (2002-2003). From 2004-2006 he was an Associate Professor for Research on Learning and Instruction at the University of Tuebingen and head of the research unit Collaborative Knowledge Construction at the Knowledge Media Research Center. Since October 2006, he is a Full Professor of Education and Educational Psychology at the University of Munich. His research has been revolving around collaborative knowledge construction in interactive learning environments. In recent research projects, he has been focusing on facilitating collaborative knowledge construction with computer-supported socio-cognitive scaffolding with collaboration scripts in school (biology and physics) and university (educational science, medicine, computer science) contexts.*

Preface

The focus on knowledge has shifted during the last decades. Nowadays, lifelong learning and the ability to work with knowledge belong to the key skills of our society. This is reflected by authors using terms like *knowledge society* (e.g., Nonaka, 1994) or *knowledge age* (e.g., Bereiter, 2002). The quantity of information, which is generated and also accessible due to the new information and communication technologies, requires new strategies of information processing and exchange. It requires the individual as well as the society to keep their knowledge up to date, which results in a continuous process of knowledge generation (see Nonaka, 1994). In this way, it is not more enough to acquire knowledge and rely on it—learners find themselves in a permanent process of knowledge construction and rebuilding. Consequently, also learning scenarios have changed. Teaching cannot be seen anymore from the perspective of a teacher who is passing his or her knowledge to students and also learning cannot be seen any more as memorizing things presented by a teacher (see Ertl, Winkler & Mandl, 2007). Such kinds of learning would rather result in inert knowledge—knowledge which is reproducible for tests but not applicable by the learners (see Renkl, Mandl & Gruber, 1996).

COLLABORATIVE KNOWLEDGE CONSTRUCTION

According to constructivist approaches, learners have to construct their knowledge *actively* to create applicable knowledge. Thus, active knowledge construction in collaborative scenarios is provided by approaches like *cognitive apprenticeship* (Collins, Brown & Newman, 1989) or *situated learning* (Lave & Wenger, 1991). Fischer, Bruhn, Gräsel, and Mandl (2002) describe four important processes for collaborative knowledge construction: Learners' *externalization* and *elicitation* of knowledge, their *conflict-oriented negotiation* and their *consensus-oriented integration*. Externalization and elicitation relate to the exchange of knowledge in which the learning partners present their knowledge and query mutually for resolving deficits. These processes are complemented by conflict-oriented negotiation and consensus-oriented integration, which describe that learning partners have to negotiate about different viewpoints and integrate them to construct a shared knowledge base for collaboration. The development of this shared knowledge base can be a goal collaborative knowledge construction as well as the fundament for further collaborative activities, for example in learning communities. In sum, collaborative knowledge construction is attributed with many benefits for learners (see e.g., Ertl, Fischer & Mandl, 2006; Lou, Abrami & d'Apollonia, 2001; Roschelle & Teasley, 1995).

AFFORDANCES FOR E-COLLABORATIVE KNOWLEDGE CONSTRUCTION

Collaborative knowledge construction requires *collaboration* in a style in which collaboration partners interact frequently with *content-specific* activities and also commitment of the collaboration partners. It means that they work together at the same (virtual) place to construct one joint product or mental artifact (see Bereiter, 2002). Such collaboration does not necessarily have to happen synchronously—however, the collaboration partners' timing and their commitment have to be solid enough for the processes of collaborative knowledge construction to take place (see Ertl, 2008). The e-collaborative setting relies furthermore on the computer, which features collaboration partners' communication (e.g., by the provision of newsgroups, chats, Wikis, instant messaging tools or audio-visual communication). Communication (and collaboration) tools enable different scenarios for e-collaborative knowledge construction, for example virtual communities of practice, virtual learning communities, situated learning environments, cased-based learning, and virtual seminars. However, providing communication and collaboration facilities itself is not enough for e-collaborative knowledge construction (ECKC) to happen. Besides this, there is at least a shared motivation necessary and some aspects of instructional design (see Kirschner, Sweller & Clark, 2006). This can be introduced by the shared screen, which sets up the virtual collaboration space (e.g., the context and introducing pages of a learning environment or virtual community or by a shared application). In the last case, learners can see the moves of their collaboration partners simultaneously (see Dillenbourg & Traum, 2006; Ertl et al., 2006).

Environments for e-collaborative knowledge construction can be improved further by dedicated support for collaboration partners. Several methods offer such support, such as visualization aids (e.g., Mayer, 1994), structures for collaboration (e.g., Fischer, Kollar, Mandl & Haake, 2007) and tutoring (e.g., Pata, Sarapuu & Lehtinen, 2005). One challenge for designing support methods is to provide as much support as necessary for learners, but without overextending their capacity by too complex tools or inappropriate simplifications. Therefore, it is important to learn about the knowledge, skills, and needs of collaboration partners to provide appropriate support (see Dobson, 1999).

STRUCTURE OF THE BOOK

This book comprises four sections which take up important aspects of e-collaborative knowledge construction. It starts with environments that give an impression about scenarios of e-collaborative knowledge construction. The second section focuses typical approaches in the context of ECKC and discusses the issue of analysing and evaluating processes and outcomes of environments for ECKC. This is followed by the third section which deals with particular mechanisms to facilitate learners' processes and outcomes in ECKC. The book concludes with broader perspectives which set ECKC back in a school and an organizational context. In the following, the sections and chapters are described in more detail. Furthermore, the contents described can be complemented by technical perspectives and good practice examples, which appeared in Ertl (2010), *Technologies and Practices for Constructing Knowledge in Online Environments: Advancements in Learning*.

Environments for E-Collaborative Knowledge Construction

The book starts with a section about environments to illustrate scenarios in the context of e-collaborative knowledge construction. Chapters of this section give an impression of what is meant by e-collaborative knowledge construction and show implementations. They focus on different goals ranging from empowering learners with 21st century skills to setting up a sustainable learning community. Thereby, authors give insights into issues that came up during planning, implementing and running these environments and provide lessons learned. The chapters discuss good practices for the design, the implementation and the application of environments for e-collaborative knowledge construction.

Clark, Sampson, Stegmann, Marttunen, Kollar, Janssen, Weinberger, Menekse, Erkens, and *Laurinen* show how working in e-collaborative environments can facilitate learners to develop *21st century skills*. By using this term, they refer to the concepts of adaptability, complex communication skills, non-routine problem-solving skills, self-management/self-development, and systems thinking. The chapter describes four different environments for e-collaborative knowledge construction, namely WISE Seeded Discussions, CASSIS, VCRI, and DREW and analyzes to which extent each environment supports the development of these skills.

Bettoni takes a community approach to e-collaborative knowledge construction. He describes how to apply the principle of communities of practice to the design and implementation of a community of research. His chapter gives insights into the design and implementation process of a community and into the activities which occurred within this community. By that, the author derives good practices and suggestions for the design, implementation and maintenance of communities.

Oehl and *Pfister* focus on applying chat for e-collaborative knowledge construction. Besides the pure chat communication, the authors also provide a shared application for enabling knowledge construction. They discuss shortcomings of chat-based scenarios and present the approach of learning protocols to facilitate it. These learning protocols provide collaboration partners means for referencing chat contributions and to classify them according to their intention. The chapter discusses which particular aspects can be facilitated by learning protocols and provides aspects which should be considered when setting up scenarios with chat communication.

Approaches in the Context of E-Collaborative Knowledge Construction

E-collaborative knowledge construction can be seen from different approaches, such as distributed cognitive processing, conceptual change, help-seeking, and expertise development. Each of them has a particular focus to build environments for the collaboration partners. All of them refer to cognitive processes and interactions that are taking place during e-collaborative knowledge construction and the assessment of its outcomes and they illustrate the process character of e-collaborative knowledge construction. This section will elaborate these approaches and their impact for e-collaborative knowledge construction.

The chapter by *Tscholl* and *Dowell* focuses on distributed cognitive processing and describes an approach for studying processes of e-collaborative knowledge construction. It illustrates this approach by examples from discourse analysis and presents evidence for a significant overlap between critical argumentation and knowledge construction. The authors provide a refined definition of co-construction that comprises of an interrelation between interaction and co-construction. The chapter concludes with implications on the analysis and evaluation of knowledge co-construction in different environments.

Harteis elaborates how e-collaborative knowledge construction is related with the development of professional expertise. He distinguishes different types of knowledge and shows how they develop individually and during collaboration. The chapter describes how information and communication technologies can facilitate these knowledge construction processes, including a discussion about challenges for e-collaborative knowledge construction.

Schworm and *Heckner* focus on the concept of help seeking that relates to an asymmetric knowledge distribution setting. Starting from the issue of interactions in academic help seeking they summarize general aspects of collaboration in settings with asymmetric expertise. They shift their attention to peculiarities of computer-based help seeking in human-human interactions as well as in human-computer scenarios. Thereby, they identify typical weaknesses of current help systems and show how far social Web can have an impact for the design of future help systems.

Liu and *Hmelo-Silver* elaborate scientific conceptual change during collaborative knowledge construction in their chapter. They present a model for collaborative scientific conceptual change (CSCC) and describe a study that was analyzed according to this model. Their analyses identified several processes of e-collaborative knowledge construction which are related to the outcomes of the collaborative setting. This enabled them to exemplify how conceptual change takes place during collaboration.

Sluijsmans and Stribos focus on the outcomes of e-collaborative knowledge construction, which is often some kind of group product that was created jointly by all members of the group. Research has shown that there are often differences in the individual contributions of each group member to the group outcome, which could result in inequalities and injustice for assessment. Sluijsmans and Strijbos focus on peer-assessment to overcome this issue. Peer-assessment facilitates instructors to evaluate the individuals' contributions to a group's outcome according to mutual estimations of the learning partners. The authors present different methods for peer-assessment and discuss their advantages and disadvantages.

Support Measures

The different settings and technologies are the key to understand how e-collaborative knowledge construction takes place and offers a starting point for the design of environments for e-collaborative knowledge construction as well as for the support of collaboration partners in these environments. Support approaches focus on instructional interventions which are applied during the process of e-collaborative knowledge construction. They help learners to work more effectively on their knowledge construction. Chapters in this section focus on particular mechanisms of the described support method (scripting, trainings, and tutoring) in the context of an environment for ECKC. They allow readers to transfer the presented support methods to other environments to provide further facilitation there.

Diziol and *Rummel* present a descriptive framework that provides dimensions for the support of collaborative e-learning. This framework allows classifying different types of support for e-collaborative knowledge construction by focussing important dimensions for support: the level of support, the domain, the mode, the timing, and the adaptivity. They exemplify their framework by the description of an adaptive domain-related assistance for a cognitive tutor algebra.

Häkkinen, Arvaja, Hämäläinen, and *Pöysa* focus on the particular support method of scripting in the context of a collaborative Web-based university course. They highlight the issue of different styles of script support, present a review of theoretical and empirical analyses and provide results of a design-based study which implemented three different styles of scripting. Based on this, they are able to present main applications for scripting and introduce the approach of flexible pedagogical scripts.

Pächter, Kreisler, and *Maier* raise the issue of how far processes and results of e-collaborative knowledge construction in videoconferencing settings may differ from face to face. They provide evidence by the presentation of an empirical study which shows that results do not differ significantly even if there are differences in the processes. Based on these results, the authors present a study about support by trainings for facilitating collaboration in videoconferencing which enable collaboration partners to reach better collaborative outcomes.

Kopp, Germ, and *Mandl* focus on the method of tutoring for providing support for e-collaborative knowledge construction. They elaborate the issue that tutors need more than just content-specific skills if they want to set beneficial conditions for learning. They further analyze which particular skills are necessary for a tutor to facilitate learning processes in e-collaborative scenarios. Their contribution is substantiated by the description of two virtual courses, one course which dealt with e-tutoring as subject matter and another course in which these tutoring strategies were applied.

Outlook

The outlook section puts e-collaborative knowledge construction in a broader context and discusses critically educational and organisational perspectives. Chapters in this section describe possible developments of e-collaborative knowledge construction in the future and driving and hindering forces.

Stevens provides in his chapter an educational perspective on the future development of e-collaborative knowledge construction. He focuses on the issue of rural education, which is characterized by small school sizes and often also by a decreasing number of students per school. Based on the exemplary situation of Newfoundland, he shows how e-collaborative knowledge construction can be applied in a school setting and how it can help schools, particularly in rural areas, to maintain their educational mission although to their small student numbers.

Moreland, Swanenburg, Flagg, and *Fetterman* take an organisational perspective on e-collaborative knowledge construction. They deal with the issue of transactive memory, which describes meta-knowledge about the skills of collaboration partners. They show prerequisites for the development of transactive memory and raise the issue, how far e-collaboration can support the development of transactive memory. Their conclusions show an ambivalent view on the role of technology for supporting e-collaborative knowledge construction.

CONCLUSION

E-collaborative knowledge construction describes an interactive process of collaborative knowledge work for the collaboration partners. The approaches and environments described in this book are therefore not restricted to the pure exchange of knowledge—learners also have the opportunity to negotiate on a collaborative knowledge base. Even if environments are very different with respect to their aims and contents, all of them facilitated these intense collaboration processes by their instructional design which was added to or included in the technical features. Technical development can promote chances for e-collaborative knowledge construction (see therefore the already mentioned book of Ertl, 2010: *Technologies and Practices for Constructing Knowledge in Online Environments: Advancements in Learning*). The increasing use of Web 2.0 technologies will be a motor for enabling intense collaboration due to their interactivity and support smooth processes of ECKC. Yet, the most interactive technology doesn't implicate processes of e-collaborative knowledge construction per se—there is always the need to contextualize the technology for example, by group rules for virtual communities or by the instructional design for learning environments (see Kirschner, Sweller & Clark, 2006).

E-collaborative knowledge construction may have links to face to face collaboration but may also be completely virtually. Currently there is just little research about interpersonal knowledge in virtual settings, which can provide motivation and prerequisite for successful processes and outcomes. Therefore, future research should also analyze the influence and contribution of social networking systems like facebook to e-collaborative knowledge construction.

Bernhard Ertl
Universität der Bundeswehr München, Germany

REFERENCES

Bereiter, C. (2002). *Education and mind in the knowledge age*. Mahwah, NJ: Erlbaum.

Collins, A., Brown, J.S., & Newman, S. (1989). Cognitive apprenticeship: Teaching the crafts of reading, writing, and mathematics. In L. B. Resnick (Ed.), *Knowing, learning, and instruction: Essays in honor of Robert Glaser*. Hillsdale, NJ: Erlbaum.

Dillenbourg, P., & Traum, D. (2006). Sharing solutions: persistence and grounding in multimodal collaborative problem solving. *Journal of the Learning Sciences, 15*(1), 121-151.

Dobson, M. (1999). Information enforcement and learning with interactive graphical systems. *Learning and Instruction, 9*(4), 365-390.

Ertl, B. (2008). E-collaborative knowledge construction. In N. Kock (Ed.), *Encyclopedia of E-Collaboration* (pp. 233-239). Hershey, PA: Information Science Reference.

Ertl, B. (Ed.). (2010). *Technologies and Practices for Constructing Knowledge in Online Environments: Advancements in Learning*. Hershey, PA: Information Science Reference.

Ertl, B., Fischer, F., & Mandl, H. (2006) Conceptual and socio-cognitive support for collaborative learning in videoconferencing environments. *Computers & Education, 47*(3), 298-315.

Ertl, B., Winkler, K., & Mandl, H. (2007). E-learning - Trends and future development. In F. M. M. Neto & F. V. Brasileiro (Eds.), *Advances in Computer-Supported Learning* (pp. 122-144). Hershey, PA: Information Science Publishing.

Fischer, F., Bruhn, J., Gräsel, C., & Mandl, H. (2002). Fostering collaborative knowledge construction with visualization tools. *Learning and Instruction, 12*, 213-232.

Fischer, F., Kollar, I., Mandl, H., & Haake, J. M. (Eds.). (2007). *Scripting computer-supported communication of knowledge - Cognitive, computational, and educational perspectives*. Berlin, Germany: Springer.

Kirschner, P. A., Sweller, J., & Clark, R. E. (2006). Why minimal guidance during instruction does not work: an analysis of the failure of constructivist, discovery, problem-based, experiential, and inquiry-based teaching. *Educational Psychologist, 41*(2), 75-86.

Lave, J., & Wenger, E. (1991). *Situated learning: Legitimate peripheral participation*. New York: Cambridge University Press.

Lou, Y., Abrami, P. C., & d'Apollonia, S. (2001). Small group and individual learning with technology: A meta-analysis. *Review of Educational Research, 71*(3), 449-521.

Mayer, R. E. (1994). Visual Aids to Knowledge Construction: Building mental representations from pictures and words. In W. K. Schnotz & R.W. Kulhavy (Eds.), *Comprehension of Graphics* (pp. 125-138). Amsterdam: North Holland.

Nonaka, I. (1994). A Dynamic Theory of Organizational Knowledge Creation. *Organization Science, 5*(1), 14-37.

Pata, K., Sarapuu, T., & Lehtinen, E. (2005) Tutor scaffolding styles of dilemma solving in network-based role-play. *Learning and Instruction, 15*, 571-587.

Renkl, A., Mandl, H., & Gruber, H. (1996). Inert knowledge: Analyses and remedies. *Educational Psychologist, 31*(2), 115-121.

Roschelle, J., & Teasley, S. D. (1995). The construction of shared knowledge in collaborative problem solving. In C. O'Malley (Ed.), *Computer Supported Collaborative Learning* (pp. 69-97). Berlin, Germany: Springer.

Acknowledgment

I would like to thank all the authors who submitted their chapter proposals, the full and revised chapters during the several stages of development of this book. I would also like to thank all the colleagues who were acting as reviewers and who provided valuable feedback for me and for the authors, which helped to select and to strengthen the chapters. My special thank is to the editorial advisory board and in particular Heinz Mandl and Frank Fischer for their advice and contributions. Last but not least, I would like to thank the staff of IGI Global and specially Ms. Elizabeth Ardner who provided extraordinary support in all the technical and organizational issues.

Bernhard Ertl
Universität der Bundeswehr München, Germany

Section 1
Environments for E–Collaborative Knowledge Construction

Chapter 1

Online Learning Environments, Scientific Argumentation, and 21st Century Skills

Douglas Clark
Vanderbilt University, USA

Victor Sampson
Florida State University, USA

Karsten Stegmann
University of Munich, Germany

Miika Marttunen
University of Jyväskylä, Finland

Ingo Kollar
University of Munich, Germany

Jeroen Janssen
Utrecht University, The Netherlands

Armin Weinberger
University of Twente, The Netherlands

Muhsin Menekse
Arizona State University, USA

Gijsbert Erkens
Utrecht University, The Netherlands

Leena Laurinen
University of Jyväskylä, Finland

ABSTRACT

A workshop held at the National Academies in the United States in 2007 highlighted five broad categories of skills that appear valuable across a range of jobs for people working in modern global economies. Engaging students in scientific argumentation can support the development of these 21st century skills. Unfortunately, opportunities are rare in typical classrooms for students to learn how to engage in scientific argumentation. Over the past ten years several online environments have been developed to support students engaging with one another in scientific argumentation. This paper considers how engaging students in scientific argumentation through the activity structures and scripts in these online environments could also support the development of 21st century skills. More specifically, the paper considers how WISE Seeded Discussions, CASSIS, VCRI, and DREW can support students' development of Adaptability, Complex Communication Skills, Non-Routine Problem-Solving Skills, Self-Management/Self-Development, and Systems Thinking.

DOI: 10.4018/978-1-61520-729-9.ch001

INTRODUCTION

The *Workshop on Research Evidence Related to Future Skill Demands* held at the National Academies in the United States in 2007 highlighted five broad categories of 21st century skills that appear valuable across a range of jobs, from low-wage service work to professional work, for people working in modern global economies. These five broad categories of skills include (1) adaptability, (2) complex communication and social skills, (3) non-routine problem solving, (4) self-management and self-development, and (5) systems thinking. Complex communication and social skills, for example, involve processing and interpreting both verbal and non-verbal information from others in order to respond appropriately. The full definition for each of these categories is provided later in this chapter. Research suggests that individuals learn and apply these broad skills within the context of specific domains and bodies of knowledge in school, the workplace, and other settings (National Research Council, 2008, 2000; Levy and Murnane, 2004). At work, development of these skills is intertwined with development of technical job content knowledge, but these skills can also potentially be developed through experiences in educational settings.

This chapter considers how engaging students in scientific argumentation in online environments inside and outside the classroom can help promote and support the development of 21st century skills. More specifically, this chapter (1) highlights the potential value and challenges of integrating scientific argumentation into school and university curricula, (2) outlines several technology enhanced learning environments that have been developed to support students engaging in argumentation (either scientific argumentation specifically or interpretations of argumentation that align well with many of the core commitments of scientific argumentation), and (3) discusses how the goals and activity structures of these environments can simultaneously support and promote the develop-

ment of each of the 21st century skills as defined by the National Academies.

WHY SCIENTIFIC ARGUMENTATION?

Inquiry is at the heart of current efforts to help students develop scientific literacy (AAAS, 1993; NRC, 2000). True scientific literacy involves understanding *how knowledge is generated, justified, and evaluated* by scientists and *how to use such knowledge to engage in inquiry* in ways that reflect the practices of the scientific community (Driver Newton, & Osborne, 2000; Duschl & Osborne, 2002). Scientific inquiry is often described in this literature as a knowledge building process in which explanations are developed to make sense of data and then presented to a community of peers so they can be critiqued, debated, and revised (Driver et al., 2000; Duschl, 2000; Sandoval & Reiser, 2004; Vellom & Anderson, 1999). The ability to engage in scientific argumentation (i.e., the ability to examine and then either accept or reject the relationships or connections between and among the evidence and the theoretical ideas invoked in an explanation or the ability to make connections between and among evidence and theory in an argument) is therefore viewed by many as an important aspect of scientific literacy (Driver et al., 2000; Duschl & Osborne, 2002; Jimenez-Aleixandre, Rodriguez, & Duschl, 2000; Kuhn, 1993; Siegel, 1989).

Learning to engage in scientific argumentation is challenging for students. For example, students are often asked to generate an explanation for why or how something happens during activities designed to engage students in scientific argumentation. To do this, students must first *make sense of the phenomenon* they are studying based on the data available to them. Current research suggests that students struggle with this process (Abell, Anderson, & Chezem, 2000; Kuhn & Reiser, 2005; Sandoval, 2003; Vellom & Anderson, 1999) and often rely on their personal beliefs or past experiences to do so (Berland & Reiser, 2009; Kollar, Fischer & Slotta, 2008; Linn & Eylon, 2006; Sampson & Clark, 2008). Another challenge that students face involves *generating a sufficient and useful explanation* or solution to a problem that is consistent with the types of explanations or solutions valued in science (Carey, Evans, Honda, Jay, & Unger, 1989; Lawson, 2003; Ohlsson, 1992; Sandoval, 2003).

Once students have generated a suitable explanation or solution, students also have difficulty *justifying their explanation using appropriate evidence and reasoning* from a scientific perspective. Research indicates that students often do not use appropriate evidence, enough evidence, or attempt to justify their choice or use of evidence in the arguments they produce (Bell & Linn, 2000; Erduran, Simon, & Osborne, 2004; Jimenez-Aleixandre et al., 2000; Kuhn & Reiser, 2005; McNeill & Krajcik, in press; Sadler, 2004; Sandoval, 2003). Finally, students often do not *evaluate the validity or acceptability of an explanation* for a given phenomenon in an appropriate manner. Current research indicates that students often do not use criteria that are consistent with the standards of the scientific community to determine which ideas to accept, reject, or modify (Hogan & Maglienti, 2001; Kuhn & Reiser, 2006) and distort, trivialize, or ignore evidence in an effort to reaffirm a misconception (Clark & Sampson, 2006; Kuhn, 1989). Overall, this literature indicates that students often struggle with many aspects of scientific argumentation in spite of the dexterity they demonstrate when supporting or refuting a viewpoint in everyday contexts (Eisenberg & Garvey, 1981; Schwarz & Glassner, 2003; Stein & Bernas, 1999; Stein & Miller, 1991).

Unfortunately, however, opportunities for students to learn how to engage in scientific argumentation in a productive manner as part of the teaching and learning of science are rare (Newton, Driver, & Osborne, 1999; Simon, Erduran, & Osborne, 2006). It is therefore not surprising that a great deal of research over the last ten years has

been devoted to the development of new curricula, instructional practices, and technology-enhanced learning environments that can be used to promote and support scientific argumentation inside the classroom (see Andriessen, Baker, & Suthers, 2003; deVries, Lund, & Baker, 2002; McNeill, Lizotte, Krajcik, & Marx, 2006; Osborne, Erduran, & Simon, 2004; Passmore & Stewart, 2002; Sandoval & Reiser, 2004 for examples).

In this chapter, we will highlight several examples of technology-enhanced learning environments that have been developed to address this need and discuss the available research that indicates that these environments are effective at improving the ways students engage in scientific argumentation or helping students develop scientific literacy. The technology-enhanced learning environments that we will focus on are WISE Seeded Discussions, CASSIS, VCRI, and DREW. After providing an overview of these four environments, this chapter considers how these technology-enhanced learning environments may also offer a promising context to help students develop 21st century skills in light of the full definitions of these 21st century skills provided by the National Academies.

OVERVIEW OF FOUR ONLINE ENVIRONMENTS DESIGNED TO SUPPORT ARGUMENTATION

Technology-enhanced learning environments can provide opportunities and support for students to learn how to engage with one another in argumentation. We will henceforth refer to these technology-enhanced learning environments that focus on supporting multiple students engaging with one another in argumentation online as "online argumentation environments," or more simply as "environments," for brevity. These environments provide several categories of affordances that can be used to foster student engagement in argumentation. These categories include scripting collaboration and activity structures, supporting communication, optimizing group composition, facilitating the co-creation and sharing of artifacts, providing awareness tools, and scaffolding the creation of individual arguments and contributions. Individual environments incorporate various configurations and combinations of these categories of affordances, but generally do not focus on all of these affordances simultaneously. None of the four focal environments in this chapter (WISE Seeded Discussions, CASSIS, VCRI, and DREW), for example, includes all of these categories of affordances. The four focal environments were selected, however, because they provide multiple examples of each category and illustrate how different affordances can be combined in a synergistic manner to promote better argumentation between students. Their inclusion in the chapter should therefore not be construed as suggesting their superiority to other excellent online argumentation environments – they have been chosen to represent the range of potential affordances that may be brought to bear in environments to support argumentation between multiple students and potentially the development of 21st century skills.

WISE (The Web-Based Inquiry Science Environment) Seeded Discussions

Overview and Similar Environments. WISE Seeded Discussions are just one type of online project that can be built with the WISE authoring environment. WISE Seeded Discussions focus on grouping students together with other students who have expressed differing perspectives or stances. This general approach can be referred to as a "conflict schema." Conflict schemas guide or structure opportunities for learners to engage in and resolve socio-cognitive conflict by forming heterogeneous groups, providing learners with divergent resources, and encouraging learners to adopt opposing roles in a discussion or debate (Dil-

lenbourg & Jermann, 2007; Kobbe, Weinberger, Dillenbourg, Harrer, Hämäläinen, & Fischer, 2007). ArgueGraph (e.g., Jermann & Dillenbourg, 2003) and WISE Seeded Discussions represent two different examples of this class of scripts that have proven successful in supporting argumentation (e.g., Clark, 2004; Clark & Sampson, 2005, 2007, 2008; Cuthbert, Clark, & Linn, 2002; Dillenbourg & Jermann, 2007; Jermann & Dillenbourg, 2003; Weinberger, 2008; Weinberger, Ertl, Fischer, & Mandl, 2005; Weinberger, Stegmann, Fischer, & Mandl, 2007).

Environment Features and Activity Structures. WISE Seeded Discussions first engage students in exploring the phenomenon to be discussed through probe-based labs and virtual simulations. Students are then scaffolded in constructing an explanation for the phenomenon. In order to help students focus on the salient issues, highlight distinctions between the ideas, and articulate clear stances, the environment provides students with an interface of pull-down menus to construct their explanation from sentence fragments identified through research on students' alternative conceptions (see Figure 1). The predefined phrases and elements in much of the research on WISE Seeded Discussions include components of inaccurate ideas that students typically use to describe heat, thermal equilibrium, and thermal conductivity that were identified through the misconceptions and conceptual change literature (e.g., Clough & Driver, 1985; Erickson & Tiberghien, 1985; Harrison, Grayson, & Treagust, 1999) and an earlier thermodynamics curriculum development project (Clark, 2000, 2006; Clark & Linn, 2003; Lewis, 1996; Linn & Hsi, 2000). In summary, this first component of the script is intended to focus students on salient issues and highlight distinctions between ideas for students by allowing them to explore the specific idea facets at the heart of the seed comments in the subsequent discussion.

Once the students have submitted their explanations, the second component of the personally-seeded script organizes students into discussion

Figure 1. The explanation construction interface. Students use a pull-down menu to construct an explanation from four sentence fragments that include common misconceptions.

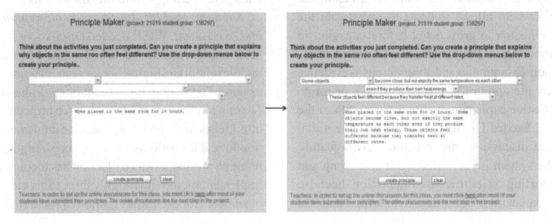

groups with other students who have created explanations conceptually different from one another. Discussion groups consist of three to five students. Organizing students with conceptually different perspectives together is intended as a "pedagogical strategy that will both initiate and support argumentation" (Osborne, Erduran, & Simon, 2004, p. 997). This is the core mechanism of the conflict schema approach and increases students' exposure to alternative interpretations of the phenomenon under discussion. The preset discussion seed comments are tailored from the original sentence fragments to represent an optimized range of student misconceptions. Students participate in an asynchronous online discussion of their explanations where they are encouraged to propose, support, critique, evaluate, and revise ideas. Finally, students reflect on how their ideas have changed through the discussion.

The design rationale for the WISE Seeded Discussions is therefore more elaborate than a less scripted discussion plan that simply directs students to evaluate one another's ideas. By asking the students to construct preliminary explanations from sentence fragments based on common misconceptions before joining the discussion, the script attempts to familiarize students with the ideas and distinctions at the heart of the upcoming debate. By grouping students with students who created conceptually different explanations, the script attempts to increase diversity of perspectives in the discussion. Thus, this activity structure is intended to go beyond typical small group work. Rather than viewing small group work as an opportunity to divide up the labor in order to finish a task quicker or as an opportunity to rely on a more knowledgeable peer (Cohen, 1994; Linn & Burbules, 1993), students must engage in genuine collaboration and consensus building.

Current and Future Research. The research program conducted with the WISE Seeded Discussions has focused on the initial structuring of online discussions. This research has focused on (1) the explanation construction interface, (2) the implementation of the conflict schema script, and (3) the nature of the initial seed comments. Future research will focus on scaffolding students' interactions within the actual discussions and helping students make connections in their comments with the simulations and hands-on data collection.

Strengths and Limitations of the Environment Design. WISE Seeded Discussions draw upon the general affordances of the WISE authoring environment to include robust access and interaction with simulations, note taking, and general access to data along with custom simulations and custom data collection and analysis software specific to the WISE Seeded Discussions. As a result, the environment allows students to investigate the phenomenon in great detail before engaging in argumentation. This strategy also enables students to use measurements and observations as evidence when attempting to support, evaluate, or refute alternative explanations. Another strength of the WISE Seeded Discussions is the way the initial online discussions are structured. This feature of the system is very effective at promoting and supporting scientific argumentation because the explanation construction interface and the automated sorting functionality that organizes discussion groups helps students focus on the main ideas and groups students who have constructed different explanations together. The environment does not, however, provide scaffolding of students' interactions with one another inside the discussions; students are only provided with a detailed set of instructions and a list of criteria to be used to evaluate the different explanations during the discussions before entering the discussion forum. Another limitation is that the environment does not provide teachers with easy-to-use analysis tools for the discussions. As a result, some teachers are inclined to just use the simulations and data exploration tools and skip or abridge the discussions because (1) they are not sure how to efficiently grade or analyze the discussions for their students and (2) they feel pressure from the national and state standards to cover content as quickly as possible and they aren't convinced that the discussions help with this.

In summary, WISE Seeded Discussions are strong for supporting student engagement in argumentation in terms of (1) providing students access and interaction with the phenomena to be discussed and (2) structuring and organizing the discussions in terms of a conflict schema script. WISE Seeded Discussions, however, would benefit from (1) more active approaches for scaffolding students' interactions within the discussions and (2) providing teachers with simple analytical tools

or reports to help them score, monitor, and analyze what is happening within the discussions.

Strengths and Limitations of Implementation and Assessment. WISE Seeded Discussions have been implemented in a broad range of public middle school and high school science classrooms as part of an overarching Technology Enhanced Learning in Science (TELS) research project (see http://telscenter.org/). The extensive implementation in real classrooms is one of the strengths of research program. Data collection has focused on implementations with roughly three to six classes of students for each study, although some studies have involved more classes (e.g., Clark, D'Angelo, & Menekse, 2009; Clark, Menekse, D'Angelo, Touchman, & Schleigh, 2008). Initial research assigned treatments to full classes, but later development allowed independent random assignment within classrooms. In the initial studies, assessment focused on analyses of students' participation within the discussions in terms of the structural quality of the argumentation occurring between students (e.g., Clark & Sampson, 2005).

Assessment then expanded to investigate conceptual quality and grounds quality as well as structural quality of students' argumentation as described by Clark and Sampson (2006, 2007, 2008). Thus the early research focused on coding aspects of students' comments within the actual discussions. These assessment rubrics have high inter-rater reliability and construct validity as described in those articles, but less is known about other aspects of validity and overall robustness. These rubrics map well onto 21st century skills in terms of the complex communications skills and non-routine problem-solving skills that will be discussed later in this chapter. One limitation of these rubrics, however, was that they rely on frequency counts and averages in terms of types of comments or features of individual comments to assess quality rather than sequences of comments or the trajectories of participation. More recent work, however, has begun to account for these trajectories by integrating sequential analysis techniques (Jeong, Clark, Sampson, & Menekse, in press). Recent studies have also analyzed content knowledge gains from pre to post discussion by comparing the explanation the students construct prior to the discussion with the explanation they construct using the same interface after the discussion (Clark, Menekse, D'Angelo, Touchman, & Schleigh, 2008; Clark, D'Angelo, & Menekse, 2009). Thus, assessment has evolved from focusing simply on levels of participation and structural quality of argumentation to also include analyses of grounds quality, conceptual normativity, sequences of comment types, and pre-post conceptual gains.

CASSIS (Computer-Supported Argumentation Supported by Scripts - Experimental Implementation System)

Overview and Goals of the Environment. CASSIS was designed to facilitate argumentation in asynchronous online discussions by using collaboration scripts. These collaboration scripts specify and sequence collaborative learning activities and distribute them among members of a collaborating group (see Kollar, Fischer & Hesse, 2006). In CASSIS, these activities were typically clustered to particular roles that were distributed among the members of a group. The scripts that were implemented in CASSIS target several different collaborative learning processes, such as homogenous participation (Weinberger, Fischer, & Mandl, 2001), epistemic activities (i.e. how knowledge is constructed; Weinberger, Reiserer, Ertl, Fischer, & Mandl, 2005), transactivity, (i.e. the degree to which learners operate on others' reasoning; Teasley, 1997; Weinberger, 2008), and argumentation (Stegmann, Weinberger, & Fischer, 2007). While CASSIS was developed for social science contexts rather than natural science contexts, it can support students engaging in scientific argumentation. Guzdial and Turns (2000) applied a similar approach in their CaMILE environment

to support and promote better asynchronous online discussions. Other tools, such as the *learning protocol-approach* by Pfister and Mühlpfordt (2002) or the work of Hron and colleagues (Hron, Hesse, Reinhard & Picard, 1997) involve applications of collaboration scripts in more synchronous scenarios such as chats.

Environment Features and Activity Structures. CASSIS engages small groups of three students in analyzing problem cases using a specific theory. Usually, the group's task is to first analyze three problem cases in a collaborative learning phase and then develop a joint solution for each case in a collaborative argument construction phase. An asynchronous, text-based discussion board is built into the environment so group members can communicate with each other as they work. Different collaboration scripts are implemented to promote and support productive collaboration between the students. A *script for the construction of single arguments,* for example, is embedded within the interface of the discussion board to help students construct a high quality argument that provides and justifies a solution for each problem case. In accordance with a simplified version of Toulmin's argument model (1958), this script consists of three text boxes that require students to input a claim, grounds, and qualifications for a co-constructed argument (see Figure 2). In order to improve the ways students engage in dialogical (or multi-voiced) argumentation, a *script for the construction of argumentation sequences* is embedded into an asynchronous, text-based discussion board to encourage students to engage in argument-counterargument-integration sequences (based on the work of Leitão, 2000). This is accomplished by automatically labeling each participant's contribution in the discussion board as an "argument," "counterargument," or "integration" depending on the role he or she was supposed to adopt in the discussion.

Current and Future Research. Computer-supported collaboration scripts are viewed as a scaffold for argumentation. In other words, the

Figure 2. The script for the construction of single arguments. Students use the textboxes labeled "Claim", "Grounds", and "Qualifications" to construct single arguments. Each single argument can then be added to the regular textbox of the online discussion by clicking the button labeled "Add".

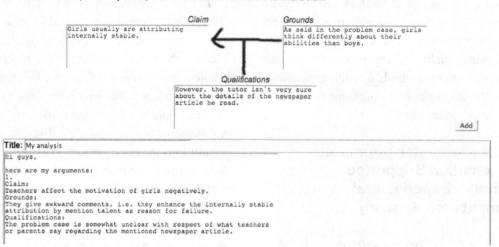

scripts are only used to temporally support an activity. Therefore, current research that focuses on the CASSIS environment examines how scripts can be removed (or "faded out"; Pea, 2004) during the collaborative learning phase and how relapses into novice strategies can be prevented (Wecker & Fischer, 2009). Current research also examines how the fading-out (as well as the fading-in) of collaboration scripts can be tailored to the current skill level of the learners. As part of this work, software that can automatically analyze the quality of the arguments crafted by the students was developed and embedded into the online environment. This software identifies low (e.g., arguments that only contain claims, but no grounds) and high quality arguments so students can be provided with a script as needed.

The CASSIS environment also enables quick implementation of different computer-supported collaboration scripts into a standardized learning environment. This flexibility and adaptability of the environment facilitates systematic research on the impact of different collaboration scripts or script components (e.g., Stegmann, Wecker, Weinberger, & Fischer, 2007; Stegmann, Weinberger, & Fischer, 2007; Wecker & Fischer, 2009; Weinberger, 2008; Weinberger, Stegmann, Fischer, in press). The stable use of the same learning materials and assessments has also enabled researchers to collect and compare data from online discussions over the last ten years. The main strength of this approach is the possibility to examine a train of consecutive research questions and to deeply understand the mechanisms of collaborative learning supported by scripts.

Strengths and Limitations of the Environment Design. Current research indicates that *construction of a single argument* and the *construction of argumentation sequences* scripts embedded in CASSIS promote and support higher quality argumentation and learning. While the effects of collaboration scripts have been found and replicated in a lab setting, more evidence needs to be collected to substantiate the script effect in other environments, domains, and cultures. Some evidence has been collected showing that scripts work across different environments. For example, Kollar and colleagues (Kollar, Fischer, & Slotta, 2007) implemented argumentative collaboration scripts into a WISE environment for science learning and successfully supported argumentative knowledge construction. This research shows that a script with a specific goal, such as facilitating the construction of argumentation sequences, can be translated to and implemented in different online environments. Scripts similar in function and structure also produce the same effects across different domains. For instance, Zottmann and colleagues (Zottmann, Diekmann, Rall, Fischer & Taraszow, 2006) showed that a collaboration script fostered simulation-based learning in medical education. Scripts designed to structure learners' (inter-)actions interact with the procedural knowledge or internal scripts learners already possess (Kollar et al., 2007). The guidance learners experience by external scripts should be adjusted to the level of detail of their internal scripts, i.e. the more learners know the less should they be guided by external scripts (Cohen, 1994; Dillenbourg, 2002). Internal scripts are regarded as culturally shared knowledge (Weinberger, Clark, Häkkinen, Tamura, & Fischer, 2007). Learners with different cultural backgrounds thus possess different internal scripts on how to learn and work together. For instance, Weinberger and colleagues (Weinberger, Laurinen, Stegmann, & Marttunen, 2009) compared the impact of a peer-review-script aiming to foster counter-argumentation on Finnish and German students. The script facilitated counter-argumentation and learning outcomes in both cultures, but the in general more conflict-oriented German groups were affected more by the script. The results point out that learning environments and collaboration scripts need to be designed in a culture-sensitive way.

Strengths and limitations of Implementation and Assessment. CASSIS is an experimental online learning environment. It therefore has not been fully integrated into the entire curriculum of a course. However, several studies have been conducted to examine the impact of CASSIS on student learning in the context of a course on Educational Science at the University of Munich. So far, several hundred students have participated in a series of experimental sessions that take the place of a three-hour lecture. In each experiment session, the students used CASSIS to develop a solution to three different authentic problem cases using attribution theory (Weiner, 1985).

The individuals' contributions to the online discussion in CASSIS served as the primary data source for assessing the quality of collaborative argumentation supported by the *script for the construction of argumentation sequences* in these studies. To assess the quality of these discussions, transcripts were generated and then analyzed using a coding scheme developed by Weinberger and Fischer (2006). This coding scheme requires a discussion to be first segmented into propositional units. These units are then coded with respect to the formal quality of each argument and with respect to the formal quality of argumentation sequences. The *formal quality of a single argument* is based on the share of segments that are coded as claims with grounds and/or qualifications. A sequence analysis is then used to assess the *formal quality of argumentation sequences*. This is accomplished by first identifying the arguments, counterarguments, and integrations in the discussion. The probability of transitions between the aforementioned message types (argument, counterargument, or integration) for each group of three is then computed using a software tool called MEPA (developed by Erkens, 1998). This coding scheme has high inter-rater reliability and evidence gathered through think aloud protocols suggest it is also a valid way to measure argumentation skills (cf. Stegmann, Wecker, Weinberger, & Fischer, 2007).

VCRI (Virtual Collaborative Research Institute)

Overview and Goals of the Environment. VCRI is a groupware program designed to support collaborative learning on inquiry tasks and research projects. Students can use VCRI to communicate with each other, access information sources, and co-author texts and essays. While working with VCRI, students share several tools. These tools are designed to support three aspects of the collaborative inquiry process: task-related or cognitive aspects (e.g., writing an essay or constructing an argumentation map), meta-cognitive aspects (e.g., planning and evaluating the inquiry process), and social aspects (e.g., monitoring the collaborative process and supporting communication). The impact of VCRI as a way to improve collaborative learning outcomes has been assessed in several different studies that examine the nature of collaboration and argumentation in different contexts, content areas, and with different age groups (e.g., Janssen, Erkens, Jaspers, & Kanselaar, 2007; Slof, Erkens, & Kirschner, 2008; Van Drie, Van Boxtel, Jaspers, & Kanselaar, 2005). Although this research has not generally focused specifically on science-related content, the features and design of this environment could be used to support scientific argumentation.

Environment Features and Activity Structures. In VCRI, students work on collaborative inquiry projects that span approximately eight lessons. Students start a project by investigating a topic by reading, collecting, and summarizing information found in various sources using the *sources-tool* (see Figure 3a). Students are able to discuss the information found in these sources with other group members as they work using the synchronous *chat-tool* (see Figure 3a). Often, the information sources contain an argument that consists of various facts, data, or other information that is used by the author in order to support or refute a particular viewpoint or position. Students use the *debate-tool* (see Figure 3b) to help them examine

and explore these arguments. This tool enables the students to co-create an *argumentative map* or a visual representation of the arguments that can be found in a source or across sources, thereby giving them a better overview of a topic or a way to explore the merits of one or more positions. To help streamline this process, students can transfer information they gather using the *sources-tool* directly to the *debate-tool*. Students can also manually add supporting or refuting information from sources outside of VCRI to their argumentative maps. Once the argumentative maps are complete, students can transfer the line(s) of reasoning in the argumentative maps to *cowriter*. Students then use *cowriter*, which is a text processor that allows simultaneous editing by multiple users (see Figure 3a), to write a final report using the line(s) of reasoning identified and highlighted with the *debate-tool* as a guide.

In addition, VCRI contains several awareness heightening tools. Through these tools, students are made aware of several important aspects of the collaborative process. The *status-bar*, for example, gives information to the students about who is online, and who is working with which tool, while the *participation-tool* gives information about the relative contributions of the group members. These tools enable the students to judge the quantity and the quality of their collaboration. The *chat-tool* also gives feedback to the students about the kind of discussions they are conducting.

Current and Future Research. The research program conducted with the VCRI environment has focused on promoting and supporting better collaboration between students as they work on inquiry projects. Initially, the program addressed support for the cognitive and meta-cognitive aspects of collaborative inquiry projects. This research included an examination of the effects of representational guidance (Janssen et al., in press; Van Drie et al., 2005) and the impact of planning tools (Erkens, Jaspers, Prangsma, & Kanselaar, 2005). More recently research efforts have concentrated on supporting the social aspect

Figure 3. Screenshot of the VCRI environment showing the chat-tool, the sources-tool, and cowriter and screenshot of the debate-tool. This tool enables students to create a visual representation of the argument found within a source or across sources.

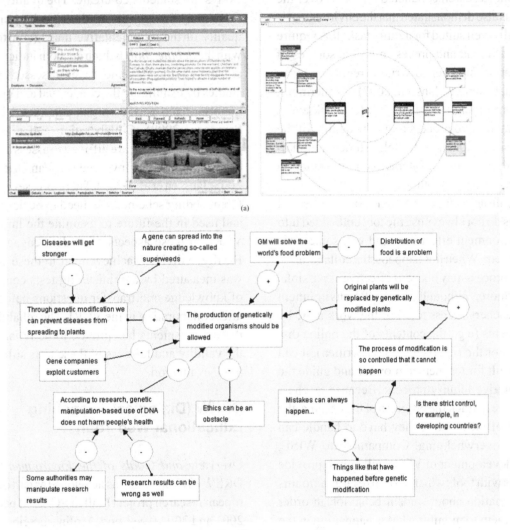

of collaborative inquiry learning (e.g., collaboration and communication, see for example Janssen, Erkens, Jaspers, et al., 2007; Janssen, Erkens, & Kanselaar, 2007). Future studies will focus on (1) the implementation and use of peer feedback tools (cf., Phielix, Prins, & Kirschner, 2009) and (2) the development, implementation, and evaluation of tools that enable teachers to monitor and guide students' collaborative inquiry process better.

Strengths and Limitations of the Environment Design. VCRI is developed as a generic environment to support collaborative inquiry learning. One advantage of the VCRI environment is that it can and has been used in several domains and subjects. VCRI also offers several tools that students may use during the collaborative inquiry process. Students are however, not obliged or forced to use these tools (Beers, Kirschner, Boshuizen, &

Gijselaers, 2007). This is another strength of VCRI because it allows students more choice and limits coercion. Research conducted on VCRI over the years has also demonstrated that the environment is especially well suited for inquiry tasks that require students to read and process multiple sources of information in order to write a report or essay (Damsa, Erkens, & Janssen, 2007). Furthermore, by incorporating tools that give feedback about the collaborative process (e.g., the quality of the online discussions), VCRI helps students capitalize on the benefits of interactive argumentation and discussion with others.

One disadvantage of VCRI, however, is that students do not always use the tool embedded into the environment effectively and will sometimes ignore them. When this happens, the collaborative inquiry process may not be as effective as possible. Furthermore, although the VCRI-environment gives teachers access to all of the work done by the students (e.g., the contents of the online discussions or the reports they have written), it can be difficult for teachers to monitor and guide the collaborative inquiry process. Because teachers often have to track the progress of 8-10 teams, the amount of information they have to handle can become overwhelming. Comparable to WISE, future development of VCRI will aim to provide teachers with tools which visualize large amounts of information about student behavior, in order to help them to monitor what is happening in the environment.

Strengths and Limitations of Implementation and Assessment. VCRI has been used and assessed in upper secondary education and in several different subject areas (e.g., history, Dutch language, social studies, economy). Assessment of the impact of VCRI as a way to support the complex nature of collaborative inquiry projects tends to focus on the nature of communication and the collaboration processes that take place between groups of students as they work. Research conducted by Janssen et al., (2007) and Janssen et al. (in press), for example, has assessed the ways student work

with VCRI, their ability to co-construct high quality argumentation maps, and the quality of the final essays the students co-create. The quality of the final essay (written using the *cowriter*) and the quality of the argumentative maps (constructed with the *debate-tool)*, which are both indicators of collaborative achievement, were assessed in these studies by examining the conceptual and grounds quality of the various arguments (see Clark & Sampson, 2008). Collaboration and reasoning processes, however, are difficult to assess because of the complexities involved (cf. Van Drie et al., 2005; Janssen et al., 2007). Therefore, several different coding schemes will need to be developed and used in the future to examine the impact of VCRI on these aspects of student engagement. Finally, individual achievement in these studies was measured by administering tests consisting of knowledge and transfer questions before and after collaboration in the VCRI. The reliability of these assessments has proven to be reliable but the validity and fairness of these tests still needs more evaluation.

DREW (Dialogical Reasoning Educational Web Tool)

Overview and Goals of the Environment. The DREW environment was developed as part of a European research project (called SCALE) between 2001 and 2004 (see Lund, Molinari, Séjourné, & Baker, 2007). The DREW environment consists of several different computer tools that are designed to support collaborative activities. These tools include a chat environment, a collaborative writing tool, and an argument diagram tool. Research conducted by Marttunen and Laurinen (2006, 2007) has focused primarily on how secondary and university students use DREW's argument diagram tool. Similar to the *debate-tool* in VCRI, this tool enables students to visualize arguments found in written materials (e.g. newspaper articles, book chapters, online recourses, etc). The diagram tool in DREW, however, also enables users to diagram the arguments in discussions. The main goal of the diagram tool is to help students learn how to identify and examine a claim, justifications for the claim, and the criticisms of the claim. This goal is shared by other environments that focus on argument diagramming such as Belvedere (Suthers, 2008; Suthers, Hundhausen, & Girardeau, 2003), Reason!Able (van Gelder, 2002), TC3 (van Amelsvoort, 2006), and VCRI. The DREW environment may also be used as a discussion forum to help promote and support more productive interactions when students engage in argumentation. DREW (like CASSIS and VCRI) was not developed specifically to help students examine arguments that focus on issues related to science but it can also be used to support students to learn how to engage in more productive scientific argumentation.

Environment Features and Activity Structures. The argument diagram tool enables users, either individually or collaboratively using a shared screen at different workstations, to construct a diagram that includes boxes for claims, arguments, and counterarguments. The boxes are connected which each other with arrows indicating whether the content of the box either supports (+ sign) or criticizes (- sign) the content of the box to which the arrow points. The construction of the diagram often proceeds in three phases. First, the main thesis of the text or discussion is defined and written into a box that is then located within the diagram. Second, all of the arguments and counterarguments that directly link to the main thesis are defined, written into boxes, and labeled with the appropriate signs. Finally, all the other arguments and counterarguments are defined and put into the diagram. The location of the various arguments and counterarguments depends on whether they support or criticize the main thesis or some other argument or counterargument in the diagram. In addition to writing arguments into boxes, the students can also elaborate on the arguments or counter arguments using "commentary boxes" that are automatically connected to the appropriate box.

A completed diagram depicts the argumentative structure of a text or discussion by indicating the main thesis of the material and showing how the thesis is supported and criticized by illustrating the other arguments and counterarguments and their interconnections. Figure 4 provides an example of an argument diagram that was constructed by secondary school students as part of a study.

Current and Future Research. Research on the Drew argument diagram tool has focused on questions relating to the use of the diagram as a way to represent development in students' argumentative thinking (Marttunen & Laurinen, 2006, 2007). In a recent study (Kiili, Laurinen & Marttunen, 2008), for example, secondary school students used the diagram tool to organize arguments and counterarguments gathered from different Internet sources and then used to the diagram in a joint essay-writing task. The diagram has also been used to analyze students' argumentative discussions (Salminen, Marttunen & Laurinen, 2007). Future research will focus more on the use of the diagram as a way to improve students' reading and writing skills. Particularly the following research questions will be investigated: 1) How can argument diagrams be used most effectively to foster strategic reading before, during, and after reading of texts? 2) How can the argument diagram tool be used to support collaborative writing either in connection with the writing tool of the DREW environment or with other word processors?

Strengths and Limitations of the Environment Design. Argument diagrams are self or group constructed representations that support better reasoning because they possess exploitable perceptual effects (see Cox, 1999). In the era of chalkboards and paper and pencils, argument diagrams would have been laborious to construct and difficult to modify; the DREW's argument diagram tool, however, makes representational formalisms easier to exploit. The construction of an argument diagram on the basis of text material also helps students to detach themselves from the surface structure of the texts. This process enables them to focus on

Figure 4. An argument diagram on genetically modified organisms created by secondary school students

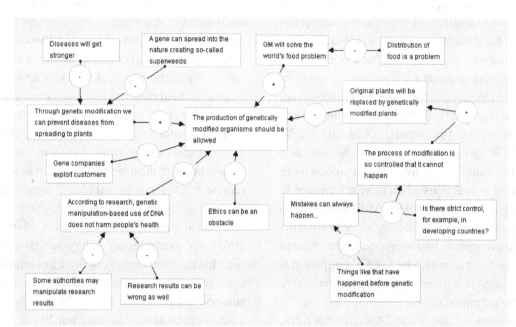

the meaning of the texts at a deep level. Further, if students are asked to use the diagram to analyze several texts from various content areas, they can begin to develop metacognitive skills and learn how to be constructive responsive readers (see Pressley & Gaskins, 2006). More precisely, the diagram directs students to search for claims, arguments, and counterarguments in the texts and to process it further; it helps students seek connections between the sentences and paragraphs inside the same text or between separate texts; and it fosters an evaluative attitude towards the content of texts. These points can be regarded as pedagogical strengths of the diagram tool. However, as the tool has been developed particularly for texts that are expository or persuasive in nature it is not very suitable for the analyses of all kinds of texts. Furthermore, a technical weakness of the tool is that the argument commentary boxes are visible for the user only one in time. For this reason the diagram tool, at its current developmental phase, cannot be recommended, for example, for constructing concept maps from texts to be learned (see Novak, 1998).

Strengths and Limitations of Implementation and Assessment. The DREW argument diagram tool has been examined in the context of both secondary and university students by researchers at the University of Jyväskylä. In the earliest studies of DREW (Marttunen & Laurinen, 2007; Salminen, Marttunen & Laurinen, 2007; Lund et al., 2007), the researchers focused on (1) the ways secondary students working in dyads engaged in chat discussions about current social issues that often involve socio-scientific aspects (e.g., genetically modified organisms, nuclear power, vivisection) and (2) how students analyzed the claims, arguments, and counterarguments in their discussions using the argument diagram tool. The diagram tool was also applied at university level when education students concentrated on the controversial issue of guided versus constructive learning in an advanced course on educational psychology. In this course the students were asked to analyze the argumentative content of two articles by creating argument diagrams using the DREW diagram tool.

Analyses of students' diagrams focus on size, breadth, depth, and branching (Marttunen & Laurinen, 2006: Salminen et al., 2007). To assess the *size* of the diagram, the total number of argument boxes and commentary boxes are tabulated. The *breadth* of the diagram, on the other hand, is assessed by counting the number of arguments and counterarguments directly linked to the main thesis. Another indicator of quality is the length of argument chains inside the diagram. Chains of arguments are formed by successive arguments and counterarguments. To assess the *depth* of the argument, the number of arguments and counterarguments successively linked to each other are counted. In addition, when arguments and counterarguments are linked around the main thesis so that they form argument chains, they are re-categorized as a secondary thesis. A secondary thesis refers to all the arguments and counterarguments that are supported by one or more new arguments or opposed by one or more new counterarguments. The *branches* of the diagram can then be evaluated by counting the number of secondary theses linked to more than one argument or counterargument. Finally, the *Counterargumentativeness* (Salminen et al., 2007) of a diagram is assessed by comparing the amount of counterarguments and rebuttals with the amount of claims and arguments. This coding scheme is a reliable way to examine the quality of both the argument diagrams students produce using DREW and students' argumentative thinking (Marttunen & Laurinen, 2006; Salminen et al., 2007). However, less is known about how well these skills transfer to other contexts.

RELATIONSHIP OF ENVIRONMENT GOALS AND EVIDENCE WITH 21ST CENTURY SKILLS

The following sections discuss the relationship of the example environments (and several other environments) to the five categories of 21st century

skills: (1) adaptability, (2) complex communication skills, (3) non-routine problem solving, (4) self-management/self-development, and (5) systems thinking. Although these environments were not designed specifically with these skills in mind, these environments can contribute to the development of these skills because of the significant overlap between the skills needed to engage in productive scientific argumentation and 21st century skills. Each section begins with the quoted definition of one of the five categories of 21st century skills developed through National Academy workshops (National Research Council, 2008). Each section then (1) highlights how online argumentation environments can support and promote the development of that category of 21st century skills and (2) outlines the empirical evidence indicating that online argumentation environments are effective at helping students develop skills relevant to that category of 21st century skills.

Adaptability

"The ability and willingness to cope with uncertain, new, and rapidly-changing conditions on the job, including responding effectively to emergencies or crisis situations and learning new tasks, technologies, and procedures. Adaptability also includes handling work stress; adapting to different personalities, communication styles, and cultures; and physical adaptability to various indoor or outdoor work environments (Houston, 2007; Pulakos, Arad, Donovan, and Plamondon, 2000)." (NRC, 2008)

Relationship to the Example Environments. We argue that all of the example environments focus on the development of skills related to adaptability in at least two senses. First, these environments are designed to help students learn how to adapt their everyday communication skills to align more closely with the values, habits of mind, and criteria involved in scientific argumentation. The development of argumentation skills, in this context, can be viewed as a task that is central to helping individuals learn how to adapt to quickly changing circumstances in their environment. The ability to respond to a counterargument to one's own claims, for example, is a competence that is of a high value in many everyday situations, both in private and in professional situations (such as emergencies or crisis situations). The ability to weigh arguments and to evaluate the relevance, significance, or validity of the facts, evidence, and other reasons that people use to support or challenge a claim enable individuals to make better decisions even in scenarios where prior knowledge is low.

Second, students can also develop adaptability skills in these environments as they learn how to communicate using new technologies and learn about the various affordances or constraints that are associated with them. Students are supported in this process by scripts embedded within these environments that are designed to scaffold students as they collaborate. These scripts help students learn how to participate in an unfamiliar context in a more productive manner and how to transition from one form of communication to another as needed. Scripts can scaffold role rotation, which can guide learners as they assume various roles and perspectives. The environments also have the potential to automatically fade this scaffolding as students become more proficient, which is very important for an internalization of the argumentation strategies (see Pea, 2004).

Evidence from the Example Environments. Individuals with highly developed argumentation skills, as noted earlier, are also able to adapt to new problems, new modes of communication, and people or cultures. Individuals with these skills can also propose, support, critique, and refine new ideas. These skills enable individuals to cope with uncertain, new, and rapidly changing conditions or evaluate the merits of new ideas, technologies, and procedures. Empirical evidence indicates that

the example environments are effective at fostering these types of skills. Research conducted on DREW (Marttunen & Laurinen, 2006: Salminen et al., 2007), for example, indicates that diagrams help individuals learn how to identify and evaluate the arguments for and against a particular position when investigating an unfamiliar topic. Research conducted by Stegmann and colleagues (Stegmann, Wecker, et al., 2007; Stegmann, Weinberger, et al., 2007) on CASSIS also provides empirical support for this claim. These studies indicate that the CASSIS environment is effective in improving students' ability to generate persuasive and convincing arguments. In these studies, the effects of two different argumentative scripts (*construction of single arguments* and *the construction of argumentation sequence)* were tested. While one script was designed to support the construction of single arguments that would match theoretical standards, the other script aimed at helping students produce argument sequences that have been described as helpful for collaborative knowledge construction. Results show that both scripts did their job: the *script for the construction of single arguments* increased the formal quality of single arguments (i.e., students more frequently provided reasons for their claims), and the *script for construction of argumentation sequences* increased the quality of argumentation sequences (i.e., the frequency of counterarguments was increased). DREW and CASSIS therefore can be used to help students learn a new mode of communication (in this case, reasoned arguments or counterarguments), which in turn, enables students to learn how to adapt their modes of communication to better align with a given context.

The environments can also provide a context that promotes and supports productive argumentation and increase participation so learners have an opportunity to hone these skills. Early empirical research on the WISE Seeded Discussion, for example, showed that the initial versions of the environment were superior to standard online discussions for promoting high quality of argumentation (in terms of structure) and increasing student participation in a discussion (Clark, 2004; Clark & Sampson, 2005; Cuthbert, Clark, & Linn, 2002). Current research in WISE suggests that much of the added value of the personally-seeded script in comparison to standard online discussions stems from (1) the initial scaffolding provided in terms of exploring the explanation fragments that encapsulate the key idea facets that will be used in the seed comments and (2) the conflict schema approach of grouping students in discussions with students who have expressed different perspectives (Clark, Menekse, et al., 2008; Clark, D'Angelo, & Menekse, 2009). In essence, this environment enables students to engage in higher quality argumentation and increases the amount of student participation by exposing students to opposing perspectives. It also increases content learning. Overall, the evidence available indicates that this environment provides a meaningful context where students can hone their argumentation skills, which in turn, helps students learn to adapt to new or changing conditions.

Empirical research also indicates that the described environments can encourage adaptability by distributing and re-distributing roles and activities to individual group members. This provides students with an opportunity to engage in collaborative argumentation independent of learners' actual perspectives and helps them learn how to cope with uncertain, new, and rapidly changing conditions. Research in CASSIS, for example, guided learners to take on and rotate the roles of case analyst and constructive critic. Each of the three learners in a group switched roles at fixed intervals to criticize the case analyses of their learning partners. This script proved to substantially facilitate learning outcomes in several lab and field studies as learners elaborated arguments and counter-arguments in a highly transactive way and shared their knowledge and perspectives in the discussions (Weinberger, 2008; Weinberger, Ertl et al., 2005). This type of approach, where students are encouraged to take on different roles

during a task designed to promote and support argumentation, can therefore not only help students learn more from an activity but it can also help students learn how to adapt to different roles in a discussion.

Empirical research also indicates that these environments can encourage adaptability by increasing students' awareness of important aspects of the collaborative process. Research in VCRI, for example, demonstrated that awareness tools such as the *participation-tool* increased students' awareness of their group members' contribution to the collaborative process. Students use this information to help regulate and coordinate the work of the group, which over time resulted in more productive group interactions and outcomes (Janssen et al., 2007). This research indicates that online learning environments can help students learn how to adapt to the complex processes involved in collaboration and argumentation by increasing their awareness of the ways they are interacting with each other.

Evidence from the Related Environments. The ArgueGraph script is another example of a conflict schema that can help students to develop adaptability skills. ArgueGraph identifies students' opinions through a questionnaire and then represents the students' positions on a graph. The software then matches pairs of opposing opinions with the largest distance on the graph into groups to construct and exchange arguments and counterarguments. Jermann and Dillenbourg (2003) examined the efficacy of this approach. Their study demonstrates that organizing groups in this manner can increase engagement in the processes of argumentation and learning, which helps students learn how to propose, support, critique, and refine new ideas. These skills enable individuals to evaluate the merits of new ideas, technologies, and procedures or cope with uncertain and rapidly changing conditions.

In an environment based on videoconferencing, a script has been applied that guides learners through specific macro-phases of diagnosing and proposing therapies for psychiatric cases, including orchestration of individual and collaborative phases as well as structuring learners to formulate and answer questions, exchange notes and discuss and revise individual ideas and converge on joint solutions (Rummel & Spada, 2005). This study shows that scripts can facilitate learners' interaction processes as well as the quality of their joint solutions.

Lastly, research on online environments demonstrates that students tend to benefit in a variety of ways when they use asynchronous and synchronous communication technologies in technology-enhanced learning environments. Asynchronous modes of communication, for example, often foster engagement in high-quality argumentative processes (e.g., de Vries, Lund & Baker, 2002; Pea, 1994). Asynchronous communication also facilitates task-oriented discussions and individual knowledge construction by allowing participants time to reflect, understand, and craft their contributions and responses (Kuhn & Goh, 2005; Marttunen, 1992; Schellens & Valcke, 2006). This expanded time allows students to construct and evaluate textual arguments more carefully than in face-to-face environments (Joiner & Jones, 2003; Marttunen & Laurinen, 2001). The text-based nature of these asynchronous online environments (as opposed to speech-based) tends to supplement the construction of complex and well-conceived arguments (e.g., de Vries et al., 2002) and helps students develop skills in processing and interpreting information from others in order to respond appropriately. Asynchronous modes may also potentially provide more equitable access and participation for students engaging in argumentation than face-to-face settings because of simultaneous access and participation opportunities (Hsi & Hoadley, 1997). Asynchronous modes that allow anonymous contributions may also increase this equitable access and participation (Hsi & Hoadley, 1997).

Synchronous chat facilities, on the other hand, offer a different set of affordances. Task-oriented synchronous chat, for example, affords simultaneous deliberation and coordination as students work together on a shared artifact (de Vries et al., 2002; Janssen, Erkens, Jaspers, & Kanselaar, 2006). Research suggests that providing ways for students to coordinate resources and negotiate how to proceed with a task can foster productive collaborative learning (Barron, 2003; Pfister, 2005; Rogoff, 1998). It also enables students to learn how to select key pieces of a complex idea to express in words in order to build shared understanding during collaborative problem solving. Finally, and perhaps most importantly, synchronous chat allows users a chance to provide immediate feedback on argumentation. This tends to facilitate co-construction of argumentation sequences and deeper discussions. A comparison study conducted by Munneke, Andriessen, Kirschner, and Kanselaar (2007), for example, showed that students in a synchronous chat condition argued in a more elaborated and deep way than students in an asynchronous forum on the same task. Students using the asynchronous forum, however, produced more accurate argumentative texts. Both asynchronous and synchronous technologies can therefore enhance the adaptability of students because they enable students to learn to communicate (1) with different types of technologies, (2) in different situations and contexts, and (3) with a wider diversity of people.

Complex Communications Skills

"Skills in processing and interpreting both verbal and non-verbal information from others in order to respond appropriately. A skilled communicator is able to select key pieces of a complex idea to express in words, sounds, and images, in order to build shared understanding (Levy and Murnane, 2004). Skilled communicators negotiate positive outcomes with customers, subordinates and superiors through social perceptiveness, persuasion, negotiation, instructing, and service orientation (Peterson et al, 1999)." (NRC, 2008)

Relationship to the Example Environments. Of the five 21st century skills, the development of complex communication and social skills is most central to these environments. All of these environments focus heavily on complex communication and social skills. Many of the environments focus on helping students learn how to work toward consensus. Students need to be able to communicate complex ideas in order to build a shared understanding. Scientific argumentation is ultimately about developing, warranting, and finally communicating a persuasive argument in terms of the processes and criteria valued in science. Argumentation skills are necessary for both the construction of valid and sound arguments as well as for the evaluation of the soundness and relevance of arguments provided by others. Argumentation skills are therefore an integral component of complex communication skills.

One important way that these environments develop and support complex communication skills is through the scripts integrated into the environments that support students in these roles. Essentially, the design of these environments can be thought of in terms of "scripts" that orchestrate and control students' interactions with each other and the environments (e.g., King, 2007; Carmien, Kollar, Fischer, & Fischer, 2007; Kopp & Mandl, 2007; Stahl, 2007; Stegmann, Weinberger, & Fischer, 2007). As Weinberger and colleagues explain, "scripts provide more or less explicit and detailed instructions for small groups of learners on what activities need to be executed, when they need to be executed, and by whom they need to be executed in order to foster individual knowledge acquisition" (Weinberger, Stegmann et al., 2007, p.195). These scripts and activity structures can help students learn complex communication and social skills in technology-enhanced learning environments.

The collaboration scripts implemented in CASSIS, for example, improve the argumentative quality of social discourse between learning partners and help learners develop a shared, well-grounded position on a topic. The WISE environment uses a script to sort students into groups with students who think differently about the phenomenon under discussion as discussed earlier in the overview of the example environments and in the section on **Adaptability**. Students begin their discussions with multiple different perspectives and reaching consensus in these discussions is often a significant challenge for students. This requires students to develop new and complex communication skills so they can better communicate with individuals with divergent perspectives.

In terms of VCRI, the *debate-tool* and the *participation-tool* also support complex communication. The *debate-tool* stimulates students to discuss and argue about a topic. Analysis of the argumentation maps students co-create using the *debate-tool* show that online learning environments can promote and support conceptually sound, and well-grounded discussions between students. Finally, the *participation-tool* gives students information about the relative contribution of the group members allowing them to judge the quality of their collaboration.

Finally, when the argument diagram tool in the DREW environment is used as a joint discussion forum for some controversial topic, the argumentative relations (i.e. arguments indicating either agreement or disagreement) of the contributions of the interlocutors become visible. Visualization of the argumentative structure of the discussion helps participants focus their discussion on the most conflicted and complex issues, which in turn, can promote the building of a shared understanding. Carr (2003), for example, found that argument diagrams produced in the QuestMap environment helped students to focus their discussion on those aspects in which they particularly disagreed with each other.

Evidence from the Example Environments. Research in CASSIS indicates that argumentative scripts facilitate the formal quality of argumentation during online discussion (cf. Stegmann, Weinberger, & Fischer, 2007). The proportion of single arguments with higher formal quality significantly increased for learners who were supported with *the script for the construction of single arguments* in these studies. The *script for the construction of argumentation sequences* also improved the formal quality of argumentation sequences by increasing the proportion of counterarguments and transitions from arguments to counterarguments in these studies. Furthermore, both scripts successfully facilitated the acquisition of knowledge on argumentation. Learners specifically acquired more knowledge on single arguments when supported by the *script for the construction of single arguments* and more knowledge on argumentation sequences when supported with the *script for the construction of argumentation sequences* as compared to learners without script support. However, the scripts did not affect domain-specific knowledge acquisition, although enhanced argumentation skills may facilitate domain-specific knowledge acquisition in the future (cf. Kollar et al., 2007). In another study (Janssen et al., in press), it was demonstrated that the *debate-tool* helps students create high quality argumentation maps and write conceptually sound historical essays. Additionally, students used the *debate-tool* to formulate well-grounded warrants for the arguments put forth in their essays. On the other hand, the debate-tool did not affect the quality of the argumentation exchanged between group members during their online collaboration.

Evidence from Related Environments. Other research has also demonstrated the value of supports for individual argument construction. Research on Belvedere (which focuses more heavily on single argument construction rather than argumentation between students) showed that students' craft better arguments when they use a Toulmin-inspired graphical template of the structural components of an argument (Suthers & Hundhausen, 2003). While support for data evaluation is a key feature of tools like Belvedere, these tools also facilitate the construction of sound arguments by visualizing respective claims, relevant evidences, and

possible qualifications (Fischer, Bruhn, Gräsel, & Mandl, 2002; Kirschner, Buckingham Shum, & Carr, 2003; Suthers & Hundhausen, 2001). Similar results have been found by Kollar et al. (2007). In Kollar et al., a script that aimed at improving both the structural and the sequential quality of arguments produced during collaboration on a WISE unit about deformed frogs led to a higher number of arguments with a high structural quality and more counterarguments. Further analyses (Kollar, Fischer, & Slotta, 2008), however, have shown that as soon as this script was removed, students resorted back to their internal scripts on how to construct arguments and argument sequences. Thus, facilitating the internalization of more sophisticated argumentation strategies through adequate scripts appears to require longer-term interventions.

Like Belvedere, research on BGuILE and SenseMaker focuses heavily on evaluation of data for single argument construction, but research on BGuILE and SenseMaker also focuses on the value of computer-mediated supports for individual argument construction (Bell, 1997, 2004; Bell & Linn, 2000; Reiser, 2002; Reiser, Tabak, Sandoval, Smith, Steinmuller, & Leone, 2001; Sandoval, 2003; Sandoval & Millwood, 2005; Sandoval & Reiser, 2004). Research on specific BGuILE software tools, such as the *ExplanationConstructor*, for example, underscores the value of these tools in helping students express their reasoning and beliefs in meaningful ways (Sandoval & Reiser, 2004). BGuILE research has also investigated inferential validity in terms of the causal coherency of students' explanations (Sandoval, 2003; Sandoval & Millwood, 2005). According to this BGuILE research, students' explanations are predominantly coherent even though they sometimes use inappropriate inferences to justify their positions.

Non-Routine Problem-Solving Skills

"A skilled problem-solver uses expert thinking to examine a broad span of information, recognize patterns, and narrow the information to reach a diagnosis of the problem. Moving beyond diagnosis to a solution requires knowledge of how the information is linked conceptually and involves metacognition—the ability to reflect on whether a problem-solving strategy is working and to switch to another strategy if the current strategy isn't working (Levy and Murnane, 2004). It includes creativity to generate new and innovative solutions, integrating seemingly unrelated information; and entertaining possibilities others may miss (Houston, 2007)." (NRC, 2008)

Relationship to the Example Environments. All of the example environments promote non-routine problem-solving skills. Negotiating consensus and critiquing ideas through a discussion in WISE, for example, where novel ideas are introduced by other students on a regular basis, requires students to use expert thinking in integrating and applying a broad span of information and data from the initial laboratory activities, simulations, and everyday experiences. This involves pattern recognition, deduction, analogical thinking, and several other key problem-solving skills in a context that is constantly shifting as students interact with one another and add new ideas to the mix. WISE scaffolds this process through helping to focus students on the salient ideas prior to the discussion. This helps students consider the breadth and range of the problem space and key issues and alternatives within the problem space. The discussions are then seeded with comments to cue these specific issues within the subsequent debate.

Within the CASSIS environment, learners are encouraged to apply a theory to solve authentic problems. CASSIS provides argumentative collaboration scripts to improve joint solutions. Thus, students more often base their final solutions

on grounds and consider different perspectives, which is facilitated by a collaboration script that asks learners to provide counterarguments to their fellow learners' contributions (which is a task that requires a great deal of metacognitive awareness with respect to the validity of the arguments produced by the learning partner). The argument diagram tool in the DREW environment can also promote non-routine problem-solving skills. This tool allows students to examine a broad span of information, recognize patterns, and narrow the information to reach a solution to a problem. The DREW argument diagram tool also encourages students to reflect on whether or not a claim is well-supported by available evidence and to weigh the pros and cons of a solution to an ill-defined or complex problem. This type of metacognition is a key element of non-routine problem solving.

Evidence from the Example Environments. The WISE Seeded Discussions help students learn how to solve non-routine problems by helping them learn to evaluate the validity or acceptability of claims, explanations, or solutions. To do this, WISE requires students to use a series of pull-down menus that students use to explore the key idea facets that will be included in the seed comments of the subsequent discussions. Current research in WISE investigates the value of the conflict schema approach and the value of this pre-exploration and focusing on the key ideas and variants at the heart of the debate prior to the discussions. The research suggests that this initial scaffolding in conjunction with the conflict schema approach increases conceptual and structural quality of the ensuing argumentation (Clark, D'Angelo, & Menekse, 2009). This environment can therefore help students focus at the salient levels of the debate, recognize distinctions between seed-comment claims, learn how to integrate seemingly unrelated information, entertain possibilities others may miss, and examine or evaluate a broad span of information.

The results on DREW thus far have shown that students deepen and broaden their knowledge of a given topic when diagrams are used across three sequential phases of students' work (Marttunen & Laurinen, 2006). The DREW diagrams have been demonstrated to provide students with a suitable tool for reflecting on their previous debate and earlier knowledge (Marttunen & Laurinen, 2007). The VCRI environment also helps both university and secondary students balance positively and negatively oriented arguments during discussions. Overall, this research indicates that the DREW and the VCRI environments can help students develop argumentation and non-routine problem-solving skills.

Current research also indicates that the CAS-SIS environment can be an effective way to foster non-routine problem-solving skills. For example, an epistemic script implemented in the CASSIS environment guided learners to engage in a series of problem-solving moves, such as identifying the relevant problem information, applying the relevant concepts to this problem information, and drawing conclusions and proposing interventions. Learners supported with an epistemic script were better able to focus on the core aspects of a problem case, but also pursued additional information and explored multiple perspectives (Mäkitalo, Weinberger, Häkkinen, Järvelä, & Fischer, 2005; Weinberger, 2008; Weinberger, Stegmann et al., 2007). This work suggests that the CASSIS environment can help students develop non-routine problem-solving skills by giving students an opportunity to learn how to analyze large amounts of information, recognize patterns, and determine whether or not a claim is well support by available evidence.

Evidence from Related Environments. The use of argument diagrams in environments comparable to the DREW argument diagram tool has produced results suggesting that argument diagrams help develop argumentation skills which, in turn, are highly useful in non-routine problem solving. Twardy (2004) found that the use of argument maps promoted critical thinking among university students. Likewise, the use of the Belvedere helps

students balance positively and negatively oriented arguments during a discussion (van Boxtel & Veerman, 2001).

Research also demonstrates that these environments can support students engaging in non-routine problem solving by providing access to data and supporting the evaluation of data. In terms of access to data, Kolodner, Schwarz, Barkai, Levy-Neumand, Tcherni, and Turbovsk (1997) developed an indexed case library that students search for examples and facts as evidence for their arguments about specific issues. The case library provides and indexes alternative solutions to support students' examination of counterarguments to their own line of argumentation. Kolodner et al. (1997) showed that the case library supports students' construction of counterarguments and refines learners' understanding of what makes a good argument.

Other research shows that enriched representations can provide significant interrelated information to students (Fisher & Larkin, 1986) and that incorporating media-rich representations of the learning task, materials that enhance the authenticity of the learning task, and contextual anchors can facilitate student learning (Bransford, Brown, & Cocking, 2000; Cognition and Technology Group at Vanderbilt, 1997). These environments can also provide access to visualizations and simulations that may allow students to explore aspects of the subject matter to support a specific claim, thereby potentially increasing the persuasiveness of their arguments (Oestermeier & Hesse, 2000).

Research on the SenseMaker tool within the KIE and WISE environments (Bell, 1997, 2004; Bell & Linn, 2000) indicates that online argumentation environments can help develop non-routine problem-solving skills. SenseMaker focuses primarily on helping students craft individual arguments. SenseMaker research showed that students' understanding of the core issues, evidence, and arguments benefited from working with a tool that helped them analyze the conflicting pieces of evidence at the core of a debate. Similarly, the

BGuILE environment helps students design and practice scientific inquiry through investigation, refine their own explanations and reasoning, and critique other students' explanations (Reiser, 2002; Reiser, Tabak, Sandoval, Smith, Steinmuller, & Leone, 2001; Sandoval, 2003; Sandoval & Millwood, 2005; Sandoval &Reiser, 2004). The BGuILE environment integrates dynamic visualizations and outlining environments to help students learn, understand, and integrate new and complex knowledge and concepts that students might not otherwise address (Reiser, 2002).

Self-Management and Self-Development

"Self-management skills include the ability to work remotely, in virtual teams; to work autonomously; and to be self motivating and self monitoring. One aspect of self-management is the willingness and ability to acquire new information and skills related to work (Houston, 2007)." (NRC, 2008)

Relationship to the Example Environments. Self-management and self-development are supported to varying degrees by these environments. The environments that include participant awareness tools, for example, help students monitor their own participation or contributions and the participation or contributions of other group members. VCRI's *participation-tool*, for example, provides students with educative feedback about how well they work in a group and how to improve their participation. Awareness tools encourage students to engage in metacognition and can help promote and support the development of the skills needed to self-monitor. Through this process students can improve their ability to work remotely or in virtual teams and to monitor their own progress.

Another approach to supporting self-management and self-development involves metacognitive prompts that encourage students to reflect on the implications of the data, the types of responses that would be appropriate in a given situation, and how their own ideas have changed. Providing these metacognitive prompts helps students learn both content (i.e., science concepts) and process (i.e., how to engage in productive scientific argumentation) and can also help students learn how to self-monitor in subsequent encounters. These prompts can be faded over time or with increased proficiency. If students fail to provide persuasive grounds supporting their own arguments, for example, the argumentative collaboration scripts within CASSIS can help students or their learning partners identify these flaws in the arguments. This in turn may engage learners in re-thinking and revising their own claims and in searching for further evidence to support or discard their claims.

Evidence from the Example Environments. In terms of supporting self-management and self-development through awareness tools, several studies with VCRI have focused on the effects of awareness tools on students' communication and collaboration (e.g., Janssen et al., 2007). These awareness tools help students to improve their collaboration process and stimulate them to engage in constructive argumentation. VCRI's *shared space*, for example, analyzes the content of the chat messages sent. This analysis establishes whether group members are conducting shallow consensual online discussions or whether they are engaged in critical exploratory discussion. The results of this analysis are then fed back to the group members. This helps students to become aware of the type of online discussions they are having with their group members. Students can use this information to adapt their collaboration and communication if necessary. Research by Janssen, Erkens, and Kanselaar (2007) showed that groups that had access to the *shared space* engaged in more critical and exploratory discussions compared to groups without access to the *shared space*. These groups were also more satisfied with the online collaborative process and performed better on a historical inquiry task. This research indicates that awareness tools can help students learn how to work in virtual teams, to work autonomously, and to be self-motivating and self-monitoring.

Research on the CASSIS environment indicates the argumentative collaborative scripts can also help promote self-management and development. A general effect of the various scripts implemented in the CASSIS environment seems to be that learners are more engaged in on-task discourse and participate more frequently and more homogeneously (Weinberger, Stegmann et al., 2007). Scripts guide learners to engage in the relevant steps for arriving at problem solutions, which makes the sometimes arduous coordination in online environments redundant. Learners seem to have less opportunity to engage in off-topic discourse and focus on the task at hand. In another study conducted within CASSIS (Wecker & Fischer, 2007), students were supported in classifying the components of the argumentation of their learning partners. Students were then supported in formulating counterarguments on the basis of the identified components. By the means of fading (i.e. reducing the instructional support by script step by step) and distributed monitoring (i.e., evaluation of the quality of counter argument by peers), students engaged in these argumentative processes on their own (i.e., without an external script that would ask them to do so). Overall, this research indicates that online environments can help students learn how to monitor their own performance as well as the performance of others.

Research on an early version of WISE (Davis, 2003; Davis & Linn, 2000) on prompts showed that generic prompts that ask students to "stop and think" will encourage greater reflection in comparison to directed prompts that provide with hints indicating potentially productive directions for their reflection. The results showed that students in the generic prompt condition developed more coherent understandings as they worked on a complex science project in the environ-

ment and that students reflect unproductively more frequently in response to directed prompts as compared to the generic prompts. Thus the structure of prompts in these environments can support students' self-monitoring.

Evidence from Related Environments. Other research also supports the value of awareness tools for increasing group members' awareness of the nature and quality of contributions and participation within the group (e.g., Dillenbourg, 2002). These tools support the self-regulating capacities of collaborative learners. Research by Jermann and Dillenbourg (2008), for example, showed that providing awareness information about the amount of communicative and task-related activities performed by group members led to increased participation in online dialogue and to more frequent and precise planning of the collaborative process. Similar results were reported by Michinov and Primois (2005). Students can also be made aware of possible strengths and deficits regarding the group's collaborative activities and of possible gaps in the group's argumentation. Based on this feedback, students can self-correct their collaborative argumentation accordingly (e.g., Hesse, 2007; Jermann, Soller, & Muehlenbrock, 2001). These tools also help students develop the skills they will need to process and interpret both verbal and non-verbal information in order to respond to other people in an appropriate manner.

Research by White and Frederiksen (1998) demonstrates the positive effects of metacognitive prompting on learning processes and learning outcomes. White and Frederiksen implemented reflection prompts in an inquiry-oriented curriculum unit on force and motion. These prompts were designed to raise the metacognitive awareness of the students to help them design more reasonable experiments and to develop higher-level conclusions from their experiments. White and Frederiksen's results demonstrate that the prompts were successful. Students in the prompting condition produced more sophisticated research designs, showed more high-level conclusions, and displayed smoother teamwork than students who had participated in regular classroom instruction. Moreover, students from the prompting condition outperformed students from regular classrooms on a subsequent transfer test in which they were supposed to develop a research plan on a different topic.

Systems Thinking

"The ability to understand how an entire system works, how an action, change, or malfunction in one part of the system affects the rest of the system; adopting a "big picture" perspective on work (Houston, 2007). It includes judgment and decision-making; systems analysis; and systems evaluation as well as abstract reasoning about how the different elements of a work process interact (Peterson, 1999)." (NRC, 2008)

Relationship to the Example Environments. Arguments are systems and chains of claims, warrants, backings, and data that can involve substantial complexity as they evolve through discussion. In order to participate in these discussions in a productive manner, students must learn how to evaluate information, make well-reasoned decisions, and examine how the various components of an argument or counterargument fit together with one another. Students must also develop appropriate criteria for evaluating what counts as warranted knowledge and how to determine if information is relevant to the phenomenon under discussion or if there is sufficient information to make a decision. Students therefore learn to adopt a "big picture" perspective on their work. In this way, these environments support students in developing the habits of mind needed to engage in systems thinking.

The argument diagram tool in DREW, for example, helps students think about how the parts of the argument fit together and weigh the pros and cons of a particular stance or viewpoint. This encourages students to think about the components as a larger system. VCRI's *debate-tool* helps students to examine information critically and create argumentation maps that focus not only on supporting information but also on information that refutes an argument or position. Similarly, the argumentative collaboration scripts within CASSIS assist learners in building networks of well-grounded arguments or counterarguments. Overall, these environments can promote the development of systems thinking by encouraging students to see how one change in a system of arguments affects the rest of the system and by improving their evaluation, judgment, and decision-making skills.

Evidence from the Example Environments. As discussed earlier, research on DREW has demonstrated positive effects on the use of diagrams during studies at the secondary level. The results suggest that students deepened and broadened their knowledge of a given topic during an intervention in which diagrams were used in three subsequent phases during students' working (Marttunen & Laurinen, 2006). Furthermore, the diagrams have proved to provide students with a suitable tool for reflecting on their previous debate and earlier knowledge (Marttunen & Laurinen, 2007). This work provides evidence that students can develop a better understanding of a complex phenomenon or a system and can help them engage in systems analysis and evaluation when they have an opportunity to use an argument-diagramming tool.

As discussed earlier, learners in the CASSIS environment analyzed complex problem cases containing information that could sometimes lead to contradictory conclusions (e.g., a student exposed to some beneficial and some detrimental attribution patterns from parents, teachers, and self). Learners who were assigned through a script to play the opposing roles of "case analyst" and "constructive critic" were better able to explore the multiple perspectives of the complex problem cases in terms of applying different theoretical concepts and principles to different aspects of complex problem cases (Weinberger, Ertl et al., 2005; Weinberger, 2008).

Evidence from Related Environments. Evidence from related environments demonstrates the value of co-creating and sharing intellectual artifacts that present or visualize arguments in promoting and supporting the development of systems thinking (e.g., Kirschner, Buckingham, Shum, & Carr, 2003). Producing these external representations engages students in proposing, supporting, evaluating, and refining their ideas and encourages students to keep the 'big picture" in mind. Furthermore, external representations can help learners identify faulty or incomplete lines of argumentation and elicit task-relevant knowledge (Fischer, Bruhn, Gräsel, & Mandl, 2002). The *DUNES* system (Schwarz & Glassner, in press), for example, encourages students to engage in dialogic argumentation as they co-construct a rich argumentation map in which shapes represent types of contributions (e.g., information, argument, comment, or question) and arrows between shapes show connections (with solid arrows signifying support and dashed arrows signifying opposition). These diagrams show how claims, arguments, and counterarguments relate to each other and the topic in general. Related work also shows that co-creating and sharing artifacts and external representations can facilitate argumentation by guiding learners' attention toward gaps and elicit task-relevant knowledge (Fischer et al., 2002; Suthers & Hundhausen, 2001). These types of external representations also seem to contribute to the development of systems thinking because they provide opportunities for students to analyze and evaluate a complex system of ideas and engage in abstract reasoning about how the different elements interact.

SYNTHESIS AND FINAL THOUGHTS

We conclude our chapter by considering issues of generalizability and possible limitations. We first consider the potential generalizability of these environments beyond the domain of science in the classroom. We then consider generalizability to other online and offline curricular media and strategies. We then consider the balance of the focus of the environments across the five categories of 21st century skills. Finally, we consider limitations to the evidence that has been collected and propose areas for future research and development to address these limitations.

Generalizability to Domains Beyond Science. Engaging students in scientific argumentation supports many of the goals for the development of 21st century skills. Taken together, the evidence discussed in this chapter suggests that these environments support students engaging in argumentation in a manner that reflects the core commitments of scientific argumentation. The applicability of these environments, however, is not limited solely to the domain of science. Several other domains share many core commitments, assumptions, values, criteria, and structures for argumentation with the forms of argumentation traditionally attributed to the domain of science. In fact, many of these environments have been used primarily in domains other than science. CASSIS, for example, has been implemented primarily in social science contexts and VCRI has been used in history and several other contexts. That is not to say that there are not domain specific aspects of argumentation in science, but to say that argumentation as enacted in these environments focuses on forms of argumentation that generalize to certain other domains (and more fundamentally to partaking in societal debates and political life within democratic societies). In fact, this generality supports the development of 21st century skills. That said, however, the national science standards of many countries place heavy emphasis on incorporating inquiry and the inherent argumentation into the curriculum. Science classrooms therefore provide an excellent opportunity to embed this type of argumentation into the curriculum.

Generalizability to Other Curricular Media and Strategies. Can the affordances of these environments be transferred or applied in other curricular media, online and offline? As discussed, many of these environments can be thought of in terms of "scripts" that orchestrate and structure students' interactions with each other and the environments (e.g., Hesse, 2007; King, 2007; Carmien, Kollar, Fischer, & Fischer, 2007; Stahl, 2007; Stegmann, Weinberger, Fischer, 2007). These scripts are highly detailed design patterns for how students' activities should be orchestrated and structured in order to support learning and promote the attainment of certain of educational outcomes. As a result, much of the research that has been conducted in these environments has focused on the comparative efficacy of various configurations and structures of these scripts. The research on CASSIS and WISE, for example, focuses specifically on these types of comparisons. Research on CASSIS and similar environments provides evidence that students can develop a broad range of collaborative learning skills when supported by computer-supported collaboration scripts. While the VCRI and DREW environments are usually not described in terms of scripts, research on VCRI and DREW tends to focus on the efficacy of clearly defined tools and activity structures that can be thought of as a scripts or design principles in a similar manner. These scripts or approaches for promoting and supporting argumentation involve clearly specified activity structures that can be used to guide the development or refinement of other online and offline learning environments or curricula.

Balance of Focus Across the Five Categories of 21st century skills. It is also important to note that all five categories of 21st century skills are not equally supported by all environments. Taken together, the environments overall support the development of complex communications skills the most strongly, followed by problem solving, self monitoring, adaptability, and systems thinking. Obviously the precise balance of focus, however, varies by environment.

Limitations of the Evidence Collected to Date and Future Research. While this chapter has considered possible affordances and evidence for these environments in terms of supporting the development of 21st century skills, there are definite limitations to the claims that can be made based on the evidence collected to date.

One major limitation is the fact that the assessments employed in the research on these environments weren't designed specifically to assess the categories of 21st century skills outlined by the National Academies. The assessments were developed or chosen from pre-existing assessments to measure specific aspects of collaboration and argumentation considered important by the researchers and field for the questions the researchers wished to pursue. There is a great deal of overlap between some these assessments and the definitions of the 21st century skills, particularly in terms of the "complex communication and social skills" category. Similarly the curricular goals of many argumentation and inquiry environments map very well onto the categories of "non-routine problem solving" and "systems thinking." The skills and habits of mind involved in "adaptability" and "self-monitoring and self development," on the other hand, are certainly valued by many developers of inquiry and argumentation environments, particularly environments that focus on awareness tools like VCRI, but few assessments have been developed specifically to document or evaluate students' self-monitoring abilities. Instead, research on these environments has focused on the quality of students' products and levels of participation as indirect measures of these abstract metacognitive skills and habits of minds. The connections between the evidence from the research on these environments and their potential to support 21st century skills, as a result, are sometimes relatively tenuous and are sometimes suggestive more than concrete. This chapter is therefore meant to outline the potential of these environments rather than to serve as final proof of their current capabilities with regard to 21st century skills.

Part of the challenge for the future in terms of gathering more definitive and conclusive evidence will in fact involve identifying, refining, and even developing appropriate assessments that target the five categories of 21st century skills and sub-skills. Good assessments have been developed in the CSCL and argumentation communities to use as a base or template for some aspects of the complex communication and social skills category. Similarly, assessments have been developed in the psychology and learning sciences communities to assess problem solving skills, systems thinking, some aspects of self-monitoring and self-development, and potentially adaptability. The challenges will be two-fold, however, in terms of refining and defining exactly what constitutes the specific 21st century skills we wish to measure and then selecting from the existing assessments, building and refining upon those assessments, and developing additional assessments or extensions of the existing assessments to provide a battery of instruments to measure these abstract skills.

This process will be somewhat daunting; but the development of assessments that can measure these general skills in a valid and reliable manner will also enable the educational systems to assess student learning and progress in ways transcending the behaviorist-inspired models of assessment that focus on atomized facts and content and drive most curricula in schools toward that model of education. Thus, while these environments may hold the potential to support the development of 21st century skills, investigating this potential directly will involve the development of new assessment approaches to measure these 21st century skills. Developing these instruments, however, will potentially provide dividends well beyond these environments by creating a system for valuing and measuring these skills that may prove more productive than the current behaviorist-driven assessment practices in schools for promoting skills and habits of mind that eclipse the current focus on atomized content coverage in schools.

Final Thoughts. Engaging students in scientific argumentation can support the development of 21st century skills. Opportunities are rare in typical classrooms for students to learn to engage in scientific argumentation, but online environments have been developed to support multiple students engaging with one another in scientific argumentation. As research on these environments continues to clarify optimal scripts and design principles to support students and teachers engaging in argumentation in the classroom, these environments will offer even more valuable resources for developing students' scientific literacy along with critical 21st century skills.

REFERENCES

Abell, S. K., Anderson, G., & Chezem, J. (2000). Science as argument and explanation: Exploring concepts of sound in third grade. In J. Minstrell & E. H. Van Zee (Eds.), *Inquiry into InquiryLearning and Teaching in Science* (pp. 100-119). Washington DC: American Association for the Advancement of Science.

American Association for the Advancement of Science. (1993). *Benchmarks for science literacy.* New York: Oxford University Press.

Andriessen, J., Baker, M., & Suthers, D. (2003). Argumentation, computer support, and the educational contexts of confronting cognitions. In J. Andriessen, M. Baker & D. Suthers (Eds.), *Arguing to learn: Confronting cognitions in computer-supported collaborative learning environments* (pp. 1-25). Dordrecht, The Netherlands: Kluwer Academic Publishers.

Barron, B. (2003). When smart groups fail. *Journal of the Learning Sciences, 12,* 307–359. doi:10.1207/S15327809JLS1203_1

Beers, P., Kirschner, P. A., Boshuizen, H. P. A., & Gijselaers, W. (2007). ICT-support for grounding in the classroom. *Instructional Science, 35,* 535–556. doi:10.1007/s11251-007-9018-5

Bell, P. (1997). Using argument representations to make thinking visible for individuals and groups. In R. Hall, N. Miyake & N. Enyedy (Eds.), *Proceedings of the Second International Conference on Computer Support for Collaborative Learning (CSCL 1997)* (pp. 10-19). Toronto: Toronto University Press.

Bell, P. (2004). Promoting students' argument construction and collaborative debate in the science classroom. In M. C. Linn, E. A. Davis & P. Bell (Eds.), *Internet environments for science education* (pp. 115-143). Mahwah, NJ: Erlbaum.

Bell, P., & Linn, M. C. (2000). Scientific arguments as learning artifacts: Designing for learning from the web with KIE. *International Journal of Science Education, 22*(8), 797–817. doi:10.1080/095006900412284

Berland, L., & Reiser, B. (2009). Making sense of argumentation and explanation. *Science Education, 93*(1), 26–55. doi:10.1002/sce.20286

Bransford, J. D., Brown, A. L., & Cocking, R. R. (2000). *How People Learn: Brain, Mind, Experience, and School*. Washington, DC: National Academic Press.

Carey, S., Evans, R., Honda, M., Jay, E., & Unger, C. (1989). An experiment is when you try it and see if it works: A study of grade 7 students' understanding of the construction of scientific knowledge. *International Journal of Science Education, 11*(Special Issue), 514–529. doi:10.1080/0950069890110504

Carmien, S., Kollar, C., Fischer, G., & Fischer, F. (2007). The interplay of internal and external scripts. In F. Fischer, H. Mandl, J. Haake & I. Kollar (Eds.), *Scripting computer-supported communication of knowledge - cognitive, computational and educational perspectives* (pp. 303-324). New York: Springer.

Carr, C. S. (2003). Using computer supported argument visualization to teach legal argumentation. In P. A. Kirschner, S. J. Buckingham Shum, & C. S. Carr (Eds.), *Visualizing argumentation. Software tools for collaborative and educational sense-making* (pp. 75–96). London: Springer.

Clark, D. B. (2004). Hands-on investigation in Internet environments: Teaching thermal equilibrium. In M. C. Linn, E. A. Davis., & P. Bell (Eds.), *Internet Environments for Science Education* (pp. 175-200). Mahwah, NJ: Lawrence Erlbaum Associates.

Clark, D. B. (2006). Longitudinal conceptual change in students' understanding of thermal equilibrium: An examination of the process of conceptual restructuring. *Cognition and Instruction, 24*(4), 467–563. doi:10.1207/s1532690xci2404_3

Clark, D. B., D'Angelo, C. M., & Menekse, M. (2009). Initial structuring of online discussions to improve learning and argumentation: Incorporating students' own explanations as seed comments versus an augmented-preset approach to seeding discussions. *Journal of Science Education and Technology, 18*(4), 321–333. doi:10.1007/s10956-009-9159-1

Clark, D. B., & Linn, M. C. (2003). Scaffolding knowledge integration through curricular depth. *Journal of the Learning Sciences, 12*(4), 451–494. doi:10.1207/S15327809JLS1204_1

Clark, D. B., Menekse, M., D'Angelo, C., Touchman, S., & Schleigh, S. (2008). *Scaffolding students' argumentation about simulations*. Paper presented as part of a symposium organized by Hsin-Yi Chang to the International Conference of the Learning Sciences (ICLS) 2008, Utrecht, Netherlands.

Clark, D. B., & Sampson, V. (2005, June). *Analyzing The Quality Of Argumentation Supported By Personally-Seeded Discussions*. Paper presented at the annual meeting of the Computer Supported Collaborative Learning (CSCL) Conference, Taipei, Taiwan.

Clark, D. B., & Sampson, V. (2006, July). *Evaluating argumentation in science: New assessment tools.* Paper presented at the International Conference of the Learning Sciences 2006, Bloomington, Indiana.

Clark, D. B., & Sampson, V. (2008). Assessing dialogic argumentation in online environments to relate structure, grounds, and conceptual quality. To appear in *Journal of Research in Science Teaching, 45*(3), 6.

Clark, D. B., Sampson, V., Weinberger, A., & Erkens, G. (2007). Analytic frameworks for assessing dialogic argumentation in online learning environments. *Educational Psychology Review, 19*(3), 343–374. doi:10.1007/s10648-007-9050-7

Clark, D. B., & Sampson, V. D. (2007). Personally-Seeded Discussions to scaffold online argumentation. *International Journal of Science Education, 29*(3), 253–277. doi:10.1080/09500690600560944

Clough, E. E., & Driver, R. (1985). Secondary students' conceptions of the conduction of heat: Bringing together scientific and personal views. *Physical Educator, 20*, 176–182. doi:10.1088/0031-9120/20/4/309

Cognition and Technology Group at Vanderbilt. (1997). *The Jasper Project: Lessons in curriculum, instruction, assessment, and professional development.* Mahwah, NJ: Erlbaum.

Cohen, E. G. (1994). Restructuring the classroom: Conditions for productive small groups. *Review of Educational Research, 64*, 1–35.

Cox, R. (1999). Representation construction, externalized cognition and individual differences. *Learning and Instruction, 9*(4), 343–363. doi:10.1016/S0959-4752(98)00051-6

Cuthbert, A. J., Clark, D. B., & Linn, M. C. (2002). WISE learning communities: Design considerations. In K.A. Renninger & W. Shumar (Eds.), *Building Virtual Communities: Learning and Change in Cyberspace* (pp. 215-246). Cambridge, MA: Cambridge University Press.

Damsa, C. I., Erkens, G., & Janssen, J. (2007). Discourse synthesis: A research study on the use of semantic information for collaborative writing in secondary education. In B. Csapo & C. Csikos (Eds.), *Proceedings of the 12th conference of the European Association for Research on Learning and Instruction (EARLI)* (pp. 713). Budapest, Hungary: Graduate School of Education, University of Szeged, Faculty of Arts.

Davis, E. A. (2003). Prompting middle school science students for productive reflection: Generic and directed prompts. *Journal of the Learning Sciences, 12*(1), 91–142. doi:10.1207/S15327809JLS1201_4

Davis, E. A., & Linn, M. C. (2000). Scaffolding students' knowledge integration: Prompts for reflection in KIE. *International Journal of Science Education, 22*(8), 819–837. doi:10.1080/095006900412293

de Vries, E., Lund, K., & Baker, M. (2002). Computer-mediated epistemic dialogue: explanation and argumentation as vehicles for understanding scientific notions. *Journal of the Learning Sciences, 11*(1), 63–103. doi:10.1207/S15327809JLS1101_3

Dillenbourg, P. (2002). Over-scripting CSCL: The risks of blending collaborative learning with instructional design. In P. A. Kirschner (Ed.), *Three worlds of CSCL: Can we support CSCL?* (pp. 61-91). Heerlen, The Netherlands: Open University of the Netherlands.

Dillenbourg, P., & Jermann, P. (2007). Designing integrative scripts. In F. Fischer, H. Mandl, J. Haake & I. Kollar (Eds.), Scripting computer-supported communication of knowledge - cognitive, computational and educational perspectives (pp. 275-301). New York: Springer.

Driver, R., Newton, P., & Osborne, J. (2000). Establishing the norms of scientific argumentation in classrooms. *Science Education*, *84*(3), 287–313. doi:10.1002/(SICI)1098-237X(200005)84:3<287::AID-SCE1>3.0.CO;2-A

Duschl, R. (2000). Making the nature of science explicit. In R. Millar, J. Leach & J. Osborne (Eds.), *Improving science education: The contribution of research*. Philadelphia, PA: Open University Press.

Duschl, R. A., & Osborne, J. (2002). Supporting and promoting argumentation discourse in science education. *Studies in Science Education*, *38*, 39–72. doi:10.1080/03057260208560187

Eisenberg, A., & Garvey, C. (1981). Children's use of verbal strategies in resolving conflict. *Discourse Processes*, *4*, 149–170. doi:10.1080/01638538109544512

Erduran, S., Simon, S., & Osborne, J. (2004). TAPping into argumentation: Developments in the application of Toulmin's argument pattern for studying science discourse. *Science Education*, *88*, 915–933. doi:10.1002/sce.20012

Erickson, G., & Tiberghien, A. (1985). Heat and temperature. In R. Driver, E. Guesne & A. Tiberghien (Eds.), *Children's ideas in science* (pp. 52-83). Philadelphia, PA: Open University Press.

Erkens, G. (1998). *Multiple episode protocol analysis (MEPA 4.0)*. Utrecht, The Netherlands: Department of Educational Sciences, Utrecht University.

Erkens, G., Jaspers, J., Prangsma, M., & Kanselaar, G. (2005). Coordination processes in computer supported collaborative writing. *Computers in Human Behavior*, *21*, 463–486. doi:10.1016/j.chb.2004.10.038

Fischer, F., Bruhn, J., Gräsel, C., & Mandl, H. (2002). Fostering collaborative knowledge construction with visualization tools. *Learning and Instruction*, *12*, 213–232. doi:10.1016/S0959-4752(01)00005-6

Fischer, F., Kollar, I., Mandl, H., & Haake, J. (Eds.). (2007). *Scripting computer-supported collaborative learning*. New York: Springer.

Fisher, C., & Larkin, J. H. (1986). *Diagrams as Working Memory for Scientific Problem Solving (Technical Report)*. Carnegie-Mellon University Department of Psychology.

Guzdial, M., & Turns, J. (2000). Effective discussion through a computer-mediated anchored forum. *Journal of the Learning Sciences*, *9*(4), 437–469. doi:10.1207/S15327809JLS0904_3

Harrison, A., G., Grayson, D., J., & Treagust, D., F. (1999). Investigating a grade 11 student's evolving conceptions of heat and temperature. *Journal of Research in Science Teaching*, *36*(1), 55–87. doi:10.1002/(SICI)1098-2736(199901)36:1<55::AID-TEA5>3.0.CO;2-P

Hesse, F. (2007). Being told to do something or just being aware of something? An alternative approach to scripting in CSCL. In F. Fischer, I. Kollar, H. Mandl, J., & Haake (Eds.), *Scripting computer-supported communication of knowledge - cognitive, computational and educational perspectives* (pp. 91-98). New York: Springer.

Hogan, K., & Maglienti, M. (2001). Comparing the epistemological underpinnings of students' and scientists' reasoning about conclusions. *Journal of Research in Science Teaching*, *38*(6), 663–687. doi:10.1002/tea.1025

Houston, J. (2007). *Future skill demands, from a corporate consultant perspective*. Presentation at the National Academies Workshop on Research Evidence Related to Future Skill Demands. Retrieved July 3, 2007, from http://www7.nationalacademies.org/cfe/Future_Skill_Demands_Presentations.html

Hron, A., Hesse, F. W., Reinhard, P., & Picard, E. (1997). Strukturierte Kooperation beim computerunterstutzten kollaborativen Lernen. *Unterrichtswissenschaft, 25*, 56–69.

Hsi, S., & Hoadley, C. M. (1997). Productive discussion in science: Gender equity through electronic discourse. *Journal of Science Education and Technology, 6*(1), 23–36. doi:10.1023/A:1022564817713

Janssen, J., Erkens, G., Jaspers, J., & Kanselaar, G. (2006, June/July). Visualizing participation to facilitate argumentation. In *Proc. of the 7th Intl. Conf. of the Learning Sciences*, Bloomington, IN.

Janssen, J., Erkens, G., Jaspers, J., & Kanselaar, G. (2007). Visualization of participation: Does it contribute to successful computer-supported collaborative learning? *Computers & Education, 49*, 1037–1065. doi:10.1016/j.compedu.2006.01.004

Janssen, J., Erkens, G., & Kanselaar, G. (2007). Visualization of agreement and discussion processes during computer-supported collaborative learning. *Computers in Human Behavior, 23*, 1105–1125. doi:10.1016/j.chb.2006.10.005

Janssen, J., Erkens, G., Kirschner, P. A., & Kanselaar, G. (in press). Effects of representational guidance during computer-supported collaborative learning. *Instructional Science*.

Jeong, A., Clark, D. B., Sampson, V. D., & Menekse, M. (in press). Sequentially analyzing dialogical scientific argumentation across asynchronous online discussion environments. In S. Puntambekar, G. Erkens, & C. Hmelo-Silver (Eds.), *Interactions in CSCL: Methodologies, Approaches and Issues*. The Netherlands: Springer.

Jermann, P., & Dillenbourg, P. (2003). Elaborating new arguments through a CSCL script. In J. Andriessen, M. Baker & D. Suthers (Eds.), *Arguing to learn: Confronting cognitions in computer-supported collaborative learning environments* (pp. 205-226). Dordrecht, NL: Kluwer Academic Publishers.

Jermann, P., & Dillenbourg, P. (2008). Group mirrors to support interaction regulation in collaborative problem solving. *Computers & Education, 51*, 279–296. doi:10.1016/j.compedu.2007.05.012

Jermann, P., Soller, A., & Muehlenbrock, M. (2001). *From mirroring to guiding: a review of state of art technology for supporting collaborative learning*. Paper presented at the European Computer Supported Collaborative Learning Conference (EU-CSCL'01), Maastricht, NL.

Jimenez-Aleixandre, M., Rodriguez, M., & Duschl, R. A. (2000). 'Doing the lesson' or 'doing science': Argument in high school genetics. *Science Education, 84*(6), 757–792. doi:10.1002/1098-237X(200011)84:6<757::AID-SCE5>3.0.CO;2-F

Joiner, R., & Jones, S. (2003). The effects of communication medium on argumentation and the development of critical thinking. *International Journal of Educational Research, 39*(8), 861–971. doi:10.1016/j.ijer.2004.11.008

Kiili, C., Laurinen, L., & Marttunen, M. (2008). *Argumentointikaavio lukiolaisten internetlukemisen apuna [Argument diagram as an aid for Internet reading among secondary school students]*. Paper presented at the annual conference of the Finnish Educational Research Association (FERA), 27.-28.11.2008, Turku, Finland.

King, A. (2007). Scripting collaborative learning processes: A cognitive perspective. In F. Fischer, H. Mandl, J. Haake & I. Kollar (Eds.), *Scripting computer-supported communication of knowledge - cognitive, computational and educational perspectives* (pp. 275-301). New York: Springer.

Kirschner, P. A., Buckingham Shum, S. J., & Carr, C. S. (Eds.). (2003). *Visualizing argumentation: software tools for collaborative and educational sense-making*. London: Springer.

Kobbe, L., Weinberger, A., Dillenbourg, P., Harrer, A., Hämäläinen, R., & Fischer, F. (2007). Specifying computer-supported collaboration scripts. *International Journal of Computer-Supported Collaborative Learning, 2*(2-3), 211–224. doi:10.1007/s11412-007-9014-4

Kollar, I., Fischer, F., & Hesse, F. W. (2006). Collaboration scripts – a conceptual analysis. *Educational Psychology Review, 18*(2), 159–185. doi:10.1007/s10648-006-9007-2

Kollar, I., Fischer, F., & Slotta, J. D. (2007). Internal and external scripts in computer-supported collaborative inquiry learning. *Learning and Instruction, 17*(6), 708–721. doi:10.1016/j.learninstruc.2007.09.021

Kollar, I., Fischer, F., & Slotta, J. D. (2008). Argumentation in web-based collaborative inquiry learning: Scripts for writing and scripts for talking aren't the same. In *Proceedings of the Conference of the International Society of the Learning Sciences*. Utrecht, The Netherlands.

Kolodner, J. L., Schwarz, B., Barkai, R. D., Levy-Neumand, E., Tcherni, A., & Turbovsk, A. (1997). Roles of a case library as a collaborative tool for fostering argumentation. In R. Hall, N. Miyake & N. Enyedy (Eds.), *Proceedings of the 1997 computer support for collaborative learning (CSCL 97)* (pp. 150-156). Hillsdale, NJ: Erlbaum.

Kopp, B., & Mandl, H. (2007). Fostering argumentation with script and content scheme in videoconferencing. In *Proceedings of the Computer Supported Collaborative Learning Conference*, 2007.

Kuhn, D. (1989). Children and adults as intuitive scientists. *Psychological Review, 96*(4), 674–689. doi:10.1037/0033-295X.96.4.674

Kuhn, D. (1993). Science as argument: Implications for teaching and learning scientific thinking. *Science Education, 77*(3), 319–337. doi:10.1002/sce.3730770306

Kuhn, D., & Goh, W. W. L. (2005). Arguing on the computer. In T. Koschmann, D. Suthers & T. W. Chan (Eds.), *Computer Supported Collaborative Learning 2005: The Next 10 Years* (pp. 125-134). Mahwah, NJ: Lawrence Erlbaum.

Kuhn, L., & Reiser, B. (2005). *Students constructing and defending evidence-based scientific explanations*. Paper presented at the annual meeting of the National Association for Research in Science Teaching, Dallas, TX.

Kuhn, L., & Reiser, B. (2006). *Structuring activities to foster argumentative discourse*. Paper presented at the annual meeting of the American Educational Research Association, San Francisco, CA.

Lawson, A. (2003). The nature and development of hypothetico-predictive argumentation with implications for science teaching. *International Journal of Science Education, 25*(11), 1387–1408. doi:10.1080/0950069032000052117

Leitão, S. (2000). The potential of argument in knowledge building. *Human Development, 43*, 332–360. doi:10.1159/000022695

Levy, F., & Murnane, R. J. (2004). *The new division of labor: How computers are creating the next job market*. Princeton, NJ: Princeton University Press.

Lewis, E. L. (1996). Conceptual change among middle school students studying elementary thermodynamics. *Journal of Science Education and Technology, 5*(1), 3–31. doi:10.1007/BF01575468

Linn, M. C., & Burbules, N. (1993). Construction of knowledge and group learning. In K. Tobin (Ed.), *The practice of constructivism in science education* (pp. 91-119). Washington, DC: American Association for the Advancement of Science.

Linn, M. C., & Eylon, B.-S. (2006). Science Education: Integrating views of learning and instruction. In P. Alexander & P. H. Winne (Eds.), *Handbook of Educational Psychology* (pp. 511-544). Mahwah, NJ: Lawrence Erlbaum Associates.

Linn, M. C., & Hsi, S. (2000). *Computers, teachers, peers: Science learning partners*. Mahwah, NJ: Lawrence Erlbaum Associates.

Lund, K., Molinari, G., Séjourné, A., & Baker, M. (2007). How do argumentation diagrams compare when student pairs use them as a means for debate or as a tool for representing debate? *Computer-Supported Collaborative Learning*, 2(2-3), 273–295. doi:10.1007/s11412-007-9019-z

Mäkitalo, K., Weinberger, A., Häkkinen, P., Järvelä, S., & Fischer, F. (2005). Epistemic cooperation scripts in online learning environments: Fostering learning by reducing uncertainty in discourse? *Computers in Human Behavior*, 21(4), 603–622. doi:10.1016/j.chb.2004.10.033

Marttunen, M. (1992). Commenting on written arguments as a part of argumentation skills: Comparison between students engaged in traditional vs on-line study. *Scandinavian Journal of Educational Research*, 36(4), 289–302. doi:10.1080/0031383920360404

Marttunen, M., & Laurinen, L. (2001). Learning of argumentation skills in networked and face-to-face environments. *Instructional Science*, 29, 127–153. doi:10.1023/A:1003931514884

Marttunen, M., & Laurinen, L. (2006). Collaborative learning through argument visualisation in secondary school. In S. N. Hogan (Ed.) *Trends in learning research* (pp. 119-138). New York: Nova Science Publishers.

Marttunen, M., & Laurinen, L. (2007). Collaborative learning through chat discussions and argument diagrams in secondary school. *Journal of Research on Technology in Education*, 40(1), 109–126.

McNeill, K. L., & Krajcik, J. (in press). Middle school students' use of appropriate and inappropriate evidence in writing scientific explanations. In M. Lovett & P. Shah (Eds.), *Thinking with data: The proceedings of 33rd Carnegie Symposium on Cognition*. Mahwah, NJ: Lawrence Erlbaum Associates, Inc.

McNeill, K. L., Lizotte, D. J., Krajcik, J., & Marx, R. W. (2006). Supporting students' construction of scientific explanations by fading scaffolds in instructional materials. *Journal of the Learning Sciences*, 15(2), 153–191. doi:10.1207/s15327809jls1502_1

Michinov, N., & Primois, C. (2005). Improving productivity and creativity in online groups through social comparison process: New evidence for asynchronous electronic brainstorming. *Computers in Human Behavior*, 21, 11–28. doi:10.1016/j.chb.2004.02.004

Munneke, L., Andriessen, J., Kirschner, P., & Kanselaar, G. (2007, July). *Effects of synchronous and asynchronous CMC on interactive argumentation*. Paper to be presented at the CSCL 2007 Conference, New Brunswick, NY.

National Research Council. (2000). *How People Learn: Brain, Mind, Experience, and School*. Washington, DC: National Academies Press.

National Research Council. (2008). *Research on Future Skill Demands: A Workshop Summary*. Washington, DC: National Academies Press.

Newton, P., Driver, R., & Osborne, J. (1999). The place of argumentation in the pedagogy of school science. *International Journal of Science Education*, 21(5), 553–576. doi:10.1080/095006999290570

Novak, J. D. (1998). *Learning, creating, and using knowledge: concept maps as facilitative tools in schools and corporations*. Mahwah, NJ: Lawrence Erlbaum Associates.

Oestermeier, U., & Hesse, F. (2000). Verbal and visual causal arguments. *Cognition, 75,* 65–104. doi:10.1016/S0010-0277(00)00060-3

Ohlsson, S. (1992). The cognitive skill of theory articulation: A neglected aspect of science education? *Science & Education, 1,* 181–192. doi:10.1007/BF00572838

Osborne, J., Erduran, S., & Simon, S. (2004). Enhancing the quality of argumentation in science classrooms. *Journal of Research in Science Teaching, 41*(10), 994–1020. doi:10.1002/tea.20035

Passmore, C., & Stewart, J. (2002). A modeling approach to teaching evolutionary biology in high schools. *Journal of Research in Science Teaching, 39*(3), 185–204. doi:10.1002/tea.10020

Pea, R. D. (1994). Seeing what we build together: Distributed multimedia learning environments for transformative communications. Special Issue: Computer support for collaborative learning. *Journal of the Learning Sciences, 3*(3), 285–299. doi:10.1207/s15327809jls0303_4

Pea, R. D. (2004). The social and technological dimensions of scaffolding and related theoretical concepts for learning, education, and human activity. *Journal of the Learning Sciences, 13*(3), 423–451. doi:10.1207/s15327809jls1303_6

Pfister, H.-R. (2005). How to support synchronous net-based learning discourses: Principles and perspectives. In R. Bromme, F. Hesse & H. Spada (Eds.), *Barriers and biases in computer-mediated knowledge communication* (pp. 39-57). New York: Springer.

Pfister, H.-R., & Mühlpfordt, M. (2002). Supporting discourse in a synchronous learning environment: The learning protocol approach. In G. Stahl (Ed.), *Proceedings of the Conference on Computer Supported Collaborative Learning (CSCL) 2002,* Erlbaum, Hillsdale (pp. 581-589).

Phielix, C., Prins, F. J., & Kirschner, P. A. (2009). *The design of peer feedback and reflection tools in a CSCL environment.* Paper to be presented at the Computer Supported Collaborative Learning Conference 2009, 8-13 June 2009, Rhodes, Greece.

Pressley, M., & Gaskins, I. W. (2006). Metacognitively competent reading comprehension is constructively responsive reading: How can such reading be developed in students? *Metacognition and Learning, 1*(1), 99–113. doi:10.1007/s11409-006-7263-7

Pulakos, E. D., Arad, S., Donovan, M. A., & Plamondon, K. E. (2000). Adaptability in the workplace: Development of a taxonomy of adaptive performance. *The Journal of Applied Psychology, 85,* 612–624. doi:10.1037/0021-9010.85.4.612

Reiser, B. J. (2002). Why scaffolding should sometimes make tasks more difficult for learners. In G. Stahl (Ed.), *Computer Support for Collaborative Learning: Foundations for a CSCL community. Proceedings of CSCL 2002* (pp. 255-264). Hillsdale, NJ: Lawrence Erlbaum Associates, Inc.

Reiser, B. J., Tabak, I., Sandoval, W. A., Smith, B. K., Steinmuller, F., & Leone, A. J. (2001). BGuILE: Strategic and conceptual scaffolds for scientific inquiry in biology classrooms. In S. M. Carver & D. Klahr (Eds.), *Cognition and instruction: Twenty-five years of progress* (pp. 263-305). Mahwah, NJ: Erlbaum.

Rogoff, B. (1998). Cognition as a collaborative process. In D. S. Kuhn & R. W. Damon (Eds.), *Cognition, perception and language* (5th ed.) (Vol. 2, pp. 679-744). New York: Wiley.

Rummel, N., & Spada, H. (2005). Learning to collaborate: An instructional approach to promoting collaborative problem-solving in computer-mediated settings. *Journal of the Learning Sciences, 14*(2), 201–241. doi:10.1207/s15327809jls1402_2

Sadler, T. (2004). Informal reasoning regarding socioscientific issues: A critical review of the research. *Journal of Research in Science Teaching, 41*(5), 513–536. doi:10.1002/tea.20009

Salminen, T., Marttunen, M., & Laurinen, L. (2007). Collaborative argument diagrams based on dyadic computer chat discussions. In Kinshuk, D.G. Sampson, J.M. Spector & P. Isaias (Eds.), *Proceedings of the IADIS International Conference on Cognition and Exploratory Learning in Digital Age,* December 7–9, 2007, Algarve, Portugal (pp. 197-204).

Sampson, V., & Clark, D. (2008). Assessment of the ways students generate arguments in science education: Current perspectives and recommendations for future directions. *Science Education, 92*(3), 447–472. doi:10.1002/sce.20276

Sandoval, W. A. (2003). Conceptual and epistemic aspects of students' scientific explanations. *Journal of the Learning Sciences, 12*(1), 5–51. doi:10.1207/S15327809JLS1201_2

Sandoval, W. A., & Millwood, K. A. (2005). The quality of students' use of evidence in written scientific explanations. *Cognition and Instruction, 23*(1), 23–55. doi:10.1207/s1532690xci2301_2

Sandoval, W. A., & Reiser, B. J. (2004). Explanation-driven inquiry: Integrating conceptual and epistemic supports for science inquiry. *Science Education, 88*, 345–372. doi:10.1002/sce.10130

Schellens, T., & Valcke, M. (2006). Fostering knowledge conctruction in university students through asynchronous discussion groups. *Computers & Education, 46*(4), 349–370. doi:10.1016/j.compedu.2004.07.010

Schwarz, B., & Glassner, A. (2003). The blind and the paralytic: Supporting argumentation in everyday and scientific issues. In *Arguing to learn: Confronting cognitions in computer-supported collaborative learning environments* (pp. 227-260). Amsterdam: Kluwer Academic Publishers.

Schwarz, B. B., & Glassner, A. (in press). The role of CSCL argumentative environments for broadening and deepening understanding of the space of debate. In R. Saljo (Ed.), *Information Technologies and Transformation of Knowledge.*

Siegel, H. (1989). The rationality of science, critical thinking and science education. *Synthese, 80*(1), 9–42. doi:10.1007/BF00869946

Simon, S., Erduran, S., & Osborne, J. (2006). Learning to teach argumentation: Research and development in the science classroom. *International Journal of Science Education, 28*(2-3), 235–260. doi:10.1080/09500690500336957

Slof, B., & Erkens, G. Kirschner, P. A. (2008). Matching model representations to task demands. In *Proceedings of the 8th International Conference of The Learning Sciences,* Utrecht, The Netherlands.

Stahl, G. (2007). Scripting group cognition. In F. Fischer, H. Mandl, J. Haake & I. Kollar (Eds.), *Scripting computer-supported communication of knowledge - cognitive, computational and educational perspectives* (pp. 327-335). New York: Springer.

Stegmann, K., Wecker, C., Weinberger, A., & Fischer, F. (2007). Collaborative Argumentation and Cognitive Processing - An Empirical Study in a Computer-Supported Collaborative Learning Environment. In C. Chinn, G. Erkens, & S. Puntambekar (Eds.), *Mice, minds, and society. CSCL 2007* (pp. 661-670). New Brunswick, CT: ISLS.

Stegmann, K., Weinberger, A., & Fischer, F. (2007). Facilitating argumentative knowledge construction with computer-supported collaboration scripts. *International Journal of Computer-Supported Collaborative Learning, 2*(4), 421–447. doi:10.1007/s11412-007-9028-y

Stein, N. L., & Bernas, R. (1999). The early emergence of argumentative knowledge and skill. In G. Rijlaarsdam, E. Esperet, J. Andriessen & P. Coirier (Eds.), *Studies in writing: Vol 5. Foundations of Argumentative text processing*. Amsterdam: University of Amsterdam Press.

Stein, N. L., & Miller, C. (1991). I win... you lose: The development of argumentative thinking. In J. F. Voss, D. N. Perkins & J. W. Segal (Eds.), *Informal reasoning and instruction*. Hillsdale, NJ: Lawrence Erlbaum.

Suthers, D. (2008). Empirical studies of the value of conceptually explicit notations in collaborative learning. In A. Okada, S. Buckingham Shum & T. Sherborne (Eds.), Knowledge Cartography. Software tools and mapping techniques (pp. 1-23). London: Springer.

Suthers, D. D., & Hundhausen, C. D. (2001). Learning by constructing collaborative representations: An empirical comparison of three alternatives. In P. Dillenbourg, A. Eurelings, & K. Hakkarainen (Eds.), *European perspectives on computer-supported collaborative learning* (pp. 577-592). Maastricht, The Netherlands: University of Maastricht.

Suthers, D. D., Hundhausen, C. D., & Girardeau, L. E. (2003). Comparing the roles of representations in face-to-face and online computer supported collaborative learning. *Computers & Education, 41*(4), 335–351. doi:10.1016/j.compedu.2003.04.001

Teasley, S. (1997). Talking about reasoning: How important is the peer in peer collaboration? In L. B. Resnick, R. Säljö, C. Pontecorvo, & B. Burge (Eds.), *Discourse, tools and reasoning: Essays on situated cognition* (pp. 361-384). Berlin, Germany: Springer.

Toulmin, S. (1958). *The uses of argument*. Cambridge, MA: Cambridge University Press.

Twardy, C. R. (2004). Argument maps improve critical thinking. *Teaching Philosophy, 27*(2), 95–116.

van Amelsvoort, M. (2006). *A space of debate. How diagrams support collaborative argumentation-based learning*. Dutch Interuniversity Center for Educational Research (ICO). Enschede, Netherlands: PrintPartners Ipskamp.

van Boxtel, C., & Veerman, A. (2001). Diagram-mediated collaborative learning. Diagrams as tools to provoke and support elaboration and argumentation. In P. Dillenbourg, A. Eurelings, & K. Hakkarainen (Eds.), *European perspective on computer-supported collaborative learning. Proceedings of the First European conference on computer-supported collaborative learning* (pp. 131–138). Universiteit Maastricht, the Netherlands.

van Drie, J., Van Boxtel, C., Jaspers, J., & Kanselaar, G. (2005). Effects of representational guidance on domain specific reasoning in CSCL. *Computers in Human Behavior, 21*, 575–602. doi:10.1016/j.chb.2004.10.024

van Gelder, T. (2002). Argument mapping with Reason!Able. *The American Philosophical Association Newsletter on Philosophy and Computers*, 85-90.

Vellom, R. P., & Anderson, C. W. (1999). Reasoning about data in middle school science. *Journal of Research in Science Teaching, 36*(2), 179–199. doi:10.1002/(SICI)1098-2736(199902)36:2<179::AID-TEA5>3.0.CO;2-T

Wecker, C., & Fischer, F. (2007). Fading Scripts in Computer-Supported Collaborative Learning: The Role of Distributed Monitoring. In C. Chinn, G. Erkens & S. Puntambekar (Hrsg.), *Mice, minds, and society. Proceedings of the CSCL 2007. Computer Supported Collaborative Learning*, Rutgers University, New Brunswick, New Jersey, USA.

Wecker, C., & Fischer, F. (2009, August). *Preventing relapses into novice strategies during the fading of instructional scripts: The role of distributed control*. Paper presented *at EARLI 2009*.

Weinberger, A. (2008). *CSCL scripts: Effects of social and epistemic scripts on computer-supported collaborative learning*. Berlin, Germany: VDM Verlag.

Weinberger, A., Clark, D. B., Häkkinen, P., Tamura, Y., & Fischer, F. (2007). Argumentative knowledge construction in online learning environments in and across different cultures: A collaboration script perspective. *Research in Comparative and International Education, 2,* 68–79. doi:10.2304/rcie.2007.2.1.68

Weinberger, A., Ertl, B., Fischer, F., & Mandl, H. (2005). Epistemic and social scripts in computer-supported collaborative learning. *Instructional Science, 33*(1), 1–30. doi:10.1007/s11251-004-2322-4

Weinberger, A., & Fischer, F. (2006). A framework to analyze argumentative knowledge construction in computer-supported collaborative learning. *Computers & Education, 46*(1), 71–95. doi:10.1016/j.compedu.2005.04.003

Weinberger, A., Fischer, F., & Mandl, H. (2001). *Scripts and scaffolds in text-based CSCL: fostering participation and transfer.* Paper presented at the 8th European Conference for Research on Learning and Instruction, Fribourg (Switzerland).

Weinberger, A., Laurinen, L., Stegmann, K., & Marttunen, M. (2009). *Inducing socio-cognitive conflict into Finnish and German groups of online learners.* Paper presented at the 13th Biennial EARLI Conference.

Weinberger, A., Reiserer, M., Ertl, B., Fischer, F., & Mandl, H. (2005). Facilitating collaborative knowledge construction in computer-mediated learning with cooperation scripts. In R. Bromme, F. Hesse & H. Spada (Eds.), *Barriers and biases in computer-mediated knowledge communication - and how they may be overcome* (pp. 15-37). Boston: Kluwer.

Weinberger, A., Stegmann, K., & Fischer, F. (in press). Learning to argue online: Scripted groups surpass individuals (unscripted groups do not). *Computers in Human Behavior.*

Weinberger, A., Stegmann, K., Fischer, F., & Mandl, H. (2007). Scripting argumentative knowledge construction in computer-supported learning environments. In F. Fischer, I. Kollar, H. Mandl, & J. Haake (Eds.), *Scripting computer-supported communication of knowledge - cognitive, computational and educational perspectives* (pp. 191-211). New York: Springer.

Weiner, B. (1985). An attributional theory of achievement motivation and emotion. *Psychological Review, 92,* 548–573. doi:10.1037/0033-295X.92.4.548

White, B. Y., & Frederiksen, J. R. (1998). Inquiry, modeling, and metacognition: Making science accessible to all students. *Cognition and Instruction, 16*(1), 3–118. doi:10.1207/s1532690xci1601_2

Zottmann, J., Dieckmann, P., Rall, M., Fischer, F., & Taraszow, T. (2006, June/July). *Fostering Simulation-based Learning in Medical Education with Collaboration Scripts.* Paper presented at the 12th Annual Meeting of the Society in Europe for Simulation Applied to Medicine (SESAM), Porto, Portugal.

AUTHOR NOTE

An earlier version of this paper was first presented at a workshop titled *Exploring the Intersection of Science Education and the Development of 21st Century Skills* at the National Academy of Science in Washington, D.C., USA, in February 2009. This material is based upon research supported by The National Science Foundation (NSF) under grant No. REC 98-05420 (TELS/WISE), The Netherlands Organization for Scientific Research under project number 411-02-121 (VCRI), The Academy of Finland (DREW), and The Deutsche Forschungsgemeinschaft (CASSIS).

Chapter 2
Negotiations of Meaning with MOODLE:
Concept, Implementation and Experiences

Marco Bettoni
Swiss Distance University of Applied Sciences, Switzerland

ABSTRACT

In this chapter we present a design for an e-collaboration environment and its implementation with MOODLE within the context of a research knowledge network at our university. In the first part, after a short introduction of our constructivist knowledge model, we present our idea of what we call a "design for meaning", explaining its theoretical foundation and developing its conceptual features. In the second part we show how we have implemented this concept with Moodle for supporting a community-based knowledge network of researchers at our university and reflect on the experiences that we have collected during this 3 years pilot project.

INTRODUCTION AND BACKGROUND

For many years after its foundation in 1998, research activities at our university – the Swiss Distance University of Applied Sciences (FFHS) – have been too much isolated in the departments; at the same time human resources were dispersed, research knowledge did not flow enough, projects were small and less recognised, know-how got easily lost and research tools' development was too slow. In fall 2005 FFHS appointed me as director of the

DOI: 10.4018/978-1-61520-729-9.ch002

research department with the most urgent task of solving this problem.

One of the first activities of my team was a simple, but powerful analysis that consisted in distinguishing defects, their causes and measures leading to these causes (Fig. 1); this tool gave us a very helpful insight in some essential reasons for the defects and lead to a set of hypotheses for a possible solution.

We found that what we had to focus on as a primary source of the defects, was the combination of 3 elements that were characteristic for our academic institution: traditional hierarchical structures,

Figure 1. Defects analysis (⇐ is caused by; has consequence ⇒)

functional divisions based on course subjects and a radically decentralized organization characterized by weak ties (Granovetter 1973, 1983) . By generating a highly dispersed set of "knowledge islands" (Probst et al. 1999) this combination had negative consequences on the flow of knowledge and this again was to a large extent responsible for the insufficient level and quality of research performances.

Based on this defects analysis, the first hypothesis was that if we could increase and improve the knowledge flow, then also research performances would improve. But how to make knowledge flow better under conditions of weak ties and given a traditional structure of the organization with hierarchical levels, functional divisions and a conventional "command & control" approach to corporate governance and management?

The objective of this chapter is to sketch the solution that we developed, an e-collaboration environment, by focusing on its central design principle and by presenting several examples of its implementation.

The discipline of Knowledge Management (KM) has been dealing with the issue of knowledge flow for almost 20 years since the end of the 1980's decade and particularly the domain of knowledge networking seemed at first sight to be most suitable to our configuration as a radically distributed organization. After some pioneering publications and many implementations in the second half of the 1990's (Schmitz & Zucker 1996), Knowledge Networking became a focus of research in the beginning of the new millennium (Graggober et al. 2003; Lembke et al. 2005; Back et al. 2006); this work covered a wide range

of issues like for example: the proposal of global knowledge networks as a way to a more equitable society, the investigation of how to institutionalize knowledge networks in companies, the analysis and design of innovation networks, the role of ICT for enabling and the collection of best practices for facilitating knowledge networks.

Unfortunately in all these and similar investigations an essential component was missing or not explicitly stated and discussed: the fundamental principle or view that every person is inseparably bound to his or her (tacit) knowledge (Bettoni & Schneider 2002, 2003, Bettoni 2005).

The problem of "knowledge islands" is usually considered a very common and well known problem. Conventional organizations rely on two complementary ways for doing well their job: hierarchical levels (task subordination) and functional sectors (task domain). Their combination leads to clearly separated organizational entities (OE): these individual entities are valuable for accomplishing tasks and limiting information overflow but they also limit (and hinder) the knowledge flow. The problem seems to be clear and knowledge networking seems a good solution; but all approaches that have been proposed have failed in recognizing one essential aspect of this problem: that tasks and information can be easily separated from a person but tacit knowledge is inseparably bound to his or her owner. As a consequence, when the dominant approach to management is transferred to knowledge networking, it creates a fundamental conflict that it cannot resolve: *"How can the employee pawn his knowledge to the enterprise without doing harm to himself?"* (Bettoni, Clases & Wehner 2004).

CONSTRUCTIVIST KNOWLEDGE MODEL

The foundation of the mentioned principle that *"every person is inseparably bound to his or her tacit knowledge"* is Radical Constructivism (von Glasersfeld, 1995), which anchors the concept of knowledge more than ever in the human being (individually and socially). Under its influence knowledge and learning theory are moving from cognitivism and instructional design towards a more human-centered view of knowing and knowledge. For example according to Wenger et. al. (2002, pp. 8-10) the essence and uniqueness of knowledge is based on four central points:

- Knowledge lives in the human act of knowing
- Knowledge is tacit as well as explicit
- Knowledge is social as well as individual
- Knowledge is dynamic.

Accordingly knowledge can't be reduced to an object, but has to be considered as a "human factor".

This approach to knowledge as a human factor and not a merely economic resource, is consistent with the findings of Radical Constructivism, according to which knowledge can be characterized by four main features:

- inseparable (tacit knowledge constitutes identity)
- autopoietic (doing creates being)
- constructive (the How determines the What)
- objective (the logic of experience validates experience)

It is by taking seriously these characteristics then we can also reach an insight of huge importance for knowledge management: that tacit knowledge must not be separated from and dispossessed to the individual or group, which are creat-ing and cultivating it. Why must the knowledge owner of tacit knowledge not be dispossessed? Because whereas explicit knowledge is some-thing we «have», tacit knowledge is something we «are» and which therefore constitutes our identity. Dispossessing knowledge is then the same as negating the individual who owned it. The owner of knowledge (individual or group) cannot and should not be dispossessed of her tacit knowledge but should instead be recognized as the central agent from which decisions influencing quality, availability, access, use and other aspects of tacit knowledge depend.

Knowledge processes therefore cannot be cultivated in the same way as working or per-forming processes. The insight into the difference between the mode of having and being in regard to knowledge shows this very clearly. In knowledge management we are facing a similar dilemma as in life dealing with both basic attitudes towards human existence (Fromm, 1976): the one of hav-ing and the one of being.

KNOWLEDGE NETWORK AS A COP

Knowledge Networks can increase and improve the knowledge flow within an organization, but in order to be successful they need an interaction and collaboration approach in which tacit knowledge is respected as a constitutive element of human iden-tity. Since, due to the mentioned reasons, we could not find in the research literature a suitable weak ties collaboration model, we developed our own approach by conceiving, creating and cultivating CoRe (an acronym for **Co**mmunity of **Re**search), an intra-organizational knowledge network of researchers (academic staff, students) organized as a community of practice (Wenger 1998, 2002) connecting its members around the common task of *collaboratively stewarding research knowledge* and modeling their interactions with a "Knowledge Cooperation" approach (Bettoni 2005; Bettoni et al. 2006, 2007, 2008).

Our work of conceiving, launching and cultivating CoRe was different from the traditional design and development work done for other organizational structures or knowledge management systems. Communities need to be approached like living things: working with a community of practice actively and systematically is more like cultivating a plant than like building a machine. A machine or other artificial systems are built in their final state by assembling separate parts; a plant on the contrary does its own growing from a seed and evolves. As Wenger et al. remark (2002, pp. 12-13): "You cannot pull the stem, leaves or petals to make a plant grow faster or taller. However … you can till the soil … supply water, secure the right amount of sun exposure …". Similarly for communities of practice you have to develop an environment in which they can prosper and "bring out the community's own internal direction, character and energy" (Wenger et al. 2002, 51). Thus a CoP, like other organisms, cannot be really "developed": working with a CoP is rather a facilitation process where an appropriate environment is created in which it can emerge, grow and flourish. For that reason we will use in the following consistently the term "cultivation" where traditionally one would speak of "development".

The new and most challenging aspect of our concept was the way in which we designed the connection between the network members: in fact our idea – based on our constructivist view of knowledge (von Glasersfeld, 1995) - was to connect them around the common task of stewarding their research knowledge in a participative way (Bettoni, 2005).

DESIGN FOR MEANING: WHAT IS IT?

This raised the new and challenging research question of how to get and maintain a lasting engagement in a community of practice whose members have to collaborate under conditions of weak ties. One of the most common approaches to engagement in organizations is to look for incentives, for motivation (Bettoni et al. 2003). This may be a useful perspective in many organisational development initiatives, but in the case of community-based knowledge initiatives we claim that is not enough: the incentives view on engagement should be extended by a complementary and at least equally important consideration of the issue of "meaning".

In fact our knowledge is of course strongly related to motivation but probably much more intimately connected and directly influenced by our experience of meaning. More specifically our claim is that if we want to get enough engagement for stewarding knowledge in a community of practice, then we need to:

- better understand the human experience of meaning (in KM tasks)
- extend our community design by a design for meaning (in KM tasks)

A basic aspect of our engagement is that we thrive for experiencing our actions, our practice as meaningful; we do not simply want to get something done (a report written, an event organized, a request answered, etc.): what counts in what we do is always more than the result, it is the experience of meaning connected with that result. In the end the meaning we produce matters even more than the product or service we deliver.

The kind of meaning involved here is an experience of everyday life, the experience that what we did, are doing or plan to do "makes sense" to us. But how do we operate to produce these meanings and to put them in relation to the histories of meanings of which they are part? In his investigation of this issue Wenger (1998, p. 53) introduces the notion of negotiation of meaning as "the process by which we experience the world and our engagement in it as meaningful." This process has the following characteristics:

- an active, dynamic, historical process
- it affects the elements which shape it
- the meaning we experience is not imposed, it is produced, but not from scratch
- the meaning we experience is not pre-existing and not simply made up
- the meaning we experience does not exist as an independent entity outside the process
- the meaning we experience exists in the process (in fieri)

Which elements are necessary for constituting a process with these characteristics? Wenger proposes a model which distinguishes two constituent processes:

1. a process embodied in human operators, called participation
2. a process embodied in an artificial operand (artefact), called reification

The human operators contribute to the negotiation of meaning by their histories of interactions in the practices of a community. The artificial operand contributes to the negotiation of meaning by reflecting aspects of the practice of the community (histories of transformations). Thus the negotiation of meaning takes place as a convergence of two histories, that of the human operators and that of the artificial operands.

In Wenger's model participation is conceived as: a) the social experience of living in the world in terms of membership in social communities; b) active involvement in social enterprises. In the same model reification is seen as the process of giving form to our understandings, experiences, practice by producing objects which express them. Writing down a law, producing a tool or even even putting back a book in a shelf are examples of this process. Participation and reification are both distinct and complementary. They cannot be considered in isolation, they come as a pair. They form a unity in their duality (Wenger 1998, p. 62).

According to this model, our experience of meaning is viewed as a duality, as an interplay of participation and reification with the following implications: a) when you understand one, you should also understand the other; b) when one is given, you should wonder where the other is; c) when you enable one, you should also enable the other; d) one comes about through the other, but they cannot replace each other.

By taking seriously Wenger's theory and appreciating its potential impact on knowledge management we can now deduce the following **main guideline for our design for meaning**:

if meaning as a constituent of a social theory of learning should be viewed as a duality of participation and reification, then engagement in stewarding knowledge should be implemented as a duality of two corresponding processes, in our case participation in knowledge and cultivation of knowledge.

The right loop, cultivation of knowledge, is the circular process by which a community collaboratively stewards its knowledge resources (by processes like acquiring, developing, making transparent, sharing and preserving knowledge) and uses them in daily work. The left loop, participation in knowledge, is the circular process by which community members build social capital (establish and take care of personal relationships, develop individual and collective identities, etc.) and "invest" this social capital in collaboratively

Figure 2. Circular processes of knowledge co-operation

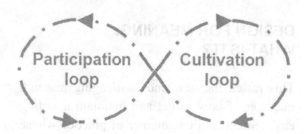

Figure 3. Navigation to the seven activity spaces of CoRe Square

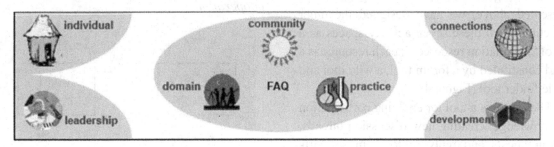

stewarding the knowledge resources of their community.

To conceive and implement participation and cultivation as a duality means that they should take place together, they should both require and enable each other. There should not be any cultivation without participation and no participation without cultivation.

Participation and cultivation should imply each other. Increasing the level of cultivation should not substitute an equal amount of participation; on the contrary it should tend to require an increase of participation. Cultivation of knowledge should always rest on participation in knowledge: applying knowledge requires a history of participation as a context for its interpretation. In turn, also participation in knowledge should rest on cultivation because it always involves words, concepts and artefacts that allow it to proceed.

Finally, the processes of participation and cultivation should not be considered just as a distinction between people (human operators) and explicit knowledge (artificial operands, things) that embody them. In terms of meaning, people and things cannot be defined independently of each other. On one hand our sense of ourselves includes the objects of our practice, on the other hand what these objects are depends on the people that shape them through their experiences.

IMPLEMENTATION & EXPERIENCES

The CoRe knowledge network has been cultivated at the Swiss Distance University of Applied Sciences for two main strategic purposes: 1) acquiring and realising major research projects; 2) integrating teaching and research (Bernhard & Bettoni, 2007). CoRe connects people doing research around the common task of stewarding their research knowledge in a participative way. Viewed as a social structure CoRe is constituted by seven basic elements, seven interaction and cooperation areas which correspond to aspects of community life. The individual elements are: 1) Community, 2) Practice, 3) Domain, 4) Leadership, 5) Individual, 6) Connections and 7) Resource Development. This concept is based on Etienne Wenger's social theory of learning and on his international online workshop "Foundations of Communities of Practice".

Since CoRe is a distributed community, interactions among its members are supported by an online collaboration platform on MOODLE called "CoRe Square", a virtual space for meeting community members and collaborate for stewarding research knowledge (Bettoni, Andenmatten & Mathieu 2006). The CoRe Square platform is designed as a "community cooperation space" for research tasks: for each aspect of community life in CoRe there is a corresponding cooperation area in CoRe Square collecting a specific set of resources that support and facilitate the activities in that area.

Following the "design for meaning" guideline presented above, we have designed the inner structure of all these seven activity spaces as a set of "negotiation resources": each resource is a triad constituted by a forum tool, a wiki tool and a file folder tool (Figure 4).

The forum is a tool for enabling participation in knowledge: creating new discussion threads, reading posts and replying to them supports participation as the social experience of being connected with other and being actively involved in a collective enterprise (stewarding research knowledge).

The wiki is a tool for enabling cultivation of knowledge that preserves the results of conversations (new ideas, insights, best practices, lessons learned, definitions, procedures, etc.) by organizing them in a structured way and independently of time.

Finally the file folder is a tool for storing the documents referenced either in the associated forum or in the associated wiki.

Following this design, in the final version of CoRe Square the seven activity spaces contained for example the following negotiation resources: a) *Core Team Meetings*: a forum for preparing and following up meetings of the community's core group and a wiki for meeting agendas, minutes and other contents related to the meetings; b) *Community Rules*: a forum for developing and reflecting about community rules and a wiki for making a systematic overview of these rules; c) *Research Strategy:* a wiki for collecting an overview of issues related to research strategy and a forum for developing a shared research strategy; d) *Conferences:* a forum for planning, preparing a contribution, reflecting about conference results and an associated wiki for a systematic collection of contents related to conference work and experiences; e) *Leadership Lounge:* a wiki where members can sign up for tasks and a forum for talking about engagement for the community; f) *Individual Hut*: an own forum ("personal blog") and an own wiki for each community member.

Figure 4. Negotiation Resource of knowledge cooperation

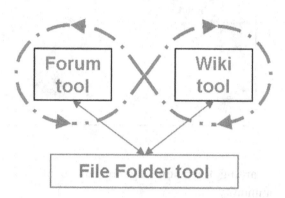

In the following sections we will present three of the most used negotiation resources (triads) of CoRe by sketching their background and components, describing the experiences we did and reflecting on the lessons learned from these experiences.

Core Group Meetings

During the community launch in June 2006 we identified 4 main topics for community cultivation in its first year: a) competence analysis, b) research strategy, c) incentives system and d) communication strategy. In my role as community coordinator my approach for addressing these topics was to build a strong core team and have its members work - with some support from the other community members - on the development of four community resources: a competence tool (Bettoni et al. 2007 b), a research strategy with a research plan draft, an incentives plan and an internet site about research at FFHS (Bettoni et al. 2007 c). Following a suggestion from Wenger et al. (2002, p. 88) I preferred to concentrate on making connections and fostering cooperation between core group members instead of involving peripheral members or recruiting new ones. In the first year (June 2006 to June 2007) the total amount of work (coordination, moderation, contributing contents, defining roles, organizing online events, etc.) that has been spent by the core group (which includes the coordinator) for keeping the group itself going, for cultivating the whole community (about 60 members) and updating the platform has been of about 0.8 FTE (full time equivalent) distributed over 6 persons: 3 of them each with 0.2 FTE and 3 of them with totally 0.2 FTE.

From the beginning of the core group development process the most important negotiation resource was that used for supporting regular "Technology Enhanced Meetings" (TEM). A TEM had typically 3 phases. First, in a pre-meeting phase, the core group members interacted to discuss a meeting place, a time and an agenda; people also could sign up for standard roles like facilitating the meeting or editing and publishing the minutes. In this stage the forum was used for announcing the coming meeting and discussing issues related to the agenda, the participants, the roles, the technology, etc. The associated wiki contained two main pages: 1) a "meeting calendar" which is a list of all previous meetings, with their dates and links to related minutes; 2) a "meeting agenda" with all the data of the current meeting (date, place, roles, etc.) followed by a structured list of topics to be discussed and their associated facilitators.

The second phase of the meeting was the synchronous phase for talking about the points listed in the agenda. Since we mostly could not meet face-to-face, we were happy to be able to use Skype technology: a meeting typically started in the chat window for coordinating participation and as soon as everybody was ready we added the Skype audio connection (VoIP). During the audio conversation the chat window was used for spelling words that were difficult to understand, for sharing URLs or other hints and for collaborating in writing the meeting minutes.

The third phase finally begun just after closing the synchronous Skype conversation: someone collected the minutes from the chat windows and produced a minutes document that included the complete chat transcript as well as a summary of the main points and a list of tasks (who does what when). When the minutes were ready the document was stored in the "meetings" files folder, an entry was added in the meeting calendar pointing to that document and an announcement was made in the forum that the minutes were ready for download. This thread in the forum became then the place for asking follow-up questions or making comments about the past meeting, its minutes and the list of tasks.

These regular technology enhanced meetings became one of the most important means for developing the core group because it provided to its members the opportunity to experience a new way of collaborating under conditions of weak ties: combining synchronous and asynchronous conversations, making summaries of conversations, storing documents, collaborating online on the development of a document and using a coordinated set of Web 2.0 tools.

Community Rules

After a few months of regular interactions within the core group of CoRe, members of this team reflected on their contributions to asynchronous conversations in forums and realized that they had collected some shared ideas about how to make the best use of this tool; this emerged when they compared formal aspects of postings (like subject line, opening posting, discussion thread, length of posting, multiple subjects in one posting, language, netiquette, etc.), discussed different use cases and identified good practices among the instances they had compared.

For example the subject line was handled basically in two ways: 1) as if it were the subject line of an email; 2) as a title in a newspaper article. In the first case a posting that was an answer to an existing posting received the same subject line as this one: this is what most people do, when they answer an email. It works well in an email box, but in the forum the consequence was that a discussion thread with say 3 sub-threads and 12 postings had 3 ramifications and 10 contributions that at first sight (when looking at the discussion in the outline format) were identical; thus orientation within the discussion and its threads became more difficult because the subject line could not be used as a navigation support. On the contrary, when each subject line was written as a title in an article, i.e. like a pointer to or a summary of the essence of what was said in the text, then the 3 ramification and 10 contributions could be easily identified and contributed by that to improve orientation and by that increase the efficiency in reading and writing.

During a core group meeting, after discussing these experiences, one member suggested that she could summarize our experiences by setting up a draft of "Forums Rules and Suggestions", a collection of policies (a standard that all members should follow) and guidelines (more advisory in nature) documenting best practices on how to write to a forum.

The first question she posted to the forum was about where to place the draft: when we work individually it is mostly easy to know where to store a document, but that is no more the case when we work in a group. In a conventional setting (for example project teams) the answer is given by some fixed, traditional practices and prescriptions about communication, organization and document management, but such prescriptions do not exist in a coalescing, self-organizing group like a new community of practice, they need to be invented and re-invented depending on the situation (who is in the group, which is the context), the shared experiences (what works best, etc.) and the shared understanding.

We agreed to create a wiki-page called "Forums Rules and Suggestions" - exactly like the forum – and to put there the first draft where everybody could read and change it. After a first period of changes and related discussions the facilitator produced a revised version of the draft. It was

now structured in 3 main parts: introduction, rules, examples. At the following core group meeting the new draft was presented and after the meeting the whole procedure began again proposals for modifications or new design ideas in the forum, changes in the wiki, revised draft. At the end of several of these cycles the core group agreed to produce a final version and to publish these "Forums Rules and Suggestions" in a HTML-page with a highly visible link in the "Topics Bar", one of two main navigation areas of the platform.

Research Strategy

Many members of CoRe where engaged not only in research but also in the development of the educational program of our university; in this context one of their main tasks in the period 2006-2007 consisted in developing solutions for the integration of teaching and research in the context of new Master degree courses planned for 2009-2010. In my role as community coordinator I saw here a chance for working on this task within the context of CoRe by offering an e-collaboration approach to strategy development.

I started a forum and in a first posting I suggested an e-collaboration approach to the definition of the research strategy for the new Master courses: asynchronous conversations in the forum, synchronous meetings on Skype (following our TEM model, see above), collaborative editing of summaries of the conversations and of other texts in the wiki and storing of documents in the related folder of CoRe Square. Initially there were only few reactions, but they were all very positive; thus the discussion started with only few participants but quickly gained visibility and a lot of discussion threads began to flourish: how to proceed, who to invite, which contents, examples from other universities, use and organization of the wiki, preparation of a synchronous meeting, vision, mission, etc.

At the same time also the wiki and the file folder began to grow with pages and documents about the profile of individual research institutes, a draft for a research vision, ideas about research fields and main research areas, links to related websites, etc. At regular intervals a summary of the conversation written by a member of the core group was posted to the forum: it was used as a milestone that closed previous discussion threads and offered to newcomers the opportunity to enter the conversation more easily.

About two months after its start the discussion came to an end when a shared draft of the research strategy for the new Master courses became available in the wiki. It was the result of a successful process of e-collaboration which had demonstrated to its participants the potential of a new way of working together but also the complexity of this way of interacting.

In a conventional meeting, face to face or virtual, the success of the meeting is measured in terms of the shared understanding that has been reached at the end; in an e-collaboration process this shared understanding is only one element of the success, the other two are shared knowledge methods (how to do the knowledge work) and shared knowledge structures (how to organize work results). And since knowledge workers (and in particular researchers) are manly very fond of their individual knowledge methods and knowledge structures, reaching an agreement in a large group can be a real challenge.

FUTURE RESEARCH DIRECTIONS AND CONCLUSION

After one year of community life, in June 2007 we took an informal check on the community's health to see whether community building was on the right track. At that time CoRe had about 60 members, 6 of them in the core team. How had their expectations been met? What should be improved or changed? We organized the "1ˢᵗ Annual CoRe Conference" where we evaluated the first year's achievements and determined how to continue. We

asked community members about their motivation, engagement, expected vs. obtained benefits, sense of belonging to CoRe, etc.

The results showed that the core team was well established and cohesive but the majority of the other members still felt rather isolated, disconnected and were frustrated that the resources they had requested at the launch event in June 2006 and that had been developed during the first year (mainly by the core team) had not led to the expected burst in participation. Many CoRe members expressed the need for less self-organization and more structure, more guidance and more directives (managing commitment) on how CoRe spaces and resources could be fuelled with life (Bettoni, Schiller & Bernhard 2008). With the help of this informal check of CoRe's health, the experience of the first year of CoRe can be summarized in the following three lessons learned:

- **The silent "novice".** When members feel that their expertise level is more that of a novice than that of a competent or proficient professional, then participation in discussions can be low if people belong to a linear-active culture (Lewis 2003) like Germans and Swiss-Germans (our case): since they highly value "facts and figures" they more easily feel uncomfortable when they cannot provide them.

- **The prototype "deadlock".** For supporting one to one interactions we had created a tool for competence analysis, visualisation and interaction called "Yellow Tool" (Bettoni, Bernhard et al. 2007b). In the first year our tool was a prototype: it needed users that *jump in* in order to be improved; CoRe members instead were *leaning back*, waiting that the tool gets improved before they use it for their interactions. Using and improving the propotype were both waiting for the other activity to finish, and thus neither ever went on: a typical deadlock that prevented people to interact, explore who is who and understand who knows what.

- **"Voluntary is not serious"**. Projects are wonderful opportunities for networking and engaging in collaborative activities that in turn can promote a strong sense of belonging. In the first year members of CoRe started a lot of research projects but did that still on an individual basis without trying to connect online with other colleagues by means of CoRe Square and thus failing to include them in their perspective. One cause for this disconnected approach could come form our Central-European education in which work and voluntary activites are strictly separated: the first considered "serious but not fun", the second "fun but not serious". As a consequence the idea of "volunteering for work" – like in CoRe - is intuitively and unawarely seen as not serious or even impossible.

In our interpretation these results showed a clear challenge for implementing a collaborative knowledge strategy at our university: that of balancing self-governance, self-organization and voluntary participation on one side and stronger guidance, obligatory interactions and mandatory use of tools (CoRe Square) on the other side. Thus we see a clear emergence of a tension between two opposing tendencies, autonomy and guidance. We in the core team were convinced that CoRe had made important steps forward and were confident that we would have been able to cope with the mentioned tension and challenge.

But our university's rector saw the whole thing in a less optimistic way. He had expected a much higher satisfaction, interaction, participation of the CoRe members and much more outcome in terms of research performances. He mistrusted our "facilitative" approach to leadership within CoRe and was worried that the community would never flourish. In line with his traditional view

of leadership as "command and control", in November 2007 our rector started the planning for a complete reorganization of research, which lasted until April 2008.

CoRe hibernated for one year and awoke again in November 2008: since then it is running under the new name of "eDolphin" with a modified approach based on bioteaming (Bettoni, Schiller & Bernhard 2008) and is undergoing some essential modifications for taking in consideration not only the lessons learned from the first year but also the new organizational structures.

In a recent article Barry Libert (2008) reflects on the changes that he has seen taking place since 2001 in the area of e-collaboration and social technologies and concludes with the belief that the future core competency will be "facilitative", not "command and control" leadership.

Our experiences with the implementation of our "design for meaning" fully confirm this belief. In future, business value will depend not only on the quality of knowledge and of its application in business processes but will also be more and more influenced by the quality of knowledge collaboration, particularly e-collaboration. In this context facilitative leadership - e.g. the ability of an organization, of a group and of a leader to follow others and meet their needs and not the reverse (Libert 2008) - will become an essential success factor.

For the moment facilitative leadership is an art: in order to develop it into a competence that can be taught, learned and applied future research is needed that will show us how to lead in a consistent way three kinds of interrelated "negotiations of knowledge": negotiations of meaning, negotiations of knowledge methods and negotiations of knowledge structures.

REFERENCES

Back, A., Enkel, E., Seufert, A., & von Krogh, G. (Eds.). (2006). *Getting real about Knowledge Networks: unlocking corporate knowledge assets.* Hampshire, UK: Palgrave MacMillan.

Bettoni, M. (2005). Wissenskooperation – Die Zukunft des Wissensmanagements. Lernende Organisation. *Zeitschrift für Systemisches Management und Organisation, 25, Mai/Juni 2005.*

Bettoni, M., Andenmatten, S., & Mathieu, R. (2007a). Knowledge Cooperation in Online Communities: A Duality of Participation and Cultivation. [Retrieved from http://www.ejkm.com/]. *Electronic Journal of Knowledge Management, 5*(1), 1–6.

Bettoni, M., & Bernhard, W. (2007c). CoRe – Linking Teaching and Research by a Community-Oriented Strategy. In G. Richards (Ed.), *Proceedings of World Conference on E-Learning in Corporate, Government, Healthcare, and Higher Education 2007* (pp. 2354-2362). Chesapeake, VA: AACE.

Bettoni, M., Bernhard, W., Borter, F., & Dönnges, G. (2007b). The Yellow Tool – Making Yellow Pages More Social and Visible. In B. Martin & D. Remenyi, (Eds.), *Proc. of the 8th European Conference on Knowledge Management, ECKM 2007, Consorci Escola Industrial de Barcelona (CEIB), Barcelona, Spain, Sept. 6-7, 2007* (pp. 118-124) Reading, MA: Academic Publishing Ltd.

Bettoni, M., Bernhard, W., & Schiller, G. (2009). Community-orientierte Strategien zur Integration von Lehre und Forschung. In P. Bergamin, H. Muralt Müller, & C.Filk (Hrsg.), *Offene Bildungsinhalte (OER), Teilen von Wissen oder Gratisbildungskultur?* Bern, Switzerland: h.e.p. Verlag.

Bettoni, M., Braun, A., & Weber, W. (2003). What motivates cooperation and sharing in communities of practice? In F. McGrath & D. Remenyi (Eds.), *Proc. of the 4th Europ. Conference on Knowledge Management, Oriel College, Oxford University, UK* (pp. 67-72) Reading, MA: Academic Publishing Ltd.

Bettoni, M., Clases, C., & Wehner, T. (2004). Communities of Practice as a Way to a More Human-Oriented Knowledge Management. In I. Svetlik & J. Nadoh (Eds.), *Proc. Intern. Conference on Human resource management in a knowledge-based economy (HRM 2004),* Ljubljana, Slovenia (CD-Rom), 2-4 June.

Bettoni, M., Schiller, G., & Bernhard, W. (2008). Weak Ties Cooperation in the CoRe Knowledge Network. In D. Harorimana & D. Watkins (Eds.), *Proc. of the 9th European Conference on Knowledge Management Southampton Solent University, Southampton, UK, 4-5 September 2008* (pp. 59-66). Reading: Academic Publishing Ltd.

Bettoni, M., & Schneider, S. (2002). Experience Management - Lessons Learned from Knowledge Engineering. In *Lecture Notes in Informatics (LNI)* (Vol P-10, pp. 117-128). Bonn, Germany: Gesellschaft für Informatik (GI).

Bettoni, M., & Schneider, S. (2003). The Essence of Knowledge Management: A Constructivist Approach. In O. Camp, J. Felipe, S. Hammoudi, & M. Piattini (Eds.), *Proc. of the Fifth Intern. Conf. on Enterprise Information Systems*, ICEIS 2003, Angers, France, April 22-26, 2003 (Vol. 2, pp. 191-196).

Fromm, E. (1976). *Haben oder Sein? Die seelischen Grundlagen einer neuen Gesellschaft.* Stuttgart, Germany: DVA.

Graggober, M. Ortner, J. & Sammer, M. (2003). *Wissensnetzwerke. Konzepte, Erfahrungen und Entwicklungsrichtungen.* Wiesbaden, Germany: DUV.

Lembke, G., Müller, M., & Schneidewind, U. (Eds.). (2005). *Wissensnetzwerke. Grundlagen, Praxisberichte, Anwendungsfelder*. Wiesbaden, Germany: LearnAct!

Lewis, R. D. (2003). *The Cultural Imperative: Global Trends in the 21st Century*. Yarmouth, ME: Intercultural Press.

Libert, B. (2008). *Social Media Change Corporate Culture*. Retrieved October 14, 2008, from http://www.mzinga.com/en/Community/Blogs/Barry-Libert/

Probst, G., & Borzillo, S. (2008). Why Communities of practice succeed and why they fail. *European Management Journal*, *26*, 335–347. doi:10.1016/j.emj.2008.05.003

Probst, G. J. B., Raub, S., & Romhardt, K. (1999). *Managing Knowledge: Building Blocks for Success*. Chichester, UK: John Wiley & Sons.

Schmitz, C., & Zucker, B. (1996). *Wissen gewinnt. Knowledge Flow Management*. Düsseldorf, Germany: Metropolitan.

von Glasersfeld, E. (1995). *Radical Constructivism: A Way of Knowing and Learning*. London: Falmer Press.

Wenger, E. (1998). *Communities of Practice. Learning, Meaning and Identity*. Cambridge, UK: Cambridge University Press.

Wenger, E., McDermott, R., & Snyder, W. (2002). *Cultivating Communities of Practice: A Guide to Managing Knowledge*. Boston, MA: Harvard Business School Press

ADDITIONAL READING

Agostini, A., Albolino, S., De Paoli, F., Grasso, A., & Hinrichs, E. (2005). Supporting Communities by Providing Multiple Views. In Van den Besselaar et al. (Eds.), *Communities and Technologies 2005. Proc. of the Second C&T Conference, Milano*. Dordrecht, NL: Springer.

Arnold, P., & Smith, J. D. (2003). Adding connectivity and losing context with ICT: Contrasting learning situations from a community of practice perspective. In M. Huysman, E. Wenger, & V. Wulf (Eds.), *Communities and Technologies. Proc. 1st Int. Conf. on Communities and Technologies* (pp. 465-484). Dordrecht, Netherlands: Kluwer.

Bendel, O. (2006). Das 1x1 der Wikis und Weblogs. *Wissensmanagement. Das Magazin für Führungskräfte*, *3*, 22–25.

Bernhard, W., & Bettoni, M. (2007). Wissensnetzwerke - Offene Zusammenarbeit im virtuellen Raum. In P. Bergamin & G. Pfander (Eds.), *Medien im Bildungswesen: Kompetenzen, Organisation, Mehrwert* (pp. 99-121). Bern, Switzerland: h.e.p. Verlag, Bettoni, M., & Borter, F. (2007). Wissenskooperation: Gemeinsam zum Erfolg. *Wissensmanagement. Das Magazin für Führungskräfte*, *3*, 28-29.

Bettoni, M. (2005). Communities of Practice as a Method for Knowledge-Oriented Cooperation. In R. Carneiro, K. Steffens, & J. Underwood (Eds.), *Proc. of the TACONET Conf. on Self-regulated Learning in Technology Enhanced Learning Environments* (pp. 92-99). Aachen, Germany: Shaker Verlag.

Bettoni, M., Andenmatten, S., & Mathieu, R. (2006). Research Networking with CoRe Square. In D. Grabe & L. Zimmermann (Eds.), *MApEC - Multimedia Applications in Education Conference Proceedings 2006* (pp. 48-55). Graz, Austria: FH JOANNEUM.

Bettoni, M., Clases, C., & Wehner, T. (2004). Communities of Practice im Wissensmanagement: Charakteristika, Initiierung und Gestaltung. In G. Reinmann & H. Mandl (Eds.), *Psychologie des Wissensmanagements. Perspektiven, Theorien und Methoden*. Göttingen, Germany: Hogrefe.

Collison, C. (2005). *Knowledge Management: Creating a Sustainable Yellow Pages System*. Retrieved October 15, 2008, from http://www.chriscollison.com/

Collison, C., & Parcell, G. (2004). *Learning to Fly. Practical knowledge management from some of the world's leading learning organizations.* Chichester, UK: Capstone.

Granovetter, M. (1973). The Strength of Weak Ties. *American Journal of Sociology, 78,* 1360–1380. doi:10.1086/225469

Granovetter, M. (1983). The Strength of Weak Ties: A Network Theory Revisited. *Sociological Theory, 1,* 201–233. doi:10.2307/202051

Jonczyk, C. (2005). Writing learning stories: The case of Telcotech. In S. Gherardi & D. Nicolini (Eds.), *The Passion for Learning and Knowing. Proc. of the 6th Intern. Conf. on Organizational Learning and Knowledge (2 vols.).* Trento: Univ. of Trento e-books.

Kavanaugh, A., Reese, D. D., Carroll, J. M., & Rosson, M. B. (2003). Weak Ties in Networked Communities. In M. Huysman, E. Wenger & V. Wulf (Eds.), *Communities and Technologies* (pp. 265-286). Dordrecht, The Netherlands: Kluwer Academic Publishers.

Lave, J., & Wenger, E. (1991). *Situated Learning. Legitimate Peripheral Participation.* Cambridge, UK: Cambridge University Press.

O'Reilly, T. (2006). *Web 2.0 Compact Definition: Trying Again.* Retrieved October 15, 2008, from http://radar.oreilly.com/archives/2006/12/web-20-compact.html

Schütt, P. (2005). Blogs und Wikis. Mehr Mitarbeit wagen. *Wissensmanagement, 7,* 14–16.

Chapter 3
E–Collaborative Knowledge Construction in Chat Environments

Michael Oehl
Leuphana University of Lüneburg, Germany

Hans-Rüdiger Pfister
Leuphana University of Lüneburg, Germany

ABSTRACT

Chat-based tools are often used for computer-supported net-based learning and knowledge construction. However, due to its media characteristics, chat-based communication frequently suffers from deficits due to incoherence of contributions, lack of coordination as well as related problems of awareness. These shortcomings of conventional chat-based communication pose severe problems for online knowledge construction and learning. We claim that these restrictions can be overcome and propose that extending the medium 'chat' with appropriate educational and conversational strategies embedded in the chat environment can actually improve the learning discourse and thus support collaborative knowledge construction. Relevant approaches and recent research will be reviewed. Conclusions for the design of chat-based CSCL environments will be discussed.

INTRODUCTION

From the beginning chat was predominantly used for casual internet communication. In the meantime it has become a common and well-established form of communication also for serious purposes in educational as well as in business contexts. Among its advantages are its easy access, its low-tech affordances, high usability and fast and flexible communication processes. A variant of chat, SMS

messaging, has met the public with unexpected popularity.

Nevertheless, due to its media properties, chat-based communication frequently suffers from deficits due to incoherence of contributions, lack of coordination and problems of awareness concerning social awareness as well as awareness of context and available knowledge (Herring, 1999; Pimentel, Fuks, & Lucena, 2003). These restrictions of conventional chat-based communication pose severe problems for online knowledge construction and learning processes in collaborative settings (Jucks, Paechter, & Tatar, 2003).

DOI: 10.4018/978-1-61520-729-9.ch003

We suggest and elaborate in this chapter that chat environments can be redesigned and enriched in a way to support serious educational needs and to meet the requirements of professional life.

Collaborative learning can be loosely defined as a learning method involving a group of learners who exchange knowledge and/or solve a problem together and interdependently, that is, under a common learning goal (Johnson & Johnson, 1992). The particular setting of computer-supported collaborative learning (CSCL) or, more precise in this case, *net-based e-collaborative knowledge construction in chat environments* implies that participants are separated physically and communication is mediated by chat tools via the internet. With respect to time, chat-based communication is synchronous with participants communicating at the same time, although chat might be located somewhat in the middle between fully synchronous communication such as phone calls and fully asynchronous tools such as mailing lists (Fuks, Pimentel, & Lucena, 2006).

This chapter focuses on e-collaborative knowledge construction in chat environments. Thus we will discuss computer-mediated net-based textual synchronous knowledge communication in groups, that is, between two or more participants. A basic assumption of collaborative knowledge construction is that learning outcomes will improve when learners need to make their current knowledge and their lack of knowledge explicit, and when they need to negotiate via arguments, critiques, and justifications with other participants during a discourse (Stahl, Koschmann, & Suthers, 2006). As a result, this is expected to lead to deeper understanding, to better retention, and knowledge should be more easily transferred and applied. Learning environments should elicit and support these kinds of genuine learning interactions that induce the emergence of knowledge and understanding (Dillenbourg & Hong, 2008). However, what actually constitutes a genuine learning interaction is still far from clear (Soller, Martinez, Jerman, & Mühlenbrock, 2005).

We argue here that the shortcomings of chat-based communication due to its media properties can be overcome, and we propose that extending the medium 'chat' with appropriate educational and conversational strategies embedded in the chat environment as tools or interface features can actually improve the learning discourse and thus support collaborative knowledge construction beyond casual everyday communication. Relevant approaches and recent research will be reviewed, and conclusions for the design of chat-based environments will be discussed both with respect to academic scenarios as well as with respect to the needs of practitioners.

BACKGROUND

Computer-supported collaborative learning requires successful communication as a prerequisite (Pfister, 2005). The collaborating learners should understand each other's contributions to the learning discourse and be able to generate a shared understanding of the content under discussion. These basic communication elements can be understood as located on a micro-level, upon which more encompassing didactical components are built comprising what might be called the macro-level. A macro-component, such as collaboratively summarizing a portion of text, will only function properly if the micro-level mechanisms, such as a coordinated exchange of messages, works out smoothly.

From a linguistic perspective communication mechanisms in chat environments share many features with oral language although it is a textual medium (Beißwenger, 2007). Nevertheless, the properties of the medium and the distinctive features of chat in particular lead to discourse structures that are very different to the ones of spoken face-to-face communication, in particular if groups of more than two learners communicate simultaneously (Bromme, Hesse, & Spada, 2005; Jucks, Paechter, & Tatar, 2003).

Figure 1. The macro- and micro-level of chat-based knowledge construction

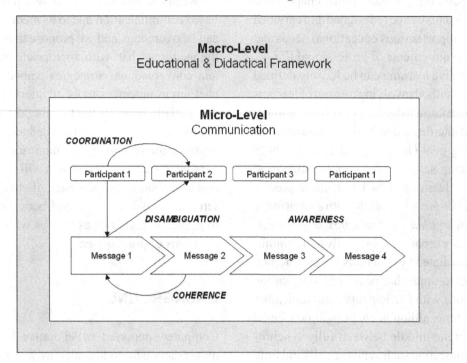

Two important distinctive properties are: (1) The *separation of production and presentation*, that is, the production of a chat message is usually not perceived by its addressee. The message is presented only after it has been sent by the contributor as a unit; grounding processes (Clark & Brennan, 1991) during production are inhibited. (2) The *decontextualisation of messages*, that is, the contributor cannot easily determine the precise position and context of where to place her or his message, and the addressee cannot easily identify a message's context from the flow of incoming messages, typically arising from several intermingled and fragmented threads (Hewitt, 2005).

Due to these properties, a number of shortcomings of chat-based communication ensue. We will briefly describe the relevant shortcomings, and discuss some findings on how users adapt to obstructive circumstances in chat-based communication. Then the micro-macro-level distinction will be elaborated.

Shortcomings of Chat-Based Communication

In general, chat-based communication suffers from deficits due to incoherence of contributions, lack of coordination, insufficient feedback, fragmented discourse threads, and related problems (Cornelius & Boos, 2003; Herring, 1999; O'Neill & Martin, 2003); as a consequence, *chat confusion* as called by Pimentel, Fuks, and de Lucena (2003) arises. Some of the most relevant facets of chat confusion refer to coordination, coherence, feedback, ambiguity, and awareness (see Figure 1).

The steady flow of incoming messages is characterized by disrupted adjacency and confused turn-taking, as a problem of *coordination* of participants' actions in chat-based communication (Hancock & Dunham, 2001). Without a human moderator, in groups of more than two learners coordination of contributions usually is a major problem.

Moreover, in chat-based communication participants are frequently not able to identify the precise relationships among individual contributions – a phenomenon called '*co-text loss*' (Pimentel, Fuks, & de Lucena, 2003). More generally, in a learning discourse, several topics are covered in parallel threads, and the problem of sustaining threads and avoiding *incoherence* among different threads emerges (Hewitt, 2005; Lipponen, Rahikainen, Lallimo, & Hakkarainen, 2003). A related problem is the lack of instantaneous *feedback*, which is particularly important for grounding strategies in spoken communication (Brennan, 1998; Clark & Brennan, 1991) in order to build up shared knowledge.

Isolated messages are often difficult to *disambiguate* with respect to the intended speech act. A message might be intended as a question or a critique, but without appropriate semantic embedding, the type of a message is frequently hard to identify (Baker & Lund, 1997).

As mentioned already, when learning groups involve more than two participants, not only problems of coordination but also problems of *awareness* arise. This refers to situational awareness, that is, what is the current task and state of knowledge, as well as to social awareness, that is, who is attending (Buder & Bodemer, 2008; Gutwin & Greenbergs, 2002).

Facing these problems, chat users try to compensate by adapting their communication strategies with growing experience to the medium (Brennan, 1998; Clark & Brennan, 1991; Herring, 1999; Werry, 1996). For instance, (1) an integrated contribution is broken down in a sequence of separate messages, indicating at the end of the message that it is continued (Herring, 1999); (2) the addressee of the message is explicitly mentioned; (3) responses to messages of parallel threads are done with different messages, trying to preserve the sequential order (O'Neill & Martin, 2003). Further adaptive communication strategies could be observed, for example, concerning task performance and communicative effort (Hollingshead, McGrath, & O'Connor, 1993; Münzer & Holmer, 2009; Newlands, Anderson, & Mullin, 2003).

However, we definitely should not rely on users' adaptive creativity when it comes to serious learning and knowledge construction. In the following we propose that extending basic chat tools with different educational and conversational strategies as well as with corresponding tools embedded in the chat environment can help to overcome the shortcomings of chat communication mentioned above, such as incoherence and lack of awareness.

Macro- and Micro-Level

Extending or enriching the medium chat means to impose some kind of structure on chat discourses, that is, to impose constraints, or rules, or scaffolds that guide and channel the ongoing discourse along educational and didactical lines assumed to be supportive. For example, a rule might refer to turn-taking in order to generate an equal proportion of contributions from each participant; or a scaffold might impose a pre-defined sequence of topics to be discussed. Constraints restrict the possible set of actions of learners, trying to prevent those which are not conducive for learning. Furthermore, extending chat means to provide some kind of relevant information about the ongoing discourse or about the status of participants; that is, one tries to extract useful information from observable discourse features and to make it explicit for participants. For example, an explicit indicator of the amount of contributions from each participant might help to create a more balanced discussion.

Unfortunately, it is highly unlikely that a productive discourse will unfold only because advanced and sophisticated communication tools are available (Kreijns, Kirschner, & Jochems, 2003). Without assistance, just being together in a virtual collaborative setting will not trigger elaborative processes automatically, and thus will generally not improve knowledge construction. A discourse setting provides an opportunity, but needs further systematic support to promote better learning. So the question is how to support groups of learners to communicate efficiently.

Useful extensions may be introduced on many levels; here, we follow the distinction between a macro-level and a micro-level as proposed by Pfister (2005) or Dillenbourg and Hong (2008) (see Figure 1).

We define the *micro-level* to comprise activities ranging from individual cognitive acts (such as remembering or attending to something) to individual learning activities (such as reading or writing in isolation) to elementary communicative activities such as exchanging and grounding a message (Clark, 1996), to particular discourse units such as providing an explanation or rephrasing an argument. The micro-level refers to the building-blocks of successful communication and discourse.

The *macro-level*, on the other hand, refers to particular aggregates of collaborative activities subordinate to a specific pedagogical goal. Aggregates of this kind usually are extended episodes of collaborative activities, composed of micro-level building-blocks. For example, trying to establish consensus about the meaning of a complex concept in a group of learners represents a macro-level episode; or collaboratively producing a summary text from a set of diverse documents is another example of a macro-level activity, targeted at a particular didactic objective.

We will only briefly discuss extensions concerning the macro-level, since extensions on the macro-level are not specific to chat communication. We will then focus on the micro-level, referring to the shortcomings identified above, and present examples of potential improvements.

The Macro-Level: Scripts and Scaffolds

Looking at a discourse as a whole, even naturally occurring learning discourses divide into typical phases. As a simple example take the phases a tutor might follow to introduce a well-defined topic: Starting with an introduction, he or she might present an overview, define the central concepts, followed by questions and explanations, and finally finish with a closing summary. Detailed analyses of such segmentations yielded a number of discourse types, which appear useful for specific didactical scenarios. In so-called *scripted cooperation* (O'Donnell & King, 1999), participants typically work in pairs to comprehend a piece of text about a scientific topic. The script starts with one learner reading the text, then recalling and summarizing it, followed by the other learner adding missing points and criticizing imprecise issues. Roles then alternate, and another section of text is read. Generally, any such scripting approach defines a succession of phases, defined by specific sub-goals, and the group of learners works through these stages, possibly with changing roles.

A large body of research has demonstrated the beneficial effects of *scripted collaboration* or *scripts* in computer-supported collaborative learning, using chat exclusively or in combination with tools such as white boards or videos (Bromme et al., 2005; Fischer, Kollar, Mandl, & Haake, 2007; Kobbe, Weinberger, Dillenbourg, Harrer, Hämäläinen et al., 2007; Kollar, Fischer, & Hesse, 2006; O'Donnell & King, 1999; Weinberger, Ertl, Fischer, & Mandl, 2005). Kollar et al. (2006) provide a detailed analysis of net-based scripted collaboration. Kobbe et al. (2007) provide a valuable framework allowing a description of collaboration scripts with a distinct number of components (participants, activities, roles, resources and groups) and mechanisms (task, distribution, group formation and sequencing). To avoid scripts that are to restrictive for learners (Dillenbourg, 2002), recent research suggests the development of flexible scripting (Dillenbourg & Tchounikine, 2007; Haake & Pfister, 2007), or to use optional scripts that allow learners to employ scripting functionalities on demand (Pfister & Oehl, 2009).

For example, Weinberger et al. (2005) studied the effect of different cooperation scripts on a problem solving task. They applied a social (focussing on the interaction of learners) and an epistemic (focussing on the task) cooperation script on a CSCL scenario based on textual communication. Results show that social cooperation scripts fostered the processes of collaborative knowledge construction, conflict-orientation of the learners as well as learning outcomes. Epistemic cooperation scripts facilitated the processes of collaborative knowledge construction as well, but they had negative effects on learning outcomes.

Related approaches are the implementation of *scaffolds*, that is, providing templates to support the acquisition of domain specific knowledge (Weinberger, Fischer, & Mandl, 2002; Wood, 2001). In contrast to scripts, which are merely targeted to support collaboration in general, scaffolds or so-called *content-schemes* represent an outline of the content of particular domains (Kopp, Ertl, & Mandl, 2006); for example, a visualisation of content topics has been shown to enhance performance in learning dyads (Fischer, Bruhn, Grasel, & Mandl, 2002).

Along similar lines, a macro-level approach is to instigate *observational learning* by providing worked-out collaboration examples (Rummel & Spada, 2005; Rummel, Spada, & Hauser, 2009). Although it is still somewhat unclear which knowledge domains and learning tasks fit to which of these methods, empirical evidence clearly shows that providing structure on the macro-level is generally superior to unstructured and unguided discourse in most cases (Derry, 1999).

The Micro-Level: Mechanisms for Grounding

On the micro-level, a chat discourse can be analyzed as consisting of atomic building-blocks, that is, the utterances (chat messages) of participants, which must be constructed, formulated, and understood. To describe the functioning of single utterances, we draw on Clark's theory of *grounding* (Clark, 1996; Clark & Brennan, 1991) which has provided an important framework to understand computer-mediated communication in general and net-based collaborative learning in particular (Baker, Hansen, Joiner, & Traum, 1999; Beers, Boshuizen, Kirschner, & Gijselaers, 2007; Dillenbourg & Traum, 2006; Pfister, 2005; Pfister & Oehl, 2009; Schooneboom, 2008).

Grounding according to Clark (1996; Clark & Brennan, 1991) is the process of collaboratively establishing common ground during communication. Common ground is the shared core of knowledge among participants, which they mutually take for granted in an ongoing discourse. The basic component of grounding in chat-based communication is a two-part exchange of chat messages. First, in the presentation phase, a participant presents a statement, expecting the addressee to respond with evidence that he or she has understood. Second, in the acceptance phase, the addressee provides evidence that she or he has understood, or, otherwise, initiates a new exchange to clarify what has not been understood, eventually trying to establish common ground. In face-to-face settings, grounding typically occurs spontaneously and without much trouble, for example, by acknowledgements ("mmh, yeah ..."), eye contact, or deictic gestures. In text-based chat, these mechanisms are not available, impeding the process of grounding seriously.

With respect to a successful learning discourse, macro-level and micro-level are not independent. A discourse designation which characterizes the type of discourse on the macro-level, for example, specifying a discourse as a critical exchange of arguments, to a large extent defines the types of contributions on the micro-level, such as the prevalence of particular adjacency pairs (question-explanation, or claim-critique). More important, the discourse type defines what Clark (1996) calls the grounding criterion, that is, the degree or strength of grounding necessary for current purposes. A casual exchange of opinions might imply a lower criterion than does the precise explanation of a complex theory. Depending on the grounding criterion, grounding activities will be more or less intense and elaborated.

This perspective implies that the macro-micro-level dependency is asymmetric, that is, discourse phases on the macro-level will be performed successfully only if grounding on the micro-level proceeds undisturbed. As the micro-level can be regarded as primarily concerned with grounding, the macro-level is primarily concerned with the achievement of an overall learning goal.

However, since collaborative learning involves successful transfer of knowledge and construction of knowledge involving several learners, this suggests that collaborative learning is to a large extent equivalent to the accumulation of common ground. We call this the *grounding-first principle* (Pfister, 2005): Supporting a learning discourse by imposing structure on the macro-level will only be accomplished if grounding of the elementary contributions on the micro-level of a discourse is warranted. Several studies investigating the micro-level of chat-based communication, strengthen this view (Baker et al., 1999; Beers et al., 2007; Fuks, Pimentel, & de Lucena, 2006; Herring, 1999; Münzer & Holmer, 2009; Pfister & Oehl, 2009; Strijbos & Stahl, 2007; Zemel, Xhafa, & Cakir, 2007). As a consequence, enriching chat tools to foster collaborative knowledge construction first and foremost implies to provide support on the micro-level; this will be elaborated in the following section.

IMPOSING STRUCTURE ON THE MICRO-LEVEL

We take up the list of shortcomings identified above, that is, coordination, incoherence, disambiguation and feedback, and awareness, and discuss proposed measures to overcome these shortcomings. Coordination and awareness mainly refers to structuring participants' interaction, co-herence mainly refers to improving the structure of contributed messages, and disambiguation and feedback mainly concerns grounding processes relating participants and their respective messages (see Figure 1 for an overview).

Coordination

Successful knowledge construction relies on a collaborative process requiring participants to *coordinate their conversational turns* (Sacks, Schegloff, & Jefferson, 1974). Clark and Brennan (1991) identified some basic methods for turn-taking in face-to-face communication, such as making gestures as feedback, or initiating turn-taking via non-verbal cues. In normal chat, however, speakers cannot rely on non-verbal cues to infer the understanding of others. Additionally, unstructured chat allows participants to submit their contributions to the ongoing chat discourse at the very same time. Hence, disrupted turn-taking in chat-based conversation is a persistent phenomenon (Herring, 1999). According to Clark (1996), communication settings disrupting the regulation of turn-taking undermine higher level language processes of grounding and knowledge communication as well as increase the frequency of meta-communication in order to coordinate the ongoing discourse.

Only a few studies have introduced turn-taking devices, but with some success. To coordinate turn-taking, Hron, Hesse, Cress, and Giovis (2000) sequenced the interaction of learners by alternately prompting learners to propose a correction of the learning partner, explain the correction, and obtain agreement from the learning partner. Hancock and Dunham (2001) analyzed the grounding process in chat-based collaborative knowledge construction depending on the possibility to control turn-taking. An explicit turn marker, that is, a signal that indicates the end of a conversational turn, facilitated the grounding process and reduced the number of verbal coordination devices required to ground communication.

Incoherence

Participants in chat-based environments are frequently not able to assign individual contributions to their appropriate threads, a phenomenon called *'co-text loss'* (Pimentel, Fuks, & de Lucena, 2003). A high degree of disrupted adjacency pairs, of overlapping exchanges, and of topic decay can be observed (Herring, 1999; Hewitt, 2005). Multiple synchronous responses are often directed at a single initiating message, and single messages may respond to more than one initiating message.

In order to enhance coherence and to decrease disrupted topic maintenance, chat environments often use a process called *threading* to impose structure on the evolving communication. A thread is a hierarchically organized collection of chat contributions. Originating from the contribution that started a discourse the ensuing chat contributions appear as associated replies in a quasi-graphical interface. These kinds of representations, well-known from mailing lists, make it easier for participants to trace the progress of the ongoing discourse.

Hewitt (2005) examined in a asynchronous chat-based communication environment how and why discussion threads died. Analyses of the threading revealed that participants usually focussed their attention on unread contributions. Hewitt argues that this effect can produce a starvation condition that accelerates the death of threads and reduces the likelihood that inactive threads will become active again. As educational implications of this finding Hewitt (2005) recommends the use of a moderator who reduces the amount of incoming chat contributions and who weights them with respect to their importance for the different discourse threads.

A second recommendation is the implementation of external representations of the ongoing chat discourse in terms of a threading graph. Participants should become aware of the different discourse threads and related contributions. For example Holmer (2008; Münzer & Holmer, 2009)

proposed the CHATLINE software to analyze automatically discourse threads and coherence in chat-based communication. In another automated approach (Cakir, Xhafa, Zhou, & Stahl, 2005), thread information was also analyzed to identify frequent interaction patterns and the conversational structure of discussion.

As an implementation of threading research, Fuks et al. (2006) provide a sophisticated chat environment using graphical depictions of the ongoing chat discourse threads. Participants are provided with a simple chronological view (simple chat history) as well as a hierarchical view (related chat contributions are connected via arrows) of message threading. They developed several versions of this mediated chat tool; at the current stage of research, earlier solutions have been revised and integrated into Mediated Chat version 6.0 – a chat tool structuring the communication and collaboration process for example by means of a session register to avoid decontextualization.

Disambiguation and Feedback

Isolated messages are often difficult to *disambiguate* with respect to the intended speech act. A message might be intended as a question or a critique, but without appropriate semantic embedding, the type of messages is frequently hard to identify (Baker & Lund, 1997). A related problem is the lack of instantaneous *feedback*, which is especially important for grounding (Brennan, 1998; Clark & Brennan, 1991).

With regard to disambiguation of chat messages, Soller (2004) analyzed knowledge exchange with a chat-based tool using sentence-openers enriched with a shared graphical workspace. The sentence-openers are implementd to help participants to clearly identify the conversational meaning of a chat contribution (for example, as a question or an answer) and thus to avoid ambiguous chat messages. Baker and Lund (1997) used a chat tool with sentence-openers as well to analyze learners' performance in a problem-solving task.

In contrast to the same chat tool without sentence-openers, the chat tool with sentence-openers promoted a more task-focussed and reflective interaction manner.

An integrated approach trying to solve several problems of chat communication simultaneously is the *learning protocol approach* (Pfister & Mühlpfordt, 2002; Pfister, Müller, & Mühlpfordt, 2003); many similar approaches along these lines have been developed (Kollar et al., 2006). We illustrate this approach as an example of a typical class of chat environments in more detail (see Figure 2).

The learning protocol approach aims at improving chat discourse by implementing a set of discourse rules in the virtual learning environment. Focusing on the significance of a coherent and meaningful discourse for collaborative learning (micro-level), learning protocols provide four

basic functionalities to increase the efficiency of chat discourses:

a. **Role assignment:** A distinctive role, such as learner, tutor, or commentator, is assigned to each participant for the duration of the learning process. This role partly constrains what activities he or she is permitted to perform.

b. **Typing of contributions:** Each textual contribution can be explicitly classified and labeled by the learner with respect to its communicative type, such as question, explanation, comment, critique, or any other category. The learner attaches a label to the message, and the label precedes the message on the screen and is visible for all participants. Thus, the primary purpose of one's contribution is unambiguously highlighted.

Figure 2. Screenshot of the learning protocol interface with the software ConcertChat (Mühlpfordt, 2006; the left pane shows the common text about the learning topic, also shown there is the pop-up menu of contribution types. The large right pane shows the chat-history with all learners' contributions to the discourse. The lower right pane depicts the input field for one's own contribution. A referencing line goes from the current contribution pane to a text fragment in the left text pane).

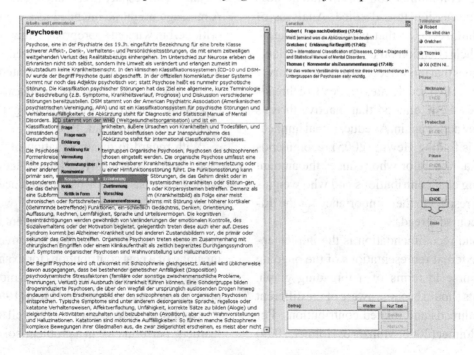

c. **Explicit referencing:** When submitting a contribution, the learner can indicate the referent of a contribution, that is, he or she can establish a reference to a previous contribution, or to a portion of a previous contribution, or to a portion of any additional material provided on-screen. The text referred to is marked with the mouse, and by a simple mouse-click the relationship is established. This relationship is visualized by an arrow pointing from the current contribution to the referred to contribution, or to the text segment referred to, being visible on the interface for all participants during the learning session. On the one hand, chat participants can thus re-read discussion threads by simply tracking back the arrows linking the single contributions. This threading functionality serves to increase discourse coherence. On the other hand, explicit referencing allows participants to provide feedback to related conversational turns in terms of efficient grounding.

d. **Turn-taking:** A specific sequence of turn-taking among participants can be defined to increase coordination processes during the chat discourse. Simple turn-taking has usually been set up as following the one-after-the-other rule.

In previous studies the potential benefits of learning with this kind of learning protocols in contrast to an unstructured chat discussion could be demonstrated. It was found that it is mainly the referencing function, that is, visualizing relationships among contributions or between a contribution and additional fragments in order to increase discourse coherence and to provide relatable conversational feedback, which is of major importance with respect to performance (Mühlpfordt & Wessner, 2005; Pfister et al., 2003; Stahl, Zemel, Sarmiento, Cakir, Weimar, et al., 2006). According to Stahl (2006), referencing is at the core of creating what he calls the "discourse fabric", that is, the shared meaning of a narrative text.

In a recent study (Pfister & Oehl, 2009), we analyzed if and when learners use discourse supporting functions such as referencing and typing during a chat-based collaborative learning session. We suggested that if learners put more effort into grounding in terms of referencing and typing this would lead to improved learning outcomes. Three context factors, which we hypothesized to systematically influence grounding and learning, were examined: Goal focus, task type, and group size. In sum, it turned out that with respect to learning outcomes learning protocols are more conducive to support collaborative learning framed as a knowledge acquisition task than a task framed as problem solving. Goal focus showed no effect on learning outcome. Furthermore, we found a significant propensity of participants to apply more referencing and typing under a group focus compared to an individual focus. Task type, in contrast, did not influence referencing and typing activities. Generally, there was a tendency that learning protocols are more beneficial, in terms of learning outcome as well as in terms of grounding, for larger groups of four participants than for groups of three participants. Finally, it could be shown that participants who use the referencing function more frequently are more likely to perform better in a final multiple choice knowledge test. In particular, it turned out that referencing plays a mediating role: When group size increases, participants are more likely to use the referencing function, and thereby to improve their learning outcomes.

Awareness

According to Buder and Bodemer (2008; see also Endsley, 1995) *awareness* can be defined as the perception of or knowledge about situational affordances of a communication setting. When learning groups are larger than two participants, problems of awareness arise. This refers to situational awareness as well as to social awareness (Buder & Bodemer, 2008; Gutwin & Greenbergs, 2002; Kimmerle & Cress, 2008; Kirschner & Kreijns, 2005).

With regard to social presence (Short, Williams, & Christie, 1976) and media richness theory (Daft & Lengel, 1984, 1986), text-based communication is often perceived as impersonal because of its lack of audio or video cues. Similarly, from the perspective of social presence, text-based communication (low in social presence) could cause de-individuation and de-personalization, hence, text-based communication is less social and more task-oriented (Rice & Love, 1987).

Up to now, only few implementations of group awareness tools in CSCL settings have been made (Soller et al., 2005). We would like to point out some recent promising attempts.

Kirschner and Kreijns (2005) introduce a group awareness widget. This tool provides the communication partners with graphic illustrations of their social interaction during their work. The group awareness widget should compensate for motivation and structure barriers by supplying adapted information, for example, if communication partners are on- or offline. However, first prototypes were not used and accepted successfully by participants as hoped. Most participants used the tool not for communication or collaboration processes, but only for spying, that is, to get information if other participants were online. This is, however, another indication that users creatively adopt available tools to their own purposes, overriding the intended purpose of the designer.

Another recent attempt is made by Buder and Bodemer (2008). They developed an augmented group awareness tool that provides communication partners with a visualisation of mutual ratings about their online discussion contributions. This confronts every participant with an average evaluation of his or her discourse contributions by the whole group. Participants rated each contribution on two dimensions, agreement and novelty. An experimental study on group deci-

sion making could show some beneficial effects of this tool: Groups which used this augmented group awareness tool performed better in terms of group decision and individual correctness than did unsupported groups.

Methodological Approaches

According to Strijbos and Stahl (2007), previous attempts to analyze communication in computer-supported chat environments on a surface-level focused on counting messages to determine students' discourse participation and on mean numbers of words as an indicator for the quality of chat messages. Later, more promising methods like thread-length analysis (e.g., Cakir et al., 2005; Holmer, 2008) and the analysis of interaction patterns in chat environments (Rosé, Wang, Arguello, Stegmann, Weinberger, et al., 2008; Soller, 2004) expanded this repertoire with more sophisticated methods. Current research on chat-based CSCL agrees that surface methods can provide a useful initial orientation, but more detailed analysis is needed to understand the underlying mechanisms.

Strijbos and Stahl (2007) as well as Zemel et al. (2007) provide valuable coding schemes and reflective guidelines for the analysis of chat-based learning and knowledge-sharing processes. Herring (1999) as well as Münzer and Holmer (2009) give guidance to analyze the coherence of contributions to chat-based discourses and knowledge construction. Beers et al. (2007) provide a detailed study on how to analyse the negotiation of common ground in CSCL.

Besides analyses of chat discourses on a linguistic level another promising current methodological development in CSCL research are *eye movement analyses*. Eye movements have proved to be a valuable source of information for the study of cognitive processes, however, they are hardly employed in the field of CSCL. Eye tracking as a new methodological approach to CSCL offers promising insights into real-time interaction processes during collaboration and the use of supportive extensions for chat discourse. For example, do the collaborators look at shared external representations within a chat environment (for example, threading or awareness visualisations) while composing or when receiving a chat message? Such questions should be examined in more detail to yield guidelines for chat-based learning environments. Only few eye tracking studies exist in research on learning and knowledge communication (Oehl & Pfister, 2009; Schwonke, Renkl, & Berthold, 2007).

This might be due to the lack of suitable observational *coding schemes* to code the continuous flow of behavioural data into meaningful discrete categories. We proposed a coding scheme for global text processing in chat-based CSCL based on established well-defined eye movement measures (Oehl, Pfister, & Gilge, 2008). Participants' eye movements were encoded according to two information categories: (i) behavior, and (ii) point of interest. The first category *behaviour* comprised possible behavioural actions of learners within chat-based scenarios (reading, searching, browsing and writing). The definitions were based on gaze patterns, that is, significant and well-defined eye movement measures in terms of fixations and saccades (e.g., Hyönä, Lorch, & Rinck, 2003; Radach & Kennedy, 2004). The second category *point of interest* indicated the point within the chat environment the behavioural category was referring to (for example, to previous discourse contributions). The codes within each category were mutually exclusive and the combination of two variables out of the two categories resulted in one definite eye movement code for global text processing. In preliminary studies, for each category of the coding scheme high inter-rater reliabilities could be obtained (Oehl et al., 2008).

Eye tracking studies and the search for appropriate coding schemes emphasize the importance of detailed process analyses, which appears to be the most fruitful path for future research. Efforts along similar lines have been made by Strijbos and Stahl (2007), Rosé et al. (2008), Zemel et al. (2007), and Meier, Spada, and Rummel (2007), among others.

FUTURE RESEARCH DIRECTIONS

A central focus of future research will probably be on *adaptive scripting*, that is, once learners begin to internalize a collaboration script, it can be useful to reduce the level of coercion and allow the learners to make more decisions themselves. The process of reducing the amount of external instruction is known as *fading* (Pea, 2004). Such collaboration scripts need mechanisms to adapt to the learners' progress and to assess the learners' evolving interactions. On the side of the designer or educator, this could be achieved by providing tools for flexible scripting, which allow to change the script as the learning process proceeds (Haake & Pfister, 2007). Also, a promising approach is automated methodological analysis. For example, Miao, Harrer, Hoeksema, and Hoppe (2007) are currently investigating the possibilities of automated adaption of collaboration scripts in combination with sequencing features embedded in a chat environment with anchored discussion.

Another prospective research focus is the *sustainability* of computer-mediated learning and knowledge communication processes and their exploitation for further learning or relearning purposes. The increasing application of computer-supported learning environments for learning and teaching processes provides a major advantage in contrast to traditional learning situations: It is a relatively trivial task to record the ongoing learning process in detail on digital media, to store it, to make it available for a large audience via the internet and, especially, to reuse it for purposes of repetition or further study. For example, chat environments make it easy to produce a complete recording of an extended online learning process, either automatically or controlled by the student or teacher. These stored learning processes may range from simple recordings of chat histories to full-fledged recordings of chat environments, including awareness tools or external knowledge representations. However, it is far from clear what kind of recordings should be used, and what kinds of replay formats might be helpful depending on the purpose of the learner. Preliminary results are reported by Oehl and Pfister (2008).

CONCLUSION

This chapter provides an overview about the possibilities and problems of chat-based collaborative knowledge construction. The most important frequently reported deficits of the medium chat were outlined. Promising approaches to overcome these deficits by extending chat communication when applied in net-based collaborative learning settings are discussed. Short-comings of chat, tolerable when chat is used for casual communication, must be overcome when used for serious learning and knowledge building. Helpful and effective design features which have the potential to promote chat-based collaborative learning and knowledge construction for different settings are described and discussed. Existing strategies and tools which augment chat environments and improve learning outcomes include possibilities to impose structure on the macro-level of a learning discourse, as well as strategies or tools supporting and enhancing micro-structural features of collaborative learning. We predict that in the future methods that foster the coherence and intuitive comprehension of multiple threaded discourses, such as referencing tools, and methods that provide visualisations of evolving knowledge building processes, such as awareness tools, will become an enriching standard in chat-based collaborative learning.

Checklist for Chat-Based Knowledge Construction Scenarios

Although full-fledged virtual environments might play an increasingly more important role in e-collaborative applications, minimalistic text-based chat communication, we maintain, will have its place in educational as well as in business areas whenever task-focused net-based knowledge construction is a vital objective. However, from what is currently known about chat-based knowledge construction, a few guiding principles can be distilled for the practitioner who wants to use chat as his or her medium of choice:

- **Provide support:** Do not rely that productive discourse will emerge automatically without further guidance; any kind of support is better than none
- **Provide domain-specific support:** If feasible, for example, overviews, visualisations, or similar schemes
- **Keep support optional:** Do not force the discourse into a straitjacket. Participants prefer to have a choice whether to use supporting measures.
- **Ensure coordination and awareness:** Facilitate the grounding process in communication by reducing costs of coordination, for example, with a turn-taking rule, as well as reducing problems of awareness, especially in larger groups, for example, with group awareness tools
- **Ensure coherence of discourse:** Use strategies and tools which support participants in relating their messages in a meaningful way, for example, referencing or threading. Coherence is crucial.
- **Ensure disambiguation:** By typing of contributions to the chat message discourse.
- **Be flexible:** Change tools as soon as it turns out they are not accepted; adapt the tool to your participants, not participants to the tool.

The consideration of these guiding principles for chat-based communication, we suggest, might unlock the potential of this medium for enhanced e-collaborative knowledge construction in chat environments.

REFERENCES

Baker, M. J., Hansen, T., Joiner, R., & Traum, D. (1999). The role of grounding in collaborative learning tasks. In P. Dillenbourg (Ed.), *Collaborative learning: Cognitive and computational approaches* (pp. 31-63). Oxford, UK: Elsevier.

Baker, M. J., & Lund, K. (1997). Promoting reflective interactions in a computer-supported collaborative learning environment. *Journal of Computer Assisted Learning, 13*, 175–193. doi:10.1046/j.1365-2729.1997.00019.x

Beers, P. J., Boshuizen, H. P. A., Kirschner, P. A., & Gijselaers, W. H. (2007). The analysis of negotiation of common ground in CSCL. *Learning and Instruction, 17*, 427–435. doi:10.1016/j.learninstruc.2007.04.002

Beißwenger, M. (2007). *Sprachhandlungskoordination in der Chat-Kommunikation*. Berlin, Germany: Walter de Gruyter.

Brennan, S. (1998). The grounding problem in conversations with and through computers. In S. R. Fussel & R. J. Kreuz (Eds.), *Social and cognitive psychological approaches to interpersonal communication* (pp. 201-225). Mahwah, NJ: Erlbaum.

Bromme, R., Hesse, F. W., & Spada, H. (2005). Barriers, biases and opportunities of communication and cooperation with computers: Introduction and overview. In R. Bromme, F. W. Hesse & H. Spada (Eds.), *Barriers and biases in computer-mediated communication - and how they may be overcome* (pp. 1-14). New York: Springer.

Buder, J., & Bodemer, D. (2008). Supporting controversial CSCL discussions with augmented group awareness tools. *Computer-Supported Collaborative Learning, 3*(2), 123–139. doi:10.1007/s11412-008-9037-5

Cakir, M., Xhafa, F., Zhou, N., & Stahl, G. (2005). Thread-based analysis of patterns of collaborative interaction in chat. *Paper presented at the international conference on AI in Education* (AI-Ed 2005). Retrieved from http://GerryStahl.net/pub/aied2005.pdf

Clark, H. H. (1996). *Using language*. Cambridge, UK: Cambridge University Press.

Clark, H. H., & Brennan, S. E. (1991). Grounding in communication. In L. B. Resnick, J. M. Levine & S. D. Teasley (Eds.), *Perspectives on socially shared cognition* (pp. 127-149). Washington, DC: APA.

Cornelius, C., & Boos, M. (2003). Enhancing mutual understanding in synchronous computer-mediated communication by training: Trade-offs in judgmental tasks. *Communication Research, 30*, 147–177. doi:10.1177/0093650202250874

Daft, R. L., & Lengel, R. H. (1984). Information richness: A new approach to managerial behavior and organisation design. In B. M. Staw, & L. L. Cummings (Eds.), *Research in organisational behaviour* (Vol. 6, pp. 191–233). Greenwhich, CT: JAI Press.

Daft, R. L., & Lengel, R. H. (1986). Organizational information requirements, media richness and structural design. *Management Science, 32*(5), 554–571. doi:10.1287/mnsc.32.5.554

Derry, S. J. (1999). A fish called peer learning: Searching for common themes. In A. M. O'Donnell & A. King (Eds.), *Cognitive perspectives on peer learning* (pp. 197-211). Mawah, NJ: Erlbaum.

Dillenbourg, P. (2002). Over-scripting CSCL: The risks of blending collaborative learning with instructional design. In P. A. Kirschner (Ed.), *Three worlds of CSCL. Can we support CSCL?* (pp. 61-91). Heerlen, The Netherlands: Open Universiteit Nederland.

Dillenbourg, P., & Hong, F. (2008). The mechanics of CSCL macro scripts. *Computer-Supported Collaborative Learning, 3*, 5–23. doi:10.1007/s11412-007-9033-1

Dillenbourg, P., & Tchounikine, P. (2007). Flexibility in macro-scripts for computer-supported collaborative learning. *Journal of Computer Assisted Learning, 23*, 1–13. doi:10.1111/j.1365-2729.2007.00191.x

Dillenbourg, P., & Traum, D. (2006). Sharing solutions: Persistence and grounding in multimodal collaborative problem solving. *Journal of the Learning Sciences, 15*(1), 121–151. doi:10.1207/s15327809jls1501_9

Endsley, M. (1995). Towards a theory of situation awareness in dynamic systems. *Human Factors and Ergonomics Society, 37*(1), 32–64. doi:10.1518/001872095779049543

Fischer, F., Bruhn, J., Grasel, C., & Mandl, H. (2002). Fostering collaborative knowledge construction with visualization tools. *Learning and Instruction, 12*(2), 213–232. doi:10.1016/S0959-4752(01)00005-6

Fischer, F., Kollar, I., Mandl, H., & Haake, J. M. (Eds.). (2007). *Scripting computer-supported collaborative learning*. New York: Springer.

Fuks, H., Pimentel, M. G., & de Lucena, C. J. P. (2006). R-U-Typing-2-Me? Evolving a chat tool to increase understanding in learning activities. *International Journal of Computer-Supported Collaborative Learning, 1*, 117–142. doi:10.1007/s11412-006-6845-3

Gutwin, C., & Greenbergs, S. (2002). A descriptive framework for workspace awareness for real-time groupware. *Computer Supported Cooperative Work, 11*, 411–446. doi:10.1023/A:1021271517844

Haake, J. M., & Pfister, H.-R. (2007). Flexible scripting in net-based learning groups. In F. Fischer, I. Kollar, H. Mandl & J. M. Haake (Eds.), *Scripting computer-supported collaborative learning* (pp. 155-175). New York: Springer.

Hancock, J. T., & Dunham, P. J. (2001). Language use in computer-mediated communication: The role of coordination devices. *Discourse Processes, 31*(1), 91–110. doi:10.1207/S15326950dp3101_4

Herring, S. (1999). Interactional coherence in CMC. *Journal of Computer-Mediated Communication, 4*. Retrieved from http://www.ascusc.org/jcmc/vol4/issue4/herring.html

Hewitt, J. (2005). Toward an understanding of how threads die in asynchronous computer conferences. *Journal of the Learning Sciences, 14*(4), 567–589. doi:10.1207/s15327809jls1404_4

Hollingshead, A. B., McGrath, J. E., & O'Connor, K. M. (1993). Group task performance and communication technology: A longitudinal study of computer-mediated versus face-to-face work groups. *Small Group Research, 24*, 307–333. doi:10.1177/1046496493243003

Holmer, T. (2008). Discourse structure analysis of chat communication. *Language@Internet, 5*. Retrieved from http://www.languageatinternet.de

Hron, A., Hesse, F. W., Cress, U., & Giovis, C. (2000). Implicit and explicit dialogue structuring in virtual learning groups. *The British Journal of Educational Psychology, 70*, 53–64. doi:10.1348/000709900157967

Hyönä, J. Lorch. R. F., & Rinck, M. (2003). Eye movement measures to study global text processing. In J. Hyönä (Ed.), *The Mind's Eye: Cognitive and Applied Aspects of Eye Movement Research* (pp. 313-334). Amsterdam: Elsevier.

Johnson, D. W., & Johnson, R. T. (1992). Positive interdependence: Key to effective cooperation. In R. Hertz-Lazarowitz & N. Miller (Eds.), *Interaction in cooperative groups: The theoretical anatomy of group learning* (pp. 174-199). New York: Cambridge University Press.

Jucks, R., Paechter, M., & Tatar, D. G. (2003). Learning and collaboration in online discourses. *International Journal of Educational Policy, Research, and Practice, 4,* 117–146.

Kimmerle, J., & Cress, U. (2008). Group awareness and self-presentation in computer-supported information exchange. *International Journal of Computer-Supported Collaborative Learning, 3*(1), 85–97. doi:10.1007/s11412-007-9027-z

Kirschner, P. A., & Kreijns, K. (2005). Enhancing sociability of computer-supported collaborative learning environments. In R. Bromme, F. W. Hesse & H. Spada (Eds.), *Barriers and biases in computer-mediated knowledge communication - and how they may be overcome* (pp. 169-192). New York: Springer.

Kobbe, L., Weinberger, A., Dillenbourg, P., Harrer, A., Hämäläinen, R., Häkkinen, P., & Fischer, F. (2007). Specifying computer-supported collaboration scripts. *International Journal of Computer-Supported Collaborative Learning, 2,* 211–224. doi:10.1007/s11412-007-9014-4

Kollar, I., Fischer, F., & Hesse, F. W. (2006). Collaboration scripts – a conceptual analysis. *Educational Psychology Review, 18,* 159–185. doi:10.1007/s10648-006-9007-2

Kopp, B., Ertl, B., & Mandl, H. (2006). Wissensschemata und Skript - Förderung der Anwendung von Theoriewissen auf Aufgabenbearbeitung in Videokonferenzen. *Zeitschrift für Entwicklungspsychologie und Pädagogische Psychologie, 38*(3), 132–138. doi:10.1026/0049-8637.38.3.132

Kreijns, K., Kirschner, P. A., & Jochems, W. (2003). Identifying the pitfalls for social interaction in computer-supported collaborative learning environments: A review of the research. *Computers in Human Behavior, 19*(3), 335–353. doi:10.1016/S0747-5632(02)00057-2

Lipponen, L., Rahikainen, M., Lallimo, J., & Hakkarainen, K. (2003). Patterns of participation and discourse in elementary students' computer-supported collaborative learning. *Learning and Instruction, 13*(5), 487–509. doi:10.1016/S0959-4752(02)00042-7

Meier, A., Spada, H., & Rummel, N. (2007). A rating scheme for assessing the quality of computer-supported collaboration processes. *Computer-Supported Collaborative Learning, 2,* 63–86. doi:10.1007/s11412-006-9005-x

Miao, Y., Harrer, A., Hoeksema, K., & Hoppe, U. H. (2007). Modeling CSCL scripts – a reflection on learning design approaches. In F. Fischer, I. Kollar, H. Mandl, & J. M. Haake (Eds.). *Scripting computer-supported collaborative learning* (pp. 117-134). New York: Springer.

Mühlpfordt, M. (2006). *ConcertChat* [Computer software]. Retrieved June 19, 2009, from http://www.ipsi.fraunhofer.de/concert/index_en.shtml?projects/chat

Mühlpfordt, M., & Wessner, M. (2005). Explicit referencing in chat supports collaborative learning. In *Proceedings of CSCL 2005,* Taipei, Taiwan, 2005.

Münzer, S., & Holmer, T. (2009). Bridging the Gap Between Media Synchronicity and Task Performance. *Communication Research, 36*, 76–103. doi:10.1177/0093650208326464

Newlands, A., Anderson, A. H., & Mullin, J. (2003). Adapting communicative strategies to computer-mediated communication: An analysis of task performance and dialogue structure. *Applied Cognitive Psychology, 17*, 325–348. doi:10.1002/acp.868

O'Donnell, A. M., & King, A. (Eds.). (1999). *Cognitive perspectives on peer learning.* Mahwah, NJ: Erlbaum.

O'Neill, J., & Martin, D. (2003). Text chat in action. In M. Pendergast, K. Schmidt, C. Simone, & M. Tremaine (Eds.), *GROUP '03. Proceedings of the Conference on Supporting Group Work* (pp. 40-49). New York: ACM.

Oehl, M., & Pfister, H.-R. (2008). Re-learning in CSCL with learning protocols: which replay formats are beneficial? In G. Richards (Ed.), *Proceedings of World Conference on E-Learning in Corporate, Government, Healthcare, and Higher Education 2008* (pp. 3046-3051). Chesapeake, VA: AACE.

Oehl, M., & Pfister, H.-R. (2009). Explicit References in Chat-Based CSCL: Do They Faciliate Global Text Processing? Evidence from Eye Movement Analysis. In A. Dimitracopoulou, C. O'Malley, D. Suthers, & P. Reimann (Eds.), *Computer Supported Collaborative Learning Practices: CSCL2009 Conference Proceedings* (Vol. 2, pp. 138-140). International Society of the Learning Sciences, Inc. (ISLS).

Oehl, M., Pfister, H.-R., & Gilge, A. (2008). Global text processing in CSCL with learning protocols: a coding scheme for eye movement analyzes. In P. A. Kirschner, F. Prins, V. Jonker, & G. Kanselaar (Eds.), *International Perspectives in the Learning Sciences: Cre8ing a learning world. Proceedings of the Eighth International Conference for the Learning Sciences – ICLS 2008* (Vol. 3, pp. 103-104). International Society of the Learning Sciences, Inc. (ISLS).

Pea, R. D. (2004). The social and technological dimensions of scaffolding and related theoretical concepts for learning, education, and human activity. *Journal of the Learning Sciences, 13*(3), 423–451. doi:10.1207/s15327809jls1303_6

Pfister, H.-R. (2005). How to support synchronous net-based learning discourses: Principles and perspectives. In R. Bromme, F. W. Hesse & H. Spada (Eds.), *Barriers and biases in computer-mediated knowledge communication - and how they may be overcome* (pp. 39-57). New York: Springer.

Pfister, H.-R., & Mühlpfordt, M. (2002). Supporting discourse in a synchronous learning environment: The learning protocol approach. In G. Stahl (Ed.), *Proceedings of CSCL 2002* (pp. 581-589). Hillsdale, NJ: Erlbaum.

Pfister, H.-R., Mühlpfordt, M., & Müller, W. (2003). Lernprotokollunterstütztes Lernen - ein Vergleich zwischen unstrukturiertem und systemkontrolliertem diskursivem Lernen im Netz. *Zeitschrift für Psychologie mit Zeitschrift für Angewandte Psychologie, 211*, 98–109. doi:10.1026//0044-3409.211.2.98

Pfister, H.-R., & Oehl, M. (2009). The Impact of Goal Focus, Task Type, and Group Size on Synchronous Net-Based Collaborative Learning Discourses. *Journal of Computer Assisted Learning, 25*, 161–176. doi:10.1111/j.1365-2729.2008.00287.x

Pimentel, M. G., Fuks, H., & de Lucena, C. J. P. (2003). Co-text loss in textual chat tools. In P. Blackburn, C. Ghidini, R. M. Turner & F. Giunchiglia (Eds.), *Modeling and using context. Lecture notes in computer science* (Vol. 2680, pp. 483-490). Berlin, Germany: Springer.

Radach, R., & Kennedy, A. (2004). Theoretical perspectives on eye movements in reading: Past controversies, current issues, and an agenda for future research. *The European Journal of Cognitive Psychology, 16*, 3–26. doi:10.1080/09541440340000295

Rice, R. E., & Love, G. (1987). Electronic emotion: Socioemotional content in a computer-mediated network. *Communication Research, 14*, 85–108. doi:10.1177/009365087014001005

Rosé, C. P., Wang, Y. C., Arguello, J., Stegmann, K., Weinberger, A., & Fischer, F. (2008). Analyzing collaborative learning processes automatically: Exploiting the advances of computational linguistics in computer-supported collaborative learning. *International Journal of Computer-Supported Collaborative Learning, 3*(3), 237–272. doi:10.1007/s11412-007-9034-0

Rummel, N., & Spada, H. (2005). Learning to collaborate: An instructional approach to promoting collaborative problem-solving in computer-mediated settings. *Journal of the Learning Sciences, 14*(2), 201–241. doi:10.1207/s15327809jls1402_2

Rummel, N., Spada, H., & Hauser, S. (2009). Learning to collaborate while being scripted or by observing a model. *Computer-Supported Collaborative Learning, 4*, 69–92. doi:10.1007/s11412-008-9054-4

Sacks, H., Schegloff, E., & Jefferson, G. (1974). A simplest systematics for the organization of turn-taking for conversation. *Language, 50*(4), 696–735. doi:10.2307/412243

Schooneboom, J. (2008). The effect of a script and a structured interface in grounding discussions. *Computer-Supported Collaborative Learning, 3*, 327–341. doi:10.1007/s11412-008-9042-8

Schwonke, R., Renkl, A., & Berthold, K. (2007). Knowledge construction with multiple external representations: What eye movements can tell us. In S. Vosniadou, D. Kayser, & A. Protopapas (Eds.). *Proceedings of the 2nd European Cognitive Science Conference* (pp. 238-243). New York, NJ: Erlbaum.

Short, J., Williams, E., & Christie, B. (1976). *The social psychology of telecommunications.* London: John Wiley & Sons.

Soller, A. (2004). Understanding knowledge sharing breakdowns: A meeting of the quantitative and qualitative minds. *Journal of Computer Assisted Learning, 20*, 212–223. doi:10.1111/j.1365-2729.2004.00081.x

Soller, A., Martinez, A., Jerman, P., & Mühlenbrock, M. (2005). From mirroring to guiding: A review of state of the art technology for supporting collaborative learning. *International Journal of Artificial Intelligence in Education, 15*, 261–290.

Stahl, G. (2006). Analyzing and designing the group cognition experience. *International Journal of Collaborative Information Systems, 15*, 157–178. doi:10.1142/S0218843006001323

Stahl, G., Koschmann, T., & Suthers, D. D. (2006). Computer-supported collaborative learning. In R. K. Sawyer (Ed.), *The Cambridge handbook of the learning sciences* (pp. 409-425). New York: Cambridge University Press.

Stahl, G., Zemel, A., Sarmiento, J., Cakir, M., Weimar, S., Wessner, M., & Mühlpfordt, M. (2006). Shared referencing of mathematical objects in online chat. In S. A. Barab, K. E. Hay, & D. T. Hickey (Eds.), *Proceedings of the 7th International Conference of the Learning Sciences (ICLS 2006)* (pp. 716-722). Mahwah, NJ: Lawrence Erlbaum Associates.

Strijbos, J.-W., & Stahl, G. (2007). Methodological issues in developing a multi-dimensional coding procedure for small-group chat communication. *Learning and Instruction, 17*, 394–404. doi:10.1016/j.learninstruc.2007.03.005

Weinberger, A., Ertl, B., Fischer, F., & Mandl, H. (2005). Epistemic and social scripts in computer-supported collaborative learning. *Instructional Science, 33*, 1–30. doi:10.1007/s11251-004-2322-4

Weinberger, A., Fischer, F., & Mandl, H. (2002). Fostering computer supported collaborative learning with cooperation scripts and scaffolds. In G. Stahl (Ed.), *Computer Support for Collaborative Learning: Foundations for a CSCL Community. Proceedings of CSCL 2002* (pp. 573-574).

Werry, C. C. (1996). Linguistic and interactional features of internet relay chat. In S. C. Herring (Ed.), *Computer-mediated communication: Linguistic, social and cross-cultural perspectives* (pp. 29–46). Amsterdam and Philadelphia: John Benjamins.

Wood, D. (2001). Scaffolding, contingent tutoring and computer-supported learning. *International Journal of Artificial Intelligence in Education, 12*, 280–292.

Zemel, A., Xhafa, F., & Cakir, M. (2007). What's in the mix? Combining coding and conversation analysis to investigate chat-based problem-solving. *Learning and Instruction, 17*, 405–415. doi:10.1016/j.learninstruc.2007.03.006

Section 2
Approaches in the Context of E–Collaborative Knowledge Construction

Chapter 4

Collaborative Knowledge Construction:
Examples of Distributed Cognitive Processing

Michael Tscholl
University College London, UK

John Dowell
University College London, UK

ABSTRACT

In discussions centered on jointly solving a problem or case, significant construction of new knowledge can occur. Several theoretical frameworks have been invoked to explain the productivity of dialogues, but questions about the relative or unique impact on learning of the multiple facets of dialogues remain. We present an analytical approach that studies small-group discussions from the perspective of joint cognitive processing of knowledge and information. We illustrate our approach through a microanalysis of two discussions that were held in a real-world educational setting. We show that knowledge construction can overlap significantly with critical argumentation, but may occur even in its absence. On the basis of these findings we propose a refined definition of co-construction, and a view of the inter-relations between interaction and co-construction. We discuss the implications of our findings for the analysis and evaluation of differences in knowledge co-construction in different environments.

INTRODUCTION

In discussions centered on jointly solving a problem or carrying out a task, significant construction of new knowledge can occur. Each problem represents a new challenge for a team and requires the use and adaptation of existing knowledge. The productivity and creativity of groups involved in joint problem solving is well known, although the processes by which groups jointly construct knowledge have only recently been studied in detail. Beyond the relevance of research studying these processes for social learning theories, more direct interest in this research is in its potential output for the evaluation of computer systems supporting virtual learning groups. In the last decade, substantial research has addressed issues such as how to support distributed

DOI: 10.4018/978-1-61520-729-9.ch004

groups, how to analyse distributed group processes and how distributed processing of knowledge relates to learning gains. This chapter contributes to this literature by presenting an analytical approach by which the joint knowledge construction processes as well as the potential learning gains from such processes are described and modeled. We rely on a microanalysis of dialogues that focuses on relations between learners' utterances in terms of how they contribute to the processing of an abstract item – such as an idea, concept or example – identifying in this way joint distributed processing of knowledge. This focus on processes rather than media-specific properties of communication renders the approach applicable to group learning and work situations mediated by computer technology.

The identification of these processes relies on an information-processing model of learning from problems, cases and examples that we compiled from the relevant cognitive science literature (the model is described in the section after next). The model allows us to analyze contributions in terms of what knowledge they introduce into the groups' cognitive environment and how they affect a change in the groups' conception, interpretation and solution of the problem. This analysis of the ideas and knowledge conveyed in contributions is combined with an analysis of the interactional processes (e.g. argumentation) of exchanges. By carrying out these parallel analyses we are able to describe not only how students interact, but also what effect interactions have on how knowledge is processed and what new knowledge is constructed. We illustrate our analyses with data collected in a real-world educational setting where groups of 1st year medical students discuss cases of professional medical ethics concerning 'the right to die'. Through this analysis we will show that a generic model capturing distributed cognitive processing can describe in detail knowledge co-construction, and that such a model can support the practical empirical analysis of dialogues. We then discuss the implications of our approach to analyse and evaluate co-construction in face-to-face and computer-mediated communication settings.

BACKGROUND

The theoretical and analytical approach we lay out and illustrate in this chapter is to be seen within the question of how new knowledge is constructed in and from social interaction and more generally, how the social and the cognitive interact. These questions have acquired greater relevance as the significance of social interaction in learning has been recognized in research on learning (e.g. Andriessen, Baker & Suthers, 2003). The consensus emerging in recent years assumes the pre-eminence of the social in conversation and collaboration while also accepting that knowledge is transformed through the social (cf. D'Andrade, 1981, Hutchins, 1995; Stahl, 2003). For example, we will show in this chapter that learners' utterances contribute to interpretation construction while they engage in an argumentation.

As a result of the dual nature of interaction, research often separates analytically the social from the knowledge-transformational. For example, while an interaction follows socially accepted conventions, contributions to an argumentation also convey and transform knowledge, and affect how a problem is recognized as such, problematised, interpreted and solved (Barron, 2003). While this analytical separation does not question the primacy of the social, contributions to a conversation carrying content and transforming knowledge affect a groups' problem conception. Suthers (Suthers et al., 2005), for example, recognizes the primacy of the social but also analyses semantic-informational relations between utterances once there is evidence for social interaction to trace the development of shared conceptions. Our analysis lies on a similar research agenda, but by studying the processing of information and knowledge in terms of their distribution over people and in terms of what knowledge they construct, we extend the notion of interaction to include dependency relations established through carrying out complex and shared cognitive operations. Our approach therefore extends earlier research on distributed reasoning, mostly carried out within a Vygotskian tradition of social constructivism (e.g. Resnick et al. 1993), and integrates it with more recent research on interaction and information uptake (e.g. Suthers, 2005).

An important contribution to capture the social as well as knowledge-transformational properties of dialogue contributions is the notion of epistemic interactions (DeVries, Lund & Baker, 2002). Similar to epistemic actions that an individual carries out in order to modify a problem space (Kirsh & Maglio, 1994), epistemic interactions modify a groups' conception and understanding of a problem that is being jointly solved.

However, most research has so far focused on identifying which kinds of interactions are conducive for learning (e.g. Schwarz, Neuman & Biezuner, 2000; Baker et. al, 2001), thus emphasising the social aspect of conversations rather than studying how each contribution to a conversation affects the conception of a problem being jointly solved. Further, this research relies on the identification of statistical correlations between particular interaction sequences and their value in terms of learning gains, an approach that is unable to capture whether a particular contribution or small exchange (e.g. one leading to an insight) had an especially important role in learning. A notable exception to this trend is Mephu-Nguifo, Baker & Dillenbourg (1999) where a dialogue is analyzed on two levels and the inter-relations between the levels studied through microanalysis. The levels are: the dynamic-conversational level that identifies the kind of dialogue moves being performed, and; the knowledge level identifying the changes in the knowledge space occurring through the conversation. The authors' analysis rests on the assumption that a strong parallelism exists between dialogue moves and knowledge-transformation moves. In their illustrative example, the authors

analyse each contribution in terms of how it modifies the knowledge space (e.g. specializing an item, or generalizing it), as well as which dialogue moves occur in parallel. Through this analysis, the authors are able to identify patterns of knowledge generation and knowledge change, enabling them to trace the development of a shared body of knowledge from collaboration.

Similarly to Memphu-Nguifo, et al. (1999) we rely on a microanalysis of dialogues to identify their structural properties, exposing in detail how the distributed processing of knowledge changes the conception, interpretation and solution of the case. In contrast with Mephu-Nguifo et al.'s (1999) work that relied on assumptions of knowledge transformation derived from artificial intelligence research, we instead rely on a generic cognitive model of learning to identify the processes that occur, and the knowledge these processes construct or modify.

Our analysis rests on the assumption that an essential parallelism exists between generic cognitive processes in individual and group knowledge construction, an assumption that has guided some important work in collaborative learning (e.g. Dillenbourg, 1996). That is, we assume that just as individuals construct abstract representations through processes that operate on representations, so also do groups. We therefore take the further step of suggesting that what is known about how individual learners learn from problem solving can be applied to a group of collaborative learners. Such processes as abstraction, generalization, comparison or analogy that have been well established in studies of individual learners may equally occur with groups of learners, distributed though over the group members. We present here a generalized model of learning from problem solving that integrates prior models and findings for application to both individuals and groups.

We make a further assumption that most of the processing of knowledge and information relevant for our understanding of how the group constructs new knowledge is visible in the group members' activities, be they utterances, chat messages or manipulations of shared epistemic representations. Individual processes occurring, as it were, 'in the mind' are strongly constrained by the external representations built up as a result of the group's construction processes (Hutchins, 1995).

To further locate our work, we will briefly outline related work on knowledge construction processes.

The general notion of co-construction, as one of the core concepts in constructivism, entails that utterances can be seen as constructing knowledge in a group learning situation: learners add knowledge, elaborate knowledge, analyse knowledge, etc. (e.g. Davies, 2003). However, this prior work does not make a commitment to *what is constructed* by these processes. Rather, the interest of this research is in characterizing the processes in a dialogue in order to make judgments about its efficacy or other qualities (cf. Hara et al., 2000; Newman et al., 1995). Other work has focused on the knowledge and information processed in a group learning situation, exploiting the concept of critical thinking (Garrison et al., 2000); however the aim has been to gauge how much a group learning environment supports a community of inquiry of which critical thinking is a core component.

Our approach posits a relation between processes and products, that is, it speculates about what knowledge is constructed by specific cognitive processes. We focus especially on how the correct abstract representation of the problem is constructed, and describe which processes are employed during the construction of that representation. This description allows us to characterise a learners' discussion of a case in terms of processes.

A GENERIC MODEL OF LEARNING FROM PROBLEMS AND CASES

Learning as Abstracting a Structure

Learning with cases and problems is fundamentally the abstraction of structure; it is the recognition of deep features that give meaning to the situation. Cognitive science has consistently viewed learning in this way, particularly in relation to episode-based problem solving (Gick & Holyoak, 1980; Forbus, 2001). Our aim is to discover which cognitive processes occur when people attempt to solve problems and which processes give rise to the structure of a case. To this end we first compiled a generalized model of learning from cases, characterizing what is learnt and how. The model delineates a set of cognitive processes and a set of cognitive products (most notably the structure of the case) that are likely to occur as a result of the tension between the case (novel information) and existing knowledge. A summary of the model is presented in the next section (for a more detailed description, see Tscholl & Dowell, 2008)

Cognitive Processes in Learning

Learning with cases and problems occurs through two main processes: first, people use their existing knowledge to interpret and conceptualize the case, refining their knowledge in the process; second, they may abstract a structure from the case. For example, they may conceptualize a particular medical negligence lawsuit as essentially an issue of whether patient consent had been obtained, and recognize in it a structural link between patient consent and actual clinical outcome. Hence the two main processes of learning with cases are intertwined: using existing knowledge to interpret the case can force recognition of new relationships within that knowledge, relationships that then represent the structure of the case. Even without acquiring structural knowledge, cases can promote learning by refining the existing knowledge because cases, consisting of specific concrete aspects, function implicitly as tests of existing knowledge. For example, people may ask whether some conceptual knowledge is really useful to interpret the case, and by verifying the applicability of that knowledge, they may learn more about when to apply that knowledge. Clearly, the process of verifying the applicability of knowledge is most pertinent with conceptual knowledge, but also models may be tested.

Research on learning from problems and examples has identified more specific processes of learning. In mathematics learning, for example, students acquire knowledge about the conditions of applicability of production rules by adding the specific features of an example to the condition part of that rule. A similar form of learning occurs when conceptual knowledge is used to interpret cases, leading to learning about the conditions under which specific concepts should be used. However, learning of concepts also entails recognising the structure of problem features, a pattern or constellation of concrete problem aspects that is representative for a specific type of problem. The literature on this form of learning is extensive, and a common theme is that experts possess a large set of domain-specific examples acquired through practice that permits them to see the structure of a problem situation beyond its surface features. Chi et al.'s (1981) research on expert/ novice differences led to the claim about the role of a conceptual system (concepts related to other concepts) in problem solving. This research emphasised that learning occurs through practice that teaches how to apply concepts to examples, how to relate concepts and how to abstract structural (relational) knowledge from examples.

The research on example-based problem solving has identified generalization over specific features of instances as the core learning mechanisms, by which those cognitive products found in the research cited above are built. Reusing an earlier example to solve a current one forces a generalization over the two: the concrete features

are abstracted and represented by more general knowledge (Ross & Kennedy, 1990). The role of earlier solved problems (memorized problem solving episodes) is hence crucial and explains why it is that expert-type knowledge is generated through practice and experience.

When earlier episodes are used, a problem may be solved through analogy, and people may abstract the structure common both to the current and the past problem (Gick & Holyoak, 1980). However, analogies are computationally complex and demand some structural knowledge about the solved problem. As a result, analogies occur only infrequently.

While the reuse of episodes is frequent in problem solving, novices are more likely to use conceptual knowledge because they still do not possess an adequate knowledge base of episodes. However when episodes are available and are used, conceptual knowledge is used at several stages of reuse: at retrieval, for the identification of similarities between the current and memorized episodes, and when transferring structural knowledge from the past to the current problem. In these stages, conceptual knowledge is both used and constructed. Knowledge abstracted in this way constitutes domain-specific knowledge in the form of principles or 'points of the story'. Individual case aspects that have been found also provide indices for the organization of episodes in memory (Kolodner, 1993) and become part of the domain-specific vocabulary. In future situations, students will rely on this vocabulary to encode new cases

THE STUDY CONTEXT: CASE-BASED-LEARNING IN MEDICAL SCHOOL

Our study involved engagement with students in a medical school where case-based-learning is practiced alongside more traditional lecture-based teaching. We gathered data from two small groups of students taking a course on professional skills development within the undergraduate medical program. The groups were given two clinical scenarios in each of which a profoundly ill patient wished to end their life. During the discussions, the students develop a shared explanation for each scenario that would take into account the relevant concepts and principles of medical ethics facing the clinicians treating the patients.

Two landmark cases (Mrs. B and Mrs. Pretty) were chosen for the sessions. The cases report the 'stories' of both patients in detail, including how their health deteriorated, the kinds of requests they made to various medical and judicial bodies, and the final decision made by a panel of judges. The cases are similar in all aspects with the crucial difference, however, that Mrs. B is able end her own life, while the physical condition of Mrs. Pretty would require the active intervention of a physician (passive versus active euthanasia). Understanding the similarities and differences between the two cases is of major importance to understanding the domain of medical ethics.

Euthanasia cases are normally understood on the basis of several general ethical principles: autonomy (the right to chose), nonmaleficience (the prohibition for physicians to harm patients) and beneficence (the duty to help and do good). Euthanasia cases raise ethical issues because these principles often are in conflict with each other. For example, a patient requesting euthanasia would emphasise that it is her right to do so under the principle of autonomy, while a physician would rely on the principle of nonmaleficience to deny her request. However, if the quality of life of the patient is very low, then the principle of beneficence may apply because a physician may help end the patient's suffering.

The students were introduced to these basic principles in an earlier lecture.

The two groups comprised three and five members, respectively and their discussions were videotaped. Two tutors were present during the discussions, but did not act as facilitators. The groups were located in the same room, either around a table or sitting in a circle in chairs.

Impressions on Learning

Here we report our impressions on learning that will come into play when we discuss the analysis of the discussion.

In general, both groups identify the ethical dilemma in the cases and relate the case aspects correctly to the relevant concepts. The identification of the dilemma occurs gradually, with individual students bringing in different viewpoints that are then argued for and against by their peers. This characteristic is somewhat puzzling because the students' own opinions of the cases are based on the principle of autonomy, i.e. they place the 'freedom to choose' above all other considerations, and none of the students places much value on other principles that conflict with it. The arguments for and against the judges' decision are hence not made on the grounds that some students agree with the judges. Rather, it appears that some students temporarily take on the view of the authorities. In this sense, many exchanges can be characterised as arguments.

DATA ANALYSIS AND INTERPRETATION

The differentiation between interactional processes and knowledge construction processes, as discussed above, can be recognised in the dialogues of the medical students. We will examine this differentiation in a series of individual contributions and exchanges within the dialogues. The examples support the argument for a dual (interactional and knowledge-transformational) approach to analysing collaborative knowledge construction.

Figure 1. An exchange (of group 2) revolving around the question whether the patient was of 'sound mind' when deciding to decline to artificially prolong her life. The question of whether her decision was made with 'sound mind' implicates the principle of autonomy.

57	E	that she has made an informed decision *** she was, she was (points to his head)
58	P	... she was stable ...
59	E	yes
60	C	she was unstable ...
61	P	she was stable at the point when she wrote the letter [6:55]

Argumentation and Knowledge Construction

Figure 1 shows just one such example. The exchange revolves around the question whether the patient was able to make an informed decision about the choices she has available in case her conditions worsen or she even enters a vegetative state. The patient discussed here indeed requested to be allowed to 'die peacefully' – and did so in writing – but the core question is whether the patient was of sound mind when she made that decision. Merely informing the patient about her choices is insufficient because the patient must also be able to understand her choice. Once it is established that the patient was indeed 'of sound mind', her decision is binding for a court of law, or so the students believe.

More generally, the exchange revolves around the question of whether the principle of autonomy is applicable to the case. This principle guides medical decisions in that it stipulates that patients have a right to decide their own treatment and are not to be paternalised by medical personnel. The principle is however only applicable if the patient is able to make decisions for herself.

When we look at the exchange, we can observe that it has the structure of an argumentation (cf. Walton, 2006). An early claim by student E (line 57) is questioned by student C (60) and, as a result of this questioning, the claim is refined (61). Students E and P collaborate in developing the initial claim (57 + 58). Student E's gesture (in 57) shifts the groups' attention to the mind of the patient, a gesture whose relatively broad reference is taken up by student P (58). P correctly re-interprets the gesture, and specialises and narrows the reference to 'state of mind', assigning, in the process, also a quality ('stable') to that state (cf. Mephu-Nguifo et al., 1999). In other words, student P takes up an idea and transforms it into a specific claim (cf. Suthers, 2005). C challenges the claim (in 60), assuming that it refers to a later state in the patient's history, namely a state where her worsened condition may have made it difficult to make an informed decision. E interprets correctly the underlying temporal reference of C's counterclaim, and points out that the original claim was meant to apply to the 'point when she wrote the letter' (61).

The exchange is significant in terms of what knowledge is constructed and how the case is interpreted. It starts with student E placing the concept of 'informed decision' into the groups' cognitive environment (cf. Sperber & Wilson, 1986). The student justifies that introduction by pointing to her head, thus almost literally drawing a relation between the concept and the 'mind'. The related but more specialised concept 'state of mind' remains implicit in the contribution, but is, as described above, made explicit by the subsequent one. Through these two contributions the concept of informed decision is, for one, related to the idea of mind, and, second, proposed as

Figure 2. An exchange (of group 2) revolving around the question whether the concept of quality of life is applicable to the cases and can be used as the basis of a decision. Once the students agree that 'quality of life' cannot be defined, student E attempts to argue again for the patients on the basis of the principle of autonomy (line 132).

125	E	are there cases where the doctors are going to push the button?
126	I	it is difficult, you can see where it is going to be very blurred, if somebody, you know, ... who judges what is quality of life
127	C	* {inaudible}
128	E	but in this case {pointing to sheet} she was sick
129	I	she was, but you know in this case I think if they said that this is legal then it could potentially open up a lot of, ... a lot of blur kind of, a lot of grey areas
130	E	...where to draw the line...
131	I	exactly
132	E	... someone has to be able to say and someone has to be able to write...

contributing to the interpretation of the case, i.e. as a building block in the overall construction of the interpretation. Thus, the concept is instantiated by the case, and, importantly, the case is structured according to the concept: one of the facts is given relevance within the overall interpretation of the case, and the temporal structure of the case is emphasised.

In this distributed processing, argumentation and interpretation construction overlap: while making and elaborating a claim and supporting it by referring to a fact, then questioning that claim and further elaborating it, the students gradually tie the facts of the case to the concept, while the concept also prompts the students to give meaning and relevance to the facts of the case. However, not only is the case structured but the concept itself is refined in the process. Indeed, the imprecise deictic reference to 'the mind' and its relation to the concept of informed decision is specialised twice: once through the adjective 'stable' (an adjective that should be further specialised into 'sound mind') and a second time by précising that it is sufficient for the patient to have been of sound mind at the time she wrote the letter for her demand to be taken seriously. Thus, the conditions of applicability of the concept of informed decision, and, by implication of the principle

of autonomy, are clarified. The stable cognitive structure constructed through this exchange is thus: in order for the principle of autonomy to apply a patient must be of sound mind at the moment she makes the decision.

Figure 2 is another example of how students refer to a fact of the case to explore whether or not a concept is to be used to interpret the case. The concept in question is 'quality of life' that is introduced into the discussion as a result of a reminding (see figure 3). The students consider quality of life a decisive criterion for selecting an appropriate action in euthanasia cases. Specifically, their view is that patients should be allowed to die if they suffer chronically and medical science is unable to provide relief to pain as well as curing the illness. This view corresponds to the idea of a 'good and gentle death' – doctors may allow (passive euthanasia) or even induce (active euthanasia) death – and is a specialisation of the principle of beneficence. In a sense, a doctor would 'do good' if he relieves a patient from unnecessary suffering. The principle contrasts with the demand that doctors should not harm their patients.

The exchange also evolves as an argumentation, with student I contending that the concept of quality of life cannot be used to make a decision in this case (126). She points out that the problem

Figure 3. An example of a student bringing a publicly known case into the discussion (a reminding). The case is 'processed' jointly by the group, without the exchange demonstrating the form of an argument.

122	I	yeah, ... there was a huge case in Canada a few years ago, were a father assisted his daughter, she was really very disabled ... and no quality of life [C and E seem to know the case] and he just suffocated her, and I think he got 12 years manslaughter.
123	E	she actually left a note writing?
124	I	no, she was actually 12 years old and very disabled

is really that no objective and universal definition of 'quality of life' exist. Student E counters I's statement pointing to the patients' condition of sickness (meaning 'extreme and persistent suffering') to support her argument that the patient should indeed be relieved of her suffering by being allowed to die (128). E's statement is also an attempt to define 'quality of life' as the absence of 'extreme and persistent suffering', thus constructing, in the attempt to counter I's statement, a relationship between a concept and a generic feature.

E's counterclaim is again countered by student I who re-emphasises that it is impossible to define what 'quality of life' is. Her arguments are particularly interesting because they embody an epistemological distinction between the definition of a concept and the nature of concepts, i.e. that concepts *do* have definitions.

The contribution in line 132 is somewhat puzzling, but considerations on the students' general view of the cases can shed some light on it. It is clear from the discussion that the students are on the patient's side and that they are in favour of granting patients who suffer from a terminal illness the option to end their life. A generic anti-establishment stance (there is evidence of this in the discussion), as well as a heightened sensibility for suffering may underlie this stance.

If we consider this stance, then E's contribution in line 132 can be interpreted as another attempt to argue for the patient, an attempt that results from the failure of the previous one (I's counter-argument in 129). Our reasoning underlying this interpretation is the following. Superficially, the

statement appears to offer a definition of 'quality of life', i.e. to say that as long as the patient "is able to say (i.e. talk) and write", she has some quality of life. However, this is a very unlikely meaning, because one could not possibly think this to be 'defining' characteristics of quality of life – the more appropriate being, for example, absence of pain, etc. The statement refers instead, in our view, to the ability to express one's wish, i.e. to "be able to say and write what I want to happen to me". The statement thus refers to the earlier exchange about the patient's decision before her condition worsened (see figure 1), and emphasises again that what should uniquely and finally be considered in a court of law is the patient's own will (the decision would be made on the basis of the principles of autonomy and non-paternalism).

While this interpretation can account for the students' overall as well as local stance (i.e. having 'lost' the argument based on quality of life), the form of the statement is still puzzling. But we think we can see it as an amalgamation of a previous idea and a form used in the immediately preceding contributions. In a sense, the statement is an idea that is *cast* in a form similar to the overall form of defining general properties of a concept. As discussed above, the concept of quality of life has been dismissed as not being definable. This *form* of argument is taken up in 132, but used to argue *for* the patient by combining it with an idea expressed in a previous exchange. Our interpretation is supported by research on pupils' talk that showed how argument stratagems (such as analogies) are, once introduced, taken up by other group members and used as general rules instantiated by particular knowledge (Anderson et al., 2001). Clearly, social learning theory, especially of Vygotskian tradition, would recognise in this exchange the development of ways of reasoning from social interaction.

Complex Distributed Processes: Remindings and Analogies

We will now describe in detail contributions based on remindings. As introduced in the model section of this chapter, remindings may result in complex reasoning and argumentation because the similarity between a known case and the current case may need to be identified, knowledge transferred, and inferences made. However, contrary to our expectations, remindings, though occurring quite frequently, do not lead to the extensive and complex processing of the cases. They nevertheless contribute to the interpretation of the case in the following ways.

Figure 3 shows a contribution (line 122) referring to a case of active euthanasia reported in the media about a severely disabled girl who was suffering from persistent pain and who was killed by a family member. The case has clear similarities with the cases of Mrs. B and Mrs. Pretty: all suffer from persistent pain, and medical science is unable to provide relief or improvement of their condition. While these similarities are apparent to the students, and some features common to all cases have already been identified earlier in the discussion, the reminding prompts emphasis on the fact that the patients have very little 'quality of life'. This feature is crucial to understand the motivation of the girl's father: he has apparently acted because he could not bear anymore to see his daughter suffer. Indeed, in contrast to the cases discussed by the students, the girl had not expressed her wish to die (she was probably unable to) and therefore the case does not revolve around the question whether the patient has made an informed decision.

The exchange is not an argumentation in a sense that different viewpoints are explored and one view is accepted on the basis of the facts of the case. Contributions 123 and 124 are not opposing the claim about the similarities between the cases, made implicitly in 122. Rather, contribution 123 is to be understood as accepting and further elaborating that similarity. That is, it asks: "which features make these cases similar and different?" The question about 'a written note (i.e. decision)' refers to the earlier identified fact that Mrs. B had made a decision in writing, a fact that implicates the concept of informed consent (and autonomy) in decision of the case. Since the Canadian girl made no such decision, the similarity between the cases rests on the absence of quality of life which, through the reminding, is *identified as another defining feature* of the cases; and possibly a feature upon which a decision should be based. Indeed, this exchange is immediately preceding the exchange shown in figure 2 where the notion of quality of life is explored further.

The way in which the reminding affects the interpretation of the case has a parallel in the processing of similar examples in individual problem solving, where features identified by mapping similar examples or problems are highlighted (e.g. Gentner & Markman, 1994). Here, the normally relatively automatic and unconscious assessment of similarities between cases is an externalised cognitive process distributed over the group members. Most interestingly, the reminding, beyond leading to the identification of a feature of the cases ('quality of life'), is incidental in directing the course of the discussion. Specifically, the newly identified feature becomes a new topic the group focuses on in the subsequent contributions (see figure 2).

These 'assessments' of similarities/differences occur quite frequently, either as a result of a reminding (i.e. bringing in a case from the outside, as it were) or by comparing the two cases. One important effect of a reminding is, as described above, the identification of distinctive descriptive

Figure 4. A contribution to the discussion of group 1. Student I brings in a case leading to dilemma similar to cases of 'the right to die.'

| 147 | I | I: because, I know someone who is a doctor and they had {referred?}, *** had a huge motorcycle accident he actually had to have blood transfusions, * but when it actually came out ** that he was a Jehovah's witness [who refuse blood transfusions] , ** how can a doctor try to preserve life *** |

Figure 5. A contribution (group 1) comparing the two cases

| 64 | C | (shakes head in disagreement) ... there is the difference, because [looks at sheet], because, basically, Mrs. Pretty, no, Mrs. B ... it is passive and they could just switch off the ventilator, because basically they are keeping her alive, without her will, ..., whereas the other one [Mrs. Pretty] was actually actively given drugs to die. So that's why it's difference there |

features. However, also the ethical dilemma of euthanasia cases themselves may be emphasised in a reminding. Figure 4 shows just one such example. Here a student talks about a case known to her about a Jehovah's Witness who refused a blood transfusion because of his religious beliefs. The reminding emphasises the contrast between autonomy (non-paternalism) and the principle of beneficence, intended as the demand that doctors need to do the utmost to help their patients. It does not affect the interpretation of the cases as such because the students had already identified the contrasting principles before this contribution. Rather, it shows how the students generalise upon the dilemma embodied in the cases to other cases, a processing of the case that helps them build up a richer knowledge base of cases.

Constructing Knowledge from Comparing the Cases

Clearly, the fact that the students were given two cases to discuss present opportunities for comparing them and abstracting similarities and differences (see figure 5 as an example).

The processes of relationing, of, comparison between and abstraction from cases are highly valuable for learning. While memorisation of cases or episodes is by itself considered to be a form of learning (cf. Kolodner, 1993), the reuse of episodes is crucially dependent on their organisation in memory. Episodes must be organized so as to permit efficient access and retrieval. Episodes that share features are normally grouped under a single header, with features not shared providing a subsequent identification opportunity if the header matches the input. Relating cases becomes a crucial mechanism in adding a case to the knowledge base, since it entails an assessment of similarities and differences, and an assessment of the relevance of the features, i.e. the identification of that or those features that represent the core of the case.

As described, the two cases represent similar situations. Active versus passive intervention is the only specific difference between them. This difference assigns different weights to beneficence and nonmaleficiance, but the validity of autonomy remains unchanged.

Relating the cases, i.e. seeing the differences and similarities (see figure 5), promote the reiteration of the application of the ethical principles, as well as the search for a solution that is applicable to both cases. It is a first step towards a deeper understanding of the principles.

NOTES ABOUT LEARNING

In this chapter, we set out to identify knowledge construction processes in dialogues. To this aim, we interpret contributions to the dialogues within the question how they generate or modify the conception, interpretation and solution of a case, and refine their conceptual knowledge. We interpret the discussions as the processing of information and knowledge that results from the tension between new information (the case) and existing conceptual and episodic knowledge. Since the members of the groups are first year students, their conceptual knowledge is rather simple, such as the general sense that cases of the 'right to die' represent, in our culture, unsolvable ethical dilemmas. When tasked to provide an interpretation and 'solution' to such cases in an educational setting, the students are confronted with the fact that their knowledge may be incomplete and too simple to provide a reasoned stance. In this sense, the cases then become concrete examples whereupon the students' conceptual knowledge is tested. From this perspective, we show how contributions lead to a more refined understanding of the case and result in the construction of more refined or new conceptual knowledge.

Given the relatively unsophisticated understanding of ethics, it is not surprising that most of the discussion revolves around the question whether and to what degree core ethics concepts are applicable to the cases. This question is decided (1) on a group level and (2) often as a result of differing viewpoints that give rise to argumentations. In particular, students check the facts of the case, as well as their personal definitions of the concepts to decide whether one or more concepts are suitable for the interpretation of the case. In these instances, argumentation and knowledge construction overlap. For example, the question whether the patient has made an informed decision is played out as an argument that is 'resolved', and results also in the progressive refinement of the concept of informed consent, in relation to

the question about its conditions of applicability. The more refined conception of the notion of informed consent is then the shared and individual take-away of the discussion.

Studies on how individuals classify examples and on the structure of concepts deriving from engaging with examples have shown that similar processes and take-aways take place on an individual level (Wisniewski & Medin, 1994). In a group situation, this processing is distributed over the members: one member introduces the concept, another questions its applicability, a third points to a fact that supports its applicability, etc. Thus our assumption about the basic similarity between individual and group-level processes is supported by the data.

Argumentations arising from different viewpoints are not necessarily the only form of interaction conducive for knowledge construction. Indeed, as figure 3 shows, the processing of new knowledge (in that specific exchange: another case) occurs at a group level and results in the identification of a new feature ('quality of life') without the exchange being an argumentation. Rather, the 'assessment' of the similarity of the cases and the identification of a common feature occurs at a group level, with the group members carrying out individual processing steps that make up the complex processing of remindings in individuals (e.g. Gentner, 1983; Ross, 1989). It appears, from this exchange, that the reminding is placed into the group's cognitive environment with the implicit 'invitation' to jointly processes it.

As concerns the overall evaluation of learning, it should be pointed out that learning is conservative in the sense that students do not radically revise their conceptual knowledge, but rather refine it. The discussions serve more as opportunities to externalise existing knowledge about the ethical dilemma rather than the dilemma being identified for the first time. It promoted a clearer recognition of the relationships between ethical principles that embody the dilemma; and further, these conceptual relations have become tied to two specific cases that may serve as the basis for conceptualisations of structurally similar cases.

The occurrence of relationing between cases is of major importance: when students discuss the similarities and differences between the cases, they develop a knowledge base of cases, with the aspects found to be different functioning as distinguishing features. These features are indices for future retrieval of cases (Kolodner, 1993). The abstraction of commonalties and differences between cases leads also to the acquisition of a domain-specific vocabulary that will be used to encode future cases of medical ethics.

The view of learning underlying our analysis as constructing a structure (a conception, an interpretation) of a case, contrasts with other views on social knowledge construction, most prominently those advocated by Activity Theory (e.g. Engeström, Miettinen & Punamäki, 1999), where learning is conceptualized as an expansion, as discovering the limits of, for example, ontologies and processes. The recognition of these limits would place people in the zone of proximal development where they develop new ontologies, processes and practices (Engeström, 1987). The students whose discussions we analyse do not question underlying ontologies nor discover new ways of understanding ethics cases. The processes uncovered through our analysis should hence be seen as being placed *between* processes where such radical re-organizations take place. That is, the educational setting intended as a learning ecology (Cobb & Steffe, 1983) comprising the students, the goals of the course, the lectures, the learning material and the tasks were overall not conducive and indeed not designed for re-organisation.

DISCUSSION AND CONCLUSION

The structure of collaborative knowledge construction discourses, as well as their quality (in terms of learning gains), has been studied extensively in the recent decade, with recognition given

to the fundamentally social nature of learning. Yet despite the attempts to develop integrated accounts of discourses (e.g. Baker et al., 2007), fundamental questions remain about the nature and the incidence of different characteristics of dialogues. In this chapter, we rely on the view of dialogues as an interactional achievement that also processes knowledge and information in a group's cognitive environment. The analysis we presented confirms the validity of our assumptions and allows us to make conclusions about how to study knowledge construction. For one, we were able to identify a substantial overlap between typical interactional structures (such as argumentations) and the elaboration of existing conceptual knowledge. Specifically, attempts to apply conceptual knowledge to the cases, something that contributes to interpretation construction, occur often within argumentations and have the effect of successfully refining the students' conceptual knowledge (figures 1 and 2). This confirms the view that argumentations are overall conducive for learning. However, we also identify distributed processing of knowledge without being able to discern typical argumentation structured in the dialogue (figure 3). Instances of remindings are particularly noticeable in this respect: cases reported in the media or drawn from students' personal experiences are processed jointly or by a single individual, both without the introduction of differing viewpoints, counter-claims, etc. Nevertheless, these kinds of processing are valuable for learning and do also influence the direction of the discussion.

If we consider the exchanges as constituted by a sequence of contributions that respond to earlier ones, and that therefore a dependency exists between subsequent contributions, we can see that the interaction between group members follows from their joint distributed processing of knowledge. Indeed, as described, the processing of knowledge is distributed over the group members, but contrary to claims about the role of socially shared scripts in establishing and maintaining interaction, our analysis leads to the claim that it is common procedural knowledge that is at the basis of the interaction. That is, the relationships between individual contributions are guided by complex cognitive operations that are part of the individuals' cognitive repertoire in a group-learning situation. This view does not invalidate the role of other interactional structures. Rather, it is to be seen as an alternative level of analysis that may bring research closer to understanding the relationship between interaction and knowledge construction.

Though our data were collected in a face-to-face learning situation, our view of interaction and the analysis deriving from it applies equally well to e-learning environments. For one, we have presented a more refined conception of co-construction. Often, co-construction is said to have occurred when people work together in solving a problem and jointly produce new knowledge (cf. Dillenbourg et al., 1995). This rather loose definition of co-construction cannot answer the question as to whether individuals respond to each others' contributions (i.e. genuinely interact) - or merely add knowledge to the common ground predating the learning session (cf. Suthers, 2005; Koschmann, 2003); nor does it study the ways in which contributions are built upon by group members and how these individual uptakes lead to a shared outcome. Our view of co-construction as the joint processing of knowledge offers a clear analytic construct that can guide analyses independently of media characteristics. Indeed, and this is our second point, we have argued that the analysis of co-construction needs to identify the way in which an utterance, written message, etc. contributes to the joint processing of knowledge. Thus, the target of this analysis, namely the content of and processing entailed by a contribution, can be found in messages written in a chat facility or other computer-based medium as well as in spoken contributions, and also in manipulations of graphical representations of knowledge on a computer interface, thus extending the applicability of our analysis to a wide variety of environ-

ments. Indeed, the notion of uptake, on which our approach is based, has been introduced as a high-level concept to study informational and processing relations between acts independently of media-specific properties (Suthers et al. 2007), where the notion of acts refers to anything learners do (talking, writing, dragging virtual objects in an interface, etc.). By carrying out analyses at this level, we can provide evidence where genuine co-construction has occurred and where not, and thus study the effects of media conditions on co-construction.

We present here a few speculations regarding the difference of co-construction in f2f and CMC environments. As is clear in our examples, the distributed processing relies on the f2f-conversation-typical tight sequentiality, where non-verbal communication is used for floor control and turn-taking. The absence of opportunities for non-verbal communication in CMC will certainly have an effect on the distribution of processes, because, for example, learners contribute to a chat in parallel or, if a chat history is available, take up and elaborate ideas conveyed in quite time-distant contributions. The typical distributed processing of knowledge (concepts or other cases) observed in the discussions here may well be absent, and individual group members may resort to more substantial individual processing rather than inviting other group members to 'jointly process' what is being said. This is all the more the case in asynchronous systems such as discussion forums where responses can be delayed and arrive out of sequence, and where learners normally present small arguments rather than short proposals. However, in order to identify these differences and to have a basis for addressing them through design, an analytical approach is needed as the basis for a common description of the cognitive implications of different conditions. It is such an approach that this chapter has attempted to provide.

ACKNOWLEDGMENT

This work was supported by the Economic and Social Research Council of the UK (grant L328 25 3013).

REFERENCES

Anderson, R. C., Nguyen-Jahiel, K., McNurlen, B., Archodidou, A., Kim, S.-Y., & Reznitskaya, A. (2001). The snowball phenomenon: spread of ways of talking and ways of thinking across groups of children. *Cognition and Instruction, 19*(1), 1–46. doi:10.1207/S1532690XCI1901_1

Andriessen, J., Baker, M., & Suthers, D. (Eds.). (2003) *Arguing to learn: Confronting cognitions in computer-supported collaborative learning environments*. Dordrecht, The Netherlands: Kluwer.

Baker, M., Andriessen, J., Lund, K., van Amelsvoort, M., & Quignard, M. (2007). Rainbow: a framework for analyzing computer-mediated pedagogical debates. *International Journal of Computer-Supported Collaborative Learning, 2*(2-3). doi:10.1007/s11412-007-9022-4

Baker, M. J., deVries, E., Lund, K., & Quignard, M. (2001). Computer-mediated epistemic interactions for co-constructing scientific notions: Lessons learned from a five-year research programme. In P. Dillenbourg, A. Eurelings & K. Hakkarainen (Eds.), *Proceedings of EuroCSCL 2001: European Perspectives on Computer-Supported Collaborative Learning* (pp. 89-96).

Barron, B. (2003). When smart groups fail. *Journal of the Learning Sciences, 12*, 307–359. doi:10.1207/S15327809JLS1203_1

Chi, M., Feltovich, P., & Glaser, R. (1981). Categorization and representation of physics problems by experts and novices. *Cognitive Science, 5*, 121–152. doi:10.1207/s15516709cog0502_2

Cobb, P., & Steffe, L. (1983). The constructivist researcher as teacher and model builder. *Journal for Research in Mathematics Education, 14*(2), 83–94. doi:10.2307/748576

D'Andrade, R. (1981). The cultural part of cognition. *Cognitive Science, 5*(3), 179–195. doi:10.1207/s15516709cog0503_1

Davies, E. (2003). Knowledge integration in science teaching: Analyzing teachers' knowledge development. *Research in Science Education, 34*, 21–53. doi:10.1023/B:RISE.0000021034.01508.b8

DeVries, E., Lund, K., & Baker, M. J. (2002). Computer-mediated epistemic dialogue: Explanation and argumentation as vehicles for understanding scientific notions. *Journal of the Learning Sciences, 11*(1), 63–103. doi:10.1207/S15327809JLS1101_3

Dillenbourg, P. (1996). Some technical implications of the distributed cognition approach on the design of interactive learning environments. *Journal of Artificial Intelligence in Education, 7*(2), 161–180.

Dillenbourg, P., Baker, M., Blaye, A., & O'Malley, C. (1995). The evolution of research on collaborative learning. In E. Spada & P. Reiman (Eds.), *Learning in Humans and Machine: Towards an interdisciplinary learning science* (pp. 189-211). Oxford, UK: Elsevier.

Engeström, Y. (1987). *Learning by expanding: an activity-theoretical approach to developmental research*. Helsinki, Finland: Orienta-Konsultit.

Engeström, Y., Miettinen, R., & Punamäki, R.-L. (Eds.). (1999). *Perspectives on Activity Theory*. Cambridge, UK: Cambridge University Press.

Forbus, K. (2001). Exploring analogy in the large. In D. Gentner, K. Holyoak, & B. Kokinov (Eds.), *The analogical mind: Perspectives from Cognitive Science*. Cambridge, MA: MIT Press.

Garrison, D. R., Anderson, T., & Archer, W. (2000). Critical thinking in a text-based environment: computer conferencing in higher education. *The Internet and Higher Education*, 2(2), 87–105. doi:10.1016/S1096-7516(00)00016-6

Gentner, D. (1983). Structure-mapping: a theoretical framework for analogy. *Cognitive Science*, 7(2), 155–170.

Gentner, D., & Markman, A. (1994). Structural alignment in comparison: no difference without similarity. *Psychological Science*, 5(3). doi:10.1111/j.1467-9280.1994.tb00652.x

Gick, M., & Holyoak, K. (1980). Analogical problem solving. *Cognitive Psychology*, 12, 306–355. doi:10.1016/0010-0285(80)90013-4

Hara, N., Bonk, C. J., & Angeli, C. (2000). Content analysis of online discussion in an applied educational psychology course. *Instructional Science*, 28, 115–152. doi:10.1023/A:1003764722829

Herring, S. (1999). Interactional coherence in CMC. *Jrnl. of Computer-Mediated Communication*, 4(4).

Hutchins, E. (1995). *Cognition in the Wild*. Cambridge: MA, MIT Press.

Kirsh, D., & Maglio, P. (1994). On distinguishing epistemic from pragmatic actions. *Cognitive Science*, 18, 513–549.

Kolodner, J. (1993). *Case-based Reasoning*. San Mateo: CA, Morgan Kaufmann.

Koschmann, T. (2002). Dewey's contribution to the foundations of CSCL research. In G. Stahl (Ed.), *Proceedings of CSCL 2002* (pp. 17-22). Mahwah, NJ: LEA.

Mephu-Nguifo, E. Baker, M.J. & Dillenbourg, P. (1999). Knowledge transformations in agents and interactions: A comparison of machine learning and dialogue operators. In P. Dillenbourg (Ed.), *Collaborative Learning: Cognitive and Computational Approaches* (122-146). Amsterdam: Pergamon / Elsevier Science.

Newman, D. R., Webb, B., & Cochrane, C. (1995). A content analysis method to measure critical thinking in face-to-face and computer supported group learning. *Interpersonal Computing and Technology*, 3(2), 56–77.

Resnick, L., Salmon, M., Zeitz, C., Wathen, S., & Holowchak, M. (1993). Reasoning in conversation. *Cognition and Instruction*, 11(3), 347–364.

Ross, B. (1989). Remindings in learning and instruction. In Vosniadou, S. & Orthony, A. (Eds.) *Similarity and Analogical Reasoning*. New York: Cambridge University Press.

Ross, B., & Kennedy, P. (1990). Generalising from the use of earlier examples in problem solving. *Journal of Experimental Psychology. Learning, Memory, and Cognition*, 16.

Schwartz, B., Neuman, Y., & Biezuner, S. (2000). Two wrongs make it right…if they argue together! *Cognition and Instruction*, 18(4), 461–494. doi:10.1207/S1532690XCI1804_2

Sperber, D., & Wilson, D. (1986). *Relevance: Communication and Cognition*. Cambridge, MA: Harvard UP.

Stahl, G. (2003). Meaning and interpretation in collaboration. In B. Wasson, S. Ludvigsen, & U. Hoppe (Eds.), *Designing For Change in Networked Learning Environments* (pp. 523-532). Dordrecht, The Netherlands: Kluwer Academic Publishers.

Suthers, D. (2005). *Technology affordances for intersubjective learning: a thematic agenda for CSCL*. Keynote at the 2005 International Conference of Computer Support for Collaborative Learning (CSCL 2005), Taipei, Taiwan.

Suthers, D. D., Dwyer, N., Medina, R., & Vatrapu, R. (2007). A framework for eclectic analysis of collaborative interaction. In C. Chinn, G. Erkens, & S. Puntambekar (Eds.), *The 2007 Computer Supported Collaborative Learning (CSCL) Conference* (pp. 694-703). New Brunswick: International Society of the Learning Sciences.

Tscholl, M., & Dowell, J. (2008). Analysing problem structuring in a collaborative explanation dialogue to capture conceptual change. In V. Sloutsky, B. Love, & K. McRae (Eds.), *Proceedings of 30th Meeting of The Cognitive Science Society*. Mahwah, NJ: LEA.

Veerman, A. L., Andriessen, J., & Kanselaar, G. (1999). Collaborative learning through computer-mediated argumentation. In C. Hoadley & J. Roschelle (Eds.), *Proceedings of CSCL99*. Mahwah, NJ: LEA.

Walton, D. (2006). *Fundamentals of Critical Argumentation*. Cambridge, UK: Cambridge University Press.

Wisniewski, E., & Medin, D. (1994). On the interaction of theory and data in concept learning. *Cognitive Science, 18*(2), 221–281.

Chapter 5
Contributions of E–Collaborative Knowledge Construction to Professional Learning and Expertise

Christian Harteis
University of Regensburg, Germany

ABSTRACT

Modern employment and work life demands employees who continuously develop and actualize their competencies. Information and computer technology (ICT) provides rich opportunities to support individuals in their professional learning. This contribution describes professional learning from the perspective of research on expertise, which analyses the development of knowledge structures on the way from novice to high performing expert. First, a general concept of competence and knowledge development is to be discussed and different types of knowledge are to be distinguished. Then this contribution discusses opportunities to support this development with e-learning scenarios on the various levels of knowledge construction. The main argument is that e-learning opportunities are an option to overcome the traditional distinction between formal and informal learning. However, crucial challenges for implementing e-collaborative knowledge construction remain – as the contribution finally will conclude.

INTRODUCTION

In order to enhance people's employability and enterprises' competitiveness, educational policy in Europe focuses heavily on lifelong learning (Grek et al., 2009; Rauner, 2008). This is a reaction to the circumstances of modern worklife in Western industries, which is often characterized as knowledge-based or knowledge-intensive work

(Cort, 2009). A crucial component for occupational success on an individual level and economic success on an organizational level is the capability to react to changes in the competition, which can be the result of technological development or customers' demands. As a consequence of market diversification, it is not possible to predict developments precisely. Moreover, it is plausible that future developments and demands cannot be foreseen. Hence, it is rational to rely on employees' capabilities and competences, which are the best and most flexible

DOI: 10.4018/978-1-61520-729-9.ch005

resources available for the enterprises. Employees are expected to develop expertise in their professional domain, in order to be capable of steadily performing on a high level (Gruber, Harteis, & Rehrl, 2008). However, it cannot be sufficient just to focus competence development on top-down strategies of human resource development programs. Sending employees to trainings and seminars are only one component of individual learning opportunities. It is the workplace environment itself which is a rich source for learning experiences (Billett, 2001, 2006a). Employees are expected to develop their competencies in a self-directed fashion.

Without a doubt, information and communication technology (ICT) is an important resource for all kinds of work-related and professional learning. Computer networks can support professional learning activities in manifold ways: they provide access to information, and they allow the distribution of knowledge and bring together individuals who are spatially distributed. In the area of educational sciences, research on professional learning investigates preconditions for the development of professional competencies. This article describes the recent understanding of professional expertise and discusses chances and challenges for e-collaborative knowledge construction as a support for professional learning as the development and the maintenance of individual professional competence and expertise.

DEVELOPING PROFESSIONAL COMPETENCE AND EXPERTISE: STATE OF RESEARCH

When discussing issues of professional learning, the core reference is professional competence. In the following sections a theoretical concept of professional competence and its development is discussed, in order to develop a precise understanding of the purposes that are followed by work-related e-collaborative knowledge construction.

This section presents a typology of professional competence as well as a consideration of the acquisition of competence from the perspective of knowledge construction. Several types of knowledge (e.g., declarative, conceptual, procedural, and negative knowledge) are distinguished in order to explain the capability to perform on a high level. Case examples of computer-mediated learning processes, which illustrate this general theory of professional competence in the area of e-collaborative knowledge construction, will be addressed in the third section.

Typology of Professional Competence

Educational research in the area of professional learning focuses on conditions, characteristics, and effects of the development of professional competence. Large parts of that body of research focus on the teaching and learning of teachers, so that teaching certainly is among the best investigated of professional domains. Ample findings exist regarding how teachers acquire knowledge, from being a teaching novice to becoming a teaching expert (Berliner, 2001). Meanwhile, professional learning research covers almost the full range of occupational activities from artists or sportsmen, managers, white collar workers through blue collar workers (e.g., Boshuizen, Bromme, & Gruber, 2004; Ericsson, Charness, Feltovich, & Hoffman, 2006; Billett, Harteis, & Eteläpelto, 2008). The most prominent approach in that field is the research on expertise, which usually compares cognitive features of persons on different levels of expertise during the solving of problems or dealing with professional tasks (Ericsson, 2006). Expertise, in this view, is defined by the capability to show excellent performance stably and repeatedly. However, often it is quite difficult to operationalize excellence in a domain, e.g., in the domains of counselling or teaching. Referring only to the year of experience, number of clients or examinations, numbers of sessions, and courses or turnover (if freelancers) would provide a quantitative measurement, but may represent only a small section out of the range of professional activities. However, most of the studies about expertise try to avoid such problems by operationalizing expertise through calculating the likely amount of experience required in the domain to develop expertise. On average, researchers assume a time span of ten years that is necessary for the acquisitions of expertise (Berliner, 2001).

Theories developed on the basis of empirical findings from the domains of medicine and counselling have received much attention, for instance the theory of knowledge encapsulation (Boshuizen & Schmidt, 1992) or the theory of learning from experience (Strasser & Gruber, 2004). These theories explain the growth of expertise by changes in the individual's repertoire and the structure of explicable or declarative knowledge. On the way from novice to expert, these theories claim that theoretical declarative knowledge is enriched by practical problem-solving and through deliberate practice. With an increasing level of expertise, declarative knowledge loses its direct relevance for practical solutions, and case-based patterns of practice emerge instead, that are more likely to be able to respond to non-routine or unfamiliar problems within the domain. At the expert level, declarative knowledge is encapsulated in experience-based memory organisation packets—the so-called "encapsulation" theory thus describes how expert knowledge changes its quality if rich experience with domain-specific cases is accessed. Subjects at the expert level, when asked about their ways of problem-solving, less frequently report about the use of declarative knowledge than do novices, who still do not have the benefit of a broad scope of practical experience. The theory of learning from experience describes cognitive processes occurring when practical reality confirms or contradicts an individual's knowledge about procedures and operations, i.e., his/her procedural knowledge. If practice confirms procedural knowledge as being appropriate for reaching action

goals, this procedural knowledge is strengthened by reflective confirmation. As a consequence, robust learning from experience occurs—as well as when procedural knowledge fails, which leads to a modification of that knowledge (Kolodner, 1983). It will be an issue of later sections to discuss the opportunities for ICT to support these processes of knowledge development.

It is plausible to describe professional competence by using expertise research, because the demand for professional performance usually is set on a high level. Professional competence is mostly based on the domain-specific knowledge of the profession that can be distinguished in declarative knowledge—knowledge explaining facts and objects—and procedural knowledge—knowledge about how things work or how things interrelate. The importance of these two kinds of knowledge changes as professional experience increases.

Accordingly, Gruber, Harteis, and Rehrl (2008) proposed a model for professional competence consisting of the following four elements: (1) competence for the adequate accomplishment of recurring tasks (routines), (2) competence to deal with novel situations (i.e., mental models of anticipated situations), (3) competence to acquire and recall well-founded domain-specific declarative knowledge, and (4) competence to become a member of a community of practice.

The Acquisition of Professional Competence

The acquisition of professional competence is a twofold process: on the one hand, the development of domain-specific theoretical knowledge occurs in institutional forms of learning (e.g., apprenticeship, trainings). In those settings, mainly declarative and general procedural knowledge is taught, in order to provide learners an occupational background and general strategies for application to the occupation. On the other hand, professional activity embeds individuals' learning in the social context of the workplace and gives access to a community of practice (Wenger, 1998). By doing so, procedural knowledge on the use of declarative and general knowledge develops in the context of the workplace, and in ways that reflect both the norms and practices of the workplace, but also individuals' expanding repertoire of experiences (Billett, 2006a). It is this dimension of competence development which shapes the potential of ICT.

The acquisition of domain-specific knowledge and the embedding in the community of practice cannot be thought of as independent, but instead as complementary (Mandl, Gruber, & Renkl, 1996). The relation between individual and sociocultural processes affects the development of professional competence continuing over the entire occupational career. Employees bring their specific experiences into a (eventually computer-generated) training setting, while they (hopefully) modify their knowledge and create new skills during and within the training setting, and finally they transfer training-content into their daily work life. When integrating experiences into training as well as when transferring training lessons into practice, it is crucial that the learners have opportunities to monitor the application of the newly generated knowledge in the context of their work activities.

Recent literature and research acknowledges the importance of the integration of formal and informal learning processes (Gruber, Harteis, Mulder, & Rehrl, 2005) and the interrelation between individual and social contributions to professional learning (Billett, 2006a; Harteis & Billett, 2008). The relation between theoretical (conceptual) and practical (procedural) knowledge is important, because the former is transformed into the latter through professional activities. That means that—apart from implicit learning processes (Reber, 1993)—the acquisition of conceptual knowledge often is a prerequisite for the development of procedural knowledge. It is the traditional distinction between formal teaching and instruction settings (school, seminar, training)

on the one hand and informal learning settings (in the context of practice) on the other hand, which usually distributes separated responsibilities: teacher-centred instruction mediates conceptual knowledge—practice has to prove applicability and by that supports the development of procedural knowledge. It is an important conclusion of current educational research as well as a major advantage of ICT to overcome this traditional distinction. Baylen and Glacken (2007) describe several networked technologies supporting lifelong learning processes between formal and informal settings (e.g., e-portfolios, social bookmarking, wikis). They conclude with the description of challenges for providing such learning opportunities from a case study in teachers' professional development. These challenges will be discussed later on.

Research on expertise, which investigates roots for excellent performance in professional domains, has generated fruitful insights on the development of professional competence. However, the way of thinking about professional expertise has dramatically changed in recent years. A few decades ago, professional competence was considered to be based on the amount of specific knowledge a person had accumulated during the professional life. This view has been replaced by a perspective differentiating dimensions of knowledge and action competence. As such, it represented a plea to integrate both individual cognitive aspects and social and cultural dimensions of growing into a community of experts (Billett, 2001). Individual cognitive processes like acquisition, storage, and retrieval of knowledge in memory systems are represented by research on expertise, whereas socio-cultural theories of professional development highlight processes of increasingly becoming integrated in communities of experts and acquiring practicable knowledge through directly participating in professional practice. Hence, there is a need to understand the repertoire of performances that are required to secure that professional knowledge and competence.

After this general discussion of professional learning processes, the following sections will firstly focus the distinctive perspectives of knowledge construction on the different stages of competence development and then discuss opportunities for ICT to simulate a social environment influencing knowledge construction.

KNOWLEDGE CONSTRUCTIONS DURING THE DEVELOPMENT OR MAINTENANCE OF EXPERTISE

From an individual perspective, different processes of knowledge construction can be distinguished. Taken together, these processes contribute to the development of professional competence. There are two forms of knowledge to be distinguished: positive and negative knowledge. Positive knowledge can be thought of as that kind of knowledge most people are aware of: it consists of information and meaning about the characteristic objects of consideration which describes equivalences with the objective reality. Or, more simply, it describes features of objects as they really are shaped. Negative knowledge, in contrast, comprises information on objects of observation as they are not shaped. It addresses features of an object by describing reverse features—information how objects are not shaped. Both forms of knowledge are important for the development of professional competence and they demand similar conditions to be constructed. This section describes processes of acquiring knowledge about objects, processes of understanding in the sense of integration of new knowledge into prior knowledge, and processes of testing applicability. Finally, success or failure provoke confirmation or rejection as a result of knowledge evaluation, which completes the development of professional competence and expertise. However, in order to maintain expertise, an embedding into a community of experts facilitates critical reflection and actualization of individual expertise. At all of these steps, ICT is an important facilitating device.

Acquisition of Conceptual Knowledge

Conceptual knowledge consists of information on objects, humans, relations, instruments, etc. If it describes relations between objects, conceptual knowledge consists of theories—thus, it also can be called theoretical knowledge. The use of terminology differs across various paradigms: the term conceptual knowledge mostly is used by representatives with socio-cultural or cultural anthropologic background (e.g., Billett, Rogoff, Lave, Wenger), whereas cognitivists use the term declarative knowledge (e.g., Anderson, de Groot). In an everyday language description, conceptual knowledge also is called "knowing that" (Fox, 2005). The acquisition of conceptual knowledge occurs by reflective and thoughtful learning—it demands an understanding of the meaning of terms and theories (Slavin, 2006). This means firstly that this kind of knowledge cannot be learnt just by rote, because there necessarily has to be a connection to a specific meaning. Secondly, awareness, concentration, and probably deliberation are necessary circumstances of the construction of conceptual knowledge. Hence, the acquisition does not occur incidentally, but as a learner's goal-oriented agency: by reading or hearing information and reflecting upon it in order to construct individual meaning. Thus, provision of information and the stimulation of reflection—either from books, humans, or documents, files—are the basic types of educational interventions to support the acquisition of conceptual knowledge. Goldberg (2006) and Taylor and Hsueh (2005) extensively describe case studies on the integration of the Internet into classroom settings in order to enlarge the scope of information and provide opportunities for individual constructions of meanings. However, the advantages of the Internet only apply if learners know what is expected, if sufficient time is allocated, and if several sources for the same topics are provided (Izumi-Taylor & Lovelace, 2007).

Integration of New Knowledge

Prior knowledge is a key factor for the acquisition of knowledge, because it controls the integration of new knowledge into the existing stock of knowledge in various respects (Alexander, Kulikowich, & Jetton, 1994; Schneider, 1993): it determines self-directed learning activities, it structures the way of understanding for new knowledge, and it is the best predictor for learning success. Computer-supported learning comprises learning processes with a high extent of self-direction. It is the opportunity of user-adaptation which provides the richest didactic potential of e-learning. However, learners should choose e-learning procedures which fit with their individual knowledge (Burgos, Tattersall, & Koper, 2007). In that sense, prior knowledge determines the learning activities. In those cases when learners know enough in order to competently decide about learning activities, learning success becomes probable—whereas in those cases where learners do not dispose of enough prior knowledge, learning success might remain elusive and tend to affirm individual assumptions. As the construction of meaning is considered to be the crucial moment of learning, prior knowledge is relevant, because it shapes the basis for understanding. The construction of meaning can be conceptualized as successful integration of new knowledge into existing knowledge structures. It is a popular saying in handbooks of teaching that teaching effort has to dock onto the learners' mental prerequisites. It is not an objective fit which results in understanding, but the learners' subjective integration of new knowledge. Thus, the learner's individual specification of prior knowledge constitutes understanding and the construction of meaning. The respectively larger and broader this stock of prior knowledge is, the better are the chances to create connections with new knowledge. Since the establishment of those connections can be understood as learning success, it becomes plausible that prior knowledge predicts learning success. An agenda for support-

ing the creation of knowledge by integration of new knowledge has to follow two main issues (Gagné, Wager, Golas, & Keller, 2004): firstly, it is important to create a stock of knowledge as large as possible. Secondly, it is important to provide a structuring scaffold in the context of the instructional setting, in order to activate prior knowledge and to provide new knowledge with many connecting factors. Therefore, the Internet in general and Wiki-systems in particular are fruitful learning resources. Even though the process of integration of new knowledge primarily is to be considered as an individual and subjective operation, it is not necessarily isolated from external stimuli which can emanate from virtual settings (e.g., simulations) as well as from real contacts mediated by computer networks.

Testing the Applicability of Knowledge

The major purpose of instruction and teaching—not only in school but also and especially in professional contexts—is enabling learners to perform competently. This means that the construction of knowledge is not the crucial criterion for learning success but the application of that knowledge. However, though from an educational point of view it is not possible to change the learners' behaviour itself (except through efforts of force), it is just possible to change learners' knowledge, beliefs, and attitudes—that is, their behaviour potential. Under these circumstances, the challenge arises to support the creation of knowledge which does not remain inert. Inert knowledge is that knowledge which should be applicable to a wide range of situations but is applied only to a very limited set of circumstances (Bransford, Burn, Delclos, & Vye, 1986). Cognitive theories claim a compilation of declarative knowledge into procedural knowledge occurs through practical problem solving (Anderson, 1982; De Jong & Ferguson-Hessler, 1996; Schmidt & Boshuizen, 1993). Situated learning and socio-psychological theories emphasize the importance of situational factors influencing the applicability of knowledge (Lave & Wenger, 1991; Resnick, 1987). To avoid inert knowledge and to support the creation of practical capabilities, cognitive theories suggest the creation of rules and their testing, mental simulations (Klein, 2003), and practicing (Ericsson, 2006). Situated learning theories suggest changes of perspectives, multiple approaches to a problem and social exchange of assumptions and commonly shared cognitions as appropriate maxims for teaching applicable knowledge. The main purpose of (practically or mentally) testing the applicability of knowledge—following the theory of dynamic memory (Kolodner, 1983)—is the development of the capability of competent decision making: in successful case, these tests end up in a confirmation and affirmation of knowledge and in cases of failing in a revision or rejection of knowledge. Orton and Mulhausen (2008) recently published an impressive study proving the effectiveness of knowledge testing for the confirmation or the modification of knowledge and behaviour by implementing virtual simulations in the area of geriatric education.

Confirmation or Rejection of Knowledge

Depending on the result of the application test, knowledge will be confirmed or rejected and stored or not in the dynamic memory (Kolodner, 1983). This memory comprises individual episodes and incidents which an individual experiences across the lifespan. It changes with each new experience which deliberately is reflected upon by the individual. Two outcomes are possible: (1) a new experience confirms or enriches the prior knowledge. In this case the original mental concept of a procedure is consolidated and will be, thus, accessed again the next time a similar situation arises. (2) A new experience contradicts previous concepts. In this case, reflection extracts the shortcomings of the prior knowledge and

ends up in a modification of the prior knowledge. Moderate errors are to be stated, knowledge is modified, and, as a consequence of fundamental errors, knowledge is rejected. In this model of memory, episodic memory organisation packets are the basic entities of knowledge, which combine generalised action concepts with singular features of succeeding and failing incidents (Kolodner, 1984). On the basis of such memory units, the integration of experience into the previous stock of procedural knowledge can be conceptualised. Hereby, failing experiences are at least as important for developing professional competence as successful experiences, because the high performance of experts cannot be attributed exclusively to positive knowledge, but has to be attributed also to negative knowledge: experts also know quite surely, what not to do in crucial situations. Otherwise they would fail and lose their attribution as expert.

Community of Experts

The four different processes of knowledge construction described in 3.1 through 3.4 comprise the mental activities of the individual which are involved in the development from novice to expert. Recent research approaches complement the individual perspective by including social considerations. Learning always occurs in a social setting—when considering professional learning, this social setting often is the workplace. That means that a large share of professional learning occurs as interplay between individual and social contributions to learning and competence development. Such an understanding of expertise implies a socio-constructivist view of knowledge creation. It is a result of social negotiation about what is to be considered the value or quality of knowledge (Valsiner & van der Veer, 2000). Thus, expertise implies an exchange of opinions and knowledge in order to socially construct knowledge which radiates reliability (Gruber, Palonen, Rehrl, & Lehtinen, 2007). In that sense, not only questions on development of expertise become relevant but also questions arise on the maintenance of expertise. As worklife, technology, and societies are supposed to change, new knowledge is generated and competences are permanently to be actualised. Hence, maintenance of expertise demands exchange and social reflection of knowledge in a community of experts. ICT can provide useful support for such an exchange, especially as experts often are spatially separated over huge distances.

OPPORTUNITIES FOR ICT TO CONTRIBUTE TO COLLABORATIVE KNOWLEDGE CONSTRUCTIONS

The earlier sections discussed the relevance of expertise research for analysing professional learning processes and distinguished various dimensions of mental processes that occur during the development of professional competence. Several hints already have been placed regarding the ways ICT provides features which can support the construction of knowledge. The focus of the discussion will point out the degree to which computers and collaboration in virtual networks can generate a social environment for the development of professional competence and expertise.

When computer technology had developed sufficiently to provide powerful and reasonably priced hardware and software solutions, e-learning developed similarly. The hope arose that technological applications would offer cheap, quick, and effective learning opportunities and that—finally—e-learning would substitute traditional learning environments (Liu, Liao, & Pratt, 2009). Meanwhile, those hopes have been replaced by a more realistic view on e-learning opportunities. In the current view of most observers, the most important role of e-learning in adult education is to supplement regular education—either as blended learning or as preparation or rework of face-to-face trainings (Breitwieser, Küpper, & Ponomareva,

2002). Recent literature on e-learning frequently refers to constructivist paradigms of learning and instruction (Slevin, 2008). Thus, the potential of e-learning in the current literature is described as offering opportunities for self-directed learning and social interaction in virtual communities aiming at socially shared construction of meaning. As virtual learning environments allow learners to create knowledge based on their individual and social background, and as ICT technology allows the embedding of procedures in learning processes, inert knowledge is less likely to emerge (Vosniadou, DeCorte, & Mandl, 1994). Thus, e-learning seems to be a fruitful learning device for professional learning.

Evidence exists that the combination of text and graphics supports the acquisition of knowledge. However, in the "generative theory of multimedia learning" (Plass, Chun, Mayer, & Leutner, 1998), it is argued that learners take profit from e-learning only if they indeed use all the sources offered. Brünken, Steinbacher, Schnotz, and Leutner (2001) showed that a combination of picture and text can improve the acquisition of knowledge especially of beginners. Multimedia systems, in which text, pictures, and sequences of videos are combined, and in which the user is able to select a preferred mode, are called "adaptive learning systems." In such systems, learners are able to adapt the learning process to their own demands by making a choice from the offered devices.

Such a kind of learning is powerful, because it leads to advantages in motivational as well as in cognitive respects. Through successful self-direction of learning processes, learners can experience autonomy and competence, which supports the development of intrinsic learning motivation (Deci, Koestner, & Ryan, 2001). Successful self-direction of learning processes also allows the adaptation of learning processes to the learner's prior knowledge (Boekaerts, 1995). However, these advantages do not occur automatically, but depend on the learners' approach to e-learning (Schunk & Zimmerman, 2003).

Social interaction between learners or between learners and an instructor/tutor addresses motivational and cognitive aspects, too. It allows the perception of social embedding which supports intrinsic learning motivation (Ryan & Deci, 2000). Further, it fosters the joint negotiation of meaning through several individuals, which is believed to be a crucial mode of understanding the complexity of the world (Valsiner & van der Veer, 2000). However, learners must explicitly search for opportunities to exchange opinions and interpretations in order to make use of these options of e-learning. This implies that learners have to have the attitude that social negotiation of meaning is an integral component of knowledge construction (Pintrich, 2002).

Tying these points of didactical potential of ICT for knowledge construction together and focusing the generation of a social environment, computers, and collaboration in virtual networks particularly can foster the following processes:

- **Provision of information:** The World Wide Web and its content management tools (e.g., Wiki-systems, searching engines) provide the richest source for information available. Even though the quality of information provided in the World Wide Web is controversially discussed and sceptically judged by teachers (Eynon, 2008), it has proved to be the quickest access to primary source materials and original resources in almost every area of knowledge construction (Su, 2009). Provided that users dispose of media competence and hypermedia literacy (Kellner & Share, 2007; Levinson & Grohe, 2001), they can autonomously investigate digital libraries and analyse virtual documents. Thus, with respect to the provision of information, ICT shapes the broadest resource and is an appropriate instrument for intrinsic motivated self-directed professional learning. The latest developments of internet applications

tend to be user-friendly enough so that "regular" users also can make use of them. Automated services for identifying news (e.g. rss-feeds) keep users up on the most recent state of information.

- **Provision of discussion fora:** As explained above, the social negotiation of meaning and knowledge is an important component of professional learning. Of course, not every communication contributes necessarily to a social construction of meaning; in some but crucial cases such a negotiation process may demand the interaction of particular persons (e.g., peers, experts, jurors). ICT provides social software which offers opportunities to integrate those persons even though they are not present. In that sense the potential scopes of discussions increase drastically. Empirical studies in the field of professional development and higher education confirm the potential of interactive webfora such as weblogs and wiki-systems (Costa, 2007; Trentin, 2009; Wheeler, Yeomans, & Wheeler, 2008). An important idea of web-based discussion fora consists of quality management by peer control. Tapscott and Williams (2006) introduced the term of "wikinomics" in order to express the commonly shared commitment between contributors and organisers which shapes mutual control and, thus, supports reliability of information provided in the contributions. Hence, these communities act in a self-directed manner and establish specific rules which also guarantee that systems of quality control apply (Staley, 2009).

- **Provision of simulations:** ICT provides the opportunity for applying simulations for complex problem-solving scenarios and has, thus, relevance for professional learning processes. The development of hardware and software makes the presentation of authentic audiovisual situations possible.

Whereas a huge optimism was observable in the 1990s regarding the didactic potential of simulations for learning purposes (e.g., Tergan, Sparkes, Hitchcock, Kaye, Hron, & Mandl, 1992), research of the last decade has provided differentiated insight regarding the prerequisites which must be fulfilled in order to foster learning success. Recent articles integrate the crucial factors of learning through simulations: students' motivation is relatively high, but only if they can operate in a self-directed manner, which again demands a certain amount of prior knowledge and intuitive guidance through the system (Adams et al., 2008). For example, in a study in the area of medical education, it could be revealed that students only profit from complex simulations when they are combined with a common reflection of experiences together with experts (Holzinger, Kickmeier-Rust, Wassertheurer, & Hessinger, 2009). The area for learning by simulations is quite broad: they can be used for training methods of complex decision making, testing effects of social interventions, testing logical, physical, or mathematical solutions, etc. However, there is convincing evidence that the simulation has to be embedded in a larger didactical arrangement (Meier, Reinhard, Carter, & Brooks, 2008).

- **Provision of networks:** An important option for collaborative knowledge construction is the provision of networks. Companies invest huge efforts in the implementation of networking communities. Almost every company operates an intranet with controlled access only for members of the organisation. More specialised enterprises strive to implement knowledge management systems which aim at the identification of crucial persons or their knowledge for cases where information or solutions are needed. The main idea of

such networks is the sharing of expertise and a free flow of information among their members (Hatala & Lutta, 2009). Even though the efforts necessary for a successful implementation of a network for collaborative knowledge constructions are high, especially as the potential participants have to be convinced (Harris, 2008), it is possible to profit from such a network and utilise individual competence collaboratively (e.g., Dealtry, 2006). From an individual point of view, networks become relevant for the maintenance of expertise as they are an option for self-actualisation of knowledge within a community of experts (Gruber, Harteis, & Rehrl, 2008).

All these options serve for the cognitive operations identified as part of the development or maintenance of expertise in the context of professional learning. As the view into the recent research literature revealed, there is a variety of chances of ICT for supporting collaboration in order to construct commonly shared knowledge. However, the potential of ICT does not automatically come into operation. Moreover, from the perspective of professional learning, there are certain core challenges for the implementation of e-collaborative knowledge construction.

CHALLENGES FOR E-COLLABORATIVE KNOWLEDGE CONSTRUCTION

This section will discuss three selected aspects of computer-mediated collaborative construction of knowledge. Firstly, the aspect of communication should be approached, as each collaborative process is based on communication processes, which are different than the regular ones when computer mediated. Secondly, the aspect of subjectivity should be analysed. Communication as well as knowledge construction is a process which is to a great extent determined by subjective interpretations. Thirdly and finally, the theory of situated learning should be addressed, as this theory provides insight into supporting the development of applicable knowledge. Addressing this theory challenges the respect to which computer-mediated knowledge construction can meet the requirements of situated learning theories.

Computer-Mediated Communication

On the one hand, ICT provides access to a huge amount of (eventually inconsistent) information, which has to be processed in order to be integrated into communication processes. On the other hand, ICT provides various options of communications which systematically differ from traditional ways of communication. Besides asynchronous communication options which might be supplemented by multimedia applications (e.g., e-mails, fora, YouTube, Facebook), ICT also provides options for location-independent but synchronous communication (e.g., chat, Skype). On this basis the didactical potential for cooperative and workplace learning arose which are no longer restricted through geographical areas or borders of organisations. This integration into a virtual community can help to prevent negative emotions and the experience of demotivation which can come along with the feeling of isolation in traditional settings of teacher instruction (Seidel, Rimmele, & Prenzel, 2005). Therefore the learners have to identify and judge relevant information in a complex pattern of mass information. The pre-filter of an instructor's or an expert's lens is not necessarily available. The use of internet information demands a different strategy of searching for information than reading a textbook. Additionally, it demands the capability to make the crucial distinction between important and unimportant, credible and noncredible, authentic and fake information. The latter capability implies the development of ethical standards of communication which immediately are to be applied for the distribution of information via ICT.

The social interactions within computer-mediated communication differ from direct face-to-face interactions in various aspects (Pfister, 2005). They are totally mediated through technology and are, thus, either text-based or screen-based. Many nonverbal components of human interaction remain hidden. This may simplify communication processes or make them more difficult. However, in every case, users have to develop new action-scripts in order to be able to smoothly participate in computer-mediated communication processes: grounding processes and sequences of establishing a commonly shared basis and understanding (Clark & Brennan, 1991) demand higher efforts and spatial distances can complicate the coordination between interaction partners. Last not least it has to be considered that inhibition thresholds may arise if the members of a computer-mediated communication process become aware that their behaviour is in a certain way public—as it is when mediated via the Internet.

Challenges from an educational perspective, thus, arise regarding an appropriate preparation of individuals for a competent participation in computer-mediated communication (Costa, 2007). The goal of such a preparation often is called "media literacy" (Baacke, 1997; Kress, 2003) which comprises various dimensions of the competence to make reasonable use of web-based information (e.g., selection, comprehension and, assessment of information, distributing information, identifying, and evaluating conditions of information distribution).

Shapes of Subjectivity

"Subjectivity comprises the conscious and non-conscious conceptions, dispositions and procedures that constitute individuals' cognitive experience" (Billett, 2006b, p. 6). This bundle of action potential determines individual behaviour in social settings and generates, thus, social reality (Valsiner & van der Veer, 2000). It is developed through an individual's experiences over the lifespan, which implies that subjectivity underlies a continuous self-actualization and development. A major challenge for understanding (and thus influencing) individual learning and acting in social contexts is related to the circumstance that subjectivity comprises conscious as well as unconscious assumptions, beliefs, and convictions. The unconscious components of subjectivity are quite difficult or even impossible to access. Thus, the interpretation of an individual's behavior always partly relies on guesses and hypotheses. Educational interventions become difficult on this basis and their prospects of success depend on the teacher's diagnostic and interpretative capabilities.

This understanding of subjectivity exceeds the constructivist concept of individual construal of sense (e.g., Glasersfeld, 1996), as it puts the individual into the central position of the genesis of a social setting. In the case of computer-mediated collaborative knowledge construction, it means that subjective beliefs about the content and about knowledge shape how individuals engage in the social construction of meaning. It is challenging to provide computer-based learning scenarios, e.g., for learners who possess a less elaborate system of epistemic beliefs, because the learning environment demands self-directed exploring activities, whereas the learner expects clear facts (Harteis, Gruber, & Hertramph, 2007). It is the lack of sensitivity of both learners and teachers towards those unconsidered and unconscious attitudes which often lead to obstacles for collaborative knowledge construction (Fenwick, 2003).

A third challenge arises in the context of debates about the didactical opportunities of e-learning scenarios: it is considered to be a major chance of e-learning to provide authentic problem situations which can be handled by learners for cooperative knowledge construction purposes (e.g., Fischer, Troendle, & Mandl, 2003). Often, the issue of authenticity is dealt with as being self-evident, but in fact the learners have their subjective pictures of authenticity. Martens, Bastiaens and Kirschner

(2007) emphasize this point in their study which revealed that learners often experience less authenticity in distance learning settings than the developers expect.

Situated Learning in Computer-Based Environments

The idea of situated learning emphasizes that much of learned content is specific to the situation in which it is learned (Brown, Collins, & Duguid, 1989). Without any doubt, each activity and every kind of learning is embedded in specific contexts. The idea behind attempts to develop theories of situated learning, however, is to make systematic use of included context factors in designing computer-based learning environments. Therefore, theories of situated learning are to be distinguished from casual learning in action (in situ), because they comprise educational intentions (Lave & Wenger, 1991). Situated learning therefore does not at all mean "learning by doing anything," but rather "intentional learning by dealing with challenges and by taking situational contexts into consideration." This notion of situated learning is based on a constructivist background. From this background, it is argued that knowledge cannot directly be transferred from one situation to another, because learners individually construct their knowledge on the basis of their interpretation of situational affordances and constraints. If learners create knowledge in simulations of authentic real-world situations, this knowledge can more easily be applied to challenges of the real world.

Discussions about the distinctions between formal learning, informal learning, and situated learning suggest that formal learning and situated learning are in principle contrarieties. Admittedly, substantial differences exist in the background of learning theories and epistemologies. When contrasting formal and situated learning, obviously the idea prevails that formal learning is related to instruction in a cognitivist view, whereas situated learning enfolds constructivist perspectives of learning.

Each computer-based learning environment is a kind of formal learning situation because it aims at providing learning opportunities. ICT offers opportunities to integrate multiple perspectives, complex problem situations, and moments of authenticity. Computer-based learning environments, thus, are formal settings following the idea of the situated learning movement. From a perspective of collaborative knowledge construction the following challenges arise: firstly, the more realistic a virtual environment is shaped, the higher is the probability that users of such an environment develop a set of experiences which is completely separated from real-world circumstances. Individuals namely are capable of developing multiple context-related identities (Oksama & Hyona, 2008). If so, the setting loses all didactical advantages of supporting the development of applicable knowledge. Secondly, it might prove to be difficult for learners to verbalize their experiences of authenticity in specific situations. However, it is this range of experiences which is considered to be the important learning effect. In cases of collaborative knowledge construction, these experiences have to be verbalized in order to share them with others.

CONCLUSION: PROFESSIONAL LEARNING AS INTERPLAY BETWEEN COLLABORATIVE KNOWLEDGE CONSTRUCTION IN COMPUTER AND REAL-WORLD SETTINGS

As mentioned above, computer learning environments provide opportunities for an integration of formal and informal learning. This concerns the hardware and software options for generating "situated aspects," even though the educational challenges for supporting sustainable collaborative knowledge constructions are manifold. For example, collaborative e-learning in a workplace setting does not always proceed smoothly, but re-

quires intensive instructional support, particularly if little expertise exists in the working team. Learning activities at workplaces, however, require time and space, and they depend on explicit rules allowing employees to pursue learning activities instead of productive ones. In the respective educational and organizational research, this topic is discussed within the concept of "learning culture" (Bauer, Rehrl, & Harteis, 2007; Harris, 1999). Attempts to establish a learning culture in an organization require both some formal regulations and opportunities to make use of context-dependent learning processes (Senge, 1993). If both requirements are fulfilled, a workplace environment provides the best conditions for professional learning and collaborative knowledge construction. In this case, professionals should have opportunities to use computer networks and software to search for solutions for problems occurring in their real-work context.

Educators and teachers who want to support e-collaborative knowledge constructions in working contexts have to cope with various tasks. A crucial issue consists of the integration of working experiences into computer-mediated social settings and vice versa. It is a tightrope walk between guiding learners and providing degrees of freedom as well as between considering individual attitudes and focusing on commonly shared beliefs. In the introductory paragraphs it was argued that professional learning is necessary across the entire span of an occupational career. The goal of professional learning is the development and the maintenance of expertise. E-collaborative knowledge construction can be an effective approach to reach this goal as it can be integrated in a workplace setting. The main argument of this chapter was that professional learning has to be considered as an individual development interrelated within a social setting. The development of expertise occurs by changing knowledge structures. Some of these changes happen intentionally and consciously, some don't. The preceding discussion has worked out how computer-based learning processes can support those changes of knowledge structures. The analysis of the literature indicates that the implementation of e-collaborative knowledge construction in workplace contexts has to integrate the individual professionals. A pure top-down implementation strategy does not seem promising as theories of subjectivity, constructivist, and situated learning suggest that the individual commitment is an important precondition for successful professional learning over the entire professional career.

REFERENCES

Adams, W. K., Reid, S., LeMaster, R., McKagan, S. B., Perkins, K. K., Dubson, M., & Wieman, C. E. (2008). A study of educational simulations – part I: Engagement and learning. *Journal of Interactive Learning Research, 19*, 397–419.

Alexander, P. A., Kulikowich, J. M., & Jetton, T. L. (1994). The role of subject-matter knowledge and interest in the processing of linear and nonlinear texts. *Review of Educational Research, 64*, 201–252.

Anderson, J. R. (1982). Acquisition of cognitive skill. *Psychological Review, 89*, 369–406. doi:10.1037/0033-295X.89.4.369

Baacke, D. (1997). *Medienpädagogik* [Media pedagogy]. Tübingen, Germany: Niemeyer.

Bauer, J., Rehrl, M., & Harteis, C. (2007). Measurement of learning culture: A motivational approach. In H. Gruber & T. Palonen (Eds.), *Learning in the workplace – new developments* (pp. 21-50). Turku, Finland: FERA.

Baylen, D. M., & Glacken, J. (2007). Promoting lifelong learning online: A case study of a professional development experience. In Y. Inoue (Ed.), *Online education for lifelong learning* (pp. 229-251). Hershey, PA: Information Science Publishing.

Berliner, D. C. (2001). Learning about and learning from expert teachers. *International Journal of Educational Research, 35*, 463–482. doi:10.1016/S0883-0355(02)00004-6

Billett, S. (2001). *Learning in the workplace. Strategies for effective practice.* Crows Nest, Australia: Allen & Unwin.

Billett, S. (2006a). *Workers, work and change.* Dordrecht, The Netherlands: Springer.

Billett, S. (2006b). Work, subjectivity and learning. In S. Billett, T. Fenwick, & M. Somerville (Eds.), *Work, subjectivity and learning. Understanding learning through working life* (pp. 1-20). Dordrecht, The Netherlands: Springer.

Billett, S., Harteis, C., & Eteläpelto, A. (Eds.). (2008). *Emerging perspectives of workplace learning.* Rotterdam, Germany: Sense Publishers.

Boekaerts, M. (1995). Self-regulated learning: Bridging the gap between metacognitive and metamotivational theories. *Educational Psychologist, 30*, 195–200. doi:10.1207/s15326985ep3004_4

Boshuizen, H. P. A., Bromme, R., & Gruber, H. (Eds.). (2004). *Professional learning: gaps and transitions on the way from novice to expert.* Dordrecht, The Netherlands: Kluwer.

Boshuizen, H. P. A., & Schmidt, H. G. (1992). On the role of biomedical knowledge in clinical reasoning by experts, intermediates and novices. *Cognitive Science, 16*, 153–184.

Bransford, J. D., Burns, M. S., Delclos, V. R., & Vye, N. J. (1986). Teaching thinking: Evaluating evaluations and broadening the data base. *Educational Leadership, 44*(2), 68–70.

Breitwieser, A., Küpper, C., & Ponomareva, N. (2002). *Akzeptanz von E-Learning.* Frankfurt am Main, Germany: Cognos.

Brown, J. S., Collins, A., & Duguid, P. (1989). Situated cognition and the culture of learning. *Educational Researcher*, *18*(1), 34–41.

Brünken, R., Steinbacher, S., Schnotz, W., & Leutner, D. (2001). Mentale Modelle und Effekte der Präsentations- und Abrufkodalität beim Lernen mit Multimedia [Mental models and effects of presentation and retrieval cue codality in multimedia learning]. *Zeitschrift fur Padagogische Psychologie*, *15*, 16–27. doi:10.1024//1010-0652.15.1.16

Burgos, D., Tattersall, C., & Koper, R. (2007). How to represent adaption in e-learning with IMS learning design. *Interactive Learning Environments*, *15*, 161–170. doi:10.1080/10494820701343736

Clark, H. H., & Brennan, S. A. (1991). Grounding in communication. In L. B. Resnick, J. M. Levine, & S. D. Teasley (Eds.), *Perspectives on socially shared cognition* (pp. 127-149). Washington, DC: AERA.

Cort, P. (2009). The EC discourse on vocational training: How a 'common vocational training policy' turned into a lifelong learning strategy. *Vocations and Learning: Studies in Vocational and Professional Education*, *2*, 87–107.

Costa, C. (2007). A professional development weblog: Supporting work-based learning in a TAFE library. *The Australian Library Journal*, *56*, 36–55.

De Jong, T., & Ferguson-Hessler, M. G. M. (1996). Types and qualities of knowledge. *Educational Psychologist*, *31*, 105–113. doi:10.1207/s15326985ep3102_2

Dealtry, R. (2006). The corporate university's role in managing an epoch in learning organisation innovation. *Journal of Workplace Learning*, *18*, 313–320. doi:10.1108/13665620610674980

Deci, E., Koestner, R., & Ryan, R. (2001). Extrinsic rewards and intrinsic motivation in education: Reconsidered once again. *Review of Educational Research*, *71*, 1–27. doi:10.3102/00346543071001001

Ericsson, K. A. (2006). The influence of experience and deliberate practice on the development of superior expert performance. In K. A. Ericsson, N. Charness, P. J. Feltovich, & R. R. Hoffman (Eds.), *The Cambridge handbook of expertise and expert performance* (pp. 683-703). Cambridge, UK: Cambridge University Press.

Ericsson, K. A., Charness, N., Feltovich, P. J., & Hoffman, R. R. (Eds.). (2006). *The Cambridge handbook of expertise and expert performance*. Cambridge, UK: Cambridge University Press.

Eynon, R. (2008). The use of the world-wide-web in learning and teaching in Higher Education: Reality and rhetoric. *Innovations in Education and Teaching International*, *45*, 15–23. doi:10.1080/14703290701757401

Fenwick, T. J. (2003). *Learning through experience: Troubling orthodoxies and intersecting questions*. Malabar, India: Krieger.

Fischer, F., Troendle, P., & Mandl, H. (2003). Using the Internet to improve university education – problem-oriented web-based learning and the MUNICS environment. *Interactive Learning Environments*, *11*(3), 193–214. doi:10.1076/ilee.11.3.193.16546

Fox, R. (2005). *Teaching and learning. Lessons from psychology*. Malden, UK: Blackwell Publishing.

Gagné, R. M., Wager, W. W., Golas, K. C., & Keller, J. M. (2004). *Principles of instructional design* (5th ed.). Florence, KY: Wadsworth.

Glasersfeld, E. v. (1996). *Radical constructivism: A way of knowing and learning*. Abingdon, UK: Falmer Press.

Goldberg, M. (2006). *Integrating the arts: An approach to teaching and learning in multicultural and multilingual settings*. Boston: Allyn & Bacon.

Grek, S., Lawn, M., Lingard, B., Ozga, J., Rinne, R., Segerholm, C., & Simola, H. (2009). National policy brokering and the construction of the European education space in England, Sweden, Finland and Scotland. *Comparative Education, 45*, 5–21. doi:10.1080/03050060802661378

Gruber, H., Harteis, C., Mulder, R. H., & Rehrl, M. (Eds.). (2005). *Bridging individual, organisational, and cultural perspectives on professional learning*. Regensburg, Germany: Roderer.

Gruber, H., Harteis, C., & Rehrl, M. (2008). Professional learning: Skill formation between formal and situated learning. In K. U. Mayer & H. Solga (Eds.), *Skill formation. Interdisciplinary and cross-national perspectives* (pp. 207-229). Cambridge, UK: Cambridge University Press.

Gruber, H., Palonen, T., Rehrl, M., & Lehtinen, E. (2007).Understanding the nature of expertise: Individual knowledge, social resources and cultural context. In H. Gruber & T. Palonen (Eds.), *Learning in the workplace – new developments* (pp.2227-250). Turku, Finland: Finnish Educational Research Association.

Harris, R. J. (1999). Lifelong learning in work contexts. *Research in Post-Compulsory Education, 4*, 161–182. doi:10.1080/13596749900200055

Harris, R. J. (2008). Developing of a collaborative learning environment through Technology Enhanced Education (TE3) support. *Education & Training, 50*, 674–686. doi:10.1108/00400910810917055

Harteis, C., & Billett, S. (2008). Workplaces as learning environment: Introduction. *International Journal of Educational Research, 47*, 209–212. doi:10.1016/j.ijer.2008.07.002

Harteis, C., Gruber, H., & Hertramph, H. (2007). Epistemological beliefs and their impact on the practice of e-learning in companies. In V. Uskov (Ed.), *Computers and advances technologies in education. Globalization of education through advanced technology* (pp. 266-271). Anaheim, CA: ACTA.

Hatala, J.-P., & Lutta, J. G. (2009). Managing information sharing within an organizational setting: A social network perspective. *Performance Improvement Quarterly, 21*, 5–33. doi:10.1002/piq.20036

Holzinger, A., Kickmeister-Rust, M. D., Wassertheurer, S., & Hessinger, M. (2009). Learning performance with interactive simulations in medical education. Lessons learned from results of learning complex physiological models with the HAEMOdynamics SIMulator. *Computers & Education, 52*, 292–301. doi:10.1016/j.compedu.2008.08.008

Izumi-Taylor, S., & Lovelace, A. F. (2007). Techknowledge: How children and early childhood education teachers develop knowledge through technology. In Y. Inoue (Ed.), *Online education for lifelong learning* (pp. 187-207). Hershey, PA: Information Science Publishing.

Kellner, D., & Share, J. (2007). Critical media literacy: Crucial policy choices for a twenty-first century democracy. *Policy Futures in Education, 5*, 59–69. doi:10.2304/pfie.2007.5.1.59

Klein, G. (2003). *Intuition at work*. New York: Currency Doubleday.

Kolodner, J. L. (1983). Towards an understanding of the role of experience in the evolution from novice to expert. *International Journal of Man-Machine Studies, 19*, 497–518. doi:10.1016/S0020-7373(83)80068-6

Kolodner, J. L. (1984). *Retrieval and organizational strategies in conceptual memory: A computer model*. Hillsdale: Erlbaum.

Kress, G. (2003). *Literacy in new media age.* London: Routledge.

Lave, J., & Wenger, E. (1991). *Situated learning. Legitimate peripheral participation.* Cambridge, UK: Cambridge University Press.

Levinson, E., & Grohe, B. (2001). Managing the internet at school: Limits and access to the greatest source. *Converge, 4*(2), 58–60.

Liu, S.-H., Liao, H.-L., & Pratt, J. A. (2009). Impact of media richness and flow on e-learning technology acceptance. *Computers & Education, 52,* 599–607. doi:10.1016/j.compedu.2008.11.002

Mandl, H., Gruber, H., & Renkl, A. (1996). Communities of practice toward expertise: Social foundation of university instruction. In P. B. Baltes & U. Staudinger (Eds.), *Interactive minds. Life-span perspectives on the social foundation of cognition* (pp. 394-411). Cambridge, UK: Cambridge University Press.

Martens, R., Bastiaens, T., & Kirschner, P. A. (2007). New learning design in distance education: The impact on student perception and motivation. *Distance Education, 28,* 81–93. doi:10.1080/01587910701305327

Meier, D. K., Reinhard, K. J., Carter, D. O., & Brooks, D. W. (2008). Simulations with worked example modeling: Beneficial effects on scheme acquisition. *Journal of Science Education and Technology, 17,* 262–273. doi:10.1007/s10956-008-9096-4

Oksama, L., & Hyona, L. (2008). Dynamic binding of identity and location information: A serial model of multiple identity tracking. *Cognitive Psychology, 56,* 237–283. doi:10.1016/j.cogpsych.2007.03.001

Orton, E., & Mulhausen, P. (2008). E-learning virtual patients for geriatric education. *Gerontology & Geriatrics Education, 28,* 73–88. doi:10.1300/J021v28n03_06

Pfister, H.-R. (2005). How to support synchronous net-based learning discourses: Principles and perspectives. In R. Bromme, F. W. Hesse, & H. Spada (Eds.), *Barriers and biases in computer-mediated knowledge communication* (pp. 39-57). New York: Springer.

Pintrich, P. R. (2002). Future challenges and directions for the theory and research on personal epistemology. In B. K. Hofer & P. R. Pintrich (Eds.), *Personal epistemology. The psychology of beliefs about knowledge and knowing* (pp. 389-414). Mahwah, NJ: Lawrence Erlbaum.

Plass, L. J., Chun, D. M., Mayer, R. E., & Leutner, D. (1998). Supporting visual and verbal learning preferences in a second language multimedia learning environment. *Journal of Educational Psychology, 90,* 25–36. doi:10.1037/0022-0663.90.1.25

Rauner, F. (2008). European vocational education and training: A prerequisite for mobility? *Journal of European Industrial Training, 32,* 85–98. doi:10.1108/03090590810861640

Reber, A. S. (1993). *Implicit learning and tacit knowledge. An essay on the cognitive unconscious.* New York: Oxford University Press.

Resnick, L. B. (1987). Learning in school and out. *Educational Researcher, 16*(9), 13–20.

Ryan, R., & Deci, E. (2000). Intrinsic and extrinsic motivations: Classic definitions and new directions. *Contemporary Educational Psychology, 25,* 54–67. doi:10.1006/ceps.1999.1020

Schmidt, H. G., & Boshuizen, H. P. A. (1993). On acquiring expertise in medicine. *Educational Psychology Review, Special Issue: European educational psychology, 5,* 205-221.

Schneider, W. (1993). Domain-specific knowledge and memory performance in children. *Educational Psychology Review, 5,* 257–273. doi:10.1007/BF01323047

Schunk, D. H., & Zimmerman, B. J. (2003). Self-regulation and learning. In W. M. Reynolds & G. E. Miller (Eds.), *Handbook on psychology: Vol. 7. Educational psychology* (pp. 59-78). Hoboken, NJ: Wiley.

Seidel, T., Rimmele, R., & Prenzel, M. (2005). Clarity and coherence of lesson goals as a scaffold for student learning. *Learning and Instruction, 15,* 539–556.

Senge, P. (1993). *The fifth discipline. The art and practice of the learning organization.* London: Random House.

Slavin, R. E. (2006). *Educational psychology. Theory and practice* (8th ed.). New York: Pearson.

Slevin, J. (2008). E-learning and the transformation of social interaction in higher education. *Learning, Media and Technology, 33,* 115–126. doi:10.1080/17439880802097659

Staley, D. J. (2009). Managing the platform: Higher education and the logic of wikinomics. *EDUCAUSE Review, 44,* 36–46.

Strasser, J., & Gruber, H. (2004). The role of experience in professional training and development of psychological counselors. In H. P. A. Boshuizen, R. Bromme, & H. Gruber (Eds.), *Professional learning: Gaps and transitions on the way from novice to expert* (pp. 11-27). Dordrecht, The Netherlands: Kluwer.

Su, M. C. (2009). Inside the web: A look at digital libraries and the invisible deep web. *Journal of Educational Technology Systems, 37,* 71–82. doi:10.2190/ET.37.1.f

Tapscott, D., & Williams, A. D. (2006). *Wikinomics: How mass collaboration changes everything.* New York: Penguin Books.

Taylor, S. L., & Hsueh, Y. (2005). Implementing a constructivist approach in higher education through technology. *Journal of Early Childhood Teacher Education, 26,* 127–132. doi:10.1080/10901020590967353

Tergan, S. O., Sparkes, J. J., Hitchcock, C., Kaye, A. R., Hron, A., & Mandl, H. (1992). Computer-based systems for open learning. State of the art. In G. Zimmer & D. Blume (Eds.), *Multimediales Lernen in der Berufsbildung, Bd. 4* (pp. 97-99). Nürnberg, Germany: Bildung und Wissen.

Trentin, G. (2009). Using a wiki to evaluate individual contribution to a collaborative learning project. *Journal of Computer Assisted Learning, 25,* 43–55. doi:10.1111/j.1365-2729.2008.00276.x

Valsiner, J., & van der Veer, R. (2000). *The social mind.* Cambridge, UK: Cambridge University Press

Vosniadou, S., DeCorte, E., & Mandl, H. (Eds.). (1994). *Technology-based learning environments.* Berlin, Germany: Springer.

Wenger, E. (1998). *Communities of practice. Learning, meaning, and identity.* Cambridge, UK: Cambridge University Press.

Wheeler, S., Yeomans, P., & Wheeler, D. (2008). The good, the bad, and the wiki: Evaluating student-generated content for collaborative learning. *British Journal of Educational Technology, 39,* 987–995. doi:10.1111/j.1467-8535.2007.00799.x

Chapter 6
E-Collaborative Help-Seeking Using Social Web Features

Silke Schworm
University of Munich, Germany

Markus Heckner
Accenture Information Management Services, Germany

ABSTRACT

Many help systems fail because users do not perceive them as helpful and refuse to use them. Obviously there is a gap between the intentions of the help content authors and the achievement of objectives concerning the perceived usefulness by help users. Current help systems show considerable weaknesses concerning (1) the comprehensibility of the help content, and (2) the format of the help output. Users are often seriously challenged with understanding the instructions given by the system, which usually is not adequately adapted to users' prior knowledge or their vocabulary. This problem is strengthened by the implementation problem of missing feedback channels. The current paper aims to address these issues by presenting an information architecture for an online help system, which constitutes the basis for a dynamic help system, gradually developed by experts and users. It combines earlier models of design patterns with features for user contribution from social software.

INTRODUCTION

Help systems of **computer-based learning environments** are designed to help learners to complete a task or to solve a problem which they cannot solve on their own. Unfortunately learners often perceive those **help systems** as not being helpful at all and they refuse to use them (Aleven, Stahl, Schworm, Fischer, & Wallace, 2003). Thus, many

current **help systems** fail due to the gap between the intentions of the **help system** designers and the objectives of the **help system** users. For a successful help-seeking process the learners have to be able to clearly formulate their help request and to look for the appropriate help. Help is appropriate if it enables the learner to complete the task (Mercier & Frederiksen, 2007). However, systems sometimes do not contain the appropriate help to enable the learners to solve their problems, since help content authors often do not know enough about the actual

DOI: 10.4018/978-1-61520-729-9.ch006

problems and tasks of the learners. Additionally content authors are domain experts and often do not share the learners' vocabulary, which makes retrieving and understanding of help difficult for the learners. One possibility to bridge this gap is to address aspects of communication between help designers and users by merging approaches from educational science and information architecture. The authors developed a **help system** which combines elements of a design pattern language, **expert-lay-communication** and **social computing** to enable feedback processes, collaborative annotation and retrieval of help artifacts. This **help system** fosters interaction between help seekers and help designers and therefore is an effective tool for e-collaborative knowledge construction.

ACADEMIC HELP-SEEKING

Academic help-seeking describes help-seeking activities within learning contexts. In learning contexts help-seeking is essential for the successful construction of knowledge as it is a necessary resource-based learning strategy (Karabenick & Newmann, 2006). In contrast to other strategies of **self-regulated learning**, it requires interaction with teachers, peers or **computer-based learning environments**. This chapter focuses on the features of effective **help systems** in computer-based settings. However, the cognitive processes underlying computer-based help-seeking processes are quite similar to those in face to face settings.

A Model of the Help-Seeking Process

Mercier and Frederiksen (2007) developed a model of the help-seeking process focusing on cognitive processes. According to them the help-seeking process can be segmented into five steps. (1) The recognition of an impasse indicates that a relevant task cannot be successfully completed, which leads to the *awareness of need for help*. (2) The diagnosis of the origin of the impasse leads to a

specification of a need for help. (3) Consequently a *help goal* is set. (4) The learner looks for appropriate help. Help is appropriate if it enables the learner to complete the task. This implies that the learner is able to *comprehend the help content*. (5) *Evaluating* the received help completes the process. However, learners might have serious difficulties in discovering an impasse and diagnosing its origin. Even if an impasse is discovered, in a computer-based setting, the learner must be able to formulate a help request using a language the **help system** understands. The interaction with the **help system** can be regarded as successful if the learners are subsequently able to complete the task, or are able to solve similar tasks on their own. However, not all ways of help-seeking are equally adequate for learning. Often, the learners' goal in seeking help may be to merely complete the task without striving for deeper understanding. This superficial kind of help-seeking is often just a short term perspective since it enables the learners to complete the current task, but does not lead to a deeper understanding which would enable them to solve similar tasks without further help of the system. Learners who want enhance their understanding show more elaborate help seeking behavior (i.e. requesting help considering understanding and future performance; Nelson-LeGall & Resnick, 1998). Thus, help just supporting learners to complete a task might be appropriate in some cases but elaborated help should be available as well. Some studies revealed that learners in **computer-based learning environments** often show rather inadequate help-seeking behavior (cf. Aleven et al., 2003). Schworm and Renkl (2006) for example showed that in a **computer-based learning environment** about instructional design principles learners' self-explanation activity decreased if they were provided with instructional explanations giving direct answers to the questions asked. Learners' self-explanation activity however is highly correlated with their learning outcome (Chi, Bassock, Lewis, Reimann, & Glaser, 1989; Renkl, 2002; Schworm & Renkl, 2006, 2007).

Collaborative learning provides useful opportunities for the development of competencies in help-interactions (i.e. purposeful help-seeking as well as help-giving activities): In **collaborative settings** learners either have to elaborate received help (i.e. self-explaining the given help), to successfully apply it, or they have to formulate explanations to react on help requests of their peers. Giving an explanation according to a help request requires the student to articulate implicit cognitive processes. They thereby organize their knowledge and gain insight into their own understanding (King, 1992; Webb, 1991; Webb et al., 2006).

However, collaborative learning does not guarantee that learners interact in a way that supports learning. Help-related interactions in those groups are often far from optimal (Webb, Ing, Kersting, & Nehmer, 2006; Webb & Palinscar, 1996).

Help-Seeking in Collaborative Settings

According to help-related behavior, Webb and colleagues (2006) stated two important factors which are crucial for a supportive help-seeking interaction. First, the given help should be specific and elaborate rather than general and nonelaborate. Second, the received help should directly be applied to a related problem. The help-seeking interaction only fosters learning outcome if it is followed by any kind of elaboration or transfer. Thereby the level of follow-up activity is correlated with the level of the received help (Vedder, 1985; Webb, Troper, & Fall, 1995; Webb & Farivar, 1999; Webb & Mastergeorge, 2003).

Research has shown that instrumental help, that means help containing explanations which foster understanding and enable the help seekers to solve the task on their own, is most likely to be given when requests are formulated directly and specifically (Webb & Mastergeorge, 2003; Webb et al., 2006; Wilkinson & Calculator, 1982; Wilkinson & Spinelli, 1983).

In the study of Webb and colleagues (2006) students fare more often asked general questions (e.g. just stating a lack of understanding) compared to specific questions. Those general questions were more likely to lead to no responses, negative socio-emotional behavior or the order to just copy the results. As one would expect, those reactions reduced further **help-seeking activities**. However, specific questions lead to elaborated answers, higher application rates and higher posttest scores. The authors identified two factors most likely influencing the level of question formulation. First, formulating only general questions may be the result of a lack of motivation or the unwillingness to seek help. Second, the ability to ask specific questions may on the other hand be influenced by the student's knowledge about the issue under consideration. Students who asked general questions and received an elaborated explanation often were not able to understand the given help and to apply it to the task.

Those studies showed that formulating an adequate help request is crucial for a successful help- seeking process and learners definitely have difficulties in doing so. If this is a problem in synchronous, oral communication, it can be considered to be even more challenging in computer-based settings.

Puustinen, Volckaert-Legrier, Coquin and Bernicot (2008) analyzed middle school students' mathematics-related help-seeking behavior in a support forum. Their results showed that only the 15-year-olds (age of the participants ranged from 11 to 15) were able to formulate help requests that contained all problem relevant information as well as context information, including opening and finishing sequences to make the post socially acceptable. Thus the competencies to formulate a written help request seem to develop with age and cannot be taken for granted in computer-mediated communication when working with forums and chats.

HELP-SEEKING AND HELP DESIGN IN COMPUTER-BASED SETTINGS

Help-seeking in computer-based settings can be divided into two categories: First, the interaction of learners with the **help system** of a **computer-based learning environment** (e.g. Aleven et al., 2006; Aleven et al., 2003; Schworm, Bradler, & Renkl, 2008), second, the computer-mediated interaction of a learner and a human tutor (e.g. Puustinen et al., 2008; Schworm & Gruber, submitted).

Computer-Mediated Help-Related Activities between Humans

A **virtual workspace** offers the opportunity to support students' learning beyond institutional or social support. Students can access additional materials like handouts, presentations, or papers. They can discuss special topics of interest in chatrooms or ask for help in forums. In a computer-based setting where help is not available through instructional explanations by the system but must be sought by posting questions and answers in forums, social aspects such as the perceived threat of help-seeking may again be relevant (Ryan et al., 2001). However, asking for help via the computer seems to be less threatening than in a face to face interaction (Anderson & Lee, 1995; Karabenick & Knapp, 1988). Research has shown that distance learning technologies foster learners' cooperation and **help-seeking activities** (Keefer & Karabenick, 1998; Kitsantas & Chow, 2007). Kitsantas and Chow (2007) for example showed that students in distributed (i.e. blended learning) and distance courses were more likely to seek help from formal sources (e.g. teachers), and felt less threatened by doing so. On the other hand meta-cognitive processes in those settings are far more relevant to the learners' ability to detect an impasse, choose the help goal and formulate adequate questions (Aleven, McLaren, Roll, & Koedinger, 2006; Mercier & Frederiksen, 2007).

Furthermore research has shown that collaborative processes in a computer-based setting are often far from optimal. Usually a relatively low number of individuals contribute very frequently while the majority does this very infrequently. This phenomenon is called the long tail distribution (Heckner & Schworm, in press; Ortega & Barahona, 2007; Tonkin, 2006).

A possible solution to this problem may be to force the students to do a minimum of contribution to the virtual discussion, to evaluate the contributions and make them part of students' credits or to employ some kind of gratification system to motivate contributions (Heckner & Schworm, in press; Littlejohn & Pegler, 2007).

Schworm and Gruber (submitted) tried to foster students' active participation, particularly their help-seeking behavior, by the implementation of prompts. They investigated students' actual help-seeking behavior in the context of a distributed course on qualitative research methods where learners worked collaboratively on a qualitative research project. Group processes were supported by a **virtual workspace** with forums and opportunities for the upload of documents. Learners' **help-seeking activities** were influenced by prompting information about the relevance of help-seeking as a strategy of **self-regulated learning**. Two prompts informed students of an experimental group about (1) the relevance of help-seeking as a strategy of **self-regulated learning**, and (2) about the inadequacy of feeling threatened by need for help or avoiding help-seeking behavior. Results confirmed the relevance of help-seeking behavior on learning outcome. The prompts had an effect on students' actual **help-seeking activities** in the **virtual workspace**. Learners of the experimental group posted more contributions which contained help requests compared to learners of the control group. Those students also reported a higher participation in the workspace which was positively related to learning outcome. Indeed, the experimental group showed a better learning outcome.

Figure 1. Classification of help systems

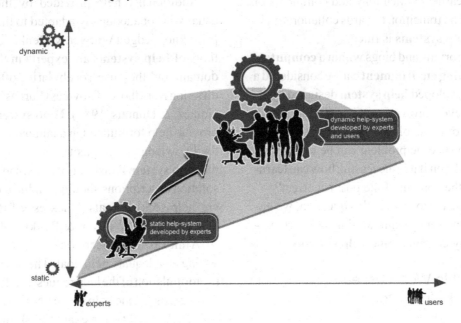

Help-Related Activities Between Learners and Help Systems

Help-seeking and help-giving within computer-based settings can be placed on a continuum according to two dimensions: (1) static versus dynamic, (2) written by experts versus written by users.

Static help systems developed by experts. Static **help systems** contain instructional explanations according to the content of the program. Those **help systems** are written by experts and, once developed, are no longer subject to change. Usually the learners have to formulate their help request in terms of system vocabulary. This query is matched against the content of the **help system** which offers a variety of help outputs. The learners have to inspect the output and select the issues possibly relevant to the given help need. Here the success of the help-seeking process is determined by the mapping of help request and output and the comprehensibility of the help content. This kind of help is often used in computer applications like for example Word or SPSS. In **computer-based learning environments help systems** usually are more context specific. The learner who has to solve a task is offered on demand help by clicking on a button. Sometimes those instructional explanations are offered in separate steps with increasing elaboration (e.g. Aleven, McLaren, & Koedinger, 2006).

*Dynamic **help systems** are gradually developed by experts and users.* Today information flow is no longer unidirectional from professional content providers towards the users as consumers of information. Since the development of blogging tools and wiki engines learners can participate in the construction process. They can write and edit articles, respectively learning content, evaluate content of other learners by rating and **tagging**, and publish their personal experiences in blogs. Blogs are frequently updated webpages which list articles they contain in reverse-chronological order (Nardi, Schiano, & Gumbrecht, 2004). A typical social web feature of blogs is that they support communication between blog authors and readers by enabling the readers (known as well as unknown ones) to leave comments on existing posts. These may be other "invited" experts who form a community of practice or also less proficient learners which may add comments or questions. The transition towards collaboratively designed **help systems** is fluent.

Posts in forums and blogs within a **computer-based learning environment** can be considered a gradually developed **help system** designed by its users. However, browsing and searching within the content of those blogs and forums to find an answer on a specific problem can be rather time consuming. Even if it is successful, how can learners be sure the content of the post is correct?

Before we try to answer this question, we approach the answer by summarizing the shortcomings of many current online **help systems**.

Considerable Weaknesses of Current Help Systems

As put by ISO-standards, software should at its best be suitable for learning and self descriptive (ISO 9241-110, 2006). This holds particularly true for **help systems** which are designed to provide users with specific information to help them reach their help-seeking goal (Xie & Cool, 2006). Thus the main problem is that the provided assistance does not meet the users' goals (Vouligny & Robert, 2005). Improvable aspects of current **help systems** can be divided into two categories: (1) Problems considering the comprehensibility of the content, and (2) problems considering the format of the help output.

Weaknesses Concerning the Comprehensibility of the Help Content

The output to a help query often includes lengthy step by step instructions. The elaboration of the output affords time and effort, and especially novices are frustrated by the irritating richness of details of the given help. **Help systems** should provide help as condensed as possible to enable the learners to quickly continue with their original task. However, an extended explanation should be available on demand (Renkl, 2002; Tidwell, 2006).

Additionally help provided by the systems usually is not adequately adapted to the learners' prior knowledge (Wittwer & Renkl, 2008). Authors of **help systems** are experts in the content domain and they use vocabularies often widely differing from those of novices (Furnas, Landauer, Gomez, & Dumais, 1987). **Help systems** should provide help formulated in a language adapted to the knowledge prerequisites of the learners and the **help systems**' instructional explanations and solution descriptions should be adjusted to learners' help-seeking goals (Nückles & Ertelt, 2006; Nückles, Ertelt, Wittwer, & Renkl, 2007).

A third aspect concerns learners' difficulties in setting an adequate help goal. The preciseness of the formulation of the help request is influenced by the expertise of the help seeker. Nückles, Wittwer and Renkl (2007), for example, showed within the context of internet-based computer support, that the successful completion of the help-seeking process is influenced by the competencies of the users in adequately formulating their help request. **Help systems** should lower the burden on learners by accepting different synonymous formulations of help requests.

Weaknesses Concerning the Format of the Help Output

In computer applications help is often presented in a separate window or even an external application (e.g. a browser). The learners have to keep in mind the concrete constellation of their problem (e.g. the relevant variables of the current task) or even worse they have to switch between several windows to map the aspects of the task to the information of the help output. This "split-source" format produces extraneous cognitive load which interferes with learning (Sweller, Merrienboer, & Paas, 1998).

Even though meanwhile a lot of research on the helpfulness of graphical representation (Mayer, 2005; Schnotz & Bannert, 2003) and on the usefulness of multiple representations for learning (Ainsworth, 2006; Berthold, Eysink,

& Renkl 2008) has been carried out, most **help systems** are still presented using plain text. The **help systems** of software applications sometimes contain screenshots to help the users allocate the relevant buttons or menu options. However, often there are more than just one or two screenshots necessary to visualize the relevant workflow. Learners' have to scroll and keep in mind all foregoing steps. This again affords irrelevant cognitive load which would better be used for understanding the content of the help.

Finally the phenomenon of being "lost in hyperspace" (Conklin, 1987) can also occur within **help systems**. **Help systems** often lack a clear navigation structure and after following the links of specific help pages getting back to the starting point is sometimes challenging.

Problems of comprehensibility accordingly have their origins either in missing congruence of help authors' intention and help users' need, which is a matter of communication, or in the representation of the help content, which is a matter of design. One possibility to address those weaknesses is to combine an adequate and user oriented information architecture with features of **social computing**. This enables help designers to bridge the gap between technical aspects, design aspects and psychological aspects and to create a **help system** that successfully fosters e-collaborative knowledge building.

The Social Web and Its Possible Relevance for Future Help Design

When the Web started to spread in the middle of the 1990s, publication was a strenuous process involving several steps which demanded a substantial level of specialized knowledge. Today Web 2.0 provides a technology that enables non programmers to easily publish content in the internet (O´Reilly, 2005).

Schauer (2005) defined, among others, *user contributed value* and *co-creation* to be two core issues of the social web. Co-creation considers a community of users who participate in the creation of content. This includes the issue of user-contribution but additionally requires the collaboration of a group of users (e.g. Wikipedia or Delicious). User-contributed value on the other hand can be realized by a one-user blog.

One of the most popular features of the social web is *blogging*. The possibility to comment on articles enables users, which were formerly reduced to the role of mere consumers of information, to actively take part in content production. With respect to help design, blogging offers the possibility to bridge the gap between the content experts and the lay persons. By commenting on a help issue the help users can give feedback on the perceived quality of the help content. They may paraphrase the content using their own vocabulary and thereby help other users to understand the help issue and the help designer to improve it. Additionally this comment function offers the opportunity for the learners to directly contact the help authors without using other channels like mail or phone.

By *rating* digital resources users' attitude towards the issue can be made explicit in a way which can easily be evaluated. According to help design, learners rating for example the perceived helpfulness of the issue may give a very informative feedback for peers and help designers.

As mentioned above, when searching within a large **help system** the learners have to adequately formulate their help requests. This affords the ability to formulate the query in terms familiar to the **help system**. When vocabularies of help content authors and help seeking users do not match, then the users' queries will yield no or non adequate results. The problem of query formulation may effectively be lowered using *tagging* as a feature of resource annotation. It offers the opportunity for the system to „learn" the users language, which enables the users to formulate their help request using the vocabulary they are familiar with. Therefore the users' tags may be used by any learner for query formulation and will further on be familiar to the **help system** (Heckner, Mühlbacher, & Wolff, 2008).

Consistency in the design of the help issues and in the navigation structure of the whole system are additional requirements which effective **help systems** should meet.

Information Architecture and Design Patterns

In 1977 Alexander defined a structure for step by step instructions to solve problems in the domain of architecture. Those instructions contained experience-based solutions for common design problems in a language easily understandable for non-experts. They build on each other and are highly cross-referenced.

Since then the concept of design patterns has frequently been adapted from different IT-domains (Borchers, 2001; Gamma, Helm, Johnson, & Vlissides, 2005; Tidwell, 2006; van Duyne, Landay, & Hong, 2003). However, the common ground has always been to make expert knowledge explicit and applicable for lay persons (Borchers, 2001). This idea is also central for using design patterns in the context of **help system** design. Each pattern is designed to solve one particular problem, but the patterns are highly interrelated to provide the learner with all knowledge relevant for task completion. The following aspects of patterns are considered to be of crucial relevance for their transfer on help design: (1) Organizing information by subject, (2) Consistent structure.

1. According to the organization principle patterns are grouped into topically related units. Headings of those units form the navigation structure.
2. Equivalent to the structure on the macronavigation level, the structure of the individual help files has to be considered. Each pattern contains the same parts in the same sequence with the same layout (Borchers, 2001; Gamma et al., 2005). An important

issue of usability is to enable the user to solve similar tasks in a consistent manner (ISO 14915-3, 2002). This requires that the same kind of information is presented in a similar way. Consistency in structure is as well a well known principle in multimedia design to reduce extraneous cognitive load (Mayer, 2005). Cognitive resources should not be bound in locating relevant information on the screen.

Help Design with Design Patterns and Social Computing: A Scenario

In the following a solution for an online **help system** for statistical software is presented which is currently empirically evaluated. Students of educational science or educational psychology are at some point of their studies confronted with the affordances of an empirical investigation. The gathered data has to be analyzed using statistical software. Those students can be expected to be novices in working with this software and they should at some point of their learning process recognize an impasse. Using the **help system** of statistical software can be rather challenging. Help topics are ordered according to expert jargon and queries within the system often do not lead to the desired output. However, those **help systems** are highly elaborated, topics are at least to some extent interrelated and they usually offer some examples to facilitate transfer. All together they are adequately comparable to the new design approach.

Overcoming Weaknesses Concerning the Comprehensibility of the Help Content
As stated above, the output to a help query often includes lengthy step by step instructions. The elaboration of the output affords time and effort and the given help often is too detailed. Our **help system** condenses the solution of a specific problem as much as possible. However, the learners have the possibility to follow an animated description

of the solution process or to choose one of the given links for additional explanations.

To adequately adapt our **help system** to the learners' prior knowledge and their specific help goal, help topics are organized according to the **design pattern approach**. That means each help topic solves a specific user problem (e.g. what to do if a questionnaire contains items with reversed polarity). A **tagging** function is included to overcome problems of **expert-lay-communication** by enabling the learners to tag the help issues to allow better retrieval for future users. Our **help system** therefore efficiently lowers the burden on learners by accepting different synonymous formulations of help requests. To continuously improve the **help system** according to difficulties in vocabulary and solution description, a blogging function is included to foster interaction between help designers and help users. The learners may leave comments concerning the specific help issue (e.g. if in the step by step description an important step was missing) or the overall adequacy of the system (e.g. if they had a statistical problem which is not adequately dealt with in the **help system**). Even teachers or instructors may leave comments including alternative solutions or more detailed information about the current or similar problems.

Overcoming Weaknesses Concerning the Format of the Help Output

As a "split-source" format produces extraneous cognitive load which interferes with learning we included animated screencaptures showing the learners the different steps of the problem solution directly within the context of the learning environment. Of course a direct implementation in the application would have been appreciable. However, the animation facilitates the location of for example menus and checkboxes when the learners solve their own problem in the application.

Additionally the animation enables the learners to visualize the relevant workflow in an integrated way. They do not have to scroll and keep in mind all foregoing steps. This again reduces irrelevant cognitive load which can be used for understanding the content of the help.

Finally the phenomenon to be "lost in hyperspace" is addressed by using the **design pattern approach**. Our **help system** has a clear navigation structure. The learners' position within the system is always highlighted and they are able to go back to the starting page of the **help system** at any point in time.

Implementation of the Help System

The **help system** introduced here was build using WordPress (http://www.wordpress.org) an open source weblog system, enriched by additional modules developed by the authors.

The system contains two navigation levels. According to the organization principle, the menu structure at the left sidebar contains the help items grouped by topics. Additionally there is a constant link at the top of the screen which directly points back to the starting page. The position of the user within the system is always highlighted in the menu bar.

Each help page is structured according to the **design pattern approach**:

1. Title
2. Problem description of the anticipated problem of the learner the help issue is written for
3. List of related problems in case the current problem does not fully meet the learners needs
4. A step by step instruction where the users can chose according to their level of prior knowledge whether (1) to see an animation of the necessary steps or (2) to simply read a textual description
5. Additional extended explanations for expert performers (Hackos & Stevens, 1997; Wittwer & Renkl, 2008)

6. A comment box that enables the learner to directly contact the help author

7. A **tagging** function to gradually improve retrieval

Figure 2 shows an example of the help page structure. For reasons of the planned experiment the page does not yet contain extended explanations for expert performers and a list of related problems.

The **help system** is intended to be used within the statistic education of students of educational sciences and psychology who use SPSS for the analysis of their empirical data. Most of the time several months or even years lie between the course on empirical data analysis and its application, for example in the context of a master thesis. Students are not totally unknowing regarding the use of SPSS. However, according to experience they do not remember in detail the applicability of the software according to their current problem. Questions derive like "How do I deal with items with reversed polarity?" or "How do I test reliability?"

Results of a First Preliminary Evaluation

To test the functionality of the system, a small group of students of educational sciences at the university of Regensburg (N = 8) was assigned to do a task on questionnaire analyses. The task required the students to (1) recode items according to their polarization, (2) build scales according to the concepts of the questionnaire (e.g. a scale on cognitive learning strategies had to be built which included the relevant items), (3) test the reliability of the scale by calculating Cronbach's alpha, (4) testing two hypotheses about relations between variables (correlational analysis) and differences between groups (t-test). The task was tested in a seminar on research methods before and is considered to be of a moderate to high difficulty. The participants were informed that this is a test of the **help system** and that they would have to judge the components of the system afterwards.

There was no posttest on learning outcome as this is planned to be part of the main experimental study. Acceptance of the learning environment was assessed by questionnaire.

All participants were able to successfully complete the task and all participants reported to have used the help facilities. Especially the **social computing** features (comments and tags) were positively evaluated, even though they were rarely used. However those features may possibly show their power with the longterm use of the system when learners use their own tags for retrieving relevant help issues. Some of the students have even asked whether they could get access to the **help system** afterwards to further use it for their study related tasks.

CONCLUSION AND FUTURE RESEARCH

When seeking help within a computer-based setting, learners apply three methods: (1) Browsing – Looking and "clicking" for information, (2) Searching – Typing a query into a search field, and Asking – when searching and browsing fail, learners need to ask a person for help (Rosenfeld & Morville, 2002). As a consequence a successful information- or **help system** should support all aspects of help seeking behavior (Bates, 1989). Information should be well structured and labeled appropriately so that learners can find and understand the content provided by the system. The search component must be designed to help learners find the information that they are looking for using the vocabulary they are familiar with. However, when learners fail in using the system features of **social computing** offer the opportunity to give feedback and ask questions within the bounds of the system, without leaving the system and consulting an external person or resource. A **help system** written by experts ensures the quality of the content. However solely presenting a static **help system** which, once having been written, is

Figure 2. Example of a help page with design pattern and features of social computing

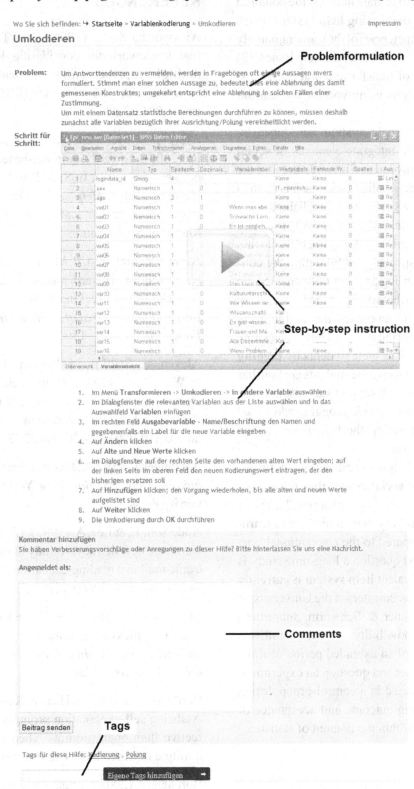

no longer subject to change neglects the potential of a dynamically developing **help system** which integrates the competencies of the learners, namely (1) diagnosing weaknesses of the help issues, (2) giving examples of transfer and practice, or (3) **tagging** the issues by using vocabulary familiar to their peers.

The exemplary **help system** introduced by the authors tries to integrate elements of **social computing** and information architecture into the design of help functionalities with the intention to use the competencies of the users to collaboratively develop a **help system** which is actively used and perceived as helpful in task completion. Such a **help system** is especially useful within the context of formal learning as it not only enables the interaction between help designers and learners but also the interaction between teachers and students within the bounds of the system. The teachers may foster help retrieval of their students by **tagging** help issues with concepts the students are familiar with. They may as well support students in using the facilities of the system in blogging additional explanations connecting the help issues to the content of the course.

Future research has to address two main aspects: (1) Are the **social computing** features of the system actively used by the learners? (2) How does the "new" **help system** contribute to learning outcome compared to the conventional one. To answer the first question a long-time study is required. An equivalent **help system** is currently implemented for webmasters at the University of Regensburg (Heckner & Schworm, submitted) which offers the possibility to assess comments and tags of users of an extended period of time. According to the second question an experimental study is conducted in a control-group design comparing learning outcome and acceptance of the **help system** within the domain of statistics.

REFERENCES

Ainsworth, S. E. (2006). DeFT: A conceptual framework for considering learning with multiple representations. *Learning and Instruction, 16*, 183–198. doi:10.1016/j.learnstruc.2006.03.001

Aleven, V., McLaren, B. M., & Koedinger, K. R. (2006). Toward computer-based tutoring of help-seeking skills. In S. A. Karabenick & R. S. Newman (Eds.), *Help seeking in academic settings: Goals, groups, and contexts* (pp. 259-296). Mahwah, NJ: Erlbaum.

Aleven, V., McLaren, B. M., Roll, I., & Koedinger, K. R. (2006). Toward meta-cognitive tutoring: A model of help-seeking with a cognitive tutor. *International Journal of Artificial Intelligence in Education, 16*, 101–130.

Aleven, V., Stahl, E., Schworm, S., Fischer, F., & Wallace, R. (2003). Help Seeking and Help Design in Interactive Learning Environments. *Review of Educational Research, 73*, 277–320. doi:10.3102/00346543073003277

Alexander, C. (1977). *A pattern language. Towns, buildings, construction.* New York: Oxford University Press.

Anderson, J., & Lee, A. (1995). Literacy teachers learning a new literacy: A study of the use of electronic mail in a reading education class. *Reading Research and Instruction, 34*, 222–238.

Bates, M. J. (1989). The Design of Browsing and Berrypicking Techniques for the Online Search Interface. *Online Review, 13*(5), 407–424. doi:10.1108/eb024320

Berthold, K., Eysink, T. H. S., & Renkl, A. (2008). Assisting self-explanation prompts are more effective than open prompts when learning with multiple representations. *Instructional Science.*

Borchers, J. (2001). *A pattern approach to interaction design.* Chichester, UK: Wiley.

Chi, M. T. H., Bassock, M., Lewis, M., Reimann, P., & Glaser, R. (1989). Self-explanations: How students study and use examples in learning to solve problems. *Cognitive Science, 13*, 145–182.

Conklin, J. (1987). Hypertext: An Introduction and Survey. *Computer, 20*(9), 17–41. doi:10.1109/MC.1987.1663693

Furnas, G. W., Landauer, T. K., Gomez, L. M., & Dumais, S. T. (1987). The vocabulary problem in human-system communication. *Communications of the ACM, 30*(11), 964–971. doi:10.1145/32206.32212

Gamma, E., Helm, R., Johnson, R., & Vlissides, J. (2005). *Design Patterns.* Boston: Addison-Wesley.

Hackos, J. T., & Stevens, D. M. (1997). *Standards for Online Communication.* New York: Wiley.

Heckner, M., Mühlbacher, S., & Wolff, C. (2008). Tagging tagging. Analysing user keywords in scientific bibliography management systems. [JODI]. *Journal of Digital Information, 9*(2).

Heckner, M., & Schworm, S. (in press). The tagblog. Exploring forms of user contribution on the Web 2.0 for encouraging students to actively engage with learning content. *International Journal of Web Based Communities.*

ISO 14915-3. (2002). *Software ergonomics for multimedia user interfaces – Part 3: Media selection and combination.* International Organization for Standardization.

ISO 9241-110. (2006). *Ergonomics of human-system interaction -- Part 110: Dialogue principles.* International Organization for Standardization.

Karabenick, S. A., & Knapp, J. R. (1988). Effects of computer privacy on help-seeking. *Journal of Applied Social Psychology, 18*, 461–472. doi:10.1111/j.1559-1816.1988.tb00029.x

Karabenick, S. A., & Newman, R. S. (2006). *Help seeking in academic settings: Goals, groups, and contexts.* Mahwah, NJ: Erlbaum.

Keefer, J. A., & Karabenick, S. A. (1998). Help-seeking in the information age. In S. A. Karabenick (Ed.), *Strategic help-seeking: Implications for learning and teaching* (pp. 219-250). Mahwah, NJ: Erlbaum.

King, A. (1992). Facilitating elaborative learning trough guided student-generated questioning. *Educational Psychologist, 27*, 111–126. doi:10.1207/s15326985ep2701_8

Kitsantas, A., & Chow, A. (2007). College students' perceived threat and preference for seeking help in traditional, distributed and distance learning environments. *Computers & Education, 48*, 383–395. doi:10.1016/j.compedu.2005.01.008

Littlejohn, A., & Pegler, C. (2007). *Preparing for blended e-learning: Understanding blended and online learning.* New York: Routledge.

Mayer, R. E. (2005). Cognitive theory of multimedia learning. In R. E. Mayer (Ed.), *The Cambridge handbook of multimedia learning* (pp. 31-48). New York: Cambridge University Press.

Mercier, J., & Frederiksen, C. H. (2007). Individual differences in graduate students' help-seeking process in using a computer coach in problem-based learning. *Learning and Instruction, 17*, 184–203. doi:10.1016/j.learninstruc.2007.01.013

Nardi, B., Schiano, D. J., & Gumbrecht, M. (2004). Blogging as social activity, or, would you let 900 million people read your diary? In *Proceedings of the 2004 ACM conference on Computer Supported Cooperative Work (CSCW).* Chicago: ACM.

Nelson-Le Gall, S., & Resnick, L. (1998). Help-seeking, achievement motivation, and the social practice of intelligence in school. In S. A. Karabenick (Ed.), *Strategic help-seeking. Implications for learning and teaching* (pp. 117-139). Mahwah, NJ: Erlbaum.

Nückles, M., & Ertelt, A. (2006). The problem of describing a problem: Supporting laypersons in presenting their queries to the Internet-based helpdesk. *International Journal of Human-Computer Studies, 64*(8), 648–669. doi:10.1016/j.ijhcs.2006.01.001

Nückles, M., Ertelt, A., Wittwer, J., & Renkl, A. (2007). Scripting Laypersons' Problem Descriptions in Internet-Based Communication with Experts. *Scripting Computer-Supported Collaborative Learning,* 73-89.

O'Reilly, T. (2005). *What is web 2.0 design patterns and business models for the next generation of software.* Retrieved March 10, 2009, from http://www.oreilly.com/pub/a/oreilly/tim/news/2005/09/30/what-is-web-20.html

Ortega, F., & Barahona, J. M. G. (2007). Quantitative analysis of the wikipedia community of users. In *Proceedings of the 2007 international symposium "WikiSym '07".* New York: ACM.

Puustinen, M., Volckaert-Legrier, O., Coquin, D., & Bernicot, J. (in press). An analysis of students' spontaneous computer-mediated help seeking: A step towards the design of ecologically valid supporting tools. *Computers & Education.*

Renkl, A. (2002). Learning from worked-out examples: Instructional explanations supplement self-explanations. *Learning and Instruction, 12,* 529–556. doi:10.1016/S0959-4752(01)00030-5

Rosenfeld, L., & Morville, P. (2002). *Information Architecture for the World Wide Web.* Sebastopol, CA: O'Reilly.

Ryan, A. M., Pintrich, P. R., & Midgley, C. (2001). Avoiding seeking help in the classroom: Who and why? *Educational Psychology Review, 13,* 93–114. doi:10.1023/A:1009013420053

Schauer, B. (2005). What put the '2' in web 2.0? Retrieved March 10, 2009 from http://adaptivepath.com/images/publications/essays/What_puts_the_2_in_Web_20.pdf

Schnotz, W., & Bannert, M. (2003). Construction and Interference in learning from multiple representations. *Learning and Instruction, 13,* 141–156. doi:10.1016/S0959-4752(02)00017-8

Schworm, S., Bradler, P., & Renkl, A. (2008). Help design in a computer-based learning environment - teaching argumentation skills through the use of double-content examples. In G. Kanselaar, V. Jonker, P. A. Kirschner & F. J. Prins (Eds.), *Proceedings of the 8th International Conference of the Learning Sciences 2008.* Utrecht: ICLS.

Schworm, S., & Gruber, H. (Manuscript submitted for publication). E-learning in university courses: Fostering participation and help-seeking in a blended learning environment. *Computers in Human Behavior.*

Schworm, S., & Renkl, A. (2006). Computer-supported example-based learning: When instructional explanations reduce self-explanations. *Computers & Education, 46,* 426–445. doi:10.1016/j.compedu.2004.08.011

Schworm, S., & Renkl, A. (2007). Learning argumentations skills through the use of prompts for self-explaining examples. *Journal of Educational Psychology, 99,* 285–296. doi:10.1037/0022-0663.99.2.285

Sweller, J., Merrienboer, J. J. G., & Paas, F. (1998). Cognitive architecture and instructional design. *Educational Psychology Review, 10,* 251–296. doi:10.1023/A:1022193728205

Tidwell, J. (2006). *Designing Interfaces.* Sebastopol, CA: O'Reilly.

Tonkin, E. (2006). Searching the long tail: Hidden structure in social tagging. In *Proceedings of the 17th Workshop of the American Society for Information Science and Technology, Special Interest Group in Classification Research 17.* Austin, TX: ASIST.

Van Duyne, D., Landay, J., & Hong, J. (2003). *The design of sites. Patterns, principles, and processes for crafting a customer-centered Web experience.* Boston: Addison Wesley.

Vedder, P. (1985). *Cooperative learning. A study on processes and effects of cooperation between primary school children.* Groningen, The Netherlands: University of Groningen.

Vouligny, L., & Robert, J. M. (2005). *Online help system design based on the situated action theory.* Proceedings of the 2005 Latin American conference on Human-computer interaction. Cuernavaca, Mexico: ACM.

Webb, N. M. (1991). Task-related verbal interaction and mathematics learning in small groups. *Journal for Research in Mathematics Education, 22,* 366–389. doi:10.2307/749186

Webb, N. M., & Farivar, S. (1999). Developing productive group interaction in middle school mathematics. In A. M. O'Donnell & A. King (Eds.), *Cognitive perspectives on peer learning* (pp. 117-150). Hillsdale: Erlbaum.

Webb, N. M., Ing, M., Kersting, N., & Nehmer, K. M. (2006). Help seeking in cooperative learning groups. In S. A. Karabenick & R. S. Newman (Eds.), *Help seeking in academic settings: Goals, groups, and contexts* (pp. 259-296). Mahwah, NJ: Erlbaum.

Webb, N. M., & Mastergeorge, A. M. (2003). The development of students' learning in peer-directed small groups. *Cognition and Instruction, 21,* 361–428. doi:10.1207/s1532690xci2104_2

Webb, N. M., & Palinscar, A. S. (1996). Group processes in the classroom. In D. Berliner & R. Calfee (Eds.), *Handbook of educational psychology* (pp. 841-873). New York: Macmillan.

Webb, N. M., Troper, J. D., & Fall, R. (1995). Constructive activity and learning in collaborative small groups. *Journal of Educational Psychology, 87,* 406–423. doi:10.1037/0022-0663.87.3.406

Wilkinson, L. C., & Calculator, S. (1982). Requests and responses in peer-directed reading groups. *American Educational Research Journal, 19,* 107–120.

Wilkinson, L. C., & Spinelli, F. (1983). Using requests effectively in peer-directed instructional groups. *American Educational Research Journal, 20,* 479–502.

Wittwer, J., & Renkl, A. (2008). Why instructional explanations often do not work: A framework for understanding the effectiveness of instructional explanations. *Educational Psychologist, 43,* 49–64.

Xie, H., & Cool, C. (2006). Toward a Better Understanding of Help Seeking Behavior: An Evaluation of Help Mechanisms in Two IR systems. Paper presented at the 69th Annual Meeting of the American Society for Information Science and Technology (ASIST).

Chapter 7

Computer–Supported Collaborative Scientific Conceptual Change:
Effects of Collaborative Processes on Student Learning

Lei Liu
University of Pennsylvania, USA

Cindy E. Hmelo-Silver
Rutgers University, USA

ABSTRACT

One problem in science education is that students neither construct in-depth conceptual understanding nor are they able to apply scientific thinking processes. A myriad of studies on conceptual change have investigated the nature and process of conceptual change, and pedagogical strategies to foster conceptual change and improve higher-level thinking. We propose a new framework - the collaborative scientific conceptual change model – to stresses the importance of high quality collaborative discourse and scientific epistemic practices in the process of conceptual change. To investigate how group interactions influence individual students' learning gains, multilevel analysis was used to analyze the hierarchically nested data and qualitative analyses were presented to compare high and low-achievement groups' discourse and their application of epistemic practices. The results found that predicting and coordinating theory and evidence were key practices that predicted students' individual posttest performance and the group interactions were related to the group understanding.

INTRODUCTION

One problem in science education is that students neither construct in-depth conceptual understanding nor are they able to analyze and apply scientific thinking processes (National Research Council, 1996). A myriad of studies on conceptual change have investigated the nature and process of conceptual change, pedagogical strategies to foster conceptual change and improve higher-level thinking. One common instructional strategy is to confront

DOI: 10.4018/978-1-61520-729-9.ch007

students with discrepant events, causing cognitive conflicts, which is widely accepted to be essential for conceptual change (Posner, Strike, Hewson, & Gertzog, 1982). However, other researchers propose that conceptual change is a gradual process and argue that adults, children and even trained scientists fail to change their theories when faced with conflicting evidence (Chinn & Brewer, 2001; Mason, 2003). Accordingly, other factors must be considered, such as peer interactions and engagement in the epistemic practices of science. We propose a new theoretical framework – the collaborative scientific conceptual change (CSCC) model – to explain conceptual change processes.

COLLABORATIVE SCIENTIFIC CONCEPTUAL CHANGE MODEL

This model proposes that conceptual change occurs when learners co-construct new knowledge and make a shift from naive ways of thinking towards the ways of thinking that scientists use to explain phenomena. The CSCC framework echoes with Sinatra's urges to use multiple theoretical spotlights to understand conceptual change. Sinatra (2002) suggested the pursuit of both internal (cognitive and motivational) and external (social and contextual) aspects of conceptual change. Thus, this framework integrates three major perspectives (i.e., cognitive, social, epistemic) to explore the conceptual change process with a particular stress on social and epistemic aspects. We explore how collaborative discourse and epistemic practices mediate conceptual change in the context of using computer simulations to learn about aquarium ecosystems.

Conceptual change is not easy to achieve because students tend to use their intuition to explain science concepts, which can lead to superficial understanding that may be resistant to instruction (Chi, 2005). Posner, Hewson, and Gertzop (1982) believe that conceptual change is a rational

process "by which people's central, organizing concepts change from one set of concepts to another set, incompatible with the first" (p. 211). On the practical level, they presented four conditions that foster conceptual change. First, learners should be dissatisfied with their existing conceptions and such dissatisfaction leads to cognitive conflict. Secondly, the new conception must be understandable to learners so that they can make accommodation in their thinking. Additionally, the new conception should appear initially plausible so that learners may use that to solve problems or construct explanations of phenomena in current context. Finally, the new conception must be fruitful so that learners can transfer the understanding to other different contexts.

In addition to the cognitive aspect, other researchers noticed that the social artifacts play a role in conceptual change. Social constructivists insist that knowledge develops through social negotiation and through the judgment of the application of the ideas of others. The distributed nature of cognition suggests that conceptual change requires communication among people (Pea, 1993). As misconception research shows, students have strong tendencies for meanings to diverge. The features of collaborative learning may help students converge differentiated meanings as they construct meanings for scientific concepts. Peer discourse may create an awareness of the need for knowledge revision and encourage the deep processing needed for conceptual change (Roschelle, 1992). In addition, the intersubjective meaning-making in peer discourse helps create joint interpretations through phases of negotiation focused on shared information (Suthers, 2006). There are several benefits of collaborative discourse in student conceptual change. First, peer interactions may stimulate students to restructure their existing knowledge, which may lead to conceptual change (Smith, diSessa, & Roschelle, 1993). In addition, Roschelle (1992) suggested that by asking learners to work together on joint problems, they are faced with challenges of establishing common references, resolving discrepancies in understanding, negotiating issues of individual and collective action, and coming to joint understanding. Roschelle (1992) reported a study in which convergent conceptual change occurred when students collaboratively used a computer-based simulation - the Envisioning Machine (EM) to learn about two physical concepts: velocity and acceleration. He proposed that *convergence* is the crux of collaboration. As misconception research shows, students have strong tendencies for meanings to diverge. Some features of collaborative learning may help students converge differentiated meanings as they construct meanings for scientific concepts. In the EM study, Roschelle (1992) applied Smith et al's knowledge reconstruction model (Smith et. al., 1993) to explain the process of collaborative conceptual change. Specifically, students restructured their "p-prims", such as commonsense metaphors, to make meaning of a scientific concept. In other words, the students successfully understood a scientific concept without using the standard scientific language.

Second, peer interactions in collaborative activities may generate the need for knowledge revision and to consider alternative perspectives from different cultural backgrounds. Duschl and Osborne (2002) suggest opportunities for discussion and argumentation could aid students in considering and evaluating other perspectives and thus helps them revise their original ideas. Scientific argumentation usually involves proposing, supporting, criticizing, evaluating, and refining ideas, some of which may conflict or compete, about a scientific subject, and engages students in using evidence and theory to support or refute ideas or claims (Simon, Erduran, & Obsorne, 2002). Peer collaboration provides opportunities for scientific argumentation to occur. It provides a rich environment for mutual discovery, reciprocal feedback, and frequent sharing of ideas (Damon & Phelps, 1989). Such an environment provides abundant opportunities to arouse dissatisfaction with existing knowledge. Crook (1994) also

pointed out three major cognitive benefits of peer collaboration: articulation, conflict, and co-construction. According to Piagetian perspectives on conceptual change, the discrepant ideas from peers may require students to explain or reflect on and then compare their original ideas with other alternative ones from their peers, thus lead to eventual conceptual change.

Finally, peer interactions may contribute to conceptual change by encouraging deep mental processing. Deep processing includes attending to contradictory information, attempting to make meaning of alternative ideas, looking for evidence to support or dispute a theory, establishing causal relations between the evidence and considering the validity of evidence (Chinn & Brewer, 1993). In collaborative learning, people have the opportunity to convince others by providing evidence to support their own theories and ask for evidence for alternative theories. Such a tendency provides opportunities to encourage deep processing, thus foster conceptual change.

However, collaborative learning is not always productive as students may not see science as a process of formulating researchable questions, conducting experiments to test ideas, and formulating evidence-based argumentation (Carey & Smith, 1993; Dillenbourg, 1999; Sandoval & Reiser, 2004). Southerland, Sinatra, and Matthews (2001) believe that knowledge is "understood to be based on an assessment of evidence (in the case of scientific knowledge, the evidence would be judged using scientific epistemic criteria)" (pp. 337-338). Both diSessa (2006) and Linn (2006) question the coherence of the criteria students use for their epistemic practices and advocate epistemic practices entailing systematic observation, argumentation, and experimentation. Vosniadou (2002) further their statements by pointing out that children begin the knowledge acquisition process by organizing their sensory experiences under the influence of everyday culture and language into narrow, but coherent, explanatory frameworks that may not be the same as currently accepted science. Students need more opportunities to develop sophisticated epistemic practices such as testing and modifying ideas through experimentation and evidence-based argumentation. Computer tools may support coordinating social interactions and provide opportunities for learners to test their ideas, and coordinate theory and evidence in coherent ways. The CSCC framework argues that on one hand, in the computer-supported collaborative learning context, collaborative discourse makes students' epistemic practices visible and available for comparison. On the other hand, the epistemic practices of science require that students use evidence to support their claims thus producing productive discourse. Such reciprocal relations between collaborative discourse and epistemic practices should foster conceptual change.

Much research has explored the roles that computers can play in student learning. Particularly, the feature of microscopic representation and simulations can make the invisible visible and track student problem-solving strategies. Many scientific phenomena include some invisible microlevel which cannot be observed in real life. However understanding the microlevel phenomena is often essential for learning science. With the affordance of computer-based technologies, students have opportunities to visualize the invisible phenomena via microscopic representation as well as to represent the dynamic phenomena. Further, simulated environments allow students to get involved with problems through visual media, which provide integrated context and can help students comprehend new ideas more easily.

Research has shown the particular effectiveness of computers in fostering conceptual change (e.g. Beichner, 1996; McDermott, 1990; White, & Horwitz, 1988; Zietsman, & Hewson, 1986). McDermott (1990) found that the interactive computer application *Graphs and Tracks* helps students make connections between motions and their graphical representations, using the example of balls rolling on tracks with varied slopes. Consistently, Beichner (1996) proposed that microcomputer-based laboratories and digital video analysis of experimental data have great potential to contribute to the development of conceptual change in science. Papert (1980) argued that computer-supported environments bring in such "mindstorms" in which students can formulate and test alternative hypotheses and reconcile the discrepancy between their ideas and the observations in a microworld. That is, the computers help students to discover the discrepancy by providing contexts for students to test out their original hypotheses and showing the consequences of their hypotheses.

In addition, research found that the computer-supported environment might help students in developing their metacognitive capabilities, the importance of which is stressed by the intentional conceptual change researchers. The ThinkerTools Inquiry Project research group found that ThinkerTools helped students' capabilities of planning in their inquiry (White, 1993).

Taken collectively, we suggest an integrated model – the collaborative scientific conceptual change model, which involves three major elements within conceptual change: the cognitive conflict, the collaborative discourse, and the epistemic practices of science. Collaborative scientific conceptual change occurs when learners co-construct new knowledge and make a shift from their previous ways of thinking towards the scientific ways of thinking that scientists are inclined to use to explain phenomena. This framework stresses two factors in student conceptual change: the effect of social interactions and the shift towards epistemic practices of science. The reciprocally facilitating relations between collaborative discourse and epistemic practices combine the two perspectives together. In collaborative discourse, students realize the need for knowledge revision. Thus knowledge discrepancies are discovered in conversations, which stimulates knowledge reconstruction to solve the discrepancy. More importantly, collaborative discourse encourages deep processing for students. The sociocultural view illuminates that the collaborative discourse may lead to a shared zone of proximal development (ZPD) among students that allows them to engage in practices that are not supported by individual learning, such as scientific observation, collaborative argumentation, and experimentation. By achieving a shared ZPD, the students in a group gradually develop the ability to do certain tasks without help or guidance from peers. Furthermore, the collaborative discourse may also make epistemic practices explicit, thus make metacognitive thinking visible and comparable. For example, during the epistemic practice of coordinating theory and evidence, the underlying criteria students use to justify their claims is exposed to other students who can monitor the coherence of criteria in the discourse.

DESCRIPTION OF THE STUDY

In this paper, we report on a classroom study using the collaborative scientific conceptual change framework to investigate trajectories of conceptual change in a simulation-supported collaborative learning context. In the study, computer simulations were used as a media to provide opportunities for students to conduct science observation, collaborative argumentation, and experimentation.

Participants

The participants were 145 middle school students from two public schools who participated in this study as part of their science instruction. Two different teachers, Teacher A and Teacher B, were experienced science teachers. The teachers randomly assigned students to groups. Twenty focal groups' interactions were videotaped.

Computer Simulations

To facilitate students' understanding of the aquarium ecosystem, we developed two NetLogo simulation models (Wilensky & Reisman, 2006). The two simulations (the fishspawn model and the nitrification process model) present system characteristics at different scales. The fishspawn model is a macro level model, simulating how fish reproduce in a natural environment (Figure 1). The nitrification process model is a micro level simulation of how chemicals reach a balance in an aquarium (Figure 2). This simulation allows students to examine how bacterial-chemical interactions affect the water quality represented in the macro level simulation.

Figure 1. Fish spawn

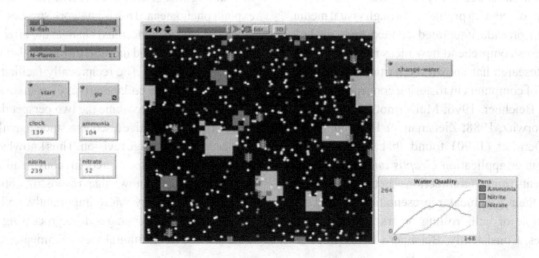

Figure 2. Nitrification process

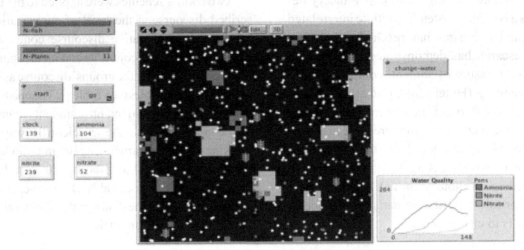

Procedures

The goal of the study was to support middle school science curriculum instruction and to promote deep scientific understanding of the aquarium ecosystem through the use of computer simulations. We collaborated with two public middle school science teachers to develop specific curriculum units. Prior to enacting instruction, the teachers participated in a two-week professional development on the content and tools.

In both classroom settings, teachers were asked to facilitate students on using computer simulations to learn about the aquarium ecosystem. Before the classroom study, both classrooms had a physical aquarium model installed and maintained for about two months. All learning activities were completed in small groups, the size of which varied from 2 to 6 students.

Both teachers used the unit for approximately two school weeks and succeeded in getting students engaged in most of the learning events. In both classrooms, before using the computer simulations, both teachers started with a class discussion on the aquarium ecosystem to activate students' prior knowledge and make connections to the physical fish tank in the classrooms. Then the teachers introduced a hypermedia introducing basic concepts about the aquarium ecosystem.

The students explored the hypermedia software in groups followed by other activities such as class discussions and construction of concept maps that connected parts of the system to their function. Then the teachers conducted a demo class to introduce students to how to use the NetLogo simulations by demonstrating one sample model unrelated to the aquarium system. The students then collaboratively explored the fish spawn simulation and the nitrification process simulation. Students took individual pre and posttests, which asked students to draw all the parts of an aquarium and label the diagram, followed by questions and problems to elicit knowledge about the aquarium ecosystem. Twenty focal groups' collaborative activities were video and audio taped and the tapes were transcribed. This paper reports the results the learning gains of all the students in both classrooms and explores the learning process of the focal groups' exploration of the computer simulations (a four-day intervention of pure group exploration and discussion).

CODING

Pre- and post-tests were scored using a structure-behavior-function (SBF) coding scheme as a measure of conceptual understanding (Hmelo-

Silver, Marathe, & Liu, 2007). SBF theory describes a complex system's multiple interrelated levels, and its dynamic nature (Goel et al., 1996). Prior research has demonstrated that this is a sensitive measure of student' complex system understanding (Hmelo-Silver et al. 2007; Liu et al., 2006). Parts of the system, such as fish or filter, were coded as structures. Mechanisms were coded as behaviors (e.g., the behavior of plants is to absorb carbon dioxide and produce oxygen through photosynthesis). Functions were coded for roles of different parts (e.g., function of filter is to clean water).

Two coding schemes were applied to the transcribed discourse at the level of conversational turns. The collaborative discourse codes were designed to uncover cognitive and metacognitive processes underlying the groups' discourse as well as the facilitators' roles (see Table 1). The epistemic practices codes examined how students engaged in the practices embodying scientific ways of thinking and how learners engage in knowledge construction (Duschl & Osborne, 2002) to build their understanding (see Table 2). An independent rater coded 20% of the data and the overall agreement was greater than 90%.

Table 1. Definitions for collaborative coding categories

Categories	Definitions
Cognitive Process	
Fact Question	Questions asked to obtain factual information
Explanation Question	Questions asked to obtain cause-effect information
Confirm Question	Questions asked to make sure one gets shared information
Directing Statement	Demanding statement for an ongoing activities
Agree	Explicit expression accepting other's ideas
Disagree	Expressing expression rejecting other's ideas
Share Knowledge	Share information with other members in the group
Describe Observation	Descriptions on what is observed in the simulations
Retrieve Prior Knowledge	Making connections to one's previously perceived knowledge or experiences
Generate Theory	Statement of a hypothetical proposal
Paraphrase	Rewording other's statements
Warranting claim	Statements to provide ground for an idea
Identify Cognitive Conflict	Realizing the discrepancies in one's or the group's reasoning
Off-topic Talking	Statement unrelated to the learning target
Metacognitive Process	
Plan	Defining the learning goals
Monitor	Reflecting on the learning process to keep track of the conceptual understanding
Review	Looking back on the strategies (e.g., designing experiments, running simulations) that lead to knowledge construction
Evaluate	Judging effectiveness of learning strategies
Facilitators' Roles	
Educational Statement	Statements related to learning content and strategies
Performance Statement	Statements related to class management and students' performance
Open Question	Questions seeking an elaborated answer or explanation
Closed Questions	Questions seeking a short, factual answer

Table 2. Definitions for epistemic practices coding categories

Categories	Definitions
Basic Knowledge Construction	Superficial meaning-making practice without reasoning or supporting evidence
Observe	Describing phenomena on the computer screen
Predict	Project results of a simulation
Design Experiment	Deciding on a simulated experiment to test hypotheses
Check Knowledge Validity	Examine the consistency or accountability of knowledge by running several experimental trials.
Coordinate Theory-Evidence	Using theories to explain data and using data to evaluate theories
Modify Knowledge	Changing previously constructed knowledge with metacognitive awareness of the reasons for the change
Exchange Knowledge	Explicit articulation of one's knowledge to others.
Give Feedback	Providing evaluative responses to other's statements or actions
Scaffold	Applying purposeful strategies to support other's understanding (teacher's conversational turns only)

RESULTS

Learning Outcomes and Descriptive Statistics

The descriptive statistics for the pre and post tests are shown in Figure 3. For both classrooms, students showed significant learning gains on all SBF (all p <.05). Frequencies for all the discourse codes are shown in Figure 4-5. Figure 4 displays that the three most frequent codes were describing observations, generating theories and warranting claims. The least frequent codes were identifying cognitive conflicts and disagreement. Figure 5 shows that the most frequently used epistemic practices were observing and exchanging knowledge, and the least frequently used practices was modifying knowledge and check knowledge validity.

Multilevel Analysis

To investigate how group interactions and teachers' facilitation influence individual students' learn-

Figure 3. Mean SBF scores of pre and posttests

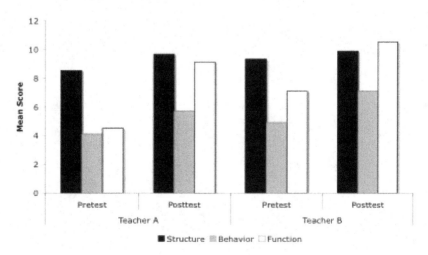

Figure 4. Mean percentage of collaborative discourse codes

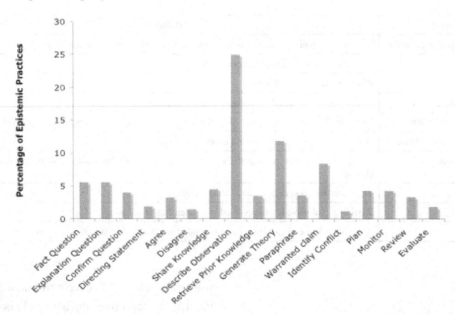

ing gains, multilevel analysis (MLA) is used to analyze the hierarchically nested data (Snijders & Bosker, 1999). MLA deals with the question of how to appropriately disentangle the effects and dependencies interplaying across the multiple levels (Strijbos & Fischer, 2007) by allowing

variance in outcome variables to be analyzed at multiple hierarchical levels. In this research, there are three levels of hierarchically nested data: individual student (Level 1), group interaction (Level 2), and teachers' facilitation (Level 3). The MLA analysis focused onidentifying the

Figure 5. Mean percentage of epistemic codes

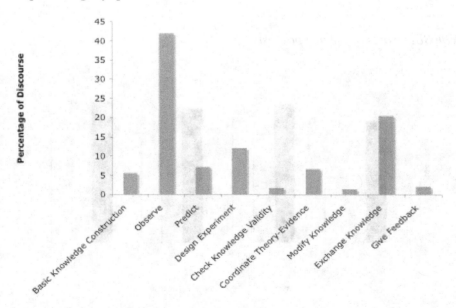

variables in collaborative discourse and epistemic practices that could predict individual student's posttest performance as a function of group-level interaction and teacher-level characteristics. We use the total behavior and function scores as the dependent variable as this accounts for variability in deep understanding.

The multilevel model was constructed using the group-level interaction categories and teachers' facilitating categories as predictors of the dependent variable – TotalBF scores in the posttest. The significant coefficient for the fixed variables demonstrates which characteristics of collaborative discourse and/or epistemic practices at the group level predict individual students' learning outcomes in the posttest.

The goal of the MLA was to explore how group-level variables affected students' learning. For the measures of collaborative discourse and teacher's facilitation, only Warranted claims significantly predicted learning outcomes (β=95.82, t(58)=2.16, p=.03). This indicates that the more warranted claims produced in the group discourse, were associated with higher learning outcomes.

Of the epistemic practices, three codes were significant predictors for TotalBF: Coordinate Theory-Evidence (β=104.19, t(72)=2.74, p=.01), Modify Knowledge (β= −144.16, t(72)= −2.11, p=.04), and Predict (β=54.80, t(72)=2.18, p=.03). This suggests that engaging in two of these three sophisticated epistemic practices within a group was associated with enhanced learning outcomes. We are not sure how to interpret the negative effect of modifying knowledge, however in inspecting the frequencies, we note that this is a very low frequency event and this may be a result of a restricted range so we would be cautious about any generalizations.

Qualitative Analysis

The qualitative analysis takes a close look at the conversational discourse within groups of students to provide further evidence for the inferences drawn from previous quantitative analysis and to identify the patterns occurred in group interactions that may have effect on the quality of collaborative activities. Four groups (including two highest-achievement and two lowest-achievement) were selected based on the group mean score of TotalBF scores and their final understanding level of the Nitrogen Cycle, which is essential for understanding the whole system.

Differences in Discourse Patterns

The results show that compared to the two lowest-achievement groups, both highest-achievement groups made more efforts to paraphrase, ask explanation questions and generate warranted claims. The lowest-achievement groups asked more fact questions. When paraphrasing, students restated peers' ideas in their own words. It allows students opportunities to clarify and check how well they understand each other, fill in gaps between the distributed knowledge, thus build on each other's knowledge to achieve shared knowledge (King, 2002). For example, in one of the high-achievement groups, Eva started to notice the function of graph in the Nitrogen Cycle simulation model, and said to the group, "The change wait a minute, the number change of the ammonia, nitrite, nitrate. The graph shows what is going on." Another student, Hima paraphrased Eva's statement by saying, "It shows us what is going on in the tank… like it shows us the ammonia and the bacteria." On the one hand, Hima parroted Eva's idea that the graph could help understand what was happening in the model. On the other hand, as Eva illustrated ammonia, nitrite and nitrate as the components included in the simulation model, Hima added his own understanding that the model was also related to bacteria, thus suggesting that he had reorganized his thinking by incorporating the concept into his existing knowledge.

Different types of questioning provide different opportunities for students to learn. Explanation questions require peer students to justify their responses, thus engage the group in the scientific practices of explanation and argumentation and provided an invitation for the group to generate warranted claims and check the accountability of proposed ideas (Duschl, Schweingruber, & Shouse, 2007). In CSCL learning environments, thought-provoking questions (i.e., explanation questions) and warranted claims are essentially important to engage students in "minds-on" activities and integrate the information delivered by the computer tools with prior knowledge thus construct new knowledge. In addition, the computer tools (e.g., simulation models) provide opportunities for students think about "why" things happen. The following excerpts from one high-achievement group illustrate how an explanation question drove warranted claims and affected the tool-based activities:

139. Brad: Look at this, why is there so many small fish?
140. Ada: Increasing the water quality increases spawning. So let's leave everything alone.
141. Ada: So you guys want to try what the higher one (water quality) does. Okay, ready?
142. Ada: Look at the spawn, is like 1460 right now.

In the dialogue above, based on what he saw in the Fish Spawn simulation model, Brad asked an explanation question (Turn 139), "why is there so many small fish?" This question drove Ada's warranted claim (Turn 140), "Increasing the water quality increases spawning." And Ada continued to run an experiment in the model to test his justification. This example illustrated how simulation models mediated students' high-level thinking by stimulating explanation questions and affording opportunities to test one's warranted claims.

In contrast to explanation questions, the answers to fact questions are straightforward and largely oriented towards retrieving declarative knowledge and engaged less cognitive activities.

That is, fact questions may only stimulate students to search information in their existing knowledge and they may fail to make causal connections. In simulation-based learning, students often come up with a lot of fact questions, such as "what is the yellow?", "what is the blue?" "What just happened?" These questions do stimulate students to describe their observation or even come up with a theory. However, the fact questions failed to help students develop causal relations between what they observed and the generated theory. The following excerpt from a low-achievement group illustrates a sequence of several fact questions and answers among students.

116. Chris: yea … yellow nitrate, the white is what?
117. Gabby: Nitrite, the yellow.
118. Chris: Red is ammonia, and that was like really high in the beginning
119. Gabby: Look at the yellow thing
120. Chris: Yea. Wait does it show the fish or no?
121. Gabby: No.
122. Chris: It just die, whatever. Oh my god.

Here in the above dialogue, Chris asked two fact questions. The question "the white is what?" (Turn 116) was not answered at all. And the answer to the second question "does it show the fish or no?" (Turn 120) was one word "No" (Turn 121) without elaboration. This example indicated that unlike explanation questions, fact questions failed to ignite discussion thus failed to arouse active engagement in thinking.

Differences in Epistemic Practices

The differences across highest-achievement and lowest-achievement groups in epistemic practices lay in predicting, designing experiment, coordinating theory-evidence, and exchanging knowledge. Specifically, the highest-achievement groups engaged in more practices like predicting, designing experiment, and coordinating theory-evidence during the collaborative activities. These are sophisticated epistemic practices that scientists use to conduct scientific exploration. To some extent, the results challenge the assertion that few students see science as a process of building and testing models and theories (Carey & Smith, 1993; Driver, et al, 1996; Linn & Songer, 1993), because both highest-achievement groups proved themselves to be able to "talk" and "do" science like a scientist.

To illustrate, an example from a high-achievement group discussion presented how this group of students used the simulation tools to explore science:

130. Ada: The water quality do nothing to the fish ...
131. Brad: I think that it will go up in like a second…
132. Ada: If you increase the number of pspawn, the water quality goes down. It's negative now.
133. Ada: The water quality decreases because of the population.
134. Brad: Try it.
135. Ada: Look at this, look at this. It goes down to zero, right?
136. Ada: Negative 400.
137. Brad: The water quality decreases.
138. Siddarth: Yes, it did make sense. If you increase the filter flow the water gets clean, and then it kills all the things that kill the fishes.

At the beginning, the students presented alternative hypotheses on "water quality". Ada at first predicted that water quality had nothing to do with fish (Turn 130). Brad predicted the water quality should go up (Turn 131), and Ada came up with a hypothesis to predict the relation between water quality and population (Turn 132). Then Brad suggested to do an experiment saying "Try it" (Turn 134). Through the observation, Siddarth concluded that increasing filter flow made the water clean and it killed all the organisms in the tank (Turn 138). Judging the content, the students presented a lot of problematic propositions. However, they were operating in the way that scientists normally do. First propose problematic hypotheses, then conduct an experiment to test them, and finally draw a conclusion that might still be problematic. An important finding from recent work is that students with more sophisticated epistemologies seem to take better advantage of inquiry-based learning opportunities (Windschitl & Andre, 1998). As theory theorists assume that even young children have their own theories to explain the world, it is important to acknowledge the capability of young students to learn science. Therefore, although the reasoning was not perfect and lacked coherence here, the group in the example did exhibit the tendency of using scientific way of thinking as well as sharing distributed cognition to co-construct conceptual understanding of the materials presented in the simulation model.

By contrast, the low-achievement groups tended to be more engaged in simple knowledge exchange without questioning and reasoning. Despite the importance of sharing knowledge among peers, to develop scientific understanding of the world, it is extremely important to provide student sufficient opportunities and experiences to develop their theories to explain the scientific phenomena. The following excerpts from one low-achievement group illustrate one typical example:

138. Robby: What did you put so far?
139. Jean: The fish urine drinks ammonia, the ammonia urine.
140. Robby: Wait, the fish water bring ammonia
141. Jean: No, the fish urine.
142. Robby: Yea, the fish urine I meant. Yeah
……
213. Robby: How everything reacts in the tank.
214. Jean: How all the acids and the fish react in the tank
215. Robby: I just put how the acids and the fish react.

It is easy to tell that the goal of Robby and Jean was to give a reasonable answer to the question. They were sharing answers without reasoning with each other. Instead, they were just mechanically copying each other's ideas. This further corroborates that the practice of knowledge exchange is not sufficient at all to foster collaborative scientific conceptual. It is essential to involve other epistemic practices such as hypothesis testing, debate and argumentation, to occur in situated and collaborative contexts.

DISCUSSION

Throughout the study, the students used computer simulations to mediate their epistemic practices. For example, they collected patterns of data through observing simulations, generated theories based on their observations, and constructed causal explanations to connect data with theories. The visualization and manipulative opportunities provided by computer-based simulation models afford students an opportunity to test and refine their hypotheses. It was such affordance that made the behavioral and functional knowledge tangible and discernable for students to construct deep understanding, which eventually led to both knowledge enrichment and revision. In addition, the collaborative discussion around the use of simulation models helped students activate and restructure the existing knowledge distributed among the group (Roschelle, 1992), and the discrepancies emerging in the conversation stimulated the need for knowledge revision (Duschl & Osborne, 2002). Given the role on student understanding, the quality of students' collaborative discussion and practices does make a difference.

The MLA analyses found that predicting and coordinating theory and evidence were key practices that predicted students' individual posttest performance. The qualitative analyses compared the high and low-achievement groups and found that the features of group discourse and the epistemic practices were related to the group understanding. These results are consistent with the CSCC framework, which stresses the importance of high quality collaborative discourse and scientific epistemic practices. Scientific knowledge is comprised of theory and empirical evidence. It is crucial to interrelate these two pieces together to understand what science is and how it works (Kuhn & Pearsall, 2000). Coordinating theory and evidences produces explanations to integrate hypothesized theories and collected evidences from the simulating activities. The results of this study implicate that students need opportunities to experience the mechanisms of collaborative scientific conceptual change and need to use the intentional and deliberate mechanisms that scientists use to restructure knowledge in a social process. These intentional mechanisms often include cycles of hypothesizing, testing hypotheses, generating theories, negotiating, and revising theories. Further research is needed to refine the theoretical framework by addressing questions such as how students' collaborative discourse and/or epistemic practice patterns evolve during the conceptual change process. In addition, further research is needed to investigate what makes some groups perform better than others and what could possibly explain differences in collaborative processes.

REFERENCES

Beichner, R. J. (1996). The impact of video motion analysis on kinematics graph interpretation skills. *American Journal of Physics, 64,* 1272–1278. doi:10.1119/1.18390

Carey, S., & Smith, C. (1993). On understanding the nature of scientific knowledge. *Educational Psychologist, 28,* 235–251. doi:10.1207/s15326985ep2803_4

Chi, M. T. H. (2005). Commonsense conceptions of emergent processes: Why some misconceptions are robust. *Journal of the Learning Sciences, 14,* 161–199. doi:10.1207/s15327809jls1402_1

Chinn, C. A., & Brewer, W. F. (2001). Models of data: A theory of how people evaluate data. *Cognition and Instruction, 19*, 323–393. doi:10.1207/ S1532690XCI1903_3

Damon, W., & Phelps, E. (1989). Critical distinction among three approaches to peer education. *International Journal of Educational Research, 13*, 9–19. doi:10.1016/0883-0355(89)90013-X

Dillenbourg, P. (1999). What do you mean by collaborative learning? In P. Dillenbourg (Ed.), *Collaborative-learning: Cognitive and Computational Approaches* (pp. 1-19). Oxford, UK: Elsevier.

diSessa, A. (2006). A history of conceptual change research: Threads and fault lines. In R. K. Sawyer (Ed.), *The Cambridge handbook of the learning Science* (pp. 265-281). New York: Cambridge University Press.

Duschl, R., & Osborne, J. (2002). Supporting and promoting argumentation discourse. *Studies in Science Education, 38*, 39–72. doi:10.1080/03057260208560187

Goel, A. K., Gomez de Silva Garza, A., Grué, N., Murdock, J. W., Recker, M. M., & Govinderaj, T. (1996). Towards designing learning environments -i: Exploring how devices work. In C. Fraisson, G. Gauthier & A. Lesgold (Eds.), *Intelligent tutoring systems: Lecture notes in computer science*. New York: Springer.

Hmelo-Silver, C. E., Marathe, S., & Liu, L. (2007). Fish swim, rocks sit, and lungs breathe: Expert-novice understanding of complex systems. *Journal of the Learning Sciences, 16*, 307–331.

Kuhn, D., & Pearsall, S. (2000). Developmental origins of scientific thinking. *Journal of Cognition and Development, 1*, 113–129. doi:10.1207/ S15327647JCD0101N_11

Linn, M. (2006). The knowledge integration perspective on learning and instruction. In R. K. Sawyer (Ed), *The Cambridge handbook of the learning Science* (pp. 243-264). New York: Cambridge University Press.

Liu, L., Marathe, S., & Hmelo-Silver, C. E. (2006). Effects of conceptual representations on learning from hypermedia. In S. A. Barab, K. E. Hay, & D. T. Hickey (Eds.). *Proceedings of 7th International Conference of the Learning Sciences* (pp. 495- 501). Mahwah, NJ: Erlbaum.

Mason, L. (2003). Personal epistemologies and intentional conceptual change. In G. M. Sinatra, & P. R. Pintrich (Eds.), *Intentional Conceptual Change* (pp. 199-237). Mahwah, NJ: Lawrence Erlbaum.

McDermott, L. C. (1990). Research and computer-based instruction: Opportunity for interaction. *American Journal of Physics, 58*, 452–462. doi:10.1119/1.16487

National Research Council. (1996). National science education standards. Washington, DC: National Academy Press.

Papert, S. (1980). *Mindstorms: Children, computers, powerful ideas*. Brighton, UK: Harvester Press.

Pea, R. D. (1993). Learning scientific concepts through material and social activities: Conversational analysis meets conceptual change. *Educational Psychology, 28*, 265–277. doi:10.1207/ s15326985ep2803_6

Posner, G., Strike, K., Hewson, P., & Gertzog, W. (1982). Accommodation of a scientific conception: Toward a theory of conceptual change. *Science Education, 66*, 211–227. doi:10.1002/ sce.3730660207

Roschelle, J. (1992). Learning by collaborating: Convergent conceptual change. *Journal of the Learning Sciences, 2*, 235–276. doi:10.1207/ s15327809jls0203_1

Sandoval, W. A., & Reiser, B. J. (2004). Explanation-driven inquiry: Integrating conceptual and epistemic scaffolds for scientific inquiry. *Science Education, 88*, 345–372. doi:10.1002/sce.10130

Simon, S., Erduran, S., & Osborne, J. (2002). *Enhancing the Quality of Argumentation in School Science.* Paper presented at the annual meeting of the National Association for Research in Science Teaching, New Orleans, LA.

Sinatra, G. M. (2002). Motivational, social, and contextual aspects of conceptual change: A commentary. In M. Limon and L. Mason (Eds.), *Reconsidering conceptual change: Issues in theory and practice* (pp. 187- 197). Dordrecht, The Netherlands: Kluwer.

Smith, J., diSessa, A., & Roschelle, J. (1993). Misconceptions reconceived: A constructive analysis of knowledge in transition. *Journal of the Learning Sciences, 3,* 115–163. doi:10.1207/s15327809jls0302_1

Snijders, T., & Bosker, R. (1999). *Multilevel Analysis. An introduction to basic and advanced multilevel modeling.* London: SAGE Publications.

Strijbos, J. W., & Fischer, F. (2007). Methodological challenges for collaborative learning research. *Learning and Instruction, 17,* 389–393. doi:10.1016/j.learninstruc.2007.03.004

Sutherland, S. A., Sinatra, G. M., & Matthews, M. R. (2001). Belief, knowledge, and science education. *Educational Psychology Review, 13,* 325–351. doi:10.1023/A:1011913813847

Suthers, D. D. (2006). Technology affordances for intersubjective meaning making. *International Journal of Computer-Supported Collaborative Learning, 1,* 315–337. doi:10.1007/s11412-006-9660-y

Vosniadou, S. (2002). Content and conceptual change: A commentary. In M. Limon & L. Mason (Eds.), *Reconsidering conceptual change: Issues in theory and practice* (pp.291-297). Dordrecht, The Netherlands: Kluwer.

White, B., & Horwitz, P. (1988). Computer microworlds and conceptual change: A new approach to science education. In P. Ramsden (Ed.), *Improving learning: New Perspectives (pp.69-80).* London: Kogan Page.

White, B. Y. (1993). ThinkerTools: Causal models, conceptual change, and science education. *Cognition and Instruction, 10,* 1–100. doi:10.1207/s1532690xci1001_1

Wilensky, U., & Reisman, K. (2006). Thinking like a wolf, a sheep or a firefly: Learning biology through constructing and testing computational theories. *Cognition and Instruction, 24,* 171–209. doi:10.1207/s1532690xci2402_1

Zietsman, A. I., & Hewson, P. W. (1986). Effect of instructing using microcomputer simulations and conceptual change strategies on science learning. *Journal of Research in Science Teaching, 23,* 27–39. doi:10.1002/tea.3660230104

Chapter 8
Flexible Peer Assessment Formats to Acknowledge Individual Contributions During (Web–Based) Collaborative Learning

Dominique M.A. Sluijsmans
HAN University & Open University of the Netherlands, The Netherlands

Jan-Willem Strijbos
Leiden University, The Netherlands

ABSTRACT

In (web-based) collaborative learning, practitioners increasingly stress the need to acknowledge individual efforts. To this end, peer assessment is regarded as a valuable tool. Research, however, shows shortcomings in the calculations and flexibility of peer assessment formats that are used to transform a group score into individual scores. This chapter proposes an innovative approach by presenting peer assessment formats that underlie sound formulas, but moreover allow flexibility in peer assessment design. Subsequently, the effects of the formats on individual scores are investigated. The results reveal that our formulas and formats outweigh 'traditional' practices to utilise peer assessment for transforming a group score into individual scores. Guidelines for practitioners on the application of peer assessment formats are presented, as well as an outline for a research agenda with a strong focus on the development of flexible peer assessment in (web-based) collaborative based learning.

THEORETICAL BACKGROUND

Collaborative learning is a common practice in education. Crucial to collaborative learning is that group members perform a fair share of the task.

Problems arise when one of more group members do not. This lack of individual effort is referred to as social loafing and free-riding. Social loafing is a tendency to reduce individual effort when working in a group, as compared to individual effort expended when working alone (Williams & Karau, 1991).

DOI: 10.4018/978-1-61520-729-9.ch008

Free-riding exists when an individual does not bear a proportional amount of the collaborative learning process and yet s/he shares the benefits of the group (Kerr & Bruun, 1983). Social loafing and free-riding are two often voiced complaints regarding unsatisfactory assessment experiences during collaborative learning (Johnston & Miles, 2004). Positive interdependence (Johnson, 1981) and individual accountability (Slavin, 1980) are crucial to any approach of collaborative learning (Strijbos, Martens, & Jochems, 2004). For a group to be successful, group members need to understand that they are each individually accountable for at least one aspect of the group task. Moreover, apart from conventional instructional approaches (e.g., scripted cooperation; O'Donnell & Dansereau, 1992), assessment can be applied to enhance both positive interdependence and individual accountability, as well as address concerns regarding a group members' below or above average contribution. However, how the group score can be supplemented with (or corrected through) an individual students' contribution to the collaborative process is precisely the tricky issue we will address in the chapter. We will first outline the lack of alignment between collaborative learning and assessment. We then introduce peer assessment as a method to reduce social loafing and free-riding in (web-based) collaborative learning. It should be noted that this chapter predominantly focuses on the design of peer assessment formats (for classroom and web-based settings) and that the technological design aspects are beyond our scope.

The Need to Align Collaborative Learning and its Assessment

In general, assessment of collaborative learning focuses on the final group product and is only conducted by the teacher. Criteria are predefined by the teacher and the assessment process is treated as a 'black box' without any involvement of the learners (Sluijsmans, Strijbos, & Van de Water-

ing, 2007; Sluijsmans, 2008). Not surprisingly a 'group score' is often applied for the group task, supplemented with one (or more) individual tasks and the final score consists of the average with a weighting factor applied (e.g., Langrish & See, 2008) – using the individual task(s) to 'correct' student grades for a possible lack of individual effort (irrespective by whom) during the group task. The approaches to such weighting vary and no overall rules exist, i.e. the percentage contributed to the final grade by the group task and individual task(s) can be each anywhere in-between 10 to 90%. Although the combination of group and individual tasks and a weighted marking procedure might be appealing, it invites for a certain degree of free-riding (because students can compensate a low group score with their individual work) and it does not reward the group member(s) that invest more effort, or in other words compensate for lack of effort by a fellow group member(s) ('sucker effect'; see Kerr, 1983, Salomon & Globerson, 1989). Moreover, Hoffmann and Rogelberg (2001) found that the extent to which a group task contributes to the course grade affects students' preferences, with low ability students being more prone to prefer a course where the group task attributes stronger to the overall grade compared to the individual task(s).

Assessment in collaborative learning has hardly evolved beyond so-called 'summative' practices. Summative assessment focuses strongly on the cognitive aspects of learning, often applies a single performance score, is decontextualised and atomic, isolated from the learning process, and takes place only at the end of a course to judge how well a student performed. Furthermore, the assessment in collaborative learning is typically disconnected from the instructional setting, i.e. a lack of 'constructive alignment' exists (Biggs, 1996). However, since assessment strongly influences learning (Frederiksen, 1984), any collaborative learning course should apply an assessment that a) reflects both the collaboration process and product, and b) promotes students' collaboration skills. The need for including the group process into assessment of collaborative learning is implicitly expressed by students: a group score is considered fair as long as all group members contributed to the group product, however if one or more group members did not perform a fair share of the group task, students who invested a lot of effort express a strong concern that their group score (or grade) should also acknowledge their contribution to the group task (Strijbos, Martens, Jochems, & Broers, 2007).

The issues of assessment of collaborative learning and alternative approaches to such assessment have only recently received more attention (Birenbaum, 2005; Meier, Spada, & Rummel, 2007). One approach to acknowledge individual contributions is by involving students through peer assessment.

The Involvement of Learners as Assessors in (Web-Based) Collaborative Learning

In collaborative learning settings the teacher typically has to divide the attention among multiple small groups simultaneously. As a consequence it is difficult for the teacher to obtain sufficient insight into the collaborative process of each group, especially when the collaboration spans several weeks and involves out-of class collaboration. Since active student participation in the assessment process corresponds with active involvement in the collaborative learning process, constructive alignment may be achieved through involvement of students by using peer assessment (Orsmond, Merry, & Reiling, 2002). During peer assessment equal status students judge a peers' performance with a rating scheme or qualitative report (Topping, 1998), and this stimulates students to share responsibility and conduct continuous dialogue with their peers (Boud, 1990; Orsmond, Merry, & Callaghan, 2004).

With regard to peer assessment of collaborative learning we distinguish intra-group assessment and inter-group assessment (Sivan, 2000). We regard intra-group assessment as the assessment where each individual group member assesses all group members, including themselves. Inter-group assessment is the process by which each individual group member assesses the performance of another group. Intra-group assessment can make students more aware of their internal group dynamics and individual contribution, whereas inter-group assessment provides the students a group-external reference to determine the quality/ progress of their own group. In both assessment settings the peer assessment is an individual activity. As such, peer assessment appears to be a valuable tool to reduce social loafing, free-riding and sucker effects, enhance students' awareness of individual accountability and promote positive interdependence, and provide the opportunity to acknowledge an individual's effort to the collaborative process as an individual score derived from the group score. From an instructional point of view, peer assessment covers the part of collaboration that a teacher has difficulty to assess, i.e. the collaborative process, and students can be involved in the construction of assessment criteria – which stimulates ownership and accountability (Sluijsmans, Brand-Gruwel, Van Merriënboer, & Martens, 2004).

The process of (web-based) collaborative learning is increasingly recognised as an important element in the assessment of collaborative learning (Lee, Chan, & van Aalst, 2006; Lopez-Real & Chan, 1999; Macdonald, 2003; Prins, Sluijsmans, Kirschner, & Strijbos, 2005; Weinberger, Stegmann, & Fischer, 2007). Whenever collaborative learning is marked solely on the basis of the group product, and not process, there can be a bias and inequities in individual marking that are unfair and unacceptable. In this chapter we argue that both process and product are important aspects for collaborative learning and need to be assessed. Hence, for successful assessment of collaborative learning both intra- and inter-group assessment need to be applied. Nevertheless, the contemporary applications of peer assessment of collaborative learning do not address the pivotal issue that has received some (rather limited) attention: computing the transformation of a group score into an individual score using peer assessment scores.

Research Questions

Based on our theoretical outline, we defined three research questions: 1) What do previous studies tell us about the measurement of individual contributions during collaborative learning? 2) Can we design peer assessment formats that reduce the current shortcomings?, and 3) What is the impact of different peer assessment formats on the transformation of group scores into individual scores?

PRIOR RESEARCH ON THE MEASUREMENT OF INDIVIDUAL CONTRIBUTIONS

To investigate the formats and formulas used to measure individual contributions in during collaborative learning, a broad literature search was conducted (see Sluijsmans, Strijbos, & Van de Watering, 2007). Eighteen studies were analysed in-depth and this analysis revealed six weaknesses in the formats and formulas that are used to transform group scores into individual scores.

A first weakness is that nearly all studies (17 out of 18) applied a rating scale to obtain peer assessment scores. Only one study applies a distribution format (Lejk & Wyvill, 2001) and only one study addressed peer ranking (Fermelis, Tucker, & Palmer, 2007). The distribution format provides each student with, for example, 100 credits to be distributed across all other group members, and the individual peer assessment score consists of the average of all credits given by fellow group members. The ranking format requires each student, for example, to rank each fellow group member from best to weakest on a number of criteria.

Secondly, all studies applied a computation formula that ties the individual's score to the group score. Consequently, a high group score yields a larger profit/loss than a low group score. This practice also narrows the variability of individual scores and limits the real goal of the peer assessment score, that is, to increase variability.

A third problem is that reciprocity effects can occur where the lack of variability in scores is often caused by friendship marking whereby students do not want to assess their peers too harshly (e.g., Freeman, 1995; Mathews, 1994; Williams, 1992). Some studies propose to conduct an anonymous peer assessment to control for reciprocity effects (cf. Cheng & Warren, 1997). Although this would be preferred when the assessment outcomes have summative or high-stake implications, the opposite would be preferred for a formative setting where the outcomes are used for reflection, and can act as input for change in individuals' contributions during the remainder of the collaboration. In this respect, self-assessment scores should be included in addition to peer assessment scores.

A fourth concern is the inclusion of a scaling down approach (Conway, Kember, Sivan & Wu, 1993), whereas peer assessment aims at increasing the variability of individual scores. The variability should be addressed by the factors of the peer assessment format, but we advocate to exclude a weighting factor in the computation. Rather we propose to utilise variability of individual scores by having students discuss these variations within their group.

Another issue is that none of the studies discussed the flexible use of peer assessment formats. The criteria and the rating scale are often defined beforehand and standardised based on the group mean, and there is limited creativity and variation in the choice and definition of criteria. Formats apply either a category or a holistic approach to weighting of criteria, and participation in peer assessment is mandatory.

Finally, the review revealed that peer assessment is predominantly approached as a measurement issue rather than an educational design issue (see for example Sharp, 2006). This originates from research on assessment being historically an area of psychometricians rather than of instructional designers. The consequence is that issues such as 'the educational value of peer assessment in collaborative learning' are hardly addressed. Hence, we advocate a stronger focus on the design aspects of peer assessment formats besides solely a psychometric perspective.

In summary, the literature review showed clear shortcomings with respect to current peer assessment formats. Therefore, we advanced our research by investigating the design of peer assessment formats that address these limitations.

THE DESIGN OF REFINED PEER ASSESSMENT FORMATS

To support teachers and students with a sound approach to use peer assessment in collaborative learning to derive individual scores from group scores, we decided to refine existing peer assessment formats (hereafter referred to as PA-format) in terms of factors that are taken into account (e.g., maximum deviation of the group score) as well as the formulas to calculate an individual score. Based on our analysis of current approaches to peer assessment of individual contributions in collaborative learning, we conclude that: 1) the individual score should not depend on the group score, 2) all scores should be included in the final computation (self-assessment (SA) and peer assessment (PA) scores), 3) there should be no scaling down or individual weighting, 4) the designer should be allowed to easily change the type of format, the criteria, the weight of each criterion, the rating scale, and the maximum deviation from the group score, and 5) the format should be user friendly and efficient for both teachers and students, which means that any variations in the design should be automatically adjusted within the scoring formulas.

Based on these five requirements, we developed three PA-formats using the functionalities of Excel™: one based on the 'traditional format' in which the students assess their peers on a rating scale, one in which students distribute a number of credits among their fellow group members, and one where the students ranks their peers from best to weakest on a number of criteria. We will first discuss our PA-rating format in conjunction with the 'traditional' scoring formulas in PA-rating formats. Subsequently we will discuss the PA-distribution and PA-ranking format.

Elaboration of the Rating Format

To illustrate the difference between 'traditional' PA-rating formats and formulas and our approach, we will use Gupta's (2004) dataset presented as an example. Figure 1 illustrates our PA-rating format. The green shaded cells (light grey in black and white print) represent the variables that can be flexibly designed by the teacher. In the PA-rating format a teacher can decide: 1) the definition and weight of the criteria, 2) the group size, 3) the maximum deviation from the group score (the maximum impact of an individual's PA-score on the final individual score), and 4) the group score (i.e., the mark on the group assignment). Each format provides the following scoring information:

- group score: final score awarded to the group by the teacher (same for each group member);
- SA-score: evaluation by student of his or her own contribution;
- PA-total: sum of ratings received by fellow group members;
- PA-score: sum of ratings received by fellow students plus a students' SA-score;
- individual score: final individual score – group score corrected by the individual PA-score;
- SA-score compared to the mean score (SA comp. mean);

Figure 1. The default rating PA-format

Peer assessment format: Rating

	Description criteria		Weight (1-4)					
Criterion1					# criteria			
Criterion2					# students			
Criterion3					medium			
Criterion4					sum of weights			
Criterion5					minimum score			
					mean score			
					maximum score			
					Maximum deviation from group score (0-100)			
					Group score (0-100)			
Student	Name	SA comp. PA	SA comp.mean	SA Score	PA total	PA score	Ind.score	
Student1								
Student2								
Student3								
Student4								
Student5								
Student6								
Student7								
Student8								
Student9								
Student10								

- SA-score compared to the PA-score (SA comp. PA).

The data are automatically inserted in the individual peer assessment forms used by students to conduct the peer assessment. The red shaded cells (dark grey in black and white print) represent variables (with embedded formulas) computed from the data in the student forms and entries in the green shaded cells.

Table 1 presents the self- and peer assessment scores of a group of five students regarding the level of contribution (the rating scale ranges from 1 (poor) to 5 (outstanding), as well as the individual scores that were derived from the group score (referred to as 'group average rating') – including the received PA-score (referred to as 'individual average rating'). This group received a group score of 75 out of 100.

The formulas applied by Gupta (2004) to compute individual scores were derived from Conway et al. (1993). We will illustrate the formulas with respect to Adam's individual score:

$$\text{Group average rating} = \frac{5 + 4.2 + 4 + 4 + 3.8}{5} = 4.2$$

$$\text{Individual weighting factor (IWF)} = \frac{ind.averagerating}{groupaveragerating} = \frac{5}{4.2} = 1.19$$

$$\text{Individual score} = \text{IWF} * \text{group score} = 1.19 * 75 = 89.3$$

The formulas of our PA-rating format (Figure 1) are presented in Appendix A. The scores of Adam are presented in the right column of Appendix A to illustrate our formulas. Subsequently, we computed the individual scores and the difference between these individual scores and the group score, using both the traditional and revised formulas for the case of a group score of 75, as well as the effect on the individual score given a hypothetical group score of 65 or 55.

Table 2 reveals three interesting findings. First of all, it illustrates the zero-sum principle underlying the Conway-formula, meaning that the overall

Table 1. Peer and self assessment within a group (derived from Gupta, 2004)

	Adam	Brett	Chris	Lyn	Maria	Individual average rating	IWF	Individual score
Adam	5	5	5	5	5	5.0	1.19	89.3
Brett	5	4	4	4	4	4.2	1.00	75.0
Chris	4	4	4	4	4	4.0	.95	71.4
Lyn	4	4	4	4	4	4.0	.95	71.4
Maria	4	3	4	4	4	3.8	.90	67.9

balance between profit and loss between group members is zero. This automatically implies that the individual score of some group members is above group score and the individual score of other members is below group score. This is rather odd, since the self- and peer assessment data in Table 1 clearly show that all ratings (except for one) are above average. This would imply that none of the individual scores can be lower than the group score. After all, each student received positive peer evaluations. In contrast, our formulas allow for a correct representation of the actual self- and peer assessment. In all cases the individual scores are above group score. Whether the positive peer evaluations accurately represent each students' contribution or indicate reciprocity, is a valid concern for the teacher (e.g., perhaps more specific criteria are needed to increase variability in ratings), but not automatically – and potentially incorrectly – controlled through formulas.

A second finding is that for students who are positively evaluated by themselves and their peers, the profit decreases as the group score decreases, whereas for students with lower self- and peer scores, the loss decreases as group score decreases. In other words, the profit or loss depends on the group score, because the IWF is multiplied by the group score. This implies that group score – which is based on an assessment of the quality of the group product – is interlinked with self- and peer assessment scores, which are based on an assessment of the group process. Since both assessments measure different constructs (product and process), we advocate in our formulas that

both assessments are treated as independent measurements, meaning that self- and peer assessment scores are constant irrespective of the group score. In sum, our formula separates the IWF-factor and the group score.

A third observation is the need for flexibility. Table 2 shows that the IWF scales down the variability and as a result the PA-scores are not optimally used to enhance variability of individual scores. In our formula, this issue is addressed by the feature to flexibly define the maximum deviation of individual scores from the group score. The maximum variation is 15 points from the group score, and this is well below the threshold of 20 points that we set in our formula for this example (see Appendix A).

Elaboration of the Distribution Format and Ranking Format

Unfortunately, Gupta's data (2004) could not be transposed to a distribution and ranking format, therefore we used a baseline peer assessment dataset of 72 fourth year teacher training students (Bachelor of Education) – 11 male and 61 female – randomly distributed over eight groups ($n1 = 7$; $n2 = 10$; $n3 = 9$; $n4 = 10$, $n5 = 10$; $n6 = 10$; $n7 = 6$; $n8 = 10$) to illustrate both PA-formats. The PA-format for ranking provides the same functionalities and scoring information as the rating format. The distribution format has one additional feature, i.e. the specification of the number of credits that can be distributed.

Table 2. Comparing the traditional and revised formulas for the rating format in terms of the differences between the individual score and the group score (individual scores are included between parentheses)

	Conway et al. formula				Sluijsmans et al. formula		
	Group 75	Group 65	Group 55		Group 75	Group 65	Group 55
	Individual	Individual	Individual		Individual	Individual	Individual
Adam	14.3 (89.3)	12.35 (77.35)	12.45 (65.45)		15 (90)	15 (80)	15 (70)
Brett	0 (75)	0 (65)	0 (55)		7 (82)	7 (72)	7 (62)
Chris	-3.6 (71.4)	-3.25 (61.75)	-2.75 (52.25)		5 (80)	5 (70)	5 (60)
Lyn	-3.6 (71.4)	-3.25 (61.75)	-2.75 (52.25)		5 (80)	5 (70)	5 (60)
Maria	-7.1 (67.9)	-6.5 (58.5)	-5.5 (49.5)		3 (78)	3 (68)	3 (58)

All students were randomly assigned to groups to prevent that students chose to collaborate with their friends. Students assessed their fellow group members and themselves on five criteria: 1) contributions to group discussions, 2) quality of contributions, 3) preparedness to be involved in tasks, 4) actual contribution to the group work, and 5) a flexible attitude towards the opinions of group members. Peers provided PA-scores of their group members by distributing 100 credits per criterion among all group members, including themselves.

Students were not allowed to use identical scores within their distribution, to allow the modelling of the ranking format without ties, based on the PA distribution scores obtained from the 72 students. We awarded the students with the most credits in the distribution PA-format with a score of 1 (best) and the students with the least credits with a 7 (weakest). Table 3 shows the self- and peer assessment scores by one student (Lesley) for her own contribution and each fellow group member's contribution, for the distribution and ranking PA-format. The underlying formulas for the distribution PA-format are illustrated in Appendix B and the formulas for the ranking PA-format are explained in Appendix C. To clarify the modelling, distribution scores on the

first criterion are presented between parentheses. For example, because Jantien received the highest score in the distribution format (20), she is ranked first in the ranking format (self-assessment scores are italicised).

Table 4 presents the self- and peer assessment scores for the entire group in which Lesley participated, for both the distribution and ranking PA-format (self-assessment scores are italicised).

When we process the data for the entire group, an overview of scores per student is generated. Figure 2 shows the scores for the distribution PA-format, and Figure 3 presents the scores for the ranking PA-format. Both Figures reveal that four students (Lesley, Jantien, Denise and Erik) received an individual score higher than the group score (individual score > 70). In the distribution format, five students (Lesley, Jantien, Jeroen, Denise, and Linda) overrate themselves compared to the received PA-scores (SA comp. PA > 1), compared to six students (Lesley, Jantien, Jeroen, Denise, Linda and Erik) in the ranking format. In each format there are two students (Jeroen and Sven) who underrate themselves compared to the mean score (SA comp. mean < 1).

Both Figures also show that individual scores can differ substantially given the PA-format used.

For example, Lesley, Jantien and Denise obtain a higher individual score in the ranking format compared to the distribution format. Linda and Erik obtain similar individual scores, whereas Jeroen and Sven receive substantially lower individual scores in the ranking format.

Table 3. Self- and peer assessment scores by Lesley in the distribution and ranking format.

Distribution format							
Criteria	*Lesley*	Jantien	Jeroen	Denise	Linda	Sven	Erik
Contribution to the discussions	16	20	10	15	9	11	19
Quality of the contribution	13	19	5	13	14	12	24
Willingness to take up tasks	21	22	6	18	7	12	14
Actual contribution	22	13	7	14	11	12	21
Flexible attitude	25	14	8	14	10	9	20
Total	97	88	36	74	51	56	98
Ranking format							
Criteria	*Lesley*	Jantien	Jeroen	Denise	Linda	Sven	**Erik**
Contribution to the discussions	3 (16)	1 (20)	6 (10)	4 (15)	7 (9)	5 (11)	**2 (19)**
Quality of the contribution	4	2	7	4	3	6	**1**
Willingness to take up tasks	2	1	7	3	6	5	**4**
Actual contribution	1	4	7	3	6	5	**2**
Flexible attitude	1	3	7	3	5	6	**2**
Total	*11*	**11**	**34**	17	27	27	**11**

Figure 2. Group overview of the distribution PA-format

Peer assessment format: Distribution

	Description criteria		Weight (1-4)				
Criterion1	Contribution to the discussions		1		# criteria	5	
Criterion2	Quality of the contribution		1		# students	7	
Criterion3	Willingness to take up tasks		1		medium	14,28571429	
Criterion4	Actual contribution to the group work		1		sum of weights	5	
Criterion5	Flexible attitude		1		minimum score	0	
					mean score	500	
					maximum score	3500	
					minimum		
					credits	100	
					Maximum deviation from group score (0-100)	20	
					Group score (0-100)	70	

Student	Name	SA comp. PA	SA comp.mean	SA Score	PA total	PA score	Ind.score
Student1	Lesley	1,16	1,36	97	501	598	70,65
Student2	Jantien	1,07	1,39	99	553	652	71,01
Student3	Jeroen	1,56	0,69	49	189	238	59,52
Student4	Denise	1,42	1,61	115	486	601	70,67
Student5	Linda	1,48	1,32	94	381	475	69,00
Student6	Sven	0,96	0,76	54	338	392	65,68
Student7	Erik	0,96	1,05	75	469	544	70,29

Table 4. Self- and peer assessment scores of Lesley's group in the distribution and ranking format

	Distribution by							
	Lesley	**Jantien**	**Jeroen**	**Denise**	**Linda**	**Sven**	**Erik**	**PA score**
Lesley	*97*	86	75	79	75	100	86	598
Jantien	88	*99*	83	96	83	95	108	652
Jeroen	36	25	*49*	24	49	30	25	238
Denise	74	89	78	*115*	78	80	87	601
Linda	51	59	94	52	*94*	65	60	475
Sven	56	59	53	58	53	*54*	59	392
Erik	98	83	68	76	68	76	*75*	544
	Ranking by							
	Lesley	Jantien	Jeroen	Denise	Linda	Sven	Erik	PA score
Lesley	*11*	16	17	17	17	5	16	99
Jantien	11	*8*	14	10	14	10	7	74
Jeroen	34	35	*33*	35	33	35	35	240
Denise	17	11	16	*5*	16	18	13	96
Linda	27	26	6	29	*6*	23	27	144
Sven	27	26	31	26	31	*29*	25	195
Erik	11	14	23	18	23	20	*17*	126

THE IMPACT OF VARIATIONS WITHIN EACH PA-FORMAT

Based on the default distribution and ranking PA-formats, we modelled two variations: a) adding extra weight to two out of five criteria (total weight sum of seven), and b) expanding the maximum deviation of an individual score from the group score with ten points (from 20 to 30). We specifically aim to investigate whether individual scores vary between students in Lesley's group for different variations, whether individual scores vary between groups for different variations, and whether the distribution and ranking PA-formats overall lead to similar individual scores?

Data-Analysis

First, we calculated the individual score for each member of Lesley's group and the mean individual scores for all other groups in the teacher training course. Subsequently, we calculated the means, standard deviations, minima, maxima and range of the individual scores per group for each variation. Due to different group scores, the individual scores were standardised. We modelled six variations: distribution default, distribution weight, distribution deviation, ranking default, ranking weight, and ranking deviation. We applied the non-parametric Kruskal-Wallis one-way analysis of variance to investigate the six variations at the group level. The overall differences between both formats at the individual level, were examined through paired t- tests.

Results

Table 5 presents the individual scores per variation for Lesley's group (see Figures 3 and 4 for the default distribution and ranking format respectively).

Table 5 reveals that the individual scores for different variations within either format do not differ

Table 5. Individual scores of Lesley's group for each distribution and ranking variation

	Distribution default	Distribution weight	Distribution deviation	Ranking default	Ranking weight	Ranking deviation
Lesley	70.65	70.71	70.98	77.81	78.44	**81.71**
Jantien	71.01	71.06	71.52	82.57	83.06	**88.86**
Jeroen	59.52	59.51	54.28	50.95	50.68	**41.43**
Denise	70.67	70.72	71.01	78.38	78.71	**82.57**
Linda	69.00	68.74	68.50	69.24	69.18	**68.86**
Sven	65.68	65.63	63.52	59.52	59.52	**54.29**
Erik	**70.29**	**70.19**	**70.44**	**72.67**	**71.50**	**74.00**

Figure 3. Group overview of the ranking PA-format

Peer assessment format: Ranking

	Description criteria	Weight (1-4)
Criterion1	Contribution to the discussions	1
Criterion2	Quality of the contribution	1
Criterion3	Willingness to take up tasks	1
Criterion4	Actual contribution to the group work	1
Criterion5	Flexible attitude	1

# criteria	5
# students	7
medium	4
sum of weights	5
minimum ranking	245
mean ranking	140
maximum ranking	35

Maximum deviation from group score (0-100)	20
Group score (0-100)	70

Student	Name	SA comp. PA	SA comp.mean	SA Score	PA total	PA score	Ind.score
Student1	Lesley	1,33	1,82	11	88	99	77,81
Student2	Jantien	1,38	2,50	8	66	74	82,57
Student3	Jeroen	1,05	0,61	33	207	240	50,95
Student4	Denise	3,03	4,00	5	91	96	78,38
Student5	Linda	3,83	3,33	6	138	144	69,24
Student6	Sven	0,95	0,69	29	166	195	59,52
Student7	Erik	1,07	1,18	17	109	126	72,67

for individual students. Table 6 presents the means and standard deviations for all eight groups.

Group level comparisons (Kruskal-Wallis test) revealed no differences for distribution default (χ^2 (1, 8) = .399, *df* = 7, ns), distribution weight (χ^2 (1, 8) = .398, *df* = 7, ns), distribution deviation (χ^2 (1, 8) = .390, *df* = 7, ns), rank default (χ^2 (1, 8) = 2.401, *df* = 7, ns), rank weight (χ^2 (1, 8) = 2.627, *df* = 7, ns), and rank deviation (χ^2 (1, 8) = 2.395, *df* = 7, ns). Subsequently we investigated possible differences between format variations for the entire sample. Table 7 provides the overall mean, standard deviation, minima, maxima and range for each variation.

Table 7 reveals that the overall scores for different variations within either format do not differ. However, the mean, SD and range in the distribution format are smaller than the mean, SD and range in the ranking format. Paired *t*-tests reveal significant differences between the default distribution and default ranking format ($t(71)$ = -3.54, $p < .001$), between the distribution weight format and the ranking weight format ($t(71)$ = -3.48, $p < .001$), and between the distribution deviation format and the ranking format deviation format ($t(71)$ =-3.54, $p <.001$).

Table 6. Group-level individual score mean and standard deviation for each distribution and ranking variation (N = 8)

	Distribution default		Distribution weight		Distribution deviation		Ranking default		Ranking weight		Ranking deviation	
Group	M	SD	M	SD	M	SD	M	SD	M	SD	M	SD
1 (n = 7)	68.12	4.22	68.08	4.22	67.18	6.33	70.16	11.32	70.16	11.57	70.25	16.98
2 (n = 10)	71.61	6.49	71.65	6.42	69.92	9.74	75.52	12.49	75.47	12.64	75.45	18.24
3 (n = 9)	76.76	5.82	76.70	5.77	75.08	8.72	80.11	11.41	80.14	11.38	80.17	17.12
4 (n = 10)	67.00	5.51	67.08	5.28	65.50	8.26	70.27	10.87	70.25	10.63	70.40	16.31
5 (n = 10)	77.21	5.31	77.34	5.07	75.82	7.96	80.32	9.84	80.34	9.54	80.48	14.75
6 (n = 10)	72.86	3.76	72.86	3.79	71.78	5.64	75.39	7.39	75.43	7.34	75.59	11.09
7 (n = 6)	73.49	2.52	73.48	2.52	72.73	3.78	75.31	8.14	75.32	8.21	75.47	12.21
8 (n = 10)	67.28	5.17	67.35	5.03	65.91	7.76	66.19	4.29	66.19	4.26	64.28	6.43

Table 7. Overall mean, standard deviation, minima, maxima and range of the individual scores for each variation in the distribution and ranking format (N = 72)

Format	Mean	SD	Minimum	Maximum	Range
Distribution default	71.77	6.22	57.84	82.40	24.56
Distribution weight	71.81	6.14	58.43	82.45	24.02
Distribution deviation	70.44	8.26	51.76	83.60	31.84
Raking default	74.18	10.47	50.95	99.89	48.94
Ranking weight	74.18	10.44	50.68	99.92	49.24
Ranking deviation	74.00	14.84	41.43	109.83	68.40

CONCLUSION

In this chapter we explored the design of several PA-formats to award individual effort in collaborative learning, by using sound calculations and affording increased flexibility. We proposed the design of three PA-formats which allow for more variance in the PA-format and calculation formulas in which the individual scores are measured independently from the group score. We also investigated the impact of variations within each format (weight of criteria and maximum deviation of the group score) on the individual score.

Two main conclusions can be drawn. Firstly, the shortcomings of current practice are tack-led in the design of the proposed flexible PA-formats: there is more variance in the PA-format (besides rating, also distribution and ranking), the individual scores are calculated independent from the group score, a maximum variation is warranted because there is no scaling down in the calculations, and flexibility in the formats is assured. Secondly, the differences in outcomes of formats were investigated. Comparisons between the distribution and ranking PA-formats reveal significant differences in individual outcomes. The distribution format appears to be the weakest format because of its asymmetry: the larger the group size, the less the above average students benefit from peer assessment in collaborative learning. Another consequence is that individual scores drop more easily for a below average student. The ranking format may be the most effective format at this stage, because it a) allows for symmetry in scores, and b) prevents students from monomaniac assessment. However, several issues remain unresolved.

First, our formulas theoretically do not prevent that an individual score exceeds the maximum possible score (in our case 100). To deal with this, we propose a refinement of our formula, for example by replacing the 'deviation * group score', by assigning the group score and then adding a weight to both the PA-score and group score. However, one can argue why a student could not pass the score of 100. Are we perhaps too conservative in our ideas of scoring systems and should consider other approaches? Furthermore, the proposed ranking and distribution formats do not fully prevent the 'zero-sum' game as highlighted by Lopez-Real and Chan (1999), which means that a gain for one student implies a loss for another student. If a students' contribution is rated as zero by all peers, the final score will also be zero. As this perspective assumes a competitive element in peer assessment, one can argue whether it hampers the goal of collaborative learning (Lopez-Real & Chan, 1999). Sharp (2006) also questions the zero-sum and proposes a 'default' value. A final issue in relation to the formats is that – in most cases – the criteria applied for determining the group score are dissimilar to the criteria used in the peer assessment. The group score criteria are mostly criteria for the group product (e.g., essay, presentation, report), whereas the peer assessment is focused on process criteria. Since two different constructs are measured, it can be argued that it is not valid to correct the group score with a PA-score to obtain the individual score, even if these two scores are regarded as independent. It might be more elegant when students and teachers apply the same criteria and assess both the collaborative product and process or either one of them.

DISCUSSION

A direction for future research regarding the formats and formulas is the quality of the assessor. In the proposed formats and calculations we assume that all student posses equal assessment skills; in practice however this will rarely be the case. A future extension of the presented formats and formulas could be to investigate how peer assessor quality could be acknowledged in the individual scores (Hamer, Ma, & Kwong, 2005; Kali & Ronen, 2008), for example a score that represents a relative comparison: rating by group member A of the contribution of group member B relative to the ratings of group members C and D. In addition, more attention could be paid to the interpretation of peer assessment criteria to assure validity. Mathews (1994) provides a nice example of how criteria can be described and interpreted. The validity could for example be strengthened by using scoring rubrics – i.e. descriptions and examples of each criterion – that guide the self- and peer assessment. A scoring rubric can then be used to stimulate discussion within the group about the evaluation criteria. A study by Cohen, Lotan, Scarloss, Schultz and Abram (2002) for example showed that clarity of evaluation criteria enhances task-focused discussions and results in better group performance.

Peer Assessment in (Web-Based) Collaborative Learning

Peer assessment is an attractive approach to transform the group score into individual scores through peer ratings of individual group members' contributions. In addition, it provides an opportunity to track the collaborative process of groups simultaneously; through students' perceptions of their collaborative experience (Sluijsmans et al., 2007) or web tracking and Social Network Analysis of the collaborative process in Web-based contexts (Martínez, Dimitriadis, Gómez-Sánchez, Rubia-Avi, Jorrín-Abellán, & Marcos,

2006; Mazzino & Gaffuri, in press). However, the apparent 'ease' of peer assessment during web-based collaborative learning might be misleading, resulting in overly simplistic implementations. Although rating is appealing in large scale web-based courses, the minimal information provided by ratings should be balanced against the learning objectives. Moreover, implementations that pertain to save instructional time may not really do so, as collaborative learning and peer assessment require a considerable amount of up-front time. We argue in line with Salomon (2000) to "(…) let technology show us what can be done, and let educational considerations determine what will be done" and that design decisions made by the teacher are central to (web-based) peer assessment of collaborative learning. Nevertheless, the interest for peer assessment is reflected by the development of computer supported and web-based peer assessment tools in recent years. Some examples are:

- Networked Peer assessment system (NetPeas; Lin, Liu, & Yuan, 2001);
- Self and Peer Asssessment Resource Kit (SPARK; Freeman & McKenzie, 2002);
- Web-based Self and Peer Assessment system (Web-SPA; Sung, Chang, Chiou, & Hou, 2005);
- Online Peer Assessment System (OPAS; Trahasch, 2004);
- Questions Sharing and Interactive Assignments (QSIA; Barak & Rafaeli, 2004);
- Question Posing and Peer Assessment system (QPPA; Yu, Liu, & Chan, 2005);
- Computerised Assessment by Peers (CAP; Davies, 2006)
- Scaffolded Writing and Rewriting in the Discipline (SWoRD; Cho & Schunn, 2007);
- Collaborative e-learning Structures (CeLS; Kali & Ronen, 2008)

Early systems go back as far as 1993 (Miao & Koper, 2007). Although an extensive discussion and comparison of system functionalities is beyond the scope of this chapter, it should be noted that peer rating is most common (Web-SPA, QSIA), usually supplemented with open ended comments (NetPeas, QSIA, QPPA, CAP, SWoRD, CeLS), and these systems typically focus on peer assessment of individual assignments. To our knowledge only CeLS allows the teacher flexibility in the design of peer assessment (choice for rating, with or without comments, individuals, groups – in isolation or a combination) for alignment with the course and the instructional format (e.g., collaborative learning), but it does not contain a module that affords automatic calculation of individual scores from group scores using peer assessment – for example as part of collaboration scripts.

Scripting Peer Assessment in (Web-Based) Collaborative Learning

In line with instructional approaches in collaborative learning that facilitate individual activity in groups to enhance the collaborative process and group performance, our PA-formats can be applied analogue to scripts. Scripts consist of at least five components: learning objectives, type of activities, sequencing, role distribution and type of representation (Kollar, Fischer, & Hesse, 2006). The activities and/or the role of the assessor and assessee can be modelled with scripts by representing the peer assessment procedure (Davies, 2006), sequencing interactivity during peer assessment (Strijbos, Ochoa, Sluijsmans, Segers, & Tillema, in press) and/or facilitate the peer assessment based revision of essays (Cho & Schunn, 2007). Furthermore, in computer-supported settings computational approaches can be used to represent and model scripts (and our PA-formats) through platform independent applications for electronic learning environments (Hernández-Leo, Ascensio-Pérez, & Dimitriadis,

2005; Joosten-ten Brinke, Van Bruggen, Hermans, Burgers, Giesbers, Koper, & Latour, 2007; Miao & Koper, 2007). In addition, computational affordances can be used to collect self- and peer assessments scores and automatically represented and inform each individual group member or the entire group on each members' effort and involvement in the collaborative process at the end, on the fly during the collaborative assignment, or even on demand. Developing and extending present applications of peer assessment through (computer-supported) scripts, including the increased flexibility in peer assessment design and calculations, is an important direction for future research on assessment of collaborative learning in general, and peer assessment in particular.

Towards Collaborative Design of (Web-Based) Peer Assessment: Some Practical Guidelines

Peer assessment by means of a PA-format on no account guarantees reflective, critical learners, although this is often voiced by researchers and practitioners as the main aim of self- and peer assessment (Boud, 1990). To avoid the risk that peer assessment in (web-based) collaborative learning discourages reflective learning and becomes solely a mechanic activity, some guidelines may be helpful:

- consider peer assessment as a complex *skill* that develops through experience and training. We strongly advocate a longitudinal approach in peer assessment, so that progress in peer assessment skill can be monitored;
- organise multiple occasions where students assess their peers during collaborative learning – preferably in different group compositions and using different criteria. In this way, students can develop their peer assessment skills by assessing peers under varying conditions;

- stimulate students to build up a portfolio on their role as assessor and assessee in both individual and collaborative learning settings. This allows for continuous monitoring of the development of assessment skills;
- evaluate the peer assessment results at all times with the students. Especially when students have very diverse perceptions of the contributions by peers, such evaluation through group discussions may introduce students to contrasting perspectives;
- include a box where the students can write their qualitative feedback (e.g., with justifications and elaborate explanations) to make the peer assessment more valuable (beyond 'cold' rating);
- design the peer assessment together with students. Although the negotiation and setting of criteria with students is stressed by many researchers (e.g., Boud, 1990; Orsmond, Merry, & Reiling, 1996; Sluijsmans, Brand-Gruwel, Van Merriënboer, & Martens, 2004), in our view this negotiation could be broadened by adding discussions on the type of PA-format, the weight, the rating scale, etc.;
- design a peer assessment that fits your goal and discuss this goal with your students before they start with the group task;
- provide training for teachers where they can discuss and exchange perspectives on assessment of collaborative learning.

A general observation is that teachers struggle with the assessment of collaborative learning. Although they notice that a group score is inadequate, sound applications for including the individual performance (and/or correcting the group score) are presently not widely available for researchers and teachers. Our PA-formats are available with all formulas embedded for each application, which makes the use of these formats very user-friendly and efficient. Therefore, we hope that our refined view on PA-formats encourages teachers and students to collaboratively apply these formats to collaborative learning from a design-based perspective, and to gain a better understanding of the importance to acknowledge individual contributions during (web-based) collaborative learning.

REFERENCES

Biggs, J. (1996). Enhancing teaching through constructive alignment. *Higher Education, 32,* 347–364. doi:10.1007/BF00138871

Birenbaum, M. (2005, October). Multidimensional assessment of computer-supported knowledge building. In [Vancouver, Canada: Association for the Advancement of Computing in Education.]. *Proceedings of E-Learn, 2005,* 1203–1208.

Boud, D. J. (1990). Assessment and promotion of academic values. *Studies in Higher Education, 15,* 101–113. doi:10.1080/03075079012331377621

Cheng, W., & Warren, M. (1997). Having second thoughts: Student perceptions before and after a peer assessment exercise. *Studies in Higher Ed., 22,* 233–239. doi:10.1080/03075079712331381064

Cho, K., & Schunn, C. D. (2007). Scaffolded writing and rewriting in the discipline: A web-based reciprocal per assessment peer review system. *Computers & Education, 48,* 409–426. doi:10.1016/j.compedu.2005.02.004

Cohen, E. G., Lotan, R., Scarloss, B., Schultz, S. E., & Abram, P. (2002). Can groups learn? *Teachers College Record, 104,* 1045–1068. doi:10.1111/1467-9620.00196

Conway, R., Kember, D., Sivan, A., & Wu, M. (1993). Peer assessment of an individual's contribution to a group project. *Assessment & Evaluation in Higher Education, 18,* 45–56. doi:10.1080/0260293930180104

Davies, P. (2006). Peer assessment: Judging the quality of students' work by comments rather than marks. *Innovations in Education and Teaching International, 43,* 69–82. doi:10.1080/14703290500467566

Fermelis, J., Tucker, R., & Palmer, S. (2007). Online self and peer assessment in large, multi-campus, multi-cohort contexts. In R. Atkinson, C. McBeath, S. K. A. Soong & C. D. Cheers (Eds.), *Providing choices for learners and learning: Proceedings ASCILITE Singapore* (pp. 271-281). Singapore: Nanyang Technological University, Centre for Educational Development.

Frederiksen, N. (1984). The real test bias: Influences of testing on teaching and learning. *The American Psychologist, 3,* 193–202. doi:10.1037/0003-066X.39.3.193

Freeman, M. (1995). Peer assessment by groups of group work. *Assessment & Evaluation in Higher Education, 20,* 289–301. doi:10.1080/0260293950200305

Freeman, M., & McKenzie, J. (2002). SPARK, a confidential web-based template for self and peer assessment of student team work: Benefits of evaluating across different subjects. *British Journal of Educational Technology, 33,* 551–569. doi:10.1111/1467-8535.00291

Gupta, M. L. (2004). Enhancing student performance through cooperative learning in physical sciences. *Assessment & Evaluation in Higher Education, 29,* 63–73. doi:10.1080/0260293032000158162

Hamer, J., Ma, K. T. K., & Kwong, H. H. F. (2005). A method of automatic grade calibration in peer assessment. In A. Young & D. Tolhurst (Eds), *Proceedings of the seventh Australasian computing education conference* (pp. 67-72). Newcastle, Australia: CRPIT.

Hernández-Leo, D., Ascensio-Pérez, J. I., & Dimitriadis, Y. A. (2005). Computational representation of collaborative learning flow patterns using IMS Learning Design. *Educational Technology & Society, 8*(4), 75–89.

Hoffman, J. R., & Rogelberg, S. G. (2001). All together now? College students' preferred project group grading procedures. *Group Dynamics, 5,* 33–40. doi:10.1037/1089-2699.5.1.33

Johnson, D. W. (1981). Student-student interaction: The neglected variable in education. *Educational Researcher, 10,* 5–10.

Johnston, L., & Miles, L. (2004). Assessing contributions to group assignments. *Assessment & Evaluation in Higher Education, 29,* 751–768. doi:10.1080/0260293042000227272

Joosten-ten Brinke, D., Van Bruggen, J., Hermans, H., Burgers, J., Giesbers, B., Koper, R., & Latour, I. (2007). Modeling assessment for re-use of traditional and new types of assessment. *Computers in Human Behavior, 23,* 2721–2741. doi:10.1016/j.chb.2006.08.009

Kali, Y., & Ronen, M. (2008). Assessing the assessors: Added value in web-based multi-cyle peer assessment in higher education. *Research and Practice in Technology Enhanced Learning, 3,* 3–32. doi:10.1142/S1793206808000434

Kerr, N. L. (1983). Motivation losses in small groups: A social dilemma analysis. *Journal of Personality and Social Psychology, 45,* 819–828. doi:10.1037/0022-3514.45.4.819

Kerr, N. L., & Bruun, S. E. (1983). Dispensability of member effort and group motivation losses: Free rider effects. *Journal of Personality and Social Psychology, 44,* 78–94. doi:10.1037/0022-3514.44.1.78

Kollar, I., Fischer, F., & Hesse, F. W. (2006). Collaboration scripts – A conceptual analysis. *Educational Psychology Review, 18,* 159–185. doi:10.1007/s10648-006-9007-2

Langrish, T., & See, H. (2008). Diverse assessment methods in group work settings. *Education for Chemical Engineers, 3,* 40–46. doi:10.1016/j.ece.2008.01.001

Lee, E. Y. C., Chan, C. K. K., & van Aalst, J. (2006). Students assessing their own collaborative knowledge building. *International Journal of Computer-Supported Collaborative Learning, 1,* 277–307. doi:10.1007/s11412-006-8997-6

Lejk, M., & Wyvill, M. (2001). Peer assessment of contributions to a group project: A comparison of holistic and category-based approaches. *Assessment & Evaluation in Higher Education, 26,* 61–72. doi:10.1080/02602930020022291

Lin, S. S. J., Liu, E. Z. F., & Yuan, S. M. (2001). Web-based peer assessment: Feedback for students with various thinking-styles. *Journal of Computer Assisted Learning, 17,* 420–432. doi:10.1046/j.0266-4909.2001.00198.x

Lopez-Real, F., & Chan, Y. P. (1999). Peer assessment of a group project in a primary mathematics education course. *Assessment & Evaluation in Higher Education, 24,* 68–79. doi:10.1080/0260293990240106

Martínez, A., Dimitriadis, Y., Gómez-Sánchez, E., Rubia-Avi, B., Jorrín-Abellán, I., & Marcos, J. A. (2006). Studying participation networks in collaboration using mixed methods. *International Journal of Computer-Supported Collaborative Learning, 1,* 383–408. doi:10.1007/s11412-006-8705-6

Mathews, B. (1994). Assessing individual contributions: Experience of peer evaluation in major group projects. *British Journal of Educational Technology, 25,* 19–28. doi:10.1111/j.1467-8535.1994.tb00086.x

Mazzoni, E., & Gaffuri, P. (in press). Monitoring activity in e-Learning: a quantitative model based on web tracking and Social Network Analysis. In A. A. Juan, T. Daradoumis, F. Xhafa, S. Caballe, J. Faulin (Eds.), *Monitoring and assessment in online collaborative environments: Emergent Computational Technologies for E-learning Support.* Hershey, PA: IGI Global.

Meier, A., Spada, H., & Rummel, N. (2007). A rating scheme for assessing the quality of computer-supported collaboration process. *International Journal of Computer-Supported Collaborative Learning, 2,* 63–86. doi:10.1007/s11412-006-9005-x

Miao, Y., & Koper, R. (2007). An efficient and flexible technical approach to develop and deliver online peer assessment. In C. Chinn, G. Erkens, & S. Puntambekar (Eds.), *Mice, minds and society: The Computer supported collaborative learning (CSCL) conference 2007* (pp. 502-510). New Brunswick, NJ: International Society of the Learning Sciences.

O'Donnell, A. M., & Dansereau, D. F. (1992). Scripted cooperation in student dyads: A method for analysing and enhancing academic learning and performance. In R. Hertz-Lazarowitz & N. Miller (Eds.), *Interaction in cooperative groups: The theoretical anatomy of group learning* (pp. 120-144). New York: Cambridge University Press.

Orsmond, P., Merry, S., & Callaghan, A. (2004). Implementation of a formative assessment model incorporating peer and self-assessment. *Innovations in Education and Teaching International, 41,* 273–290. doi:10.1080/14703290410001733294

Orsmond, P., Merry, S., & Reiling, K. (1996). The importance of marking criteria in the use of peer assessment. *Assessment & Evaluation in Higher Education, 21,* 239–249. doi:10.1080/0260293960210304

Orsmond, P., Merry, S., & Reiling, K. (2002). The use of exemplars and formative feedback when using student-derived marking criteria in peer and self-assessment. *Assessment & Evaluation in Higher Education, 22,* 357–367. doi:10.1080/0260293970220401

Salomon, G. (2000, June 28). *It's not just the tool, but the educational rationale that counts.* Keynote address at the 2000 ED-MEDIA Meeting, Montreal, Canada. Retrieved February 13, 2009, from http://www.aace.org/conf/edmedia/00/salomonkeynote.htm

Salomon, G., & Globerson, T. (1989). When teams do not function the way they ought to. *International Journal of Educational Research, 13,* 89–99. doi:10.1016/0883-0355(89)90018-9

Sharp, S. (2006). Deriving individual student marks from a tutor's assessment of group work. *Assessment & Evaluation in Higher Education, 31,* 329–343. doi:10.1080/02602930500352956

Sivan, A. (2000). The implementation of peer assessment: An action research approach. *Assessment in Education: Principles . Policy & Practice, 7,* 193–213.

Slavin, R. E. (1980). Cooperative learning in teams: State of the art. *Educational Psychologist, 15,* 93–111. doi:10.1080/00461528009529219

Sluijsmans, D. M. A. (2008, June 6). *Betrokken bij beoordelen* [Involved in assessment]. Lectoral address, HAN University, the Netherlands.

Sluijsmans, D. M. A., Brand-Gruwel, S., Van Merriënboer, J., & Martens, R. (2004). Training teachers in peer-assessment skills: Effects on performance and perceptions. *Innovations in Education and Teaching International, 41,* 59–78. doi:10.1080/1470329032000172720

Sluijsmans, D. M. A., Strijbos, J. W., & Van de Watering, G. (2007, August). *Designing flexible and fair peer-assessment formats to award individual contributions in group-based learning.* Paper presented at the biannual meeting of the European Association for research on Learning and Instruction (EARLI), Budapest, Hungary.

Strijbos, J. W., Martens, R. L., & Jochems, W. M. G. (2004). Designing for interaction: Six steps to designing computer-supported collaborative learning. *Computers & Education, 42,* 403–424. doi:10.1016/j.compedu.2003.10.004

Strijbos, J. W., Martens, R. L., Jochems, W. M. G., & Broers, N. J. (2007). The effect of functional roles on perceived group efficiency during computer-supported collaborative learning: A matter of triangulation. *Computers in Human Behavior, 23,* 353–380. doi:10.1016/j.chb.2004.10.016

Strijbos, J. W., Ochoa, T. A., Sluijsmans, D. M. A., Segers, M. S. R., & Tillema, H. H. (in press). Fostering interactivity through formative peer assessment in (web-based) collaborative learning environments. In C. Mourlas, N. Tsianos, & P. Germanakos (Eds.), *Cognitive and emotional processes in web-based education: Integrating human factors and personalization.* Hershey, PA: IGI Global.

Sung, Y. T., Chang, K. E., Chiou, S. K., & Hou, H. T. (2005). The design and application of a web-based self- and peer-assessment system. *Computers & Education, 45,* 187–202. doi:10.1016/j.compedu.2004.07.002

Topping, K. (1998). Peer assessment between students in colleges and universities. *Review of Educational Research, 68,* 249–276.

Weinberger, A., Stegmann, K., & Fischer, F. (2007). Knowledge convergence in collaborative learning: Concepts and assessment. *Learning and Instruction, 17,* 416–426. doi:10.1016/j.learninstruc.2007.03.007

Williams, E. (1992). Student attitudes towards approaches to learning and assessment. *Assessment & Evaluation in Higher Education, 17,* 45–58.

Williams, K. D., & Karau, S. J. (1991). Social loafing and social compensation: The effects of expectations of co-worker performance. *Journal of Personality and Social Psychology, 61,* 570–581. doi:10.1037/0022-3514.61.4.570

APPENDIX A

Table 8. Scoring formulas in the rating format

Scoring formula	Example derived from Gupta (2004)
Medium score = mean of the rating scale	Medium score = 3
Minimum score = $\sum students$ * sum of weights * minimum of rating scale	Minimum score = 5 * 1 * 1 = 5
Maximum score = $\sum students$ * sum of weights * maximum of rating scale	Maximum score = 5 * 1 * 5 = 25
Mean score = $\sum students$ * sum of weights * medium	Mean score = 5 * 1 * 3 = 15
SA compared to received PA scores = SA score * $\dfrac{\sum students - 1}{PAtotal - SAscore}$	SA compared to received PA scores = $5 * \dfrac{5-1}{25-5} = 1.00$ (a score of 1 means that Adam assessed himself the same way as his peers assessed him)
SA compared to mean = $\dfrac{SAscore}{medium * sumofweights}$	SA compared to mean = $\dfrac{5}{3*1} = 1.67$ (a score > 1 means that Adam assessed himself higher compared to the mean of the group)
PA score = received PA scores including SA scores (PA-total are only the received PA scores)	PA total of Adam = 5 (Adam) + 5 (Brett) + 5 (Chris) + 5 (Lyn) + 5 (Maria) = 25
Individual score = $\dfrac{PAtotalscore - mean}{\max imum - mean}$ * deviation + group score	Individual score = $\dfrac{25-15}{25-15} * 20 + 70 = 90$

APPENDIX B

Table 9. Scoring formulas and examples for the distribution format

Scoring formula	Example derived from the fictitious data presented in Table 3 and 4
Medium score = $\dfrac{\sum credits}{\sum students}$	Medium score = $\dfrac{100}{7} = 14.29$
Minimum score = 0	Minimum score = always 0 in a distribution format because theoretically a student can give a score of 0 to one of the peers or her/himself
Maximum score = $\sum credits$ * sum of weights * $\sum students$	Maximum score = 100 * 5 (= there are five criteria with a weight of one each) * 7 = 3500
Mean score = sum of weights * $\sum students$ * $\dfrac{\sum credits}{\sum students}$	Mean score = $5 * 7 * \dfrac{100}{7} = 500$

Scoring formula	Example derived from the fictitious data presented in Table 3 and 4
PA score = received PA scores including SA scores (PA-total are only the received PA scores)	PA total of Lesley = 97 (SA score) + 86 (Janice) + 75 (Jeremy) + 79 (Denise) + 75 (Linda) + 100 (Sven) + 86 (Eric) = 598
SA compared to received PA scores = SA score * $$\frac{\sum students - 1}{PA total - SA score}$$	SA compared to received PA scores = $97 \times \dfrac{7-1}{598-97} = 1.16$ (a score > 1 means that Lesley assessed herself higher than her peers assessed her)
SA compared to mean = $$\frac{SA score}{medium * sumofweights}$$	SA compared to mean = $\dfrac{97}{14.29 * 5} = 1.36$ (a score > 1 means that Lesley assessed herself higher compared to the mean of the group)
Individual score (if PA total < mean) = $\dfrac{PA total - mean}{mean}$ * deviation + group score	Individual score (if PA score < mean, as is in the case of Jeremy) = $\dfrac{238 - 500}{500}$ * 20 + 70 (the group of Jeremy received a score of 70 for the group work) = 59.52
Individual score (if PA score > mean) = $\dfrac{PA total - mean}{max - mean}$ * deviation + group score	Individual score (if PA score > mean, as is in the case of Lesley) = $\dfrac{598 - 500}{3500 - 500}$ * 20 + 70 = 70.65

APPENDIX C

Table 10. Scoring formulas and examples for the ranking format

Scoring formula	Example derived from the data presented in Table 3 and 4
Medium = $\dfrac{\sum students}{2} + 0.5$	Medium = $\dfrac{7}{2} = 4$
Minimum score = sum of weights * $\sum students$ * $\sum students$	Minimum score = 5 * 7 * 7 = 245
Maximum ranking = sum of weights * $\sum students$	Maximum ranking = 5 * 7 = 35
Mean ranking = sum of weights * medium * $\sum students$	Mean ranking = 5 * 4 * 7 = 140
PA score = received PA scores including SA scores (PA-total are only the received PA scores)	PA total of Lesley = 11 (SA score) + 16 (Janice) + 17 (Jeremy) + 17 (Denise) + 17 (Linda) + 5 (Sven) + 16 (Eric) = 99

Scoring formula	Example derived from the data presented in Table 3 and 4
SA compared to received PA scores = $\dfrac{1}{SAscore}$ $\dfrac{PAtotal - SAscore}{\sum students - 1}$ *	SA compared to received PA scores = $\dfrac{99-11}{7-1} * \dfrac{1}{11} = 1.34$ (a score > 1 means that Lesley assessed herself higher than her peers assessed her)
SA compared to mean = $\dfrac{sumofweights * medium}{SAscore}$	SA compared to mean = $\dfrac{5*4}{11} = 1.82$ (a score > 1 means that Lesley assessed herself higher compared to the mean of the group)
Individual score = $\dfrac{PAtotalscore - meanranking}{\max imum - mean}$ * deviation + group score	Individual score = $\dfrac{99-140}{35-140} * 20 + 70 = 77.81$

Section 3
Support Measures

Chapter 9
How to Design Support for Collaborative E-Learning:
A Framework of Relevant Dimensions

Dejana Diziol
University of Freiburg, Germany

Nikol Rummel
University of Freiburg, Germany

ABSTRACT

Research on collaborative e-learning has often shown the effectiveness of students' interaction on their group performance and their individual learning outcomes. However, these positive effects cannot always be found. Collaboration assistance such as pre-collaboration training and collaboration scripts have been shown to support student interaction and problem-solving. When developing assistance for collaboration, teachers and designers must make decisions concerning the processes the support should target, the timing of support, and the interplay of support on multiple levels. The framework we introduce in this book chapter describes these dimensions in detail. We present advantages and disadvantages of different design options, and give an example from our own research to exemplify the design of an e-learning environment that provides collaboration support. We discuss how the circumstances of any particular learning situation might influence which type of support is optimal, and conclude the book chapter with a discussion of possible future developments.

INTRODUCTION

Picture the following scenario: In a science class, groups of three students are asked to research advantages and disadvantages of different options for energy supply for a little village in the Swiss Alps. Using the internet, they collect information on the geographical site, on costs for the different options (e.g. solar panels, windmills, and power plants), and on expected energy outcome. They are instructed to exchange their findings on a wiki page and develop recommendations for the village that they are supposed to present during classroom instruction. The goals of the exercise are to increase student knowledge on prerequisites for, and advantages and disadvantages of, environmentally friendly energy systems. In group 1, Lynn, Marc and Tom are collaborating. Lynn is not very moti-

DOI: 10.4018/978-1-61520-729-9.ch009

vated to participate in the group work and hardly contributes to the wiki page. When Marc realizes that Lynn takes advantage of her partners' efforts, he as well decides to cease his efforts. In the end, Tom mainly works on the wiki page on his own. While he increases his knowledge on the subject, his partners do not show any learning gains.

In another group, the three students Sandy, Bob and Mike are actively engaged in the team work. They split the task between themselves, each student being responsible for a different type of energy supply. Sandy is responsible for finding out information on energy gained from windmills. She is very enthusiastic about this technology and thus encourages her partners to choose this option. However, in her search, she ignores facts about the geographical site of the village and thus does not realize that the site is too calm for windmills to be efficient. Bob mistakenly believes that solar energy cannot be used during night time and thus encourages his partners not to take this option. After several rounds of discussion, the group agrees on advising the village to build windmills. Due to the missing information on Sandy's part and the erroneous knowledge of Bob, the group has reached a less-than-optimal decision. Additionally, Sandy and Mike might have even adopted erroneous knowledge from Bob during their interaction.

Promises and Challenges of Collaborative Knowledge-Construction

Both in school settings and in adult education, there is a trend towards employing collaborative e-learning. There are a variety of different e-learning environments ranging from computer-supported face-to-face interaction, chat, and video-conferencing to asynchronous environments such as wiki pages or knowledge forums. As research on collaborative learning in general, and on collaborative e-learning in particular, has shown, student interaction often positively influences the

group performance and the individual learning outcomes (e.g. Lou, Abrami, & d'Appolonia, 2001). The largest effects can be found when comparing individual and collaborative learning for dyadic and small group settings (three to four students, cf. Lou et al., 1996). Positive effects of collaboration have been found in a variety of domains, including reading (Hythecker, Dansereau, & Rocklin, 1988), mathematics (Hooper, 1992), and science (Ploetzner, Fehse, Kneser, & Spada, 1999). The positive impact of interaction on student learning is generally ascribed to an increased processing of the learning content through collaborative activities, such as mutual elaboration, and asking for and giving help (Hausmann, Chi & Roy, 2004; Webb, Troper, & Fall, 1995). However, it has also grown apparent that students often do not exhibit beneficial collaborative behaviors spontaneously. The scenarios presented in the introduction point at several challenges students might encounter in a collaborative e-learning scenario and demonstrate the necessity to support student collaboration in order to yield positive learning outcomes. Two main reasons for students failing to benefit from the learning opportunities of a collaborative e-learning scenario can be identified: challenges of collaborative problem-solving, that is, challenges related to student interaction; and challenges related to the learning domain and the specific learning content. As research has shown, students often do not benefit from collaboration due to unequal engagement in the collaborative learning activity: While a few students in the group take responsibility for the problem-solving, the other students engage in social loafing or free-riding and are not motivated to interact with their partners (Kerr, 1983; O'Donnell, 1999). Unequal participation can particularly be found in larger groups and has detrimental effects on student learning. But even if students are equally engaged in the interaction, they might not show the types of collaborative behaviors that are positively related to learning. Particularly, they often do not engage in sufficient elaboration, which is one of the learning mechanisms most relevant for collaborative knowledge construction. For instance, studies by Webb and colleagues (Webb, 1989; Webb et al., 1995) have shown that students tend to answer their partner's question by telling them the correct solution. Yet, telling the answer has been shown to impede the partner's learning, while explaining the solution steps could improve it. Secondly, students might fail to benefit from the interaction because the knowledge of the collaborators is not sufficient to master the group task. As we have exemplified in the second scenario above, collaboration might even lead to the acquisition of incorrect knowledge if a misconception held by one learning partner is taken on by the whole group.

In order to yield the potential benefits of collaboration, students therefore need to be supported on several fronts, ranging from assistance with fruitful, reciprocal interaction to domain-related assistance. Several different instructional methods have been developed to support student collaboration. Earlier approaches such as pre-collaboration training or teacher instruction gave instructions to students prior to their interaction (e.g. King, 1991). While these instructional methods provided little support for students during their actual interaction, many recent approaches to collaboration assistance have focused on the effects of giving students online assistance. For example, computer-supported collaboration scripts provide students with designated roles and activities as they work together (Fischer, Kollar, Mandl, & Haake, 2007). Compared to the earlier approaches, this direct implementation of collaboration assistance in the e-learning environment makes it possible to provide step by step instruction and thus reduces coordination costs (Rummel & Spada, 2005). However, particularly for students who are capable of regulating their own learning, fixed script instruction may give too much structure, requiring students to engage in additional activities that might not be directly relevant for their learning outcome. In other words, the support may increase the "extraneous collaborative load" and reduce

students' capacities that should be directed towards the learning content. In research on collaboration scripts, this phenomenon has been referred to as *overscripting* (Dillenbourg, 2002). For instance, if two students that are already skilled in giving explanations and monitoring their partner's actions are instructed to alternate the role of explainer and checker, the role alternation might actually distract the students rather than supporting their interaction. Therefore, more recently there has been a movement toward developing adaptive assistance for collaborative e-learning, where collaborative interactions are modelled as they occur, and the results of the analysis determine the content of the assistance given (Kumar, Rosé, Wang, Joshi, & Robinson, 2007; Rummel & Weinberger, 2008).

The question of the adaptivity of collaboration support is only one of several questions that have to be taken into account when developing instruction for a collaborative e-learning environment. For instance, one also has to decide which level the support should target, and when and in which manner it should be delivered to students. In the remainder of the chapter, we will introduce a descriptive framework for collaboration support that highlights the issues one has to bear in mind when designing a collaborative e-learning environment. We will further give an example of collaborative e-learning support from our own research that we have tested in an empirical classroom study. The book chapter concludes with a discussion of possible future developments.

SUPPORT FOR COLLABORATIVE E-LEARNING: A DESCRIPTIVE FRAMEWORK

Teachers and designers developing support for collaborative e-learning have to decide on the aspects of the interaction they want to support, and on how to best deliver this support to students. Our descriptive framework for collaboration support in e-learning (see Table 1) consists of five

Table 1. A framework for collaboration support in e-learning

Level of support	- social processes (e.g. student participation) - cognitive processes (e.g. elaboration) - metasocial processes (e.g. reflection on the interaction) - metacognitive processes (e.g. monitoring of the problem-solving)
Domain	- interaction as domain - learning content
Mode of support	- direct (i.e. tell students what to do) - indirect (i.e. design enabling conditions)
Timing	- prior to the collaboration - during the collaboration - at fixed points: time- or task-related - adaptively: immediate or delayed - after the collaboration
Adaptivity	- fixed support - adaptive support

dimensions: the *level* and the *domain* the support targets, the *mode* in which the support is delivered, the *timing* of support, and its level of *adaptivity*. On the one hand, the framework can serve to classify existing systems; on the other hand, it can be of help when designing a collaborative e-learning environment. For each dimension, we present different design options for collaboration assistance that have shown to be beneficial, and discuss their advantages and disadvantages.

Level of Support

A main question when developing support for collaborative e-learning environments is which level the support should target. Four main processes can be distinguished that existing instructional support methods for collaborative e-learning aim to improve. First, many approaches target *social processes*, such as the amount or balance of student participation during the interaction. As discussed earlier, unequal participation can be detrimental for students' learning outcomes. One example of support on the social level are mirroring tools, such as the ones developed by Jermann and Dillenbourg (2008), which provide visual feedback on

student interaction based on an online assessment of student chat contributions and problem-solving actions. The aim of these tools is to help students identify differences in their engagement and to yield a more balanced interaction. In the work by Jermann and Dillenbourg (2008), one mirroring tool displayed the amount of chat contributions and problem-solving actions of two students participating in collaborative problem-solving. A second mirroring tool additionally provided information on the proportion of chat contributions to problem-solving actions for each participating student, and compared this information to an external standard, thus enabling students to diagnose the quality of their interaction. The first tool did not show an effect on student interaction and problem-solving, however, the second tool yielded increased student participation and a higher amount of planning behavior. While support of social processes aims first and foremost at promoting student interaction in general, it can set the stage for fruitful collaborative behaviors and can thereby also affect student problem-solving and learning. To foster student learning more specifically, collaborative e-learning support often explicitly targets *cognitive processes*. For example, many script approaches contain prompts that instruct students to engage in mutual elaboration. By guiding student interaction with questions or sentence starters, some approaches even prompt particular content-related activities such as providing evidence to support a position (e.g. "It was found that ..."; Kollar, Fischer, & Slotta, 2005). These "epistemic scripts" (Weinberger, Reiserer, Ertl, Fischer, & Mandl, 2005) explicitly encourage cognitive behaviors that have proven beneficial for student problem-solving and learning. It is not always possible to distinguish between systems that target social processes, and systems that target cognitive processes. Indeed, often support for both levels is intertwined. One example is the jigsaw script approach that was first introduced by Aronson, Blaney, Sikes, Stephan, and Snapp (1978; for a discussion of the jigsaw schema in computer-supported environments see Dillenbourg & Jermann, 2007). In a jigsaw script, the learning material is distributed between interaction partners. Each student is responsible for preparing his or her part of the learning material in order to explain it to the group. This increases the individual accountability of each student and thus promotes overall participation; additionally, the necessity to explain one's own material to the learning partner stimulates cognitive processes. Similarly, script approaches that assign roles to students increase student participation, while the specific role instruction encourages improved processing of the learning content. To support student interaction in an asynchronous learning environment, De Wever, Keer, Schellens, and Valcke (2007), for instance, assigned roles such as theoretician, moderator, and summarizer to improve student discussions of the course topic. The summarizer role significantly improved students' learning outcome compared to students who did not receive a role assignment, while the other roles did not have a significant impact. According to De Wever et al. (2007), taking the role of a summarizer requires the student to compare different viewpoints and to reach a general overview of what has been discussed so far. These elaboration activities support students' knowledge construction and thus explain the positive impact of the role assignment. The analyses of De Wever et al. (2007) also exemplify the importance of alternating student roles in order for each student to capitalize on the beneficial aspects that a role provides.

Support of social and cognitive processes is typically rather directive and mainly targets the current interaction. In order to enable students to show better interaction in the future, it might also be beneficial to improve students' self-regulatory processes. Therefore, a few instructional methods for collaboration support foster meta-processes such as reflection on the interaction or the problem-solving. For instance, in a study by Yager, Johnson, Johnson, and Snider (1986),

the collaboration support targeted *metasocial processes*: Following each session, students were asked to evaluate the quality of their interaction and to discuss how to improve it subsequently. Likewise, one of the roles employed in De Wever et al.'s (2007) script approach prompted *metacognitive* activities. The student was instructed to summarize the viewpoints of his learning partners and to identify inconsistencies in their messages that had to be resolved. Similarly, King (1991) developed a set of metacognitive questions that instructed students to plan, monitor and evaluate their problem-solving process. Both instructions on metasocial and on metacognitive activities have been shown to promote student learning. Yager et al. (1986) found a positive impact on student knowledge construction compared to a collaborative control condition without group processing, and an individual control condition. Also in the study by King (1991), the questioning technique had a positive impact on students' post test results.

In summary, support features that target social and metasocial processes mainly aim at promoting student interaction in general and serve to ensure that difficulties such as social loafing will not occur. Social support targets the current interaction, while metasocial support is concerned with the quality of the interaction in the long term. In contrast, support features that target cognitive and metacognitive processes mainly serve to foster student problem-solving, ensuring that students will engage in cognitive activities that are fruitful for learning. Support for cognitive processes targets students' current problem-solving, while metacognitive support aims at improving students' self-regulatory processes to increase the likelihood that fruitful collaborative problem-solving behaviors also occur in future interactions. For collaboration support to be most successful, it is important that the collaboration assistance stimulates both (meta-)social and (meta-)cognitive processes: The collaboration will not be conducive to student learning if only one student is engaged in the learning activity; likewise, equal interaction might not be sufficient if the collaboration partners do not engage in deep cognitive processing.

Domain of Support

Assistance in collaborative e-learning environments mostly targets student problem-solving and interaction (i.e. interaction as domain, see Table 1). However, as the second example that we presented in the introduction already pointed out, this may not be sufficient to guarantee student success. Often, learners struggle with the learning content itself. Due to gaps in their content knowledge, they may not be able to benefit from the collaborative learning activity. Also, students might adopt misconceptions from their learning partners if erroneous information is not corrected.

In some cases, collaboration assistance that targets cognitive processes already provides some content-related assistance as well. For instance, sentence starters in epistemic scripts ensure that students consider important aspects of the learning content, and thus can yield improved performance and learning (Kollar et al., 2005). However, in epistemic scripts, the support still does not target problems specifically related to missing domain knowledge. An example for a collaborative e-learning environment in which content-related support is implemented in a more specific, adaptive fashion is the system developed by Baghaei, Mitrovic, and Irwin (2007). This system gives feedback regarding the correctness and the quality of student solutions. Recent approaches to collaborative e-learning assistance have gone one step further by leveraging methods of intelligent tutoring technology in order to provide adaptive content-related support to collaborating students (Rummel, Diziol, & Spada, 2009; Walker, Rummel, & Koedinger, 2008). Intelligent tutoring systems observe students' problem-solving actions and compare them to a model of successful student performance; if an error is detected, the systems provide feedback to students; often, the systems

also allow students to actively request for help (Koedinger, Anderson, Hadley, & Mark, 1997).

Mode of Support

In addition to the level and the domain the support targets, assistance for collaborative e-learning can also vary regarding the mode of support. Collaboration assistance can either *directly* instruct students on the behavior they should engage in, or it can provide conditions that *indirectly* support the desired behavior. For instance, to reach equal contribution of all learning partners, the collaboration assistance can directly instruct students on how many contributions they have to post, or indirectly ensure equal contribution, for instance by mirroring differences in their participation (Jermann & Dillenbourg, 2008). Also in supporting students' cognitive processes, the mode of support may vary: Giving a student the explainer role indirectly fosters cognitive processes that might improve student learning (e.g. giving explanations), while sentence starters foster specific cognitive processes more directly. Similarly, as we have argued above, sentence starters can already provide some content-related support; however, domain support as offered in intelligent tutoring systems targets students' content-related problems more directly.

Both direct and indirect collaboration support have advantages and difficulties. For instance, while students might not capitalize on the conditions provided by indirect support, direct support might be too coercive and thus demotivating for students (overscripting, Dillenbourg, 2002).

Timing

Collaboration support can be given either prior, during, or after the interaction. Particularly in earlier approaches support was provided prior to the collaboration. For instance, in a study by King (1991), students received a set of questions at the beginning of the interaction that they were then supposed to apply throughout the interaction. In a few collaborative learning scenarios support was implemented after student interaction with the goal to improve subsequent collaborations. For instance, in Yager et al. (1986), students were guided to reflect on the quality of their interaction after each collaborative session. Collaborative e-learning settings have made it easier to provide support through the computer at fixed points during the collaboration, either after a specified time, or as an introduction to a new phase of interaction. More recent approaches to providing adaptive, intelligent support during the collaboration have yielded additional timing options: Adaptive systems can give support immediately after a suboptimal student action, or delay it until a pre-defined time interval has passed or a problem-solving sequence is finished. For instance, in a collaborative e-learning environment for peer-tutoring developed by Walker et al. (2008), the system provides immediate feedback following inappropriate student behavior. In contrast, Baghaei et al. (2007) provide delayed adaptive support: The system evaluates the rate of student participation at pre-defined times during the interaction and gives feedback if student participation is not sufficient.

On the one hand, the decision on the timing of assistance may be based on practical considerations. For instance, giving students a set of questions they should apply during their interaction is easier to implement than automated guidance by a software tool that provides support at specific points during the interaction. Also, some types of support can only be realized with certain timing options. For instance, the homogeneity of participation can only be evaluated in a valid way after students spent some time interacting with each other, while the correctness of student statements or their problem-solving actions can be evaluated on a constant basis. Finally, different timing options can serve to attain different goals. Mathan and Koedinger (2005) compared immediate and delayed error feedback in an in-

telligent tutoring setting for individual learning. They conclude that the question of which timing option is best may not be appropriate; rather, the question should be which timing option is optimal to reach the desired goals. While immediate feedback ensures that students do not get stuck in problem-solving and thus often is shown to be more effective and efficient, delayed feedback enables students to practice their monitoring skills and allows them to self-regulate their learning; thus, the two timing options serve different goals. The tutoring system developed by Mathan and Koedinger (2005) employs delayed feedback and combines the feedback with metacognitive support. It withholds the immediate error feedback to enable the students to detect the error on their own. However, if the error is not detected, the system intervenes and guides the students through error detection and error correction. Students who worked with the system showed better conceptual understanding and improved learning transfer. This indicates that delayed feedback that supports students' metacognitive activities can encourage students to learn from their errors and to correct their misconceptions and thus can improve their knowledge construction.

Adaptivity

As became apparent in the previous section, the issue of timing support is interrelated with the adaptivity of collaboration assistance. So far, most scripts for collaborative e-learning support the interaction in a *fixed manner*; in other words, they do not dynamically change based on the behavior of the students. However, students skilled at collaborating might already have fairly good internal collaboration scripts, and thus they might not need so much external support (see Kollar et al., 2005). Also, overly coercive external control of the collaboration could reduce student motivation to interact, in other words, overscripting the interaction (Dillenbourg, 2002). On the other hand, if interaction support is too weak, it may not lead to the desired interactions (Dillenbourg & Tchounikine, 2007). Thus, it has been suggested that it might be optimal if collaboration support *adaptively* responded to the individual needs of students (Dillenbourg & Tchounikine, 2007; Rummel & Weinberger, 2008). Adaptive support approaches only intervene in response to pre-defined situations or student behaviors, for example, when difficulties or ineffective behaviors occur, and thus enable students to increasingly self-regulate their learning. First evaluations of adaptive support for collaborative e-learning alluded to a positive impact of adaptive assistance on student interaction and learning. The effectiveness of adaptive support has so far primarily been evaluated with a Wizard of Oz approach (e.g. Tsovaltzi et al., in press; Meier & Spada, in press), where a confederate of the experimenter or a teacher observes the interaction and gives adaptive support in pre-defined situations. Implemented in this manner, adaptive assistance has been shown to be better than no assistance (Gweon, Rosé, Carey, & Zaiss, 2006) and fixed assistance (Meier & Spada, in press) at increasing learning. Further, the few automated systems for adaptive collaborative learning support that were evaluated experimentally have shown promising results. For instance, Kumar et al. (2007) found that adaptive support to collaborating pairs was better than no support to collaborating pairs and adaptive support to individual learning. Similarly, the adaptive support in Walker et al. (2008) showed positive impact on students' learning behavior as it facilitated the peer tutors to notice the peer tutees' errors. The error detection encouraged peer tutors to elaborate on their knowledge and on common misconceptions in order to help the tutees repair the errors, and thus fostered student learning.

One main challenge when developing adaptive collaboration support is defining and detecting appropriate and inappropriate collaborative behavior. Going back to the example presented in the introduction, we can see that there are several indications for need of support: when students meet impasses concerning the learning content; when students show insufficient participation; or when they do not engage in beneficial collaborative behaviors. So far, most systems for adaptive collaboration support detect need for support based on the first two cases, that is, by observing the collaborative *problem-solving actions* or the *metrics of the social interaction*. For instance, when students submit a group solution in COLLECT-UML, a system developed by Baghaei et al. (2007), the intelligence evaluates the solution using a constraint-based model. Depending on the quality of the solution, the system provides assistance on how to improve problem-solving. Similarly, in the peer tutoring approach developed by Walker et al. (2008), the system evaluates the peer tutor's feedback to the peer tutee's problem-solving actions. If it detects an error, for instance, an incorrect solution approach was marked correct, the peer tutor receives an adaptive feedback prompt. Adaptive assistance to students' social interaction, based on an automatic analysis of interactions as they occur, poses big challenges for designers of collaborative e-learning environments. Most adaptive systems detect need for support based on metrics of participation, for example, by looking at the contributions collaborators make to a shared workspace or to a dialogue. The adaptive assistance then supports social processes by directly encouraging the non-contributors to participate more (Constantino-Gonzalez, Suthers, & de los Santos, 2003; Jermann & Dillenbourg, 2008). Other systems have looked at patterns of dialogue acts, comparing them to a model of ideal dialogue, and providing feedback based on the discrepancy. Usually those dialogue acts have been detected by asking participants to select sentence starters before they speak. More recent work has been directed towards automatically assessing the *content of student interaction* to give feedback on the type of collaborative behaviors students should engage in. These systems use a simple keyword analysis to detect the types of contributions people make (Israel & Aiken,

2007; Tedesco, 2003). Future developments in automating the analysis of verbal interaction data (e.g., Rosé et al., 2008) will provide us with the opportunity to investigate in more detail the effects of adaptive collaboration support that is based on the analysis of the content rather than the amount of student statements.

The above discussion indicates that it is not always easy to define which student behavior would indicate need for support, and how this could be detected by a computer system. Even if one were able to define good diagnostic criteria to evaluate student interaction on the fly, the technical implementation is still very time- and resource-intensive and requires a substantial programming effort. Thus, so far, it often may not be possible for teachers and designers to provide adaptive feedback in a collaborative e-learning environment. Furthermore, it is not yet clear if adaptive support is always the best way to go. For instance, particularly for students with minor experience with collaborative e-learning, it may be beneficial to have a collaboration script with fixed script elements that provide a general structure to students' interaction, and additional adaptive script elements that support the interaction when specific difficulties occur.

In the following section, we give an example for collaborative e-learning support from our own research. In order to provide assistance towards both student interaction and the learning content, the system consisted of several support components, each addressing a different aspect of the collaboration. We will describe these components based on the dimensions of the framework introduced above.

IMPLEMENTATION OF SUPPORT FOR COLLABORATIVE E-LEARNING: AN EXAMPLE

In a recent project (Diziol, Rummel, Spada, & McLaren, 2007; Rummel, Diziol, & Spada, 2009)

we developed support for a collaborative e-learning environment in mathematics. We extended an already existing intelligent tutoring system that has commonly been used for individual instruction to a collaborative scenario. The implementation of the collaboration support in the existing system had several advantages: The integration of the collaboration support with intelligent tutoring made it possible to provide adaptive content-related assistance within the collaborative environment. This is an advantage over other collaboration support approaches so far, which have only supported student problem-solving by structuring the learning tasks or providing guidance (e.g. by employing epistemic scripts), but were not able to react to errors or provide context-sensitive help. Second, by leveraging the student models already present in the tutoring system, the integration enabled us to implement some of the interaction support adaptively. Extending an already existing system might limit the type of adaptive collaboration support that can be provided by the system. On the other hand, it enables a researcher or instructor to implement adaptive collaboration support that could not be realized if the system would have to be built from scratch, as the development of intelligent tutoring behavior is very cost- and time-intensive and often difficult to implement (Murray, 2003). The Cognitive Tutor Algebra, the intelligent tutoring system employed in this study, is a particularly sophisticated system for adaptive content-related assistance, which has been developed and iteratively improved over the last twenty years. In the following sections, we will first shortly introduce the Cognitive Tutor Algebra; then, we will describe the collaboration support we implemented in the system, based on the descriptive framework presented in the previous section. Finally, we will give a short overview of its evaluation in a classroom study.

The Cognitive Tutor Algebra (CTA) is a cognitive tutoring system for mathematics at the high-school level that has been developed and tested at Carnegie Mellon University in Pittsburgh

(Koedinger et al., 1997). In a number of studies, it was shown to improve learning by about one standard deviation compared to traditional classroom instruction (Koedinger et al., 1997). The CTA evaluates student problem-solving actions by comparing them to a cognitive model of successful student performance, represented using a set of production rules. If an error is detected, the CTA immediately marks it as incorrect and provides context-sensitive feedback. In addition, students can actively request help from the CTA. These on-demand hints are tailored to the student's current focus of attention. Hints are presented in a hierarchical sequence with increasing levels of detail: By making repeated help requests, students receive more and more detailed information and are finally provided with the correct answer in the "bottom-out hint", that is, the final hint of the sequence (Koedinger, 1998). Classroom courses following the Algebra Tutor curriculum alternate between different modes of instruction: In three of five course periods a week, student instruction is based on classroom activities; during the remaining two periods, students work on the CTA in the computer lab. According to teachers working with the CTA, a main advantage of the curriculum is that they can concentrate their assistance to weaker students as the CTA provides sufficient support for the average and strong students during lab instruction. In our study, students collaborated on the CTA in pairs, sitting next to each other at one computer. The learning content was a unit on system of equations. In this unit, students solved story problems that asked them to compare two linear equations such as two mobile contracts with different phone charges. Students were requested to derive the algebraic equation, answer several questions, and plot the graph in a coordinate grid.

When designing support for this setting, challenges resulting from the required interaction and challenges resulting from the learning content had to be taken into account. To support both levels, our collaboration support consisted of multiple elements (see Table 2). First, in order to *support student interaction*, we implemented a collaboration script that followed a jigsaw schema (Dillenbourg & Jermann, 2007), i.e., it distributed expertise for solving the collaborative problem between the learning partners. We adapted the common jigsaw script (Aronson, et al., 1978) for a dyadic setting in the following way: During an individual phase, each student solved one linear equation on the CTA; during the subsequent collaborative phase, students moved together on one computer to solve the system of equations problem that combined the two linear equations. During the collaboration, each student was responsible for explaining his or her part of the problem to the learning partner. Again, students' problem-solving was supported by the CTA. The fixed assistance indirectly targeted beneficial cognitive and social processes: As the knowledge of both learning partners was necessary to solve the collaborative problem, the script stimulated deeper elaboration on the learning content and increased the need for interaction. Students received the script instruction at fixed points during their interaction, based on the task they solved. In this collaborative e-learning environment, students only had minor experiences with collaborative learning in mathematics. By providing the support for social processes in a fixed manner, we set the stage for fruitful interaction.

In addition to the fixed assistance towards cognitive and social processes, the collaboration support implemented in the CTA contained fixed assistance for meta-level processes. In a reflection phase following each collaborative phase, students received instruction that prompted metasocial processes. Students were instructed to rate the quality of their interaction with regard to eight collaboration skills and to set goals for which three skills they wanted to improve during the subsequent collaboration. Directly prompting these metasocial processes served two goals: First, it aimed at improving students' interaction during the subsequent collaborative problem-solving phase. Second, it

Table 2. Implementation of collaboration support for multiple processes

	Jigsaw script	**Reflection phase**	**CTA-assistance (feedback and hints)**	**Adaptive prompting**
Level of support	cognitive / social	metasocial	cognitive	social / cognitive
Domain	interaction	interaction	learning content	interaction
Mode of support	indirect	direct	direct	direct / indirect
Timing	at fixed points during the collaboration: task-related	after the collaboration	during the collaboration: immediate feedback	during the collaboration: immediate feedback
Adaptivity	fixed support	fixed support	adaptive support	adaptive support

aimed at enabling students to self-regulate their collaborative learning even when script support was no longer available (cf., script as objective, Dillenbourg & Jermann, 2007).

For *content-related assistance,* the CTA provided just-in-time feedback and on-demand hints as in individual use of the system. Studies on individual learning with the CTA have shown that students do not always use this problem-solving support in a productive way to advance their learning. Often, students apply shallow learning strategies to solve the problems and use the system's feedback and hint facilities ineffectively. There are two common behaviors that may prevent students from capitalizing on the cognitive tutor support. First, students have been found to engage in a *trial and error strategy* in order to perform well and to advance in the cognitive tutor curriculum (Baker, Corbett, & Koedinger, 2004). Trial and error is indicated by multiple errors within a short time interval. Second, students "abuse" the on-demand hints (Aleven, McLaren, Roll, & Koedinger, 2004). Hint abuse refers to students' tendency to click through the hint hierarchy and copy the answer given in the bottom-out hint. Both trial and error and hint abuse are connected to low elaboration and thus are detrimental for students' knowledge construction. These inefficient student behaviors can be seen as additional content-related challenges students encounter in this learning environment, and thus, we decided to address them with our collaboration support. Since not all students show these behaviors, we addressed them in an adaptive way.

First, when the tutoring system detected "trial and error", a script message prompted collaborative elaboration, in other words, it encouraged deeper cognitive processes (e.g. "Don't forget to consult with your partner. If you both don't know how to find the solution, ask for a hint."). When the collaboratively enhanced CTA detected hint abuse, that is, students clicked "next" on the penultimate hint to receive the bottom out hint and to copy the answer, a prompt encouraged the learning partners to use the information given so far to find the answer on their own (see Figure 1). In both cases, the need for support was detected based on students' problem-solving actions, and the support was given immediately after the inefficient behavior. By directly addressing students' social processes, this support element indirectly aimed at improving students' cognitive processes when learning with the CTA.

To evaluate the collaborative CTA extension, we conducted a classroom study that compared collaborative learning with support to unsupported collaborative learning and to individual learning with the CTA (Rummel et al., 2009). In the collaboration condition with support, student interaction was guided by the collaboration script described above. In the collaboration condition without support, two students joined in front of one computer to solve the system of equations problems without further guidance. In the individual condition, students worked on the CTA on their own. A total of eight classes (106 students) participated in the study, which took place on three

Figure 1. Screenshot of adaptive hint prompt © 2009, Carnegie Learning. Used with permission.

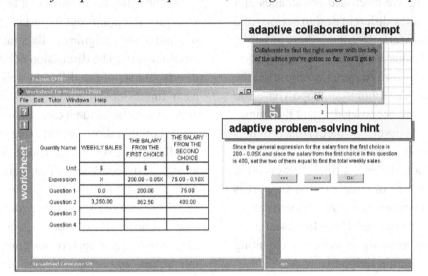

days over the course of a week. After a two-day learning phase, we assessed the learning outcome concerning three aspects of robust learning (cf. VanLehn, Koedinger, Rummel, & Liu, 2007): reproduction, transfer, and future learning. There were no differences in the *collaborative* and the *individual reproduction test* between conditions. In the *transfer test*, the collaboration condition with support reached highest test scores, though the differences did not reach significance. It should be noted, however, that the test performance of students in the supported collaborative condition was comparable or better than the performance of students in the control conditions even though they had solved significantly fewer problems (i.e., had had less practice) during the learning phase – in other words, their learning was more efficient. Furthermore, in the *future learning test,* which was solved collaboratively, we found a positive effect of the collaboration support on student interaction. Dyads that had received collaboration support during instruction made significantly fewer errors when compared to dyads in the unsupported collaboration condition.

A qualitative analysis disclosed the positive influence of the adaptive collaboration support after trial and error and hint abuse. The analy-sis compared two contrasting cases: a dyad of the supported collaboration condition that had shown higher learning gains, and a dyad of the unsupported collaboration condition that had shown lower learning gains. As hypothesized, the adaptive prompts yielded a decreased amount of trial and error behavior and increased reflection on the CTA hints in the dyad that had received collaboration assistance. In contrast, the dyad that had not received collaboration assistance frequently engaged in trial and error and hint abuse. Remarkably, the improved interaction behavior was even transferred to the collaborative post tests (i.e. collaborative reproduction and future learning) where collaboration support was no longer available. The improved collaborative behavior supported students' problem-solving: The dyad that had received collaboration support mastered the most challenging tasks faster, while the dyad that had learned without support still had difficulties during the post tests.

CONCLUSION

In this chapter, we introduced a framework that describes relevant dimensions of e-collaborative learning support. We discussed advantages and disadvantages of the different design options and demonstrated their effectiveness, where possible, by referring to evaluation studies. The application example from our own research exemplified the implementation of collaboration support based on the framework. We acknowledge that the framework is not a fully-developed model that provides clear guidelines for how to optimize collaborative e-learning support. Indeed, a final answer to the question which type of collaboration support is most effective cannot yet be given. Nevertheless, the framework can be useful both for researchers and instructors who are interested in implementing collaborative e-learning support.

First, the framework can serve to advance *research* on collaboration support in e-learning environments. By mapping out the design space, it provides insights in the types of research questions that have yet to be answered. For instance, only few studies directly compared design options within one dimension: Mathan & Koedinger (2005) investigated different timing options by comparing immediate vs. delayed feedback, and Walker et al. (2008) investigated the impact of adaptivity by comparing an adaptive with a fixed feedback condition. Future research should evaluate more explicitly the specific effects of the different design options within each dimension, such as the differential impact of support targeting social, cognitive, metasocial, or metacognitive processes (see Table 1: level of support), or the differential impact of support targeting the interaction or the learning content (see Tabel 1: domain). Moreover, the interactions between design options on different dimensions should be investigated in-depth. For instance, it is possible that support targeting meta-level processes is most beneficial when provided at fixed points during the interaction, while support targeting cognitive processes is most beneficial when provided in an adaptive fashion. Finally, future research will have to develop guidelines for how best to integrate multiple forms of assistance in case they were needed at a single time.

Second, the framework can be useful for *instructors* as it points out important aspects to bear in mind when designing collaborative e-learning environments. The discussion of advantages and disadvantages of the different design options on each dimension can already provide some guidance. But it also made it clear that there is not one single collaboration support design that is optimal for all learning situations. The design needs to be adapted to the conditions of any particular learning environment. First, the level and mode of support should be adapted towards the *goal of the instruction.* For instance, if support is mainly aimed at improving student performance during the current interaction, supporting students' problem-solving in a direct mode, for example by providing immediate feedback to the learning content, can be beneficial. If the goal is rather to promote long-term student learning and knowledge transfer, collaboration support that indirectly targets cognitive processes, for example, by prompting elaborative behavior, may be more fruitful. And if the goal is to increase students' self-regulatory skills, the support should particularly target metacognitive and metasocial processes of the interaction. Second, optimal collaboration support may also depend on *learner characteristics.* For instance, if most students working with a collaborative e-learning environment have already had a lot of experience with collaborative learning, fixed assistance may demotivate students, while collaboration support that adaptively reacts to student participation and interaction could be more beneficial.

In our own research, we aimed at customizing the collaboration support towards the conditions of our particular learning environment. For instance, as the learning environment was developed for students with low experiences in collaborative knowledge construction, we implemented a fixed collaboration script to set the stage for fruitful interaction. To address specific challenges in the learning environment, we additionally implemented adaptive assistance for common ineffective learning behaviors. Finally, to ensure long-term effects of the collaboration assistance on future interactions, we implemented a support element that prompted metasocial processes.

While we concentrated the book chapter on collaborative e-learning in a school context, the framework might also be of interest for other areas of application. For instance, the framework could be applied to design support for collaborative e-learning in adult education. One example might be a blended learning course that trains teachers to employ e-learning in their regular classroom instruction. As part of the distance-learning activities, teachers could be asked to exchange information about their experiences with e-learning applications in an online discussion forum. To ensure mutual benefit of all participants, the activity could be supported by the learning management system that the instructor employs for the distance-learning course units. The framework's dimensions could be a guideline to develop that support. For example, the instructor could decide to use the system in order to provide fixed direct instruction that asks the course participants first to describe at least one e-learning application, and then to share their experiences with the applications introduced by the others. Additionally, the system could be designed to intervene adaptively if there was too little elaboration on one of the applications.

Above and beyond the educational context, our framework could inform the development of support for e-collaborative interactions in a corporate context. A typical challenge of companies is how to achieve effective knowledge management: Each co-worker has different expertise, and to reach the best outcome, the group has to pool the distributed knowledge. This can be accomplished by using a shared database that allows co-workers to enter their expertise and to read the contributions provided by others. However, group members are often reluctant to share information as the person contributing knowledge in the database has to invest time and energy, but does not receive a direct benefit (Cress & Hesse, 2004). This is a typical instance of a social dilemma: While for each

individual it is more beneficial not to contribute their knowledge, the group as a whole reaches a lower outcome if all members withhold their information than if all shared their expertise. A similar phenomenon occurring in such settings has been studied extensively in social psychology: the information pooling paradigm. As Stasser and Titus observed already in 1985, groups that are composed of members with different knowledge background focus their discussion on the shared information, while information that is only known to some group members is not presented and can thus not be taken into account. As the information is not effectively pooled, groups often do not reach an optimal solution. With interaction support that targets these problems, the group interaction and, consequently, the group solution, can be improved significantly (Cress & Hesse, 2004; Meier & Spada, in press). Again, our framework could be used to provide guidelines for how to optimize the support for the given setting. For instance, one approach could be to provide direct instruction on the minimum amount of participation required by each co-worker. Another approach could be to target social processes indirectly by providing feedback on the amount of teammate contribution, similarly to the mirroring tools introduced in this chapter. Finally, interaction support implemented in the shared data base could also provide adaptive instruction that targets metacognitive processes: If several group members contributed extensively to a particular topic while a group member from a different area of expertise did not yet enter information, the system could prompt this person to elaborate on the issue based on his knowledge background in order to identify aspects that might still be missing and to add this information subsequently.

To reiterate: This chapter highlighted the need for support in collaborative e-learning environments and introduced collaboration support approaches that have been shown to be effective in order to promote student interaction and learning. We introduced a descriptive framework that classifies the different design options on five dimensions. While we cannot yet provide a ready-made recipe for optimal interaction support, we reviewed advantages and disadvantages of the different options and discussed the importance of adapting the support to the goal of the instruction and the learner characteristics. The guidelines provided in this chapter – while still on a rather coarse level – can assist instructors in the development and implementation of effective collaboration support. By thoroughly comparing the different design options mapped out in our framework and by evaluating their interactions, future research will enable us to further specify these guidelines in order to implement collaboration support even more effectively in the future.

ACKNOWLEDGMENT

This work was supported by the Pittsburgh Science of Learning Center, NSF Grant # 0354420, by the Landesstiftung Baden-Württemberg, and by the Virtual PhD Programm, VGK (DFG). Many thanks go to Erin Walker for her contributions concerning the development of the framework.

REFERENCES

Aleven, V., McLaren, B., Roll, I., & Koedinger, K. R. (2004). Toward tutoring help seeking: Applying cognitive modelling to meta-cognitive skills. In J. C. Lester, R. M. Vicari & F. Paraguaçu (Eds.), *Proceedings of Seventh International Conference on Intelligent Tutoring Systems, ITS 2004* (pp. 227-239). Berlin: Springer

Aronson, E., Blaney, N., Sikes, J., Stephan, C., & Snapp, M. (1978). *The jigsaw classroom.* Beverly Hills, CA: Sage.

Baghaei, N., Mitrovic, T., & Irwin, W. (2007). Supporting collaborative learning and problem solving in a constraint-based CSCL environment for UML class diagrams. *International Journal of Computer-Supported Collaborative Learning, 2*(2-3), 159–190. doi:10.1007/s11412-007-9018-0

Baker, R. S., Corbett, A. T., & Koedinger, K. R. (2004). *Detecting student misuse of intelligent tutoring systems.* Paper presented at the 7th International Conference on Intelligent Tutoring Systems.

Constantino-Gonzalez, M. A., Suthers, D., & Escamilla de los Santos, J. (2003). Coaching web-based collaborative learning based on problem solution differences and participation. *Artificial Intelligence in Education, 13*(2-4), 263–299.

Cress, U., & Hesse, F. W. (2004). Knowledge sharing in groups: Experimental findings of how to overcome a social dilemma. In Y. Kafai, W. Sandoval, N. Enydey, A. S. Nixon, & F. Herrera (Eds.), *Proceedings of the Sixth International Conference of the Learning Sciences* (pp. 150-157). Mahwah, NJ: Lawrence Erlbaum.

De Wever, B., Van Keer, H., Schellens, T., & Valcke, M. (2007). Applying multilevel modelling on content analysis data: Methodological issues in the study of the impact of role assignment in asynchronous discussion groups. *Learning and Instruction, 17*, 436–447. doi:10.1016/j.learninstruc.2007.04.001

Dillenbourg, P. (2002). Over-scripting CSCL: The risks of blending collaborative learning with instructional design. In P. A. Kirschner (Ed.), *Three worlds of CSCL. Can we support CSCL* (pp. 61-91). Heerlen, The Netherlands: Open Univeriteit Nederland.

Dillenbourg, P., & Jermann, P. (2007). Designing integrative scripts. In F. Fischer, I. Kollar, H. Mandl, & J. Haake (Eds.), *Scripting computer-supported collaborative learning. Cognitive, computational, and educational perspectives* (pp. 275-301). New York: Springer.

Dillenbourg, P., & Tchounikine, P. (2007). Flexibility in macro-scripts for CSCL. *Journal of Computer Assisted Learning, 23*(1), 1–13. doi:10.1111/j.1365-2729.2007.00191.x

Diziol, D., Rummel, N., Spada, H., & McLaren, B. (2007). Promoting learning in mathematics: Script support for collaborative problem solving with the Cognitive Tutor Algebra. In C. A. Chinn, G. Erkens, & S. Puntambekar (Eds.), *Mice, minds and society. Proceedings of the Computer Supported Collaborative Learning (CSCL) Conference 2007,* (Vol 8, pp. 39-41). International Society of the Learning Sciences.

Fischer, F., Kollar, I., Mandl, H., & Haake, J. M. (Eds.). (2007). *Scripting computer-supported collaborative learning – cognitive, computational, and educational perspectives.* New York: Springer.

Gweon, G., Rosé, C., Carey, R., & Zaiss, Z. (2006). Providing support for adaptive scripting in an on-line collaborative learning environment. In *Proceedings of the SIGCHI Conference on Human Factors in Computing Systems* (pp. 251-260). New York: ACM Press.

Hausmann, R. G. M., Chi, M. T. H., & Roy, M. (2004). Learning from collaborative problem solving: An analysis of three hypothesized mechanisms. In K. D. Forbus, D. Gentner, & T. Regier (Eds.), *26nd Annual Conference of the Cognitive Science Society* (pp. 547-552). Mahwah, NJ: Lawrence Erlbaum.

Hooper, S. (1992). Effects of peer interaction during computer-based mathematics instruction. *The Journal of Educational Research, 85*(3), 180–189.

Hythecker, V. I., Dansereau, D. F., & Rocklin, T. R. (1988). An analysis of the processes influencing the structured dyadic learning environment. *Educational Psychologist, 23*(1), 23–37. doi:10.1207/s15326985ep2301_2

Israel, J., & Aiken, R. (2007). Supporting collaborative learning with an intelligent web-based system. *International Journal of Artificial Intelligence in Education, 17*(1), 3–40.

Jermann, P., & Dillenbourg, P. (2008). Group mirrors to support interaction regulation in collaborative problem solving. *Computers & Education, 51*(1), 279–296. doi:10.1016/j.compedu.2007.05.012

Kerr, N. L. (1983). Motivation losses in small groups: A social dilemma analysis. *Journal of Personality and Social Psychology, 45*(4), 819–828. doi:10.1037/0022-3514.45.4.819

King, A. (1991). Effects of training in strategic questioning on children's problem-solving performance. *Journal of Educational Psychology, 83*(3), 307–317. doi:10.1037/0022-0663.83.3.307

Koedinger, K. R. (1998). *Intelligent cognitive tutors as modeling tool and instructional model.* Paper presented at the NCTM Standards 2000 Technology Conference.

Koedinger, K. R., Anderson, J. R., Hadley, W. H., & Mark, M. A. (1997). Intelligent tutoring goes to school in the big city. *International Journal of Artificial Intelligence in Education, 8*, 30–43.

Kollar, I., Fischer, F., & Slotta, J. D. (2005). Internal and external collaboration scripts in webbased science learning at schools. In T. Koschmann, D. Suthers, & T.-W. Chan (Eds.), *The next 10 years! Proceedings of the International Conference on Computer Support for Collaborative Learning 2005* (pp. 331-340). Mahwah, NJ: Lawrence Erlbaum Associates.

Kumar, R., Rosé, C. P., Wang, Y. C., Joshi, M., & Robinson, A. (2007). Tutorial dialogue as adaptive collaborative learning support. In R. Luckin, K. R. Koedinger, & J. Greer (Eds.), *Proceedings of Artificial Intelligence in Education* (pp. 383-390). IOS Press.

Lou, Y., Abrami, P. C., & d'Apollonia, S. (2001). Small group and individual learning with technology: A meta-analysis. *Review of Educational Research, 71*(3), 449–521. doi:10.3102/00346543071003449

Lou, Y., Abrami, P. C., Spence, J. C., Poulsen, C., Chambers, B., & d'Appolonia, S. (1996). Within-class grouping: A meta-analysis. *Review of Educational Research, 66*(4), 423–458.

Mathan, S. A., & Koedinger, K. R. (2005). Fostering the intelligent novice: Learning from errors with metacognitive tutoring. *Educational Psychologist, 40*(4), 257–265. doi:10.1207/s15326985ep4004_7

Meier, A., & Spada, H. (in press). Developing adaptive collaboration support: The example of an effective training for collaborative inferences. *Educational Psychology Review.*

Murray, T. (2003). An overview of intelligent tutoring system authoring tools: Updated analysis of the state of the art. In: T. Murray, S. Blessing, & S. Ainsworth (Eds.) *Authoring tools for advanced learning environments.* (pp. 491-544). Dordrecht, The Netherlands: Kluwer Academic Publishers.

O'Donnell, A. M. (1999). Structuring dyadic interaction through scripted cooperation. In A. M. O'Donnell & A. King (Eds.), *Cognitive perspectives on peer learning.* (pp. 179-196). Mahwah, NJ: Lawrence Erlbaum Associates, Publishers.

Ploetzner, R., Fehse, E., Kneser, C., & Spada, H. (1999). Learning to relate qualitative and quantitative problem representations in a model-based setting for collaborative problem-solving. *Journal of the Learning Sciences, 8*, 177–214. doi:10.1207/s15327809jls0802_1

Rosé, C. P., Wang, Y. C., Cui, Y., Arguello, J., Stegmann, K., Weinberger, A., & Fischer, F. (2008). Analyzing collaborative learning processes automatically: Exploiting the advances of computational linguistics in computer-supported collaborative learning. *International Journal of Computer-Supported Collaborative Learning, 3*(3), 237–271. doi:10.1007/s11412-007-9034-0

Rummel, N., Diziol, D., & Spada, H. (2009). *Collaborative learning with the Cognitive Tutor Algebra. An experimental classroom study.* Manuscript in preparation.

Rummel, N., & Spada, H. (2005). Learning to Collaborate: An Instructional Approach to Promoting Collaborative Problem Solving in Computer-Mediated Settings. *Journal of the Learning Sciences, 14*(2), 201–241. doi:10.1207/s15327809jls1402_2

Rummel, N., & Weinberger, A. (2008). New challenges in CSCL: Towards adaptive script support. In G. Kanselaar, V. Jonker, P.A. Kirschner, & F. Prins, (Eds.), *International perspectives of the learning sciences: Cre8ing a learning world. Proceedings of the Eighth International Conference of the Learning Sciences (ICLS 2008)* (Vol. 3, pp. 338-345). International Society of the Learning Sciences.

Stasser, G., & Titus, W. (1985). Pooling of unshared information in group decision making: Biased information sampling during discussion. *Journal of Personality and Social Psychology, 48*, 1467–1478. doi:10.1037/0022-3514.48.6.1467

Tedesco, P. (2003). MArCo: Building an artificial conflict mediator to support group planning interactions. *International Journal of Artificial Intelligence in Education, 13*, 117–155.

Tsovaltzi, D., Rummel, N., McLaren, B., Pinkwart, N., Scheuer, O., Harrer, A., & Braun, I. (in press). Extending a Virtual Chemistry Laboratory with a Collaboration Script to Promote Conceptual Learning. [IJTEL]. *International Journal of Technology Enhanced Learning*.

VanLehn, K., Koedinger, K. R., Rummel, N., & Liu, Y. (2007, August). Understanding robust learning via in vivo experimentation. In *the 12th European Conference for Research on Learning and Instruction (EARLI) 2007*, Budapest, Hungary.

Walker, E., Rummel, N., & Koedinger, K. (2008). To tutor the tutor: Adaptive domain support for peer tutoring. In B. Woolf, E. Aimeur, R. Nkambou, S. Lajoie (Eds), *Proceedings of the 9th International Conference on Intelligent Tutoring Systems* (LNCS 5091, pp. 626-635). Berlin, Germany: Springer.

Webb, N. M. (1989). Peer interaction and learning in small groups. *International Journal of Educational Research, 13*, 21–39. doi:10.1016/0883-0355(89)90014-1

Webb, N. M., Troper, J. D., & Fall, R. (1995). Constructive activity and learning in collaborative small groups. *Journal of Educational Psychology, 87*(3), 406–423. doi:10.1037/0022-0663.87.3.406

Weinberger, A., Reiserer, M., Ertl, B., Fischer, F., & Mandl, H. (2005). Facilitating collaborative knowledge construction in computer-mediated learning environments with cooperation scripts. In R. Bromme, F. W. Hesse, & H. Spada (Eds.), *Barriers and biases in computer-mediated knowledge communication and how they may be overcome*. Dodrecht, NL: Kluwer Academic Publishers.

Yager, S., Johnson, R. T., Johnson, D. W., & Snider, B. (1986). The impact of group processing on achievement in cooperative learning groups. *The Journal of Social Psychology, 126*(3), 389–397.

Chapter 10

Scripting Computer–Supported Collaborative Learning:
A Review of SCORE Studies

Päivi Häkkinen
University of Jyväskylä, Finland

Maarit Arvaja
University of Jyväskylä, Finland

Raija Hämäläinen
University of Jyväskylä, Finland

Johanna Pöysä
University of Jyväskylä, Finland

ABSTRACT

In this chapter, we will present a review of theoretical and empirical analyses of Web-based collaboration processes used during a scripted university course. The results refer to a design-based study that involved first-year teacher-education students (N = 30) studying pedagogy over a period of three months. The intervention involved structuring the subjects' collaborative actions with three different pedagogical scripts. According to the findings, the scripts guided students' activities by helping them find resources for knowledge construction and work together through a series of steps. However, there were variations among groups in terms of quality of collaboration, and the students mostly cumulatively shared or constructed knowledge from similar perspectives. On the basis of the challenges raised in the SCORE and related studies, future prospects are outlined for the design of flexible pedagogical scripts.

INTRODUCTION

Computer-supported collaborative learning (CSCL) is a complex phenomenon and is often difficult to realize in authentic educational settings (e.g.,

Häkkinen, Arvaja, & Mäkitalo, 2004). It is evident that successful collaboration is not a spontaneous phenomenon. Earlier studies on collaborative interaction in CSCL environments have reported several problems and challenges (Häkkinen & Järvelä, 2006; Schellens & Valcke, 2005; Vonderwell, 2003). According to Häkkinen and Järvelä (2006), a common

DOI: 10.4018/978-1-61520-729-9.ch010

feature of CSCL environments is the production of descriptive and surface-level knowledge, instead of deeper explanations for the phenomena under examination. Thus, a crucial problem for such collaboration is the difficulty of developing inquiries that evoke more elaborate explanations (Lipponen, Hakkarainen, & Paavola, 2004). Other particular challenges are related to the achievement of reciprocal understanding and shared values and goals in networked learning environments (Järvelä & Häkkinen, 2002).

Particularly in minimally structured learning environments, students may struggle to become engaged in productive interactions, such as questioning, explaining and justifying opinions, reasoning, elaborating, and reflecting upon their knowledge (Kobbe et al., 2007). Therefore, recent research has focused on how to make collaboration more frequent and more effective by introducing collaboration scripts as a particular kind of instructional support, both to trigger productive collaborative activities and to provide structure and support to otherwise open learning environments (e.g., Dillenbourg, 2002; Weinberger, Ertl, Fischer, & Mandl, 2005).

Collaboration scripts are rooted in the scripted cooperation approach (e.g., O'Donnell, 1999). In this approach, learners engage in specific activities that are assumed to lead to higher level cognitive processing and therefore to better learning outcomes (Kobbe et al., 2007). Collaboration scripts thus serve as scaffolds to improve collaboration by structuring the interactions of two or more learning partners (Kollar, Fischer, & Hesse, 2006). The core design principle through which scripts are expected to trigger specific interactions can vary. For instance, a script could lean on the jigsaw method (Aronson, Blaney, Stephan, Sikes, & Snapp, 1978) and form pairs of participants with complementary knowledge, providing each with complementary information or roles. Alternatively, a script might aim to create sociocognitive conflict (e.g., Doise 1985) or might assign and alternate roles to foster reciprocal activities, such as questioning or tutoring (Palincsar & Brown, 1984).

The goal of a script may vary from structuring small-group interactions to orchestrating collaborative and individual activities—some of which may be computerized and others not—into a consistent whole over a longer period of time (Dillenbourg & Jermann, 2006). There are also various possible solutions with regard to the type of technology used to support scripting; thus, scripts can be differentiated according to whether collaboration is supported by specific instructional means or by technology (Hämäläinen, 2008). In line with this notion, Lipponen (2001) has drawn a distinction between the *collaborative use of technology* (in which software alone does not scaffold collaboration) and use of *collaborative technology* (in which software is designed specifically to support collaborative knowledge construction). Our SCORE studies (Pedagogical Structuring of Collaboration and Self-Regulated Learning: Individual and Group-Level Perspectives) have focused on collaborative use of existing technology via sequences of instructions.

Although several research groups have designed learning environments for single studies using specific experimental scripts (Dillenbourg & Jermann, 2006; Hämäläinen, Manninen, Järvelä, & Häkkinen, 2006; Schellens & Valcke, 2005; Stegmann, Weinberger, Fischer, & Mandl, 2005), very little long-term empirical research has considered the effects of these scripts in authentic educational settings. Most recent studies have focused on *micro-scripts* that structure the interaction process per se by providing prompts, sentence starters, and so on (Dillenbourg & Jermann, 2006). In this line of research, scripting learners' social interactions (e.g., with the aid of an argumentative script) is seen as an effective way to provide instructional support for group activities (Stegmann et al., 2005). However, some contradictory results suggest that scripting content-related (epistemic) activities might lead to better individual learning outcomes under relatively unscripted rather than minutely scripted conditions (Mäkitalo, Weinberger, Häkkinen, Fischer, & Järvelä, 2005). It seems evident that scripted collaboration is not without its challenges, as different learners need various kinds of support (e.g., Hämäläinen & Arvaja, 2009) and various groups will act differently given the same instructional interventions (Arvaja, 2007; Hämäläinen, Oksanen, & Häkkinen, 2009). Therefore, our approach to scripting collaboration is based on pedagogical scripts that set up conditions under which favorable activities and productive interaction should occur, while leaving the details of the interaction itself unconstrained. In other words, this study employs collaboration scripts as a pedagogical method to facilitate learners' group work towards shared problem solving. Such scripts may be referred to as *macro-scripts* (Dillenbourg & Jermann, 2006) and emphasize a sociocultural approach that focuses on the role of mutual engagement and shared-knowledge construction in collaboration (Lipponen, 2001).

CONTEXT OF THE STUDY

In this chapter, we will present a review of theoretical and empirical analyses of Web-based collaboration processes used during a scripted university course. The results synthesized here are based on empirical studies in the context of the SCORE project (Arvaja, 2007; Arvaja, Salovaara, Häkkinen, & Järvelä, 2007; Arvaja & Hämäläinen, 2008; Hämäläinen & Arvaja, 2009; Hämäläinen & Häkkinen, in press). The SCORE project was a design-based study in which the participants were first-year teacher-education students ($N=30$) studying pedagogy over a period of three months. Students worked in seven small groups assigned by the teacher and researchers. Data were collected using a mixed-method approach (Hmelo-Silver, 2003). Complementary methods were utilized in the analysis of the data (Arvaja, 2007; Arvaja & Hämäläinen, 2008; Arvaja, Salovaara, Häkkinen, & Järvelä, 2007; Hämäläinen & Arvaja, 2009; Hämäläinen & Häkkinen, in press).

Role of the Technological Environment

The intervention structured students' collaborative actions using various pedagogical scripts, and one of the crucial phases took place in an asynchronous Web-based learning environment (Optima). As the students participated in an authentic university course, the selection of the technology environment was directed by the official choice of the university. The asynchronous Optima environment was the most commonly used and supported. Using Optima, students worked in a Web-based learning environment comprising an asynchronous discussion tool; a tool for creating text documents; folders containing course material, such as the teacher's lecture notes; articles in PDF format; and hyperlinks to Web sites. Hence, the students' communication can be characterized mainly as text-based collaborative use of technology, rather than use of collaborative technology as a scaffold for knowledge construction (Lipponen, 2001).

Pedagogical Scripts

As technology did not directly scaffold collaboration, three different pedagogical scripts (*case, grid,* and *open-problem*) were employed to enhance the probability of particular kinds of collaboration processes (see Table 1). The scripts varied with respect to how much responsibility groups had for directing their own learning processes. In general, the scripts gave guidance on how to proceed through and solve the learning task, but they did not interfere with the details of social interactions.

In the case script, the main idea was to solve an *authentic learning problem* (e.g., Brown, Collins, & Duguid, 1989; Zualkernan, 2006) with *complementary knowledge* construction (e.g., Perkins, 1993). It was expected that by assigning students *reciprocal roles*, the script would create positive interdependency between collaborators (Arvaja,

Table 1. Pedagogical scripts used for structuring collaboration process

TYPE OF SCRIPT		
Case (Hämäläinen & Arvaja, 2009)	**Grid (Hämäläinen & Häkkinen, in press)**	**Open problem (Arvaja & Hämäläinen, 2008)**
Core theoretical/design principle • An authentic learning problem (e.g., Brown, Collins, & Duguid, 1989; Zualkernan, 2006) • Complementary knowledge construction (Perkins, 1993) • Reciprocal roles (Arvaja et al., 2003; Hämäläinen et al., 2006; Weinberger et al., 2005) Activities and resources • Small-group preparation of an individualized teaching plan for a particular learner • Theoretical background material • Reciprocal roles -> interdependency of group members • Discussion (and reciprocal teaching) • Shared plan for curriculum	Core theoretical/design principle • A combination of ConceptGrid (Dillenbourg & Jermann, 2006) and the idea of cognitive conflict (e.g., Doise 1985) • Contradictory perspectives and interdependency through different learning materials (Dillenbourg, 2002) Activities and resources • A controversial education policy topic concerning whether pre-primary education should be organized at school or at kindergarten • Groups of 4 (each with different background information) • Filling the table • Discussion (argumentation expected) • Conflict resolution as a group • Final discussion	Core theoretical/design principle • Ill-defined and open-ended problems (Simon, 1973) Activities and resources • Creation and solution of a problem related to "Differentiation in teaching reading" • Theoretical background material • Creation of the problem (about teaching reading) • Solution of the problem based on background material • Final output/lesson plan for teaching reading

Rasku-Puttonen, Häkkinen, & Eteläpelto, 2003; Hämäläinen, Manninen, Järvelä, & Häkkinen, 2006; Weinberger, Ertl, Fischer, & Mandl, 2005). Explanation and elaboration activities were also anticipated. According to the script, participants worked in small groups to prepare an individualized teaching plan for one particular learner, "Matti," who had special needs with respect to the teaching plan (Hämäläinen & Arvaja, 2009). The case script lasted for four weeks and comprised five phases. Firstly, students familiarized themselves with an authentic learning problem concerning the learning readiness of two different learners, Matti and Timo. In this phase, each group read a comic in which Matti and Timo work together. Secondly, the groups read theoretical background material about Matti's case. After this, they entered the third phase of the script, a shared Web discussion about constructing a shared plan for Matti's personal curriculum. Based on this discussion, the students moved on to the fourth phase, planning this personal curriculum within their groups. Finally, each group commented on other groups' curriculum plans and evaluated how realistic each plan was with regard to supporting the learning readiness of the learner in question. The case script

guided the students step by step through the task and also offered necessary background material, but it neither gave instructions for student interaction as such nor penalized students if they failed to follow the scripted phases.

The aim of the grid script, meanwhile, was to promote collaboration among team members and prevent *free-rider effects* (see Kerr & Bruun, 1983) by requiring individual work as part of the script. The script leaned on the ConceptGrid structure (cf. Dillenbourg & Jermann, 2006), especially the role of *mutual explanation* and the idea of resolving *cognitive conflicts* (e.g., Doise, 1985). Several modifications were made to the original ConceptGrid; instead of concepts, for example, students were expected to work on a controversial education policy topic, regarding whether pre-primary education should be organized at school or at kindergarten (Hämäläinen & Häkkinen, in press). The aim was to make use of contradictory perspectives and interdependency by giving students different learning materials (Dillenbourg, 2002). In many studies, differences in students' knowledge and perspectives are stressed as prerequisites for cognitive conflicts and their resolution (e.g., Dillenbourg, 1999) and thus for learning (Kneser & Ploetzner, 2001). Following the script, students were expected to go through five different phases: First, groups received different sets of theoretical background information and allocated one to each participant. The aim of this procedure was to create interdependence among group members by providing opposite but complementary resources to individual students (see Kobbe et al., 2007). In the second phase, each student read his or her theory material and visited a relevant site of pre-primary education (a school or a kindergarten). The aim of this phase was to gain authentic experiences and add meaning to the personal roles established in the first phase (e.g., Brown, Collins, & Duguid, 1989). In the third phase, each student filled in a table with his or her views and definitions of the topic on the basis of the background information and the visit. These tables were then made visible to the other group members. In the fourth phase, each group had a shared discussion in which students formulated final statements about the topic, taking into account the others' distinct and possibly conflicting points of view. In the final phase, group members had an analytical discussion about how well they had been able to construe the task and complete a final statement. Movement from one phase to the next presupposed that the previous task had been completed. However, students were not penalized in any way if they failed to complete a phase in the script.

In the last script, the students were set an *open problem,* in which they had to create and resolve a problem relating to the theme "differentiation in teaching reading" (Arvaja & Hämäläinen, 2008). The students' subsequent tasks were to discuss the problem they had created in an asynchronous discussion forum and, finally, to prepare a joint lesson plan to teach reading. The lesson plan was to be written in a document based in the online learning environment. This script was the most open of the three with respect to how much responsibility groups were given to structure their own learning process.

QUALITY OF SCRIPTED COLLABORATION

Next, we will discuss what we have learned from our SCORE studies focusing on structuring collaboration processes in authentic higher education contexts, with an emphasis on answers to the following questions: How did groups' activities vary, despite being given apparently similar instructional support? What was the quality of collaboration? What were the core challenges in macro-scripted collaborations? In addition, on the basis of the challenges revealed by the SCORE project and related studies, we will outline future prospects for the design of flexible pedagogical scripts.

In the SCORE project, we mainly analyzed collaborative interactions as a means of gaining insight into the process of collaborative learning in various macro-scripted settings. According to our results, the benefit of these scripts was that they guaranteed that students found resources for their knowledge construction activity and were able to work together. The major challenges were related to group-by-group variation and the achievement of high-level collaboration. We found that, despite apparently similar instructional support, the level and quality of collaborative activities varied drastically among groups, in terms of number, length, and content of interactions; group members' satisfaction with the group's work; degree of collaboration; and roles assumed and attitudes displayed in a group (Hämäläinen, 2008). The level of participation also varied among the steps of a given script. Groups differed in terms of the quality and the actual realization of the discursive processes of shared meaning-making activities (e.g., Arvaja & Hämäläinen, 2008).

In relation to quality of collaboration, several studies have demonstrated that certain activities in collaborative discourse are particularly beneficial to learning (Kobbe et al., 2007; Weinberger & Fischer, 2006). Dillenbourg (1999) has stated that collaborating participants learn if they generate certain collaborative activities (e.g., argumentation, explanation, elaboration, mutual regulation, etc.) that trigger learning mechanisms, such as knowledge elicitation and reduced cognitive load. In the ideal script, the teacher or designer intends to promote some particular collaborative activities that are seen as desirable in each case. Each actual script then refers to the emerging pattern: that is, what really happens in a scripted learning situation (Dillenbourg & Jermann, 2006).

How, then, were the SCORE scripts described above (see Table 1) realized by the students? Our work revealed how differently various groups of learners may enact the same educational design, through an analysis of the functions of discussions (e.g., Arvaja, 2007; Arvaja & Hämäläinen, 2008) and the study of social formations (Pöysä, 2006). Furthermore, the results of our studies showed a gap between ideal script design and realization in all three scripts. According to our findings, scripting generally enhanced the completion of the tasks (Hämäläinen, 2008). However, several challenges became evident in terms of the level of participation and quality of collaboration. Our results indicate that the level of Web-based discussions in the scripted tasks was not very high. The grid script, for example, was aimed to trigger mutual explanation and resolution of cognitive conflict. The reality was that mutual explanations and active conflict situations with critical argumentation and counter-argumentation were rare (Hämäläinen & Häkkinen, in press).

Looking at the case script, all the groups completed the task successfully and produced shared curriculum plans for the given case. However, use of the script did not guarantee equal or high-level collaboration within all teams (e.g., Baker, 2002). The results indicated that the groups differed in terms of quality of discussion (Arvaja & Hämäläinen, 2008). Moreover, these differences were deeply intertwined throughout the process of accomplishing the task and further crystallized as diverse routes for shared understanding. The case script was quite open with respect to assigning or allocating roles, with different roles distributed among students. Based on our analysis of the case and open-problem scripts in two selected groups, the findings for each script were similar. For both scripts, the students mostly cumulatively shared or constructed knowledge based on similar perspectives (Arvaja & Hämäläinen, 2008). Mercer's (1996) *exploratory talk*—involving different perspectives, critical evaluation, and reasoning together—was lacking from the discussions. Although students following both scripts reasoned and justified their thoughts, asked questions and elaborated, and thus participated in activities that have been found beneficial for learning (e.g., Weinberger & Fischer, 2006; Van Boxtel et al., 2000), these functions were not among the main functions of communication. While following the open-problem script, for example, members of both of the analyzed groups engaged mainly in content-based activities by providing knowledge to each other. In following the case script, one group primarily focused on sharing knowledge and reasoning, while the other focused on organizing activities and giving social support. The focus on organizational issues seemingly decreased the quality of students' content-based activities and collaboration (Arvaja, Hämäläinen, & Rasku-Puttonen, 2009).

WHAT EXPLAINS QUALITY OF COLLABORATION?

Our SCORE research has revealed several features that may harm scripted collaboration. Here, we will discuss some of the main explanations for the differing quality of students' collaborations, despite similarities in the macro-scripts provided to them. We will particularly focus on the roles students adopt, their engagement in collaboration, and the nature of the learning task.

Different Roles in Collaboration

The results indicate that the case, grid, and open-problem scripts guided students' activities at the content level by helping them find resources for their knowledge construction activity and proceed through different steps. However, when we look at one phase of the script—namely, Web-based discussions in the open-problem and case scripts—the findings showed that the groups' activities differed in terms of functional and participatory roles. Arvaja and Hämäläinen (2008) observed that some students within the groups had a strong social orientation in their activities, shown in communicative functions such as commenting, giving social support, or organizing activities. Other students focused on content-based goals, by providing and reasoning through information. The functional roles of the students differed, resulting in asymmetrical knowledge construction activities (e.g., Baker, 2002). Furthermore, several challenges became apparent at the social level, particularly in terms of uneven participation in collaborative work (Arvaja & Hämäläinen, 2008; Hämäläinen & Arvaja, 2009). It is obvious that uneven participation both impedes construction of shared goals and reduces motivation and engagement among virtual group members. Our results indicate that collaborating groups may face multiple types of social challenges that interfere with the social process of learning and task completion (Webb & Palincsar, 1996).

Quality of collaboration was also hampered by differences in individual learners' contributions during scripted collaboration (Hämäläinen & Arvaja, 2009). In particular, it proved challenging for students to sustain roles that focused equally on shared knowledge construction and problem solving. As described above, students readily took on and maintained either content-oriented or social-oriented roles (Arvaja & Hämäläinen, 2008). The different participatory roles that appeared in our studies (Hämäläinen & Arvaja, 2009) included *free riders* (members who seek the maximum benefit from a group task with a minimum of personal input; Kerr & Bruun, 1983) and *ghosts* (members with high individual learning goals but passive attitudes toward group work; Strijbos & De Laat, 2007), who hampered collaboration in their groups; *overriders* (members who dominate a group's work); and supportive *captains* (members who facilitate teamwork and increase team cohesion). Our SCORE studies indicated that it was relatively easy for individual participants to free-ride and be invisible within the virtual community in fairly open tasks, such as in the open-problem and case scripts (Hämäläinen & Arvaja, 2009). Introducing a higher level of control (e.g., in the grid script) prevented free-riding, but because all students were forced to participate, some members ended up hindering rather than promoting collaboration (Hämäläinen & Häkkinen, in press).

Engagement in Collaboration

Collaboration is often defined as engagement in a coordinated effort to solve a problem or perform a task together. Consequently, it is evident that successful collaboration depends on participants' willingness to work together. Therefore, a script should not be seen as a way to force students to collaborate. If students are forced to participate, scripting might increase the quasi-activity of disengaged students (e.g., copying and pasting from tables in the grid script) and lead to simplistic discussions or even prevent more active members' collaboration (Hämäläinen, 2008). To really engage students to participate equally in shared work in a CSCL environment has been a common problem, according to many similar studies (e.g., Arvaja & Hämäläinen, 2008; Hämäläinen & Arvaja, 2009; Oliver & Shaw, 2003; Strijbos & De Laat, 2007). One step toward this goal involves determining core design principles that motivate students and trigger high-level engagement (e.g., Järvelä, Veermans, & Leinonen, 2008; Volet, Summers, & Thurman, 2008) in collaborative knowledge construction. The question of how to prestructure collaboration through task design to guarantee learners' equal participation and engagement is seen as a particular challenge.

Nature of the Learning Task and Instructional Support

One crucial determinant of successful collaboration is related to the nature of the learning task. Compared with fact-seeking questions and unambiguous tasks, ill-defined tasks (Cohen, 1994) are more likely to promote productive collaborative activities by leaving space for disagreements, misunderstandings, questions, negotiations, explanations, and arguments. Our results indicated that shared knowledge construction in Web-based discussion occurs when the task itself triggers reasoning (Arvaja, 2007; Hämäläinen, 2008). The results of our SCORE studies presented several challenges derived from scripts that were either too open or too controlled and in this way did not guarantee high-level collaboration. Jeong and Chi (1997) have pointed out that to facilitate co-construction in computer-mediated settings, participants must feel a social obligation to engage in active interaction. In this study, students were not obligated to participate in Web-based discussions. The learning tasks were too open, and none of the three scripts guaranteed participation and engagement. Thus, it was fairly easy for individual participants to free-ride in the discussions (Hämäläinen & Arvaja, 2009; Strijbos, Kirschner, & Martens, 2004). To fully engage students in Web-based collaborative activity, the students must need to make contact and collaborate with other participants (Mäkitalo, Häkkinen, Leinonen, & Järvelä, 2002). Therefore, one of main requirements of instructional design and support of CSCL is to provide real group tasks and contexts that enhance questioning, explaining, and other forms of knowledge articulation. In designing group tasks, we should also keep in mind that face-to-face tasks cannot be directly

transferred into virtual environments. Our SCORE findings indicated, for example, that a task that would create a conflict in a face-to-face situation does not necessarily achieve the same effect in a virtual environment (Hämäläinen & Häkkinen, in press). It may be that in virtual environments, students do not enter conflict situations as easily as in face-to-face discussions (Baker, 2003).

Another problem in the SCORE studies was the lack of regulation and supervision during the collaboration process (Arvaja, Hämäläinen, & Rasku-Puttonen, 2009). During the Web-based phases of the script, the teacher's role was minimal. Even with the script and shared background knowledge, though, some learners would have benefited from additional support or supervision, as during the case script (Hämäläinen, 2008). It is evident that a teacher's support is important in facilitating equal participation and higher level discussions. In finding the balance between sufficient guidance and overscripting, then, one must consider the optimal integration of pre-structuring activities (such as task design) through scripting and reactive monitoring by the teacher during the collaboration process.

CONCLUSION

According to our findings, the scripts defined above succeeded in guiding students to work together, but they did not equally guarantee high-level collaboration in all the groups under study. Rather than sharing different perspectives and engaging in critical analysis, the students mostly shared or constructed knowledge based on similar perspectives. Several studies have demonstrated that collaborative learning as a phenomenon is neither easy nor unproblematic (Häkkinen & Järvelä, 2006; Schellens & Valcke, 2005). Instead, as described in this chapter, challenges to collaboration derive from the intertwined nature of participants' cognitive, social, and emotional sides. One might ask how much high-level collaboration it is realistic to expect during a long-term university course that enrolls participants with different backgrounds, different levels of work experience, and different social and physical environments. Among the central concerns in computer-supported collaboration is why some groups perform better than others. On the basis of several substudies pertaining to our SCORE project, we would point out that collaborative learning is always achieved under unique circumstances that are interactively constructed by the learners and whose significance cannot be directly predicted or prescribed (Arvaja, 2007; Hämäläinen & Arvaja, 2009; Stahl, 2006). As a result, definitions of collaboration must derive from the context of each situation, and its educational value must be judged against the goals and norms to be facilitated in each case. The scripts used in this study were macro-scripts that did not interfere with detailed interaction processes, but instead focused on setting up favorable situations for collaboration with the aid of pedagogical core ideas. Subsequently, there is not a simple recipe for transferring these scripts into different learning scenarios or online environments. When considering whether scripts can be transferred to different learning scenarios, the focus should be on judging the suitability of these core ideas against the goals of the learning task, the subject domain, the social context, and the variety of appropriate technological tools.

One of the primary challenges revealed through the SCORE studies is the difficulty of responding to the different needs of individuals and groups of varying backgrounds. In particular, the backgrounds of various groups of students may influence the way in which the collaborative context is created and the learning task was interpreted (Arvaja, 2007). Comparisons among groups in our study indicated differences and similarities in communicative functions and contextual resources in their discussions (Arvaja, 2007). These factors influenced discussion quality and resources used in knowledge construction. For example, in the open-problem script situation, the task was a real problem-solving task for one group (a novice group), and the students appeared to need each other as resources, leading to co-construction of knowledge; by contrast, students in the other group (an expert group) appeared to perceive no significant challenges and merely reproduced their shared knowledge based on past experience, without the need to co-construct knowledge (Arvaja, 2007).

Based on our results in regard to the productivity of collaboration, there is a need to pay more attention to the composition of collaborative learning groups. On the one hand, groups with varying compositions benefit from the opportunity to share diverse perspectives; on the other hand, such heterogeneous groups may suffer from misunderstandings and coordination difficulties when working on tasks together (Häkkinen, Arvaja, & Mäkitalo, 2004). Consequently, some degree of shared focus and coordination seems to be a prerequisite for effective collaboration in Web-based settings (Fischer & Mandl, 2005). Groups that are heterogeneous with respect to knowledge in hand thus can be offered material that creates common ground (Mäkitalo, Häkkinen, Leinonen, & Järvelä, 2002) and shared conceptual space (Kopp, Schnurer, & Mandl, 2006; Roschelle & Teasley, 1995) among participants, while at the same time making use of the collaborative value of participants' different perspectives. Similarly, in many studies, differences in students' knowledge or perspectives have been pointed out as prerequisites for productive cognitive conflict (e.g., Dillenbourg, 1999) and learning (Kneser & Ploetzner, 2001). Therefore, groups that are homogeneous with respect to knowledge can be offered the means to create variations in perspectives or knowledge—thus enhancing cognitive conflict—by assigning different material to each participant, for example (cf., modifications of jigsaw; Dillenbourg, 2002; Miyake, Masukawa, & Shirouzou, 2001).

FUTURE RESEARCH DIRECTIONS

Scripting collaborative interactions is a complicated challenge with a danger of either too much (e.g., Dillenbourg, 2002) or too little guidance (e.g., Hämäläinen et al., 2006). With insufficient guidance, students might not reach the goals set for their interactions, but when too much guidance is provided, there is a risk of overstructuring learners' interactions. If the degree of freedom is reduced to a very fine-grained level, natural interactions and problem-solving processes may be disturbed, interactions may become too didactic, the learners' cognitive load may increase too much, or the learning task may be oversimplified, at a cost of motivational frustration (Dillenbourg, 2002; Dillenbourg & Jermann, 2006; Hämäläinen & Arvaja, 2009). In order to avoid overscripting, scripts should not be interpreted as implementable action plans, but rather as resources for knowledge construction (Stahl, 2006). In other words, the design of scripts should support productive and situated collaboration. The focus of research, then, needs to shift to a micro level of analysis regarding how participants make sense of such resources in detailed interactions (Stahl, 2006). Furthermore, script design should be based on actual examples of the kinds of situated action for which the scripts are intended.

Following Dillenbourg and Jermann (2006), scripts should, moreover, be better interpreted as flexible resources and as design metaphors for finding the delicate balance between too little control to be helpful and too much control to allow for flexible group interactions. Adopting Schwartz' (1995) conclusion that the power of collaborative learning comes from the effort necessary for the group to build a shared understanding, Dillenbourg and Jermann (2006) used scripts to set up situations in which groups were forced to construct such an understanding. In this view, collaboration scripts are instructional sequences that prepare for and then reflect upon, but do not interfere with, detailed interaction. Detailed interaction is too complex and too unpredictable to be supported by a script that is written in advance (Stahl, 2006). In practice, flexible collaboration scripts mean that students can deal with unanticipated problems (e.g., by modifying the distribution of roles or by splitting tasks into subtasks). Teachers and students are granted flexibility in selecting new tools that become relevant for their activity (Dillenbourg & Tchounikine, 2007). Ideally, instructional support and structure should be interpreted as a combination of pre-structuring activities, such as task design, and the teacher's reactive support and monitoring activities.

The role of the teacher recently has been interpreted as that of a conductor who orchestrates the designed activities, integrates them into the overall classroom activity, changes them on the fly, and coordinates supportive interventions across multiple learning activities (Fischer & Dillenbourg, 2006). According to Dillenbourg and Jermann (2006), *integrated learning* refers to this intertwining of computerized activities (Web 2.0 tools, mobile devices, simulations) with face-to-face activities (small-group work, lectures, field trips). These activities are integrated together with the aid of a pedagogical script that may include activities from multiple social levels (individual, group, classroom). Instead of focusing purely on either individual use of learning technology or computer-supported collaborative learning, we should shift to integrating all activities that are relevant to the intended learning objectives (Dillenbourg & Jermann, 2006). At its best, the teacher's role in this process involves coordinating activities at various social, contextual, and media-based levels, as well as providing scaffolding at different social levels.

In the optimal situation, scripts could be gradually faded in or out, depending on the needs of learners and the degree of scaffolding needed (Kollar, Fischer, & Hesse, 2006; Kobbe et al., 2007). The teacher's role is crucial in the determination of how and when external scripts should be gradually replaced by self-regulation. Furthermore, as our

SCORE results indicated, several challenges in scripted collaboration involve social and emotional aspects. In the future, socioemotional regulation could perhaps be embedded into scripts in order to increase the probability of engaging students in productive collaboration processes. However, this presupposes the integration of research on socioemotional regulation (Järvenoja & Järvelä, in press) with research on collaboration scripts. In addition to focusing on research in these areas, it remains important to develop tools to support teachers in monitoring scripted activities (Arvaja, Hämäläinen, & Rasku-Puttonen, 2009). Although we have presented a number of challenges for scripted collaboration in this chapter, we believe that directing future research and development work toward scripts as flexible resources, meant to be integrated into the wider learning context, has the potential to support situated collaboration and knowledge construction.

ACKNOWLEDGMENT

This research was supported by the Academy of Finland (Projects 121097 & 108488).

REFERENCES

Aronson, E., Blaney, N., Sikes, J., Stephan, C., & Snapp, M. (1978). *The jigsaw classroom*. Beverly Hills, CA: Sage.

Arvaja, M. (2007). Contextual perspective in analysing collaborative knowledge construction of two small groups in Web-based discussion. *Int. Jrnl. of Computer-Supported Collaborative Learning*, *2*(2/3), 133–158. doi:10.1007/s11412-007-9013-5

Arvaja, M., & Hämäläinen, R. (2008). Collaborative knowledge construction during structured tasks in an online course at higher education context. In G. Ollington (Ed.), *Teachers and teaching: Strategies, innovations and problem solving*. New York: Nova Science.

Arvaja, M., Hämäläinen, R., & Rasku-Puttonen, H. (2009). Challenges for the teacher's role in promoting productive knowledge construction in computer-supported collaborative learning contexts. In J. O. Lindberg & A. D. Olofsson (Eds.), *Online Learning Communities and Teacher Professional Development: Methods for Improved Education Delivery* (pp. 263-280). Hershey, PA: IGI Global.

Arvaja, M., Rasku-Puttonen, H., Häkkinen, P., & Eteläpelto, A. (2003). Constructing knowledge through a role-play in a Web-based learning environment. *Journal of Educational Computing Research*, *28*(4), 319–341. doi:10.2190/4FAV-EK1T-XV4H-YNXF

Arvaja, M., Salovaara, H., Häkkinen, P., & Järvelä, S. (2007). Combining individual and group-level perspectives for studying collaborative knowledge construction in context. *Learning and Instruction*, *17*(4), 448–459. doi:10.1016/j.learninstruc.2007.04.003

Baker, M. (2002). Forms of cooperation in dyadic problem-solving. In P. Salembier & H. Benchekroun (Eds.). *Socio-technical systems: Vol. 16. Cooperation and complexity* (pp. 587–620). Paris: Hermès.

Baker, M. (2003). Computer-mediated argumentative interactions for the co-elaboration of scientific notions. In J. Andriessen, M. Baker, & D. Suthers (Eds.), *Arguing to learn: Confronting cognitions in computer-supported collaborative learning environments* (pp. 1–25). Dordrecht, the Netherlands: Kluwer Academic.

Brown, J. S., Collins, A., & Duguid, P. (1989). Situated cognition and the culture of learning. *Educational Researcher*, *18*, 32–42.

Cohen, E. (1994). Restructuring the classroom: Conditions for productive small groups. *Review of Educational Research*, *64*(1), 1–35.

Dillenbourg, P. (1999). Introduction: What do you mean by collaborative learning? In P. Dillenbourg (Ed.), *Collaborative learning: Cognitive and computational approaches* (pp. 1–19). Oxford, UK: Pergamon.

Dillenbourg, P. (2002). Over-scripting CSCL: The risks of blending collaborative learning with instructional design. In P. A. Kirschner (Ed.), *Three worlds of CSCL: Can we support CSCL?* (pp. 61–91). Heerlen, The Netherlands: Open Universiteit Nederland.

Dillenbourg, P., & Jermann, P. (2006). Designing integrative scripts. In F. Fischer, H. Mandl, J. Haake, & I. Kollar (Eds.), *Scripting computer-supported collaborative learning: Cognitive, computational and educational perspectives* (pp. 275–301). New York: Springer.

Dillenbourg, P., & Tchounikine, P. (2007). Flexibility in macro-scripts for computer-supported collaborative learning. *Journal of Computer Assisted Learning, 23*(1), 1–13. doi:10.1111/j.1365-2729.2007.00191.x

Doise, W. (1985). Social regulations in cognitive development. In R. Hinde, A.-N. Perret-Clermont, & J. Stevenson-Hinde (Eds.), *Social relationships and cognitive development* (pp. 294–308). Oxford, UK: Oxford University Press.

Fischer, F., & Dillenbourg, P. (2006). *Challenges of orchestrating computer-supported collaborative learning*. Paper presented at the 87th annual meeting of the American Educational Research Association (AERA), San Francisco, CA.

Fischer, F., & Mandl, H. (2005). Knowledge convergence in computer-supported collaborative learning—the role of external representation tools. *Journal of the Learning Sciences, 14*(3), 405–441. doi:10.1207/s15327809jls1403_3

Häkkinen, P., Arvaja, M., & Mäkitalo, K. (2004). Prerequisites for CSCL: Research approaches, methodological challenges and pedagogical development. In K. Littleton, D. Faulkner, & D. Miell (Eds.), *Learning to collaborate and collaborating to learn* (pp. 161–175). New York: Nova Science.

Häkkinen, P., & Järvelä, S. (2006). Sharing and constructing perspectives in Web-based conferencing. *Computers & Education, 47*(1/2), 433–447. doi:10.1016/j.compedu.2004.10.015

Hämäläinen, R. (2008). *Designing and investigating pedagogical scripts to facilitate computer-supported collaborative learning*. University of Jyväskylä, Finnish Institute for Educational Research.

Hämäläinen, R., & Arvaja, M. (2009). Scripted collaboration and group-based variations in a higher education CSCL context. *Scandinavian Journal of Educational Research, 53*(1), 1–16. doi:10.1080/00313830802628281

Hämäläinen, R., & Häkkinen, P. (in press). Teacher's instructional planning for computer-supported collaborative learning: Macro-scripts as a pedagogical method to facilitate collaborative learning. *Teaching and Teacher Education*.

Hämäläinen, R., Manninen, T., Järvelä, S., & Häkkinen, P. (2006). Learning to collaborate: Designing collaboration in a 3-D game environment. *The Internet and Higher Education, 9*(1), 47–61. doi:10.1016/j.iheduc.2005.12.004

Hämäläinen, R., Oksanen, K., & Häkkinen, P. (2008). Designing and analyzing collaboration in a scripted game for vocational education. *Computers in Human Behavior, 24*(6), 2496–2506. doi:10.1016/j.chb.2008.03.010

Hmelo-Silver, C. (2003). Analyzing collaborative knowledge construction: Multiple methods for integrated understanding. *Computers & Education, 41*, 397–420. doi:10.1016/j.compedu.2003.07.001

Järvelä, S., & Häkkinen, P. (2002). Web-based cases in teaching and learning—the quality of discussion and a stage of perspective taking in asynchronous communication. *Interactive Learning Environments, 10*(1), 1–22. doi:10.1076/ilee.10.1.1.3613

Järvelä, S., Veermans, M., & Leinonen, P. (2008). Investigating student engagement in computer-supported inquiry: A process-oriented analysis. *Social Psychology of Education, 11*, 299–322. doi:10.1007/s11218-007-9047-6

Järvenoja, H., & Järvelä, S. (in press). Emotion control in collaborative learning situations: Do students regulate emotions evoked from social challenges? *The British Journal of Educational Psychology*.

Jeong, H., & Chi, M. T. H. (2007). Knowledge convergence during collaborative learning. *Instructional Science, 35*, 287–315. doi:10.1007/s11251-006-9008-z

Kerr, N. L., & Bruun, S. E. (1983). Dispensability of member effort and group motivation losses: Free rider effects. *Journal of Personality and Social Psychology, 44*, 78–94. doi:10.1037/0022-3514.44.1.78

Kneser, C., & Ploetzner, R. (2001). Collaboration on the basis of complementary domain knowledge: Observed dialogue structures and their relation to learning success. *Learning and Instruction, 11*(1), 53–83. doi:10.1016/S0959-4752(00)00015-3

Kobbe, L., Weinberger, A., Dillenbourg, P., Harrer, A., Hämäläinen, R., Häkkinen, P., & Fischer, F. (2007). Specifying computer-supported collaboration scripts. *International Journal of Computer-Supported Collaborative Learning, 2*(2/3), 211–234. doi:10.1007/s11412-007-9014-4

Kollar, I., Fischer, F., & Hesse, F. W. (2003). Cooperation scripts for computer-supported collaborative learning. In B. Wasson, R. Baggetun, U. Hoppe, & S. Ludvigsen (Eds.), *Proceedings of the International Conference on Computer Support for Collaborative Learning: CSCL 2003 Community Events—Communication and Interaction* (pp. 59–61). Bergen, Norway: InterMedia.

Kopp, B., Schnurer, K., & Mandl, H. (2006). Collaborative learning in virtual seminars: Evaluation data and process-product-analyses. In V. Uskov (Ed.), *Proceedings of computers and advanced technology in education* (pp. 528–811). Calgary, Canada: Acta.

Lipponen, L. (2001). *Computer-supported collaborative learning: From promises to reality*. Unpublished doctoral dissertation, University of Turku.

Lipponen, L., Hakkarainen, K., & Paavola, S. (2004). Practices and orientations of CSCL. In J.-W. Strijbos, P. Kirschner, R. Martens & P. Dillenbourg (Eds.), *What we know about CSCL and implementing it in higher education* (pp. 31–59). Norwell, MA: Kluwer Academic.

Mäkitalo, K., Häkkinen, P., Leinonen, P., & Järvelä, S. (2002). Mechanisms of common ground in case-based Web-discussions in teacher education. *The Internet and Higher Education, 5*(3), 247–265. doi:10.1016/S1096-7516(02)00112-4

Mäkitalo, K., Weinberger, A., Häkkinen, P., Järvelä, S., & Fischer, F. (2005). Epistemic cooperation scripts in online learning environments: Fostering learning by reducing uncertainty in discourse. *Computers in Human Behavior, 21*(4), 603–622. doi:10.1016/j.chb.2004.10.033

Mercer, N. (1996). The quality of talk in children's collaborative activity in classroom. *Learning and Instruction, 6*(4), 359–377. doi:10.1016/S0959-4752(96)00021-7

Miyake, N., Masukawa, H., & Shirouzou, H. (2001). The complex jigsaw as an enhancer of collaborative knowledge building in undergraduate introductory science courses. In P. Dillenbourg, A. Eurelings, & K. Hakkarainen (Eds.), *European perspectives on computer-supported collaborative learning: Proceedings of the 1st European Conference on Computer-Supported Collaborative Learning* (pp. 454–461). Maastricht: Maastricht University.

O'Donnell, A. M. (1999). Structuring dyadic interaction through scripted cooperation. In A.M. O'Donnell & A. King (Eds.), *Cognitive perspectives on peer learning* (pp.179–196). Mahwah, NJ: Erlbaum.

Oliver, M., & Shaw, G. (2003). Asynchronous discussion in support of medical education. *Journal of Asynchronous Learning Networks, 7*(1), 56–67.

Palincsar, A., & Brown, A. (1984). Reciprocal teaching of comprehension-fostering and comprehension-monitoring activities. *Cognition and Instruction, 1*(2), 117–175. doi:10.1207/s1532690xci0102_1

Perkins, D. (1993). Person-plus: A distributed view of thinking and learning. In G. Salomon (Ed.), *Distributed cognitions: Psychological and educational considerations* (pp. 88–110). New York: Cambridge University Press.

Pöysä, J. (2006). University students' experiences in the early phases of community building in virtual learning environment: The contents of shared intellectual activity. In C. Clarebout & J. Elen (Eds.), *Avoiding simplicity, confronting complexity: Advances in studying and designing (computer-based) powerful learning environments* (pp. 255–264). Rotterdam, Germany: Sense.

Roschelle, J., & Teasley, S. (1995). The construction of shared knowledge in collaborative problem solving. In C. O'Malley (Ed.), *NATO ASO Series F: Computer and System Sciences, Vol. 128. Computer supported collaborative learning* (pp. 69–97). Berlin, Germany: Springer-Verlag.

Schellens, T., & Valcke, M. (2005). Collaborative learning in asynchronous discussion groups: What about the impact on cognitive processing? *Computers in Human Behavior, 21*, 957–975. doi:10.1016/j.chb.2004.02.025

Simon, H. A. (1973). The structure of ill-structured problems. *Artificial Intelligence, 4*, 181–204. doi:10.1016/0004-3702(73)90011-8

Stahl, G. (2006). Scripting group cognition: The problem of guiding situated collaboration. In F. Fischer, H. Mandl, J. Haake, & I. Kollar (Eds.), *Scripting computer-supported collaborative learning: Cognitive, computational and educational perspectives*. Dordrecht, the Netherlands: Kluwer-Springer Verlag.

Stegmann, K., Weinberger, A., Fischer, F., & Mandl, H. (2005). Scripting argumentation in computer-supported learning environments. In P. Gerjets, P. A. Kirschner, J. Elen, & R. Joiner (Eds.), *Instructional design for effective and enjoyable computer-supported learning. Proceedings of the first joint meeting of the EARLI SIGs "Instructional Design" and "Learning and Instruction with Computers"* (pp. 320–330) [CD-ROM]. Tübingen, Germany: Knowledge Media Research Center.

Strijbos, J. W., & De Laat, M. F. (2007). Prototypical roles in computer-supported collaborative learning: A conceptual framework for the design of a tool for teachers. In J. W. Strijbos & A. Weinberger (Chairs), *Facilitating and analyzing roles in computer-supported collaborative learning, Symposium conducted at the 12th biennial EARLI conference*, Budapest, Hungary.

van Boxtel, C., van der Linden, J., & Kanselaar, G. (2000). Collaborative learning tasks and the elaboration of conceptual knowledge. *Learning and Instruction*, *10*(4), 311–330. doi:10.1016/S0959-4752(00)00002-5

Volet, S., Summers, M., & Thurman, J. (in press). High-level co-regulation in collaborative learning: How does it emerge and how is it sustained? *Learning and Instruction*.

Vonderwell, S. (2003). An examination of asynchronous communication experiences and perspectives of students in an online course: A case study. *The Internet and Higher Education*, *6*(1), 77–90. doi:10.1016/S1096-7516(02)00164-1

Webb, N., & Palincsar, A. (1996). Group processes in the classroom. In D. Berliner & R. Calfee (Eds.), *Handbook of educational psychology* (pp. 841–873). New York: Simon & Schuster Macmillan.

Weinberger, A., Ertl, B., Fischer, F., & Mandl, H. (2005). Epistemic and social scripts in computer-supported collaborative learning. *Instructional Science*, *33*(1), 1–30. doi:10.1007/s11251-004-2322-4

Weinberger, A., & Fischer, F. (2006). A framework to analyze argumentative knowledge construction in computer-supported collaborative learning. *Computers & Education*, *46*, 71–95. doi:10.1016/j.compedu.2005.04.003

Zualkernan, I. (2006). A framework and a methodology for developing authentic constructivist e-learning environments. *Educational Technology & Society*, *9*(2), 198–212.

Chapter 11
Supporting Collaboration and Communication in Videoconferences

Manuela Paechter
Karl-Franzens-University Graz, Austria

Mareike Kreisler
Karl-Franzens-University Graz, Austria

Brigitte Maier
Karl-Franzens-University Graz, Austria

ABSTRACT

Working together in a group may lead to advantages such as a higher task performance, gains in individual knowledge or social skills, or a higher motivation. In many situations of our daily life, the members of a group cannot meet face-to-face to work together but have to rely on communication media. This paper focuses on collaboration with the support of specific communication media, namely videoconferences. Two empirical studies will be described. The first study shows that groups which communicate via videoconferences for solving a task can achieve the same results as face-to-face groups. In order to achieve results equivalent to face-to-face groups, videoconference groups have to adapt their communication behavior to the specific characteristics of videoconferences. In the second study presented in this chapter, different trainings for collaboration in videoconferences will be investigated. One of the trainings in which students learned rules for collaborative problem-solving proved to be successful: Students who had obtained such a training achieved better problem solutions than students without a training.

INTRODUCTION

Computer networks bring people together who otherwise would not be able to communicate and collaborate with each other. Over the last years, computer-mediated communication tools have also become more and more powerful. Technologies such as videoconferences provide a communication setting that closely resembles face-to-face communication allowing team members to see each other, to listen and to talk to each other. Yet, little is known about how people organize their communication and collaboration in such a communication setting.

DOI: 10.4018/978-1-61520-729-9.ch011

At the beginning of this chapter, a framework of communication media will be described. Then, the advantages and a model of collaboration in communities of practice or communities of learners will be discussed. In the following parts of the chapter, two studies on communication and collaboration in videoconferences are introduced. The first study focuses on group performance and communication in videoconferences compared to face-to-face settings. It investigates whether and how group members adapt their communication behavior to different communication settings. The second study investigates how communication and collaboration in videoconferences can be supported by a training of group members. Different trainings and their effects on group performance in videoconferences will be described.

COMMUNICATION WITH MEDIA

Communication can be understood as an ongoing process of coordination and interaction which may serve many purposes: Developing an impression of each other, exchanging information, working together, giving mutual support, etc. It can be regarded as a collective activity in which the participants have to coordinate on content as well as on process. The communication partners continually ensure that they are attending to, hearing, and trying to understand what a communication partner is saying. Therefore, they use means such as positive or negative evidences, visual and verbal back-channeling cues, or references to former contributions. In this way they ensure a common ground of mutual understanding (Clark & Brennan, 1996).

Communication partners try to minimize their collaborative effort to ensure understanding. They behave economically and try to invest only as much effort as necessary while being as clear and informative as possible. Clark and Brennan (1996, p. 135) describe this behavior as the principle of the "least collaborative effort". The effort that is needed to ensure mutual understanding may change with the communication medium. Communication behavior that can be applied efficiently in one medium may not be applicable in another one or may cost more effort. Media vary on different dimensions that influence communication behavior.

Various theories of communication with media agree on several media characteristics that may influence the communication between two people or a group of people (Clark & Brennan, 1996; Dennis & Valacich, 1999):

- *Copresence* describes whether the communication partners share the same physical environment (as in a face-to-face communication). In a shared environment, the communication partners can carry out actions together, e.g., pointing to or manipulating an object.
- *Visibility* describes whether the communication partners can see each other (as in a face-to-face communication or in videoconferences).
- *Audibility* describes whether the communication partners can hear each other and take note of paraverbal cues such as intonation. In communication settings in which the communication partners cannot talk to each other they have to rely on written communication.
- *Synchronicity* (also cotemporality) describes whether there is a delay between the production of a message and its arrival at the recipient. E.g., in a face-to-face communication, a contribution is produced just about when it is received and understood, without delay. In e-mail conversation, messages may arrive only some time after their production.
- *Simultaneity* describes whether messages can be sent and received by different communication partners at once. E.g., in a chat, a communication partner may compose a

Figure 1. Characteristics of face-to-face, videoconference and chat communication

	Face-to-face communication	Videoconference communication	Chat communication
Copresence	X	--	--
Visibility	X	X (with constraints)	--
Audibility	X	X	--
Synchronicity	X	X	X
Simultaneity	X	X	X
Sequentiality	X	X	--
Reviewability	--	--	X
Revisability	--	--	X

message while receiving one. In face-to-face communication, messages can also be sent and received simultaneously when a communication partners gives a nonverbal information (e.g., by smiling) while listening to the utterance of a communication partner.

- *Sequentiality* describes whether the turns of the communication partners may get out of sequence. E.g., in face-to-face communication, turns usually form a sequence that does not include intervening turns from other conversations. In chat communication, turn-taking may be impaired because the communication partners are writing messages simultaneously and have no means to coordinate the sequence of messages.
- *Reviewability* describes whether contributions are recorded and can be reviewed later by one of the communication partners. E.g., in e-mail conversation, messages can be recorded whereas in spoken communication settings (e.g., face-to-face communication, videoconferences) contributions usually are not recorded.
- *Revisability* describes whether a person can revise her or his contributions before sending it to another person. In most written communication settings (e.g., e-mail), messages can be revised.

Every communication setting can be described by a unique profile of these eight characteristics. Figure 1 gives an overview of the characteristics of three settings, face-to-face, videoconference, and chat communication.

At first sight, communication in videoconferences seems to resemble face-to-face communication to a high degree. In both communication settings the communication partners can see each other and speak to each other (visibility and audibility). There is no delay between the production and the reception of a message (synchronicity).

Yet, face-to-face communication and videoconference communication differ in many aspects from each other. In videoconferences, the communication partners do not share the same physical environment (copresence). This may lead to constraints in communication and interaction, e.g., when a person wants to demonstrate an action or a manipulation of an object to another person. E.g., constraints in visibility may occur in desktop videoconferences when mainly the face of the partner is filmed (similar to a portrait). In that case, only cues about the facial expression and upper body movements can be conveyed whereas cues about specific gestures or posture are missing in the communication. Besides, it is not possible to look at someone as a way of designating 'you', an important means for coordinating turn-taking or for indicating one's attention to a speaker.

These differences between communication settings do not mean that communication and collaboration are inevitably impaired in a specific setting. Communication settings can be described by a profile of various characteristics which may encompass facilitations as well as impairments for communication. However, not only features that are inherent to media influence collaborative learning and working; also the users' experience or their motivation to use a medium may have an influence. In media based communication (Bruinsma, 2004), the media users obtain a crucial role. They may adapt their behavior to the respective communication setting and develop new routines in order to ensure an effective and pleasant collaboration (Cohen, 1984; Cornelius & Boos, 2003; Dickey, Wasko, Chudoba, & Thatcher, 2006).

COMMUNICATION AND COLLABORATION IN GROUPS

In many situations of their daily lives people rely on the collaboration with others: Students at school or at university acquire knowledge together or colleagues in a company work together on a new product. When groups collaborate for a longer period of time one also speaks of "communities of practice" (Wenger, 1998, p. 5).

A community of practice can be described by three characteristics: (1) Community, i.e. a set of people who interact and communicate with each other and who develop relationships with each other in the ongoing process of interaction; (2) domain, i.e. a specific area of knowledge or expertise that the members of a community share; and (3) practice, i.e. routines of working on tasks and problems in the respective domain which develop over time (DeCagna, 2001; Wenger, 1998, 2001). Such a community can also be concerned with constructing and sharing knowledge and, in that case, is called a community of learning. Communities of learning may be regarded as a special form of communities of practice, namely communities whose practice is learning itself (Zieger & Pulichino, 2004).

In comparison to a person who learns or works alone on a task a community of practice or a community of learning may experience different benefits (Jucks, Paechter, & Tatar, 2003):

- **Higher performance:** A group may achieve a higher performance than a single person or than all group members working individually. There are different explanations for this advantage. A group of several people usually has a wider range of knowledge and skills at its disposal than a single person. This explanation emphasizes the cognitive resources of a group and its members. Another explanation concerns the motivation and the commitment of the group members. When the group members share their knowledge and motivate each other they may perform better than the same number of people working individually.

- **Gains in individual knowledge and skills:** Through collaboration group members may acquire a deeper knowledge that incorporates multiple perspectives (Ertl, Fischer, & Mandl, 2006). There are different explanations for this effect. Vygotsky (1978, 1986) assumes that less knowledgeable group members learn from more knowledgeable ones. He defines a zone of proximal development, i.e. the distance between the actual individual development level and the level of potential development, which can be reached through problem-solving under the guidance of an experienced person or a more capable group member. In contrast to this explanation, Wittrock (1978) places more emphasis on the individual group members' activities. In the process of explaining issues or demonstrating their skills to others, a person must engage in cognitive structuring, restructuring, or elaboration and develops a more elaborated and deeper knowledge.

- **Development of social skills (Webb, 1992):** If a group's success relies on successful learning and on the commitment of the individual members the group members' activities should focus on helping each other, explaining concepts to each other, and encouraging each other to achieve. In the process of working together, supportive social behavior can be learned (Slavin, 1992).

- **Gains in motivation:** Cohen (1986) assumes that when faced with challenging and interesting tasks, group members will experience the process of group work itself as highly rewarding. Group work may increase an individual member's motivation and raise his or her efforts to achieve.

These considerations indicate various advantages of collaboration. Especially, when groups work together for a longer time period and when they form a community of practice they may experience these advantages.

Yet, collaboration does not work by itself. Simply placing individuals into groups and telling them to work together does not create the effective conditions that result in the aforementioned advantages of collaboration. Communities of practice and communities of learning may also encounter difficulties in collaboration: Members of a community may experience a lack of motivation and therefore only few members take part in joint learning or working activities (Reimer, 2001; Renkl & Mandl, 1995); They may also experience problems in communication and collaboration which may lead to inefficiencies in achievement, e.g., when the members of a community do not share their knowledge or when they do not succeed in coordinating their joint activities (Paechter, 2003).

Whether the advantages of collaboration can be realized or not depends also strongly on how the group members structure the exchange of information and the collaboration (Resnick,

1991). Research on the communication in a group assumes that certain communication contents are indicators for the cognitive processes that take place in the speaker and manifest themselves in the talk during the interaction (Chinn, O'Donnell, & Jinks, 2000). In their communication, the group members share information, connect pieces of information, draw conclusions, decide on a task solution, etc. (Costa & O'Leary, 1992). Typically, studies on communication and collaboration investigated the frequency of specific contributions in communication and its relation to group outcomes such as performance or individual knowledge acquisition. Among other aspects, a group's performance is related to the frequency of contributions in which information is elaborated (conclusions, connections of pieces of information, etc; Webb, 1992).

When working together on a task different cognitive processes have to be performed by the group members and to be manifested in the communication. Therefore, an analysis of the communication in a group should consider the complexity and variety of cognitive processes and of discourse contributions. Collaboration and communication in a group can be described from the viewpoint of problem-solving (Larson & Christensen, 1993; Paechter, 2003). Such group-level problem-solving goes beyond individual problem-solving. It requires social cognition in the sense that individuals communicate their perceptions and cognitions and that they coordinate their joint activities (Gruenfeld & Hollingshead, 1993; Ickes & Gonzales, 1996).

Different cognitive processes have to be carried out by the group and to be brought into group discussion (Hirokawa, 1990):

- **Identification and definition of a problem or a task:** At the beginning of their collaboration, groups may have to start with the identification of a problem or a task and its conceptualization. They have to identify and define the starting conditions and task objectives. It is especially important that the group members develop a shared understanding about the task and the objectives they want to achieve in their collaboration (Paechter, 2003). Sometimes, however, the task and its objectives can already be outlined for the group members, e.g., in a learning situations such as a university seminar.

- **Collecting and conveying task-relevant information:** When working together on a task the group members have to collect and to distribute information that might be relevant for task solution. In collecting task-relevant information groups can be more efficient than a single person as they dispose of more resources such as temporal resources or cognitive resources and skills (Argote, Gruenfeld, & Naqin, 2001).

Groups, however, also show limitations in their communication and interaction. Such limitations mainly concern the conveyance of information. In their communication, group members often refer to information which is already known to each group member, i.e. shared information (Wittenbaum & Stasser, 1996). Often information that is only known to one or a few group members, i.e. unshared information, is not mentioned in the group discourse. Even if unshared information is mentioned it has fewer chances to be picked up again in the ongoing discourse.

- **Elaboration and structuring of information:** In order to solve a task it is usually not sufficient just to collect information. Different pieces of information have to be combined together, to be elaborated, to be structured, and to be applied to the task. The group members have to develop a joint understanding and an appropriate representation of the task and possible solution paths (Gruenfeld & Hollingshead, 1993; Resnick, Salmon, Zeitz, Wathen, &

Holowchak, 1993). Communication plays an important role in that process. In various investigations, the complexity of the group members' contributions influenced the quality of the task solution (Peterson & Swing, 1985; Webb, 1982, 1992). Especially metacognitive contributions such as plans or evaluations of possible solutions paths are important for task solution. Often, however, groups show deficits in their communication processes. They discuss information on a rather superficial level, do not develop a shared representation of the task and possible solution paths, or fail to evaluate the quality of task relevant information (Costa & O'Leary, 1992).

- **Coordination of the communication and the task execution:** Collaboration in a group is more complex than individual task completion because it requires the coordination of the resources and activities of different group members. In the ongoing process of communication, the group members have to coordinate the exchange and elaboration of information, they have to identify personal skills and resources and to decide how to solve the task (Kraut, Egido, & Galegher, 1990). The success of collaboration also depends on the group's accumulation of information about the individual knowledge and skills of its members. Based on this information, tasks can be allocated to single group members according to their specific knowledge and skills (Cooke, Salas, Cannon-Bowers, & Stout, 2000). In an ongoing process of collaboration the coordination of the group members needs less explicit verbalization. Successful groups develop tacit coordination routines and are able to coordinate the group members' actions implicitly without verbalization (Wittenbaum, Stasser, & Merry, 1996; Michinov, & Michinov, 2009).

Figure 2. Communication in groups

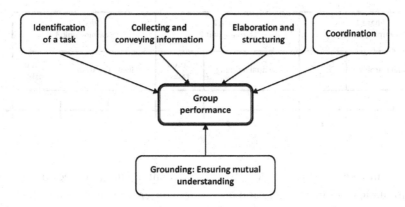

This description offers a categorization scheme for a group's task-oriented communication processes. Discourse contributions of the group members can be assigned to the categories described above. It can be analyzed how discourse contributions in different categories contribute to group outcomes such as individual gains in knowledge or group performance.

Up to now, however, communication and collaboration have been described from the viewpoint of task-related processes that take place in a group and that are represented in the communication. These processes depend on a basic requirement, namely the group members' mutual understanding of each other's concepts and contributions. It is essential for a communication process that the members maintain and ensure a mutual understanding.

Group members who work together on a task may have to meet several basic requirements in their communication processes: They may have to outline the task and possible solution paths. They have to exchange and to elaborate information that is needed for the solution of the group task. They have to coordinate the activities and contributions of the group members. Additionally, they have to ensure a common ground throughout their communication. From these assumptions the above model of communication in task-oriented groups can be derived (cf. Figure 1). It explains which requirements have to be met if groups are exchanging knowledge and working together.

A STUDY ON COLLABORATION IN VIDEOCONFERENCES

In an empirical long-term study, we investigated how learners organize communication and collaboration in different types of communication settings over a range of several group meetings (Paechter, 2003).

Four communication settings which differ with regard to the media characteristics of synchronicity, audibility, and copresence were investigated: Newsgroups, chats, videoconferences, and face-to-face settings. Newsgroups can be characterized as asynchronous, written communication without copresence of the communication partners, chats as synchronous, written communication without copresence, videoconferences as synchronous, spoken communication without copresence, and face-to-face communication as synchronous, spoken communication with copresence of the communication partners. In this paper, we will focus on the investigation of videoconferences and face-to-face settings. These settings are very similar to each other as the participants may talk to each other and can see each other. They, however, differ with regard to copresence and partly to

Figure 3. Time schedule of the online seminar

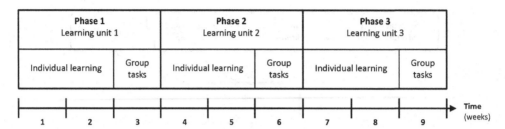

visibility of the communication partners. A comparison of the communication and cooperation in both settings may render useful information how small differences in two communication settings may influence the behavior of group members.

Two research questions were investigated: Is there a difference between academic work performance of groups in videoconferences and in face-to-face settings? How important are various discourse contributions for academic work performance in videoconferences and face-to-face settings?

Research Design of the Study

The study was carried out in an online seminar, an introduction into the Psychology of Learning, at the University of the Federal Armed Forces, Munich (Germany). Altogether, 96 male students, all German, took part. The students were between 20 and 26 years old (mean=21.87) and studied different subjects (business administration, computer sciences, education, engineering, and others). All students were in their first academic year and had no prior knowledge of the seminar subjects. They were obliged to attend the online seminar as part of their studies. In the seminar, all students were assigned to groups of four people who worked together for one term (three months). Students who had been assigned to a group did not know each other before the start of the study. The groups were randomly assigned to one of the four communication settings.

There were six groups (24 students) who met via a videoconference and six groups (24

students) who met face-to-face. Students in videoconferences used a desktop videoconference. Each group member worked separately at his computer and was connected to the others by a headset and microphone. Thus, the group members could talk to each other and see each other. Besides, six groups met in a newsgroup and six in a chat setting. The results of these groups are not reported in our paper.

All groups received online hypertexts as learning material. The learning material varied within a group: Partly, all group members received the same hypertexts (shared material), partly the group members received different hypertexts which referred to a common topic (unshared material; e.g., different theories to a specific research question). The hypertext material covered different topics of Cognitive Psychology and Psychology of Learning (knowledge structures, learning with text material, learning with pictures). Unshared learning material could consist of different aspects of a theory or of a practical problem (e.g. different material on the functions of pictures for learning).

The groups had to answer questions about the learning contents and to solve tasks. The questions and tasks differed with regard to their complexity. They could demand the recall of learning contents (e.g., to give the name of a theory), the elaboration and combination of learning contents (e.g, to explain the differences between two theories), the application of knowledge, or the development of new models and theories based on the learning contents (e.g., to develop a model that explains the functions of pictures for learning). All tasks required that the groups described their answers in an essay which could be one or few sentences or several paragraphs long. The tasks referred to the shared and to the unshared learning material. In the case of unshared material, achievement in a group depended on the degree to which the group members succeeded in exchanging their knowledge and developing a shared understanding of the learning contents. The videoconference groups used a shared document space for the composition of their essays. The face-to-face groups met in a seminar room of the university and used a notebook for the composition of their essays.

With regard to its time schedule, the seminar was divided into three phases of which each lasted three weeks. In each phase, a hypertext learning unit with shared and unshared material was distributed to the students. After distribution, each student had two weeks time to study the learning material alone. In the third week, the students met in their group and solved a set of tasks (cf. Figure 3).

RESULTS

In order to determine group performance, the essays were analyzed by a content analysis. For each essay, the number of correct arguments was determined. An argument could be a repetition from the learning material, a new idea, a combination of two ideas, a conclusion, etc. The number of arguments in an essay was compared to the total amount of possible arguments which had been determined beforehand by experienced raters. Then the percentage of arguments in all essays compared to all possible arguments was calculated. For the analyses reported here, the mean percentage of all group essays which the students finished in their three meeting was calculated. Besides, the time needed for completion of the group tasks was recorded (minutes).

A multivariate analysis of variance was carried out to investigate whether performance or time needed for task completion differed in videocon-

ferences and face-to-face settings. The analysis showed no differences between both groups ($p \geq 0.05$). On an average, the mean percentage of arguments was 35.12% in videoconferences and 37.79% in face-to-face settings. There were no differences with regard to the time needed for task completion. On an average, videoconference groups needed 53.76 minutes and face-to-face groups 58.31 minutes for task completion.

All group meetings had been recorded on videotape so that the contents, number, and percentages of discourse contributions could be determined. Two aspects of communication and collaboration were investigated, namely ensuring mutual understanding and the organization of the collaboration in the groups' discourse.

Ensuring mutual understanding by references: One possibility to indicate and to ensure mutual understanding in a group discussion is to establish coherence (Tomlin, Forrest, Pu, & Kim, 1997). In a content analysis, each group member's contributions were analyzed whether they contained a reference to one of the last five discourse contributions. The group members could make different kinds of references: They could refer to a former contribution by giving the name of the speaker, by repeating a sequence or a whole discourse contribution, by asking a question, or by giving an answer. It was recorded how many contributions a group member made in a meeting and how many of these contributions contained a reference to a former contribution. For each group member, the percentage of references in comparison to his total number of contributions was calculated. In this paper, the mean percentage of references in all three meetings is used.

Communication processes with regard to collaboration: All discourse contributions were analyzed and, if possible, allocated to one of the following categories.

- **Conveyance of information:** A contribution was coded into that category if a group

Figure 4. Percentage/frequency of discourse contributions (mean of all group meetings)

	Videoconferences	Face-to-face setting
Explicit references (%)	11.46%	7.53%
Conveyance of information [x]	41.62	54.03
Elaboration of information [x]	15.37	11.51
Coordination and task execution [x]	12.61	7.50

[x] number of contributions

Figure 5. Correlation between the percentage/frequency of contributions and group performance

	Videoconferences	Face-to-face setting
Explicit references (%)	-0.03 (0.08%)	-0.05 (0.25%)
Conveyance of information [x]	0.50 (24.60%) *	0.27 (7.51%)
Elaboration of information [x]	0.59 (34.61%) **	0.68 (46.93%) **
Coordination and task execution [x]	0.42 (17.98%) *	0.74 (54.88%) **

member described information in the learning material or asked for information

- **Elaboration of information:** Elaborations encompass a combination of arguments, an evaluation of arguments, conclusions, or solutions. They go beyond the description of information in the learning material.

- **Coordination and task execution:** These contributions refer to group resources such as the members' knowledge and skills or to the allocation of tasks to group members

Not all contributions in a group's discourse could be allocated to one of the three categories. In this paper, however, we report only the results of contributions referring to the framework of communication and collaboration described before. For each group member the frequency of contributions in the three categories was calculated. For the following analyses, the mean value of the frequency of contributions in all three meetings is used.

Figure 4 shows the mean values of the percentages respectively frequencies of contributions in videoconferences and face-to-face settings.

A univariate analysis of variance was calculated to investigate differences between videoconfer-

ences and face-to-face settings with regard to the percentage of references. No significant difference was found for this variable.

A multivariate analysis of variance for the last three discourse contributions showed a significant difference between videoconferences and face-to-face settings (Pillais $F(15, 270)=29.86$, $p \leq 0.01$). Videoconferences differ from face-to-face settings with regard to contributions concerning coordination and task execution. These topics are more often verbalized in videoconferences.

The importance of the different types of contributions for group performance was investigated by correlation analyses (cf. Figure 5).

Significant correlations were found for three variables, conveyance of information, elaboration of information, and coordination. As Figure 5 shows, the correlation coefficients differ in videoconferences and face-to-face settings. The contributions are of different importance in the two settings.

Discussion of the Results

Academic work performance in videoconferences did not differ from performance in face-to-face settings. Videoconferences were equally suitable

Figure 6. Design of the study (number of participants and groups)

		Coherence training			
		+	−		
Collaboration training	+	24 (8)	24 (8)	48 (16)	
	−	24 (8)	24 (8)	48 (16)	
		48 (16)	48 (16)	96 (32)	

as face-to-face settings for supporting collaboration of learners. It seems that the main characteristic which distinguishes videoconferences from face-to-face settings, namely copresence, has no influence on the groups' achievements.

Discourse in videoconferences and face-to-face settings differed with regard to the frequency of specific contributions. In videoconferences, coordination and task execution are more often verbalized than in face-to-face settings. Probably, this result can be explained by impairments in turn-taking in videoconferences. As eye gaze cannot be employed as means of indicating a turn the group members probably have to verbalize coordination in videoconferences more often than in face-to-face settings (e.g., in order to determine who of the group is to frame an answer).

The correlation analyses show the importance of different types of contributions for group performance. In videoconferences, the conveyance of information is especially important. This result can be explained by the distribution of discourse contributions in videoconferences. Compared to face-to-face settings, videoconference groups showed fewer contributions in which information was distributed: The mean number of contributions in which information is distributed is 41.62 in videoconferences and 54.03 in face-to-face settings. Probably, the group members were less redundant in videoconferences and, therefore, each contribution redounds highly to group achievement.

In our study, coherence was not correlated with group performance. Coherence, however, was only measured by references of one discourse contribution to a former one. Other means of establishing coherence could not be measured. For future investigation, it seems to be useful to consider further measures of coherence and to analyze their potential impact on videoconferences.

COMMUNICATION TRAININGS FOR COLLABORATION IN VIDEOCONFERENCES

Based on the empirical long-term study described before, different trainings for communication and collaboration in videoconferences were developed: a training for maintaining coherence and a training for collaboration in a problem-solving task (Kreisler, 2007).

Coherence training: Several studies emphasize the importance of coherence in computer-mediated communication (Cornelius, 2001; Cornelius & Boos, 2003; Schweizer, Paechter, & Weidenmann, 2007; Yom, Wilhelm, & Holzmüller, 2003). In videoconferences, coherence may be impaired because turn-taking cannot be coordinated by means of eye contact. Turn-taking, however, is important to structure a conversation and to facilitate coherence. An individual turn ideally relates locally to the previous turn, and globally to the discourse topic (Herring, 1999). In the coherence training, the communication partners learned rules which facilitate local and global coherence (Cornelius & Boos, 2003): to refer explicitly to a former contribution by using key words from that contribution or the last speaker's name, to ensure a joint understanding by inquiries, or to avoid deviations from the topic and side conversations.

Figure 7. Performance in the experimental conditions (mean values, standard deviation)

	Collaboration training	Coherence training	Combined training	Control group
Performance (max. 215 points)	202.75 (8.75)	191.38 (13.98)	197.50 (9.94)	183.88 (22.52)
Time on task (minutes)	19.88 (7.02)	20.88 (4.26)	21.38 (5.04)	20.38 (7.19)

Collaboration training: In our analyses of communication in videoconferences, three types of discourse contributions correlated positively with achievement in a group, specifically the conveyance of task-relevant information, the elaboration of information (e.g. drawing inferences or conclusions), and the coordination of the task execution. In the collaboration training, the communication partners learned rules which facilitate collaborative problem-solving: to collect task-related information in the group, to structure and to coordinate the task by dividing it into subtasks, or to determine steps necessary for a task solution.

Research Design of the Study

In an empirical study, we investigated how group members in a videoconference benefit from different trainings. A two-factorial design was chosen: Groups of three people received either a training for coherence, a training for collaborative problem-solving, a combined training for coherence and collaborative problem-solving, or no training at all (control group).

The study was carried out at Karl-Franzens University Graz (Austria). Altogether, 96 students took part in the study, all between 19 and 52 years old (mean=25). The majority studied Psychology (76%); 79 (82%) students were female, 17 (18%) were male. Students worked in groups of three, i.e., 32 groups took part in the study. Each group was allocated to one of the four experimental conditions.

At the beginning of the experiment, the groups received one of the three trainings and applied the

rules in a communication task in which they had to find out job-related characteristics of the group members and to discuss a specific topic. Students in the control group received no training but carried out the same communication tasks.

After the introductory training, all groups had to solve a complex problem-solving task which is typically used in assessment centers (Beitz & Loch, 1997). The task demanded to develop a time schedule for a person who has to carry out different activities at different places (e.g., obtaining a new passport, visiting a person in a hospital, going to the grocery). For the development of the time schedule, one had to take into account that the activities had to be carried out at different locations, that each activity needs a specific amount of time, and that all the activities had to be handled in a specific time. Task performance was analyzed by several criteria such as the number and the importance of activities that were considered in the time schedule, the order of the activities, time spent for the activities or overall time needed for accomplishment of the tasks. Overall performance was measured by the number of points which were given for fulfillment of the different criteria. The highest number of points was 215. The task was chosen as it is a standardized task which is widely employed for measuring performance in assessment centers.

Results

A multivariate analysis of variance with performance and time on task was carried out to investigate differences between the experimental groups. Even though the multivariate analysis was

Figure 8. Variation in performance in the experimental conditions

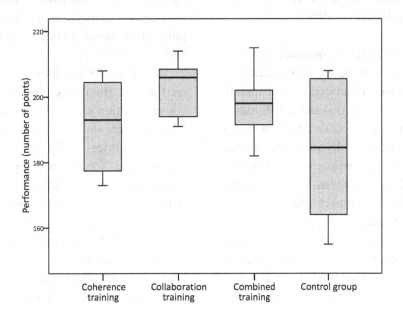

not significant (*F*(6, 56)=1.188, *n.s.*), the test of between-subject effects showed significant differences for group performance (*F*(3, 28)=2.416, *p*<.05). Groups with a collaboration training performed better than the control groups without training. The groups did not differ with regard to time on task.

A closer look at the performance in the experimental conditions reveals an especially interesting result with regard to the standard deviation in the experimental conditions (cf. Figure 8).

Performance varies most in the control condition. There are groups with a very high performance as well as groups with a very low performance. More or less the same applies for the coherence training condition which also shows a relatively high variation in performance. One may assume that there are groups which already use successful communication strategies whereas other groups use rather inefficient strategies. In the collaboration training condition and in the combined training condition, group performance is much more homogeneous and the mean performance values lie above those of the other two conditions.

Discussion of the Results

The results show that collaboration and problem-solving in videoconferences can be supported by a training of the group members. Groups with a collaboration training showed a higher performance than groups without a training. The collaboration training included rules concerning different communication strategies: collecting task-related information, structuring and coordinating the task by dividing it into subtasks, defining objectives and steps necessary for task solution, and developing a final solution. These processes that have to be carried out by the group and to be brought into group communication are essential for group performance (cf. Figure 2). Additionally, the results show large differences between the investigated groups: Some groups dispose of efficient communication and collaboration strategies whereas other groups dispose of rather inefficient strategies. Especially the latter groups benefit from a collaboration training to support their communication, collaboration, and consequently their performance.

CONCLUSION AND FUTURE RESEARCH DIRECTIONS

Based on previous results on computer-mediated communication and collaboration in groups, two empirical studies were described in this paper. In the first study, communication and collaboration in videoconferences were observed over a longer time period in an ecologically valid setting: Participants in a university seminar worked together over the course of several months. The study shows that groups in videoconferences achieve the same results as groups in a face-to-face setting. Generally, groups in videoconferences, i.e. in a setting without copresence, were able to solve complex problems without any losses in performance. The groups, however, had to adapt their communication behavior to the videoconference setting and develop new routines (in order to ensure grounding). They had to apply those communication strategies which take specific characteristics of videoconferences into consideration (such as problems in establishing eye contact) and lead to a successful performance. In our study, these strategies referred mainly to the coordination among group members and task execution. By the adaption of the communication behavior, restrictions of the medium can be overcome and groups can benefit from collaboration.

Theories on computer-mediated communication assume that various characteristics of media may influence group communication and therefore also collaboration and performance. Face-to-face and videoconference communication differ mainly with regard to two characteristics, the copresence of the communication partners and the visibility. In videoconferences, the communication partners may encounter impairments in visibility, e.g., difficulties in establishing eye contact or restrictions because only the face of the communication partner is visible. These restrictions may lead to impairments in turn-taking and hence in coordination (Clark and Brennan, 1996; Dennis & Valacich, 1999). The results of the first empirical study could confirm these assumptions. In videoconference communication, the coordination of the joint activities was an important factor for group performance.

Based on the results of the first study and on findings from other research, trainings for communication and collaboration in videoconferences were developed and investigated in a second empirical study. One type of training, the problem solving training, places specific emphasis on the coordination of joint activities (and of course on other discourse activities such as conveying relevant information). Overall, the training proved to be successful and led to higher group performance.

The results, however, also show that some groups are already able to identify successful strategies for a communication setting and to apply those strategies without a prior training. These groups would not necessarily need a training. However, groups who are not able to identify these successful strategies benefit from a training for collaboration.

In both studies, new insights into communication and collaboration in videoconferences could be gained. Yet, further investigations seem to be necessary. Altogether, the following aspects should be considered in future research on communication and collaboration in videoconferences:

- Empirical studies should take a potential novelty effect into consideration. Users may initially prefer new and innovative settings to traditional ones. They may be very enthusiastic and motivated when an unknown communication setting is introduced. Such novelty effects can be avoided by observing communication and collaboration over a longer time period.
- Communication and collaboration with media may influence different outcome variables. There is especially a lack of research on socio-emotional and motivational variables. Outcomes such as group

cohesion, the group members' motivation, and the relation of these variables to cognitive variables should also be considered in future research. Not only task-related discourse contributions but also socio-emotional discourse contributions should be investigated. These contributions may influence outcomes such as motivation or group cohesion and thus also contribute to individual or group performance.

REFERENCES

Argote, L., Gruenfeld, D., & Naqin, C. (2001). Group learning in organziations. In M. E. Turner (Ed.), *Groups at work* (pp. 369-411). London: Lawrence Erlbaum.

Beitz, H., & Loch, A. (1997). *Assessment Center. Erfolgstipps und Übungen für Bewerberinnen und Bewerber.* Niederhausen, Germany: Falken.

Bruinsma, M. (2004). Motivation, cognitive processing and achievement in higher education. *Learning and Instruction, 14*, 549–568. doi:10.1016/j.learninstruc.2004.09.001

Chinn, C. A., O'Donnell, A. M., & Jinks, T. S. (2000). The structure of discourse in collaboration learning. *Journal of Experimental Education, 69*, 77–97. doi:10.1080/00220970009600650

Clark, H. H., & Brennan, S. E. (1996). Grounding in communication. In L. B. Resnick, J. M. Levine, & S. D. Teasley (Eds.), *Perspectives on socially shared cognition* (pp. 127-149). Washington, DC: American Psychological Association.

Cohen, E. G. (1984). Talking and working together: Status interaction and learning. In P. Peterson, L. C. Wilkinson, & M. Halliman (Eds.), *Instructional groups in the classroom: Organization and processes* (pp.171-188). Orlando, FL: Academic Press.

Cohen, E. G. (1986). *Designing groups works: Strategies for heterogeneous classrooms.* New York: Teachers College Press.

Cooke, N. J., Salas, E., Cannon-Bowers, J. A., & Stout, R. J. (2000). Measuring team knowledge. *Human Factors, 42*, 151–173. doi:10.1518/001872000779656561

Cornelius, C. (2001). *Gegenseitiges Verständnis in Computerkonferenzen.* Münster, Germany: Waxmann.

Cornelius, C., & Boos, M. (1999). Es lohnt sich kohärent zu sein! In U. Reips (Hrsg.), *Aktuelle Online-Forschung. Trends, Techniken, Ergebnisse, Tagungsband der German Online Research.* Retrieved January 29, 2009, from http://www.gor.de/gor99/tband99/pdfs/a_h/cornelius.pdf

Cornelius, C., & Boos, M. (2003). Enhancing mutual understanding in synchronous computer-mediated communication by training. Trade-offs in judgmental tasks. *Communication Research, 30*(2), 147–177. doi:10.1177/0093650202250874

Costa, A. L., & O'Leary, P. W. (1992). Co-cognition. The cooperative development of the intellect. In N. Davidson & T. Worsham (Eds.), *Enhancing thinking through cooperative learning* (pp.41-65). New York: Teachers College Press.

DeCagna, J. (2001). Interview – Tending the garden of knowledge: A look at communities of practice with Etienne Wenger. *Information Outlook, 5*(7), 6–12.

Dennis, A. R., & Valacich, J. S. (1999). Rethinking media richness: Towards a theory of media synchonicity. In *Proceedings of the Hawaii International Conference on System Sciences,* USA (Vol. 32, pp. 1-10).

Dickey, M. H., Wasko, M. M., Chudoba, K. M., & Thatcher, J. B. (2006). Do you know what I know? A shared understandings perspective on text-based communication. *Journal of Computer-Mediated Communication, 12*(1), article 4. http://jcmc.indiana.edu/vol12/issue1/dickey.html

Ertl, B., Fischer, F., & Mandl, H. (2006). Conceptual and socio-cognitive support for collaborative learning in videoconferencing environments. *Computers & Education, 47*, 298–315. doi:10.1016/j.compedu.2004.11.001

Gruenfeld, D. H., & Hollingshead, A. B. (1993). Sociocognition in work groups: the evolution of group integrative complexity and its relation to task performance. *Small Group Research, 24*, 383–405. doi:10.1177/1046496493243006

Herring, S. (1999). Interactional coherence in CMC. In *Proceedings of the 32nd Hawaii International Conference on System Science*. Retrieved January 29, 2009, from http://jcmc.indiana.edu/vol4/issue4/herring.html

Hirokawa, R. Y. (1990). The role of communication in group decision making efficacy. *Small Group Research, 21*, 190–204. doi:10.1177/1046496490212003

Ickes, W., & Gonzales, R. (1996). Social cognition: From the subjective to the intersubjective. In J. L. Nye & A.M. Brower (Eds.), *What's social about social cognition? Research on socially shared cognition in small groups* (pp.285-309). Newbury Park, CA: Sage.

Jucks, R., Paechter, M., & Tatar, D. (2003). Learning and collaboration in online discourses. *International Journal of Educational Policy, Research, and Practice, 4*, 117–146.

Kraut, R. E., Egido, C., & Galegher, J. (1990). Communication in scientific research. In J. Galegher, R. E. Kraut, & C. Egido (Eds.), *Intellectual teamwork. Social and technological foundations of cooperative work* (pp. 149-171). Hillsdale: Lawrence Erlbaum.

Kreisler, M. (2007). *Förderung der Kommunikationskompetenz "Konversationale Kohärenz" im Medium Videokonferenz*. Unpublished diploma thesis, Karl-Franzens Universität Graz.

Larson, R. L., & Christensen, C. (1993). Groups as problem-solving units: Toward a new meaning of social cognition. *The British Journal of Social Psychology, 32*, 5–30.

Michinov, N., & Michinov, E. (2009). Investigating the relationship between transactive memory and performance in collaborative learning. *Learning and Instruction, 19*, 43–54. doi:10.1016/j.learninstruc.2008.01.003

Paechter, M. (2003). *Wissenskommunikation, Kooperation und Lernen in virtuellen Gruppen*. Lengerich, Germany: Pabst.

Peterson, P., & Swing, S. (1985). Students' cognition as mediators of the effectiveness of small-group learning. *Journal of Educational Psychology, 77*, 299–312. doi:10.1037/0022-0663.77.3.299

Reimer, T. (2001). Kognitive Ansätze zur Vorhersage der Gruppenleistung. Distraktion, Kompensation und Akzentuierung. *Zeitschrift für Sozialpsychologie, 32*, 107–128. doi:10.1024//0044-3514.32.2.107

Renkl, A., & Mandl, H. (1995). Kooperatives Lernen: Die Frage nach dem Notwendigen und dem Ersetzbaren. *Unterrichtswissenschaft, 25*, 292–300.

Resnick, L., Salmon, M., Zeitz, C. M., Wathen, S. H., & Holowchak, M. (1993). Reasoning in conversation. *Cognition and Instruction, 11*, 347–364.

Resnick, L. B. (1991). Shared cognition: Thinking as social practice. In L. B. Resnick, J. M. Levine, & S.D. Teasley (Eds.), *Perspectives on socially shared cognition* (pp.1-20). Washington, DC: American Psychological Association.

Schweizer, K., Paechter, M., & Weidenmann, B. (2007). Coherence in knowledge communication: How do online groups communicate? In P. Mayring, G. Huber, L. Guertler, & M. Kiegelmann (Eds.), *Mixed methodology in Psychological research* (pp. 101-112). Rotterdam, Germany & Taipei, Taiwan: Sense Publishers.

Slavin, R. E. (1992). When and why does cooperative learning increase academic achievement? Theoretical and empirical perspectives. In R. Hertz-Lazarowitz & N. Miller (Eds.), *Interaction in cooperative learning groups. The theoretical anatomy of group learning* (pp.145-173). Cambridge, USA: Cambridge University Press.

Tomlin, R. S., Forrest, L., Pu, M. M., & Kim, M. H. (1997). Discourse semantics. In T. A. van Dijk (Ed.), *Discourse as structure and process* (pp.63-111). London: Sage.

Vygotsky, L. S. (1978). *Mind in society. The development of higher psychological processes.* Cambridge, USA: Harvard University Press.

Vygotsky, L. S. (1986). *Thought and language.* Cambridge: MIT Press.

Webb, N. M. (1982). Student interaction and learning in small groups. *Review of Educational Research, 52*, 421–445.

Webb, N. M. (1992). Testing a theoretical model of student interaction and learning in small groups. In R. Hertz-Lazarowitz & N. Miller (Eds.), *Interaction in cooperative learning groups. The theoretical anatomy of group learning* (pp.102-119). New York: Cambridge University Press.

Wenger, E. (1998). *Communities of practice. Learning, meaning, and identity.* Cambridge, USA: Cambridge University Press.

Wenger, E. (2001). *Supporting communities of practice. A survey of community-oriented technologies.* Retrieved February 12, 2009, from http://www.nmc.org/projects/dkc/Technology_Survey.doc

Wittenbaum, G. M., & Stasser, G. (1996). Management of information in small groups. In J. L. Nye & A. M. Brower (Eds.), *What's social about social cognition? Research on socially shared cognition in small groups* (pp.3-28). Thousand Oaks, CA: Sage.

Wittenbaum, G. M., Stasser, G., & Merry, C. J. (1996). Tacit coordination in anticipation of small group task completion. *Journal of Experimental Social Psychology, 32*, 129–152. doi:10.1006/jesp.1996.0006

Wittrock, M. C. (1978). The cognitive movement in instruction. *Educational Psychologist, 13*, 15–29. doi:10.1080/00461527809529192

Yom, M., Wilhelm, T., & Holzmüller, H. (2003). Online-Fokusgruppen als innovative Methode zur nutzerbasierten Beurteilung der Web Usability. In G. Szwillus & J. Ziegler (Hrsg.), *Mensch & Computer 2003: Interaktion in Bewegung* (S.207-218). Stuttgart, Germany: B.G. Teubner.

Zieger, L., & Pulichino, J. (2004, Spring). Establishing a Community of Learners: A Case Study of a University Graduate Orientation Program for Online Learners. *The Journal of Interactive Online Learning, 2* (4). Retrieved January 29, 2009, from http://www.ncolr.org/jiol/issues/PDF/2.4.4.pdf

KEY TERMS AND DEFINITIONS

Coherence: Mutual product of participants' abilities and motivation to refer to each other and to develop topics

Collaboration: Recursive process where two or more people or organizations work together to accomplish common goals by sharing knowledge, learning and building consensus

Communication: An ongoing process of coordination and interaction

Community of Learning: Communities whose practice is learning itself

Community of Practice: When groups collaborate for a long period of time

Copresence: The communication partners share the same physical environment

Grounding: Ensuring mutual understanding

Least Collaborative Effort: Minimal effort that is needed to ensure mutual understanding, this effort may change with the communication medium

Chapter 12
Supporting Virtual Learning Through E–Tutoring

Birgitta Kopp
Ludwig-Maximilians-University, Germany

Melanie Germ
Ludwig-Maximilians-University, Germany

Heinz Mandl
Ludwig-Maximilians-University, Germany

ABSTRACT

E-tutoring is a hot topic in the context of virtual learning. As such learning environments become more prevalent in schools, universities or vocational training, providing adequate support for learners is becoming increasingly important – not only for individual, but also for collaborative learning. Therefore, there has been a lot of interest in using e-tutoring to foster learning processes and improve the performance of learners. Furthermore, an e-tutor can help prevent phenomena which are common in e-learning environments, such as feeling anonymous and isolated. In this chapter, we would like to first provide a theoretical introduction to e-tutoring that includes the definition, tasks and competencies of an e-tutor. Secondly, we will discuss the e-tutor in action, illustrated by a training for e-tutors and a virtual seminar which was supported by an e-tutor.

E-TUTORING: A THEORETICAL INTRODUCTION

E-tutoring is a hot topic in the context of virtual learning. Virtual learning environments are becoming increasingly common in different contexts – in schools, universities and vocational training (for on overview of this development see Rudestam & Schoenholtz-Read, 2002). Therefore, the adequate support of learners is also becoming increasingly important. Furthermore, the use of collaborative learning is also increasing, which places higher demands on learners – especially when the collaboration is designed and tailored to improve learning processes and learning outcomes. As designing e-collaborative learning units is a central task of the e-tutor, e-tutoring is closely related to e-collaboration. But what exactly is e-tutoring? What are the tasks of an e-tutor and which competencies does he need?

DOI: 10.4018/978-1-61520-729-9.ch012

In the first three sections, we will answer these three theory-related questions by giving a definition of e-tutoring as well as by describing the tasks and competencies of an e-tutor. We will then show the e-tutor in action in two steps: First, we will describe a training on e-tutoring with its content and evaluation data. Second, we will discuss the actions of an e-tutor during a virtual seminar and examine the evaluation data on these specific interventions.

Defining E-Tutoring

Online learning is increasing in everyday work and further education contexts as well as in schools, universities and vocational training. But oftentimes the e-learning environments are designed such that learners are not able to learn with them effectively – because of technical problems, an overly complex structure of the learning environment, content that is too demanding or due to individual problems with self-directed learning and motivation. In such cases, an e-tutor is essential for handling such problems when learning in an e-learning environment.

But what is an e-tutor? There are a wide range of different names that are almost used interchangeably, but do not always mean the same thing. Rautenstrauch (2001) lists different names for an e-tutor, e. g. Tele-tutor, Online-Coach, E-Moderator, Tele-Teacher, Online-Facilitator or E-Trainer. All these names are used to describe the same phenomenon, namely the support of e-learners, even though the range of tasks may differ depending on the respective name. In order to avoid misunderstandings, our terminology describes an e-tutor as a person who supports the individual and collaborative online learning processes of his/her learners. In this definition, e-tutoring comprises all the activities of a teacher that support a learner in constructively and actively dealing with the learning environment. Thus, the e-tutor's main function is to supervise his learners.

The tasks of an e-tutor are even more demanding since the communicative situation greatly differs between e-learning and face-to-face communication due to missing non-verbal signals and extra-linguistic signs. Furthermore, an e-tutor should be competent not only in content-specific knowledge and social skills, but also in knowledge about the functioning of the Internet, technical skills and knowledge on net-based communication (Salmon, 2000). Especially the last three competencies are relevant when learning online.

To gain deeper insight into the tasks and competencies of an e-tutor, we will describe them in greater detail in the next section.

Tasks of an E-Tutor

E-tutoring specifically comprises two main tasks: Tasks for preparing and organizing the learning unit and tasks for supporting the learning processes. While the first tasks are especially relevant before starting the learning unit, the second tasks are necessary during the learning unit.

Tasks for Preparing and Organizing the Learning Unit

The *e-learning environment* is a key aspect to consider before starting the learning unit. Even though e-tutors do not design the learning environment in terms of content, tasks or didactical design, they must be familiar with them before starting the learning unit. As the learning objectives and the learning material mostly determine the chosen methods and media, the e-tutor can evaluate whether the design of the learning environment is valuable from a didactical perspective.

One main focus should be on the learning tasks which provide learners an opportunity to acquire and apply their knowledge. Tasks should spark the interest and motivation of the learners by using inspiring descriptions or by incorporating the learners' own experiences (Deci, & Ryan, 1993; Hidi, & Harackiewicz, 2000). Furthermore, dividing tasks into sub-tasks may simplify the learning process. When learning collaboratively, the task must be a "real" group task which demands active discussion and participation of the learners (Cohen, 1994).

Another focus must be on the blending of online and face-to-face phases (Kopp & Mandl, 2008). Especially when learning exclusively online, a kind of anonymous and therefore de-motivating learning may occur. In this context, it is necessary for participants get to know each other and discuss specific issues and topics not only online, but in person. While online-phases are adequate for disseminating information and basic knowledge, face-to-face phases are necessary for the more in-depth processing of the acquired knowledge through discussions and extension tasks.

Organizing the learning unit specifically involves defining the schedule for diverse tasks, methods and media which are elements of the e-learning environment. Furthermore, it is also necessary to coordinate and supervise learners. Offering additional learning material, structuring and organizing the learning processes, and assigning learners to groups are also part of the organization of the e-learning environment (Haussmann, 2001). In this context, specifying group size is essential to prevent social loafing or free-riding (Salomon, & Globerson, 1989). Two to five people learning together seems to be most effective (Lou, Abrami, D'Appollonia, 2001).

All activities for preparing and organizing the class are necessary to stimulate elaborations and direct the learning process in ways that give consideration to the learning objectives (De Grave, Dolmans & Vleuten, 1999).

Tasks for Supporting the Learning Process

An e-tutor must perform several tasks to support the learning process. The support should be focused on social, cognitive, and motivational aspects of the learning. But there is no consistent description of the different tasks. Roscoe and Chi

(2007) classify the tasks as explaining, asking, evaluating and giving feedback. De Grave et al. (1999) describe stimulating knowledge integration and taking individual responsibility. Geyken, Mandl and Reiter (1995) highlight diagnosing the difficulties of the learners and counseling. Therefore, we will focus on four main tasks for supporting learning processes: fostering collaborative learning, stimulating more in-depth understanding, promoting learning motivation, and providing feedback.

Fostering Collaborative Learning

The first important task of an e-tutor is fostering of collaborative learning since groups do not spontaneously learn effectively. To guide groups in their learning, an e-tutor has two main options: adequate structuring before collaborative learning and continuous supervision during the learning process. *Structuring* involves e. g. the size of the learning group (between 2 and 5 people) (Lou, et al., 2001), assigning specific roles, providing an adequate task for creating social interdependence (Cohen, 1994; Johnson & Johnson, 1989, 1992, 1998) or defining group rules.

Another kind of structuring is provided by scripts and schemata. These support methods are useful for initiating social and cognitive processes. Social processes are fostered by collaboration scripts and cognitive processes are fostered by content schemes (Ertl, Kopp, & Mandl, 2007). Collaboration scripts "mainly structure collaborative learning by assigning specific activities to learners" (Ertl, et al., 2007, p. 216). These activities or roles are mainly content-independent. Collaboration scripts actually stem from face-to-face learning, e.g. scripted cooperation (O'Donnell & King, 1999) or cooperative teaching (O'Donnell & Dansereau, 2000), but are being increasingly used in virtual learning environments. There are different contexts in which collaboration scripts are used: cognitive, computational and educational perspectives (Fischer, Kollar, Mandl & Haake, 2007). (1) "From the perspective of cognitive psychology, scripts are culturally shared as well as personal knowledge and memory structures that help people act and understand actions and action sequences in specific every-day situations" (Fischer, Kollar, Haake & Mandl, 2007, p. 3). Based on the script definition of Schank and Abelson (1977), it is assumed that repeating specific procedures results in individuals internalizing the sequence of such procedures as a fixed script in memory, e. g. the restaurant script (Schank & Abelson, 1977). (2) From a computer science perspective, scripts are used to "support developers in defining, configuring and adapting system behavior" (Fischer et al., 2007, p. 5). In this context, collaborative learning is closely connected to Artificial Intelligence. (3) From an educational perspective, scripts are used to improve learning processes and individual as well as collaborative learning outcomes in formal and informal educational settings (Fischer et al., 2007). From the educational perspective, scripts are also used for collaborative learning to show learners a specific sequencing they should follow to improve their collaboration. Over time, learners internalize these sequences when performing a particular learning task and may solve them better in future situations. A script can also serve as a model for learners to perform the task like an expert (see Collins, Brown, & Newman, 1989).

One script realized in a videoconferencing scenario structured the collaborative task-solving unit into four phases that alternated between individual and collaborative phases (Kopp & Mandl, 2007). Each phase consisted of specific activities the learners had to follow for their collaborative task-solving. The first individual phase consisted of reading a text and extracting relevant information. In the second collaborative phase, learners had to exchange their different information concerning the task. As the information of the perspectives differed in certain ways, it was necessary for participants to discuss them. All issues which were relevant for the solution of the task were to be transferred into a document template.

After mentioning and noting all the main issues, the learners used the third phase to reflect on the appropriateness of the jointly developed notes. In the fourth and final phase, learners had time to discuss specific issues they reflected on in the third phase and had to develop a final version of the task solution.

Content schemes focus learners on certain content-specific aspects. They are based on the concept of mental schemata (Brewer & Nakamura, 1984) and include an expert meta-structure of important dimensions of the content and placeholders for adding content-specific aspects. They are permanently displayed during the learning situation (e.g. Brooks & Dansereau, 1983) or given as a sample solution. In the context of structuring, it is of utmost important to show the relationship between the individual components of the content (Lambiotte, Skaggs, & Dansereau, 1993). This meta-structure makes key components of the content salient so that learners are focused on missing or existing parts of the content (Suthers, 2001; Suthers & Hundhausen, 2001). Learners become aware of which concepts and categories of the specific content are important for the task solution and the subject matter. Zhang and Norman (1994) name this phenomenon representational guidance. The representation of specific concepts can guide and focus learners in their task-solving process, because it modifies the representational context of a task (Zhang & Norman, 1994). The assumption is that content schemes "change learners' subjective representation of the task and influence their ability to solve the task" (Ertl, et al., 2007, p. 217). This effect is not only present when using this external schema, but also without the schema. Research on using content schemes in videoconferencing shows a beneficial effect on learning processes and learning outcome (Kopp, 2005; Kopp, Ertl, & Mandl, 2006).

The second kind of support for group collaboration is *balanced participation*. An e-tutor has to supervise learners to avoid dysfunctional group phenomena, such as free riding or social loafing (Salomon & Globerson, 1989). Especially in virtual learning scenarios, it is easier for learners not to contribute to the group solution as communication takes place virtually and not face-to-face. Furthermore, ignoring minorities (Moscovici, 1980) must be avoided. Minorities can promote a deeper scrutiny of information (Moscovici, 1980), encourage creative and divergent thinking (Nemeth, 1986), or promote knowledge transfer and the generalization of learning (Quiamzade & Mugny, 2001). Minorities are able to influence the decision of the group when they constantly express the same point of view, albeit not in a static, but in a flexible way (Maass, West, & Clark, 1993).

Closely related to this is the phenomenon of status differences. Status differences occur because of e.g. race, sex, age, culture, or job tenure. Group members with lower status often have no influence on the collaboration process and therefore on group decisions or task solutions. This is because the other group members do not accept their opinion in the same way they accept the points of view of members with higher status (Cohen, 1994; Webb, 1989). The problem is that learners with lower status do not profit from collaboration in the same way as higher status learners do. It had been assumed that status differences would not be a problem in virtual collaboration, but research to date has not substantiated this assumption (Hollingshead, 1996). In fact, Hollingshead (1996) showed that status differences are also present in virtual learning environments. Paying attention to peer- or lower-status partners in interaction has been shown to reduce confirmatory bias (Butera, & Buchs, 2005), whereas interaction with expert sources, high-status sources, expert or majorities increase such bias. Supervision is necessary to ensure that group members do not ignore lower-status members when considering or seeking out alternative points of view.

To avoid such phenomena, the e-tutor has to look for balanced participation, reduce status differences and consider the contributions of minorities.

Stimulating In-Depth Understanding

A second main task of the e-tutor is to enable more in-depth understanding of the learning material. This is closely connected to the elaboration of knowledge. "The depth of processing and its elaboration are important because deeper, more elaborated processes leave more traces that can later be recovered. Variable encoding leaves traces that can be matched by more retrieval cues. Thus, the nature of the encoding processes makes a great deal of difference for how well some experience will be recalled later: Elaborate, semantic, meaningful encoding and the embedding of experiences in a rich, accessible matrix ensure memorability." (van Dijk, & Kintsch, 1983, p. 335). That means that elaborating knowledge guarantees deep information processing which is an important antecedent for a sustainable increase in knowledge.

Elaborating on knowledge means that a learner connects his prior knowledge with the new knowledge so that he has several associations to recall the information and the knowledge he has learned. Thus, the danger of forgetting knowledge is reduced. Talking in terms of schema theory, elaborations serve to enrich prior schemata or knowledge with new information to create a new, more elaborated schema (Kopp & Mandl, 2006).

Support is helpful in building such schemata, not only by providing content schemes (see paragraph above), but also through direct intervention such as an e-tutor asking meaningful questions. Research shows that this has a positive influence on the performance of the learners (Graesser & Person, 1994). There are ten key activities which specifically encourage a closer examination of the learning material (Graesser, Person & Magliano, 1995).

1. Splices in a complete or partial answer: The tutor pushes the students to elaborate more on their answers or asks for further clarification.

2. Summarizes answer: When group members give different answers on a specific task, the tutor could summarize them and generate one coherent contribution.

3. Gives hints concerning the task solution, self-directed or collaborative learning.

4. Pumps the students for more information: As soon as learners forget important information, the tutor could point them to that missing information.

5. Traces explanation or justification: When individual contributions are not very well explained or justified, the tutor may encourage students to explain their points of view in more detail or to complete the statements with data to generate fully justified arguments.

6. Elaborates on answer: The tutor elaborates on individual contributions by giving explanations, information or justifications to reduce cognitive overtaxing.

7. Asks question to elaborate on answer: The tutor focuses the learner's attention on elaborative activities.

8. Presents an example to show students expected activities.

9. Corrects a misconception: If learners possess an incorrect idea about a specific phenomenon, the tutor may correct it through further explanation.

10. Issues a command or indirect request for students to complete an activity: When learners forget to finish a specific task or process, the tutor may point it out and encourage them to complete it.

All these activities are helpful in the sense of elaborating knowledge, developing schemata and thus stimulating more in-depth understanding to help prevent knowledge gaps or the loss of knowledge.

Promoting Learning Motivation

The third task of an e-tutor is to motivate students to learn. Learning motivation is the key factor for successful learning (Pekrun & Schiefele, 1996). Defined as the desire or intention to learn more about a specific issue or topic (Deci & Ryan, 1985), learners have to activate specific behavioral patterns and processes in order to acquire new knowledge (Deci & Ryan, 1992). Reasons for motivation are mainly the learning object itself or the consequences which result from learning.

There are two main theoretical models on motivation: The ARCS-Model of Keller (1983) and Keller and Kopp (1987) and the self-determination theory of Deci and Ryan (1985; Ryan & Deci, 2000). In the *ARCS Model*, four main aspects are relevant for evoking motivation: *A*ttention, *R*elevance, *C*onfidence, and *S*atisfaction. In the beginning, learners' attention and interest for the learning object is necessary. This could be achieved by steering the learners' attention to specific interesting aspects. In the second step, the learner must be convinced that the learning object is relevant to his situation. In this context, helpful methods include using familiar examples and contexts, showing clear objectives, and adapting the content to the respective performance (Astleitner, 2006). The third step focuses on the learner's self-confidence that he can be successful. Providing learning aids (such as structuring the content or showing the objectives), adapting the tasks to the learner's level of knowledge so that the learner is successful in solving tasks, and assigning personal responsibility are adequate methods for evoking self-confidence (Astleitner, 2006). Lastly, learners should be satisfied with their learning success. Extrinsic rewards or intrinsic amplification using transfer tasks could be used in this context.

According to the *self-determination theory* of Deci and Ryan (1985), there are especially three needs which are relevant for motivation: Competence, autonomy and social embeddedness (Ryan & Deci, 2000). Competence means that a learner feels competent in doing a specific task, and is not bored and not overtaxed. Autonomy is related to the learner's sense of being self-determined and independent. Social embeddedness is connected to the idea that every human being wants to be socially integrated. When these three needs are satisfied, self-motivation and mental health result. When thwarted, they lead to diminished motivation and well-being (Ryan & Deci, 2000).

To promote intrinsic motivation, the e-tutor can focus on each specific aspect of the self-determination theory (Deci & Ryan, 1985): supporting competence, autonomy and social embeddedness. To foster competence, the e-tutor has four main options (Schiefele & Streblow, 2007): (1) The e-tutor can provide feedback and confirmation during the task solving process even though the learner is not always successful. Learners must be affirmed in their work to feel competent. (2) The e-tutor can support active participation and the practical application of the learned knowledge. This is helpful for learners to immediately see their success. (3) The e-tutor can present the content in a clear, structured and concrete manner so that learners understand the instructions easily. (4) The e-tutor may provide well-suited tasks that have been adapted to the state of knowledge of the learners so that they are not bored or overtaxed.

Four interventions are also suggested to support autonomy (Schiefele & Streblow, 2007): (1) The e-tutor can allow co-management in the choice of the learning matter and the objectives, (2) increase the freedom of action regarding specific learning methods, (3) allow self-evaluation to track one's own learning success and (4) connect uninteresting but necessary learning material to personally meaningful and practically relevant objectives.

Social embeddedness is the last main aspect of the self-determination theory. A learner may feel socially integrated when the e-tutor offers group work so that there is an extensive exchange of ideas between the group members. Furthermore, the e-tutor can act more as a partner than as a teacher so that learners are not afraid to ask the e-tutor for help.

The e-tutor can use all these methods to promote the intrinsic motivation of his learners. This is a very important task because motivation guarantees the learners' active participation.

Providing Feedback

Providing feedback is the fourth main way that an e-tutor can support the teaching and learning processes (Krause, Stark & Mandl, 2008). According to Hattie and Timperley (2007) feedback "is conceptualized as information provided by an agent (e.g., teacher, peer, book, parent, self, experience) regarding aspects of one's performance or understanding" (p. 81). The objective of giving feedback is to reduce the discrepancies between the student's current understanding and a desired goal. Research in classroom settings has shown that teaching with feedback is more effective than teaching without feedback. In e-learning contexts, feedback provided by the e-tutor is very helpful to avoid the student's sense of being totally alone and unguided (Schweizer, Paechter, & Weidenmann, 2001).

In classroom contexts, effective feedback specifically answers three questions:

1. Where am I going (Feed Up)? This aspect concerns feedback about the information given to students about the attainment of learning goals related to the task or performance. A clear definition of goals is the main component in this question. Important antecedents in this context are the appropriate challenge and commitment of tutors and students to the goal.

2. How am I going (Feed Back)? This kind of feedback consists of information about progress, and/or about how to proceed.

3. Where to next (Feed Forward)? In this context, feedback is a way of providing information that leads to greater possibilities for learning. "These include enhanced challenges, more self-regulation over the learning process, greater fluency and automaticity,

more strategies and processes to work on the tasks, deeper understanding, and more information about what is and what is not understood." (Hattie, & Timperley, 2007, p. 90). These meta-cognitive aspects of feedback are helpful as they foster reflection on the learning process and the associated consequences as part of self-regulation, e.g. changing learning strategies.

There are four main kinds of feedback: Feedback (1) on the task level, (2) on the process level, (3) on the self-regulation level, and (4) on the self level.

Feedback on the task includes how well the tasks are understood or performed (Hattie & Timperley, 2007). This corrective feedback is related to the concrete accomplishment of the task. It is the kind of feedback used most often. Meta-analyses of feedback on the task showed a very high effect size (e. g. Walberg, 1982; Tenenbaum & Goldring, 1989). Feedback on the task may differ in its elaboration. Giving only feedback on correct or incorrect answers is not as helpful for the learning process as giving detailed and elaborated feedback (Krause, et al., 2008) on faulty interpretations, detailed instructions or successful task-solving strategies.

Feedback about the processing of the task refers to the processes that take place during the task-solving and especially concerns aspects of deep understanding (Hattie & Timperley, 2007). In this context, it is important to provide strategies for error detection that provide information on how to improve and change activities to solve a task correctly or cueing mechanisms that provide information about the processes underlying the task.

Feedback about self-regulation "addresses the way students monitor, direct, and regulate actions toward the learning goal." (Hattie, & Timperley, 2007, p. 93). This includes all meta-cognitive activities learners use in their learning process to plan, monitor and evaluate their learning (King, 2007).

Feedback on the self as person such as "great effort" expresses positive evaluations and affects the student. Often realized as praise, this feedback is helpful for the development of the learner's personality. It is often mixed with feedback about the task, the processing and the self-regulation so that is not detailed enough and too uninformative about performing the task.

The different activities of the tutor mentioned above could influence social, cognitive, and motivational processes of the learners. When we look at one possible method of fostering learning processes, namely giving an example, all three processes could be supported. Regarding social processes, an example on pro-social behavior such as helping group members may foster e.g. the cohesion in groups and therefore improve collaboration. Concerning cognitive processes, the e-tutor may model a correct argumentation sequence using argument, counter-argument and reply provided with adequate justifications. Looking at motivational processes, using empathetic comments helps the group learn to create a feeling of relevance for every group member that again increases their self-efficacy.

Competencies of an E-Tutor

Which competencies does an e-tutor need to deal with all these tasks? In various sources, a number of different preconditions are mentioned for specific competencies. When we summarize them, we essentially have three kinds of knowledge (Lepper, Drake, & O'Donnell-Johnson, 1997; Salmon, 2000; Schmidt & Moust, 1995):

1. Content-specific knowledge to support more in-depth understanding on a cognitive level, and
2. Pedagogical knowledge
   a. to initiate and keep up adequate learning processes on a motivational level
   b. to adequately cope with difficulties of the learners on a social level.

3. Technical knowledge about the functioning of the Internet, technical skills and knowledge on net-based communication. This kind of knowledge refers to the "e" in the term "e-tutor".

Starting from these three kinds of knowledge, four main competencies are required of a professional e-tutor:

1. Content-specific competence comprises content-specific knowledge and skills to teach and explain content-specific knowledge.
2. Pedagogical competence contains at first the didactical knowledge and skills to adequately design teaching and learning material (didactics, media use). This is necessary for evaluating the learning environment according to the specific didactical aspects the e-tutor has to handle. A second aspect of pedagogical competence includes methods for supporting learning processes. These must be fostered on a cognitive level, such as stimulating deeper understanding or problem solving, on a motivational level to promote intrinsic learning motivation as an antecedent for active participation and successful learning in a virtual learning environment, and on a social level in giving feedback on fostering collaborative learning.
3. Social competence refers to the tutors' interaction with the learners. Schmidt and Moust (1995) specify this competence in "social congruence" and "cognitive congruence". Social congruence "refers to a tutor's willingness to act informally with students and display a caring attitude" (Schmidt & Moust, 1995, p.710). "Cognitive congruence was defined as the ability to express oneself in the language of the students, using the concepts they use and explaining things in ways easily grasped by students" (Schmidt & Moust, 1995, p.709).

4. Technical competence includes knowledge and skills about technical affairs and issues which are relevant for an e-learning environment.

E-Tutoring in Action

In the second part, we would like to present two different types of e-tutoring in action – a specific training for e-tutors and the interventions of an e-tutor in a virtual seminar with its evaluation data.

A Professional Training for E-Tutors

As stated above, it is becoming increasingly relevant for e-tutors to support collaborative learning. Since the communication and learning situation in virtual learning environments differ from normal face-to-face environments, it is a key prerequisite to provide e-tutors with pro-fessional training. The objective of a professional training is to prepare e-tutors for the different tasks involving the preparation and organization of the virtual learning environment as well to enable them to support the individual and collaborative learning processes.

Since 2005, the virtual University of Bavaria offers online trainings for e-tutors to provide basic knowledge in e-tutoring. This course has been developed and organized by the Ludwig-Maximilians-University of Munich. Its curriculum covers the tasks and competencies mentioned above.

One hundred and seventy-five e-tutors have been trained since 2005. All participants have to work collaboratively in small groups for the duration of the course, which is 6 weeks. The didactical design is based on a blended learning scenario with face-to-face workshops at the beginning and in the end of the training and virtual phases in between (Kopp & Mandl, 2008). The virtual phases are key for providing the prospective e-tutors (through the learner's perspective) with practical experience in the field in which they will work. Furthermore, the course is based on a problem-based didactic which fosters the direct application of the knowledge learned (Reinmann & Mandl, 2006). The content of the training must be applied to case-based tasks through small group work.

Content of the Training

In this section, we would like to illustrate the content of the e-tutoring training based on the theoretical considerations mentioned in the first chapter. In this training, the design and structure of the content comprise the tasks and the competencies of an e-tutor, which are consistent with the theory.

The training comprises five modules: Module 1 introduces the tasks of an e-tutor (chapter 1, section 2). Modules 2 to 5 focus on the competencies of the e-tutor (chapter 1, section 3). Modules 2 and 3 cover pedagogical competencies (didactics, media use, support methods), module 4 discusses the social competence (collaborative learning) and module 5 covers technical competence which is specific for e-tutors.

- **Module 1:** Tasks of an e-tutor. The participants acquire basic knowledge on the tasks and competencies of an e-tutor. In a group assignment, they summarize their own projects and introduce their supervision concepts.
- **Module 2:** Basics on media didactics. In this module, learners receive an introduction to different didactical designs, especially systematic and problem-based learning environments. In the learner's task, they have to describe the didactical design of their own courses and collaboratively discuss the effects of the different design criteria on their practice as e-tutors.
- **Module 3:** Individual learning. This module focuses on specific aspects and problems of individual virtual learning. The module

provides different support methods for individual learners. As a group assignment, learners have to work on problems relating to their support of individual learners and propose solutions for prevention and intervention in virtual learning environments.

- **Module 4:** Collaborative learning. The support of virtual learning groups is the main focus of this module. Problems of virtual learning groups are also part of this module as well as how to intervene when group conflicts arise. The collaborative task includes additional problems when supporting small groups and the whole learning group and involves proposing solutions for prevention and intervention.
- **Module 5:** Technical aspects. This module includes basics in HTML-programming and an introduction to different types and functionalities of learning platforms. The group has to critically examine various communication tools (asynchronous discussion boards, chat, videoconferencing, wikis) with regard to their practical application in their courses and their support for collaborative learning and exchange processes.

Instructional Support

As the prospective e-tutors should gain practical experience in the field in which they will work, as learners they receive specific instructional support from an e-tutor. These support methods are used as models for how to foster learning processes and learning outcomes. These are:

- A rotating moderator who changes every week and coordinates the group work
- Moderation reports for describing the experiences of the respective collaborative learning phase and for reflection
- Feedback after every task on the quality of the task solution and the virtual collaboration

Figure 1. Results of the evaluation of the individual modules

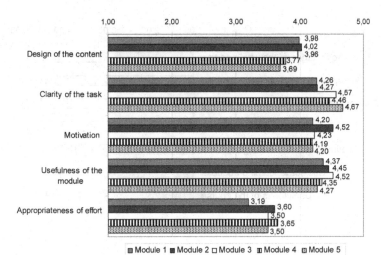

- Forum for questions provided in the learning platform where answers and support is given within a 24 hour period
- News about the learners' current level of knowledge at periodic intervals
- Further literature and basic literature for deepening and extending knowledge
- PDF-versions of the five modules

Evaluation

To steadily improve the training for e-tutors, the individual modules and the course as a whole are evaluated by the participants. The evaluation of the individual modules in all dimensions (design of the content, clarity of the task, motivation, usefulness of the module, appropriateness of the effort) reveals a predominantly positive rating (see Figure 1).

Furthermore, the final evaluation of the training as a whole indicates a high degree of acceptance and satisfaction of the participants. This is a key pre-condition for being able to apply the acquired knowledge to practice (see Figure 2) (see Bürg, 2005).

In future, further research is needed on how the e-tutors concretely transfer their knowledge to the courses after the training. Furthermore, it would be of interest to find out how e-tutors are

further supported in their work by e.g. initiating a community of practice. This would be of great importance for ensuring the continued application of the knowledge they learned in the training.

E-Tutoring in a Virtual Seminar

When implementing tutorial support in a virtual learning environment, the question becomes relevant how this support is realized and evaluated by the learners themselves. To gain further insight into these two questions, we want to present the evaluation data from a virtual seminar regarding the support of a tutor. The evaluation criteria correspond to the four main tasks of an e-tutor to support learning processes mentioned in the theoretical part: fostering collaboration, stimulating more in-depth understanding, promoting learning motivation, and providing feedback.

Virtual Seminar

The virtual seminar which was the object of investigation took place in the summer term from mid April 2008 to mid July 2008 at the Ludwig-Maximilians-University in Germany. The title of the seminar was "Attachment Theory". The main objective was to acquire knowledge on this specific theory and to apply this knowledge

Figure 2. Results of the evaluation of the training as a whole

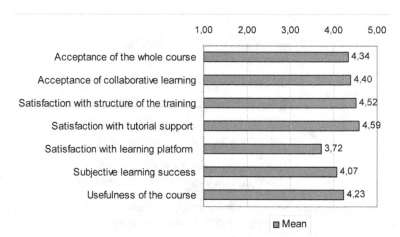

to specific cases so that knowledge transfer was guaranteed.

Thirty-three undergraduates majoring in Education participated in the seminar. These 33 participants were randomly assigned to 8 groups with roughly 4 members per group. These groups had to collaborate over the course of the semester and solve different collaborative tasks together.

The content of the seminar was delivered weekly with a detailed and in-depth PowerPoint version of the main content of the respective topic and further literature illustrating and providing more depth to the excerpt. All materials were web-based, so that the participants were able to download them after logging in to the virtual learning environment.

The seminar was didactically designed in a blended learning scenario with face-to-face and virtual phases. There were 4 face-to-face phases: One in the beginning as a kick-off and then three every four weeks during the semester after each main topic was completed. The evaluation was also conducted after finishing one main topic (therefore, it was used at three points in time).

Furthermore, the principles of problem-based learning were realized. These included authentic problems which started every learning unit and which had to be solved collaboratively during the course of one week. Different perspectives were included in the problem description. The social context was realized with group work and instructional support was given with further literature, discussion boards for questions and a 24h feedback guarantee for important questions.

The learners were supported by four main methods as mentioned in the theoretical part:

1. Collaboration was fostered by group rules and a student moderator who rotated each week
2. Answering questions helped promote more in-depth understanding
3. Learning motivation was promoted by face-to-face meetings and continuous e-mail contact
4. Weekly feedback was provided on task solutions

Experience with the Virtual Seminar

To measure the tutorial support, a questionnaire with a six-point Likert scale was used three times over the period of the whole semester. Referring to the main tasks of an e-tutor in supporting the learning process, we asked participants about the four main support dimensions mentioned in the theoretical part: (1) fostering collaboration, (2) stimulating more in-depth understanding, (3) promoting learning motivation, and (4) providing feedback.

Figure 3. Results of the evaluation of E-tutoring in a virtual seminar

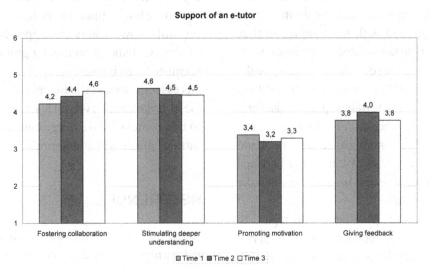

Four items were used for the elaboration of fostering collaboration, e.g. "The definition of group rules was helpful". Stimulating deeper understanding was measured with six items, e.g. "The tutor answered my questions in detail." Five items were used to obtain data on the dimension "promoting learning motivation" (e.g. "The tutor motivated us to learn."). We again used five items for the dimension "giving feedback", e.g. "The tutor provided elaborated feedback on the task solutions." All reliabilities were satisfactory (see Milekic, 2007).

The results showed that specifically fostering collaborative learning and stimulating deeper understanding was consistently evaluated to be at a very high level (see figure 3). Promoting motivation was evaluated as lowest and giving feedback on an average level. Interestingly, independent of the time, the evaluations stayed on the same level – so the e-tutor acted in a consistent manner throughout the duration of the course.

Aside from the dimension "promoting motivation", all dimensions were evaluated as above average. Therefore, participants were satisfied with the e-tutor's actions. This is also reflected in the fact that there was no participant who did not complete the seminar. Regarding participa-

tion, the actions of the tutor in supporting the learning process of the seminar's participants were helpful.

CONCLUSION AND PRACTICAL IMPLICATIONS

In light of this paper, we can see that e-tutoring is very important in the context of the increasing number of virtual learning environments, but also very demanding with respect to the tasks and competencies of an e-tutor. There are several aspects to consider, especially when looking at the key task of the e-tutor, which is to support individual and collaborative learning processes. An e-tutor requires not only content-specific competencies, but also pedagogical, social and technical competencies to cope with the complex system involved in a virtual learning environment.

Therefore, training for e-tutors is not only meaningful, but also necessary. The problem is that there are a lot of e-tutors who are working without any further training. As we have seen above, this training must comprise all relevant tasks and competencies of an e-tutor so that prospective e-tutors gain a deeper insight into their work from a theoretical and practical point of view. Our evaluation data shows that the e-tutors were overall very satisfied with the training as they received theoretical knowledge and practical hints for their own e-learning courses. To guarantee the long-term usage of the knowledge the e-tutors learned in the training, further support in the form of communities of practice could be of great importance. In such a community, experiences and knowledge could be shared – not only between the trainer and the trainees, but also between the trainees themselves.

The evaluation of the e-tutor with regard to the learning processes shows almost all high ratings. This indicates that – aside from promoting motivation – the participants were satisfied with the tutor's actions. These especially related to being available within 24 hours, giving feedback on the task-solving process as well as on the task solution, and offering face-to-face discussions every four weeks. This also could be seen in the fact that no participant left the seminar. Promoting motivation seems to be a very demanding task in virtual e-collaborative learning environments. As learners have to spend most of their time using the e-learning environment without face-to-face contact, they are more likely to feel isolated or unsupported. Therefore, the motivational component is of even greater importance.

In general, more investigation is necessary on the topic of e-tutoring – on a theoretical, empirical and practical basis. The theoretical considerations are often derived from face-to-face settings. Furthermore, there is little empirical data on e-tutoring in the sense of one human e-tutor supporting several learners in a virtual learning environment. This is due to the fact that such data is mostly carried out in real-life situations and not in an experimental design. Furthermore, research on how e-tutor practitioners could be supported in their profession by e.g. participating in a community of practice or in an e-tutors' knowledge network would also be of interest. As virtual learning increases over time, this deficit in research must be overcome and more field and

experimental studies should be conducted – firstly, regarding how e-tutors support their students and secondly, how e-tutors are supported in their profession. Collaboration among groups of e-tutors seems to be of interest here. On a practical basis, it is essential to specifically train more e-tutors on the affordances of a virtual learning environment. In this context, e-coaching as applied in business settings also plays a major role.

REFERENCES

Astleitner, H. (2006). Motivationsförderung im E-Learning: Stand der Forschung zum ARCS-Modell. *Salzburger Beiträge zur Erziehungswissenschaft*, *10*(2), 17–29.

Brewer, W. F., & Nakamura, G. V. (1984). The nature and functions of schemas. Center for the Study of Reading, Technical Report Bo. 325. In R. S. Wyer, & T. K. Krull (Eds.), *Handbook of social cognition* (Vol. 1, pp. 119-160). Hillsdale, NJ: Erlbaum.

Brooks, L. W., & Dansereau, D. F. (1983). Effects of structural schema training and text organization on expository prose processing. *Journal of Educational Psychology*, *75*(6), 811–820. doi:10.1037/0022-0663.75.6.811

Buchs, C., Butera, F., Mugny, G., & Darnon, C. (2004). Conflict Elaboration and Cognitive Outcomes. *Theory into Practice*, *43*(1), 23–30. doi:10.1207/s15430421tip4301_4

Bürg, O. *(2005)*. Akzeptanz von E-Learning in Unternehmen. Die Bedeutung von institutionellen Rahmenbedingungen, Merkmalen des Individuums und Merkmalen der Lernumgebung für die Akzeptanz von E-Learning. *Berlin, Germany: Logos.*

Butera, F., & Buchs, C. (2005), Reasoning together: From focusing to decentering. In V. Girotto & P. N. Johnson-Laird (Eds.), *The shape of reason* (pp. 193-203). Hove, England: Psychology Press.

Cohen, E. G. (1986). *Designing group work.* New York: Teachers College Press.

Collins, A., Brown, J. S., & Newman, S. (1989). Cognitive apprenticeship: Teaching the crafts of reading, writing, and mathematics. In L. B. Resnick (Ed.), *Knowing, learning, and instruction: Essays in the honour of Robert Glaser* (pp. 453-494). Hillsdale, NJ: Erlbaum.

De Grave, W. S., Dolmans, D. H. J. M., & Vleuten, C. P. M. (1999). Profiles of effective tutors in problem-based learning: scaffolding student learning. *Medical Education, 33,* 901–906. doi:10.1046/j.1365-2923.1999.00492.x

Deci, E. L., & Ryan, R. M. (1985). *Intrinsic motivation and self-determination in human behavior.* New York: Plenum.

Deci, E. L., & Ryan, R. M. (1992). Beyond the intrinsic-extrinsic dichotomy: Self-determination in motivation and learning. *Motivation and Emotion, 16*(3), 165–185. doi:10.1007/BF00991650

Ertl, B., Kopp, B., & Mandl (2007). Supporting collaborative learning in videoconferencing using collaboration scripts and content schemes. In F. Fischer, I. Kollar, H. Mandl & J. M. Haake (Eds.), *Scripting computer-supported communication of knowledge – cognitive, computational and educational perspectives* (pp. 212-236). Berlin, Germany: Springer.

Fischer, F., Kollar, I., Haake, J. M., & Mandl, H. (2007). Introduction. In F. Fischer, I. Kollar, H. Mandl & J. M. Haake (Eds.), *Scripting computer-supported communication of knowledge – cognitive, computational and educational perspectives* (pp. 1-10). Berlin, Germany: Springer.

Fischer, F., Kollar, I., Mandl, H., & Haake, J. M. (2007). *Scripting computer-supported communication of knowledge–Cognitive, computational, and educational perspectives.* New York: Springer.

Geyken, A., Mandl, H. & Reiter, W. (1995). *Selbstgesteuertes Lernen mit Tele-Tutoring.* Orientierungshilfen für Trainer/innen und Tutor/innen.

Graesser, A. C., & Person, N. K. (1994). Question asking during tutoring. *American Educational Research Journal, 31*(1), 104–137.

Graesser, A. C., Person, N. K., & Magliano, J. P. (1995). Collaborative dialogue patterns in naturalistic one-to-one tutoring. *Applied Cognitive Psychology, 9,* 495–522. doi:10.1002/acp.2350090604

Hattie, J., & Timperley, H. (2007). The power of feedback. *Review of Educational Research, 77*(1), 81–112. doi:10.3102/003465430298487

Haussmann, B. (2001). Nicht ohne meinen Tutor [Not without my tutor]. *Wirtschaft und Weiterbildung, 6,* 50–53.

Hidi, S., & Harackiewicz, J. (2000). Motivating the academically unmotivated. A critical issue for the 21st century. *Review of Educational Research, 70,* 151–179.

Hollingshead, A. B. (1996). Information suppression and status persistence in group decision making. The effects of communication media. *Human Communication Research, 23*(2), 193–219. doi:10.1111/j.1468-2958.1996.tb00392.x

Johnson, D. W., & Johnson, R. T. (1989). *Cooperation and competition: Theory and research.* Edina, MN: Interaction Book.

Johnson, D. W., & Johnson, R. T. (1992). Positive interdependence: Key to effective cooperation. In R. Hertz-Lazarowitz (Ed.), *Interaction in cooperative groups: The theoretical anatomy of group learning* (pp. 174-199). New York: Cambridge University Press.

Johnson, D. W., & Johnson, R. T. (1998). Co-operative learning and social interdependence theory. In R. S. Tindale, L. Heath, J. Edwards, E.Jj. Posavac, F. B. Bryant, Y. Suarez-Balcazar, E. Henderson-King & J. Myers (Eds.), *Theory and research on small groups* (pp. 9-35). New York: Plenum.

Keller, J. M. (1983). Motivational design of instruction. In C. M. Reigeluth (Ed.), *Instructional design theories and models: An overview of their current studies.* Hillsdale, NJ: Erlbaum.

Keller, J. M., & Kopp, T. W. (1987). An application of ARCS model of motivational design. In C. M. Reigeluth (Ed.), *Instructional theories in action. Lessons illustrating selected theories and models* (pp. 289-320). Hillsdale, NJ: Erlbaum.

King, A. (2007). Scripting collaborative learning process: A cognitive perspective. In F. Fischer, I. Kollar, H. Mandl, & J. M. Haake (Eds.), *Scripting computer-supported communication of knowledge - Cognitive, computational, and educational perspectives* (pp. 13-37). Berlin, Germany: Springer.

Kopp, B. (2005). *Effekte schematheoretischer Unterstützung auf Argumentation und Lernerfolg beim kooperativen Lernen in Videokonferenzen* [Effects of schema-theoretic support on argumentation and performance in collaborative learning with videoconferencing]. Berlin, Germany: Logos.

Kopp, B., Ertl, B., & Mandl, H. (2006). Wissensschemata und Skript - Förderung der Anwendung von Theoriewissen auf Aufgabenbearbeitung in Videokonferenzen [Content scheme and script – Fostering the application of theoretical knowledge on task solving in videoconferencing]. *Zeitschrift für Entwicklungspsychologie und Pädagogische Psychologie, 38*(3), 132–138. doi:10.1026/0049-8637.38.3.132

Kopp, B., & Mandl, H. (2006). Wissensschemata. In H. Mandl, & H. F. Friedrich (Eds.), *Handbuch Lernstrategien* (pp. 127-124). Göttingen, Germany: Hogrefe.

Kopp, B., & Mandl, H. (2007). Fostering Argumentation with Script and Content Scheme in Videoconferencing. In C. Chinn, G. Erkens, & S. Puntambekar (Eds.), *Mice, Minds and Society – The Computer Supported Collaborative Learning Conference, 8* (pp. 382-392). New Jersey: International Society of the Learning Sciences.

Kopp, B., & Mandl, H. (2008). Blended Learning. Forschungsfragen und Perspektiven. [Blended Learning. Research questions and perspectives] In J. Issing & P. Klimsa (Hrsg.), *Online-Lernen* (S. 139-150). Weinheim, Germany: Beltz PVU.

Kuhn, D. (1991). *The skills of argument.* Cambridge, NY: Cambridge University Press.

Lambiotte, J. G., Skaggs, L. P., & Dansereau, D. F. (1993). Learning from lectures: effects of knowledge maps and cooperative review strategies. *Applied Cognitive Psychology, 7*, 483–497. doi:10.1002/acp.2350070604

Lepper, M. R., Drake, M. F., & O'Donnell-Johnson, T. (1997). Scaffolding techniques of expert human tutors. In K. Hogan & M. Pressley (Eds.), *Scaffolding Student Learning: instructional approaches and issues* (pp. 108-144). Cambridge, UK: Brookline Books.

Lou, Y., Abrami, P. C., & d'Apollonia, S. (2001). Small group and individual learning with technology: A meta-analysis. *Review of Educational Research, 71*(3), 449–521. doi:10.3102/00346543071003449

Maass, A., West, S. G., & Clark, R. D. (1993). Soziale Einflüsse von Minoritäten in Gruppen [Social influences of minorities in groups]. In D. Frey, & M. Irle (Eds.), *Gruppen- und Lerntheorien* (Bd. 2, pp. 65-122). Göttingen, Germany: Hogrefe.

Mandl, H. (2008). *Ausbildung von E-Learning-Tutoren zur Betreuung von Studierenden der Virtuellen Hochschule Bayern*. Virtuelles Kursangebot: Lehrstuhl für Empirische Pädagogik und Pädagogische Psychologie.

Milekic, D. (2007). *Auswirkung der tutoriellen Unterstützung auf Akzeptanz, Lernprozess und Lernerfolg* [Effects of tutorial support on acceptance, learning process and learning outcome]. Unpublished Master Theses, Ludwig-Maximilians-Universität, Munich.

Moscovici, S. (1980). Toward a theory of conversion behavior. In L. Berkowitz (Ed.), *Advances in Experimental Social Psychology, 13*, 209-239.

Nemeth, C. J. (1986). Differential contributions of majority and minority influence. *Psychological Review, 93*(11), 23–32. doi:10.1037/0033-295X.93.1.23

O'Donnell, A. M., & Dansereau, D. F. (2000). Interactive effects of prior knowledge and material format on cooperative teaching. *Journal of Experimental Education, 68*(2), 101–118. doi:10.1080/00220970009598497

Pekrun, R., & Schiefele, U. (1996). Emotions- und motivationspsychologische Bedingungen der Lernleistung. In: Weinert, F. H. (Hrsg.): *Enzyklopädie der Psychologie D / I Psychologie des Lernens und der Instruktion* (pp. 153–180). Göttingen, Germany: Hogrefe.

Quiamzade, A., & Mugny, G. (2001). Social influence dynamics in aptitude tasks. *Social Psychology of Education, 4*, 311–334. doi:10.1023/A:1011388821962

Rautenstrauch, Ch. (2001). Tele-tutoring. Zur Didaktik des kommunikativen Handelns im virtuellen Lernraum. *ISKO*, Berlin.

Reinmann, G., & Mandl, H. (2006). Unterrichten und Lernumgebungen gestalten. In A. Krapp & B. Weidenmann (Hrsg.), *Lehrbuch Pädagogische Psychologie* (S. 613-658). Weinheim, Germ.: Beltz.

Roscoe, R. D., & Chi, M. T. H. (2007). Understanding Tutor Learning: Knowledge-Building and Knowledge-Telling in Peer Tutors' Explanations and Questions. *Review of Educational Research, 77*(4), 534–574. doi:10.3102/0034654307309920

Rudestam, K. E., & Schoenholtz-Read, J. (2002). Overview: the coming of age of adult online education. In K.E. Rudestam & J. Schoenholtz-Read (Eds.), *Handbook of online learning: innovations in higher education and corporate training* (pp. 3-28). Thousand Oaks, CA:Sage.

Rummel, N., & Spada, H. (2007). Can people learn computer-mediated collaboration by following a script? In F. Fischer, I. Kollar, H. Mandl & J. M. Haake (Eds.), *Scripting computer-supported communication of knowledge – cognitive, computational and educational perspectives* (pp. 39-55). Berlin: Springer.

Ryan, R. M., & Deci, D. L. (2000). Self-determination theory and the facilitation of intrinsic motivation, social development, and well-being. *The American Psychologist, 55*(1), 68–78. doi:10.1037/0003-066X.55.1.68

Salmon, G. (2000). *E-Moderating – The Key to Teaching and Learning Online*. London: Taylor and Francis.

Salomon, G., & Globerson, T. (1989). When teams do not function the way they ought to. *International Journal of Educational Research, 13*(1), 89–99. doi:10.1016/0883-0355(89)90018-9

Schank, R. C., & Abelson, R. P. (1977). *Scripts, plans, goals and understanding*. Hillsdale, NJ: Erlbaum.

Schiefele, U., & Streblow, L. (2007). Motivation aktivieren [Activate Motivation]. In H. Mandl & H. F. Friedrich (Eds.), *Handbuch Lernstrategien* [Handbook on learning strategies] (pp. 232-247). Göttingen, Germany: Hogrefe.

Schmidt, H. G., & Moust, J. H. C. (1995). What Makes a Tutor Effective? A Structural-equations Modeling Apporach to Learning in Problem-based Curricula. *Academic Medicine, 70,* 708–714. doi:10.1097/00001888-199508000-00015

Schweizer, K., Pächter, M., & Weidenmann, B. (2001). A field study on distance education and communication: Experiences of a virtual tutor. *Journal of Computer-Mediated Communication, 6*(2).

Stark, R., Tyroller, M., Krause, U.-M., & Mandl, H. (2008). Effekte einer metakognitiven Promptingmaßnahme beim situierten, beispielbasierten Lernen im Bereich Korrelationsrechnung. *Zeitschrift für Padagogische Psychologie, 22*(H. 1), 59–71. doi:10.1024/1010-0652.22.1.59

Suthers, D. (2001). Towards a systematic study of representational guidance for collaborative learning discourse. *Journal of Universal Computer Science, 7*(3), 254–277.

Suthers, D., & Hundhausen, C. D. (2001). Learning by constructing collaborative representations: An empirical comparison of three alternatives. In P. Dillenbourg, A. Eurelings, & K. Hakkarainen (Eds.), *Proceedings of the First European Conference on Computer-Supported Collaborative Learning (euroCSCL)* (pp. 577-584). Maastricht, The Netherlands: McLuhan Institute.

Tenenbaum, G., & Goldring, E. (1989). A meta-analysis of the effect of enhanced instructions: Cues, participation, reinforcement and feedback and correctives on motor skill learning. *Journal of Research and Development in Education, 22,* 53–64.

van Dijk, T. A., & Kintsch, W. (1983). *Strategies of discourse comprehension.* New York: Academic Press.

Walberg, H. J. (1982). What makes schooling effective? *Contemporary Education Review, 1,* 1–34.

Webb, N. M. (1989). Peer interaction and learning in small groups. *International Journal of Educational Research, 13*(1), 21–39. doi:10.1016/0883-0355(89)90014-1

Zhang, J., & Norman, D. A. (1994). Representations in distributed cognitive tasks. *Cognitive Science, 18,* 87–122.

Section 4
Outlook

Chapter 13

Three Stages in the Social Construction of Virtual Learning Environments

Ken Stevens
Memorial University of Newfoundland, Canada
Victoria University of Wellington, New Zealand

ABSTRACT

Schools located in rural communities are often physically small in terms of the number of students who attend them in person on a daily basis, but through the introduction of e-learning partnerships, they can become large educational institutions based on the enhanced range of teaching and learning they can provide. Small school capacities can be enhanced by e-learning and the creation of virtual learning environments. Structurally, the capacity of schools can be enhanced by internet-based inter-institutional collaboration. Pedagogically, e-learning can enable schools to share teaching and learning within virtual learning environments spanning participating sites to facilitate student engagement with ideas, people and places in new, interactive ways. Three stages are identified in the development of teaching and learning in the virtual structures that complement traditional schools.

INTRODUCTION

Schools have traditionally enrolled their own students, appointed their own teachers and been organized to serve designated communities and it is not uncommon for them to be named after the town, suburb or community in which they are located. Some schools take pride in the preservation of their traditions and culture and instilling in students a strong sense of identity with the

institution in which they are educated. It is possible to consider traditional schools as closed learning institutions in that they are autonomous organizations, distinct not only from other forms of institutional life but also from other schools. This traditional school model has been around for a long time and almost everyone will be familiar with it. The closed model of educational provision, based on traditional schools, has been challenged by the introduction of the Internet, expansion in information and communication technologies, a growing range of educational software and the integration

DOI: 10.4018/978-1-61520-729-9.ch013

of computers, particularly laptops, in both teaching and learning. It could be argued that the most distinctive feature of the changes being brought to classrooms by the Internet and technologies associated with it is their inherently collaborative nature. Computers are communication tools that facilitate new ways of interacting between teachers and students as well as providing efficient ways of accessing information. With increasing use of computers and the Internet in schools, the closed model of education is changing and an increasingly open approach to teaching, learning and classroom life based on individual and institutional collaboration has emerged. Nowhere is the move from closed to open teaching and learning more apparent than in rural schools in developed societies. The changes that have taken place in some rural schools encourage re-examination of the educational significance of physical isolation in terms of time, space, organization and school capacity. In a growing number of small schools in rural communities the introduction of virtual teaching and learning environments to traditional closed classrooms challenges perceptions of school size, location and the delivery of curriculum options. Above all, the integration of actual (or physical) and virtual classrooms has the potential to address long-standing policy issues of equality of access to educational opportunities by students who live beyond major centres of population.

BACKGROUND: SMALL SCHOOLS IN RURAL COMMUNITIES

In almost every society there are families who live beyond major centres of population. In Australia (Henry, 1989; Jarvis, 1990; Stevens, 2007), New Zealand (Starkey & Stevens, 2006; Stevens, 1999b; 1994) and Canada (Healey & Stevens, 2002; Stevens, 1999a; Tucker & Stevens, 1999) access to educational opportunities by students, particularly those in rural high schools, has been a long-standing policy issue. In Australia, for ex-

ample, the federal government has sought answers why young people from rural areas of that country enter universities and other institutions of higher learning in proportionally fewer numbers than their urban counterparts (Abbott-Chapman, 2001; Commonwealth Schools Commission, 1988; Goulding, 2001; James, et.al., Stewart, 2003). It has been common for rural high school students to either board at urban residential schools or be bussed to larger institutions where they can be taught by specialist teachers (Baker & Andrews, 1991). The development of rural school intranets has transformed many schools located in rural communities that are physically small in terms of the number of students who attend them, in person, on a daily basis, but, through the introduction of internet-based e-learning partnerships, have become larger and more comprehensive educational institutions based on the enhanced range of teaching and learning they can provide.

Rural Education in the Canadian Province of Newfoundland and Labrador

Atlantic Canada consists of four provinces: New Brunswick, Prince Edward Island, Nova Scotia and Newfoundland and Labrador. Newfoundland and Labrador covers by far the largest area of Atlantic Canada and, particularly in Labrador, there is very sparse population settlement. Newfoundland and Labrador's small population of approximately 500,000 residents in a large geographic area (156,185 square miles) presents challenges for the delivery of education, particularly at senior high school level. Newfoundland and Labrador has many small coastal communities, a predominantly rural lifestyle in most of the province and a distinctive history and culture.

In Newfoundland, the island portion of the province, almost all of the population lives in coastal settlements, including the capital, St John's. A decade ago approximately two thirds of schools in the province were located in rural communities but with continuing out-migration most small schools in Newfoundland and Labrador have decreased in size and during the last decade many have closed and local students have had to travel to larger centres to continue their education. Thirty one percent of educational institutions in the Canadian province of Newfoundland and Labrador are designated "small rural schools" (N=122) and 75 of these have fewer than 100 students. Seventy of the small rural schools in this province are classified as "all-grade" (K–12) which means that they must offer a senior high school program. The large proportion of small schools located in rural communities required special consideration in the development of electronic educational structures.

In the last decade there has been considerable re-organization of the school system in Newfoundland and Labrador, largely because of rural to urban migration together with a net outflow of people from the province. Small schools are not only getting smaller; many of them have been closed permanently. In 1996 ten Anglophone school district boards were created in the province together with one province-wide Francophone board - a reduction from 26 school boards. With continued reduction in school size in most rural Newfoundland and Labrador communities, the provincial administration of schools was further reorganized in 2003 to create four Anglophone and one Francophone school board.

The changes that have taken place in the organization and administration of education in rural Newfoundland and Labrador have influenced classroom structures and processes. In 1998 the first intranet was established in which eight schools in the same rural district were academically and administratively integrated, through the local school board, so that teaching and learning could be shared between the dispersed rural sites. The eight participating schools had to coordinate senior classes in those areas of the curriculum that were taught across multiple sites. Some schools received instruction for senior classes from teachers located

on other sites (schools) within the network. Collaboration between schools, teachers and students in the initial teaching and learning network was essential. Classrooms that had previously been closed to one another began to open to classes located in other parts of the district network for both teaching and learning. The autonomy of teachers within their own classrooms as well as their isolation from other members of the profession was challenged by this initiative. Students struggled with the concept of discussing their work with peers they did not know who participated in shared lessons taught from other locations. The traditional closed, or autonomous, model of the school was challenged by an increasingly open teaching and learning environment.

The initial intranet initiative challenged the notion that senior students in small schools have to leave home to complete their education at larger schools in urban areas. By participating in open classes in real (synchronous) time, combined with a measure of independent (asynchronous) learning, senior students were able to interact with one another through audio, video and electronic whiteboards. The initial electronic linking of eight sites within a school district to collaborate in the teaching of senior Biology, Chemistry, Mathematics and Physics initiated a series of open classes in rural Newfoundland and Labrador. The creation of the first intranet was an attempt to use information and communication technologies to provide geographically-isolated students with extended educational and, indirectly, vocational opportunities.

Stage One: Awareness of New Learning Environments

Adjustments had to be made in each participating site in the initial Newfoundland and Labrador intranet administratively and academically so that classes could be taught. While technological and administrative changes supported this initiative, adjustments were needed in the professional education of teachers. The structural changes that have taken place in Newfoundland and Labrador since the inception of the first intranet, within which initial senior science courses were developed and taught, has advanced to become a system that provides online instruction to almost all schools in the province. The provincial government, after a ministerial inquiry (Government of Newfoundland and Labrador, 2000) expanded the linking of schools through the creation of the Centre for Distance Learning and Innovation (CDLI) within the Newfoundland and Labrador Department of Education. Today CDLI develops and administers online learning that complements traditional classes in schools throughout the province. Awareness of what was taking place in the delivery of education in the province has had to be fostered in both pre-service as well as practicing teachers who have traditionally been prepared to teach in autonomous, or closed, teaching and learning environments known as classrooms. While many members of the profession will continue to provide instruction in traditional closed environments, an increasing number will teach in open, collaborative, internet-based learning spaces.

There are challenges in finding appropriate ways of using technology in an e-learning classroom (Cavanaugh, 2001). A major challenge is that teachers have had to learn to teach collaboratively from one site to another, using a range of technologies simultaneously.

Stage Two: New Roles for Teachers and Administrators

The introduction of intranets and the integration of face-to-face and virtual learning in rural Newfoundland and Labrador led to the creation of new roles for teachers and administrators in Newfoundland and Labrador. The relationship of e-teachers to traditional face to face teachers had to be considered, the creation of m-teachers and, subsequently, m-teams developed and administrative and technical support for virtual educational environments had to be provided.

i.   Face-to-Face and E-Teachers

A challenge facing many traditional face-to-face teachers is finding effective ways of integrating information and communication technologies (ICT), including the internet, into teaching and learning. It is not difficult to add information and communication technologies to any classroom but it requires considerable planning to integrate ICT into curricula so that both teaching and learning are enhanced.

E-teachers in Newfoundland and Labrador are experienced face-to-face classroom practitioners from the public school system who have elected to teach online. These full time teachers are subject area specialists with proven records of teaching excellence and curriculum development work. CDLI has grouped e-teachers into subject-specific or subject-related "pods" (e.g., mathematics teachers) to encourage collaborative learning and facilitate the virtual school's administrative structure (Furey & Stevens, 2008). Class sizes for e-teachers are generally kept to a maximum of twenty students who may be situated throughout the province, or even nationally or internationally depending on individual student circumstances.

Principals and teachers appointed to the closed, autonomous learning environments of face-to-face schools frequently discover that their role requires the development of open structures within which they are increasingly expected to collaborate with their peers located across a range of distant sites (Furey, 2008). Many now find that the positions to which they were appointed in face-to-face (i.e., traditional or closed) schools have become, in effect, locations within new virtual (i.e., open) electronic schools. In Newfoundland and Labrador the integration of traditional schools (most of which are located in rural areas) and virtual classes is now a challenge for educational administrators seeking to maximize the potential of on-site and on-line teaching and learning (Stevens and Stewart, 2005).

ii.   M-teachers and M-Teams

In the initial stages of e-learning in rural Newfoundland and Labrador mediating teachers (m-teachers) were appointed to manage on-site problems faced by e-learners being taught from a distant location. Usually m-teachers were face-to-face classroom teachers with the extra, mediating responsibility, of liaising with e-teachers on behalf of e-learners in their schools. In a concept paper that compared m-teachers and m-teams, Coffin (2002, p.2) pointed out that

"The benefits of a technology-enabled school will not be realized unless the human resources in those schools also possess the knowledge and skills needed to function effectively in those technologies. Technologically advanced schools need to prepare and organize their human resources so as to support an alternative delivery method which operates not as a competitor to traditional face to face (teaching and learning), but as a complement to it. Assigning one individual as a school's only resource to mediate between e-teachers and e-learners is far from sufficient to realize that vision."

Coffin argued against the practice of appointing m-teachers to support e-teachers and e-learners by creating a team approach. He suggested that m-teams be established, with specific responsibilities, to replace m-teachers in rural schools in Newfoundland and Labrador:

"The report *Supporting Learning* (Government of Newfoundland and Labrador, 2000) envisioned a teaching role to provide school-based support for students who were instructed by an off-site e- teacher. Initially conceived of as a singular role, that is, one performed by a single teacher, evolving research ...suggests that a team concept is perhaps better suited to fulfilling CDLI's vision of small schools as 'beacons of technological innovation' with respect to distance learning. Conceptually, then, e-learning needs the support of a team of people providing four sets of skills: technical, coaching, administrative and resource

advisor. We can attach an order of priority to those tasks as well, based on research. We have noted that students in e-learning courses have a high dependence on the technology used to deliver the courses. The higher the dependency, the greater the requirement that the technology be reliable. This feature is so important that it deserves the highest ranking among tasks performed by m-teams. Using students' assessments of the role of m-teachers, the coaching function is the next most helpful role, followed by administrative and, then, that of the resource teacher. Teams may be real or virtual or a combination of both.

By that we mean the expertise can reside on-site in the form of a teacher or staff person or it can exist apart from the school, e.g., a content -area web-site maintained by a teacher in another school or province. So the idea of a team doesn't have to imply people getting together periodically to plan strategy or solve problems. The team represents more of a bank of resources easily accessible to on-line students which can be used to facilitate their learning (Coffin, 2002, p.1).

The m-team typically consists of a technology teacher, a technician, help line desk, advanced computer studies student(s), a coach (another teacher with an interest in distance learning), the school secretary, the resource teacher and an administrator. Each person on the team is responsible for specific support services. The technology teacher, the technician and the help-line desk and students manage technical problems according to an agreed set of protocols. The coach provides the nurturing, encouragement and advice that students need to persist in their studies. The technology teacher could also be the coach who will be the school-based contact for the e-teacher when necessary. These two professionals together handle most of the pedagogical functions associated with on-line learning. Coaches are assigned to students, rather than courses, because the services they need to provide are client oriented rather than content oriented. The school secretary takes responsibility for conveying hard-copy correspondence between the e-teacher and students and other clerical functions. The resource teacher provides services similar to those made available to classroom instructed students. This person catalogues, stores and controls the distribution of the learning resources for the on-line courses. The administrator provides the administrative support services that ensure the smooth and efficient operation of on-line learning (including supervision of instruction). In the Coffin model the m-team could be the whole staff of a small school in a rural community, consisting of teachers, support staff, and administration. The configuration of small schools varies considerably, so it is not appropriate to consider a single model for m-teams in all schools. This approach to supporting e-learning in rural schools has been adopted in Newfoundland and Labrador by the Centre for Distance Learning and Innovation and m-teams replaced m-teachers. In the province of Newfoundland and Labrador, CDLI provides the professional development for each of these m-team members to fulfill their roles through initial training days and ongoing support. However, some schools that engage in e-learning have small numbers of students and staff, and in some instances all of the above m-team roles may be assumed by only one or two individuals.

iii.   Virtual School Administrators and Technical Support

CDLI has a director who has a liaison role between the government Department of Education of Newfoundland and Labrador and CDLI. Beneath the director there are five key administrators. An administrator for program delivery and school services acts as the principal for the virtual school establishing student demand for course offerings and assigning teaching duties. An administrator responsible for program development works as an instructional designer with curriculum developers and consultants to enrich existing high school courses and develop new ones. An administrator responsible for school technology integration works to facilitate technology initiatives with face-to-face teachers and students in grades Kindergarten to nine. An administrator responsible for communication and connectivity services is the chief technician who ensures the stability and growth of the CDLI intranet, investigating new and effective technologies. An administrator responsible for face-to-face and e-teacher professional development facilitates the development and delivery of opportunities and resources.

Instructional designers are responsible for adapting the form of provincial government curricula, as specified in course curriculum guides, to a web-based environment. They ensure that the digital offering of prescribed high school courses enable e-learners to fulfill all of the prescribed provincial government's learning outcomes. However, in fulfilling this role, instructional designers have created many useful new learning resources to support the e-teaching and e-learners. Many of these resources have been made available to teachers and students engaged in face-to-face learning.

Technical support for the delivery of virtual courses was initially envisioned as a collaborative effort between CDLI technicians, school district technicians, and locally-based school teachers who had technical expertise. However, the task of providing the specific expertise needed for the technologies introduced by CDLI quickly became the domain of technicians while teachers adopted a troubleshooting role between students and technicians. District technicians are trained by CDLI on a regular basis and as new technologies are introduced. The provision of technical support for face-to-face schools willing to offer their students distance education courses is critical to the success of e-learning in rural Newfoundland and Labrador.

Stage Three: Collaboration and the Preparation of Teachers

To prepare teachers for emerging collaborative teaching and learning environments, three initiatives have been implemented at the pre-service level in the Faculty of Education in the province's only university, based on communities of practice.

The first step in the introduction of online communities of practice for high school teachers has been the development of awareness of recent changes in school organization in the province, particularly in the majority of schools that are located beyond major centres of population. Most of these institutions are physically small but are networked with other schools both academically and administratively. Teachers in Newfoundland and Labrador are increasingly expected to provide instruction between sites as well as in traditional classrooms. This reality has had to be included in courses for new teachers.

The second step in the creation of online communities of practice for pre-service high school teachers has been an introduction to collaboration at the internship level during pre-service teacher education between those undertaking initial teaching practice and professors in the Faculty of Education. By sharing the realities of initial contact by new teachers in classrooms with one another and with their professors, mutual understandings developed during the semester-length internship in schools.

A third step in the development of online communities of practice for the integration of virtual and actual teaching and learning at the conclusion of the internship has been collaboration within learning circles in courses at the university. Pre-service teachers are required to reflect on and critique one another's recent classroom experiences in schools and relate their critiques and reflections to educational research.

i. Development of Awareness of Collaborative Teaching and Learning Structures

To be professionally prepared for the reality of new, virtual educational structures and processes in Newfoundland and Labrador it has been necessary to introduce pre-service teachers to institutional as well as professional collaboration. The contradiction of teaching in closed learning spaces (or traditional classrooms) located in collaborative networks of schools challenges students to re-examine the changed nature of education in the province. Pre-service teachers are asked to consider research on the use of computers in education (Mathiasen, 2004) and their potential for collaborative teaching as well as shared learning between dispersed sites (Cavanaugh, 2001; Ertl and Plante, 2004; Hawkes and Halverson, 2002). In initial courses in the Faculty of Education online learning communities for teachers are being developed that include practicing teachers, pre-service teachers and teacher-educators so that they can collaborate and, in doing so, learn from one another. Students have been provided with opportunities to discuss, in groups, educational theory from lectures with recent graduates who are now teaching in schools and have volunteered to participate in pre-service courses from diverse sites. Pre-service teachers are provided with access to schools and practicing teachers are kept in touch with what is happening in the Faculty of Education in terms of research, new publications and the exploration of ideas.

ii. Collaborative Teaching and Learning During the Internship

Poole (2000) noted that pre-service teacher development is an ideal time to introduce teacher candidates to the larger community of their profession and to the tools that can provide them with access to continued learning within an online community of practice. A salient benefit of communities of practice is the bridging of formal organizational boundaries in order to increase the collective knowledge, skills, and professional trust and reciprocity of practitioners who serve in these organizations. Ingersol & Kralik (2004) found evidence to indicate that beginning teachers who participated in an induction program with experienced teachers during their first year of teaching were less likely to leave the profession.

Following the introduction of pre-service teachers in the Faculty of Education to schools, a complementary program has been developed to further assist their induction into the profession through the internship. In the secondary teacher education program at Memorial University that consists of three semesters, the middle semester is spent in schools as interns under the guidance of a co-operating teacher. While in schools as interns, pre-service teachers are required to engage with one another in a further online community of practice in completing academic assignments related to their classroom work. However, not all students return from the intern experience to the university aware of the changes that are taking place in the delivery of education in the province, particularly if they spent their time in urban schools.

iii.   Learning Circles

A challenge for teacher educators engaging new members of the profession is linking the practice of teaching and learning in schools to educational theory. In post-internship learning circles students are asked to bring to their discussions appropriate reading from academic journals and books that complement their discussions about recent teaching practice as interns. Pre-service teachers in their final semester are encouraged to consider the sociological implications of classroom issues they encountered in initial teacher education courses and then met in schools as interns and, if possible, to locate them within an appropriate theoretical perspective. Discourse about shared experience between students and between practicing teachers

facilitates the creation of new realities as participants discover common perceptions, experiences and problems. Learning Circles encourage the development of awareness in pre-service teachers that members of their profession have traditionally been isolated from one another in their classroom spaces but that this is not always appropriate in an internet-based network of schools.

THEORETICAL IMPLICATIONS: THE INTEGRATION OF ACTUAL AND VIRTUAL LEARNING ENVIRONMENTS THROUGH CYBERCELLS

The development of shared realities through cybercells - face-to-face groups whose members extend their discussion to include virtual visitors (Stevens & Stewart, 2005) - challenge teacher and student isolation as intranets have challenged the physical isolation of rural schools in Newfoundland and Labrador over the last decade. In a cybercell teachers who collaborate on an actual site (or school) can share their discussions with virtual colleagues from other sites located within their internet-based network and beyond it. Cybercells enable shared realities to be created both on site, for example, in a particular school, as well as virtually, by enabling participants at a distance to engage in discourse with colleagues or peers in a given, physical location. The development of collaborative structures and, within them, engagement by teachers and students in cybercells, facilitate the social construction of knowledge through shared understandings.

The changes that have taken place in the provision of education in rural Newfoundland and Labrador are underpinned by the move from closed to open teaching and learning that has been made possible by the internet. The emergence of intranets, within which collaborative teaching and learning can develop, has provided extended educational opportunities for young people who live beyond major centres of population (Stevens, 2003). Small school capacities in Newfoundland and Labrador have been extended by e-learning and the creation of virtual learning environments in three ways: *structurally*, the capacity of small schools in rural Atlantic communities has been enhanced by the development of collaborative learning environments based on intranets; *pedagogically*, new roles for teachers have been created that complement traditional classroom instruction while facilitating e-learning, and *collaboration* has been encouraged between teachers, learners and schools by the integration of physical and virtual learning spaces

From Closed to Open Learning Environments

Traditionally, schools in rural communities have been closed, autonomous institutions, characterized by physical isolation. In the Canadian province of Newfoundland and Labrador the distance between small schools has, increasingly, been used as educational space as intranets have formed and cybercells have facilitated the creation of open, collaborative, teaching and learning environments. The development of open learning environments to complement small schools has implications for the provision of rural education in terms of space, time, organization and capacity. In the move from closed to open teaching and learning environments in rural Newfoundland and Labrador, there are several outstanding features:

- Virtual learning environments in Newfoundland and Labrador have been developed to support existing schools by using the space between rural sites to form intranets.
- The creation of open environments has enabled resources to be shared between sites, including specialized teacher expertise, thereby enhancing the educational capacity of schools that form sites within intranets.

- Learners in the open learning environments that have been established by using spaces between rural schools in Newfoundland and Labrador have been provided with access to more than one teacher. Increasingly, students in rural Newfoundland and Labrador have both on-site and on-line teachers.
- With access to teachers from multiple sites that constitute open educational environments, students in rural Newfoundland and Labrador have been provided with enhanced learning opportunities.
- Collaboration has been essential in the move from closed to open educational environments. Structurally, schools have been encouraged to collaborate through the creation of intranets. Pedagogically, teachers and students have been encouraged to collaborate through the formation of classes between sites within intranets.
- The creation of open teaching and learning environments in rural Newfoundland and Labrador has provided a local response to the global policy issue of enhancing educational opportunities for students in small schools in remote locations. Within open teaching and learning environments senior students in small rural high schools in Newfoundland and Labrador have been provided with access to specialized areas of the curriculum.

FUTURE RESEARCH DIRECTIONS

In Newfoundland and Labrador, and possibly in other places that have rural schools with internet access, research into ways educational opportunities at the community level could be developed would enhance school intranets. It is possible that the creation of electronic educational structures and processes has weakened small communities by providing young rural people with enhanced pathways to urban educational and vocational opportunities. A possible next step for internet-enhanced rural schools is to extend virtual learning environments to local homes so that parents and adult citizens can also be provided with enhanced educational opportunities.

CONCLUSION

Structural and pedagogical change in the provision of education in rural Newfoundland and Labrador has been a local response to the international problem of providing extended educational opportunities for young people regardless of the location of their homes or the size of their community schools. In resource-based economies such as Canada's, in which a large part of a nation's wealth is based on mining, forestry, fishing and agriculture, sustainable rural schools are fundamental to economic well-being. However, the well-being of the most geographically-isolated people in any society, including the rural population of Newfoundland and Labrador, increasingly depends on the extent to which physical isolation can be challenged through classrooms that facilitate e-collaboration.

REFERENCES

Abbott-Chapman, J., & Patterson, C. (2001). Improving post-school outcomes of rural school leavers. *Australian Journal of Education*, *45*(1), 35–47.

Baker, R., & Andrews, J. (1991). Parental reasons for sending children to a rural day and boarding school. *Education in Rural Australia*, *1*(1), 21–25.

Cavanaugh, C. (2001). The effectiveness of interactive distance education technologies in K-12 learning: a meta-analysis. *International Journal of Educational Telecommunications*, *7*(1), 73–88.

Coffin, G. (2002). *Mediating E-learning: M-teacher or M-team?* St John's, Centre for Distance Learning and Innovation, Department of Education of Newfoundland and Labrador.

Commonwealth Schools Commission. (1988). *Schooling In Rural Australia*. Canberra, Australia: Curriculum Development Centre.

Ertl, H., & Plante, J. (2004). *Connectivity and Learning in Canada's Schools*, Ottawa, Canada: Government of Canada.

Furey, D. (2008). *From radio broadcasts to virtual reality: A case study of distance education in Hermitage Bay Schools.* Paper presented May 2, 2008 at Symposium 2008, From the Rhetoric to the Reality, Fifty Years of Educational Change in Newfoundland and Labrador. St. John's: Memorial University of Newfoundland.

Furey, D., & Stevens, K. (2008). New Systemic Roles Facilitating the Integration of Face-to-Face and Virtual Learning. *Online Journal of Distance Learning Administration*, 11(4). Retrieved from http://www.westga.edu/~distance/ojdla/

Golding, B. (2001). *Great Divides in Learning: Youth Pathways in Rural and Remote Australian Towns.* Camberwell, Australia: Australian Council for Educational Research Government of Newfoundland and Labrador. (2000). *Supporting Learning: Report on the Ministerial Panel on Educational Delivery in the Classroom.* St John's, Department of Education.

Hawkes, M., & Halverson, P. (2002). Technology Facilitation in the Rural School: An Analysis of Options. *Journal of Research in Rural Education*, *17*(3), 162–170.

Healey, D., & Stevens, K. (2002). Student Access to Information Technology and Perceptions of Future Opportunities in Two Small Labrador Communities. *Canadian Journal of Learning and Technology / La Revue Canadienne de l'Apprentissage et de la Technologie*, 28(1), 7-18.

Henry, M. (1989). The functions of schooling: Perspectives from rural Australia. *Discourse: The Australian Jrnl. of Educational Studies, 9*(2), 5–21.

Ingersoll, R., & Kralik, J. M. (2004). *The Impact of Mentoring on Teacher Retention: What the Research Says.* Denver, CO: Education Commission of the States.

James, R., Wyn, J., Baldwin, G., Hepworth, G., McInnis, C., & Stephanou, A. (1999). *Rural and Isolated School Students and their Higher Education School Choices.* Canberra, Australia: National Board of Employment, Education and Training, Higher Education Council.

Jarvis, S. (1990). *Rural Students and Post Grade 10 Education in Tasmania: A Study for the Country Areas Program.* Hobart, Department of Education and the Arts, Tasmania.

Mathiasen, H. (2004). Expectations of Technology: When the Intensive Application of IT in Teaching Becomes a Possibility. *Journal of Research on Technology in Education, 36*(3), 273–294.

Poole, M. J. (2000). *Developing Online Communities of Practice in Preservice Teacher Education.* Retrieved September 27, 2006, from http://citeseer.ist.psu.edu/update/508413

Starkey, L. & Stevens, K. (2006). Three Stages in the Digital Integration of New Zealand Schools. *New Zealand Ann. Rev. of Education - Te Arotake a Tau o te Ao o te Matauranga i Aotearoa, 16,* 105-117.

Stevens, K. J. (2007, August). Objective and Subjective Engagement with the Non-Local World by Rural School Leavers. *International Journal of Rural Psychology,* 1-13. Retrieved from http://www.ruralpsych.com/page3.html

Stevens, K. J. (2003). E-Learning and the Development of Open Classes for Rural Students in Atlantic Canada. In J. Bradley (Ed.), *The Open Classroom – Distance Learning In and Out of Schools* (pp. 149-157). London: Kogan Page.

Stevens, K. J. (1999a). A New Model for Teaching in Rural Communities – The Electronic Organization of Classes As Intranets. *Prism – Journal of The Newfoundland and Labrador Teachers'. Association, 6*(1), 23–26.

Stevens, K. J. (1999b). Telecommunications technologies, teleLearning and the development of virtual classes for rural New Zealanders. *Open Praxis,* (1), 12-14.

Stevens, K. J. (1994). Some applications of distance education technologies and pedagogies in rural schools in New Zealand. *Distance Education, 15*(4), 318–326. doi:10.1080/0158791940150210

Stevens, K. J., & Stewart, D. (2005). *Cybercells – Learning in Actual and Virtual Groups.* Melbourne, Australia: Thomson-Dunmore Press.

Stewart, A. E. (2003). *Post School Outcomes for 'The Island' Students and their Views on Place and Identity: Year 10 to Year 11 in a Rurally Remote Area.* Unpublished Ph.D. Thesis, Hobart, University of Tasmania.

Tucker, C., & Stevens, K. (1999). Where Do We Go From Here? Post-High School Educational and Vocational Choices of Students Leaving a Small Rural Canadian Community. *Journal of Critical Inquiry into Curriculum and Instruction, 1*(3), 22–24.

ADDITIONAL READING

Furey, D., & Stevens, K. (2008). New Systemic Roles Facilitating the Integration of Face-to-Face and Virtual Learning. *Online Journal of Distance Learning Administration,* 11(4). Retrieved from http://www.westga.edu/~distance/ojdla/

Stevens, K. J., & Stewart, D. (2005). *Cybercells – Learning in Actual and Virtual Groups.* Melbourne, Australia: Thomson-Dunmore Press.

KEY TERMS AND DEFINITIONS

Cybercell: Face-to-face groups whose members extend their discussions to include virtual visitors

E-Teachers: Teachers who teach through the internet

Intranet: Schools that are academically and administratively linked through the internet for collaborative teaching and learning.

M-Teachers: Mediating teachers who support e-teachers

Open Classes: Classes that are academically and administratively integrated within intranets to facilitate collaboration

Rural: Country or non-urban schools.

Chapter 14
Transactive Memory and Technology in Work Groups and Organizations

Richard L. Moreland
University of Pittsburgh, USA

Kristina L. Swanenburg
University of Pittsburgh, USA

Jeffrey J. Flagg
University of Pittsburgh, USA

Joshua D. Fetterman
University of Pittsburgh, USA

ABSTRACT

Transactive memory is a shared awareness among individuals about who knows what. Many studies show that work groups can develop transactive memory systems, and that groups whose systems are stronger perform better. Although organizations have been studied less often in this regard, the available evidence suggests that they can develop transactive memory systems too, and that stronger systems improve their performance as well. Technology can be a tool for strengthening transactive memory systems in work groups and (especially) organizations. Unfortunately, workers often resist using such technology, which limits its effectiveness. Several explanations for that resistance are considered, but the major problem is that workers simply prefer to locate and share their knowledge using interpersonal rather than technological methods. Instead of attempting to overcome this preference, it might be wiser for organizations to explore ways to strengthen interpersonal methods of sharing knowledge among workers.

INTRODUCTION

Scholars from many disciplines are interested in improving the performance of work groups and organizations. Although there are several possible ways to achieve this goal, there has been a focus in recent years on intellectual capital as an important factor (see Stewart, 1999; 2001). Intellectual capital includes all of the relevant knowledge that

DOI: 10.4018/978-1-61520-729-9.ch014

workers possess – knowledge that can help them do their jobs. No worker can know everything a job requires, especially if the job is complex and dynamic, as many jobs are today. So, knowledge must often be sought by workers. That knowledge might well be available within a worker's own group or organization. But people are often unaware of exactly where the knowledge that they need resides, so they waste time, energy, and other valuable resources by seeking that knowledge from outsiders, or (re)generating it on their own. As a result, intellectual capital loses some of its value – much knowledge is wasted because its location is unknown.

This problem arises, in large part, from weak transactive memory systems. Wegner (1986; see also Wegner, Giuliano, & Hertel, 1985; Wegner, 1995) was among the first to analyze such systems. Although Wegner focused on dyads (e.g., romantic couples), his analysis is relevant to work groups and organizations as well. Wegner noted that people often try to supplement their own memories, which are limited and can be unreliable, with various external aids. These aids include objects, such as calendars or address books, and other people, such as coworkers or partners. Wegner was intrigued by the use of people as memory aids. According to Wegner, transactive memory systems develop in many social settings to ensure that useful information is remembered. These systems combine the knowledge of individual group members with a shared awareness of who knows what. When group members need information, but cannot remember it on their own or worry that their own memories are inaccurate, they can thus turn to one another for assistance. In this way, transactive memory systems provide group members with access to more and better information than any one of them could remember alone.

The potential benefits of transactive memory for work group performance are clear. When group members know more about each other, they can plan their work together more sensibly, assigning tasks to the people who will perform them best.

Coordination ought to improve as well, because workers can anticipate one another's behavior, rather than simply react to it (see Wittenbaum, Vaughan, & Stasser, 1998). This would help them work together more efficiently, even if their task assignments were vague. Finally, problems should be solved more quickly and easily, because workers can match them with the people who are most likely to solve them (see Moreland & Levine, 1992). Once those people were identified, they could be asked for help, or the problems could just be given to them to solve. Analogous performance benefits might occur in an organization as well. For example, a greater awareness of who knows what could improve how work groups are staffed. Workers with relevant knowledge could be assigned to groups that require such knowledge for their work. Those groups could thus be smaller, because redundant knowledge is minimized, and problems associated with a lack of knowledge should occur less often. What if unexpected problems occurred? A greater awareness of who knows what would allow knowledgeable workers within the organization to be located more readily and then asked or instructed to help. As a result, the problems might be solved more efficiently than if group members attempted to solve them on their own, or if they sought help without knowing exactly where to find it.

All of this suggests that the performance of work groups and organizations could be improved by helping workers to develop stronger transactive memory systems -- systems that are more accurate and shared more widely. Technology might aid in this endeavor. Our major goal in this chapter is to consider whether and how technology could be used to support transactive memory systems. We will begin by summarizing prior research on transactive memory systems in work groups and organizations, then review efforts to strengthen transactive memory systems through the use of technology, and finally draw some conclusions about the value of such efforts (and how they might be improved).

The Origins of Transactive Memory Systems

How do transactive memory systems arise in work settings? Job titles are the most obvious source of information about who knows what, but they often change too slowly to reflect current expertise, and they may not encompass all of the relevant knowledge anyway. That is, workers sometimes possess knowledge that is not implied by their job titles, and/or they do not possess knowledge that is implied by those titles. Some of the knowledge that could be useful can thus "fall between the cracks," in the sense that it is not clearly linked to any job titles. Of course, a manager might assign specific workers the responsibility for particular kinds of knowledge, but once again, it would be difficult to cover all the knowledge that workers might need, especially if their needs changed over time. And what would be the bases for such assignments? How could they be made fairly? Workers might try to negotiate responsibilities for knowledge directly with one another, but the same issues would probably arise and conflicts might again occur.

Beliefs about who knows what can also arise naturally, regardless of job titles, managerial assignments, and negotiated responsibilities. A variety of cues can be used by workers in this regard (Wegner, 1986), including stereotypes (e.g., women are more likely than men to know something about a task), and primacy/recency effects (e.g., the first or last person who performed the task is more likely than others to know something about it). Unfortunately, such cues may not be available to everyone, or credible to them, which could produce diverging beliefs about who knows what. And some cues are misleading, so they produce erroneous beliefs about who knows what. Divergent and erroneous beliefs about expertise could harm the performance of a work group or organization. In fact, a weak transactive memory system may actually be worse than no system at all.

Transactive memory systems can also arise through shared experience. As workers spend time together, working with one another on various projects, they obtain direct evidence of expertise. Certain tasks are performed better by some people than by others, due in part to variability in relevant knowledge. This suggests that groups whose members have worked together longer should perform better. Many researchers, studying different kinds of work groups, have indeed observed that effect (e.g., Berman, Down, & Hill, 2002; Goodman & Shah, 1992; Kanki & Foushee, 1989; Reagans, Argote, & Brooks, 2005). As people work together, and evidence of their relative expertise accumulates, informal roles may also develop, so that some people expect (and are expected by others) to be better at particular tasks. Such roles are also likely to improve the performance of a work group or an organization (see Stasser, Stewart, & Wittenbaum, 1995).

The natural emergence of a transactive memory system is often tacit, in the sense that workers do not discuss what is happening – they may not even be aware that it has happened. But the system itself, once it has formed, can be made explicit by producing a written summary of everyone's beliefs about who knows what. Those beliefs could be measured by asking workers to describe their own strengths and weaknesses, and/or the strengths and weaknesses of their colleagues. A summary of everyone's beliefs can then be made available to anyone who needs such information. Technology could be helpful in this regard – a summary of workers' expertise could be digitized and made available on a computer system as a searchable database. Later on, we will describe and evaluate some efforts of this sort.

RESEARCH ON TRANSACTIVE MEMORY

Work Groups

Much of the research on transactive memory systems in groups has been done by just a few researchers. Three major clusters of researchers can be identified, namely ourselves (with Linda Argote), Kyle Lewis and her colleagues, and social network analysts (especially Ed Palazzolo).

Our own research. Over the past few years, we have done several laboratory experiments (in collaboration with Linda Argote) to learn how the transactive memory systems of small groups can be strengthened, in order to improve the performance of those groups. More detailed descriptions of this research can be found elsewhere (see Liang, Moreland, & Argote, 1995; Moreland, 1999; Moreland, Argote, & Krishnan, 1996; 1998; Moreland & Myaskovsky, 2000). Here, we will offer only a general description of our methodology and an overview of our findings.

In our research, transactive memory systems are created primarily through shared experience. We manipulate such experience by training group members in different ways. Everyone learns to perform a rather complex task – building a transistor radio from a kit that contains dozens of parts. Although treatment conditions vary from one experiment to another, we usually train the participants in one condition individually (three persons are in the same room, at the same time, but they have limited contact and cannot interact), while the participants in another condition are trained together (in three-person groups). The latter condition creates a shared experience that helps people to develop a transactive memory system by observing one another and gathering direct evidence of who knows what.

The content of training is the same for all participants, regardless of their treatment condition. At the training session, the experimenter first demonstrates how to build the radio, answering any questions participants may have as he or she works. Participants are then asked to build a radio themselves. In the individual training condition, each person builds a radio alone, out of sight of the other group members. In the group training condition, all three group members build a radio together. The experimenter answers any questions the participants may have while they work on the radios. Once they are done, he or she inspects their radios and provides feedback about any mistakes that were made.

One week later, a second session is held. All of the participants are tested in three-person groups to see how well they learned to build the radios. In the individual training condition, group members are the three people who were trained separately at the same session the previous week. In the group training condition, group members are the three people who were trained together the previous week. We first ask the members of each group to recall, working together, as much as they can about building the radios. Then we ask each group to actually build a radio together, working within a time limit and without any help from the experimenter. Modest cash prizes are offered to the groups that perform best.

Three measures of group performance are obtained during the testing session, namely how much a group can recall about building radios, how many errors a group makes while building its radio, and how quickly a group's radio is built. Measures of transactive memory are derived from evaluations of videotapes made of the groups while they work on their radios during the testing session. Trained judges carefully examine participants' behavior for three signs that transactive memory systems are operating. The first of these is memory differentiation – the tendency for group members to specialize at remembering different aspects of building a radio. There should be more memory differentiation in groups with stronger transactive memory systems. A second sign is task coordination – the ability of group members to work together on their radio smoothly and efficiently.

Groups with stronger transactive memory systems should display better task coordination. Finally, the third sign is task credibility – the level of trust within the group about whether everybody knows what he or she is doing while working on the radio. Task credibility should be higher in groups with stronger transactive memory systems.

What have our experiments shown? First, group training (shared experience) can indeed strengthen transactive memory systems. When group members are trained together, rather than apart, they behave quite differently while building their radios – levels of memory differentiation, task coordination, and task credibility are significantly higher in such groups. Second, group performance is significantly better when group members are trained together, rather than apart. Group training helps members to recall more about building the radios and to make fewer mistakes in the radios that they build. Third, statistical analyses and variations in treatment conditions both show that the performance benefits of group training are due to transactive memory, and not to any other factors that might be associated with group training (e.g., stronger motivation, cohesion, or social identity; faster group development; generic learning about how to build radios in any group, or improved communication). To put it differently, there seems to be nothing else about group training, *other* than the creation of a transactive memory system, that improves group performance.

Along the way, several other findings worth noting have emerged from our research. First, turnover weakens transactive memory systems and thus harms the performance of groups whose members are trained together. Second, group training does not seem to produce social loafing (Latane, 1981) – the tendency for people to devote less effort to tasks when they work in groups rather than alone. Some might argue that group training is risky because it allows (or even encourages) people to learn their tasks less well. Yet when we tested people individually, rather than in groups, we found no differences in the

performance of those who received group versus individual training. Finally, the behavioral signs of transactive memory that we derive from the videotapes of our groups are valid – they correlate strongly with other, more direct measures of who knows what.

Lewis' Research. Lewis and her colleagues have also done extensive research on transactive memory systems in groups. One of her first studies (Lewis, 2003) involved the development (with careful attention to psychometric issues) of a brief pencil-and-paper, self-report scale that can be used to assess the transactive memory system of almost any group. This scale measures three general aspects of transactive memory, namely specialization, coordination, and credibility. Separate scores can be computed for each of these components, and an overall score can be computed as well. Across several studies, Lewis found that her scale had good reliability (at the component and the overall levels), and both convergent and discriminant validity. Regarding convergent validity, there were strong positive correlations (in a laboratory experiment) between scores on the scale and behavioral measures of transactive memory (similar to those used in our own research). Regarding discriminant validity, scores on the scale were not correlated with group autonomy, cohesion, or motivation. Finally, the scale's criterion validity was impressive as well. Scale scores correlated positively with both group performance and with functional communication among group members (see Leathers, 1972). Many other researchers have since used this scale (see Michinov, Olivier-Shiron, Rusch, & Chiron, 2008; Peltokorpi & Manka, 2008; Zhang, Hempel, Han, & Tjosvold, 2007); it has become a valuable asset for transactive memory research, especially research involving natural groups in field settings.

Another important contribution by Lewis was a 2004 paper on the development of transactive memory systems. Groups of MBA students, as part of a course, carried out actual consulting projects for businesses facing management problems. These projects were ultimately evaluated by both the clients and the students themselves. At the start of the term, data were collected on the demographic characteristics of group members, their prior familiarity with one another, and variability in their expertise. At two later time points, the members of each group also completed Lewis' transactive memory scale and then described how often and in what ways they had communicated with one another. Transactive memory systems early in the term were stronger in groups with greater variability in member expertise (especially if members were already familiar with one another), and in groups whose members communicated more often. However, only face-to-face communication was important in that regard; telephone calls and e-mails had no impact. Transactive memory systems strengthened, and communication levels among members increased, as the term went on. At the end of the term, stronger transactive memory systems were again found in groups whose members communicated more often, but once again, only face-to-face communication was important. Finally, project evaluations showed that groups performed better when their transactive memory systems were stronger.

More recently, Lewis, Lange, and Gillis (2005) explored how changes in the membership of a group, and in its task, can affect the group's transactive memory system and performance. At issue was whether the benefits of transactive memory for performing one task might generalize to another task. Small (three-person) groups were trained to build telephones using kits. In an initial training session, each group first watched an experimenter demonstrate how to build the telephone. Afterward, the group was given the chance to build a telephone itself. Everyone was then asked to return a week later for a second, testing session, at which they fully expected to work on the same task with the same partners.

At the second session, some groups indeed remained intact, but others were broken apart and their members reassigned to new groups, each containing three strangers. Every group was then given a kit and asked to build a telephone as quickly and accurately as possible. Afterward, group members completed a questionnaire that included Lewis' (2003) transactive memory scale. Questions were also asked about the perceived task expertise of everyone in the group. After completing the questionnaires, participants were asked to return a week later for a final session, at which they again expected to work on the same task with the same partners (from the second session).

Many surprises awaited participants at that third session, however. For example, the earlier membership manipulation was repeated, so that within each of the conditions created the week before (intact vs. reassigned), some of the groups remained intact, but others were broken apart and their members reassigned to new groups. A completely new task was then assigned to every group, namely the assembly of a small personal stereo, again from a kit. After examining a fully assembled stereo briefly, each group was given a kit and asked to build a new stereo as quickly and accurately as possible. After that, group members completed a questionnaire that asked again about everyone's task expertise. Membership was then manipulated once more, so that within each of the conditions created earlier in this session, some of the groups remained intact, but others were broken apart and their members reassigned to new groups. Finally, each group was given an electric stapler to examine briefly, then asked to write (as a group) a strategy for assembling that machine. These strategy statements were later evaluated by the researchers for "integrative quality" – a statement that went beyond trivial assembly details to address deeper, underlying electronic issues, was judged to have more integrative quality.

Analyses of data from the second session showed that intact groups had stronger transactive memory systems, and better task performance, than reassigned groups. Analyses of the data collected during the third session produced a variety of results, some of them unexpected. The researchers expected task performance to be better among groups that remained intact throughout the first two sessions (and thus kept their transactive memory system) than among groups whose members were twice reassigned (and thus never developed a transactive memory system), but no such difference was found. Nor did the researchers find, despite their expectations, any better performance among the latter groups than among groups whose members remained together at first, but were later reassigned, (and thus lost their transactive memory system). An ancillary set of analyses involving stability and changes in the task expertise of group members clarified these anomalies. Stability in the special skills of group members (revealed through a careful review of questionnaire responses about everyone's expertise) was a better predictor of group performance than was stability in group membership.

Other analyses of data from the second session focused on the integrative quality of the stapler assembly statements written by the groups. Groups whose members remained together throughout the experiment (and thus kept their transactive memory systems) produced statements of better quality than did groups whose members were consistently reassigned (and thus never developed a transactive memory system). And the latter groups produced better quality statements than did groups whose members remained together during the first session, but then were reassigned in the second and third sessions (thereby losing their transactive memory systems). These findings, which the authors expected, showed that experience with more than just one task could create a transactive memory system whose benefits are generalizable to new tasks.

Finally, Lewis, Belliveau, Herndon, and Keller (2007) later performed an experiment to learn more about the effects of membership change on transactive memory systems. Small (three-person) groups were again trained to build telephones

using kits. In an initial training session, each group watched an experimenter demonstrate how to build the telephone. Afterward, the group was given its own kit and the chance to build a telephone itself. Group members then completed a brief questionnaire, on which they described both their own task expertise and the expertise of their fellow group members. Finally, they were asked to return a week later for a second, testing session, at which everyone expected to work with the same partners.

At that later testing session, however, the composition of the groups was manipulated. In a stable groups condition, participants indeed remained in the same groups where they were trained. But in a reconstituted groups condition, the original groups were broken apart and their members were reassigned to new groups, each containing three strangers. Finally, there was a partially intact groups condition, in which one person from each group was removed and replaced by someone from another group. Each group in this condition thus contained two "oldtimers" and one "newcomer." During the testing session, participants were first asked to recall (on their own, then with their partners) everything they could about how to build the telephones. Each group was then given a kit and asked to build a telephone as quickly and accurately as possible, within a time limit. Finally, everyone completed another questionnaire, on which they again described both their own task expertise and that of their fellow (current) group members.

The speed and accuracy with which groups built their telephones were important dependent measures. But two unusual measures involving transactive memory were developed as well. One was the stability of each group's transactive memory system. The researchers reviewed the task expertise of each group member (as evaluated by that person and his or her partners) at the testing session, and then identified any particular skills that the person possessed. Those skills were then compared with the expertise structure (the total set of skills possessed by all members) of the group where that person was trained. To the extent that group members, at the testing session, retained the same "specialties" that they had during the training session, the group's transactive memory system was viewed as more stable. The other unusual measure was the "efficiency" of each group's transactive memory system. The researchers reviewed what each group collectively recalled (at the testing session) about how to build the telephones, and then compared that with what the group's members recalled on their own. To the extent that there was no loss of member knowledge by the group, its transactive memory system was said to be efficient.

What were the results? A group's transactive memory system was more stable and efficient, and its performance was better, when its membership was stable, rather than reconstituted, and both of these effects were mediated by transactive memory. The most interesting results, however, involved groups whose membership remained only partially intact. Although the transactive memory systems of these groups were just as stable as those of the groups whose membership remained the same, the efficiency of their transactive memory systems was lower and their performance was worse (comparable in both ways to the reconstituted groups). A detailed analysis of changes in member specialties from training to testing revealed the reasons for these problems. Oldtimers in the groups that were reconstituted attempted to preserve the specialties they had developed during training, whereas newcomers attempted to adapt by changing their specialties to fit the apparent needs of the groups that they joined. In some cases, those changes were maladaptive, in the sense that the newcomers did not possess the appropriate skills, and this harmed the performance of the reconstituted groups. In a separate, subsidiary study, Lewis and her colleagues tried to solve this problem by encouraging oldtimers (at the start of the testing session, before they met the newcomers) to consider carefully the special skills of everyone in their group. This tactic was

successful – the oldtimers were later more likely to change their own specialties, rather than counting on newcomers to adapt, and this led to healthier transactive memory systems, and better performance in their groups (comparable in both ways to the stable groups in the original experiment).

Social Network Researchers. A third cluster of studies comes from several social network researchers (e.g., Garner, 2006; Palazzolo, 2005; Palazzolo, Serb, She, Su, & Contractor, 2006; Yuan, Fulk, & Monge, 2007). Social networks are complex webs of relationships among actors (see Freeman, 2006). The actors are usually individuals, and their relationships (which can be unidirectional or bidirectional) represent different levels of interdependence. Interdependence can take any of several forms, such as communication, commerce, or social support. Networks based on different forms of interdependence, even among the same individuals, may or may not be similar. Although there are several methods for mapping social networks, one typically needs data on the relationships between every possible pair of actors.

Some social network researchers have studied transactive memory systems in work groups (or organizations) by examining information exchange relationships. They measure who asks whom for information, who gives information to whom, and when people have questions, how choices are made about which group member to ask, and whether those choices are wise. Consider, for example, a study by Palazzolo (2005), who asked the members of a dozen work groups to answer (on an Internet survey) questions about their own expertise, the expertise of their colleagues, and who typically asked whom for information on various topics relevant to the group's work. These data were then used to test several hypotheses suggested by a transactive memory analysis of work group behavior.

Some of those hypotheses were supported. For example, when different members of a group had similar questions, they tended to ask them of the same person, someone who was viewed by the group as having relevant expertise. Other hypotheses were not supported. For example, the researchers expected requests for information about a given knowledge area to be unidirectional – if Mary asked Nancy questions about accounting, then Nancy would not ask accounting questions of Mary. Instead, there was evidence of bidirectionality in information requests – people often asked one another similar kinds of questions, perhaps due to a reciprocity norm. Another unexpected result involved the choices group members made about whom to ask for information. The researchers expected people to ask for information from group members who viewed themselves as having more relevant expertise, and for people to prefer those group members to one another as sources of such information. Yet neither of these predictions was supported, maybe because group members do not always perceive (or report) their own expertise accurately. Also, people who know a lot about a topic may be reluctant to admit or claim their expertise, and people who actually know little about a topic may exaggerate their expertise, with the goal of private self-enhancement or public impression management (or both).

Palazzolo, Serb, She, Su, and Contractor (2006) reported a later analysis of transactive memory systems in work groups that was especially intriguing. Rather than collecting actual data, they relied on computational modeling (see Hyatt, Contractor, & Jones, 1997), a methodology that other researchers (e.g., Ren, Carley, & Argote, 2006) have also used to explore transactive memory. In research of this type, the first step is to embody some theory about people's behavior in a set of mathematical equations. Using those equations, software can be developed to create a simulated social "world" in the computer, one where the variables within the equations can interact with one another over a specified period of "time." A researcher sets each of those variables to some initial value of interest, then allows the software to run until that time has passed, when the final

values of the variables are noted. These results can then be compared with the results from a comparable study of actual people and their behavior. To the extent that the two sets of results match, the simulation is viewed as valid. Mismatches are often interesting, however, because they sometimes reveal important theoretical issues that ought to be addressed. After a simulation has been validated, it can also be used to generate "new" results, for which no relevant studies have yet been done in the real world. This can be quite valuable, especially in areas of research where data collection is difficult and such studies might never (or could never) be done.

For their computational modeling, Palazzolo and his colleagues wrote mathematical equations that embodied several of Wegner's ideas about transactive memory. These nonlinear difference equations involved three "generative mechanisms" described by Wegner (1995) – mechanisms involving communication related to directory updating (group members develop/revise beliefs about who knows what), information allocation (group members send new information to people who are viewed as having relevant expertise), and information retrieval (group members who need information seek it from people who are viewed as having relevant expertise). These equations were then incorporated into "Blanche" – flexible software that helps researchers do agent-based modeling, a common form of computational modeling. Agents are entities, such as "workers," each of whom can be assigned different attributes, such as "knowledge" about some topic. A set of rules relates the agents to one another. They might, for example, "communicate" with one another frequently or infrequently. Rules can also specify how agent attributes and relations change, and how they affect one another, over time. Palazzolo and his colleagues built into Blanche the transactive memory equations they had developed, then used the software to test several propositions about the operation of transactive memory systems in work groups. These propositions involved three attributes, namely how much each "worker" knew about the task; how accurately each worker perceived the task expertise of other "group" members, and how large the group was. Each of those attributes could take a high or low value, which allowed the researchers to carry out a 2 x 2 x 2 experiment. In each of the resulting eight cells, they created 400 networks and then observed their development. Every network was allowed to change until all attribute values (which the rules could change) stabilized. The three outcomes of interest were how often workers communicated with one another, how much they knew (at the end of the simulation) about one another's expertise, and how much knowledge differentiation they showed. Knowledge differentiation was the extent to which workers became "experts" on particular topics.

Initial support for the five propositions was unimpressive, so some corrective changes in the simulation were made. In the end, it was possible to draw some general conclusions about the apparent impact of the initial attributes on the final outcomes. Communication proved to be a key factor; it helped group members to learn more about one another's expertise and to develop better knowledge differentiation. Greater communication occurred in (a) smaller groups; (b) groups whose members knew more at first about one another's expertise; and (c) groups whose members initially knew more overall. Regardless of communication levels, there were also direct, positive effects of initial overall knowledge on final knowledge about the expertise of group members, and direct, negative effects on knowledge differentiation of initial knowledge about the expertise of group members and of group size. Many of these findings were consistent with the results of other, more conventional research on transactive memory. They also suggested some interesting new directions for future research.

Summary. It was not possible to review here all of the other research that has been done on transactive memory systems in work groups. Other research that might have been reviewed includes Akgun, Bryne, Keskin, and Lynn (2006), Austin (2003), Ellis (2006), Faraj and Sproull (2000), Michinov and Michinov (2009), Prichard and Ashleigh (2007); Rau (2005, 2006); and Srivastava, Bartol, and Locke (2006). Given the research that we did review, however, several conclusions are warranted. First, whenever people work together in a group, they are likely to develop a transactive memory system, especially if they interact often, depend on one another to do their jobs, possess different knowledge and skills, and work at jobs that are complex and difficult. Second, transactive memory systems are clearly helpful – the stronger a group's transactive memory system becomes, the better the group is likely to perform. This is especially true to the extent that workers' beliefs about who knows what are accurate and shared. Finally, transactive memory systems may have other benefits as well, for both a group and its members (e.g., collective and personal efficacy, group cohesion).

Organizations

Do organizations also possess transactive memory systems, and if so, then do such systems improve organizational performance? Many analysts would answer "yes" to both questions. Of course, there are important differences between work groups and organizations, some of which seem likely to have an impact on transactive memory systems and their effects.

Organizations are certainly larger than work groups, and so their transactive memory systems must contain more (and more varied) sources of knowledge. As a result, it is probably harder for workers to identify who knows what in organizations than it is in work groups. And there is probably a greater diffusion of responsibility among workers in organizations; everyone puts less effort into sharing what they know with others, believing that somebody else will share their knowledge instead (Latane, 1981). Organizations are also less cohesive than work groups and often evoke weaker commitment from their members (Moreland & Levine, 2000). "Safety" climates (see Edmondson, 1996;1999), where workers are not especially embarrassed to ask for information from colleagues, and do not necessarily look down on colleagues who make such requests, may also be weaker in organizations than in work groups. And trust among workers is often weaker in organizations than it is in work groups. Cohesion, commitment, safety, and trust have all been shown to affect the operation of transactive memory systems – transactive memory systems work best when those qualities are stronger (see Constant, Sproull, & Kiesler, 1996; Cruz, Perez, & Ramos, 2007; Kanawattanachai & Yoo, 2007; Peltokorpi, 2004; Van Zolingen, Streumer, & Stooker, 2001).

What is the evidence regarding transactive memory systems in organizations? That evidence is quite limited, if we stick to the claim that such systems involve a shared awareness among workers about who knows what. The best evidence that such systems exist in organizations may be a recent study by Jackson and Klobas (2008). They interviewed workers in a large division of a major technology organization. Each worker was asked to describe what kinds of knowledge existed within the organization and how such knowledge was usually created, stored, and shared. For example, where was knowledge kept in the organization, how often and in what ways did workers share it, and what factors inhibited that sharing? Transcripts of the workers' responses to these questions were examined by trained coders who looked for examples of directory updating, information allocation, and retrieval coordination – the transactive memory processes that Wegner (1995) described. Examples of all three processes were indeed found. Some of these examples involved the use of technology, but most involved interpersonal experiences, often of an informal, spontaneous type. For example, although various electronic tools (e.g., a searchable database of vitas) were

available and could be used for directory updating, workers said that much of their knowledge about colleagues came from working with them on different projects, and gossiping with or telling stories to them about work-related issues at the water cooler or during lunch.

If we loosen the concept of a transactive memory system somewhat, so that shared awareness is no longer a critical feature, then further evidence that such systems exist in organizations can be found in other studies as well. [One might also consider studies of information exchange among workers in social units that are larger than work groups, but not complete organizations – units such as social circles (e.g., Verbeke & Wuyts, 2007) and communities of practice (e.g., Vaast, 2004; Wenger & Snyder, 2000)]. At issue in these studies is whether workers display behaviors that could be viewed as evidence of transactive memory systems – behaviors that involve (for example) directory updating, information allocation, and retrieval coordination. Such behaviors have indeed been observed in several organizations (see Borgatti & Cross, 2003; Cross & Sproull, 2004; O'Reilly, 1982; Van Zolingen, Streumer, & Stooker, 2001).

Consider, for example, Borgatti and Cross (2003), who proposed and then tested a model of interpersonal information seeking in organizations. According to their model, someone who is thinking about asking a colleague for information will first try to discover what that colleague actually knows. Next, that person's knowledge will be evaluated to determine its usefulness. Issues of access must then be considered – how difficult will it be to contact the colleague and (if necessary) discuss the problem with him or her? Finally, the information seeker will consider the costs that might have to be paid to obtain the necessary information. Those costs could include expenditures of time and energy, possible embarrassment and/or reputational damage, and the need to repay the colleague in some way.

The researchers asked workers in large divisions of pharmaceutical organizations to complete anonymous surveys (administered electronically). In those surveys, the workers first identified all of the colleagues from whom they had requested information recently. Then, for each colleague, they indicated how often information was requested from that person, how valuable the information proved to be, how difficult it was to access the person, and how costly interaction(s) with the person were. Analyses of these data, using social network techniques, produced good support for the proposed model, except for the consideration of costs. When a worker knew more about someone's knowledge (indicating that directory updating had already occurred), expected that knowledge to be valuable, and had better access to the person, the worker was more likely to seek that person's knowledge. Why weren't costs important? Maybe, the researchers speculated, workers only sought information from others when it was absolutely necessary to do so (e.g., an emergency), and when that was the case, costs of the kind measured by the survey did not matter.

Another good example of research on how workers in organizations seek information from others is a study by Cross and Sproull (2004), who began by interviewing a small sample of workers in a large accounting organization. These workers were first asked to think about a recent, major consulting project in which they were involved, and then to list any people that gave them information during that project. Next, workers chose from that list the three people whose help was most valuable. Detailed information about their experiences with each of those persons was then solicited.

The researchers found that nearly all of the workers could quickly and spontaneously name specific persons who served as knowledge sources for them (indicating once again that directory updating had already occurred). Few of those sources were "experts" from the organization's viewpoint. Instead, they were viewed by the workers as informal "knowledge partners," people from whom they often sought information. The most valuable knowledge partners, according to the workers, were people who had a personal, as well as a professional, connection with them. For example, a good partner was someone who had attended the same university as the worker, lived in the same neighborhood, or shared recreational interests. These connections made it seem "safer" to confess ignorance to a partner and then ask that person for help. Connections also made it more likely that partners would actually provide the help that was needed, even if it meant considerable effort on their part. Effort was often an issue because many workers wanted more than simple solutions to their problems. What they wanted instead (or maybe as well) was "actionable knowledge." Such knowledge included referrals from the partner to other possible sources of information; reformulation of the problem by (or in collaboration with) the partner; validation (the partner's approval of the approach a worker was already taking to the problem); and legitimation (permission to tell others, inside or outside the organization, that the partner knew and endorsed the worker's approach).

To explore these issues in more detail, Cross and Sproull (2004) later surveyed another, larger sample of workers from the same organization. These workers were sent a questionnaire that first asked them to name any colleagues that had given information to them during a recent project, and then to identify the five people whose help was most valuable. Questions were then asked about the workers' characteristics (e.g., their gender, education, experience, expertise), the characteristics of the people who helped them most (e.g., their perceived expertise, willingness to "engage" while working on the problem with the worker), and the kinds of relationships that the workers had with each of those persons (e.g., weak or strong personal ties, membership in the same or different work group, sense of "safety"). Finally, the workers indicated what kinds of actionable knowledge each colleague provided for them.

The results showed that workers were more likely to obtain solutions to problems when their partners had higher job levels (than the workers), greater (perceived) expertise, belonged to a different work group than the workers, and had weak ties with them. Referrals were more likely when the workers had higher job levels and greater expertise, and when partners were more willing to "engage" with the workers on the problem. Problem reformulations were more likely when the workers had greater expertise and stronger ties with their partners, and when partners were more willing to "engage." Validation was more likely when the workers and their partners had greater expertise, partners had higher job levels and were more willing to engage, and ties between workers and partners were strong. Finally, legitimation was more likely when partners had greater expertise and higher job levels.

Studies such as these, which examine more closely how transactive memory systems actually work, have revealed the importance of at least two factors that were ignored by Wegner in his initial description of transactive memory, and by many of the researchers who have since studied transactive memory systems, especially in small groups. First, it is not enough for a worker to simply know that someone in a group or organization has relevant knowledge about a problem. It is also important to consider whether that person will share his or her knowledge, and if so, then what costs might have to be paid to obtain it. Second, a search for knowledge by a worker may begin from several starting points and with various goals. Sometimes workers have a specific question and simply want to know the answer. But at other times, they already know the answer (or an answer) to their question and want others to reassure them that their answer is correct, or to provide an authoritative "stamp of approval" for their answer that can be shown to others. Finally, workers sometimes are unsure (or mistaken) about what a problem really entails, so what they need most is for someone to help them clarify it.

TECHNOLOGICAL SUPPORT FOR TRANSACTIVE MEMORY

We turn now to the possible role of technology in transactive memory. Are there any ways in which technology can strengthen transactive memory systems in work groups or organizations, improving performance as a result? Many practitioners believe that technology can indeed be useful in this regard, but what is the evidence?

Work Groups

Examples of computer hardware and software developed for the purpose of improving work group performance are easy to find (DeSanctis & Gallupe, 1987; Fjermestad, 2004; Fjermestad & Hiltz, 1999; Jessup & Valacich, 1993). Consider Lotus Notes, for example. Many organizations use this software to help work group members interact more productively with one another. The software provides workers with email, instant messaging, web browsing, calendar/appointment, and collaboration services. But neither Lotus Notes, nor any other such "groupware" (so far as we know) was specifically designed to support the transactive memory systems of work groups. Some of this technology might strengthen such systems anyway, of course. Any technology that improves communication among group members, for example, could strengthen the transactive memory system in that group by helping members learn more about who knows what.

A simple form of technology that might affect transactive memory systems is e-mail (along with newer, related technologies, such as instant messaging). Recall, however, that Lewis (2004) found that neither telephone conversations nor e-mail messages were helpful for the development of transactive memory systems in work groups. Why? Maybe members of the groups that she studied just didn't communicate as often by telephone or e-mail as they did face-to-face (and why should they, when face-to-face communication with each other was also possible?). Or maybe people communicated about different things on the telephone or by e-mail than they did face-to-face. For example, telephone conversations and e-mail messages may have been more about fun than about business. And Lewis relied on group members' self-reports to assess both communication practices and transactive memory systems, so questions can be asked about the validity of her communication findings. Maybe people misremembered their communication practices, or they reported those practices in biased ways, in an effort to manage impressions about themselves and/or their groups.

A more worrisome explanation is that telephone conversations and e-mail messages are both inherently flawed when it comes to supporting transactive memory systems, because neither method of communication conveys enough of the cues that people want or need to make accurate judgments about who knows what. Those cues include a person's sex, race, and age; clothing and accessories (e.g., watch, glasses, pens), demeanor (e.g., stance, tone of voice, speech fluidity); social skills around other group members; and of course, actual work behaviors. It is at least possible to obtain some of these cues by upgrading telephone or e-mail technology in certain ways. Rather than using regular telephones, for example, group members could participate in conference calls or use virtual meeting rooms (Majchrzak, Malhotra, Stamps, & Lipnack, 2004; see also Kraut, Fish, Root, & Chalfonte, 1990), which simulate face-to-face group meetings to varying degrees. These technological alternatives are more complex, though, and thus less likely to operate correctly every time they are used. And some people just don't enjoy communicating in these ways, maybe because it's a novel experience that seems somewhat artificial. As a result, such persons may speak less often during group "meetings," or not attend them at all.

This issue has become salient recently with the growing popularity of virtual work groups (see Bell & Kozlowski, 2002; Martins, Gilson, & Maynard, 2004; Romano, Lowry, & Roberts, 2007). Most or all the communication within such groups occurs via telephone conversations or e-mail messages. Virtual groups often experience more and different problems than do groups whose members meet face-to-face (see Armstrong & Cole, 2002; Espinosa, Slaughter, Kraut, & Herbsleb, 2007). In particular, they may have problems with transactive memory systems. If telephone conversations and e-mail messages indeed offer poor support for transactive memory (and given that virtual groups are often larger than face-to-face work groups and experience lower levels of trust among members, both of which can weaken transactive systems), then virtual group members may find it especially difficult to learn who knows what, or to use that knowledge wisely (see Jackson & Klobas, 2008; Mannix, Griffith, & Neale, 2002).

To our knowledge, only two studies on transactive memory sytems in virtual groups have been done. Yoo and Kanawattanachai (2001) studied MBA students from several universities during a management course that the students were all taking together. As part of this course, students were assigned to four-person groups that played a complex computer game. This game simulated the operation of a company. Weekly group decisions about the company had to be made and entered into the computer. The computer then generated feedback about the effects of those decisions on the company's performance. While they were playing the game, group members could send e-mail messages to each other using a special web-based interface that was built into the simulation. Three times during the course (after the first, fifth, and eighth weeks), researchers assessed the level of communication in each group (number of e-messages sent by members); its transactive memory system (an index reflecting responses to questions about how much members thought they knew about one another's expertise); collective mind (an index reflecting members' responses to questions about whether they played the game more as a group or as a set of individuals), and performance (a composite of several measures produced by the simulation).

Communication levels dropped dramatically from Week 1 to Week 5, and then again (though less so) from Week 5 to Week 8. Transactive memory systems at Week 1 grew much stronger by Week 5, but changed little thereafter. Few changes in collective mind or group performance were observed over time.

Analyses of the relationships among measures produced complex results. At Week 1, there was a positive relationship between communication and both transactive memory systems and group performance, but communication was unrelated to collective mind. Transactive memory systems were related positively to collective mind, but unrelated to group performance, and no relationship between collective mind and group performance was found either. Several changes were apparent, however, by Week 5. At that time, communication had a positive relationship with collective mind, but was unrelated to transactive memory systems or group performance. Transactive memory systems were still related positively to collective mind, and now they had a positive relationship with group performance. There was still no relationship between collective mind and group performance. Finally, by Week 8, relationships among the measures changed yet again. Communication was now unrelated to any of the other measures. Transactive memory systems still related positively to collective mind, but were unrelated to group performance. And now, for the first time, there was a positive relationship between collective mind and group performance.

What did these results mean? The researchers argued that e-mail communication early in a virtual group's life can indeed contribute to the development of its transactive memory system. In fact, qualitative data indicated that early e-mail messages among group members were often devoted to expertise – some students revealed past work experience that implied expertise in certain topic areas, while others confessed that they lacked expertise in certain areas and would thus need help from other members of the group if relevant problems arose. It is worth noting that the game itself might have helped to clarify the students' expertise as well – each student was assigned a special functional role in the company, and the web-based interface that students used to play the game organized their inputs according to those roles. The researchers argued that later on in a virtual group's life, after its transactive memory system has developed, there may be no further need for communication about expertise. Maybe group members decide early on who knows what (correctly or not), and then resist changing their minds about such things. Once a transactive memory system has developed, it begins to improve a group's performance and contributes to the development of a collective mind. Once that mind has developed, it can improve the group's performance as well. In fact, it may eventually become more important than the transactive memory system in that regard.

A later study, by Kanawattanachai and Yoo (2007), was very similar – comparable students, taking the same course and using the same computer simulation, were again studied. And with a few exceptions, this study produced results similar to those of the earlier study. Taken together, the two studies suggest that transactive memory systems can indeed develop in virtual groups, although more than simple e-mails may be needed (remember that special web-based interface built into the computer game) for the development of those systems. Nevertheless, there is a clear need for more research on this issue – two studies (by the same researchers, using a similar methodology) do not offer a firm foundation for strong conclusions. One option might be to collect more data on work groups that can communicate in several ways (cf. Lewis, 2004), and then examine how different forms of communication affect the transactive memory systems of those groups (see Peltokorpi, 2004). It would also be useful, though difficult, to do experiments in which the transactive memory systems of (otherwise similar) work groups that are virtual or not are compared. Experiments could also be done to investigate any changes that occur in the transactive memory systems of work groups whose primary communication practices are altered (e.g., electronic to face-to-face, or face-to-face to electronic). The results of such research could be valuable for workers and for organizations, given how common virtual groups are becoming.

Organizations

Much of the communication among workers within organizations involves either telephone conversations or e-mail messages. The available evidence on virtual groups suggests that these methods of communication could indeed help workers learn who knows what, especially when their opportunities for communicating face-to-face are limited.

Consider, for example, a well-known study by Orr (1996), who investigated how the repair technicians working for a large copy machine organization interacted with each other and with customers as they performed their jobs. Orr found, through interviews with the technicians, that repairing a copy machine can be stressful - - the technician is usually alone, at the customer's office, facing a problem that may be unfamiliar and thus difficult to solve. It embarrasses the technician, and annoys the customer, if the technician must travel elsewhere to consult copy machine documentation, then return to the office later to try again. Orr also discovered, though, that technicians often exchange valuable information with one another, on the few occasions when they meet and talk together (e.g., before or after work, or at lunches), about how to solve repair problems. It occurred to Orr that it might help technicians to perform their jobs better if they could speak to one another while they were actually repairing copy machines. Orr thus persuaded the organization to give portable

radios to the technicians, so that they could call one another and ask for advice immediately when problems arose. This improved the technicians' performance, maybe because it not only gave them easier access to one another's expertise, but also because it helped them learn more about who knew what (so they knew the best person to call for advice about a particular problem).

E-mail might also be helpful for building transactive memory systems in large organizations. Constant, Sproull, and Kiesler (1996) studied the use of e-mail as a way to obtain knowledge in a computer manufacturing organization. Workers there used an internal network to send a variety of e-mail messages. Many messages were sent by one person to another, but others could be sent (and often were sent) by one person to everyone else in the organization. The latter messages were the focus on the study. Over a period of six weeks, dozens of e-mail messages were sent out by workers who asked for help with a problem (always work-related and usually technical). The researchers sent electronic surveys to the authors of these messages, asking them for information about themselves, and urging them to keep copies of any responses their requests evoked. Later on, these workers were also asked to evaluate those responses. Meanwhile, the researchers also sent an electronic questionnaire to the people who responded to the requests for help, asking them for information about themselves (e.g., location, job level, work experience, past usage of e-mail to seek or provide information, relationships with the people to whom they had responded, and motivation for helping those persons).

The results of the study were rather surprising. When workers asked for help, they received it, sometimes a lot of it. Much of that help, which included both answers to the problems that were posed and referrals to other places or people where the answers might be found, came from strangers – people who had no relationships at all with those they were helping, other than the fact that they worked for the same organization.

The messages that helpers sent were brief, but nearly always valuable, at least in the eyes of their recipients. Messages offering useful advice came more often from people with greater expertise (higher job levels, greater work experience), but messages that actually solved the problems came more often from people who worked at the organization's headquarters. Finally, the reasons that people gave for helping focused more on organizational benefits (e.g., wanting to be a good organizational citizen, hoping to help the organization succeed) than on personal benefits (e.g., enjoying the challenge of problem solving, wanting to be a helpful person, hoping to be rewarded somehow for helping).

Although transactive memory systems were not measured in this research, it seems likely that such systems would grow stronger to the extent that workers send, receive, and read the kinds of e-mail messages that Constant and his colleagues studied. In fact, there are many organizations that try to use e-mail in this way (see Stewart, 1995a).

Of course, technology involves much more than e-mail, and by now an impressive variety of technological solutions is available (thanks to the "knowledge management" movement) to help workers in organizations learn more about who knows what. Earl (2001) and Ruggles (1998) have offered broad taxonomies of such technology. And Moreland (1999) described several technological options for knowledge sharing in organizations. One option involves the use of "Yellow Pages" (see Stewart, 1995a). An organization's Yellow Pages can contain information that ranges from personal resumes to instructions or guidelines for performing certain tasks, and from frequently asked questions to news items. An important advantage of such pages is that all the information is organized using keywords, so when a particular kind of knowledge is needed, the relevant keywords can be entered into a computer, allowing workers to find that knowledge directly, or to identify colleagues who may possess it (a trans-

active memory outcome). This all works best, of course, when the information in the Yellow Pages is comprehensive and accurate, an optimal set of keywords was used to organize the information, and workers who need certain information know the best keywords with which to search for it. As they grow larger, Yellow Pages can become confusing, so some organizations offer workers personalized assistance with their use.

Another option involves complex software with the ambitious goal of helping workers learn everything that is known by anyone in their organization about a given set of topics (see Stewart, 1997). Organizational intranets are often part of such software (see, for example, Green, 2007). These intranets let workers jump quickly and easily from one web page to another, following associational links among people or work groups, tasks, procedures, equipment, and so on. Of course, simply following a path through some web pages need not involve transactive memory - - workers might find the information that they need directly on the intranet itself. But if a worker, using an intranet, identifies another person who has the information that he or she needs, then a transactive memory process has occurred.

A few other, recent developments are worth noting as well. First, a new technological option involves software (or consultants) that can map out the social networks within an organization (see Hindo, 2007; McGregor, 2006; Reingold & Yang, 2007). Often, the resulting map includes information about what each person in the network knows or can do. Such a map would clearly strengthen the organization's transactive memory system. But even without information about knowledge and skills, a network map could be helpful. For example, if a person is known (by some other means) to be knowledgeable about some topic, but he or she is unavailable or seems difficult to approach, then the map might suggest someone else to contact, someone linked on the map to the first person chosen, maybe as a work associate, friend, or someone with comparable training or interests (depending on the network's nature).

A second noteworthy development involves better ways to carry out all the work of entering and editing information about the knowledge and skills of workers within an organization, information that might appear in the organization's Yellow Pages, intranet web pages, and so on. This is an enormously difficult task, especially in large organizations. One must first identify all the knowledge and skills that *ought* to be recorded, because of their potential value. Ideally, a broad net should be cast in this regard, because it is often difficult to predict what might become important in the future (note that "tacit" knowledge, which is often important to workers, cannot be included at all). Information must then be entered into the appropriate software, a task that can take a great deal of time and effort. Finally, as time goes by, the resulting summary must be updated on a regular basis, not only because new workers enter and current workers leave the organization, but also because ongoing workers learn some things and forget others. Also, new kinds of knowledge and skills may become important for workers' performance, and so those must also be assessed and then recorded. It is possible to ask, or maybe force, workers to enter and edit their own information, but workers often drag their feet in this regard, or even refuse to comply altogether. Finally, entering and editing the necessary information could be made into a job that a few workers in the organization (or outside contractors) are paid to do, but that can be expensive. What to do? Some organizations have begun to use "expertise mining" software (see Cross & Parker, 2004; Garner, 2006; Totty, 2006), which automatically scans computer files, e-mail messages, and other electronic material for evidence of who might know what. Summaries of apparent expertise can then be produced and made available to workers, strengthening the organization's transactive memory system. Such software is sometimes unpopular with workers, who worry about invasions of their privacy, but it can save

considerable time and money (after the initial costs associated with the software are paid).

Does any of this technology *actually* strengthen transactive memory systems among workers within organizations? No one really knows, because little research on that issue has been done. This is a critical problem, in our opinion. Of course, one could use performance (by workers, work groups, or organizations) as a proxy variable and argue that if performance improves in organizations where such technology is used, then stronger transactive memory systems deserve some of the credit. But that would be a weak argument. And anyway, research of this sort is scarce. What we have, instead, are "testimonials" by people whose opinions are probably biased because they have personal stakes in the organization and/or the technology described. In these testimonials, stories are told about the performance benefits of technology. Little real evidence is provided to support the claims that are made in these stories. Moreover, stories of the opposite kind can also be found. Many organizations (see Koudsi, 2000; Stewart, 2000) have tried, but failed, to implement technology that might support the development of transactive memory systems. This has happened not just in business organizations, but also in organizations of other sorts, including non-profit organizations such as universities (our own university is an example). In fact, there is a growing skepticism about the whole technological approach to knowledge management, given its expense and the engineering problems that are often associated with it (see Goodman & Darr, 1998; Gray, 2001; Green, 2007; Jian & Jeffres, 2006; Ruggles, 1998).

What goes wrong in organizations that rely on technology to help workers learn who knows what? Let us assume (although that assumption is often unwarranted) that the technology itself is well-designed, operates with few problems, and is easy for workers to use. Why wouldn't everyone use it, then? Well, some workers may just be reluctant to ask for help from others, especially when that involves the use of technology that keeps records of their requests. And workers may not always know just what to ask, because they are unsure about what they need to know (see Cross & Sproull, 2004). So they decide not to ask for help at all, because they do not want to waste anyone's time. Asking for help could also weaken a worker's self-esteem (Fisher, Nadler, & Whitcher-Alagna, 1982) and might make the worker appear stupid to others, which could damage the worker's status (see Flynn, Reagans, Amanatullah, & Ames, 2006; Lee, 1997; 2002). Workers may also avoid asking for information because they doubt that others will be willing to provide it. A recent study by Flynn and Lake (2008) showed that people often underestimate the chances that another person will comply with a direct request from them for help. Why? Apparently because people seeking help focus on the costs (e.g., time and energy) that someone must pay to help them, rather than on the costs that person might have to pay for refusing to help. Finally, workers may not ask others for help because they do not want to be indebted to them (Greenberg, 1980), or because they fear that while helping them, others will behave harshly, maybe even in critical or demeaning ways (see Cross & Sproull, 2004).

Matters may be even worse among workers who *could* provide information to others, if only they chose to cooperate with the implementation and use of relevant technology. Yet workers are often uncooperative in this regard (see Kankanhalli, Tan, & Wei, 2005). That is somewhat surprising -- there are several reasons to expect that knowledgeable workers would help others when asked to do so (see Cabrera & Cabrera, 2002; Constant, Sproull, & Kiesler, 1996; Flynn, Reagans, Amanatullah, & Ames, 2006; Kankanhalli, Tan, & Wei, 2005; Wasko & Faraj, 2005). After all, helping others might improve the status of these workers and make them feel proud, virtuous, or valuable to the organization. Another potential benefit is an improvement in the helper's own understanding of whatever knowledge that is shared – a person

that "teaches" something to others often learns something in the process, especially when the "students" ask challenging questions (see Smith, 1993; Wasko & Faraj, 2000). Finally, a selfish worker might hope that after sharing knowledge with others, they can later be asked for favors in return (see Cabrera & Cabrera, 2002).

Unfortunately, there are many more (and often more powerful) reasons for workers *not* to be helpful. The most obvious of these is that helping requires time and energy that a worker might put to better use (Cress, Kimmerle, & Hesse, 2006). And a worker might imagine that someone needing help could easily find it elsewhere, so why should the worker take all the responsibility for helping that person? In fact, helping others within an organization can be viewed as a social dilemma, specifically a public goods problem (see Cabrera & Cabrera, 2002; Connolly & Thorn, 1990; Connolly, Thorn, & Heminger, 1992; Cress, Kimmerie, & Hesse, 2006; Goodman & Darr, 1998; Hollingshead, Fulk, & Monge, 2002; Yuan, Fulke, & Monge, 2007). If a worker makes his or her knowledge widely available, say by posting it on a webpage within the organization's intranet, then anyone can access that knowledge. Few organizations reward workers directly for access by others to their web pages, and even in organizations that provide such rewards, greater access may not produce correspondingly larger rewards. Under these conditions, many workers are likely to become selfish – they turn into "free riders" who take advantage of any knowledge that is shared by others, but do not share much knowledge themselves.

Several other reasons for workers to avoid helping others, by not sharing knowledge with them, can also be identified. For example, some people may be shy or modest, so they do not share their knowledge because that would seem almost like bragging. Others may worry about a possible weakening of their status and influence. After all, knowledge is a form of power, so if it is "given away" to others, then that might make those who share it less important or influential in the organization (see Cabrera & Cabrera, 2002; Gray, 2001). Other concerns that can make workers reluctant to share knowledge (see Connolly, Thorn, & Heminger, 1992; Cross & Parker, 2004) include doubts about the quality of that knowledge (workers would feel embarrassed, and might be sanctioned, if they share knowledge that proves to be false or misleading); fears that the knowledge might be misused by others who are less skilled or have different goals; and anxiety that the knowledge will encourage others to seek personal contact with them, trying to learn even more by asking detailed questions, seeking collaboration, and so on. Too much contact of this sort could overburden the worker who provided the knowledge that prompted it.

As all of this suggests, the "human factor" may have played a major role in the disappointing outcomes of many efforts by organizations to make better use of their intellectual capital through technology. Workers who need to know something seldom seek it technologically, and workers who have knowledge seldom provide it to others technologically. How, then, do workers share knowledge within organizations, assuming they share it at all? There is overwhelming evidence that sharing does occur, and that workers prefer an interpersonal over a technological approach to knowledge sharing (see Allen, 1995; Cross, Parker, & Prusak, & Borgatti, 2001; Earl, 2001; Hertzum, 2002; Jackson & Klobas, 2008; Kraut, Fish, Root, & Chalfonte, 1990; Nardi & Whittaker, 2002; Peltokorpi, 2004; Von Seggern & Jourdain, 1996; Zipperer, 1993; see also Dingfelder, 2006; Peltokorpi & Manka, 2008; Ruggles, 1998; Swap, Leonard, Shields, & Abrams, 2001; Verbeke & Wuyts, 2007). Why? The answer is unclear. Many of the reasons that we just reviewed for why workers do not seek or provide knowledge through technology are relevant to interpersonal experiences too. Some of those reasons are probably *more* relevant to technology, or maybe even *only* relevant to technology, but the strong preference among workers for sharing knowledge through interpersonal methods is still puzzling. Maybe the technological approach is less attractive to workers because it is less familiar to them, or seems more artificial and sterile. Maybe the technological approach is less attractive because it often takes longer, requires more specialized skills, or generates less satisfying outcomes. Workers might also feel a kind of "reactance" – they purposely resist doing something that their organizations clearly want them to do (see Brehm & Brehm, 1981). There is some evidence that technology developed by workers themselves, to share information within a "community of practice," is more likely to be successful than technology that workers are asked to use by their organizations (see O'Dell & Grayson, 1998; Vaast, 2004; Wenger & Snyder, 2000). Finally, workers may be reluctant to engage in knowledge sharing when they know relatively little about the people involved and thus are somewhat unsure about whether those persons can be trusted.

We will have more to say about the interpersonal approach in a moment, but for now, let us consider what could be done to salvage the technological approach. Some of its problems might be due to simple discomfort with technology, which is novel to many workers and may seem (at least initially) difficult to use. Some studies have shown, in fact, that technology for knowledge sharing is used more often by workers who are less wary of computers (see Jarvenpaa & Staples, 2000). Each new generation of workers should include fewer technophobes, which bodes well for the future of the technological approach. Maybe some of the problems with that approach will thus weaken on their own, after sufficient time has passed…

But are there any interventions that could be carried out right now to help to solve some of the problems with knowledge sharing technology and its use? Several suggestions have been made in this regard (see Cabrera & Cabrera, 2002; Cress, Himmerle, & Hesse, 2006; Hollingshead, Fulk, & Monge, 2002; Kankanhalli, Tan, & Wei, 2005;

Koudsi, 2000; Nebus, 2006; O'Dell & Grayson, 1998; Van Zolingen, Streumer, & Stooker, 2001; Wasko & Faraj, 2000). Three broad sets of ideas can be identified. First, workers might use such technology more often if it were made more rewarding and less costly for them to do so. Suppose, for example, the technology were faster, simpler to use, less likely to malfunction, or (ironically) made knowledge sharing a more social experience. Administrative changes in the organization could also be helpful, such as arranging for workers to have more time to learn about and use the technology, offering them more and better training in its use, or hiring someone to manage the technology (ensuring that information about workers' knowledge is recorded correctly and updated promptly, and that the technology itself always works properly). Finally, a system could be set up to reward workers whose knowledge is sought out and used by others in the organization (but see Wasko & Faraj, 2000, on the potential dangers of this idea). The salaries of such workers could be raised, for example, they could be paid bonuses, or they could receive various forms of special recognition, such as public praise.

A second set of ideas involves creating an organizational norm that encourages the use of knowledge sharing technology. If workers believe that others are using such technology, and benefitting from it, then they are more likely to use the technology themselves. One way to create a norm might be to incorporate knowledge sharing into the socialization process for new workers, perhaps by assigning to them mentors who use the technology regularly and appreciate its benefits. Another tactic might be to find workers with greater status (formal or informal) who use the technology, and then induce those workers to use their influence to persuade others to use the technology as well. Even without such persuasion, others might imitate the behavior of high-status workers in an effort to gain more status for themselves (see Coleman, Katz, & Menzel, 1966). Finally, stories that reflect successful use

of the technology could also be communicated within the organization by means of e-mail or through articles published in a newsletter.

A final set of ideas involves strengthening workers' identification with organizations (see Riketta, 2004; Van Dick, Grojean, Christ, & Wieseke, 2006). When workers identify strongly with an organization, they view its outcomes almost like personal outcomes. So, they are more willing to use any means available (including knowledge sharing technology) to improve the performance of that organization (cf. Constant, Sproull, & Kiesler, 1996), whether such behavior is personally costly or not.

Many of these interventions are now underway in various organizations, and time will tell if they are effective or not. But we are skeptical – the preference among workers for interpersonal over technological methods of sharing knowledge seems very strong and may thus be difficult, perhaps impossible, to overcome. What, exactly, are these interpersonal methods? They derive from direct, personal contacts in a wide variety of situations. Such contacts occur naturally over the course of daily activities within any organization. Some contacts are formal, as when someone works with the members of his or her own group, works with people from other parts of the organization (on special projects, for example), or attends meetings and presentations of various kinds. Other contacts are more informal and can often be quite spontaneous. One worker may pass another walking down a hallway; meet someone in the mailroom, the snack room, or near the copy machines; or stand beside others during a brief elevator trip. In all of these situations, people are likely to exchange greetings and may speak briefly to one another about what they have been doing lately. A bit of gossip may also occur, gossip that involves other people that work for the organization as well (see Dingfelder, 2006; Stambor, 2006; Winerman, 2006). All of these experiences, slowly and surely, help to build relationships and can transmit information about who knows what within the organization. As Swap and his colleagues (Swap, Leonard, Shields, & Abrams, 2001) noted, workers appear to "...drink in knowledge informally, and at times unconsciously (p. 98)" when they interact with each other.

How is an interpersonal approach to knowledge sharing implemented? Imagine a worker who needs some information for his job. It's likely, through his or her personal contacts, that this worker already knows someone within the organization who could be helpful. If so, then that person could be approached directly. Or the worker might rely on his or her work group, using that group's transactive memory system to identify which member can be most helpful.

A work group could be useful in other ways too, even if none of its members possessed exactly the knowledge that the person needed. Someone in the group might well know others within the organization (or even outside of it – see Austin, 2003) who could be helpful. Given the "small world" phenomenon, the personal networks of the people who belong to a small work group could (if combined) reach far (see Milgram, 1967). Moreover, Ancona and her colleagues (see Ancona & Bresman, 2007) have shown that successful work groups try to manage the flow of information (and other resources) across their boundaries through special activities and roles. Ancona and Caldwell (1988) found, for example, that groups were more likely to succeed when one or more of their members played the role of "scout" – seeking out and then bringing back to the group information about what was happening elsewhere in the organization. This could strengthen the transactive memory system of an organization by helping group members learn more about who knows what throughout the organization.

There are, of course, other ways in which a worker could obtain information about where to find knowledge within an organization. For example, most organizations publish newsletters that are sent to every worker. These often contain stories about the accomplishments of various workers/work groups, thereby offering clues about who is likely to know what. Presenting such information in the form of stories, which are especially easy for people to encode and process (see Martin, 1982), could draw more attention to that information and help workers to remember it better. Special events, such as parties and retreats, can also help workers learn more about others within their organization. Sutton and Hargadon (1996), for example, studied a project design firm in which brainstorming sessions were often held. Although the major purpose of those sessions was to produce ideas, the researchers found that brainstorming had other benefits as well, including the development and maintenance of organizational memories, many of which included information about who knew what within the organization. Finally, workers may find it easier to learn who knows what in organizations that have certain special structural features (e.g., linking or matrix arrangements) or practices (e.g., job rotation, cross-functional teams) that bring people from different parts of the organization into contact with one another more often.

Finally, some workers have broader knowledge than others about what is happening within their organizations (see Gladwell, 2000). That knowledge often includes information about who knows what. Burt (1992), for example, studied workers who occupied "structural holes" in the social networks of their organizations. These workers had weak ties with people and/or groups that might not otherwise have come into contact with one another. As a result, they could offer guidance for anyone seeking knowledge from people operating in other parts of the organization. Some organizations have even tried to formalize such activities by creating special roles, such as an ombudsman or "knowledge concierge," whose purpose is to help workers reach people who know what they need to know. In other organizations, special units (see Stewart, 1995b) have been created for the same reason.

Because the preference among workers for sharing knowledge by interpersonal means is so strong, maybe organizations should consider offering more support for that approach. The main goal of such support would be to help workers collect more information on their own, through more frequent contacts with a wider variety of people, about the expertise of others within their organizations.

One means of achieving that goal involves the design of workspaces. Such spaces should allow, and even encourage, informal interaction among workers (see Borgatti & Cross, 2003; Cross & Parker, 2004). Privacy (especially acoustic privacy) is certainly important to workers, but good workspaces should also incorporate "circulation systems" that encourage informal interactions among workers and provide them with places to "hang out" informally (see Brill, Keable, & Fabiniak, 2000). (It might also be helpful if workers were allowed to gather and speak to one another informally without risking disapproval from managers).

Organizations could also provide more support for the interpersonal approach to knowledge sharing through some of the special activities and arrangements mentioned earlier. Efforts to keep everyone better informed about what is happening in different parts of the organization would be helpful, for example. Such efforts might involve newsletters that reveal activities about which many workers are unaware, and special events of various kinds, especially events that bring together people that do not normally encounter one another in the course of a typical workday.

Finally, and somewhat ironically, technology itself could be used to support an interpersonal approach to knowledge sharing. For example, it might be possible to help workers who are physically isolated, or whose mobility is restricted, to have brief, spontaneous interactions with colleagues located elsewhere using special software designed for that purpose (see Kraut, Fish, Root, Chalfonte, 1990). And what about all that knowl-edge management technology described earlier? Telephone messages and e-mails are not restricted to work issues—they can also help workers to speak with one another about what they (and others) are doing, both at work and off work, even when face-to-face conversations about such matters are difficult or impossible. Organizational intranets can also offer a wide range of information about workers, including personal qualities, activities, and relationships whose relevance to work might seem weak. A recent trend in some organizations, for example, is to incorporate Facebook, Twitter, Yelp, and other commercially available social networking software into their intranets (see Baker, 2009; Green, 2007). This tactic requires little financial investment from the organization, and can link workers not only to colleagues within the organization, but also to outsiders. Of course, the latter links can create "leakage" of valuable and/or sensitive information about the organization (see Conlin & MacMillan, 2009). A few organizations have thus adopted a more expensive, but safer tactic by developing their own social networking software, meant only for internal use (see, for example, IBM's Beehive). But it is important to note that in all these cases, the main value of social networking software for the organization is not that it leads directly to the sharing of work-related knowledge. Instead, such software is valuable because it encourages the development and maintenance of closer personal relationships among workers, which has the indirect effect of making them more willing to request and provide work-related knowledge to one another later on.

Another example of how the interpersonal approach to knowledge sharing can be supported by technology involves recent efforts to create and use "maps" of the social networks within organizations. A careful review of such maps can sometimes reveal gaps in networks that might be restricting knowledge sharing among workers. These gaps can then be filled by introducing unconnected workers to one another, arranging for them to spend more time together, and so on (see Cross & Parker, 2004; Reingold & Yang, 2007). An exciting opportunity in this regard is the work of Watts and Strogatz (1998), who have developed a mathematical model that can be used to analyze any social network and identify the smallest number of new links among the people in that network that would produce (if such links were added to the network) the greatest improvement in overall connectivity. The potential benefits of such an effort for the transactive memory system of an organization seem clear (see Andreeva, 1998).

CONCLUSION

Transactive memory systems involve a shared awareness of who knows what among some set of people. There is clear evidence that such systems exist in work groups and that groups with stronger systems perform better. Research has also revealed several ways in which a group's transactive memory system can be strengthened. There is at least some evidence that transactive memory systems exist in organizations as well, and once again, stronger systems are associated with better performance. It may be possible to support the development and operation of a group or organizational transactive memory system through various kinds of technology. This issue has hardly been studied at all in work groups, and thus deserves more attention. More evidence on the issue can be found for organizations, but that evidence is not encouraging. Workers do not seem to use the technology that is offered to them by organizations that are trying to improve their performance through greater knowledge sharing. Workers that need knowledge seldom use such technology to obtain it, while workers that have knowledge seldom use such technology to provide it. This problem may eventually solve itself, as better technology emerges and workers become more comfortable with the technology. However, there is clear evidence that workers generally prefer an interpersonal, rather than a technological approach to knowledge sharing. In our opinion, organizations would thus be wise to devote more of their resources to support for the interpersonal sharing of knowledge among workers, even if that means that fewer resources are available for the technological support of knowledge sharing.

REFERENCES

Akgun, A. E., Byrne, J. C., Keskin, H., & Lynn, G. S. (2006). Transactive memory systems in new product development teams. *IEEE Transactions on Engineering Management, 53*(1), 95–111. doi:10.1109/TEM.2005.857570

Allen, T. (1995). *Managing the flow of technology*. Cambridge, MA: MIT Press.

Ancona, D. G., & Bresman, H. (2007). *X-teams: How to build teams that lead, innovate, and succeed.* Boston, MA: Harvard Business School.

Ancona, D. G., & Caldwell, D. F. (1988). Beyond task and maintenance: Defining external functions in groups. *Group and Organizational Studies, 13*(4), 468–494. doi:10.1177/105960118801300405

Andreeva, N. (1998, August 17). Do the math – it is a small world. *Business Week*, 54–55.

Armstrong, D. J., & Cole, P. (2002). Managing distances and differences in geographically distributed workgroups. In P. Hinds & S. Kiesler (Eds.), *Distributed work* (pp. 167-186). Cambridge, MA: MIT Press.

Austin, J. R. (2003). Transactive memory in organizational groups: The effects of contents, consensus, specialization, and accuracy on group performance. *The Journal of Applied Psychology, 88*(5), 866–878. doi:10.1037/0021-9010.88.5.866

Baker, S. (2009, June 1). What's a friend worth? *Business Week*, 32–36.

Bell, B. S., & Kozlowski, S. W. J. (2002). A typology of virtual teams: Implications for effective leadership. *Group & Organization Management, 27*(1), 14–49. doi:10.1177/1059601102027001003

Berman, S. L., Down, J., & Hill, C. W. L. J. (2002). Tacit knowledge as a source of competitive advantage in the National Basketball Association. *Academy of Management Journal, 45*(1), 13–31. doi:10.2307/3069282

Borgatti, S. P., & Cross, R. (2003). A relational view of information seeking and learning in social networks. *Management Science, 49*(4), 432–445. doi:10.1287/mnsc.49.4.432.14428

Brehm, S. S., & Brehm, J. W. (1981). *Psychological reactance: A theory of freedom and control.* New York: Academic Press.

Brill, M., Keable, E., & Fabiniak, J. (2000). The myth of open plan. *Facilities Design and Management, 19*(2), 36–39.

Burt, R. S. (1992). *Structural holes: The social structure of competition.* Boston, MA: Harvard University Press.

Cabrera, A., & Cabrera, E. F. (2002). Knowledge-sharing dilemmas. *Organization Studies, 23*(5), 687–710. doi:10.1177/0170840602235001

Cambridge, MA.: MIT Press.

Coleman, J. S., Katz, E., & Menzel, H. (1966). *Medical innovation: A diffusion study.* New York: Bobbs-Merrill.

Conlin, M., & MacMillan, D. (2009, June 1). Managing the tweets. *Business Week*, 20–21.

Connolly, T., & Thorn, B. K. (1990). Discretionary databases: Theory, data, and implications. In J. Fulk & C. Steinfeld (Eds.), *Organizations and communication technology* (pp. 219-233). London: Sage.

Connolly, T., Thorn, B. K., & Heminger, A. (1992). Discretionary databases as social dilemmas. In L. Liebrand, D. Messick, & H. Wilke (Eds.), *Social dilemmas: Theoretical issues and research findings* (pp. 199-208). Oxford, UK: Pergamon Press.

Constant, D., Sproull, L., & Kiesler, S. (1996). The kindness of strangers: The usefulness of weak electronic ties for technical advice. *Organization Science, 7*(2), 119–135. doi:10.1287/orsc.7.2.119

Cress, U., Kimmerle, J., & Hesse, F. W. (2006). Information exchange with shared databases as a social dilemma: The effect of metaknowledge, bonus systems, and costs. *Communication Research, 33*(5), 370–390. doi:10.1177/0093650206291481

Cross, R., & Parker, A. (2004). *The hidden power of social networks: Understanding how work really gets done in organizations.* Boston, MA: Harvard Business School.

Cross, R., Parker, A., Prusak, L., & Borgatti, S. P. (2001). Knowing what we know: Supporting knowledge creation and sharing in social networks. *Organizational Dynamics, 30*(2), 100–120. doi:10.1016/S0090-2616(01)00046-8

Cross, R., & Sproull, L. (2004). More than an answer: Information relationships for actionable knowledge. *Organization Science, 15*(4), 446–462. doi:10.1287/orsc.1040.0075

Cruz, N. M., Perez, V. M., & Ramos, Y. F. (2007). Transactive memory processes that lead to better team results. *Team Performance Management, 13*(7/8), 192–205. doi:10.1108/13527590710842529

DeSanctis, G., & Gallupe, R. B. (1987). A foundation for the study of group decision support systems. *Management Science, 33*(5), 589–608. doi:10.1287/mnsc.33.5.589

Dingfelder, S. F. (April, 2006). Learned it through the grapevine. *APA Monitor on Psychology,* 60-61.

Earl, M. (2001). Knowledge management strategies: Toward a taxonomy. *Journal of Management Information Systems, 18*(1), 215–233.

Edmondson, A. (1999). Psychological safety and learning behavior in work teams. *Administrative Science Quarterly, 44*(2), 350–383. doi:10.2307/2666999

Edmondson, A. C. (1996). Learning from mistakes is easier said than done: Group and organizational influences on the detection and correction of human error. *The Journal of Applied Behavioral Science, 32*, 5–28. doi:10.1177/0021886396321001

Ellis, A. P. J. (2006). System breakdown: The role of mental models and transactive memory in the relationship between acute stress and team performance. *Academy of Management Journal, 49*(3), 576–589.

Espinosa, J. A., Slaughter, S. A., Kraut, R. E., & Herbsleb, J. D. (2007). Team knowledge and coordination in geographically distributed software development. *Journal of Management Information Systems, 24*(1), 135–169. doi:10.2753/MIS0742-1222240104

Faraj, S., & Sproull, L. (2000). Coordinating expertise in software development teams. *Management Science, 46*(12), 1554–1568. doi:10.1287/mnsc.46.12.1554.12072

Fisher, J. D., Nadler, A., & Whitcher-Alagna, S. (1982). Recipient reactions to aid. *Psychological Bulletin, 91*(1), 27–54. doi:10.1037/0033-2909.91.1.27

Fjermestad, J. (2004). An analysis of communication mode in group support systems research. *Decision Support Systems, 37*(2), 239–263.

Fjermestad, J., & Hiltz, S. R. (1999). An assessment of group support systems experimental research: Methodology and results. *Journal of Management Information Systems, 15*(3), 7–149.

Flynn, F. J., & Lake, V. K. B. (2008). If you need help, just ask: Underestimating compliance with direct requests for help. *Journal of Personality and Social Psychology, 95*(1), 128–143. doi:10.1037/0022-3514.95.1.128

Flynn, F. J., Reagans, R. E., Amanatullah, E. T., & Ames, D. R. (2006). Helping one's way to the top: Self-monitors achieve status by helping others and knowing who knows whom. *Journal of Personality and Social Psychology, 91*(6), 1123–1137. doi:10.1037/0022-3514.91.6.1123

Freeman, L. (2006). *The development of social network analysis.* Vancouver, Canada: Empirical Press.

Garner, J. T. (2006). It's not what you know: A transactive memory analysis of knowledge networks at NASA. *Journal of Technical Writing and Communication, 36*(4), 329–351. doi:10.2190/U636-4844-2323-W071

Gladwell, M. (2000). *The tipping point: How little things can make a bid difference.* Boston: Little-Brown.

Goodman, P. S., & Darr, E. D. (1998). Computer-aided systems and communities: Mechanisms for organizational learning in distributed environments. *MIS Quarterly, 22*(4), 417–440. doi:10.2307/249550

Goodman, P. S., & Shah, S. (1992). Familiarity and work group outcomes. In S. Worchel, W. Wood, & J. A. Simpson (Eds.), *Group process and productivity* (pp. 276-298). Newbury Park, CA: Sage.

Gray, P. H. (2001). The impact of knowledge repositories on power and control in the workplace. *Information Technology & People, 14*(4), 368–384. doi:10.1108/09593840110411167

Green, H. (2007, October 1). The water cooler is now on the web. *Business Week,* 78–79.

Greenberg, M. S. (1980). A theory of indebtedness. In K. Gergen, M.S. Greenberg, & R.H. Willis (Eds.), *Social exchange: Advances in theory and research* (pp. 2–26). New York: Plenum.

Hertzum, M. (2002). The importance of trust in software engineers' assessment and choice of information sources. *Information and Organization, 12*(1), 1–18. doi:10.1016/S1471-7727(01)00007-0

Hindo, B. (2007, November 15). Mapping the crowd: Software that maps who is working on common problems is shaving years off research and honing corporate strategies. *Business Week*, 19–20.

Hinds & S. Kiesler (Ed.). *Distributed work* (pp. 335-355). Cambridge, MA: MIT Press.

Hollingshead, A. B., Fulk, J., & Monge, P. (2002). Fostering intranet knowledge sharing: An integration of transactive memory and public goods approaches. In P.

Hyatt, A., Contractor, N. S., & Jones, P. (1997). Computational organizational network modeling: Strategies and an example. *Computational & Mathematical Organization Theory, 2*(4), 285–300. doi:10.1007/BF00132313

Jackson, P., & Klobas, J. (2008). Transactive memory systems in organizations: Implications for knowledge directories. *Decision Support Systems, 44*(2), 409–424. doi:10.1016/j.dss.2007.05.001

Jarvenpaa, S. L., & Staples, D. S. (2000). The use of collaborative electronic media for information sharing: An exploratory study of determinants. *The Journal of Strategic Information Systems, 9*(2/3), 129–254. doi:10.1016/S0963-8687(00)00042-1

Jessup, L. M., & Valacich, J. S. (1993). *Group support systems: New perspectives*. New York: Plenum Press.

Jian, G., & Jeffres, L. W. (2006). Understanding employees' willingness to contribute to shared electronic databases: A three-dimensional framework. *Communication Research, 3*(4), 3, 242–261.

Kanawattanachai, P., & Yoo, Y. (2007). The impact of knowledge coordination on virtual team performance over time. *MIS Quarterly, 31*(4), 783–808.

Kankanhalli, A., Tan, B. C., & Wei, K. (2005). Contributing knowledge to electronic knowledge repositories: An empirical investigation. *MIS Quarterly, 29*(1), 113–143.

Kanki, B. G., & Foushee, H. C. (1989). Communication as group process mediator of aircrew performance. *Aviation, Space, and Environmental Medicine, 20*(2), 402–410.

Koudsi, S. (2000, March 20). Actually, it is like brain surgery. *Fortune*, 233–234.

Kraut, R. E., Fish, R. S., Root, R. W., & Chalfonte, B. L. (1990). Informal communication in organizations: Form, function, and technology. In S. Oskamp & S. Spacapan (Eds.), *Human reactions to technology* (pp. 145-199). Beverly Hills, CA: Sage.

Latane, B. (1981). The psychology of social impact. *The American Psychologist, 36*(4), 343–351. doi:10.1037/0003-066X.36.4.343

Leathers, D. G. (1972). Quality of group communication as a determinant of group product. *Speech Monographs, 39*(3), 166–173. doi:10.1080/03637757209375754

Lee, F. (1997). When the going gets tough, do the tough ask for help? Help seeking and power motivation in organizations. *Organizational Behavior and Human Decision Processes, 72*(3), 336–363. doi:10.1006/obhd.1997.2746

Lee, F. (2002). The social costs of seeking help. *The Journal of Applied Behavioral Science*, *38*(1), 17–35. doi:10.1177/0021886302381002

Lewis, K. (2003). Measuring transactive memory systems in the field: Scale development and validation. *The Journal of Applied Psychology*, *88*(4), 587–604. doi:10.1037/0021-9010.88.4.587

Lewis, K. (2004). Knowledge and performance in knowledge-worker teams: A longitudinal study of transactive memory systems. *Management Science*, *50*(11), 1519–1533. doi:10.1287/mnsc.1040.0257

Lewis, K., Belliveau, M., Herndon, B., & Keller, J. (2007). Group cognition, membership change, and performance: Investigating the benefits and detriments of collective knowledge. *Organizational Behavior and Human Decision Processes*, *103*(2), 159–178. doi:10.1016/j.obhdp.2007.01.005

Lewis, K., Lange, D., & Gillis, L. (2005). Transactive memory systems, learning, and learning transfer. *Organization Science*, *16*(6), 581–598. doi:10.1287/orsc.1050.0143

Liang, D. W., Moreland, R. L., & Argote, L. (1995). Group versus individual training and group performance: The mediating role of transactive memory. *Personality and Social Psychology Bulletin*, *21*(4), 384–393. doi:10.1177/0146167295214009

Majchrzak, A., Malhotra, A., Stamps, J., & Lipnack, J. (2004, May). Can absence make a team grow stronger? *Harvard Business Review*, 131–137.

Mannix, E. A., Griffith, T., & Neale, M. A. (2002). The phenomenology of conflict in distributed work teams. In P. Hinds & S. Kiesler (Eds.), *Distributed work* (pp. 213-233). Cambridge, MA: MIT Press.

Martin, J. (1982). Stories and scripts in organizational settings. In A. Hastorf & I. Isen (Eds.), *Cognitive social psychology* (pp. 255-305). New York: Elsevier.

Martins, L. L., Gilson, L. L., & Maynard, M. (2004). Virtual teams: What do we know and where do we go from here? *Journal of Management*, *30*(6), 805–835. doi:10.1016/j.jm.2004.05.002

McGregor, J. (2006, February 27). The office chart that really counts. *Business Week*, 48–49.

Michinov, E., Olivier-Chiron, E., Rusch, E., & Chiron, B. (2008). Influence of transactive memory on perceived performance, job satisfaction, and identification in anaesthesia teams. *British Journal of Anaesthesia*, *100*(3), 327–332. doi:10.1093/bja/aem404

Michinov, N., & Michinov, E. (2009). Investigating the relationship between transactive memory and performance in collaborative learning. *Learning and Instruction*, *19*(1), 43–54. doi:10.1016/j.learninstruc.2008.01.003

Milgram, S. (1967). The small-world problem. *Psychology Today*, *2*, 60–67.

Moreland, R. L. (1999). Transactive memory: Learning who knows what in work groups and organizations. In L. Thompson, D. Messick, & J. Levine (Eds.), *Shared cognition in organizations: The management of knowledge* (pp. 3-31). Mahwah, N.J.: Erlbaum.

Moreland, R. L., Argote, L., & Krishnan, R. (1996). Socially shared cognition at work: Transactive memory and group performance. In J. L. Nye & A. M. Brower (Eds.), *What's social about social cognition? Research on socially shared cognition in small groups* (pp. 57-84). Thousand Oaks, CA.: Sage.

Moreland, R. L., Argote, L., & Krishnan, R. (1998). Training people to work in groups. In R. S. Tindale & Colleagues (Eds.), *Theory and research on small groups* (pp. 36-60). New York: Plenum Press.

Moreland, R. L., & Levine, J. M. (1992). Problem identification by groups. In S. Worchel, W. Wood, & J. A. Simpson (Eds.), *Group process and productivity* (pp. 17-47). Newbury Park, CA.: Sage.

Moreland, R. L., & Levine, J. M. (2000). Socialization in organizations and work groups. In M. Turner (Ed.), *Groups at work: Theory and research* (pp. 69-112). Mahwah, N.J.: Erlbaum.

Moreland, R. L., & Myaskovsky, L. (2000). Explaining the performance benefits of group training: Transactive memory or improved communication? *Organizational Behavior and Human Decision Processes, 82*(1), 117–133. doi:10.1006/obhd.2000.2891

Mullen, I. B., & Goethals, G. R. (Eds.). *Theories of group behavior* (pp. 185-208). New York: Springer-Verlag.

Nardi, B. A., & Whittaker, S. (2002). The place of face-to-face communication in distributed work. In P. Hinds & S. Kiesler (Eds.), *Distributed work* (pp. 83-110).

Nebus, J. (2006). Building collegial information networks: A theory of advice network generation. *Academy of Management Review, 31*(3), 615–537.

O'Dell, C., & Grayson, C. J. (1998). If only we knew: Identification and transfer of internal best practices. *California Management Review, 40*(3), 154–174.

O'Reilly, C. A. (1982). Variations in decision makers' use of information sources: The impact of quality and accessibility of information. *Academy of Management Journal, 25*(4), 756–771. doi:10.2307/256097

Orr, J. E. (1996). *Talking about machines: An ethnography of a modern job*. Ithaca, NY: Cornell University Press.

Palazzolo, E. T. (2005). Organizing for information retrieval in transactive memory systems. *Communication Research, 32*(6), 726–761. doi:10.1177/0093650205281056

Palazzolo, E. T., Serb, D. A., She, Y., Su, C., & Contractor, N. S. (2006). Coevolution of communication and knowledge networks in transactive memory systems: Using computational models for theoretical development. *Communication Theory, 16*(2), 223–250. doi:10.1111/j.1468-2885.2006.00269.x

Peltokorpi, V. (2004). Transactive memory directories in small work units. *Personnel Review, 33*(4), 446–462. doi:10.1108/00483480410539515

Peltokorpi, V., & Manka, M. (2008). Antecedents and the performance outcomes of transactive memory in daycare work groups. *European Psychology, 13*(2), 103-113. Prichard, J., & Ashleigh, M. (2007). The effects of team-skills training on transactive memory and performance. *Small Group Research, 38*(6), 696–726.

Rau, D. (2005). The influence of relationship conflict and trust on the transactive memory-performance relation in top management teams. *Small Group Research, 36*(6), 746–771. doi:10.1177/1046496405281776

Rau, D. (2006). Top management team transactive memory, information gathering, and perceptual accuracy. *Journal of Business Research, 59*(4), 416–424. doi:10.1016/j.jbusres.2005.07.001

Reagans, R., Argote, L., & Brooks, D. (2005). Individual experience and experience working together: Predicting learning rates from knowing what to do and knowing who knows what. *Management Science, 51*(6), 869–881. doi:10.1287/mnsc.1050.0366

Reingold, J., & Yang, J. C. (2007, July 18). The hidden workplace. *Fortune*, 98–102.

Ren, Y., Carley, K. M., & Argote, L. (2006). The contingent effects of transactive memory: When is it more beneficial to know what others know? *Management Science, 52*(5), 671–682. doi:10.1287/mnsc.1050.0496

Riketta, M. (2004). Organizational identification: A meta-analysis. *Journal of Vocational Behavior*, *66*(2), 358–384. doi:10.1016/j.jvb.2004.05.005

Romano, N. C., Lowry, P. B., & Roberts, T. L. (2007). Technology-supported small group interaction: Extending a tradition of leading research for virtual teams and global organizations. *Small Group Research*, *38*(1), 3–11. doi:10.1177/1046496406297483

Ruggles, R. (1998). The state of the notion: Knowledge management in practice. *California Management Review*, *4*(3), 80–89.

Smith, T. E. (1993). Growth in academic achievement and teaching younger siblings. *Social Psychology Quarterly*, *56*(1), 77–85. doi:10.2307/2786647

Srivastava, A., Bartol, K. M., & Locke, E. A. (2006). Empowered leadership in management teams: Effects on knowledge sharing, efficacy, and performance. *Academy of Management Journal*, *49*(6), 1239–1251.

Stambor, Z. (2006, April). Brooding over others' business. *APA Monitor on Psychology*, 58-59.

Stasser, G., Stewart, D. D., & Wittenbaum, G. M. (1995). Expert roles and information exchange during discussion: The importance of knowing who knows what. *Journal of Experimental Social Psychology*, *31*(3), 244–255. doi:10.1006/jesp.1995.1012

Stewart, T. A. (1995a, October 30). Mapping corporate brainpower. *Fortune*, 209–211.

Stewart, T. A. (1995b, November 27). Getting real about brainpower. *Fortune*, 201–203.

Stewart, T. A. (1997, September 29). Does anyone around here know…? *Fortune*, 279–280.

Stewart, T. A. (1999). *Intellectual capital: The new wealth of organizations.* New York: Doubleday.

Stewart, T. A. (2000, September 4). Software preserves knowledge, people pass it on. *Fortune*, 390–393.

Stewart, T. A. (2001). *The wealth of knowledge: Intellectual capital and the twenty-first century organization.* London: Nicholas Brealey

Sutton, R. J., & Hargadon, A. (1996). Brainstorming groups in context: Effectiveness in a product-design firm. *Administrative Science Quarterly*, *41*(4), 685–718. doi:10.2307/2393872

Swap, W., Leonard, D., Shields, M., & Abrams, L. (2001). Using mentoring and storytelling to transfer knowledge in the workplace. *Journal of Management Systems*, *18*(1), 95–114.

Totty, M. (2006, February 13). Technology: The dangers within. *Wall Street Journal*, R1.

Vaast, E. (2004). O Brother, where art thou? From communities to networks of practice through intranet use. *Management Communication Quarterly*, *18*(1), 5–44. doi:10.1177/0893318904265125

Van Dick, R., Grojean, M. W., Christ, O., & Wieseke, J. (2006). Identity and the extra mile: Relationships between organizational identification and organizational citizenship behavior. *British Journal of Management*, *17*, 283–301. doi:10.1111/j.1467-8551.2006.00520.x

Van Zolingen, S. J., Streumer, J. N., & Stooker, M. (2001). Problems in knowledge management: A case study of a knowledge-intensive company. *International Journal of Training and Development*, *5*(3), 168–184. doi:10.1111/1468-2419.00130

Verbeke, W., & Wuyts, S. (2007). Moving in social circles – social circle membership and performance implications. *Journal of Organizational Behavior*, *28*(4), 357–379. doi:10.1002/job.423

Von Seggern, M., & Jourdain, J. M. (1996). Technical communities in engineering and science: The practices within a government defense laboratory. *Special Libraries*, *87*(2), 98–119.

Wasko, M. M., & Faraj, S. (2000). It is what one does: Why people participate in and help others in electronic communities of practice. *The Journal of Strategic Information Systems*, *9*, 155–173. doi:10.1016/S0963-8687(00)00045-7

Wasko, M. M., & Faraj, S. (2005). Why should I share? Examining social capital and knowledge contributions in electronic networks of practice. *MIS Quarterly*, *29*(1), 35–79.

Watts, D. J., & Strogatz, S. H. (1998). Collective dynamics of "small world" networks. *Nature*, *393*, 409–410. doi:10.1038/30918

Wegner, D. M. (1986). Transactive memory: A contemporary analysis of the group mind.

Wegner, D. M. (1995). A computer network model of human transactive memory. *Social Cognition*, *13*(3), 1–21.

Wegner, D. M., Giuliano, T., & Hertel, P. (1985). Cognitive interdependence in close relationships. In W. J. Ickes (Ed.), *Compatible and incompatible relationships* (pp. 253-276). New York: Springer-Verlag.

Wenger, E. C., & Snyder, W. M. (2000, January/February). Communities of practice: The organizational frontier. *Harvard Business Review*, 139–145.

Winerman, L. (2006, April). Have you heard the latest? *APA Monitor on Psychology*, 56-57.

Wittenbaum, G. M., Vaughan, S. I., & Stasser, G. (1998). Coordination in task-performing groups. In R. S. Tindale & Colleagues (Eds.), *Theory and research on small groups* (pp. 177-204). New York: Plenum.

Yoo, Y., & Kanawattanachai, P. (2001). Development of transactive memory systems and collective mind in virtual teams. *The International Journal of Organizational Analysis*, *9*(2), 187–208. doi:10.1108/eb028933

Yuan, Y. C., Fulk, J., & Monge, P. R. (2007). Access to information in connective and communal transactive memory systems. *Communication Research*, *34*(2), 131–155. doi:10.1177/0093650206298067

Zhang, Z.-X., Hempel, P. S., Han, Y.-L., & Tjosvold, D. (2007). Transactive memory systems link work team characteristics and performance. *The Journal of Applied Psychology*, *92*(6), 1722–1730. doi:10.1037/0021-9010.92.6.1722

Zipperer, L. (1993). The creative professional and knowledge. *Special Libraries*, *84*(2), 69–78.

Compilation of References

Abbott-Chapman, J., & Patterson, C. (2001). Improving post-school outcomes of rural school leavers. *Australian Journal of Education*, *45*(1), 35–47.

Abell, S. K., Anderson, G., & Chezem, J. (2000). Science as argument and explanation: Exploring concepts of sound in third grade. In J. Minstrell & E. H. Van Zee (Eds.), *Inquiry into InquiryLearning and Teaching in Science* (pp. 100-119). Washington DC: American Association for the Advancement of Science.

Adams, W. K., Reid, S., LeMaster, R., McKagan, S. B., Perkins, K. K., Dubson, M., & Wieman, C. E. (2008). A study of educational simulations – part I: Engagement and learning. *Journal of Interactive Learning Research*, *19*, 397–419.

Ainsworth, S. E. (2006). DeFT: A conceptual framework for considering learning with multiple representations. *Learning and Instruction*, *16*, 183–198. doi:10.1016/j.learninstruc.2006.03.001

Akgun, A. E., Byrne, J. C., Keskin, H., & Lynn, G. S. (2006). Transactive memory systems in new product development teams. *IEEE Transactions on Engineering Management*, *53*(1), 95–111. doi:10.1109/TEM.2005.857570

Aleven, V., McLaren, B. M., & Koedinger, K. R. (2006). Toward computer-based tutoring of help-seeking skills. In S. A. Karabenick & R. S. Newman (Eds.), *Help seeking in academic settings: Goals, groups, and contexts* (pp. 259-296). Mahwah, NJ: Erlbaum.

Aleven, V., McLaren, B. M., Roll, I., & Koedinger, K. R. (2006). Toward meta-cognitive tutoring: A model of help-seeking with a cognitive tutor. *International Journal of Artificial Intelligence in Education*, *16*, 101–130.

Aleven, V., McLaren, B., Roll, I., & Koedinger, K. R. (2004). Toward tutoring help seeking: Applying cognitive modelling to meta-cognitive skills. In J. C. Lester, R. M. Vicari & F. Paraguaçu (Eds.), *Proceedings of Seventh International Conference on Intelligent Tutoring Systems, ITS 2004* (pp. 227-239). Berlin: Springer

Aleven, V., Stahl, E., Schworm, S., Fischer, F., & Wallace, R. (2003). Help Seeking and Help Design in Interactive Learning Environments. *Review of Educational Research*, *73*, 277–320. doi:10.3102/00346543073003277

Alexander, C. (1977). *A pattern language. Towns, buildings, construction*. New York: Oxford University Press.

Alexander, P. A., Kulikowich, J. M., & Jetton, T. L. (1994). The role of subject-matter knowledge and interest in the processing of linear and nonlinear texts. *Review of Educational Research*, *64*, 201–252.

Allen, T. (1995). *Managing the flow of technology*. Cambridge, MA: MIT Press.

American Association for the Advancement of Science. (1993). *Benchmarks for science literacy*. New York: Oxford University Press.

Ancona, D. G., & Bresman, H. (2007). *X-teams: How to build teams that lead, innovate, and succeed*. Boston, MA: Harvard Business School.

Ancona, D. G., & Caldwell, D. F. (1988). Beyond task and maintenance: Defining external functions in groups.

Group and Organizational Studies, 13(4), 468–494. doi:10.1177/105960118801300405

Anderson, J. R. (1982). Acquisition of cognitive skill. *Psychological Review, 89*, 369–406. doi:10.1037/0033-295X.89.4.369

Anderson, J., & Lee, A. (1995). Literacy teachers learning a new literacy: A study of the use of electronic mail in a reading education class. *Reading Research and Instruction, 34*, 222–238.

Anderson, R. C., Nguyen-Jahiel, K., McNurlen, B., Archodidou, A., Kim, S.-Y., & Reznitskaya, A. (2001). The snowball phenomenon: spread of ways of talking and ways of thinking across groups of children. *Cognition and Instruction, 19*(1), 1–46. doi:10.1207/S1532690XCI1901_1

Andreeva, N. (1998, August 17). Do the math – it is a small world. *Business Week*, 54–55.

Andriessen, J., Baker, M., & Suthers, D. (2003). Argumentation, computer support, and the educational contexts of confronting cognitions. In J. Andriessen, M. Baker & D. Suthers (Eds.), *Arguing to learn: Confronting cognitions in computer-supported collaborative learning environments* (pp. 1-25). Dordrecht, The Netherlands: Kluwer Academic Publishers.

Andriessen, J., Baker, M., & Suthers, D. (Eds.). (2003) *Arguing to learn: Confronting cognitions in computer-supported collaborative learning environments*. Dordrecht, The Netherlands: Kluwer.

Argote, L., Gruenfeld, D., & Naqin, C. (2001). Group learning in organziations. In M. E. Turner (Ed.), *Groups at work* (pp. 369-411). London: Lawrence Erlbaum.

Armstrong, D. J., & Cole, P. (2002). Managing distances and differences in geographically distributed workgroups. In P. Hinds & S. Kiesler (Eds.), *Distributed work* (pp. 167-186). Cambridge, MA: MIT Press.

Aronson, E., Blaney, N., Sikes, J., Stephan, C., & Snapp, M. (1978). *The jigsaw classroom*. Beverly Hills, CA: Sage.

Arvaja, M. (2007). Contextual perspective in analysing collaborative knowledge construction of two small groups in Web-based discussion. *Int. Jrnl. of Computer-Supported Collaborative Learning, 2*(2/3), 133–158. doi:10.1007/s11412-007-9013-5

Arvaja, M., & Hämäläinen, R. (2008). Collaborative knowledge construction during structured tasks in an online course at higher education context. In G. Ollington (Ed.), *Teachers and teaching: Strategies, innovations and problem solving*. New York: Nova Science.

Arvaja, M., Hämäläinen, R., & Rasku-Puttonen, H. (2009). Challenges for the teacher's role in promoting productive knowledge construction in computer-supported collaborative learning contexts. In J. O. Lindberg & A. D. Olofsson (Eds.), *Online Learning Communities and Teacher Professional Development: Methods for Improved Education Delivery* (pp. 263-280). Hershey, PA: IGI Global.

Arvaja, M., Rasku-Puttonen, H., Häkkinen, P., & Eteläpelto, A. (2003). Constructing knowledge through a role-play in a Web-based learning environment. *Journal of Educational Computing Research, 28*(4), 319–341. doi:10.2190/4FAV-EK1T-XV4H-YNXF

Arvaja, M., Salovaara, H., Häkkinen, P., & Järvelä, S. (2007). Combining individual and group-level perspectives for studying collaborative knowledge construction in context. *Learning and Instruction, 17*(4), 448–459. doi:10.1016/j.learninstruc.2007.04.003

Astleitner, H. (2006). Motivationsförderung im E-Learning: Stand der Forschung zum ARCS-Modell. *Salzburger Beiträge zur Erziehungswissenschaft, 10*(2), 17–29.

Austin, J. R. (2003). Transactive memory in organizational groups: The effects of contents, consensus, specialization, and accuracy on group performance. *The Journal of Applied Psychology, 88*(5), 866–878. doi:10.1037/0021-9010.88.5.866

Baacke, D. (1997). *Medienpädagogik* [Media pedagogy]. Tübingen, Germany: Niemeyer.

Back, A., Enkel, E., Seufert, A., & von Krogh, G. (Eds.). (2006). *Getting real about Knowledge Networks: un-*

locking corporate knowledge assets. Hampshire, UK: Palgrave MacMillan.

Baghaei, N., Mitrovic, T., & Irwin, W. (2007). Supporting collaborative learning and problem solving in a constraint-based CSCL environment for UML class diagrams. *International Journal of Computer-Supported Collaborative Learning, 2*(2-3), 159–190. doi:10.1007/s11412-007-9018-0

Baker, M. (2002). Forms of cooperation in dyadic problem-solving. In P. Salembier & H. Benchekroun (Eds.). *Socio-technical systems: Vol. 16. Cooperation and complexity* (pp. 587–620). Paris: Hermès.

Baker, M. (2003). Computer-mediated argumentative interactions for the co-elaboration of scientific notions. In J. Andriessen, M. Baker, & D. Suthers (Eds.), *Arguing to learn: Confronting cognitions in computer-supported collaborative learning environments* (pp. 1–25). Dordrecht, the Netherlands: Kluwer Academic.

Baker, M. J., & Lund, K. (1997). Promoting reflective interactions in a computer-supported collaborative learning environment. *Journal of Computer Assisted Learning, 13*, 175–193. doi:10.1046/j.1365-2729.1997.00019.x

Baker, M. J., deVries, E., Lund, K., & Quignard, M. (2001). Computer-mediated epistemic interactions for co-constructing scientific notions: Lessons learned from a five-year research programme. In P. Dillenbourg, A. Eurelings & K. Hakkarainen (Eds.), *Proceedings of EuroCSCL 2001: European Perspectives on Computer-Supported Collaborative Learning* (pp. 89-96).

Baker, M. J., Hansen, T., Joiner, R., & Traum, D. (1999). The role of grounding in collaborative learning tasks. In P. Dillenbourg (Ed.), *Collaborative learning: Cognitive and computational approaches* (pp. 31-63). Oxford, UK: Elsevier.

Baker, M., Andriessen, J., Lund, K., van Amelsvoort, M., & Quignard, M. (2007). Rainbow: a framework for analyzing computer-mediated pedagogical debates. *International Journal of Computer-Supported Collaborative Learning, 2*(2-3). doi:10.1007/s11412-007-9022-4

Baker, R. S., Corbett, A. T., & Koedinger, K. R. (2004). *Detecting student misuse of intelligent tutoring systems.* Paper presented at the 7th International Conference on Intelligent Tutoring Systems.

Baker, R., & Andrews, J. (1991). Parental reasons for sending children to a rural day and boarding school. *Education in Rural Australia, 1*(1), 21–25.

Baker, S. (2009, June 1). What's a friend worth? *Business Week*, 32–36.

Barron, B. (2003). When smart groups fail. *Journal of the Learning Sciences, 12*, 307–359. doi:10.1207/S15327809JLS1203_1

Bates, M. J. (1989). The Design of Browsing and Berrypicking Techniques for the Online Search Interface. *Online Review, 13*(5), 407–424. doi:10.1108/eb024320

Bauer, J., Rehrl, M., & Harteis, C. (2007). Measurement of learning culture: A motivational approach. In H. Gruber & T. Palonen (Eds.), *Learning in the workplace – new developments* (pp. 21-50). Turku, Finland: FERA.

Baylen, D. M., & Glacken, J. (2007). Promoting lifelong learning online: A case study of a professional development experience. In Y. Inoue (Ed.), *Online education for lifelong learning* (pp. 229-251). Hershey, PA: Information Science Publishing.

Beers, P. J., Boshuizen, H. P. A., Kirschner, P. A., & Gijselaers, W. H. (2007). The analysis of negotiation of common ground in CSCL. *Learning and Instruction, 17*, 427–435. doi:10.1016/j.learninstruc.2007.04.002

Beers, P., Kirschner, P. A., Boshuizen, H. P. A., & Gijselaers, W. (2007). ICT-support for grounding in the classroom. *Instructional Science, 35*, 535–556. doi:10.1007/s11251-007-9018-5

Beichner, R. J. (1996). The impact of video motion analysis on kinematics graph interpretation skills. *American Journal of Physics, 64*, 1272–1278. doi:10.1119/1.18390

Beißwenger, M. (2007). *Sprachhandlungskoordination in der Chat-Kommunikation.* Berlin, Germany: Walter de Gruyter.

Beitz, H., & Loch, A. (1997). *Assessment Center. Erfolgstipps und Übungen für Bewerberinnen und Bewerber.* Niederhausen, Germany: Falken.

Bell, B. S., & Kozlowski, S. W. J. (2002). A typology of virtual teams: Implications for effective leadership. *Group & Organization Management, 27*(1), 14–49. doi:10.1177/1059601102027001003

Bell, P. (1997). Using argument representations to make thinking visible for individuals and groups. In R. Hall, N. Miyake & N. Enyedy (Eds.), *Proceedings of the Second International Conference on Computer Support for Collaborative Learning (CSCL 1997)* (pp. 10-19). Toronto: Toronto University Press.

Bell, P. (2004). Promoting students' argument construction and collaborative debate in the science classroom. In M. C. Linn, E. A. Davis & P. Bell (Eds.), *Internet environments for science education* (pp. 115-143). Mahwah, NJ: Erlbaum.

Bell, P., & Linn, M. C. (2000). Scientific arguments as learning artifacts: Designing for learning from the web with KIE. *International Journal of Science Education, 22*(8), 797–817. doi:10.1080/095006900412284

Berland, L., & Reiser, B. (2009). Making sense of argumentation and explanation. *Science Education, 93*(1), 26–55. doi:10.1002/sce.20286

Berliner, D. C. (2001). Learning about and learning from expert teachers. *International Journal of Educational Research, 35,* 463–482. doi:10.1016/S0883-0355(02)00004-6

Berman, S. L., Down, J., & Hill, C. W. L. J. (2002). Tacit knowledge as a source of competitive advantage in the National Basketball Association. *Academy of Management Journal, 45*(1), 13–31. doi:10.2307/3069282

Berthold, K., Eysink, T. H. S., & Renkl, A. (2008). Assisting self-explanation prompts are more effective than open prompts when learning with multiple representations. *Instructional Science.*

Bettoni, M. (2005). Wissenskooperation – Die Zukunft des Wissensmanagements. Lernende Organisation. *Zeitschrift für Systemisches Management und Organisation, 25, Mai/Juni 2005.*

Bettoni, M., & Bernhard, W. (2007). CoRe – Linking Teaching and Research by a Community-Oriented Strategy. In G. Richards (Ed.), *Proceedings of World Conference on E-Learning in Corporate, Government, Healthcare, and Higher Education 2007* (pp. 2354-2362). Chesapeake, VA: AACE.

Bettoni, M., & Schneider, S. (2002). Experience Management - Lessons Learned from Knowledge Engineering. In *Lecture Notes in Informatics (LNI)* (Vol P-10, pp. 117-128). Bonn, Germany: Gesellschaft für Informatik (GI).

Bettoni, M., & Schneider, S. (2003). The Essence of Knowledge Management: A Constructivist Approach. In O. Camp, J. Felipe, S. Hammoudi, & M. Piattini (Eds.), *Proc. of the Fifth Intern. Conf. on Enterprise Information Systems,* ICEIS 2003, Angers, France, April 22-26, 2003 (Vol. 2, pp. 191-196).

Bettoni, M., Andenmatten, S., & Mathieu, R. (2007). Knowledge Cooperation in Online Communities: A Duality of Participation and Cultivation. [Retrieved from http://www.ejkm.com/]. *Electronic Journal of Knowledge Management, 5*(1), 1–6.

Bettoni, M., Bernhard, W., & Schiller, G. (2009). Community-orientierte Strategien zur Integration von Lehre und Forschung. In P. Bergamin, H. Muralt Müller, & C.Filk (Hrsg.), *Offene Bildungsinhalte (OER), Teilen von Wissen oder Gratisbildungskultur?* Bern, Switzerland: h.e.p. Verlag.

Bettoni, M., Bernhard, W., Borter, F., & Dönnges, G. (2007). The Yellow Tool – Making Yellow Pages More Social and Visible. In B. Martin & D. Remenyi, (Eds.), *Proc. of the 8th European Conference on Knowledge Management, ECKM 2007, Consorci Escola Industrial de Barcelona (CEIB), Barcelona, Spain, Sept. 6-7, 2007* (pp. 118-124) Reading, MA: Academic Publishing Ltd.

Bettoni, M., Braun, A., & Weber, W. (2003). What motivates cooperation and sharing in communities of practice? In F. McGrath & D. Remenyi (Eds.), *Proc. of the 4th Europ. Conference on Knowledge Management,*

Oriel College, Oxford University, UK (pp. 67-72) Reading, MA: Academic Publishing Ltd.

Bettoni, M., Clases, C., & Wehner, T. (2004). Communities of Practice as a Way to a More Human-Oriented Knowledge Management. In I. Svetlik & J. Nadoh (Eds.), *Proc. Intern. Conference on Human resource management in a knowledge-based economy (HRM 2004)*, Ljubljana, Slovenia (CD-Rom), 2-4 June.

Bettoni, M., Schiller, G., & Bernhard, W. (2008). Weak Ties Cooperation in the CoRe Knowledge Network. In D. Harorimana & D. Watkins (Eds.), *Proc. of the 9th European Conference on Knowledge Management Southampton Solent University, Southampton, UK, 4-5 September 2008* (pp. 59-66). Reading: Academic Publishing Ltd.

Biggs, J. (1996). Enhancing teaching through constructive alignment. *Higher Education, 32*, 347–364. doi:10.1007/BF00138871

Billett, S. (2001). *Learning in the workplace. Strategies for effective practice.* Crows Nest, Australia: Allen & Unwin.

Billett, S. (2006). *Workers, work and change.* Dordrecht, The Netherlands: Springer.

Billett, S. (2006). Work, subjectivity and learning. In S. Billett, T. Fenwick, & M. Somerville (Eds.), *Work, subjectivity and learning. Understanding learning through working life* (pp. 1-20). Dordrecht, The Netherlands: Springer.

Billett, S., Harteis, C., & Eteläpelto, A. (Eds.). (2008). *Emerging perspectives of workplace learning.* Rotterdam, Germany: Sense Publishers.

Birenbaum, M. (2005, October). Multidimensional assessment of computer-supported knowledge building. In [Vancouver, Canada: Association for the Advancement of Computing in Education.]. *Proceedings of E-Learn, 2005*, 1203–1208.

Boekaerts, M. (1995). Self-regulated learning: Bridging the gap between metacognitive and metamotivational theories. *Educational Psychologist, 30*, 195–200. doi:10.1207/s15326985ep3004_4

Borchers, J. (2001). *A pattern approach to interaction design.* Chichester, UK: Wiley.

Borgatti, S. P., & Cross, R. (2003). A relational view of information seeking and learning in social networks. *Management Science, 49*(4), 432–445. doi:10.1287/mnsc.49.4.432.14428

Boshuizen, H. P. A., & Schmidt, H. G. (1992). On the role of biomedical knowledge in clinical reasoning by experts, intermediates and novices. *Cognitive Science, 16*, 153–184.

Boshuizen, H. P. A., Bromme, R., & Gruber, H. (Eds.). (2004). *Professional learning: gaps and transitions on the way from novice to expert.* Dordrecht, The Netherlands: Kluwer.

Boud, D. J. (1990). Assessment and promotion of academic values. *Studies in Higher Education, 15*, 101–113. doi:10.1080/03075079012331377621

Bransford, J. D., Brown, A. L., & Cocking, R. R. (2000). *How People Learn: Brain, Mind, Experience, and School.* Washington, DC: National Academic Press.

Bransford, J. D., Burns, M. S., Delclos, V. R., & Vye, N. J. (1986). Teaching thinking: Evaluating evaluations and broadening the data base. *Educational Leadership, 44*(2), 68–70.

Brehm, S. S., & Brehm, J. W. (1981). *Psychological reactance: A theory of freedom and control.* New York: Academic Press.

Breitwieser, A., Küpper, C., & Ponomareva, N. (2002). *Akzeptanz von E-Learning.* Frankfurt am Main, Germany: Cognos.

Brennan, S. (1998). The grounding problem in conversations with and through computers. In S. R. Fussel & R. J. Kreuz (Eds.), *Social and cognitive psychological approaches to interpersonal communication* (pp. 201-225). Mahwah, NJ: Erlbaum.

Brewer, W. F., & Nakamura, G. V. (1984). The nature and functions of schemas. Center for the Study of Reading, Technical Report Bo. 325. In R. S. Wyer, & T. K. Krull (Eds.), *Handbook of social cognition* (Vol. 1, pp. 119-160). Hillsdale, NJ: Erlbaum.

Brill, M., Keable, E., & Fabiniak, J. (2000). The myth of open plan. *Facilities Design and Management, 19*(2), 36–39.

Bromme, R., Hesse, F. W., & Spada, H. (2005). Barriers, biases and opportunities of communication and cooperation with computers: Introduction and overview. In R. Bromme, F. W. Hesse & H. Spada (Eds.), *Barriers and biases in computer-mediated communication - and how they may be overcome* (pp. 1-14). New York: Springer.

Brooks, L. W., & Dansereau, D. F. (1983). Effects of structural schema training and text organization on expository prose processing. *Journal of Educational Psychology, 75*(6), 811–820. doi:10.1037/0022-0663.75.6.811

Brown, J. S., Collins, A., & Duguid, P. (1989). Situated cognition and the culture of learning. *Educational Researcher, 18*, 32–42.

Bruinsma, M. (2004). Motivation, cognitive processing and achievement in higher education. *Learning and Instruction, 14*, 549–568. doi:10.1016/j.learninstruc.2004.09.001

Brünken, R., Steinbacher, S., Schnotz, W., & Leutner, D. (2001). Mentale Modelle und Effekte der Präsentations- und Abrufkodalität beim Lernen mit Multimedia [Mental models and effects of presentation and retrieval cue codality in multimedia learning]. *Zeitschrift fur Padagogische Psychologie, 15*, 16–27. doi:10.1024//1010-0652.15.1.16

Buchs, C., Butera, F., Mugny, G., & Darnon, C. (2004). Conflict Elaboration and Cognitive Outcomes. *Theory into Practice, 43*(1), 23–30. doi:10.1207/s15430421tip4301_4

Buder, J., & Bodemer, D. (2008). Supporting controversial CSCL discussions with augmented group awareness tools. *Computer-Supported Collaborative Learning, 3*(2), 123–139. doi:10.1007/s11412-008-9037-5

Bürg, O. *(2005).* Akzeptanz von E-Learning in Unternehmen. Die Bedeutung von institutionellen Rahmenbedingungen, Merkmalen des Individuums und Merkmalen der Lernumgebung für die Akzeptanz von E-Learning. *Berlin, Germany: Logos.*

Burgos, D., Tattersall, C., & Koper, R. (2007). How to represent adaption in e-learning with IMS learning design. *Interactive Learning Environments, 15*, 161–170. doi:10.1080/10494820701343736

Burt, R. S. (1992). *Structural holes: The social structure of competition.* Boston, MA: Harvard University Press.

Butera, F., & Buchs, C. (2005), Reasoning together: From focusing to decentering. In V. Girotto & P. N. Johnson-Laird (Eds.), *The shape of reason* (pp. 193-203). Hove, England: Psychology Press.

Cabrera, A., & Cabrera, E. F. (2002). Knowledge-sharing dilemmas. *Organization Studies, 23*(5), 687–710. doi:10.1177/0170840602235001

Cakir, M., Xhafa, F., Zhou, N., & Stahl, G. (2005). Thread-based analysis of patterns of collaborative interaction in chat. *Paper presented at the international conference on AI in Education* (AI-Ed 2005). Retrieved from http://GerryStahl.net/pub/aied2005.pdf

Cambridge, MA.: MIT Press.

Carey, S., & Smith, C. (1993). On understanding the nature of scientific knowledge. *Educational Psychologist, 28*, 235–251. doi:10.1207/s15326985ep2803_4

Carey, S., Evans, R., Honda, M., Jay, E., & Unger, C. (1989). An experiment is when you try it and see if it works: A study of grade 7 students' understanding of the construction of scientific knowledge. *International Journal of Science Education, 11*(Special Issue), 514–529. doi:10.1080/0950069890110504

Carmien, S., Kollar, C., Fischer, G., & Fischer, F. (2007). The interplay of internal and external scripts. In F. Fischer, H. Mandl, J. Haake & I. Kollar (Eds.), *Scripting computer-supported communication of knowledge - cognitive, computational and educational perspectives* (pp. 303-324). New York: Springer.

Carr, C. S. (2003). Using computer supported argument visualization to teach legal argumentation. In P. A. Kirschner, S. J. Buckingham Shum, & C. S. Carr (Eds.), *Visualizing argumentation. Software tools for collaborative and educational sense-making* (pp. 75–96). London: Springer.

Cavanaugh, C. (2001). The effectiveness of interactive distance education technologies in K-12 learning: a meta-analysis. *International Journal of Educational Telecommunications, 7*(1), 73–88.

Cheng, W., & Warren, M. (1997). Having second thoughts: Student perceptions before and after a peer assessment exercise. *Studies in Higher Ed., 22*, 233–239. doi:10.1080/03075079712331381064

Chi, M. T. H. (2005). Commonsense conceptions of emergent processes: Why some misconceptions are robust. *Journal of the Learning Sciences, 14*, 161–199. doi:10.1207/s15327809jls1402_1

Chi, M. T. H., Bassock, M., Lewis, M., Reimann, P., & Glaser, R. (1989). Self-explanations: How students study and use examples in learning to solve problems. *Cognitive Science, 13*, 145–182.

Chi, M., Feltovich, P., & Glaser, R. (1981). Categorization and representation of physics problems by experts and novices. *Cognitive Science, 5*, 121–152. doi:10.1207/s15516709cog0502_2

Chinn, C. A., & Brewer, W. F. (2001). Models of data: A theory of how people evaluate data. *Cognition and Instruction, 19*, 323–393. doi:10.1207/S1532690XCI1903_3

Chinn, C. A., O'Donnell, A. M., & Jinks, T. S. (2000). The structure of discourse in collaboration learning. *Journal of Experimental Education, 69*, 77–97. doi:10.1080/00220970009600650

Cho, K., & Schunn, C. D. (2007). Scaffolded writing and rewriting in the discipline: A web-based reciprocal per assessment peer review system. *Computers & Education, 48*, 409–426. doi:10.1016/j.compedu.2005.02.004

Clark, D. B. (2004). Hands-on investigation in Internet environments: Teaching thermal equilibrium. In M. C. Linn, E. A. Davis, & P. Bell (Eds.), *Internet Environments for Science Education* (pp. 175-200). Mahwah, NJ: Lawrence Erlbaum Associates.

Clark, D. B. (2006). Longitudinal conceptual change in students' understanding of thermal equilibrium: An examination of the process of conceptual restructuring. *Cognition and Instruction, 24*(4), 467–563. doi:10.1207/s1532690xci2404_3

Clark, D. B., & Linn, M. C. (2003). Scaffolding knowledge integration through curricular depth. *Journal of the Learning Sciences, 12*(4), 451–494. doi:10.1207/S15327809JLS1204_1

Clark, D. B., & Sampson, V. (2005, June). *Analyzing The Quality Of Argumentation Supported By Personally-Seeded Discussions.* Paper presented at the annual meeting of the Computer Supported Collaborative Learning (CSCL) Conference, Taipei, Taiwan.

Clark, D. B., & Sampson, V. (2006, July). *Evaluating argumentation in science: New assessment tools.* Paper presented at the International Conference of the Learning Sciences 2006, Bloomington, Indiana.

Clark, D. B., & Sampson, V. (2008). Assessing dialogic argumentation in online environments to relate structure, grounds, and conceptual quality. To appear in *Journal of Research in Science Teaching, 45*(3), 6.

Clark, D. B., & Sampson, V. D. (2007). Personally-Seeded Discussions to scaffold online argumentation. *International Journal of Science Education, 29*(3), 253–277. doi:10.1080/09500690600560944

Clark, D. B., D'Angelo, C. M., & Menekse, M. (2009). Initial structuring of online discussions to improve learning and argumentation: Incorporating students' own explanations as seed comments versus an augmented-preset approach to seeding discussions. *Journal of Science Education and Technology, 18*(4), 321–333. doi:10.1007/s10956-009-9159-1

Clark, D. B., Menekse, M., D'Angelo, C., Touchman, S., & Schleigh, S. (2008). *Scaffolding students' argumentation about simulations.* Paper presented as part of a symposium organized by Hsin-Yi Chang to the International Conference of the Learning Sciences (ICLS) 2008, Utrecht, Netherlands.

Clark, D. B., Sampson, V., Weinberger, A., & Erkens, G. (2007). Analytic frameworks for assessing dialogic argumentation in online learning environments. *Educational Psychology Review, 19*(3), 343–374. doi:10.1007/s10648-007-9050-7

Clark, H. H. (1996). *Using language*. Cambridge, UK: Cambridge University Press.

Clark, H. H., & Brennan, S. A. (1991). Grounding in communication. In L. B. Resnick, J. M. Levine, & S. D. Teasley (Eds.), *Perspectives on socially shared cognition* (pp. 127-149).Washington, DC: AERA.

Clark, H. H., & Brennan, S. E. (1996). Grounding in communication. In L. B. Resnick, J. M. Levine, & S. D. Teasley (Eds.), *Perspectives on socially shared cognition* (pp. 127-149). Washington, DC: American Psychological Association.

Clough, E. E., & Driver, R. (1985). Secondary students' conceptions of the conduction of heat: Bringing together scientific and personal views. *Physical Educator, 20,* 176–182. doi:10.1088/0031-9120/20/4/309

Cobb, P., & Steffe, L. (1983). The constructivist researcher as teacher and model builder. *Journal for Research in Mathematics Education, 14*(2), 83–94. doi:10.2307/748576

Coffin, G. (2002). *Mediating E-learning: M-teacher or M-team?* St John's, Centre for Distance Learning and Innovation, Department of Education of Newfoundland and Labrador.

Cognition and Technology Group at Vanderbilt. (1997). *The Jasper Project: Lessons in curriculum, instruction, assessment, and professional development*. Mahwah, NJ: Erlbaum.

Cohen, E. (1994). Restructuring the classroom: Conditions for productive small groups. *Review of Educational Research, 64*(1), 1–35.

Cohen, E. G. (1984). Talking and working together: Status interaction and learning. In P. Peterson, L. C. Wilkinson, & M. Halliman (Eds.), *Instructional groups in the classroom: Organization and processes* (pp.171-188). Orlando, FL: Academic Press.

Cohen, E. G. (1986). *Designing groups works: Strategies for heterogeneous classrooms*. New York: Teachers College Press.

Cohen, E. G. (1994). Restructuring the classroom: Conditions for productive small groups. *Review of Educational Research, 64*, 1–35.

Cohen, E. G., Lotan, R., Scarloss, B., Schultz, S. E., & Abram, P. (2002). Can groups learn? *Teachers College Record, 104*, 1045–1068. doi:10.1111/1467-9620.00196

Coleman, J. S., Katz, E., & Menzel, H. (1966). *Medical innovation: A diffusion study*. New York: Bobbs-Merrill.

Collins, A., Brown, J. S., & Newman, S. (1989). Cognitive apprenticeship: Teaching the crafts of reading, writing, and mathematics. In L. B. Resnick (Ed.), *Knowing, learning, and instruction: Essays in the honour of Robert Glaser* (pp. 453-494). Hillsdale, NJ: Erlbaum.

Commonwealth Schools Commission. (1988). *Schooling In Rural Australia*. Canberra, Australia: Curriculum Development Centre.

Conklin, J. (1987). Hypertext: An Introduction and Survey. *Computer, 20*(9), 17–41. doi:10.1109/MC.1987.1663693

Conlin, M., & MacMillan, D. (2009, June 1). Managing the tweets. *Business Week*, 20–21.

Connolly, T., & Thorn, B. K. (1990). Discretionary databases: Theory, data, and implications. In J. Fulk & C. Steinfeld (Eds.), *Organizations and communication technology* (pp. 219-233). London: Sage.

Connolly, T., Thorn, B. K., & Heminger, A. (1992). Discretionary databases as social dilemmas. In L. Liebrand, D. Messick, & H. Wilke (Eds.), *Social dilemmas: Theoretical issues and research findings* (pp. 199-208). Oxford, UK: Pergamon Press.

Constant, D., Sproull, L., & Kiesler, S. (1996). The kindness of strangers: The usefulness of weak electronic ties for technical advice. *Organization Science, 7*(2), 119–135. doi:10.1287/orsc.7.2.119

Constantino-Gonzalez, M. A., Suthers, D., & Escamilla de los Santos, J. (2003). Coaching web-based collaborative learning based on problem solution differences and participation. *Artificial Intelligence in Education, 13*(2-4), 263–299.

Conway, R., Kember, D., Sivan, A., & Wu, M. (1993). Peer assessment of an individual's contribution to a group project. *Assessment & Evaluation in Higher Education, 18*, 45–56. doi:10.1080/0260293930180104

Cooke, N. J., Salas, E., Cannon-Bowers, J. A., & Stout, R. J. (2000). Measuring team knowledge. *Human Factors, 42*, 151–173. doi:10.1518/001872000779656561

Cornelius, C. (2001). *Gegenseitiges Verständnis in Computerkonferenzen.* Münster, Germany: Waxmann.

Cornelius, C., & Boos, M. (1999). Es lohnt sich kohärent zu sein! In U. Reips (Hrsg.), *Aktuelle Online-Forschung. Trends, Techniken, Ergebnisse, Tagungsband der German Online Research.* Retrieved January 29, 2009, from http://www.gor.de/gor99/tband99/pdfs/a_h/cornelius.pdf

Cornelius, C., & Boos, M. (2003). Enhancing mutual understanding in synchronous computer-mediated communication by training. Trade-offs in judgmental tasks. *Communication Research, 30*(2), 147–177. doi:10.1177/0093650202250874

Cort, P. (2009). The EC discourse on vocational training: How a 'common vocational training policy' turned into a lifelong learning strategy. *Vocations and Learning: Studies in Vocational and Professional Education, 2*, 87–107.

Costa, A. L., & O'Leary, P. W. (1992). Co-cognition. The cooperative development of the intellect. In N. Davidson & T. Worsham (Eds.), *Enhancing thinking through cooperative learning* (pp.41-65). New York: Teachers College Press.

Costa, C. (2007). A professional development weblog: Supporting work-based learning in a TAFE library. *The Australian Library Journal, 56*, 36–55.

Cox, R. (1999). Representation construction, externalized cognition and individual differences. *Learning and Instruction, 9*(4), 343–363. doi:10.1016/S0959-4752(98)00051-6

Cress, U., & Hesse, F. W. (2004). Knowledge sharing in groups: Experimental findings of how to overcome a social dilemma. In Y. Kafai, W. Sandoval, N. Enydey, A. S. Nixon, & F. Herrera (Eds.), *Proceedings of the Sixth International Conference of the Learning Sciences* (pp. 150-157). Mahwah, NJ: Lawrence Erlbaum.

Cress, U., Kimmerle, J., & Hesse, F. W. (2006). Information exchange with shared databases as a social dilemma: The effect of metaknowledge, bonus systems, and costs. *Communication Research, 33*(5), 370–390. doi:10.1177/0093650206291481

Cross, R., & Parker, A. (2004). *The hidden power of social networks: Understanding how work really gets done in organizations.* Boston, MA: Harvard Business School.

Cross, R., & Sproull, L. (2004). More than an answer: Information relationships for actionable knowledge. *Organization Science, 15*(4), 446–462. doi:10.1287/orsc.1040.0075

Cross, R., Parker, A., Prusak, L., & Borgatti, S. P. (2001). Knowing what we know: Supporting knowledge creation and sharing in social networks. *Organizational Dynamics, 30*(2), 100–120. doi:10.1016/S0090-2616(01)00046-8

Cruz, N. M., Perez, V. M., & Ramos, Y. F. (2007). Transactive memory processes that lead to better team results. *Team Performance Management, 13*(7/8), 192–205. doi:10.1108/13527590710842529

Cuthbert, A. J., Clark, D. B., & Linn, M. C. (2002). WISE learning communities: Design considerations. In K.A. Renninger & W. Shumar (Eds.), *Building Virtual Communities: Learning and Change in Cyberspace* (pp. 215-246). Cambridge, MA: Cambridge University Press.

D'Andrade, R. (1981). The cultural part of cognition. *Cognitive Science, 5*(3), 179–195. doi:10.1207/s15516709cog0503_1

Daft, R. L., & Lengel, R. H. (1984). Information richness: A new approach to managerial behavior and organisation design. In B. M. Staw, & L. L. Cummings (Eds.), *Research in organisational behaviour* (Vol. 6, pp. 191–233). Greenwhich, CT: JAI Press.

Daft, R. L., & Lengel, R. H. (1986). Organizational information requirements, media richness and structural design. *Management Science, 32*(5), 554–571. doi:10.1287/mnsc.32.5.554

Damon, W., & Phelps, E. (1989). Critical distinction among three approaches to peer education. *International Journal of Educational Research, 13,* 9–19. doi:10.1016/0883-0355(89)90013-X

Damsa, C. I., Erkens, G., & Janssen, J. (2007). Discourse synthesis: A research study on the use of semantic information for collaborative writing in secondary education. In B. Csapo & C. Csikos (Eds.), *Proceedings of the 12th conference of the European Association for Research on Learning and Instruction (EARLI)* (pp. 713). Budapest, Hungary: Graduate School of Education, University of Szeged, Faculty of Arts.

Davies, E. (2003). Knowledge integration in science teaching: Analyzing teachers' knowledge development. *Research in Science Education, 34,* 21–53. doi:10.1023/B:RISE.0000021034.01508.b8

Davies, P. (2006). Peer assessment: Judging the quality of students' work by comments rather than marks. *Innovations in Education and Teaching International, 43,* 69–82. doi:10.1080/14703290500467566

Davis, E. A. (2003). Prompting middle school science students for productive reflection: Generic and directed prompts. *Journal of the Learning Sciences, 12*(1), 91–142. doi:10.1207/S15327809JLS1201_4

Davis, E. A., & Linn, M. C. (2000). Scaffolding students' knowledge integration: Prompts for reflection in KIE. *International Journal of Science Education, 22*(8), 819–837. doi:10.1080/095006900412293

De Grave, W. S., Dolmans, D. H. J. M., & Vleuten, C. P. M. (1999). Profiles of effective tutors in problem-based learning: scaffolding student learning. *Medical Education, 33,* 901–906. doi:10.1046/j.1365-2923.1999.00492.x

De Jong, T., & Ferguson-Hessler, M. G. M. (1996). Types and qualities of knowledge. *Educational Psychologist, 31,* 105–113. doi:10.1207/s15326985ep3102_2

de Vries, E., Lund, K., & Baker, M. (2002). Computer-mediated epistemic dialogue: explanation and argumentation as vehicles for understanding scientific notions. *Journal of the Learning Sciences, 11*(1), 63–103. doi:10.1207/S15327809JLS1101_3

De Wever, B., Van Keer, H., Schellens, T., & Valcke, M. (2007). Applying multilevel modelling on content analysis data: Methodological issues in the study of the impact of role assignment in asynchronous discussion groups. *Learning and Instruction, 17,* 436–447. doi:10.1016/j.learninstruc.2007.04.001

Dealtry, R. (2006). The corporate university's role in managing an epoch in learning organisation innovation. *Journal of Workplace Learning, 18,* 313–320. doi:10.1108/13665620610674980

DeCagna, J. (2001). Interview – Tending the garden of knowledge: A look at communities of practice with Etienne Wenger. *Information Outlook, 5*(7), 6–12.

Deci, E. L., & Ryan, R. M. (1985). *Intrinsic motivation and self-determination in human behavior.* New York: Plenum.

Deci, E. L., & Ryan, R. M. (1992). Beyond the intrinsic-extrinsic dichotomy: Self-determination in motivation and learning. *Motivation and Emotion, 16*(3), 165–185. doi:10.1007/BF00991650

Deci, E., Koestner, R., & Ryan, R. (2001). Extrinsic rewards and intrinsic motivation in education: Reconsidered once again. *Review of Educational Research, 71,* 1–27. doi:10.3102/00346543071001001

Dennis, A. R., & Valacich, J. S. (1999). Rethinking media richness: Towards a theory of media synchonicity. In *Proceedings of the Hawaii International Conference on System Sciences,* USA(Vol. 32, pp. 1-10).

Derry, S. J. (1999). A fish called peer learning: Searching for common themes. In A. M. O'Donnell & A. King (Eds.), *Cognitive perspectives on peer learning* (pp. 197-211). Mawah, NJ: Erlbaum.

DeSanctis, G., & Gallupe, R. B. (1987). A foundation for the study of group decision support systems. *Management Science, 33*(5), 589–608. doi:10.1287/mnsc.33.5.589

DeVries, E., Lund, K., & Baker, M. J. (2002). Computer-mediated epistemic dialogue: Explanation and argumentation as vehicles for understanding scientific notions. *Journal of the Learning Sciences, 11*(1), 63–103. doi:10.1207/S15327809JLS1101_3

Dickey, M. H., Wasko, M. M., Chudoba, K. M., & Thatcher, J. B. (2006). Do you know what I know? A shared understandings perspective on text-based communication. *Journal of Computer-Mediated Communication, 12*(1), article 4. http://jcmc.indiana.edu/vol12/issue1/dickey.html

Dillenbourg, P. (1996). Some technical implications of the distributed cognition approach on the design of interactive learning environments. *Journal of Artificial Intelligence in Education, 7*(2), 161–180.

Dillenbourg, P. (1999). Introduction: What do you mean by collaborative learning? In P. Dillenbourg (Ed.), *Collaborative learning: Cognitive and computational approaches* (pp. 1–19). Oxford, UK: Pergamon.

Dillenbourg, P. (2002). Over-scripting CSCL: The risks of blending collaborative learning with instructional design. In P. A. Kirschner (Ed.), *Three worlds of CSCL: Can we support CSCL?* (pp. 61-91). Heerlen, The Netherlands: Open University of the Netherlands.

Dillenbourg, P., & Hong, F. (2008). The mechanics of CSCL macro scripts. *Computer-Supported Collaborative Learning, 3*, 5–23. doi:10.1007/s11412-007-9033-1

Dillenbourg, P., & Jermann, P. (2006). Designing integrative scripts. In F. Fischer, H. Mandl, J. Haake, & I. Kollar (Eds.), *Scripting computer-supported collaborative learning: Cognitive, computational and educational perspectives* (pp. 275–301). New York: Springer.

Dillenbourg, P., & Tchounikine, P. (2007). Flexibility in macro-scripts for computer-supported collaborative learning. *Journal of Computer Assisted Learning, 23*, 1–13. doi:10.1111/j.1365-2729.2007.00191.x

Dillenbourg, P., & Traum, D. (2006). Sharing solutions: Persistence and grounding in multimodal collaborative problem solving. *Journal of the Learning Sciences, 15*(1), 121–151. doi:10.1207/s15327809jls1501_9

Dillenbourg, P., Baker, M., Blaye, A., & O'Malley, C. (1995). The evolution of research on collaborative learning. In E. Spada & P. Reiman (Eds.), *Learning in Humans and Machine: Towards an interdisciplinary learning science* (pp. 189-211). Oxford, UK: Elsevier.

Dingfelder, S. F. (April, 2006). Learned it through the grapevine. *APA Monitor on Psychology,* 60-61.

diSessa, A. (2006). A history of conceptual change research: Threads and fault lines. In R. K. Sawyer (Ed.), *The Cambridge handbook of the learning Science* (pp. 265-281). New York: Cambridge University Press.

Diziol, D., Rummel, N., Spada, H., & McLaren, B. (2007). Promoting learning in mathematics: Script support for collaborative problem solving with the Cognitive Tutor Algebra. In C. A. Chinn, G. Erkens, & S. Puntambekar (Eds.), *Mice, minds and society. Proceedings of the Computer Supported Collaborative Learning (CSCL) Conference 2007,* (Vol 8, pp. 39-41). International Society of the Learning Sciences.

Doise, W. (1985). Social regulations in cognitive development. In R. Hinde, A.-N. Perret-Clermont, & J. Stevenson-Hinde (Eds.), *Social relationships and cognitive development* (pp. 294–308). Oxford, UK: Oxford University Press.

Driver, R., Newton, P., & Osborne, J. (2000). Establishing the norms of scientific argumentation in classrooms. *Science Education, 84*(3), 287–313. doi:10.1002/(SICI)1098-237X(200005)84:3<287::AID-SCE1>3.0.CO;2-A

Duschl, R. (2000). Making the nature of science explicit. In R. Millar, J. Leach & J. Osborne (Eds.), *Improving science education: The contribution of research.* Philadelphia, PA: Open University Press.

Duschl, R., & Osborne, J. (2002). Supporting and promoting argumentation discourse. *Studies in Science Education, 38*, 39–72. doi:10.1080/03057260208560187

Earl, M. (2001). Knowledge management strategies: Toward a taxonomy. *Journal of Management Information Systems, 18*(1), 215–233.

Edmondson, A. (1999). Psychological safety and learning behavior in work teams. *Administrative Science Quarterly, 44*(2), 350–383. doi:10.2307/2666999

Edmondson, A. C. (1996). Learning from mistakes is easier said than done: Group and organizational influences on the detection and correction of human error. *The Journal of Applied Behavioral Science, 32*, 5–28. doi:10.1177/0021886396321001

Eisenberg, A., & Garvey, C. (1981). Children's use of verbal strategies in resolving conflict. *Discourse Processes, 4*, 149–170. doi:10.1080/01638538109544512

Ellis, A. P. J. (2006). System breakdown: The role of mental models and transactive memory in the relationship between acute stress and team performance. *Academy of Management Journal, 49*(3), 576–589.

Endsley, M. (1995). Towards a theory of situation awareness in dynamic systems. *Human Factors and Ergonomics Society, 37*(1), 32–64. doi:10.1518/001872095779049543

Engeström, Y. (1987). *Learning by expanding: an activity-theoretical approach to developmental research.* Helsinki, Finland: Orienta-Konsultit.

Engeström, Y., Miettinen, R., & Punamäki, R.-L. (Eds.). (1999). *Perspectives on Activity Theory.* Cambridge, UK: Cambridge University Press.

Erduran, S., Simon, S., & Osborne, J. (2004). TAPping into argumentation: Developments in the application of Toulmin's argument pattern for studying science discourse. *Science Education, 88*, 915–933. doi:10.1002/sce.20012

Erickson, G., & Tiberghien, A. (1985). Heat and temperature. In R. Driver, E. Guesne & A. Tiberghien (Eds.), *Children's ideas in science* (pp. 52-83). Philadelphia, PA: Open University Press.

Ericsson, K. A. (2006). The influence of experience and deliberate practice on the development of superior expert performance. In K. A. Ericsson, N. Charness, P. J. Feltovich, & R. R. Hoffman (Eds.), *The Cambridge handbook of expertise and expert performance* (pp. 683-703). Cambridge, UK: Cambridge University Press.

Ericsson, K. A., Charness, N., Feltovich, P. J., & Hoffman, R. R. (Eds.). (2006). *The Cambridge handbook of expertise and expert performance.* Cambridge, UK: Cambridge University Press.

Erkens, G. (1998). *Multiple episode protocol analysis (MEPA 4.0).* Utrecht, The Netherlands: Department of Educational Sciences, Utrecht University.

Erkens, G., Jaspers, J., Prangsma, M., & Kanselaar, G. (2005). Coordination processes in computer supported collaborative writing. *Computers in Human Behavior, 21*, 463–486. doi:10.1016/j.chb.2004.10.038

Ertl, B., Fischer, F., & Mandl, H. (2006). Conceptual and socio-cognitive support for collaborative learning in videoconferencing environments. *Computers & Education, 47*, 298–315. doi:10.1016/j.compedu.2004.11.001

Ertl, B., Kopp, B., & Mandl (2007). Supporting collaborative learning in videoconferencing using collaboration scripts and content schemes. In F. Fischer, I. Kollar, H. Mandl & J. M. Haake (Eds.), *Scripting computer-supported communication of knowledge – cognitive, computational and educational perspectives* (pp. 212-236). Berlin, Germany: Springer.

Ertl, H., & Plante, J. (2004). *Connectivity and Learning in Canada's Schools,* Ottawa, Canada: Government of Canada.

Espinosa, J. A., Slaughter, S. A., Kraut, R. E., & Herbsleb, J. D. (2007). Team knowledge and coordination in geographically distributed software development. *Journal of Management Information Systems, 24*(1), 135–169. doi:10.2753/MIS0742-1222240104

Eynon, R. (2008). The use of the world-wide-web in learning and teaching in Higher Education: Reality and rhetoric. *Innovations in Education and Teaching International, 45*, 15–23. doi:10.1080/14703290701757401

Faraj, S., & Sproull, L. (2000). Coordinating expertise in software development teams. *Management Science, 46*(12), 1554–1568. doi:10.1287/mnsc.46.12.1554.12072

Fenwick, T. J. (2003). *Learning through experience: Troubling orthodoxies and intersecting questions.* Malabar, India: Krieger.

Fermelis, J., Tucker, R., & Palmer, S. (2007). Online self and peer assessment in large, multi-campus, multi-cohort contexts. In R. Atkinson, C. McBeath, S. K. A. Soong & C. D. Cheers (Eds.), *Providing choices for learners and learning: Proceedings ASCILITE Singapore* (pp. 271-281). Singapore: Nanyang Technological University, Centre for Educational Development.

Fischer, F., & Dillenbourg, P. (2006). *Challenges of orchestrating computer-supported collaborative learning*. Paper presented at the 87th annual meeting of the American Educational Research Association (AERA), San Francisco, CA.

Fischer, F., & Mandl, H. (2005). Knowledge convergence in computer-supported collaborative learning—the role of external representation tools. *Journal of the Learning Sciences*, *14*(3), 405–441. doi:10.1207/s15327809jls1403_3

Fischer, F., Bruhn, J., Grasel, C., & Mandl, H. (2002). Fostering collaborative knowledge construction with visualization tools. *Learning and Instruction*, *12*(2), 213–232. doi:10.1016/S0959-4752(01)00005-6

Fischer, F., Kollar, I., Haake, J. M., & Mandl, H. (2007). Introduction. In F. Fischer, I. Kollar, H. Mandl & J. M. Haake (Eds.), *Scripting computer-supported communication of knowledge – cognitive, computational and educational perspectives* (pp. 1-10). Berlin, Germany: Springer.

Fischer, F., Kollar, I., Mandl, H., & Haake, J. (Eds.). (2007). *Scripting computer-supported collaborative learning*. New York: Springer.

Fischer, F., Troendle, P., & Mandl, H. (2003). Using the Internet to improve university education – problem-oriented web-based learning and the MUNICS environment. *Interactive Learning Environments*, *11*(3), 193–214. doi:10.1076/ilee.11.3.193.16546

Fisher, C., & Larkin, J. H. (1986). *Diagrams as Working Memory for Scientific Problem Solving (Technical Report)*. Carnegie-Mellon University Department of Psychology.

Fisher, J. D., Nadler, A., & Whitcher-Alagna, S. (1982). Recipient reactions to aid. *Psychological Bulletin*, *91*(1), 27–54. doi:10.1037/0033-2909.91.1.27

Fjermestad, J. (2004). An analysis of communication mode in group support systems research. *Decision Support Systems*, *37*(2), 239–263.

Fjermestad, J., & Hiltz, S. R. (1999). An assessment of group support systems experimental research: Methodology and results. *Journal of Management Information Systems*, *15*(3), 7–149.

Flynn, F. J., & Lake, V. K. B. (2008). If you need help, just ask: Underestimating compliance with direct requests for help. *Journal of Personality and Social Psychology*, *95*(1), 128–143. doi:10.1037/0022-3514.95.1.128

Flynn, F. J., Reagans, R. E., Amanatullah, E. T., & Ames, D. R. (2006). Helping one's way to the top: Self-monitors achieve status by helping others and knowing who knows whom. *Journal of Personality and Social Psychology*, *91*(6), 1123–1137. doi:10.1037/0022-3514.91.6.1123

Forbus, K. (2001). Exploring analogy in the large. In D. Gentner, K. Holyoak, & B. Kokinov (Eds.), *The analogical mind: Perspectives from Cognitive Science*. Cambridge, MA: MIT Press.

Fox, R. (2005). *Teaching and learning. Lessons from psychology*. Malden, UK: Blackwell Publishing.

Frederiksen, N. (1984). The real test bias: Influences of testing on teaching and learning. *The American Psychologist*, *3*, 193–202. doi:10.1037/0003-066X.39.3.193

Freeman, L. (2006). *The development of social network analysis*. Vancouver, Canada: Empirical Press.

Freeman, M. (1995). Peer assessment by groups of group work. *Assessment & Evaluation in Higher Education*, *20*, 289–301. doi:10.1080/0260293950200305

Freeman, M., & McKenzie, J. (2002). SPARK, a confidential web-based template for self and peer assessment of student team work: Benefits of evaluating across different subjects. *British Journal of Educational Technology*, *33*, 551–569. doi:10.1111/1467-8535.00291

Fromm, E. (1976). *Haben oder Sein? Die seelischen Grundlagen einer neuen Gesellschaft*. Stuttgart, Germany: DVA.

Fuks, H., Pimentel, M. G., & de Lucena, C. J. P. (2006). R-U-Typing-2-Me? Evolving a chat tool to increase understanding in learning activities. *International Journal of Computer-Supported Collaborative Learning, 1*, 117–142. doi:10.1007/s11412-006-6845-3

Furey, D. (2008). *From radio broadcasts to virtual reality: A case study of distance education in Hermitage Bay Schools.* Paper presented May 2, 2008 at Symposium 2008, From the Rhetoric to the Reality, Fifty Years of Educational Change in Newfoundland and Labrador. St. John's: Memorial University of Newfoundland.

Furey, D., & Stevens, K. (2008). New Systemic Roles Facilitating the Integration of Face- to-Face and Virtual Learning. *Online Journal of Distance Learning Administration, 11*(4). Retrieved from http://www.westga.edu/~distance/ojdla/

Furnas, G. W., Landauer, T. K., Gomez, L. M., & Dumais, S. T. (1987). The vocabulary problem in human-system communication. *Communications of the ACM, 30*(11), 964–971. doi:10.1145/32206.32212

Gagné, R. M., Wager, W. W., Golas, K. C., & Keller, J. M. (2004). *Principles of instructional design* (5th ed.). Florence, KY: Wadsworth.

Gamma, E., Helm, R., Johnson, R., & Vlissides, J. (2005). *Design Patterns.* Boston: Addison-Wesley.

Garner, J. T. (2006). It's not what you know: A transactive memory analysis of knowledge networks at NASA. *Journal of Technical Writing and Communication, 36*(4), 329–351. doi:10.2190/U636-4844-2323-W071

Garrison, D. R., Anderson, T., & Archer, W. (2000). Critical thinking in a text-based environment: computer conferencing in higher education. *The Internet and Higher Education, 2*(2), 87–105. doi:10.1016/S1096-7516(00)00016-6

Gentner, D. (1983). Structure-mapping: a theoretical framework for analogy. *Cognitive Science, 7*(2), 155–170.

Gentner, D., & Markman, A. (1994). Structural alignment in comparison: no difference without similarity. *Psy-chological Science, 5*(3). doi:10.1111/j.1467-9280.1994.tb00652.x

Geyken, A., Mandl, H. & Reiter, W. (1995). *Selbstgesteuertes Lernen mit Tele-Tutoring.* Orientierungshilfen für Trainer/innen und Tutor/innen.

Gick, M., & Holyoak, K. (1980). Analogical problem solving. *Cognitive Psychology, 12*, 306–355. doi:10.1016/0010-0285(80)90013-4

Gladwell, M. (2000). *The tipping point: How little things can make a big difference.* Boston: Little-Brown.

Glasersfeld, E. v. (1996). *Radical constructivism: A way of knowing and learning.* Abingdon, UK: Falmer Press.

Goel, A. K., Gomez de Silva Garza, A., Grué, N., Murdock, J. W., Recker, M. M., & Govinderaj, T. (1996). Towards designing learning environments -i: Exploring how devices work. In C. Fraisson, G. Gauthier & A. Lesgold (Eds.), *Intelligent tutoring systems: Lecture notes in computer science.* New York: Springer.

Goldberg, M. (2006). *Integrating the arts: An approach to teaching and learning in multicultural and multilingual settings.* Boston: Allyn & Bacon.

Golding, B. (2001). *Great Divides in Learning: Youth Pathways in Rural and Remote Australian Towns.* Camberwell, Australia: Australian Council for Educational Research Government of Newfoundland and Labrador. (2000). *Supporting Learning: Report on the Ministerial Panel on Educational Delivery in the Classroom.* St John's, Department of Education.

Goodman, P. S., & Darr, E. D. (1998). Computer-aided systems and communities: Mechanisms for organizational learning in distributed environments. *MIS Quarterly, 22*(4), 417–440. doi:10.2307/249550

Goodman, P. S., & Shah, S. (1992). Familiarity and work group outcomes. In S. Worchel, W. Wood, & J. A. Simpson (Eds.), *Group process and productivity* (pp. 276-298). Newbury Park, CA: Sage.

Graesser, A. C., & Person, N. K. (1994). Question asking during tutoring. *American Educational Research Journal, 31*(1), 104–137.

Graesser, A. C., Person, N. K., & Magliano, J. P. (1995). Collaborative dialogue patterns in naturalistic one-to-one tutoring. *Applied Cognitive Psychology, 9*, 495–522. doi:10.1002/acp.2350090604

Graggober, M. Ortner, J. & Sammer, M. (2003). *Wissensnetzwerke. Konzepte, Erfahrungen und Entwicklungsrichtungen*. Wiesbaden, Germany: DUV.

Gray, P. H. (2001). The impact of knowledge repositories on power and control in the workplace. *Information Technology & People, 14*(4), 368–384. doi:10.1108/09593840110411167

Green, H. (2007, October 1). The water cooler is now on the web. *Business Week*, 78–79.

Greenberg, M. S. (1980). A theory of indebtedness. In K. Gergen, M.S. Greenberg, & R.H. Willis (Eds.), *Social exchange: Advances in theory and research* (pp. 2–26). New York: Plenum.

Grek, S., Lawn, M., Lingard, B., Ozga, J., Rinne, R., Segerholm, C., & Simola, H. (2009). National policy brokering and the construction of the European education space in England, Sweden, Finland and Scotland. *Comparative Education, 45*, 5–21. doi:10.1080/03050060802661378

Gruber, H., Harteis, C., & Rehrl, M. (2008). Professional learning: Skill formation between formal and situated learning. In K. U. Mayer & H. Solga (Eds.), *Skill formation. Interdisciplinary and cross-national perspectives* (pp. 207-229). Cambridge, UK: Cambridge University Press.

Gruber, H., Harteis, C., Mulder, R. H., & Rehrl, M. (Eds.). (2005). *Bridging individual, organisational, and cultural perspectives on professional learning*. Regensburg, Germany: Roderer.

Gruber, H., Palonen, T., Rehrl, M., & Lehtinen, E. (2007). Understanding the nature of expertise: Individual knowledge, social resources and cultural context. In H. Gruber & T. Palonen (Eds.), *Learning in the workplace – new developments* (pp.2227-250). Turku, Finland: Finnish Educational Research Association.

Gruenfeld, D. H., & Hollingshead, A. B. (1993). Sociocognition in work groups: the evolution of group integrative complexity and its relation to task performance. *Small Group Research, 24*, 383–405. doi:10.1177/1046496493243006

Gupta, M. L. (2004). Enhancing student performance through cooperative learning in physical sciences. *Assessment & Evaluation in Higher Education, 29*, 63–73. doi:10.1080/0260293032000158162

Gutwin, C., & Greenbergs, S. (2002). A descriptive framework for workspace awareness for real-time groupware. *Computer Supported Cooperative Work, 11*, 411–446. doi:10.1023/A:1021271517844

Guzdial, M., & Turns, J. (2000). Effective discussion through a computer-mediated anchored forum. *Journal of the Learning Sciences, 9*(4), 437–469. doi:10.1207/S15327809JLS0904_3

Gweon, G., Rosé, C., Carey, R., & Zaiss, Z. (2006). Providing support for adaptive scripting in an on-line collaborative learning environment. In *Proceedings of the SIGCHI Conference on Human Factors in Computing Systems* (pp. 251-260). New York: ACM Press.

Haake, J. M., & Pfister, H.-R. (2007). Flexible scripting in net-based learning groups. In F. Fischer, I. Kollar, H. Mandl & J. M. Haake (Eds.), *Scripting computer-supported collaborative learning* (pp. 155-175). New York: Springer.

Hackos, J. T., & Stevens, D. M. (1997). *Standards for Online Communication*. New York: Wiley.

Häkkinen, P., & Järvelä, S. (2006). Sharing and constructing perspectives in Web-based conferencing. *Computers & Education, 47*(1/2), 433–447. doi:10.1016/j.compedu.2004.10.015

Häkkinen, P., Arvaja, M., & Mäkitalo, K. (2004). Prerequisites for CSCL: Research approaches, methodological challenges and pedagogical development. In K. Littleton, D. Faulkner, & D. Miell (Eds.), *Learning to collaborate and collaborating to learn* (pp. 161–175). New York: Nova Science.

Hämäläinen, R. (2008). *Designing and investigating pedagogical scripts to facilitate computer-supported collaborative learning.* University of Jyväskylä, Finnish Institute for Educational Research.

Hämäläinen, R., & Arvaja, M. (2009). Scripted collaboration and group-based variations in a higher education CSCL context. *Scandinavian Journal of Educational Research, 53*(1), 1–16. doi:10.1080/00313830802628281

Hämäläinen, R., & Häkkinen, P. (in press). Teacher's instructional planning for computer-supported collaborative learning: Macro-scripts as a pedagogical method to facilitate collaborative learning. *Teaching and Teacher Education.*

Hämäläinen, R., Manninen, T., Järvelä, S., & Häkkinen, P. (2006). Learning to collaborate: Designing collaboration in a 3-D game environment. *The Internet and Higher Education, 9*(1), 47–61. doi:10.1016/j.iheduc.2005.12.004

Hämäläinen, R., Oksanen, K., & Häkkinen, P. (2008). Designing and analyzing collaboration in a scripted game for vocational education. *Computers in Human Behavior, 24*(6), 2496–2506. doi:10.1016/j.chb.2008.03.010

Hamer, J., Ma, K. T. K., & Kwong, H. H. F. (2005). A method of automatic grade calibration in peer assessment. In A. Young & D. Tolhurst (Eds), *Proceedings of the seventh Australasian computing education conference* (pp. 67-72). Newcastle, Australia: CRPIT.

Hancock, J. T., & Dunham, P. J. (2001). Language use in computer-mediated communication: The role of coordination devices. *Discourse Processes, 31*(1), 91–110. doi:10.1207/S15326950dp3101_4

Hara, N., Bonk, C. J., & Angeli, C. (2000). Content analysis of online discussion in an applied educational psychology course. *Instructional Science, 28*, 115–152. doi:10.1023/A:1003764722829

Harris, R. J. (1999). Lifelong learning in work contexts. *Research in Post-Compulsory Education, 4*, 161–182. doi:10.1080/13596749900200055

Harris, R. J. (2008). Developing of a collaborative learning environment through Technology Enhanced Education

(TE3) support. *Education & Training, 50*, 674–686. doi:10.1108/00400910810917055

Harrison, A., G., Grayson, D., J., & Treagust, D., F. (1999). Investigating a grade 11 student's evolving conceptions of heat and temperature. *Journal of Research in Science Teaching, 36*(1), 55–87. doi:10.1002/(SICI)1098-2736(199901)36:1<55::AID-TEA5>3.0.CO;2-P

Harteis, C., & Billett, S. (2008). Workplaces as learning environment: Introduction. *International Journal of Educational Research, 47*, 209–212. doi:10.1016/j.ijer.2008.07.002

Harteis, C., Gruber, H., & Hertramph, H. (2007). Epistemological beliefs and their impact on the practice of e-learning in companies. In V. Uskov (Ed.), *Computers and advances technologies in education. Globalization of education through advanced technology* (pp. 266-271). Anaheim, CA: ACTA.

Hatala, J.-P., & Lutta, J. G. (2009). Managing information sharing within an organizational setting: A social network perspective. *Performance Improvement Quarterly, 21*, 5–33. doi:10.1002/piq.20036

Hattie, J., & Timperley, H. (2007). The power of feedback. *Review of Educational Research, 77*(1), 81–112. doi:10.3102/003465430298487

Hausmann, R. G. M., Chi, M. T. H., & Roy, M. (2004). Learning from collaborative problem solving: An analysis of three hypothesized mechanisms. In K. D. Forbus, D. Gentner, & T. Regier (Eds.), *26nd Annual Conference of the Cognitive Science Society* (pp. 547-552). Mahwah, NJ: Lawrence Erlbaum.

Haussmann, B. (2001). Nicht ohne meinen Tutor [Not without my tutor]. *Wirtschaft und Weiterbildung, 6*, 50–53.

Hawkes, M., & Halverson, P. (2002). Technology Facilitation in the Rural School: An Analysis of Options. *Journal of Research in Rural Education, 17*(3), 162–170.

Healey, D., &Stevens, K. (2002). Student Access to Information Technology and Perceptions of Future Opportunities in Two Small Labrador Communities.

Canadian Journal of Learning and Technology / La Revue Canadienne de l'Apprentissage et de la Technologie, 28(1), 7-18.

Heckner, M., & Schworm, S. (in press). The tagblog. Exploring forms of user contribution on the Web 2.0 for encouraging students to actively engage with learning content. *International Journal of Web Based Communities*.

Heckner, M., Mühlbacher, S., & Wolff, C. (2008). Tagging tagging. Analysing user keywords in scientific bibliography management systems. [JODI]. *Journal of Digital Information, 9*(2).

Henry, M. (1989). The functions of schooling: Perspectives from rural Australia. *Discourse: The Australian Jrnl. of Educational Studies, 9*(2), 5–21.

Hernández-Leo, D., Ascensio-Pérez, J. I., & Dimitriadis, Y. A. (2005). Computational representation of collaborative learning flow patterns using IMS Learning Design. *Educational Technology & Society, 8*(4), 75–89.

Herring, S. (1999). Interactional coherence in CMC. *Journal of Computer-Mediated Communication, 4.* Retrieved from http://www.ascusc.org/jcmc/vol4/issue4/herring.html

Hertzum, M. (2002). The importance of trust in software engineers' assessment and choice of information sources. *Information and Organization, 12*(1), 1–18. doi:10.1016/S1471-7727(01)00007-0

Hesse, F. (2007). Being told to do something or just being aware of something? An alternative approach to scripting in CSCL. In F. Fischer, I. Kollar, H. Mandl, J., & Haake (Eds.), *Scripting computer-supported communication of knowledge - cognitive, computational and educational perspectives* (pp. 91-98). New York: Springer.

Hewitt, J. (2005). Toward an understanding of how threads die in asynchronous computer conferences. *Journal of the Learning Sciences, 14*(4), 567–589. doi:10.1207/s15327809jls1404_4

Hidi, S., & Harackiewicz, J. (2000). Motivating the academically unmotivated. A critical issue for the 21st century. *Review of Educational Research, 70*, 151–179.

Hindo, B. (2007, November 15). Mapping the crowd: Software that maps who is working on common problems is shaving years off research and honing corporate strategies. *Business Week*, 19–20.

Hinds & S. Kiesler (Ed.). *Distributed work* (pp. 335-355). Cambridge, MA: MIT Press.

Hirokawa, R. Y. (1990). The role of communication in group decision making efficacy. *Small Group Research, 21*, 190–204. doi:10.1177/1046496490212003

Hmelo-Silver, C. (2003). Analyzing collaborative knowledge construction: Multiple methods for integrated understanding. *Computers & Education, 41*, 397–420. doi:10.1016/j.compedu.2003.07.001

Hmelo-Silver, C. E., Marathe, S., & Liu, L. (2007). Fish swim, rocks sit, and lungs breathe: Expert-novice understanding of complex systems. *Journal of the Learning Sciences, 16*, 307–331.

Hoffman, J. R., & Rogelberg, S. G. (2001). All together now? College students' preferred project group grading procedures. *Group Dynamics, 5*, 33–40. doi:10.1037/1089-2699.5.1.33

Hogan, K., & Maglienti, M. (2001). Comparing the epistemological underpinnings of students' and scientists' reasoning about conclusions. *Journal of Research in Science Teaching, 38*(6), 663–687. doi:10.1002/tea.1025

Hollingshead, A. B. (1996). Information suppression and status persistence in group decision making. The effects of communication media. *Human Communication Research, 23*(2), 193–219. doi:10.1111/j.1468-2958.1996.tb00392.x

Hollingshead, A. B., Fulk, J., & Monge, P. (2002). Fostering intranet knowledge sharing: An integration of transactive memory and public goods approaches. In P.

Hollingshead, A. B., McGrath, J. E., & O'Connor, K. M. (1993). Group task performance and communication technology: A longitudinal study of computer-mediated versus face-to-face work groups. *Small Group Research, 24*, 307–333. doi:10.1177/1046496493243003

Holmer, T. (2008). Discourse structure analysis of chat communication. *Language@Internet, 5*. Retrieved from http://www.languageatinternet.de

Holzinger, A., Kickmeister-Rust, M. D., Wassertheurer, S., & Hessinger, M. (2009). Learning performance with interactive simulations in medical education. Lessons learned from results of learning complex physiological models with the HAEMOdynamics SIMulator. *Computers & Education, 52*, 292–301. doi:10.1016/j.compedu.2008.08.008

Hooper, S. (1992). Effects of peer interaction during computer-based mathematics instruction. *The Journal of Educational Research, 85*(3), 180–189.

Houston, J. (2007). *Future skill demands, from a corporate consultant perspective.* Presentation at the National Academies Workshop on Research Evidence Related to Future Skill Demands. Retrieved July 3, 2007, from http://www7.nationalacademies.org/cfe/Future_Skill_Demands_Presentations.html

Hron, A., Hesse, F. W., Cress, U., & Giovis, C. (2000). Implicit and explicit dialogue structuring in virtual learning groups. *The British Journal of Educational Psychology, 70*, 53–64. doi:10.1348/000709900157967

Hron, A., Hesse, F. W., Reinhard, P., & Picard, E. (1997). Strukturierte Kooperation beim computerunterstutzten kollaborativen Lernen. *Unterrichtswissenschaft, 25*, 56–69.

Hsi, S., & Hoadley, C. M. (1997). Productive discussion in science: Gender equity through electronic discourse. *Journal of Science Education and Technology, 6*(1), 23–36. doi:10.1023/A:1022564817713

Hutchins, E. (1995). *Cognition in the Wild*. Cambridge: MA, MIT Press.

Hyatt, A., Contractor, N. S., & Jones, P. (1997). Computational organizational network modeling: Strategies and an example. *Computational & Mathematical Organization Theory, 2*(4), 285–300. doi:10.1007/BF00132313

Hyönä, J. Lorch. R. F., & Rinck, M. (2003). Eye movement measures to study global text processing. In J. Hyönä (Ed.), *The Mind's Eye: Cognitive and Applied Aspects of Eye Movement Research* (pp. 313-334). Amsterdam: Elsevier.

Hythecker, V. I., Dansereau, D. F., & Rocklin, T. R. (1988). An analysis of the processes influencing the structured dyadic learning environment. *Educational Psychologist, 23*(1), 23–37. doi:10.1207/s15326985ep2301_2

Ickes, W., & Gonzales, R. (1996). Social cognition: From the subjective to the intersubjective. In J. L. Nye & A.M. Brower (Eds.), *What's social about social cognition? Research on socially shared cognition in small groups* (pp.285-309). Newbury Park, CA: Sage.

Ingersoll, R., & Kralik, J. M. (2004). *The Impact of Mentoring on Teacher Retention: What the Research Says.* Denver, CO: Education Commission of the States.

ISO 14915-3. (2002). *Software ergonomics for multimedia user interfaces – Part 3: Media selection and combination.* International Organization for Standardization.

ISO 9241-110. (2006). *Ergonomics of human-system interaction -- Part 110: Dialogue principles.* International Organization for Standardization.

Israel, J., & Aiken, R. (2007). Supporting collaborative learning with an intelligent web-based system. *International Journal of Artificial Intelligence in Education, 17*(1), 3–40.

Izumi-Taylor, S., & Lovelace, A. F. (2007). Tech-knowledge: How children and early childhood education teachers develop knowledge through technology. In Y. Inoue (Ed.), *Online education for lifelong learning* (pp. 187-207). Hershey, PA: Information Science Publishing.

Jackson, P., & Klobas, J. (2008). Transactive memory systems in organizations: Implications for knowledge directories. *Decision Support Systems, 44*(2), 409–424. doi:10.1016/j.dss.2007.05.001

James, R., Wyn, J., Baldwin, G., Hepworth, G., McInnis, C., & Stephanou, A. (1999). *Rural and Isolated School Students and their Higher Education School Choices.* Canberra, Australia: National Board of Employment, Education and Training, Higher Education Council.

Janssen, J., Erkens, G., & Kanselaar, G. (2007). Visualization of agreement and discussion processes during computer-supported collaborative learning. *Computers in Human Behavior, 23*, 1105–1125. doi:10.1016/j.chb.2006.10.005

Janssen, J., Erkens, G., Jaspers, J., & Kanselaar, G. (2006, June/July). Visualizing participation to facilitate argumentation. In *Proc. of the 7th Intl. Conf. of the Learning Sciences*, Bloomington, IN.

Janssen, J., Erkens, G., Jaspers, J., & Kanselaar, G. (2007). Visualization of participation: Does it contribute to successful computer-supported collaborative learning? *Computers & Education, 49*, 1037–1065. doi:10.1016/j.compedu.2006.01.004

Janssen, J., Erkens, G., Kirschner, P. A., & Kanselaar, G. (in press). Effects of representational guidance during computer-supported collaborative learning. *Instructional Science*.

Järvelä, S., & Häkkinen, P. (2002). Web-based cases in teaching and learning—the quality of discussion and a stage of perspective taking in asynchronous communication. *Interactive Learning Environments, 10*(1), 1–22. doi:10.1076/ilee.10.1.1.3613

Järvelä, S., Veermans, M., & Leinonen, P. (2008). Investigating student engagement in computer-supported inquiry: A process-oriented analysis. *Social Psychology of Education, 11*, 299–322. doi:10.1007/s11218-007-9047-6

Järvenoja, H., & Järvelä, S. (in press). Emotion control in collaborative learning situations: Do students regulate emotions evoked from social challenges? *The British Journal of Educational Psychology*.

Jarvenpaa, S. L., & Staples, D. S. (2000). The use of collaborative electronic media for information sharing: An exploratory study of determinants. *The Journal of Strategic Information Systems, 9*(2/3), 129–254. doi:10.1016/S0963-8687(00)00042-1

Jarvis, S. (1990). *Rural Students and Post Grade 10 Education in Tasmania: A Study for the Country Areas Program.* Hobart, Department of Education and the Arts, Tasmania.

Jeong, A., Clark, D. B., Sampson, V. D., & Menekse, M. (in press). Sequentially analyzing dialogical scientific argumentation across asynchronous online discussion environments. In S. Puntambekar, G. Erkens, & C. Hmelo-Silver (Eds.), *Interactions in CSCL: Methodologies, Approaches and Issues*. The Netherlands: Springer.

Jeong, H., & Chi, M. T. H. (2007). Knowledge convergence during collaborative learning. *Instructional Science, 35*, 287–315. doi:10.1007/s11251-006-9008-z

Jermann, P., & Dillenbourg, P. (2003). Elaborating new arguments through a CSCL script. In J. Andriessen, M. Baker & D. Suthers (Eds.), *Arguing to learn: Confronting cognitions in computer-supported collaborative learning environments* (pp. 205-226). Dordrecht, NL: Kluwer Academic Publishers.

Jermann, P., & Dillenbourg, P. (2008). Group mirrors to support interaction regulation in collaborative problem solving. *Computers & Education, 51*, 279–296. doi:10.1016/j.compedu.2007.05.012

Jermann, P., Soller, A., & Muehlenbrock, M. (2001). *From mirroring to guiding: a review of state of art technology for supporting collaborative learning.* Paper presented at the European Computer Supported Collaborative Learning Conference (EU-CSCL'01), Maastricht, NL.

Jessup, L. M., & Valacich, J. S. (1993). *Group support systems: New perspectives.* New York: Plenum Press.

Jian, G., & Jeffres, L. W. (2006). Understanding employees' willingness to contribute to shared electronic databases: A three-dimensional framework. *Communication Research, 3*(4), 3, 242–261.

Jimenez-Aleixandre, M., Rodriguez, M., & Duschl, R. A. (2000). 'Doing the lesson' or 'doing science': Argument in high school genetics. *Science Education, 84*(6), 757–792. doi:10.1002/1098-237X(200011)84:6<757::AID-SCE5>3.0.CO;2-F

Johnson, D. W. (1981). Student-student interaction: The neglected variable in education. *Educational Researcher, 10*, 5–10.

Johnson, D. W., & Johnson, R. T. (1989). *Cooperation and competition: Theory and research.* Edina, MN: Interaction Book.

Johnson, D. W., & Johnson, R. T. (1992). Positive interdependence: Key to effective cooperation. In R. Hertz-Lazarowitz & N. Miller (Eds.), *Interaction in cooperative groups: The theoretical anatomy of group learning* (pp. 174-199). New York: Cambridge University Press.

Johnson, D. W., & Johnson, R. T. (1998). Cooperative learning and social interdependence theory. In R. S. Tindale, L. Heath, J. Edwards, E.Jj. Posavac, F. B. Bryant, Y. Suarez-Balcazar, E. Henderson-King & J. Myers (Eds.), *Theory and research on small groups* (pp. 9-35). New York: Plenum.

Johnston, L., & Miles, L. (2004). Assessing contributions to group assignments. *Assessment & Evaluation in Higher Education, 29,* 751–768. doi:10.1080/0260293042000227272

Joiner, R., & Jones, S. (2003). The effects of communication medium on argumentation and the development of critical thinking. *International Journal of Educational Research, 39*(8), 861–971. doi:10.1016/j.ijer.2004.11.008

Joosten-ten Brinke, D., Van Bruggen, J., Hermans, H., Burgers, J., Giesbers, B., Koper, R., & Latour, I. (2007). Modeling assessment for re-use of traditional and new types of assessment. *Computers in Human Behavior, 23,* 2721–2741. doi:10.1016/j.chb.2006.08.009

Jucks, R., Paechter, M., & Tatar, D. (2003). Learning and collaboration in online discourses. *International Journal of Educational Policy, Research, and Practice, 4,* 117–146.

Kali, Y., & Ronen, M. (2008). Assessing the assessors: Added value in web-based multi-cyle peer assessment in higher education. *Research and Practice in Technology Enhanced Learning, 3,* 3–32. doi:10.1142/S1793206808000434

Kanawattanachai, P., & Yoo, Y. (2007). The impact of knowledge coordination on virtual team performance over time. *MIS Quarterly, 31*(4), 783–808.

Kankanhalli, A., Tan, B. C., & Wei, K. (2005). Contributing knowledge to electronic knowledge repositories: An empirical investigation. *MIS Quarterly, 29*(1), 113–143.

Kanki, B. G., & Foushee, H. C. (1989). Communication as group process mediator of aircrew performance. *Aviation, Space, and Environmental Medicine, 20*(2), 402–410.

Karabenick, S. A., & Knapp, J. R. (1988). Effects of computer privacy on help-seeking. *Journal of Applied Social Psychology, 18,* 461–472. doi:10.1111/j.1559-1816.1988.tb00029.x

Karabenick, S. A., & Newman, R. S. (2006). *Help seeking in academic settings: Goals, groups, and contexts.* Mahwah, NJ: Erlbaum.

Keefer, J. A., & Karabenick, S. A. (1998). Help-seeking in the information age. In S. A. Karabenick (Ed.), *Strategic help-seeking: Implications for learning and teaching* (pp. 219-250). Mahwah, NJ: Erlbaum.

Keller, J. M. (1983). Motivational design of instruction. In C. M. Reigeluth (Ed.), *Instructional design theories and models: An overview of their current studies.* Hillsdale, NJ: Erlbaum.

Keller, J. M., & Kopp, T. W. (1987). An application of ARCS model of motivational design. In C. M. Reigeluth (Ed.), *Instructional theories in action. Lessons illustrating selected theories and models* (pp. 289-320). Hillsdale, NJ: Erlbaum.

Kellner, D., & Share, J. (2007). Critical media literacy: Crucial policy choices for a twenty-first century democracy. *Policy Futures in Education, 5,* 59–69. doi:10.2304/pfie.2007.5.1.59

Kerr, N. L. (1983). Motivation losses in small groups: A social dilemma analysis. *Journal of Personality and Social Psychology, 45,* 819–828. doi:10.1037/0022-3514.45.4.819

Kerr, N. L., & Bruun, S. E. (1983). Dispensability of member effort and group motivation losses: Free rider effects. *Journal of Personality and Social Psychology, 44,* 78–94. doi:10.1037/0022-3514.44.1.78

Kiili, C., Laurinen, L., & Marttunen, M. (2008). *Argumentointikaavio lukiolaisten internetlukemisen apuna [Argument diagram as an aid for Internet reading among secondary school students]*. Paper presented at the annual conference of the Finnish Educational Research Association (FERA), 27.-28.11.2008, Turku, Finland.

Kimmerle, J., & Cress, U. (2008). Group awareness and self-presentation in computer-supported information exchange. *International Journal of Computer-Supported Collaborative Learning, 3*(1), 85–97. doi:10.1007/s11412-007-9027-z

King, A. (1991). Effects of training in strategic questioning on children's problem-solving performance. *Journal of Educational Psychology, 83*(3), 307–317. doi:10.1037/0022-0663.83.3.307

King, A. (1992). Facilitating elaborative learning trough guided student-generated questioning. *Educational Psychologist, 27*, 111–126. doi:10.1207/s15326985ep2701_8

King, A. (2007). Scripting collaborative learning process: A cognitive perspective. In F. Fischer, I. Kollar, H. Mandl, & J. M. Haake (Eds.), *Scripting computer-supported communication of knowledge - Cognitive, computational, and educational perspectives* (pp. 13-37). Berlin, Germany: Springer.

Kirschner, P. A., & Kreijns, K. (2005). Enhancing sociability of computer-supported collaborative learning environments. In R. Bromme, F. W. Hesse & H. Spada (Eds.), *Barriers and biases in computer-mediated knowledge communication - and how they may be overcome* (pp. 169-192). New York: Springer.

Kirschner, P. A., Buckingham Shum, S. J., & Carr, C. S. (Eds.). (2003). *Visualizing argumentation: software tools for collaborative and educational sense-making*. London: Springer.

Kirsh, D., & Maglio, P. (1994). On distinguishing epistemic from pragmatic actions. *Cognitive Science, 18*, 513–549.

Kitsantas, A., & Chow, A. (2007). College students' perceived threat and preference for seeking help in traditional, distributed and distance learning environments.

Computers & Education, 48, 383–395. doi:10.1016/j.compedu.2005.01.008

Klein, G. (2003). *Intuition at work*. New York: Currency Doubleday.

Kneser, C., & Ploetzner, R. (2001). Collaboration on the basis of complementary domain knowledge: Observed dialogue structures and their relation to learning success. *Learning and Instruction, 11*(1), 53–83. doi:10.1016/S0959-4752(00)00015-3

Kobbe, L., Weinberger, A., Dillenbourg, P., Harrer, A., Hämäläinen, R., Häkkinen, P., & Fischer, F. (2007). Specifying computer-supported collaboration scripts. *International Journal of Computer-Supported Collaborative Learning, 2*, 211–224. doi:10.1007/s11412-007-9014-4

Koedinger, K. R. (1998). *Intelligent cognitive tutors as modeling tool and instructional model*. Paper presented at the NCTM Standards 2000 Technology Conference.

Koedinger, K. R., Anderson, J. R., Hadley, W. H., & Mark, M. A. (1997). Intelligent tutoring goes to school in the big city. *International Journal of Artificial Intelligence in Education, 8*, 30–43.

Kollar, I., Fischer, F., & Hesse, F. W. (2003). Cooperation scripts for computer-supported collaborative learning. In B. Wasson, R. Baggetun, U. Hoppe, & S. Ludvigsen (Eds.), *Proceedings of the International Conference on Computer Support for Collaborative Learning: CSCL 2003 Community Events—Communication and Interaction* (pp. 59–61). Bergen, Norway: InterMedia.

Kollar, I., Fischer, F., & Hesse, F. W. (2006). Collaboration scripts – a conceptual analysis. *Educational Psychology Review, 18*(2), 159–185. doi:10.1007/s10648-006-9007-2

Kollar, I., Fischer, F., & Slotta, J. D. (2005). Internal and external collaboration scripts in webbased science learning at schools. In T. Koschmann, D. Suthers, & T.-W. Chan (Eds.), *The next 10 years! Proceedings of the International Conference on Computer Support for Collaborative Learning 2005* (pp. 331-340). Mahwah, NJ: Lawrence Erlbaum Associates.

Kollar, I., Fischer, F., & Slotta, J. D. (2007). Internal and external scripts in computer-supported collaborative inquiry learning. *Learning and Instruction, 17*(6), 708–721. doi:10.1016/j.learninstruc.2007.09.021

Kollar, I., Fischer, F., & Slotta, J. D. (2008). Argumentation in web-based collaborative inquiry learning: Scripts for writing and scripts for talking aren't the same. In *Proceedings of the Conference of the International Society of the Learning Sciences.* Utrecht, The Netherlands.

Kolodner, J. (1993). *Case-based Reasoning.* San Mateo: CA, Morgan Kaufmann.

Kolodner, J. L. (1983). Towards an understanding of the role of experience in the evolution from novice to expert. *International Journal of Man-Machine Studies, 19*, 497–518. doi:10.1016/S0020-7373(83)80068-6

Kolodner, J. L. (1984). *Retrieval and organizational strategies in conceptual memory: A computer model.* Hillsdale: Erlbaum.

Kolodner, J. L., Schwarz, B., Barkai, R. D., Levy-Neumand, E., Tcherni, A., & Turbovsk, A. (1997). Roles of a case library as a collaborative tool for fostering argumentation. In R. Hall, N. Miyake & N. Enyedy (Eds.), *Proceedings of the 1997 computer support for collaborative learning (CSCL 97)* (pp. 150-156). Hillsdale, NJ: Erlbaum.

Kopp, B. (2005). *Effekte schematheoretischer Unterstützung auf Argumentation und Lernerfolg beim kooperativen Lernen in Videokonferenzen* [Effects of schematheoretic support on argumentation and performance in collaborative learning with videoconferencing]. Berlin, Germany: Logos.

Kopp, B., & Mandl, H. (2006). Wissensschemata. In H. Mandl, & H. F. Friedrich (Eds.), *Handbuch Lernstrategien* (pp. 127-124). Göttingen, Germany: Hogrefe.

Kopp, B., & Mandl, H. (2007). Fostering argumentation with script and content scheme in videoconferencing. In *Proceedings of the Computer Supported Collaborative Learning Conference, 2007.*

Kopp, B., & Mandl, H. (2007). Fostering Argumentation with Script and Content Scheme in Videoconferencing.

In C. Chinn, G. Erkens, & S. Puntambekar (Eds.), *Mice, Minds and Society – The Computer Supported Collaborative Learning Conference, 8* (pp. 382-392). New Jersey: International Society of the Learning Sciences.

Kopp, B., & Mandl, H. (2008). Blended Learning. Forschungsfragen und Perspektiven. [Blended Learning. Research questions and perspectives] In J. Issing & P. Klimsa (Hrsg.), *Online-Lernen* (S. 139-150). Weinheim, Germany: Beltz PVU.

Kopp, B., Ertl, B., & Mandl, H. (2006). Wissensschemata und Skript - Förderung der Anwendung von Theoriewissen auf Aufgabenbearbeitung in Videokonferenzen [Content scheme and script – Fostering the application of theoretical knowledge on task solving in videoconferencing]. *Zeitschrift für Entwicklungspsychologie und Pädagogische Psychologie, 38*(3), 132–138. doi:10.1026/0049-8637.38.3.132

Kopp, B., Schnurer, K., & Mandl, H. (2006). Collaborative learning in virtual seminars: Evaluation data and process-product-analyses. In V. Uskov (Ed.), *Proceedings of computers and advanced technology in education* (pp. 528–811). Calgary, Canada: Acta.

Koschmann, T. (2002). Dewey's contribution to the foundations of CSCL research. In G. Stahl (Ed.), *Proceedings of CSCL 2002* (pp. 17-22). Mahwah, NJ: LEA.

Koudsi, S. (2000, March 20). Actually, it is like brain surgery. *Fortune,* 233–234.

Kraut, R. E., Egido, C., & Galegher, J. (1990). Communication in scientific research. In J. Galegher, R. E. Kraut, & C. Egido (Eds.), *Intellectual teamwork. Social and technological foundations of cooperative work* (pp. 149-171). Hillsdale: Lawrence Erlbaum.

Kraut, R. E., Fish, R. S., Root, R. W., & Chalfonte, B. L. (1990). Informal communication in organizations: Form, function, and technology. In S. Oskamp & S. Spacapan (Eds.), *Human reactions to technology* (pp. 145-199). Beverly Hills, CA: Sage.

Kreijns, K., Kirschner, P. A., & Jochems, W. (2003). Identifying the pitfalls for social interaction in computer-supported collaborative learning environments: A review of the research. *Computers in Human Behavior, 19*(3), 335–353. doi:10.1016/S0747-5632(02)00057-2

Kreisler, M. (2007). *Förderung der Kommunikationskompetenz "Konversationale Kohärenz" im Medium Videokonferenz*. Unpublished diploma thesis, Karl-Franzens Universität Graz.

Kress, G. (2003). *Literacy in new media age*. London: Routledge.

Kuhn, D. (1989). Children and adults as intuitive scientists. *Psychological Review, 96*(4), 674–689. doi:10.1037/0033-295X.96.4.674

Kuhn, D. (1991). *The skills of argument*. Cambridge, NY: Cambridge University Press.

Kuhn, D. (1993). Science as argument: Implications for teaching and learning scientific thinking. *Science Education, 77*(3), 319–337. doi:10.1002/sce.3730770306

Kuhn, D., & Goh, W. W. L. (2005). Arguing on the computer. In T. Koschmann, D. Suthers & T. W. Chan (Eds.), *Computer Supported Collaborative Learning 2005: The Next 10 Years* (pp. 125-134). Mahwah, NJ: Lawrence Erlbaum.

Kuhn, D., & Pearsall, S. (2000). Developmental origins of scientific thinking. *Journal of Cognition and Development, 1*, 113–129. doi:10.1207/S15327647JCD0101N_11

Kuhn, L., & Reiser, B. (2005). *Students constructing and defending evidence-based scientific explanations*. Paper presented at the annual meeting of the National Association for Research in Science Teaching, Dallas, TX.

Kuhn, L., & Reiser, B. (2006). *Structuring activities to foster argumentative discourse*. Paper presented at the annual meeting of the American Educational Research Association, San Francisco, CA.

Kumar, R., Rosé, C. P., Wang, Y. C., Joshi, M., & Robinson, A. (2007). Tutorial dialogue as adaptive collaborative learning support. In R. Luckin, K. R. Koedinger, & J. Greer (Eds.), *Proceedings of Artificial Intelligence in Education* (pp. 383-390). IOS Press.

Lambiotte, J. G., Skaggs, L. P., & Dansereau, D. F. (1993). Learning from lectures: effects of knowledge maps and cooperative review strategies. *Applied Cognitive Psychology, 7*, 483–497. doi:10.1002/acp.2350070604

Langrish, T., & See, H. (2008). Diverse assessment methods in group work settings. *Education for Chemical Engineers, 3*, 40–46. doi:10.1016/j.ece.2008.01.001

Larson, R. L., & Christensen, C. (1993). Groups as problem-solving units: Toward a new meaning of social cognition. *The British Journal of Social Psychology, 32*, 5–30.

Latane, B. (1981). The psychology of social impact. *The American Psychologist, 36*(4), 343–351. doi:10.1037/0003-066X.36.4.343

Lave, J., & Wenger, E. (1991). *Situated learning. Legitimate peripheral participation*. Cambridge, UK: Cambridge University Press.

Lawson, A. (2003). The nature and development of hypothetico-predictive argumentation with implications for science teaching. *International Journal of Science Education, 25*(11), 1387–1408. doi:10.1080/0950069032000052117

Leathers, D. G. (1972). Quality of group communication as a determinant of group product. *Speech Monographs, 39*(3), 166–173. doi:10.1080/03637757209375754

Lee, E. Y. C., Chan, C. K. K., & van Aalst, J. (2006). Students assessing their own collaborative knowledge building. *International Journal of Computer-Supported Collaborative Learning, 1*, 277–307. doi:10.1007/s11412-006-8997-6

Lee, F. (1997). When the going gets tough, do the tough ask for help? Help seeking and power motivation in organizations. *Organizational Behavior and Human Decision Processes, 72*(3), 336–363. doi:10.1006/obhd.1997.2746

Lee, F. (2002). The social costs of seeking help. *The Journal of Applied Behavioral Science, 38*(1), 17–35. doi:10.1177/0021886302381002

Leitão, S. (2000). The potential of argument in knowledge building. *Human Development, 43*, 332–360. doi:10.1159/000022695

Lejk, M., & Wyvill, M. (2001). Peer assessment of contributions to a group project: A comparison of holistic and category-based approaches. *Assessment & Evaluation in Higher Education*, 26, 61–72. doi:10.1080/02602930020022291

Lembke, G., Müller, M., & Schneidewind, U. (Eds.). (2005). *Wissensnetzwerke. Grundlagen, Praxisberichte, Anwendungsfelder*. Wiesbaden, Germany: LearnAct!

Lepper, M. R., Drake, M. F., & O'Donnell-Johnson, T. (1997). Scaffolding techniques of expert human tutors. In K. Hogan & M. Pressley (Eds.), *Scaffolding Student Learning: instructional approaches and issues* (pp. 108-144). Cambridge, UK: Brookline Books.

Levinson, E., & Grohe, B. (2001). Managing the internet at school: Limits and access to the greatest source. *Converge*, 4(2), 58–60.

Levy, F., & Murnane, R. J. (2004). *The new division of labor: How computers are creating the next job market*. Princeton, NJ: Princeton University Press.

Lewis, E. L. (1996). Conceptual change among middle school students studying elementary thermodynamics. *Journal of Science Education and Technology*, 5(1), 3–31. doi:10.1007/BF01575468

Lewis, K. (2003). Measuring transactive memory systems in the field: Scale development and validation. *The Journal of Applied Psychology*, 88(4), 587–604. doi:10.1037/0021-9010.88.4.587

Lewis, K. (2004). Knowledge and performance in knowledge-worker teams: A longitudinal study of transactive memory systems. *Management Science*, 50(11), 1519–1533. doi:10.1287/mnsc.1040.0257

Lewis, K., Belliveau, M., Herndon, B., & Keller, J. (2007). Group cognition, membership change, and performance: Investigating the benefits and detriments of collective knowledge. *Organizational Behavior and Human Decision Processes*, 103(2), 159–178. doi:10.1016/j.obhdp.2007.01.005

Lewis, K., Lange, D., & Gillis, L. (2005). Transactive memory systems, learning, and learning transfer.

Organization Science, 16(6), 581–598. doi:10.1287/orsc.1050.0143

Lewis, R. D. (2003). *The Cultural Imperative: Global Trends in the 21st Century*. Yarmouth, ME: Intercultural Press.

Liang, D. W., Moreland, R. L., & Argote, L. (1995). Group versus individual training and group performance: The mediating role of transactive memory. *Personality and Social Psychology Bulletin*, 21(4), 384–393. doi:10.1177/0146167295214009

Libert, B. (2008). *Social Media Change Corporate Culture*. Retrieved October 14, 2008, from http://www.mzinga.com/en/Community/Blogs/Barry-Libert/

Lin, S. S. J., Liu, E. Z. F., & Yuan, S. M. (2001). Web-based peer assessment: Feedback for students with various thinking-styles. *Journal of Computer Assisted Learning*, 17, 420–432. doi:10.1046/j.0266-4909.2001.00198.x

Linn, M. (2006). The knowledge integration perspective on learning and instruction. In R. K. Sawyer (Ed), *The Cambridge handbook of the learning Science* (pp. 243-264). New York: Cambridge University Press.

Linn, M. C., & Burbules, N. (1993). Construction of knowledge and group learning. In K. Tobin (Ed.), *The practice of constructivism in science education* (pp. 91-119). Washington, DC: American Association for the Advancement of Science.

Linn, M. C., & Eylon, B.-S. (2006). Science Education: Integrating views of learning and instruction. In P. Alexander & P. H. Winne (Eds.), *Handbook of Educational Psychology* (pp. 511-544). Mahwah, NJ: Lawrence Erlbaum Associates.

Linn, M. C., & Hsi, S. (2000). *Computers, teachers, peers: Science learning partners*. Mahwah, NJ: Lawrence Erlbaum Associates.

Lipponen, L. (2001). *Computer-supported collaborative learning: From promises to reality*. Unpublished doctoral dissertation, University of Turku.

Lipponen, L., Hakkarainen, K., & Paavola, S. (2004). Practices and orientations of CSCL. In J.-W. Strijbos, P.

Kirschner, R. Martens & P. Dillenbourg (Eds.), *What we know about CSCL and implementing it in higher education* (pp. 31–59). Norwell, MA: Kluwer Academic.

Lipponen, L., Rahikainen, M., Lallimo, J., & Hakkarainen, K. (2003). Patterns of participation and discourse in elementary students' computer-supported collaborative learning. *Learning and Instruction, 13*(5), 487–509. doi:10.1016/S0959-4752(02)00042-7

Littlejohn, A., & Pegler, C. (2007). *Preparing for blended e-learning: Understanding blended and online learning.* New York: Routledge.

Liu, L., Marathe, S., & Hmelo-Silver, C. E. (2006). Effects of conceptual representations on learning from hypermedia. In S. A. Barab, K. E. Hay, & D. T. Hickey (Eds.). *Proceedings of 7th International Conference of the Learning Sciences* (pp. 495- 501). Mahwah, NJ: Erlbaum.

Liu, S.-H., Liao, H.-L., & Pratt, J. A. (2009). Impact of media richness and flow on e-learning technology acceptance. *Computers & Education, 52*, 599–607. doi:10.1016/j.compedu.2008.11.002

Lopez-Real, F., & Chan, Y. P. (1999). Peer assessment of a group project in a primary mathematics education course. *Assessment & Evaluation in Higher Education, 24*, 68–79. doi:10.1080/0260293990240106

Lou, Y., Abrami, P. C., & d'Apollonia, S. (2001). Small group and individual learning with technology: A meta-analysis. *Review of Educational Research, 71*(3), 449–521. doi:10.3102/00346543071003449

Lou, Y., Abrami, P. C., Spence, J. C., Poulsen, C., Chambers, B., & d'Appolonia, S. (1996). Within-class grouping: A meta-analysis. *Review of Educational Research, 66*(4), 423–458.

Lund, K., Molinari, G., Séjourné, A., & Baker, M. (2007). How do argumentation diagrams compare when student pairs use them as a means for debate or as a tool for representing debate? *Computer-Supported Collaborative Learning, 2*(2-3), 273–295. doi:10.1007/s11412-007-9019-z

Maass, A., West, S. G., & Clark, R. D. (1993). Soziale Einflüsse von Minoritäten in Gruppen [Social influences of minorities in groups]. In D. Frey, & M. Irle (Eds.), *Gruppen- und Lerntheorien* (Bd. 2, pp. 65-122). Göttingen, Germany: Hogrefe.

Majchrzak, A., Malhotra, A., Stamps, J., & Lipnack, J. (2004, May). Can absence make a team grow stronger? *Harvard Business Review*, 131–137.

Mäkitalo, K., Häkkinen, P., Leinonen, P., & Järvelä, S. (2002). Mechanisms of common ground in case-based Web-discussions in teacher education. *The Internet and Higher Education, 5*(3), 247–265. doi:10.1016/S1096-7516(02)00112-4

Mäkitalo, K., Weinberger, A., Häkkinen, P., Järvelä, S., & Fischer, F. (2005). Epistemic cooperation scripts in online learning environments: Fostering learning by reducing uncertainty in discourse? *Computers in Human Behavior, 21*(4), 603–622. doi:10.1016/j.chb.2004.10.033

Mandl, H. (2008). *Ausbildung von E-Learning-Tutoren zur Betreuung von Studierenden der Virtuellen Hochschule Bayern.* Virtuelles Kursangebot: Lehrstuhl für Empirische Pädagogik und Pädagogische Psychologie.

Mandl, H., Gruber, H., & Renkl, A. (1996). Communities of practice toward expertise: Social foundation of university instruction. In P. B. Baltes & U. Staudinger (Eds.), *Interactive minds. Life-span perspectives on the social foundation of cognition* (pp. 394-411). Cambridge, UK: Cambridge University Press.

Mannix, E. A., Griffith, T., & Neale, M. A. (2002). The phenomenology of conflict in distributed work teams. In P. Hinds & S. Kiesler (Eds.), *Distributed work* (pp. 213-233). Cambridge, MA: MIT Press.

Martens, R., Bastiaens, T., & Kirschner, P. A. (2007). New learning design in distance education: The impact on student perception and motivation. *Distance Education, 28*, 81–93. doi:10.1080/01587910701305327

Martin, J. (1982). Stories and scripts in organizational settings. In A. Hastorf & I. Isen (Eds.), *Cognitive social psychology* (pp. 255-305). New York: Elsevier.

Martínez, A., Dimitriadis, Y., Gómez-Sánchez, E., Rubia-Avi, B., Jorrín-Abellán, I., & Marcos, J. A. (2006). Studying participation networks in collaboration using mixed methods. *International Journal of Computer-Supported Collaborative Learning, 1,* 383–408. doi:10.1007/s11412-006-8705-6

Martins, L. L., Gilson, L. L., & Maynard, M. (2004). Virtual teams: What do we know and where do we go from here? *Journal of Management, 30*(6), 805–835. doi:10.1016/j.jm.2004.05.002

Marttunen, M. (1992). Commenting on written arguments as a part of argumentation skills: Comparison between students engaged in traditional vs on-line study. *Scandinavian Journal of Educational Research, 36*(4), 289–302. doi:10.1080/0031383920360404

Marttunen, M., & Laurinen, L. (2001). Learning of argumentation skills in networked and face-to-face environments. *Instructional Science, 29,* 127–153. doi:10.1023/A:1003931514884

Marttunen, M., & Laurinen, L. (2006). Collaborative learning through argument visualisation in secondary school. In S. N. Hogan (Ed.) *Trends in learning research* (pp. 119-138). New York: Nova Science Publishers.

Marttunen, M., & Laurinen, L. (2007). Collaborative learning through chat discussions and argument diagrams in secondary school. *Journal of Research on Technology in Education, 40*(1), 109–126.

Mason, L. (2003). Personal epistemologies and intentional conceptual change. In G. M. Sinatra, & P. R. Pintrich (Eds.), *Intentional Conceptual Change* (pp. 199-237). Mahwah, NJ: Lawrence Erlbaum.

Mathan, S. A., & Koedinger, K. R. (2005). Fostering the intelligent novice: Learning from errors with metacognitive tutoring. *Educational Psychologist, 40*(4), 257–265. doi:10.1207/s15326985ep4004_7

Mathews, B. (1994). Assessing individual contributions: Experience of peer evaluation in major group projects. *British Journal of Educational Technology, 25,* 19–28. doi:10.1111/j.1467-8535.1994.tb00086.x

Mathiasen, H. (2004). Expectations of Technology: When the Intensive Application of IT in Teaching Becomes a Possibility. *Journal of Research on Technology in Education, 36*(3), 273–294.

Mayer, R. E. (2005). Cognitive theory of multimedia learning. In R. E. Mayer (Ed.), *The Cambridge handbook of multimedia learning* (pp. 31-48). New York: Cambridge University Press.

Mazzoni, E., & Gaffuri, P. (in press). Monitoring activity in e-Learning: a quantitative model based on web tracking and Social Network Analysis. In A. A. Juan, T. Daradoumis, F. Xhafa, S. Caballe, J. Faulin (Eds.), *Monitoring and assessment in online collaborative environments: Emergent Computational Technologies for E-learning Support.* Hershey, PA: IGI Global.

McDermott, L. C. (1990). Research and computer-based instruction: Opportunity for interaction. *American Journal of Physics, 58,* 452–462. doi:10.1119/1.16487

McGregor, J. (2006, February 27). The office chart that really counts. *Business Week,* 48–49.

McNeill, K. L., & Krajcik, J. (in press). Middle school students' use of appropriate and inappropriate evidence in writing scientific explanations. In M. Lovett & P. Shah (Eds.), *Thinking with data: The proceedings of 33rd Carnegie Symposium on Cognition.* Mahwah, NJ: Lawrence Erlbaum Associates, Inc.

McNeill, K. L., Lizotte, D. J., Krajcik, J., & Marx, R. W. (2006). Supporting students' construction of scientific explanations by fading scaffolds in instructional materials. *Journal of the Learning Sciences, 15*(2), 153–191. doi:10.1207/s15327809jls1502_1

Meier, A., & Spada, H. (in press). Developing adaptive collaboration support: The example of an effective training for collaborative inferences. *Educational Psychology Review.*

Meier, A., Spada, H., & Rummel, N. (2007). A rating scheme for assessing the quality of computer-supported collaboration processes. *Computer-Supported Collaborative Learning, 2,* 63–86. doi:10.1007/s11412-006-9005-x

Meier, D. K., Reinhard, K. J., Carter, D. O., & Brooks, D. W. (2008). Simulations with worked example modeling: Beneficial effects on scheme acquisition. *Journal of Science Education and Technology, 17,* 262–273. doi:10.1007/s10956-008-9096-4

Mephu-Nguifo, E. Baker, M.J. & Dillenbourg, P. (1999). Knowledge transformations in agents and interactions: A comparison of machine learning and dialogue operators. In P. Dillenbourg (Ed.), *Collaborative Learning: Cognitive and Computational Approaches* (122-146). Amsterdam: Pergamon / Elsevier Science.

Mercer, N. (1996). The quality of talk in children's collaborative activity in classroom. *Learning and Instruction, 6*(4), 359–377. doi:10.1016/S0959-4752(96)00021-7

Mercier, J., & Frederiksen, C. H. (2007). Individual differences in graduate students' help-seeking process in using a computer coach in problem-based learning. *Learning and Instruction, 17,* 184–203. doi:10.1016/j.learninstruc.2007.01.013

Miao, Y., & Koper, R. (2007). An efficient and flexible technical approach to develop and deliver online peer assessment. In C. Chinn, G. Erkens, & S. Puntambekar (Eds.), *Mice, minds and society: The Computer supported collaborative learning (CSCL) conference 2007* (pp. 502-510). New Brunswick, NJ: International Society of the Learning Sciences.

Miao, Y., Harrer, A., Hoeksema, K., & Hoppe, U. H. (2007). Modeling CSCL scripts – a reflection on learning design approaches. In F. Fischer, I. Kollar, H. Mandl, & J. M. Haake (Eds.). *Scripting computer-supported collaborative learning* (pp. 117-134). New York: Springer.

Michinov, E., Olivier-Chiron, E., Rusch, E., & Chiron, B. (2008). Influence of transactive memory on perceived performance, job satisfaction, and identification in anaesthesia teams. *British Journal of Anaesthesia, 100*(3), 327–332. doi:10.1093/bja/aem404

Michinov, N., & Michinov, E. (2009). Investigating the relationship between transactive memory and performance in collaborative learning. *Learning and Instruction, 19,* 43–54. doi:10.1016/j.learninstruc.2008.01.003

Michinov, N., & Primois, C. (2005). Improving productivity and creativity in online groups through social comparison process: New evidence for asynchronous electronic brainstorming. *Computers in Human Behavior, 21,* 11–28. doi:10.1016/j.chb.2004.02.004

Milekic, D. (2007). *Auswirkung der tutoriellen Unterstützung auf Akzeptanz, Lernprozess und Lernerfolg* [Effects of tutorial support on acceptance, learning process and learning outcome]. Unpublished Master Theses, Ludwig-Maximilians-Universität, Munich.

Milgram, S. (1967). The small-world problem. *Psychology Today, 2,* 60–67.

Miyake, N., Masukawa, H., & Shirouzou, H. (2001). The complex jigsaw as an enhancer of collaborative knowledge building in undergraduate introductory science courses. In P. Dillenbourg, A. Eurelings, & K. Hakkarainen (Eds.), *European perspectives on computer-supported collaborative learning: Proceedings of the 1st European Conference on Computer-Supported Collaborative Learning* (pp. 454–461). Maastricht: Maastricht University.

Moreland, R. L. (1999). Transactive memory: Learning who knows what in work groups and organizations. In L. Thompson, D. Messick, & J. Levine (Eds.), *Shared cognition in organizations: The management of knowledge* (pp. 3-31). Mahwah, N.J.: Erlbaum.

Moreland, R. L., & Levine, J. M. (1992). Problem identification by groups. In S. Worchel, W. Wood, & J. A. Simpson (Eds.), *Group process and productivity* (pp. 17-47). Newbury Park, CA.: Sage.

Moreland, R. L., & Levine, J. M. (2000). Socialization in organizations and work groups. In M. Turner (Ed.), *Groups at work: Theory and research* (pp. 69-112). Mahwah, N.J.: Erlbaum.

Moreland, R. L., & Myaskovsky, L. (2000). Explaining the performance benefits of group training: Transactive memory or improved communication? *Organizational Behavior and Human Decision Processes, 82*(1), 117–133. doi:10.1006/obhd.2000.2891

Moreland, R. L., Argote, L., & Krishnan, R. (1996). Socially shared cognition at work: Transactive memory and group performance. In J. L. Nye & A. M. Brower (Eds.), *What's social about social cognition? Research on socially shared cognition in small groups* (pp. 57-84). Thousand Oaks, CA.: Sage.

Moreland, R. L., Argote, L., & Krishnan, R. (1998). Training people to work in groups. In R. S. Tindale & Colleagues (Eds.), *Theory and research on small groups* (pp. 36-60). New York: Plenum Press.

Moscovici, S. (1980). Toward a theory of conversion behavior. In L. Berkowitz (Ed.), *Advances in Experimental Social Psychology, 13,* 209-239.

Mühlpfordt, M. (2006). *ConcertChat* [Computer software]. Retrieved June 19, 2009, from http://www.ipsi.fraunhofer.de/concert/index_en.shtml?projects/chat

Mühlpfordt, M., & Wessner, M. (2005). Explicit referencing in chat supports collaborative learning. In *Proceedings of CSCL 2005*, Taipei, Taiwan, 2005.

Mullen, I. B., & Goethals, G. R. (Eds.). *Theories of group behavior* (pp. 185-208). New York: Springer-Verlag.

Munneke, L., Andriessen, J., Kirschner, P., & Kanselaar, G. (2007, July). *Effects of synchronous and asynchronous CMC on interactive argumentation.* Paper to be presented at the CSCL 2007 Conference, New Brunswick, NY.

Münzer, S., & Holmer, T. (2009). Bridging the Gap Between Media Synchronicity and Task Performance. *Communication Research, 36,* 76–103. doi:10.1177/0093650208326464

Murray, T. (2003). An overview of intelligent tutoring system authoring tools: Updated analysis of the state of the art. In: T. Murray, S. Blessing, & S. Ainsworth (Eds.) *Authoring tools for advanced learning environments.* (pp. 491-544). Dordrecht, The Netherlands: Kluwer Academic Publishers.

Nardi, B. A., & Whittaker, S. (2002). The place of face-to-face communication in distributed work. In P. Hinds & S. Kiesler (Eds.), *Distributed work* (pp. 83-110).

Nardi, B., Schiano, D. J., & Gumbrecht, M. (2004). Blogging as social activity, or, would you let 900 million people read your diary? In *Proceedings of the 2004 ACM conference on Computer Supported Cooperative Work (CSCW).* Chicago: ACM.

National Research Council. (1996). National science education standards. Washington, DC: National Academy Press.

National Research Council. (2000). *How People Learn: Brain, Mind, Experience, and School.* Washington, DC: National Academies Press.

National Research Council. (2008). *Research on Future Skill Demands: A Workshop Summary.* Washington, DC: National Academies Press.

Nebus, J. (2006). Building collegial information networks: A theory of advice network generation. *Academy of Management Review, 31*(3), 615–537.

Nelson-Le Gall, S., & Resnick, L. (1998). Help-seeking, achievement motivation, and the social practice of intelligence in school. In S. A. Karabenick (Ed.), *Strategic help-seeking. Implications for learning and teaching* (pp. 117-139). Mahwah, NJ: Erlbaum.

Nemeth, C. J. (1986). Differential contributions of majority and minority influence. *Psychological Review, 93*(11), 23–32. doi:10.1037/0033-295X.93.1.23

Newlands, A., Anderson, A. H., & Mullin, J. (2003). Adapting communicative strategies to computer-mediated communication: An analysis of task performance and dialogue structure. *Applied Cognitive Psychology, 17,* 325–348. doi:10.1002/acp.868

Newman, D. R., Webb, B., & Cochrane, C. (1995). A content analysis method to measure critical thinking in face-to-face and computer supported group learning. *Interpersonal Computing and Technology, 3*(2), 56–77.

Newton, P., Driver, R., & Osborne, J. (1999). The place of argumentation in the pedagogy of school science. *International Journal of Science Education, 21*(5), 553–576. doi:10.1080/095006999290570

Novak, J. D. (1998). *Learning, creating, and using knowledge: concept maps as facilitative tools in schools and corporations.* Mahwah, NJ: Lawrence Erlbaum Associates.

Nückles, M., & Ertelt, A. (2006). The problem of describing a problem: Supporting laypersons in presenting their queries to the Internet-based helpdesk. *International Journal of Human-Computer Studies, 64*(8), 648–669. doi:10.1016/j.ijhcs.2006.01.001

Nückles, M., Ertelt, A., Wittwer, J., & Renkl, A. (2007). Scripting Laypersons' Problem Descriptions in Internet-Based Communication with Experts. *Scripting Computer-Supported Collaborative Learning*, 73-89.

O'Dell, C., & Grayson, C. J. (1998). If only we knew: Identification and transfer of internal best practices. *California Management Review, 40*(3), 154–174.

O'Donnell, A. M. (1999). Structuring dyadic interaction through scripted cooperation. In A. M. O'Donnell & A. King (Eds.), *Cognitive perspectives on peer learning.* (pp. 179-196). Mahwah, NJ: Lawrence Erlbaum Associates, Publishers.

O'Donnell, A. M., & Dansereau, D. F. (1992). Scripted cooperation in student dyads: A method for analysing and enhancing academic learning and performance. In R. Hertz-Lazarowitz & N. Miller (Eds.), *Interaction in cooperative groups: The theoretical anatomy of group learning* (pp. 120-144). New York: Cambridge University Press.

O'Donnell, A. M., & Dansereau, D. F. (2000). Interactive effects of prior knowledge and material format on cooperative teaching. *Journal of Experimental Education, 68*(2), 101–118. doi:10.1080/00220970009598497

O'Donnell, A. M., & King, A. (Eds.). (1999). *Cognitive perspectives on peer learning.* Mahwah, NJ: Erlbaum.

O'Neill, J., & Martin, D. (2003). Text chat in action. In M. Pendergast, K. Schmidt, C. Simone, & M. Tremaine (Eds.), *GROUP'03. Proceedings of the Conference on Supporting Group Work* (pp. 40-49). New York: ACM.

O'Reilly, C. A. (1982). Variations in decision makers' use of information sources: The impact of quality and accessibility of information. *Academy of Management Journal, 25*(4), 756–771. doi:10.2307/256097

O'Reilly, T. (2005). *What is web 2.0 design patterns and business models for the next generation of software.* Retrieved March 10, 2009, from http://www.oreilly.com/pub/a/oreilly/tim/news/2005/09/30/what-is-web-20.html

Oehl, M., & Pfister, H.-R. (2008). Re-learning in CSCL with learning protocols: which replay formats are beneficial? In G. Richards (Ed.), *Proceedings of World Conference on E-Learning in Corporate, Government, Healthcare, and Higher Education 2008* (pp. 3046-3051). Chesapeake, VA: AACE.

Oehl, M., & Pfister, H.-R. (2009). Explicit References in Chat-Based CSCL: Do They Faciliate Global Text Processing? Evidence from Eye Movement Analysis. In A. Dimitracopoulou, C. O'Malley, D. Suthers, & P. Reimann (Eds.), *Computer Supported Collaborative Learning Practices: CSCL2009 Conference Proceedings* (Vol. 2, pp. 138-140). International Society of the Learning Sciences, Inc. (ISLS).

Oehl, M., Pfister, H.-R., & Gilge, A. (2008). Global text processing in CSCL with learning protocols: a coding scheme for eye movement analyzes. In P. A. Kirschner, F. Prins, V. Jonker, & G. Kanselaar (Eds.), *International Perspectives in the Learning Sciences: Cre8ing a learning world. Proceedings of the Eighth International Conference for the Learning Sciences – ICLS 2008* (Vol. 3, pp. 103-104). International Society of the Learning Sciences, Inc. (ISLS).

Oestermeier, U., & Hesse, F. (2000). Verbal and visual causal arguments. *Cognition, 75*, 65–104. doi:10.1016/S0010-0277(00)00060-3

Ohlsson, S. (1992). The cognitive skill of theory articulation: A neglected aspect of science education? *Science & Education, 1*, 181–192. doi:10.1007/BF00572838

Oksama, L., & Hyona, L. (2008). Dynamic binding of identity and location information: A serial model of multiple identity tracking. *Cognitive Psychology, 56*, 237–283. doi:10.1016/j.cogpsych.2007.03.001

Oliver, M., & Shaw, G. (2003). Asynchronous discussion in support of medical education. *Journal of Asynchronous Learning Networks, 7*(1), 56–67.

Orr, J. E. (1996). *Talking about machines: An ethnography of a modern job*. Ithaca, NY: Cornell University Press.

Orsmond, P., Merry, S., & Callaghan, A. (2004). Implementation of a formative assessment model incorporating peer and self-assessment. *Innovations in Education and Teaching International, 41*, 273–290. doi:10.1080/14703 290410001733294

Orsmond, P., Merry, S., & Reiling, K. (1996). The importance of marking criteria in the use of peer assessment. *Assessment & Evaluation in Higher Education, 21*, 239–249. doi:10.1080/0260293960210304

Orsmond, P., Merry, S., & Reiling, K. (2002). The use of exemplars and formative feedback when using student-derived marking criteria in peer and self-assessment. *Assessment & Evaluation in Higher Education, 22*, 357–367. doi:10.1080/0260293970220401

Ortega, F., & Barahona, J. M. G. (2007). Quantitative analysis of the wikipedia community of users. In *Proceedings of the 2007 international symposium "WikiSym '07"*. New York: ACM.

Orton, E., & Mulhausen, P. (2008). E-learning virtual patients for geriatric education. *Gerontology & Geriatrics Education, 28*, 73–88. doi:10.1300/J021v28n03_06

Osborne, J., Erduran, S., & Simon, S. (2004). Enhancing the quality of argumentation in science classrooms. *Journal of Research in Science Teaching, 41*(10), 994–1020. doi:10.1002/tea.20035

Paechter, M. (2003). *Wissenskommunikation, Kooperation und Lernen in virtuellen Gruppen*. Lengerich, Germany: Pabst.

Palazzolo, E. T. (2005). Organizing for information retrieval in transactive memory systems. *Communication Research, 32*(6), 726–761. doi:10.1177/0093650205281056

Palazzolo, E. T., Serb, D. A., She, Y., Su, C., & Contractor, N. S. (2006). Coevolution of communication and knowledge networks in transactive memory systems: Using computational models for theoretical development. *Communication Theory, 16*(2), 223–250. doi:10.1111/j.1468-2885.2006.00269.x

Palincsar, A., & Brown, A. (1984). Reciprocal teaching of comprehension-fostering and comprehension-monitoring activities. *Cognition and Instruction, 1*(2), 117–175. doi:10.1207/s1532690xci0102_1

Papert, S. (1980). *Mindstorms: Children, computers, powerful ideas*. Brighton, UK: Harvester Press.

Passmore, C., & Stewart, J. (2002). A modeling approach to teaching evolutionary biology in high schools. *Journal of Research in Science Teaching, 39*(3), 185–204. doi:10.1002/tea.10020

Pea, R. D. (1993). Learning scientific concepts through material and social activities: Conversational analysis meets conceptual change. *Educational Psychology, 28*, 265–277. doi:10.1207/s15326985ep2803_6

Pea, R. D. (1994). Seeing what we build together: Distributed multimedia learning environments for transformative communications. Special Issue: Computer support for collaborative learning. *Journal of the Learning Sciences, 3*(3), 285–299. doi:10.1207/s15327809jls0303_4

Pea, R. D. (2004). The social and technological dimensions of scaffolding and related theoretical concepts for learning, education, and human activity. *Journal of the Learning Sciences, 13*(3), 423–451. doi:10.1207/s15327809jls1303_6

Pekrun, R., & Schiefele, U. (1996). Emotions- und motivationspsychologische Bedingungen der Lernleistung. In: Weinert, F. H. (Hrsg.): *Enzyklopädie der Psychologie D / I Psychologie des Lernens und der Instruktion* (pp. 153–180). Göttingen, Germany: Hogrefe.

Peltokorpi, V. (2004). Transactive memory directories in small work units. *Personnel Review, 33*(4), 446–462. doi:10.1108/00483480410539515

Peltokorpi, V., & Manka, M. (2008). Antecedents and the performance outcomes of transactive memory in daycare work groups. *European Psychology, 13*(2), 103-113. Prichard, J., & Ashleigh, M. (2007). The effects of team-skills training on transactive memory and performance. *Small Group Research, 38*(6), 696–726.

Perkins, D. (1993). Person-plus: A distributed view of thinking and learning. In G. Salomon (Ed.), *Distributed* cognitions: *Psychological and educational considerations* (pp. 88–110). New York: Cambridge University Press.

Peterson, P., & Swing, S. (1985). Students' cognition as mediators of the effectiveness of small-group learning. *Journal of Educational Psychology, 77*, 299–312. doi:10.1037/0022-0663.77.3.299

Pfister, H.-R. (2005). How to support synchronous net-based learning discourses: Principles and perspectives. In R. Bromme, F. Hesse & H. Spada (Eds.), *Barriers and biases in computer-mediated knowledge communication* (pp. 39-57). New York: Springer.

Pfister, H.-R., & Mühlpfordt, M. (2002). Supporting discourse in a synchronous learning environment: The learning protocol approach. In G. Stahl (Ed.), *Proceedings of CSCL 2002* (pp. 581-589). Hillsdale, NJ: Erlbaum.

Pfister, H.-R., & Oehl, M. (2009). The Impact of Goal Focus, Task Type, and Group Size on Synchronous Net-Based Collaborative Learning Discourses. *Journal of Computer Assisted Learning, 25*, 161–176. doi:10.1111/j.1365-2729.2008.00287.x

Pfister, H.-R., Mühlpfordt, M., & Müller, W. (2003). Lernprotokollunterstütztes Lernen - ein Vergleich zwischen unstrukturiertem und systemkontrolliertem diskursivem Lernen im Netz. *Zeitschrift fur Psychologie mit Zeitschrift fur Angewandte Psychologie, 211*, 98–109. doi:10.1026//0044-3409.211.2.98

Phielix, C., Prins, F. J., & Kirschner, P. A. (2009). *The design of peer feedback and reflection tools in a CSCL environment.* Paper to be presented at the Computer Supported Collaborative Learning Conference 2009, 8-13 June 2009, Rhodes, Greece.

Pimentel, M. G., Fuks, H., & de Lucena, C. J. P. (2003). Co-text loss in textual chat tools. In P. Blackburn, C. Ghidini, R. M. Turner & F. Giunchiglia (Eds.), *Modeling and using context. Lecture notes in computer science* (Vol. 2680, pp. 483-490). Berlin, Germany: Springer.

Pintrich, P. R. (2002). Future challenges and directions for the theory and research on personal epistemology. In B. K. Hofer & P. R. Pintrich (Eds.), *Personal epistemology.*

The psychology of beliefs about knowledge and knowing (pp. 389-414). Mahwah, NJ: Lawrence Erlbaum.

Plass, L. J., Chun, D. M., Mayer, R. E., & Leutner, D. (1998). Supporting visual and verbal learning preferences in a second language multimedia learning environment. *Journal of Educational Psychology, 90*, 25–36. doi:10.1037/0022-0663.90.1.25

Ploetzner, R., Fehse, E., Kneser, C., & Spada, H. (1999). Learning to relate qualitative and quantitative problem representations in a model-based setting for collaborative problem-solving. *Journal of the Learning Sciences, 8*, 177–214. doi:10.1207/s15327809jls0802_1

Poole, M. J. (2000). *Developing Online Communities of Practice in Preservice Teacher Education.* Retrieved September 27, 2006, from http://citeseer.ist.psu.edu/update/508413

Posner, G., Strike, K., Hewson, P., & Gertzog, W. (1982). Accommodation of a scientific conception: Toward a theory of conceptual change. *Science Education, 66*, 211–227. doi:10.1002/sce.3730660207

Pöysä, J. (2006). University students' experiences in the early phases of community building in virtual learning environment: The contents of shared intellectual activity. In C. Clarebout & J. Elen (Eds.), *Avoiding simplicity, confronting complexity: Advances in studying and designing (computer-based) powerful learning environments* (pp. 255–264). Rotterdam, Germany: Sense.

Pressley, M., & Gaskins, I. W. (2006). Metacognitively competent reading comprehension is constructively responsive reading: How can such reading be developed in students? *Metacognition and Learning, 1*(1), 99–113. doi:10.1007/s11409-006-7263-7

Probst, G. J. B., Raub, S., & Romhardt, K. (1999). *Managing Knowledge: Building Blocks for Success.* Chichester, UK: John Wiley & Sons.

Probst, G., & Borzillo, S. (2008). Why Communities of practice succeed and why they fail. *European Management Journal, 26*, 335–347. doi:10.1016/j.emj.2008.05.003

Pulakos, E. D., Arad, S., Donovan, M. A., & Plamondon, K. E. (2000). Adaptability in the workplace: Development of a taxonomy of adaptive performance. *The Journal of Applied Psychology, 85*, 612–624. doi:10.1037/0021-9010.85.4.612

Puustinen, M., Volckaert-Legrier, O., Coquin, D., & Bernicot, J. (in press). An analysis of students' spontaneous computer-mediated help seeking: A step towards the design of ecologically valid supporting tools. *Computers & Education.*

Quiamzade, A., & Mugny, G. (2001). Social influence dynamics in aptitude tasks. *Social Psychology of Education, 4*, 311–334. doi:10.1023/A:1011388821962

Radach, R., & Kennedy, A. (2004). Theoretical perspectives on eye movements in reading: Past controversies, current issues, and an agenda for future research. *The European Journal of Cognitive Psychology, 16*, 3–26. doi:10.1080/09541440340000295

Rau, D. (2005). The influence of relationship conflict and trust on the transactive memory-performance relation in top management teams. *Small Group Research, 36*(6), 746–771. doi:10.1177/1046496405281776

Rau, D. (2006). Top management team transactive memory, information gathering, and perceptual accuracy. *Journal of Business Research, 59*(4), 416–424. doi:10.1016/j.jbusres.2005.07.001

Rauner, F. (2008). European vocational education and training: A prerequisite for mobility? *Journal of European Industrial Training, 32*, 85–98. doi:10.1108/03090590810861640

Rautenstrauch, Ch. (2001). Tele-tutoring. Zur Didaktik des kommunikativen Handelns im virtuellen Lernraum. *ISKO*, Berlin.

Reagans, R., Argote, L., & Brooks, D. (2005). Individual experience and experience working together: Predicting learning rates from knowing what to do and knowing who knows what. *Management Science, 51*(6), 869–881. doi:10.1287/mnsc.1050.0366

Reber, A. S. (1993). *Implicit learning and tacit knowledge. An essay on the cognitive unconscious.* New York: Oxford University Press.

Reimer, T. (2001). Kognitive Ansätze zur Vorhersage der Gruppenleistung. Distraktion, Kompensation und Akzentuierung. *Zeitschrift für Sozialpsychologie, 32*, 107–128. doi:10.1024//0044-3514.32.2.107

Reingold, J., & Yang, J. C. (2007, July 18). The hidden workplace. *Fortune*, 98–102.

Reinmann, G., & Mandl, H. (2006). Unterrichten und Lernumgebungen gestalten. In A. Krapp & B. Weidenmann (Hrsg.), *Lehrbuch Pädagogische Psychologie* (S. 613-658). Weinheim, Germ.: Beltz.

Reiser, B. J. (2002). Why scaffolding should sometimes make tasks more difficult for learners. In G. Stahl (Ed.), *Computer Support for Collaborative Learning: Foundations for a CSCL community. Proceedings of CSCL 2002* (pp. 255-264). Hillsdale, NJ: Lawrence Erlbaum Associates, Inc.

Reiser, B. J., Tabak, I., Sandoval, W. A., Smith, B. K., Steinmuller, F., & Leone, A. J. (2001). BGuILE: Strategic and conceptual scaffolds for scientific inquiry in biology classrooms. In S. M. Carver & D. Klahr (Eds.), *Cognition and instruction: Twenty-five years of progress* (pp. 263-305). Mahwah, NJ: Erlbaum.

Ren, Y., Carley, K. M., & Argote, L. (2006). The contingent effects of transactive memory: When is it more beneficial to know what others know? *Management Science, 52*(5), 671–682. doi:10.1287/mnsc.1050.0496

Renkl, A. (2002). Learning from worked-out examples: Instructional explanations supplement self-explanations. *Learning and Instruction, 12*, 529–556. doi:10.1016/S0959-4752(01)00030-5

Renkl, A., & Mandl, H. (1995). Kooperatives Lernen: Die Frage nach dem Notwendigen und dem Ersetzbaren. *Unterrichtswissenschaft, 25*, 292–300.

Resnick, L. B. (1987). Learning in school and out. *Educational Researcher, 16*(9), 13–20.

Resnick, L. B. (1991). Shared cognition: Thinking as social practice. In L. B. Resnick, J. M. Levine, & S.D. Teasley (Eds.), *Perspectives on socially shared cognition* (pp.1-20). Washington, DC: American Psychological Association.

Resnick, L., Salmon, M., Zeitz, C. M., Wathen, S. H., & Holowchak, M. (1993). Reasoning in conversation. *Cognition and Instruction, 11*, 347–364.

Rice, R. E., & Love, G. (1987). Electronic emotion: Socioemotional content in a computer-mediated network. *Communication Research, 14*, 85–108. doi:10.1177/009365087014001005

Riketta, M. (2004). Organizational identification: A meta-analysis. *Journal of Vocational Behavior, 66*(2), 358–384. doi:10.1016/j.jvb.2004.05.005

Rogoff, B. (1998). Cognition as a collaborative process. In D. S. Kuhn & R. W. Damon (Eds.), *Cognition, perception and language* (5th ed.) (Vol. 2, pp. 679-744). New York: Wiley.

Romano, N. C., Lowry, P. B., & Roberts, T. L. (2007). Technology-supported small group interaction: Extending a tradition of leading research for virtual teams and global organizations. *Small Group Research, 38*(1), 3–11. doi:10.1177/1046496406297483

Roschelle, J. (1992). Learning by collaborating: Convergent conceptual change. *Journal of the Learning Sciences, 2*, 235–276. doi:10.1207/s15327809jls0203_1

Roschelle, J., & Teasley, S. (1995). The construction of shared knowledge in collaborative problem solving. In C. O'Malley (Ed.), *NATO ASO Series F: Computer and System Sciences, Vol. 128. Computer supported collaborative learning* (pp. 69–97). Berlin, Germany: Springer-Verlag.

Roscoe, R. D., & Chi, M. T. H. (2007). Understanding Tutor Learning: Knowledge-Building and Knowledge-Telling in Peer Tutors' Explanations and Questions. *Review of Educational Research, 77*(4), 534–574. doi:10.3102/0034654307309920

Rosé, C. P., Wang, Y. C., Arguello, J., Stegmann, K., Weinberger, A., & Fischer, F. (2008). Analyzing collaborative learning processes automatically: Exploiting the advances of computational linguistics in computer-supported collaborative learning. *International Journal of Computer-Supported Collaborative Learning, 3*(3), 237–272. doi:10.1007/s11412-007-9034-0

Rosenfeld, L., & Morville, P. (2002). *Information Architecture for the World Wide Web*. Sebastopol, CA: O'Reilly.

Ross, B. (1989). Remindings in learning and instruction. In Vosniadou, S. & Orthony, A. (Eds.) *Similarity and Analogical Reasoning*. New York: Cambridge University Press.

Ross, B., & Kennedy, P. (1990). Generalising from the use of earlier examples in problem solving. *Journal of Experimental Psychology. Learning, Memory, and Cognition, 16*.

Rudestam, K. E., & Schoenholtz-Read, J. (2002). Overview: the coming of age of adult online education. In K.E. Rudestam & J. Schoenholtz-Read (Eds.), *Handbook of online learning: innovations in higher education and corporate training* (pp. 3-28). Thousand Oaks, CA:Sage.

Ruggles, R. (1998). The state of the notion: Knowledge management in practice. *California Management Review, 4*(3), 80–89.

Rummel, N., & Spada, H. (2005). Learning to collaborate: An instructional approach to promoting collaborative problem-solving in computer-mediated settings. *Journal of the Learning Sciences, 14*(2), 201–241. doi:10.1207/s15327809jls1402_2

Rummel, N., & Spada, H. (2007). Can people learn computer-mediated collaboration by following a script? In F. Fischer, I. Kollar, H. Mandl & J. M. Haake (Eds.), *Scripting computer-supported communication of knowledge – cognitive, computational and educational perspectives* (pp. 39-55). Berlin: Springer.

Rummel, N., & Weinberger, A. (2008). New challenges in CSCL: Towards adaptive script support. In G. Kanselaar, V. Jonker, P.A. Kirschner, & F. Prins, (Eds.), *International perspectives of the learning sciences: Cre8ing a learning world. Proceedings of the Eighth International*

Conference of the Learning Sciences (ICLS 2008) (Vol. 3, pp. 338-345). International Society of the Learning Sciences.

Rummel, N., Diziol, D., & Spada, H. (2009). *Collaborative learning with the Cognitive Tutor Algebra. An experimental classroom study.* Manuscript in preparation.

Rummel, N., Spada, H., & Hauser, S. (2009). Learning to collaborate while being scripted or by observing a model. *Computer-Supported Collaborative Learning, 4,* 69–92. doi:10.1007/s11412-008-9054-4

Ryan, A. M., Pintrich, P. R., & Midgley, C. (2001). Avoiding seeking help in the classroom: Who and why? *Educational Psychology Review, 13,* 93–114. doi:10.1023/A:1009013420053

Ryan, R. M., & Deci, D. L. (2000). Self-determination theory and the facilitation of intrinsic motivation, social development, and well-being. *The American Psychologist, 55*(1), 68–78. doi:10.1037/0003-066X.55.1.68

Ryan, R., & Deci, E. (2000). Intrinsic and extrinsic motivations: Classic definitions and new directions. *Contemporary Educational Psychology, 25,* 54–67. doi:10.1006/ceps.1999.1020

Sacks, H., Schegloff, E., & Jefferson, G. (1974). A simplest systematics for the organization of turn-taking for conversation. *Language, 50*(4), 696–735. doi:10.2307/412243

Sadler, T. (2004). Informal reasoning regarding socioscientific issues: A critical review of the research. *Journal of Research in Science Teaching, 41*(5), 513–536. doi:10.1002/tea.20009

Salminen, T., Marttunen, M., & Laurinen, L. (2007). Collaborative argument diagrams based on dyadic computer chat discussions. In Kinshuk, D.G. Sampson, J.M. Spector & P. Isaias (Eds.), *Proceedings of the IADIS International Conference on Cognition and Exploratory Learning in Digital Age,* December 7–9, 2007, Algarve, Portugal (pp. 197-204).

Salmon, G. (2000). *E-Moderating – The Key to Teaching and Learning Online.* London: Taylor and Francis.

Salomon, G. (2000, June 28). *It's not just the tool, but the educational rationale that counts.* Keynote address at the 2000 ED-MEDIA Meeting, Montreal, Canada. Retrieved February 13, 2009, from http://www.aace.org/conf/edmedia/00/salomonkeynote.htm

Salomon, G., & Globerson, T. (1989). When teams do not function the way they ought to. *International Journal of Educational Research, 13,* 89–99. doi:10.1016/0883-0355(89)90018-9

Sampson, V., & Clark, D. (2008). Assessment of the ways students generate arguments in science education: Current perspectives and recommendations for future directions. *Science Education, 92*(3), 447–472. doi:10.1002/sce.20276

Sandoval, W. A. (2003). Conceptual and epistemic aspects of students' scientific explanations. *Journal of the Learning Sciences, 12*(1), 5–51. doi:10.1207/S15327809JLS1201_2

Sandoval, W. A., & Millwood, K. A. (2005). The quality of students' use of evidence in written scientific explanations. *Cognition and Instruction, 23*(1), 23–55. doi:10.1207/s1532690xci2301_2

Sandoval, W. A., & Reiser, B. J. (2004). Explanation-driven inquiry: Integrating conceptual and epistemic supports for science inquiry. *Science Education, 88,* 345–372. doi:10.1002/sce.10130

Schank, R. C., & Abelson, R. P. (1977). *Scripts, plans, goals and understanding.* Hillsdale, NJ: Erlbaum.

Schauer, B. (2005). What put the '2' in web 2.0? Retrieved March 10, 2009 from http://adaptivepath.com/images/publications/essays/What_puts_the_2_in_Web_20.pdf

Schellens, T., & Valcke, M. (2005). Collaborative learning in asynchronous discussion groups: What about the impact on cognitive processing? *Computers in Human Behavior, 21,* 957–975. doi:10.1016/j.chb.2004.02.025

Schellens, T., & Valcke, M. (2006). Fostering knowledge conctruction in university students through asynchronous discussion groups. *Computers & Education, 46*(4), 349–370. doi:10.1016/j.compedu.2004.07.010

Schiefele, U., & Streblow, L. (2007). Motivation aktivieren [Activate Motivation]. In H. Mandl & H. F. Friedrich (Eds.), *Handbuch Lernstrategien [Handbook on learning strategies]* (pp. 232-247). Göttingen, Germany: Hogrefe.

Schmidt, H. G., & Boshuizen, H. P. A. (1993). On acquiring expertise in medicine. *Educational Psychology Review, Special Issue: European educational psychology, 5,* 205-221.

Schmidt, H. G., & Moust, J. H. C. (1995). What Makes a Tutor Effective? A Structural-equations Modeling Apporach to Learning in Problem-based Curricula. *Academic Medicine, 70,* 708–714. doi:10.1097/00001888-199508000-00015

Schmitz, C., & Zucker, B. (1996). *Wissen gewinnt. Knowledge Flow Management.* Düsseldorf, Germany: Metropolitan.

Schneider, W. (1993). Domain-specific knowledge and memory performance in children. *Educational Psychology Review, 5,* 257–273. doi:10.1007/BF01323047

Schnotz, W., & Bannert, M. (2003). Construction and Interference in learning from multiple representations. *Learning and Instruction, 13,* 141–156. doi:10.1016/S0959-4752(02)00017-8

Schooneboom, J. (2008). The effect of a script and a structured interface in grounding discussions. *Computer-Supported Collaborative Learning, 3,* 327–341. doi:10.1007/s11412-008-9042-8

Schunk, D. H., & Zimmerman, B. J. (2003). Self-regulation and learning. In W. M. Reynolds & G. E. Miller (Eds.), *Handbook on psychology: Vol. 7. Educational psychology* (pp. 59-78). Hoboken, NJ: Wiley.

Schwartz, B., Neuman, Y., & Biezuner, S. (2000). Two wrongs make it right…if they argue together! *Cognition and Instruction, 18*(4), 461–494. doi:10.1207/S1532690XCI1804_2

Schwarz, B. B., & Glassner, A. (in press). The role of CSCL argumentative environments for broadening and deepening understanding of the space of debate. In R.

Saljo (Ed.), *Information Technologies and Transformation of Knowledge.*

Schwarz, B., & Glassner, A. (2003). The blind and the paralytic: Supporting argumentation in everyday and scientific issues. In *Arguing to learn: Confronting cognitions in computer-supported collaborative learning environments* (pp. 227-260). Amsterdam: Kluwer Academic Publishers.

Schweizer, K., Pächter, M., & Weidenmann, B. (2001). A field study on distance education and communication: Experiences of a virtual tutor. *Journal of Computer-Mediated Communication, 6*(2).

Schweizer, K., Paechter, M., & Weidenmann, B. (2007). Coherence in knowledge communication: How do online groups communicate? In P. Mayring, G. Huber, L. Guertler, & M. Kiegelmann (Eds.), *Mixed methodology in Psychological research* (pp. 101-112). Rotterdam, Germany & Taipei, Taiwan: Sense Publishers.

Schwonke, R., Renkl, A., & Berthold, K. (2007). Knowledge construction with multiple external representations: What eye movements can tell us. In S. Vosniadou, D. Kayser, & A. Protopapas (Eds.). *Proceedings of the 2nd European Cognitive Science Conference* (pp. 238-243). New York, NJ: Erlbaum.

Schworm, S., & Gruber, H. (Manuscript submitted for publication). E-learning in university courses: Fostering participation and help-seeking in a blended learning environment. *Computers in Human Behavior.*

Schworm, S., & Renkl, A. (2006). Computer-supported example-based learning: When instructional explanations reduce self-explanations. *Computers & Education, 46,* 426–445. doi:10.1016/j.compedu.2004.08.011

Schworm, S., & Renkl, A. (2007). Learning argumentation skills through the use of prompts for self-explaining examples. *Journal of Educational Psychology, 99,* 285–296. doi:10.1037/0022-0663.99.2.285

Schworm, S., Bradler, P., & Renkl, A. (2008). Help design in a computer-based learning environment - teaching argumentation skills through the use of double-content examples. In G. Kanselaar, V. Jonker, P. A. Kirschner &

F. J. Prins (Eds.), *Proceedings of the 8th International Conference of the Learning Sciences 2008*. Utrecht: ICLS.

Seidel, T., Rimmele, R., & Prenzel, M. (2005). Clarity and coherence of lesson goals as a scaffold for student learning. *Learning and Instruction, 15*, 539–556.

Senge, P. (1993). *The fifth discipline. The art and practice of the learning organization*. London: Random House.

Sharp, S. (2006). Deriving individual student marks from a tutor's assessment of group work. *Assessment & Evaluation in Higher Education, 31*, 329–343. doi:10.1080/02602930500352956

Short, J., Williams, E., & Christie, B. (1976). *The social psychology of telecommunications*. London: John Wiley & Sons.

Siegel, H. (1989). The rationality of science, critical thinking and science education. *Synthese, 80*(1), 9–42. doi:10.1007/BF00869946

Simon, H. A. (1973). The structure of ill-structured problems. *Artificial Intelligence, 4*, 181–204. doi:10.1016/0004-3702(73)90011-8

Simon, S., Erduran, S., & Osborne, J. (2002). *Enhancing the Quality of Argumentation in School Science*. Paper presented at the annual meeting of the National Association for Research in Science Teaching, New Orleans, LA.

Simon, S., Erduran, S., & Osborne, J. (2006). Learning to teach argumentation: Research and development in the science classroom. *International Journal of Science Education, 28*(2-3), 235–260. doi:10.1080/09500690500336957

Sinatra, G. M. (2002). Motivational, social, and contextual aspects of conceptual change: A commentary. In M. Limon and L. Mason (Eds.), *Reconsidering conceptual change: Issues in theory and practice* (pp. 187- 197). Dordrecht, The Netherlands: Kluwer.

Sivan, A. (2000). The implementation of peer assessment: An action research approach. *Assessment in Education: Principles . Policy & Practice, 7*, 193–213.

Slavin, R. E. (1980). Cooperative learning in teams: State of the art. *Educational Psychologist, 15*, 93–111. doi:10.1080/00461528009529219

Slavin, R. E. (1992). When and why does cooperative learning increase academic achievement? Theoretical and empirical perspectives. In R. Hertz-Lazarowitz & N. Miller (Eds.), *Interaction in cooperative learning groups. The theoretical anatomy of group learning* (pp.145-173). Cambridge, USA: Cambridge University Press.

Slavin, R. E. (2006). *Educational psychology. Theory and practice* (8th ed.). New York: Pearson.

Slevin, J. (2008). E-learning and the transformation of social interaction in higher education. *Learning, Media and Technology, 33*, 115–126. doi:10.1080/17439880802097659

Slof, B., & Erkens, G. Kirschner, P. A. (2008). Matching model representations to task demands. In *Proceedings of the 8th International Conference of The Learning Sciences*, Utrecht, The Netherlands.

Sluijsmans, D. M. A. (2008, June 6). *Betrokken bij beoordelen* [Involved in assessment]. Lectoral address, HAN University, the Netherlands.

Sluijsmans, D. M. A., Brand-Gruwel, S., Van Merriënboer, J., & Martens, R. (2004). Training teachers in peer-assessment skills: Effects on performance and perceptions. *Innovations in Education and Teaching International, 41*, 59–78. doi:10.1080/1470329032000172720

Sluijsmans, D. M. A., Strijbos, J. W., & Van de Watering, G. (2007, August). *Designing flexible and fair peer-assessment formats to award individual contributions in group-based learning*. Paper presented at the biannual meeting of the European Association for research on Learning and Instruction (EARLI), Budapest, Hungary.

Smith, J., diSessa, A., & Roschelle, J. (1993). Misconceptions reconceived: A constructive analysis of knowledge in transition. *Journal of the Learning Sciences, 3*, 115–163. doi:10.1207/s15327809jls0302_1

Smith, T. E. (1993). Growth in academic achievement and teaching younger siblings. *Social Psychology Quarterly, 56*(1), 77–85. doi:10.2307/2786647

Snijders, T., & Bosker, R. (1999). *Multilevel Analysis. An introduction to basic and advanced multilevel modeling*. London: SAGE Publications.

Soller, A. (2004). Understanding knowledge sharing breakdowns: A meeting of the quantitative and qualitative minds. *Journal of Computer Assisted Learning, 20,* 212–223. doi:10.1111/j.1365-2729.2004.00081.x

Soller, A., Martinez, A., Jerman, P., & Mühlenbrock, M. (2005). From mirroring to guiding: A review of state of the art technology for supporting collaborative learning. *International Journal of Artificial Intelligence in Education, 15,* 261–290.

Sperber, D., & Wilson, D. (1986). *Relevance: Communication and Cognition*. Cambridge, MA: Harvard UP.

Srivastava, A., Bartol, K. M., & Locke, E. A. (2006). Empowered leadership in management teams: Effects on knowledge sharing, efficacy, and performance. *Academy of Management Journal, 49*(6), 1239–1251.

Stahl, G. (2003). Meaning and interpretation in collaboration. In B. Wasson, S. Ludvigsen, & U. Hoppe (Eds.), *Designing For Change in Networked Learning Environments* (pp. 523-532). Dordrecht, The Netherlands: Kluwer Academic Publishers.

Stahl, G. (2006). Analyzing and designing the group cognition experience. *International Journal of Collaborative Information Systems, 15,* 157–178. doi:10.1142/S0218843006001323

Stahl, G. (2006). Scripting group cognition: The problem of guiding situated collaboration. In F. Fischer, H. Mandl, J. Haake, & I. Kollar (Eds.), *Scripting computer-supported collaborative learning: Cognitive, computational and educational perspectives*. Dordrecht, the Netherlands: Kluwer-Springer Verlag.

Stahl, G. (2007). Scripting group cognition. In F. Fischer, H. Mandl, J. Haake & I. Kollar (Eds.), *Scripting computer-supported communication of knowledge - cognitive, computational and educational perspectives* (pp. 327-335). New York: Springer.

Stahl, G., Koschmann, T., & Suthers, D. D. (2006). Computer-supported collaborative learning. In R. K. Sawyer (Ed.), *The Cambridge handbook of the learning sciences* (pp. 409-425). New York: Cambridge University Press.

Stahl, G., Zemel, A., Sarmiento, J., Cakir, M., Weimar, S., Wessner, M., & Mühlpfordt, M. (2006). Shared referencing of mathematical objects in online chat. In S. A. Barab, K. E. Hay, & D. T. Hickey (Eds.), *Proceedings of the 7th International Conference of the Learning Sciences (ICLS 2006)* (pp. 716-722). Mahwah, NJ: Lawrence Erlbaum Associates.

Staley, D. J. (2009). Managing the platform: Higher education and the logic of wikinomics. *EDUCAUSE Review, 44,* 36–46.

Stambor, Z. (2006, April). Brooding over others' business. *APA Monitor on Psychology,* 58-59.

Stark, R., Tyroller, M., Krause, U.-M., & Mandl, H. (2008). Effekte einer metakognitiven Promptingmaßnahme beim situierten, beispielbasierten Lernen im Bereich Korrelationsrechnung. *Zeitschrift für Pädagogische Psychologie, 22*(H. 1), 59–71. doi:10.1024/1010-0652.22.1.59

Starkey, L. & Stevens, K. (2006). Three Stages in the Digital Integration of New Zealand Schools. *New Zealand Ann. Rev. of Education - Te Arotake a Tau o te Ao o te Matauranga i Aotearoa, 16,* 105-117.

Stasser, G., & Titus, W. (1985). Pooling of unshared information in group decision making: Biased information sampling during discussion. *Journal of Personality and Social Psychology, 48,* 1467–1478. doi:10.1037/0022-3514.48.6.1467

Stasser, G., Stewart, D. D., & Wittenbaum, G. M. (1995). Expert roles and information exchange during discussion: The importance of knowing who knows what. *Journal of Experimental Social Psychology, 31*(3), 244–255. doi:10.1006/jesp.1995.1012

Stegmann, K., Wecker, C., Weinberger, A., & Fischer, F. (2007). Collaborative Argumentation and Cognitive Processing - An Empirical Study in a Computer-Supported Collaborative Learning Environment. In C. Chinn, G. Erkens, & S. Puntambekar (Eds.), *Mice, minds, and society. CSCL 2007* (pp. 661-670). New Brunswick, CT: ISLS.

Stegmann, K., Weinberger, A., & Fischer, F. (2007). Facilitating argumentative knowledge construction with computer-supported collaboration scripts. *International Journal of Computer-Supported Collaborative Learning, 2*(4), 421–447. doi:10.1007/s11412-007-9028-y

Stegmann, K., Weinberger, A., Fischer, F., & Mandl, H. (2005). Scripting argumentation in computer-supported learning environments. In P. Gerjets, P. A. Kirschner, J. Elen, & R. Joiner (Eds.), *Instructional design for effective and enjoyable computer-supported learning. Proceedings of the first joint meeting of the EARLI SIGs "Instructional Design" and "Learning and Instruction with Computers"* (pp. 320–330) [CD-ROM]. Tübingen, Germany: Knowledge Media Research Center.

Stein, N. L., & Bernas, R. (1999). The early emergence of argumentative knowledge and skill. In G. Rijlaarsdam, E. Esperet, J. Andriessen & P. Coirier (Eds.), *Studies in writing: Vol 5. Foundations of Argumentative text processing.* Amsterdam: University of Amsterdam Press.

Stein, N. L., & Miller, C. (1991). I win... you lose: The development of argumentative thinking. In J. F. Voss, D. N. Perkins & J. W. Segal (Eds.), *Informal reasoning and instruction.* Hillsdale, NJ: Lawrence Erlbaum.

Stevens, K. J. (1994). Some applications of distance education technologies and pedagogies in rural schools in New Zealand. *Distance Education, 15*(4), 318–326. doi:10.1080/0158791940150210

Stevens, K. J. (1999). A New Model for Teaching in Rural Communities – The Electronic Organization of Classes As Intranets. *Prism – Journal of The Newfoundland and Labrador Teachers'. Association, 6*(1), 23–26.

Stevens, K. J. (1999). Telecommunications technologies, teleLearning and the development of virtual classes for rural New Zealanders. *Open Praxis,* (1), 12-14.

Stevens, K. J. (2003). E-Learning and the Development of Open Classes for Rural Students in Atlantic Canada. In J. Bradley (Ed.), *The Open Classroom – Distance Learning In and Out of Schools* (pp. 149-157). London: Kogan Page.

Stevens, K. J. (2007, August). Objective and Subjective Engagement with the Non-Local World by Rural School Leavers. *International Journal of Rural Psychology,* 1-13. Retrieved from http://www.ruralpsych.com/page3. html

Stevens, K. J., & Stewart, D. (2005). *Cybercells – Learning in Actual and Virtual Groups.* Melbourne, Australia: Thomson-Dunmore Press.

Stewart, A. E. (2003). *Post School Outcomes for 'The Island' Students and their Views on Place and Identity: Year 10 to Year 11 in a Rurally Remote Area.* Unpublished Ph.D. Thesis, Hobart, University of Tasmania.

Stewart, T. A. (1995, October 30). Mapping corporate brainpower. *Fortune,* 209–211.

Stewart, T. A. (1995, November 27). Getting real about brainpower. *Fortune,* 201–203.

Stewart, T. A. (1997, September 29). Does anyone around here know...? *Fortune,* 279–280.

Stewart, T. A. (1999). *Intellectual capital: The new wealth of organizations.* New York: Doubleday.

Stewart, T. A. (2000, September 4). Software preserves knowledge, people pass it on. *Fortune,* 390–393.

Stewart, T. A. (2001). *The wealth of knowledge: Intellectual capital and the twenty-first century organization.* London: Nicholas Brealey

Strasser, J., & Gruber, H. (2004). The role of experience in professional training and development of psychological counselors. In H. P. A. Boshuizen, R. Bromme, & H. Gruber (Eds.), *Professional learning: Gaps and transitions on the way from novice to expert* (pp. 11-27). Dordrecht, The Netherlands: Kluwer.

Strijbos, J. W., & De Laat, M. F. (2007). Prototypical roles in computer-supported collaborative learning: A conceptual framework for the design of a tool for teachers. In J. W. Strijbos & A. Weinberger (Chairs), *Facilitating and analyzing roles in computer-supported collaborative learning, Symposium conducted at the 12th biennial EARLI conference*, Budapest, Hungary.

Strijbos, J. W., & Fischer, F. (2007). Methodological challenges for collaborative learning research. *Learning and Instruction, 17*, 389–393. doi:10.1016/j.learninstruc.2007.03.004

Strijbos, J. W., Martens, R. L., & Jochems, W. M. G. (2004). Designing for interaction: Six steps to designing computer-supported collaborative learning. *Computers & Education, 42*, 403–424. doi:10.1016/j.compedu.2003.10.004

Strijbos, J. W., Martens, R. L., Jochems, W. M. G., & Broers, N. J. (2007). The effect of functional roles on perceived group efficiency during computer-supported collaborative learning: A matter of triangulation. *Computers in Human Behavior, 23*, 353–380. doi:10.1016/j.chb.2004.10.016

Strijbos, J. W., Ochoa, T. A., Sluijsmans, D. M. A., Segers, M. S. R., & Tillema, H. H. (in press). Fostering interactivity through formative peer assessment in (web-based) collaborative learning environments. In C. Mourlas, N. Tsianos, & P. Germanakos (Eds.), *Cognitive and emotional processes in web-based education: Integrating human factors and personalization*. Hershey, PA: IGI Global.

Strijbos, J.-W., & Stahl, G. (2007). Methodological issues in developing a multi-dimensional coding procedure for small-group chat communication. *Learning and Instruction, 17*, 394–404. doi:10.1016/j.learninstruc.2007.03.005

Su, M. C. (2009). Inside the web: A look at digital libraries and the invisible deep web. *Journal of Educational Technology Systems, 37*, 71–82. doi:10.2190/ET.37.1.f

Sung, Y. T., Chang, K. E., Chiou, S. K., & Hou, H. T. (2005). The design and application of a web-based self- and peer-assessment system. *Computers & Education, 45*, 187–202. doi:10.1016/j.compedu.2004.07.002

Sutherland, S. A., Sinatra, G. M., & Matthews, M. R. (2001). Belief, knowledge, and science education. *Educational Psychology Review, 13*, 325–351. doi:10.1023/A:1011913813847

Suthers, D. (2001). Towards a systematic study of representational guidance for collaborative learning discourse. *Journal of Universal Computer Science, 7*(3), 254–277.

Suthers, D. (2005). *Technology affordances for intersubjective learning: a thematic agenda for CSCL*. Keynote at the 2005 International Conference of Computer Support for Collaborative Learning (CSCL 2005), Taipei, Taiwan.

Suthers, D. (2008). Empirical studies of the value of conceptually explicit notations in collaborative learning. In A. Okada, S. Buckingham Shum & T. Sherborne (Eds.), Knowledge Cartography. Software tools and mapping techniques (pp. 1-23). London: Springer.

Suthers, D. D. (2006). Technology affordances for intersubjective meaning making. *International Journal of Computer-Supported Collaborative Learning, 1*, 315–337. doi:10.1007/s11412-006-9660-y

Suthers, D. D., & Hundhausen, C. D. (2001). Learning by constructing collaborative representations: An empirical comparison of three alternatives. In P. Dillenbourg, A. Eurelings, & K. Hakkarainen (Eds.), *European perspectives on computer-supported collaborative learning* (pp. 577-592). Maastricht, The Netherlands: University of Maastricht.

Suthers, D. D., Dwyer, N., Medina, R., & Vatrapu, R. (2007). A framework for eclectic analysis of collaborative interaction. In C. Chinn, G. Erkens, & S. Puntambekar (Eds.), *The 2007 Computer Supported Collaborative Learning (CSCL) Conference* (pp. 694-703). New Brunswick: International Society of the Learning Sciences.

Suthers, D. D., Hundhausen, C. D., & Girardeau, L. E. (2003). Comparing the roles of representations in face-to-face and online computer supported collaborative learning. *Computers & Education, 41*(4), 335–351. doi:10.1016/j.compedu.2003.04.001

Sutton, R. J., & Hargadon, A. (1996). Brainstorming groups in context: Effectiveness in a product-design firm. *Administrative Science Quarterly, 41*(4), 685–718. doi:10.2307/2393872

Swap, W., Leonard, D., Shields, M., & Abrams, L. (2001). Using mentoring and storytelling to transfer knowledge in the workplace. *Journal of Management Systems, 18*(1), 95–114.

Sweller, J., Merrienboer, J. J. G., & Paas, F. (1998). Cognitive architecture and instructional design. *Educational Psychology Review, 10*, 251–296. doi:10.1023/A:1022193728205

Tapscott, D., & Williams, A. D. (2006). *Wikinomics: How mass collaboration changes everything.* New York: Penguin Books.

Taylor, S. L., & Hsueh, Y. (2005). Implementing a constructivist approach in higher education through technology. *Journal of Early Childhood Teacher Education, 26*, 127–132. doi:10.1080/10901020590967353

Teasley, S. (1997). Talking about reasoning: How important is the peer in peer collaboration? In L. B. Resnick, R. Säljö, C. Pontecorvo, & B. Burge (Eds.), *Discourse, tools and reasoning: Essays on situated cognition* (pp. 361-384). Berlin, Germany: Springer.

Tedesco, P. (2003). MArCo: Building an artificial conflict mediator to support group planning interactions. *International Journal of Artificial Intelligence in Education, 13*, 117–155.

Tenenbaum, G., & Goldring, E. (1989). A meta-analysis of the effect of enhanced instructions: Cues, participation, reinforcement and feedback and correctives on motor skill learning. *Journal of Research and Development in Education, 22*, 53–64.

Tergan, S. O., Sparkes, J. J., Hitchcock, C., Kaye, A. R., Hron, A., & Mandl, H. (1992). Computerbased systems for open learning. State of the art. In G. Zimmer & D. Blume (Eds.), *Multimediales Lernen in der Berufsbildung, Bd. 4* (pp. 97-99). Nürnberg, Germany: Bildung und Wissen.

Tidwell, J. (2006). *Designing Interfaces.* Sebastopol, CA: O'Reilly.

Tomlin, R. S., Forrest, L., Pu, M. M., & Kim, M. H. (1997). Discourse semantics. In T. A. van Dijk (Ed.), *Discourse as structure and process* (pp.63-111). London: Sage.

Tonkin, E. (2006). Searching the long tail: Hidden structure in social tagging. In *Proceedings of the 17th Workshop of the American Society for Information Science and Technology, Special Interest Group in Classification Research 17.* Austin, TX: ASIST.

Topping, K. (1998). Peer assessment between students in colleges and universities. *Review of Educational Research, 68*, 249–276.

Totty, M. (2006, February 13). Technology: The dangers within. *Wall Street Journal*, R1.

Toulmin, S. (1958). *The uses of argument.* Cambridge, MA: Cambridge University Press.

Trentin, G. (2009). Using a wiki to evaluate individual contribution to a collaborative learning project. *Journal of Computer Assisted Learning, 25*, 43–55. doi:10.1111/j.1365-2729.2008.00276.x

Tscholl, M., & Dowell, J. (2008). Analysing problem structuring in a collaborative explanation dialogue to capture conceptual change. In V. Sloutsky, B. Love, & K. McRae (Eds.), *Proceedings of 30th Meeting of The Cognitive Science Society.* Mahwah, NJ: LEA.

Tsovaltzi, D., Rummel, N., McLaren, B., Pinkwart, N., Scheuer, O., Harrer, A., & Braun, I. (in press). Extending a Virtual Chemistry Laboratory with a Collaboration Script to Promote Conceptual Learning. [IJTEL]. *International Journal of Technology Enhanced Learning.*

Tucker, C., & Stevens, K. (1999). Where Do We Go From Here? Post-High School Educational and Vocational Choices of Students Leaving a Small Rural Canadian Community. *Journal of Critical Inquiry into Curriculum and Instruction, 1*(3), 22–24.

Twardy, C. R. (2004). Argument maps improve critical thinking. *Teaching Philosophy, 27*(2), 95–116.

Vaast, E. (2004). O Brother, where art thou? From communities to networks of practice through intranet use. *Management Communication Quarterly, 18*(1), 5–44. doi:10.1177/0893318904265125

Valsiner, J., & van der Veer, R. (2000). *The social mind.* Cambridge, UK: Cambridge University Press

van Amelsvoort, M. (2006). *A space of debate. How diagrams support collaborative argumentation-based learning.* Dutch Interuniversity Center for Educational Research (ICO). Enschede, Netherlands: PrintPartners Ipskamp.

van Boxtel, C., & Veerman, A. (2001). Diagram-mediated collaborative learning. Diagrams as tools to provoke and support elaboration and argumentation. In P. Dillenbourg, A. Eurelings, & K. Hakkarainen (Eds.), *European perspective on computer-supported collaborative learning. Proceedings of the First European conference on computer-supported collaborative learning* (pp. 131–138). Universiteit Maastricht, the Netherlands.

van Boxtel, C., van der Linden, J., & Kanselaar, G. (2000). Collaborative learning tasks and the elaboration of conceptual knowledge. *Learning and Instruction, 10*(4), 311–330. doi:10.1016/S0959-4752(00)00002-5

Van Dick, R., Grojean, M. W., Christ, O., & Wieseke, J. (2006). Identity and the extra mile: Relationships between organizational identification and organizational citizenship behavior. *British Journal of Management, 17*, 283–301. doi:10.1111/j.1467-8551.2006.00520.x

van Dijk, T. A., & Kintsch, W. (1983). *Strategies of discourse comprehension.* New York: Academic Press.

van Drie, J., Van Boxtel, C., Jaspers, J., & Kanselaar, G. (2005). Effects of representational guidance on domain specific reasoning in CSCL. *Computers in Human Behavior, 21*, 575–602. doi:10.1016/j.chb.2004.10.024

Van Duyne, D., Landay, J., & Hong, J. (2003). *The design of sites. Patterns, principles, and processes for crafting a customer-centered Web experience.* Boston: Addison Wesley.

van Gelder, T. (2002). Argument mapping with Reason!Able. *The American Philosophical Association Newsletter on Philosophy and Computers,* 85-90.

Van Zolingen, S. J., Streumer, J. N., & Stooker, M. (2001). Problems in knowledge management: A case study of a knowledge-intensive company. *International Journal of Training and Development, 5*(3), 168–184. doi:10.1111/1468-2419.00130

VanLehn, K., Koedinger, K. R., Rummel, N., & Liu, Y. (2007, August). Understanding robust learning via in vivo experimentation. In *the 12th European Conference for Research on Learning and Instruction (EARLI) 2007,* Budapest, Hungary.

Vedder, P. (1985). *Cooperative learning. A study on processes and effects of cooperation between primary school children.* Groningen, The Netherlands: University of Groningen.

Veerman, A. L., Andriessen, J., & Kanselaar, G. (1999). Collaborative learning through computer-mediated argumentation. In C. Hoadley & J. Roschelle (Eds.), *Proceedings of CSCL99.* Mahwah, NJ: LEA.

Vellom, R. P., & Anderson, C. W. (1999). Reasoning about data in middle school science. *Journal of Research in Science Teaching, 36*(2), 179–199. doi:10.1002/(SICI)1098-2736(199902)36:2<179::AID-TEA5>3.0.CO;2-T

Verbeke, W., & Wuyts, S. (2007). Moving in social circles – social circle membership and performance implications. *Journal of Organizational Behavior, 28*(4), 357–379. doi:10.1002/job.423

Volet, S., Summers, M., & Thurman, J. (in press). High-level co-regulation in collaborative learning: How does it emerge and how is it sustained? *Learning and Instruction.*

von Glasersfeld, E. (1995). *Radical Constructivism: A Way of Knowing and Learning.* London: Falmer Press.

Von Seggern, M., & Jourdain, J. M. (1996). Technical communities in engineering and science: The practices within a government defense laboratory. *Special Libraries, 87*(2), 98–119.

Vonderwell, S. (2003). An examination of asynchronous communication experiences and perspectives of students in an online course: A case study. *The Internet and Higher Education, 6*(1), 77–90. doi:10.1016/S1096-7516(02)00164-1

Vosniadou, S. (2002). Content and conceptual change: A commentary. In M. Limon & L. Mason (Eds.), *Reconsidering conceptual change: Issues in theory and practice* (pp.291-297). Dordrecht, The Netherlands: Kluwer.

Vosniadou, S., DeCorte, E., & Mandl, H. (Eds.). (1994). *Technology-based learning environments.* Berlin, Germany: Springer.

Vouligny, L., & Robert, J. M. (2005). *Online help system design based on the situated action theory.* Proceedings of the 2005 Latin American conference on Human-computer interaction. Cuernavaca, Mexico: ACM.

Vygotsky, L. S. (1978). *Mind in society. The development of higher psychological processes.* Cambridge, USA: Harvard University Press.

Vygotsky, L. S. (1986). *Thought and language.* Cambridge: MIT Press.

Walberg, H. J. (1982). What makes schooling effective? *Contemporary Education Review, 1,* 1–34.

Walker, E., Rummel, N., & Koedinger, K. (2008). To tutor the tutor: Adaptive domain support for peer tutoring. In B. Woolf, E. Aimeur, R. Nkambou, S. Lajoie (Eds), *Proceedings of the 9th International Conference on Intelligent Tutoring Systems* (LNCS 5091, pp. 626-635). Berlin, Germany: Springer.

Walton, D. (2006). *Fundamentals of Critical Argumentation.* Cambridge, UK: Cambridge University Press.

Wasko, M. M., & Faraj, S. (2000). It is what one does: Why people participate in and help others in electronic communities of practice. *The Journal of Strategic Information Systems, 9,* 155–173. doi:10.1016/S0963-8687(00)00045-7

Wasko, M. M., & Faraj, S. (2005). Why should I share? Examining social capital and knowledge contributions in electronic networks of practice. *MIS Quarterly, 29*(1), 35–79.

Watts, D. J., & Strogatz, S. H. (1998). Collective dynamics of "small world" networks. *Nature, 393,* 409–410. doi:10.1038/30918

Webb, N. M. (1982). Student interaction and learning in small groups. *Review of Educational Research, 52,* 421–445.

Webb, N. M. (1989). Peer interaction and learning in small groups. *International Journal of Educational Research, 13,* 21–39. doi:10.1016/0883-0355(89)90014-1

Webb, N. M. (1991). Task-related verbal interaction and mathematics learning in small groups. *Journal for Research in Mathematics Education, 22,* 366–389. doi:10.2307/749186

Webb, N. M. (1992). Testing a theoretical model of student interaction and learning in small groups. In R. Hertz-Lazarowitz & N. Miller (Eds.), *Interaction in cooperative learning groups. The theoretical anatomy of group learning* (pp.102-119). New York: Cambridge University Press.

Webb, N. M., & Farivar, S. (1999). Developing productive group interaction in middle school mathematics. In A. M. O'Donnell & A. King (Eds.), *Cognitive perspectives on peer learning* (pp. 117-150). Hillsdale: Erlbaum.

Webb, N. M., & Mastergeorge, A. M. (2003). The development of students' learning in peer-directed small groups. *Cognition and Instruction, 21,* 361–428. doi:10.1207/s1532690xci2104_2

Webb, N. M., & Palinscar, A. S. (1996). Group processes in the classroom. In D. Berliner & R. Calfee (Eds.), *Handbook of educational psychology* (pp. 841-873). New York: Macmillan.

Webb, N. M., Ing, M., Kersting, N., & Nehmer, K. M. (2006). Help seeking in cooperative learning groups. In S. A. Karabenick & R. S. Newman (Eds.), *Help seeking in academic settings: Goals, groups, and contexts* (pp. 259-296). Mahwah, NJ: Erlbaum.

Webb, N. M., Troper, J. D., & Fall, R. (1995). Constructive activity and learning in collaborative small groups. *Journal of Educational Psychology, 87,* 406–423. doi:10.1037/0022-0663.87.3.406

Webb, N., & Palincsar, A. (1996). Group processes in the classroom. In D. Berliner & R. Calfee (Eds.), *Handbook of educational psychology* (pp. 841–873). New York: Simon & Schuster Macmillan.

Wecker, C., & Fischer, F. (2007). Fading Scripts in Computer-Supported Collaborative Learning: The Role of Distributed Monitoring. In C. Chinn, G. Erkens & S. Puntambekar (Hrsg.), *Mice, minds, and society. Proceedings of the CSCL 2007. Computer Supported Collaborative Learning*, Rutgers University, New Brunswick, New Jersey, USA.

Wecker, C., & Fischer, F. (2009, August). *Preventing relapses into novice strategies during the fading of instructional scripts: The role of distributed control.* Paper presented *at EARLI 2009.*

Wegner, D. M. (1986). Transactive memory: A contemporary analysis of the group mind.

Wegner, D. M. (1995). A computer network model of human transactive memory. *Social Cognition, 13*(3), 1–21.

Wegner, D. M., Giuliano, T., & Hertel, P. (1985). Cognitive interdependence in close relationships. In W. J. Ickes (Ed.), *Compatible and incompatible relationships* (pp. 253-276). New York: Springer-Verlag.

Weinberger, A. (2008). *CSCL scripts: Effects of social and epistemic scripts on computer-supported collaborative learning.* Berlin, Germany: VDM Verlag.

Weinberger, A., & Fischer, F. (2006). A framework to analyze argumentative knowledge construction in computer-supported collaborative learning. *Computers & Education, 46*(1), 71–95. doi:10.1016/j.compedu.2005.04.003

Weinberger, A., Clark, D. B., Häkkinen, P., Tamura, Y., & Fischer, F. (2007). Argumentative knowledge construction in online learning environments in and across different cultures: A collaboration script perspective. *Research in Comparative and International Education, 2*, 68–79. doi:10.2304/rcie.2007.2.1.68

Weinberger, A., Ertl, B., Fischer, F., & Mandl, H. (2005). Epistemic and social scripts in computer-supported collaborative learning. *Instructional Science, 33*(1), 1–30. doi:10.1007/s11251-004-2322-4

Weinberger, A., Fischer, F., & Mandl, H. (2001). *Scripts and scaffolds in text-based CSCL: fostering participation and transfer.* Paper presented at the 8th European Conference for Research on Learning and Instruction, Fribourg (Switzerland).

Weinberger, A., Fischer, F., & Mandl, H. (2002). Fostering computer supported collaborative learning with cooperation scripts and scaffolds. In G. Stahl (Ed.), *Computer Support for Collaborative Learning: Foundations for a CSCL Community. Proceedings of CSCL 2002* (pp. 573-574).

Weinberger, A., Laurinen, L., Stegmann, K., & Marttunen, M. (2009). *Inducing socio-cognitive conflict into Finnish and German groups of online learners.* Paper presented at the 13th Biennial EARLI Conference.

Weinberger, A., Reiserer, M., Ertl, B., Fischer, F., & Mandl, H. (2005). Facilitating collaborative knowledge construction in computer-mediated learning with cooperation scripts. In R. Bromme, F. Hesse & H. Spada (Eds.), *Barriers and biases in computer-mediated knowledge communication - and how they may be overcome* (pp. 15-37). Boston: Kluwer.

Weinberger, A., Stegmann, K., & Fischer, F. (2007). Knowledge convergence in collaborative learning: Concepts and assessment. *Learning and Instruction, 17*, 416–426. doi:10.1016/j.learninstruc.2007.03.007

Weinberger, A., Stegmann, K., & Fischer, F. (in press). Learning to argue online: Scripted groups surpass individuals (unscripted groups do not). *Computers in Human Behavior.*

Weinberger, A., Stegmann, K., Fischer, F., & Mandl, H. (2007). Scripting argumentative knowledge construction in computer-supported learning environments. In F. Fischer, I. Kollar, H. Mandl, & J. Haake (Eds.), *Scripting computer-supported communication of knowledge - cognitive, computational and educational perspectives* (pp. 191-211). New York: Springer.

Weiner, B. (1985). An attributional theory of achievement motivation and emotion. *Psychological Review, 92*, 548–573. doi:10.1037/0033-295X.92.4.548

Wenger, E. (1998). *Communities of Practice. Learning, Meaning and Identity.* Cambridge, UK: Cambridge University Press.

Wenger, E. (2001). *Supporting communities of practice. A survey of community-oriented technologies.* Retrieved February 12, 2009, from http://www.nmc.org/projects/dkc/Technology_Survey.doc

Wenger, E. C., & Snyder, W. M. (2000, January/February). Communities of practice: The organizational frontier. *Harvard Business Review*, 139–145.

Wenger, E., McDermott, R., & Snyder, W. (2002). *Cultivating Communities of Practice: A Guide to Managing Knowledge.* Boston, MA: Harvard Business School Press

Werry, C. C. (1996). Linguistic and interactional features of internet relay chat. In S. C. Herring (Ed.), *Computer-mediated communication: Linguistic, social and cross-cultural perspectives* (pp. 29–46). Amsterdam and Philadelphia: John Benjamins.

Wheeler, S., Yeomans, P., & Wheeler, D. (2008). The good, the bad, and the wiki: Evaluating student-generated content for collaborative learning. *British Journal of Educational Technology, 39*, 987–995. doi:10.1111/j.1467-8535.2007.00799.x

White, B. Y. (1993). ThinkerTools: Causal models, conceptual change, and science education. *Cognition and Instruction, 10*, 1–100. doi:10.1207/s1532690xci1001_1

White, B. Y., & Frederiksen, J. R. (1998). Inquiry, modeling, and metacognition: Making science accessible to all students. *Cognition and Instruction, 16*(1), 3–118. doi:10.1207/s1532690xci1601_2

White, B., & Horwitz, P. (1988). Computer microworlds and conceptual change: A new approach to science education. In P. Ramsden (Ed.), *Improving learning: New Perspectives (pp.69-80).* London: Kogan Page.

Wilensky, U., & Reisman, K. (2006). Thinking like a wolf, a sheep or a firefly: Learning biology through constructing and testing computational theories. *Cognition and Instruction, 24*, 171–209. doi:10.1207/s1532690xci2402_1

Wilkinson, L. C., & Calculator, S. (1982). Requests and responses in peer-directed reading groups. *American Educational Research Journal, 19*, 107–120.

Wilkinson, L. C., & Spinelli, F. (1983). Using requests effectively in peer-directed instructional groups. *American Educational Research Journal, 20*, 479–502.

Williams, E. (1992). Student attitudes towards approaches to learning and assessment. *Assessment & Evaluation in Higher Education, 17*, 45–58.

Williams, K. D., & Karau, S. J. (1991). Social loafing and social compensation: The effects of expectations of co-worker performance. *Journal of Personality and Social Psychology, 61*, 570–581. doi:10.1037/0022-3514.61.4.570

Winerman, L. (2006, April). Have you heard the latest? *APA Monitor on Psychology*, 56-57.

Wisniewski, E., & Medin, D. (1994). On the interaction of theory and data in concept learning. *Cognitive Science, 18*(2), 221–281.

Wittenbaum, G. M., & Stasser, G. (1996). Management of information in small groups. In J. L. Nye & A. M. Brower (Eds.), *What's social about social cognition? Research on socially shared cognition in small groups* (pp.3-28). Thousand Oaks, CA: Sage.

Wittenbaum, G. M., Stasser, G., & Merry, C. J. (1996). Tacit coordination in anticipation of small group task completion. *Journal of Experimental Social Psychology, 32*, 129–152. doi:10.1006/jesp.1996.0006

Wittenbaum, G. M., Vaughan, S. I., & Stasser, G. (1998). Coordination in task-performing groups. In R. S. Tindale & Colleagues (Eds.), *Theory and research on small groups* (pp. 177-204). New York: Plenum.

Wittrock, M. C. (1978). The cognitive movement in instruction. *Educational Psychologist, 13*, 15–29. doi:10.1080/00461527809529192

Wittwer, J., & Renkl, A. (2008). Why instructional explanations often do not work: A framework for understanding the effectiveness of instructional explanations. *Educational Psychologist, 43*, 49–64.

Wood, D. (2001). Scaffolding, contingent tutoring and computer-supported learning. *International Journal of Artificial Intelligence in Education, 12*, 280–292.

Xie, H., & Cool, C. (2006). Toward a Better Understanding of Help Seeking Behavior: An Evaluation of Help Mechanisms in Two IR systems. Paper presented at the 69th Annual Meeting of the American Society for Information Science and Technology (ASIST).

Yager, S., Johnson, R. T., Johnson, D. W., & Snider, B. (1986). The impact of group processing on achievement in cooperative learning groups. *The Journal of Social Psychology, 126*(3), 389–397.

Yom, M., Wilhelm, T., & Holzmüller, H. (2003). Online-Fokusgruppen als innovative Methode zur nutzerbasierten Beurteilung der Web Usability. In G. Szwillus & J. Ziegler (Hrsg.), *Mensch & Computer 2003: Interaktion in Bewegung* (S.207-218). Stuttgart, Germany: B.G. Teubner.

Yoo, Y., & Kanawattanachai, P. (2001). Development of transactive memory systems and collective mind in virtual teams. *The International Journal of Organizational Analysis, 9*(2), 187–208. doi:10.1108/eb028933

Yuan, Y. C., Fulk, J., & Monge, P. R. (2007). Access to information in connective and communal transactive memory systems. *Communication Research, 34*(2), 131–155. doi:10.1177/0093650206298067

Zemel, A., Xhafa, F., & Cakir, M. (2007). What's in the mix? Combining coding and conversation analysis to investigate chat-based problem-solving. *Learning and Instruction, 17*, 405–415. doi:10.1016/j.learninstruc.2007.03.006

Zhang, J., & Norman, D. A. (1994). Representations in distributed cognitive tasks. *Cognitive Science, 18*, 87–122.

Zhang, Z.-X., Hempel, P. S., Han, Y.-L., & Tjosvold, D. (2007). Transactive memory systems link work team characteristics and performance. *The Journal of Applied Psychology, 92*(6), 1722–1730. doi:10.1037/0021-9010.92.6.1722

Zieger, L., & Pulichino, J. (2004, Spring). Establishing a Community of Learners: A Case Study of a University Graduate Orientation Program for Online Learners. *The Journal of Interactive Online Learning, 2* (4). Retrieved January 29, 2009, from http://www.ncolr.org/jiol/issues/PDF/2.4.4.pdf

Zietsman, A. I., & Hewson, P. W. (1986). Effect of instructing using microcomputer simulations and conceptual change strategies on science learning. *Journal of Research in Science Teaching, 23*, 27–39. doi:10.1002/tea.3660230104

Zipperer, L. (1993). The creative professional and knowledge. *Special Libraries, 84*(2), 69–78.

Zottmann, J., Dieckmann, P., Rall, M., Fischer, F., & Taraszow, T. (2006, June/July). *Fostering Simulation-based Learning in Medical Education with Collaboration Scripts*. Paper presented at the 12th Annual Meeting of the Society in Europe for Simulation Applied to Medicine (SESAM), Porto, Portugal.

Zualkernan, I. (2006). A framework and a methodology for developing authentic constructivist e-learning environments. *Educational Technology & Society, 9*(2), 198–212.

About the Contributors

Bernhard Ertl is senior researcher at the Universität der Bundeswehr München. He has realized several research projects in the context of video-mediated learning, Internet collaboration and online-courses with a particular focus on the support of collaborative knowledge construction by the methods of scripts and structured communication interfaces. A further focus of research is the issue of gender in computer and science teaching which includes projects with national and EU funding. Bernhard Ertl earned his Diploma in computer science from the Ludwig Maximilian University Munich in 1998 and his Doctorate in education 2003. From 1999 to 2006, he was researcher at the Department Psychology of Ludwig Maximilian University of Munich and worked with Professor Heinz Mandl in DFG-funded research projects focusing on collaborative learning, e.g. "*Collaborative Learning in Graphics-enhanced Tele-learning Environments*" and "*Collaborative Knowledge Construction in Desktop Videoconferencing*".

* * *

Maarit Arvaja is currently working as a senior researcher at the Institute for Educational Research in University of Jyväskylä, Finland. She completed her doctoral work at the field of Educational sciences in 2005. Her main research area comprises collaborative learning in technology-enhanced learning environments. Her research is especially focused on studying the interplay between social and cognitive aspects of collaborative knowledge construction process and the ways in which the context (e.g. conceptual and physical tools) mediates that process. Her research also deals with pedagogical design of technology-enhanced learning environments and developing qualitative research methods for studying the process of collaborative learning. She has actively published in international and national journals and books and acted in related scientific activities (e.g. reviewer and editorial board member in scientific journals). Her recent publications have appeared in *International Journal of Educational Research, Learning and Instruction*, and *International Journal of Computer-Supported Collaborative Learning*.

Marco C Bettoni. Director of Research & Consulting at the Swiss Distance University of Applied Sciences (FFHS). From 1977 to 2005 researcher, engineer and lecturer with industrial and academic organisations in the domains of machine design, engineering education, IT development, knowledge engineering and knowledge management. My main research interest is e-collaboration, especially online community development. I like to learn and share knowledge with everyone. Besides that I am interested in pretty much everything and my areas of knowledge are knowledge technologies (especially knowledge engineering), knowledge management (focusing on human aspects) and knowledge cooperation (focusing on communities of practice), distance cooperation, distance- and e-learning. Finally since 1981 I do research in knowledge theory, especially Radical Constructivism, Operational Methodology and Kantian Criticism. I enjoy reading ancient Greek philosophy, sailing, walking, cooking (italian, greek) and dinner with friends, especially in Greek restaurants. Motto: We need to be the change we wish to see in the world.

Douglas Clark completed his doctoral and postdoctoral work at UC Berkeley and his masters and teaching credential at Stanford. Clark's recent publications and in-press work include articles in Cognition & Instruction, Educational Psychology Review, International Journal of Science Education, Journal of the Learning Sciences, and the Journal of Research in Science Teaching. His current research continues to investigate supporting students' conceptual change processes through argumentation in technology-enhanced environments. In particular his current work focuses on supporting students engaging in argumentation in online learning environments and supporting students learning physics in game environments. His work has been funded by the National Science Foundation and the National Academy of Education/Spencer Foundation.

Dejana Diziol, Dipl.-Psych, is a doctoral student at the Institute of Psychology, University of Freiburg, Germany. From 2000 to 2006, she studied Psychology at the University of Freiburg and worked as a student research assistant in several projects on computer-supported collaborative learning. In 2004, she received an Erasmus scholarship to study at the University of Bergen, Norway. For her diploma thesis, she spent six months as a research scholar at the Pittsburgh Science of Learning Center (PSLC) at Carnegie Mellon University in Pittsburgh, USA, supported by a scholarship from the German Academic Exchange Program (DAAD). In October 2006, she received her Diploma in Psychology, with honors, from the University of Freiburg. From 2006 to 2008, she was a doctoral student in the Virtual PhD Program "Knowledge Acquisition and Knowledge Exchange with New Media". Currently, she has a teaching position at the University of Freiburg.

John Dowell is a Senior Lecturer in Human Factors and Information Systems at the Computer Science department, University College London. He obtained his PhD in Human Factors in 1993 at the Psychology department, UCL. His research interests are in collaborative learning and learning technology, particularly in relation to case based learning in professional and complex decision-making domains. The work characteristically exploits models and methods from Cognitive Science to the development of novel user interfaces for training systems. His research has been supported by UK government research councils, government agencies in Europe and by industry.

Gijsbert Erkens is Associate Professor at the Research Centre Learning in Interaction of the Department of Pedagogical and Educational Sciences at Utrecht University (the Netherlands). He received his MSc in Developmental Psychology at the University of Amsterdam, and a PhD in Social Sciences from Utrecht University. His dissertation was on computer-supported cooperative problem solving in education. He is now involved in research on computer-supported collaborative learning, dialogues in learning, and collaborative argumentative writing. He has developed the MEPA program (Multiple Episode Protocol Analysis) for analyzing dialogue protocols in collaborative learning.

Joshua Fetterman received his B.S. degree in Psychology from York College of Pennsylvania in 2003. Joshua is currently a graduate student in the Social Psychology Department at the University of Pittsburgh, where he recently completed his M.S. and is currently working to complete his PhD. Joshua's research interests include transactive memory, power, and entitativity.

Jeffrey Flagg received his B.S. degree from the University of Pittsburgh in 2001 and is currently a graduate student at that university. His research interests focus on the relationships between prospective members and groups, including such phenomena as social exclusion, entitativity perceptions, newcomer entry tactics and socialization, and group development. He is also interested in various aspects of group performance, including information sharing and transactive memory.

Melanie Germ, Dr. phil, is member of the Institute of Empirical Pedagogic and Pedagogical Psychology at the Ludwig-Maximilians-University of Munich since 2004. She did her PhD in 2008 on "Using learning strategies in a virtual course at the university". Her research focus includes e-tutoring, design and evaluation of learning environments and self-regulated learning. She works in several projects funded by companies and organisations – e.g. the Virtual University of Bavaria or the City Council of Munich.

Christian Harteis holds a senior researcher position at the Institute of Educational Science of the Regensburg University (Germany). His research field is on the field of workplace learning and professional development. The topic of his dissertation was on Competence Supporting Working Conditions and the topic of his habilitation was on Professional Learning – Theoretical and Empirical Analyses. He has conducted several German and international research projects on individual and organisational features of work related learning (e.g. motivation, epistemological beliefs, organisational learning, and learning from mistakes). He has published two monographs as well as several edited books about work related learning and is Associate Editor of the journal *Vocations and Learning – Studies in Vocational and Professional Education*. He is member of the AERA-SIG „Workplace Learning" and member of the EARLI-SIG „Learning and Professional Development".

Päivi Häkkinen is a professor of educational technology at the Institute for Educational Research in University of Jyväskylä. Her main research areas are related to computer-supported collaborative learning; particularly to the quality of collaborative knowledge construction, to structuring of interaction in computer-supported environments as well as to design and evaluation of virtual learning environments. Päivi Häkkinen has actively published in national and international journals, and she has also been invited to many national and international scientific tasks (e.g. evaluator of project proposals, member in international programme committees of conferences and reviewer in journals). Professor Häkkinen has intensive research collaboration with leading research groups particularly in Europe. From 1996-99 she participated the European Science Foundation's 'Learning in Humans and Machines' programme, and from 1998-99 she worked as a visiting Research Fellow at the Institute of Educational Technology in the Open University (UK).

Raija Hämäläinen is a researcher at the Finnish Institute for Educational Research, University of Jyväskylä, Finland. Her main research interest deal with collaborative learning processes in technology-based and virtual learning environments, design of the 3D-game environments for collaborative learning and scripted computer-supported collaborative learning. Her recent publications include articles in Computers & Education, Scandinavian Journal of Educational Research and Computers in Human Behavior.

Markus Heckner studied Information Science with a focus on Media Computing. After graduating in 2005, he worked as a research scientist at the University of Regensburg. In his PhD thesis he investigated different forms of user contributions on the social web and their role for web-based information management and information retrieval. Currently, Markus Heckner is working as a consultant within Accenture Information Management Services. Applying social web applications to support collaboration, knowledge management and learning still remains among his major interests. Markus Heckner is a member of the German Computing Society (Gesellschaft für Informatik) and of the ACM (SIG on Computer Human Interaction).

Cindy E. Hmelo-Silver is an associate professor of Educational Psychology at Rutgers, the State University of New Jersey in the United States. She received her Ph.D. from Vanderbilt University in 1994. She served postdoctoral fellowships at the Georgia Institute of Technology and University of Pittsburgh's Learning Research and Development Center. Her research interests focus on how people learn about complex phenomena and how technology can help support that learning. As part of this work, she studies problem-based learning, collaborative knowledge construction, and computer supported collaborative learning. Prof. Hmelo-Silver has published numerous journal articles, book chapters, and edited two books in these areas and is co-editor in chief of Journal of the Learning Sciences.

Jeroen Janssen studied Educational Sciences at Nijmegen University, The Netherlands before he started working on his Ph.D. at Utrecht University in 2004. He completed his dissertation on the use of visualizations in computer-supported collaborative learning environments in 2008. He now works as a post doctoral researcher and assistant professor at the Research Centre Learning in Interaction of Utrecht University. His research interests include CSCL, visualizations, cooperative and collaborative learning, and the use of multilevel analysis.

Ingo Kollar earned his master degree in Education in 2002. After that, he received a scholarship by Deutsche Forschungsgemeinschaft (DFG) and was a member of the Virtual Graduate School "Knowledge Acquisition and Knowledge Exchange with New Media" at the Knowledge Media Research Center in Tübingen (Germany). In 2006, he earned his Ph.D. at the Faculty of Cognitive and Information Science at the University of Tübingen. Since October 2006, he holds a post-doc research position at the University of Munich, Germany.

Birgitta Kopp, Dr. phil, is member of the Institute of Empirical Pedagogic and Pedagogical Psychology at the Ludwig-Maximilians-University of Munich since 2001. She did her PhD in 2005 on "Effects of schema-based support on argumentation and performance in collaborative learning in videoconferencing". She worked in several projects which were funded by the German Research Foundation, the Federal Ministry of Education and Research and the European Commission. Furthermore, research in companies – e.g. the German Railway System or BMW – is also part of her work. In all these projects, her research focus includes collaborative learning, learning with new media, blended learning, support methods, design of virtual learning environments, evaluations.

Mareike Kreisler, Mag., studied Psychology at the University of Graz (Austria). Her diploma thesis focused on fostering conversational coherence in videoconferences (2007; cf. article by Paechter, Kreisler & Maier). Since 2008, she is a research assistant at the department of Psychology at Karl-Franzens University Graz and works on a project concerning the development and empirical testing of standards in vocational education. In her doctoral thesis she develops an assessment to measure social competences and socially competent behavior in vocational education. Currently, she is enrolled in a psychotherapist and mediator training. Over the past years, she worked for different organizations in the psychosocial field.

Leena Laurinen (PhD, professor in Education, special field: Research on learning and development) has been working at the Department of Education in the University of Jyväskylä since year 1989. She started her research activity in 1976 in the University of Helsinki concerning psycholinguistic research on sentence elaboration (i.e. verbal inferences) and text understanding. She completed her dissertation on this topic in 1985. On the basis of her results she developed and studied teaching methods for schools concerning reading strategies in mother tongue (Finnish) and foreign language learning. Thereafter she has concentrated on collaborative learning and writing as well as argumentative interaction both in secondary school classrooms and in university lecture rooms. Recently she has also studied new literacy skills and collaborative reading on the Internet.

Lei Liu is a post doctoral fellow in Graduate School of Education at University of Pennsylvania, Philadelphia, Pennsylvania, USA. She received her Ph.D. in 2008 from Rutgers, the State University of New Jersey. She is the project director of an NSF-funded ITEST project at Penn's Graduate School of Education. Her research interest lies in investigating the affordances of technology in science learning and learning about complex systems. Her dissertation developed a new framework – the collaborative scientific conceptual change framework, to study trajectories of conceptual change in CSCL learning environments through the lens of collaborative discourse, epistemic practices and cognitive development. She has also experiences in designing technology-rich learning environment to facilitate middle and high school science learning and teaching and applying complex systems approaches in both constructing curricula for students and teacher professional development programs. She has been actively involved in research communities such as CSCL, ICLS, NARST, EARLI, AERA.

Brigitte Maier, Mag., is a teaching and research assistant at the Department of Psychology (Educational Psychology Section) at Karl-Franzens University Graz. She studied Psychology at the University of Graz and received her M.Sc. in 2005. Currently she is enrolled in the doctoral program of Natural Sciences/Psychology (main subject: Educational Psychology, minor subject: Social Psychology). In her dissertation, she focuses on knowledge communication and problem solving in virtual teams. Since 2005, she has been working on several research projects on quality assurance and evaluation in higher education, school development and quality assurance in vocational schools, and on communication and learning with digital media.

Heinz Mandl. Dr. phil., Dipl.-Psych., Professor of Education an Educational Psychology at the Ludwig-Maximilians-University of Munich, Dean of the Faculty of Psychology and Education (1995-2000). President of the European Association for Research on Learning and Instruction (1989 –1991). Oevre Award for Outstanding Contributions to the Science of Learning & Instruction (EARLI, 2003).

Fellow of the American Psychological Association. Main research areas are knowledge management, acquisition and use of knowledge, learning with new media, netbased knowledge communication, design of virtual learning environments. Co-Editor of several journals and book series. Co-Initiator of several research programmes of Deutsche Forschungsgemeinschaft (DFG): Knowledge Psychology, Knowledge and Action, Teaching-Learning-Processes in Initial Business Education, Netbased Knowledge Communications in Groups. Applied research and development projects in knowledge management and e-learning with Siemens AG, BMW, Telekom, VW, Linde, Deutsche Bahn, Allianz.

Miika Marttunen (D.Ed.) is working as a professor at the Department of Education in the University of Jyväskylä, Finland. Previously he has been working as a senior researcher of the Academy of Finland. He started his research activity in 1990, and completed his dissertation in 1997 on the use of e-mail in teaching argumentation skills in higher education. During the last ten years he has participated in several research projects on educational technology, collaborative learning and argumentation. Currently he leads a research project funded by the academy of Finland concentrating on collaborative writing, network-based argument visualization, problem-solving, and the pedagogical use of Internet both in secondary and higher education studies.

Muhsin Menekse is a third year graduate student pursuing a PhD degree in the Science Education program and a master's degree in Measurement, Statistics and Methodological Studies at Arizona State University. Muhsin also completed BS and MS degrees in Teaching Physics from the Bogazici University. He has worked as a graduate research assistant for the NSF funded projects in the areas of argumentation in computer supported learning environments, conceptual change and educational video games under the supervision of Dr. Douglas Clark. Muhsin is currently working as an instructor of the elementary science methods course for teacher candidates at Arizona State University.

Richard Moreland received his B.A. degree from the University of Colorado in 1973, and his Ph.D. from the University of Michigan in 1978. Both degrees were in social psychology. He accepted a faculty position in the Department of Psychology at the University of Pittsburgh In 1978, where he is currently a Professor. He also has a secondary appointment there at the Joseph Katz School of Business. He is interested in many aspects of groups and their members, including entitativity, reflexivity, and transactive memory. Much of his work, however, has focused on temporal changes in groups. Such changes include group formation and dissolution, group development, and group socialization.

Michael Oehl graduated from University of Konstanz, Germany in 2001 and from RWTH Aachen University, Germany in 2004. Currently he works as researcher at the Leuphana University of Lüneburg, Institute of Experimental Industrial Psychology, Germany and he is a PhD candidate at the Technical University of Berlin, Germany. His research interests focus on psychological aspects of human-computer interaction, especially net-based and computer-supported collaborative learning (CSCL). In this research line, he has been an invited scholar at Beijing Normal University, P.R. China. Further lines of research are psychological aspects of human-maschine systems as well as traffic psychology.

Manuela Paechter is a professor for Educational Psychology at Karl-Franzens University Graz (Austria). She studied Psychology at the University of Darmstadt (Germany) (Diploma in Psychology) and at the University of Hull (UK) (M.Sc. in Industrial Psychology). In her Ph.D. thesis (1996; Technical

University of Braunschweig, Germany), she focused on learning with digital media. She received her post-doctoral lectureship qualification in 2003 (Technical University of Braunschweig) for her work on knowledge communication and learning in virtual groups. In her research she focuses on the quality in schools, mainly vocational schools, on the development of competences, and on learning and teaching with digital media.

Hans-Rüdiger Pfister received his PhD from the Technical University of Berlin in 1990, where he worked as Assistant Professor until 1996. After positions as a senior researcher at the German Research Center for Information Technology (GMD) and at the Knowledge Media Research Center (IWM), he is currently Professor of Business Psychology at the Leuphana University of Lüneburg, Germany, and adjunct professor at the University of Bergen. His research interests focus on human-computer interaction, E-learning, especially net-based collaborative learning. A further line of research concerns behavioural decision making, the role of emotions in decision making, and cognitive, emotional, and moral factors in behavioral economics and risk perception.

Johanna Pöysä completed her Ph.D. in Educational Sciences at Katholieke Universiteit Leuven in Belgium in 2006, at the Centre for Instructional Psychology and Technology CIP&T and currently, she holds an associated member status of CIP &T. In 2007, she was awarded a post-doctoral fellowship of Academy of Finland. She is currently working at the Finnish Institute for Educational Research at the University of Jyväskylä, as a member of the research group "Human-Centred ICT in Learning and Working Environments". Her substantive areas of expertise include research on computer-supported collaborative learning (CSCL) and technology-rich learning communities in higher education context, and additionally, research-based evaluation of collective activity in technology-rich learning environments. Her methodological areas of expertise comprise qualitative research methodologies and case study methodologies. Much of her research is ethnographic and actor-sensitive, applied and developed for technology-rich, distributed fields of study.

Nikol Rummel is an Assistant Professor in the Institute of Psychology at the University of Freiburg, Germany, and an Adjunct Assistant Professor in the Human Computer Interaction Institute at Carnegie Mellon University, Pittsburgh, USA. She holds a Ph.D. and a Diploma in psychology, both with honors, from the University of Freiburg. She further received a M.Sc. degree in educational psychology from the University of Wisconsin – Madison, USA as a Fulbright scholar. Dr. Rummel has published more than twenty book chapters and journal papers in major journals, such as the Journal of Educational Psychology and the Journal of the Learning Sciences. She has conducted several national and international research projects, for example in cooperation with researchers at the Pittsburgh Science of Learning Center (PSLC), USA.

Victor Sampson is an Assistant Professor in the Science Education Program and the FSU-Teach Program at Florida State University in Tallahassee, Florida (USA). He earned a Bachelor's degree in Zoology at the University of Washington, a Master's degree in Secondary Science Education from Seattle University, and a Ph.D. in Curriculum and Instruction with a concentration in Science Education in 2007 from Arizona State University. He specializes in argumentation, assessment, and teacher education. His research focuses on ways to promote and support scientific argumentation in technology enhanced learning environments and in the classroom by developing innovative instructional materials and strategies that emphasize argumentation as part of the doing, teaching, and learning of science. He also examines how teachers' knowledge and beliefs about science, learning, and science teaching affect how they teach.

Silke Schworm received her Ph.D. in 2004 Freiburg. She has served as assistant professor at the University of Regensburg and currently holds a temporary professorship for instructional psychology at the University of Munich. Her research interests include cognitive learning processes and learning in computer-based environments. She is especially interested in help design and the implementation of social web applications in higher education to support collaborative learning.

Dominique Sluijsmans studied Educational Sciences at the Radboud University of Nijmegen. In 2002, she finished her thesis on *Student involvement in assessment* at the Centre for Learning Sciences and Technologies (CELSTEC) of the Open University of the Netherlands. For her thesis, she was awarded by the Netherlands Educational Research Association (NERA). Besides her work as a Ph.D.-student, she also advised teacher teams in higher education in the design of various forms of assessment. From March 2002 until May 2009 she has been working as an educational technologist at CELSTEC. Currently, she holds a position as an associate professorship at HAN University in Nijmegen and at Maastricht University (unpaid), which focuses on sustainable assessment. Her main interests include peer assessment, self assessment, and the effects of assessment on long term learning.

Karsten Stegmann is an assistant professor at the Chair of Education and Educational Psychology at the University of Munich (Germany). His research revolves around collaborative knowledge construction through argumentation in interactive learning environments. He examines the mutual relations between individual cognitive processes, collaborative argumentation, and knowledge acquisition. Thereby, he focus on facilitating argumentative knowledge construction by means of computer- supported socio-cognitive scaffolding (so-called computer-based collaboration scripts). With respect to methodology, he is interested in contributing to the development of methods for efficient and valid analyses of collaborative learning, e.g., measuring cognitive processes during collaboration, sequence analyses, automatic coding of natural language data, or quantification of knowledge convergence.

Ken Stevens is a New Zealander and a Professor of Education at Memorial University of Newfoundland where he was appointed to a chair in e-learning, funded by Industry Canada. His previous appointments were at James Cook University in Queensland, Australia, and at Victoria University of Wellington in New Zealand. In Australia, New Zealand and Canada he has specialized in the provision of education in rural communities and the application of information technologies for teaching and learning in and between schools in sparsely-populated areas. He recently co-authored with David Stewart *Cybercells – Learning in Actual and Virtual Groups*, Thompson-Dunmore Press, Melbourne, 2005. Currently he is cross-appointed from Memorial University of Newfoundland as Adjunct Professor of Education at Victoria University of Wellington. He lives in Canada and New Zealand.

Jan-Willem Strijbos (postdoctoral research fellow, Leiden University, the Netherlands). He received his Ph.D. on *The effect of roles in computer-supported collaborative learning* (summa cum laude) in 2004 at the Open University of the Netherland. His fields of expertise are collaborative learning, peer assessment, and peer feedback – in face-to-face and computer-supported settings. He has published widely in the area of computer-supported collaborative learning (CSCL), for example, editing the third volume in the Springer computer-supported collaborative learning (CSCL) book series *What we know about CSCL: And implementing it in higher education* (2004) and a Learning Instruction special issue on *Methodological challenges for collaborative learning research* (2007).

Kristina Swanenburg graduated with both a B.S. and a B.A. degree from the University of Pittsburgh in 2004. She is currently enrolled in the social psychology Ph.D. program at the same school. Her main research interested relate to group dynamics in virtual environments and applications of evolutionary psychology to groups.

Michael Tscholl is a Research Associate at the Centre for Applied Research in Educational Technology (CARET) at the University of Cambridge, UK. He obtained his PhD in Cognitive Science in 2008 at the Computer Science Department, University College London, under the supervision of Dr. John Dowell. His research interests are in cognitive and interactional aspects of collaborative learning, particularly in case- and problem-based learning practices. He has contributed to the study of the co-construction of knowledge in groups, as well developed models of the interrelation between interaction and knowledge construction. As one o the researchers of the ENSEMBLE project, he is currently studying how to improve case-based-learning practices with the emerging Semantic Web.

Armin Weinberger is associate professor at the Chair of Instructional Technology, Faculty of Behavioral Sciences, University of Twente, The Netherlands. His main research interests are CSCL scripts, argumentative knowledge construction, cross-cultural education, and methodological issues in small group learning. Formerly, he was lecturer and investigator at the University of Munich, the University of Tübingen, and the Knowledge Media Research Center, Germany. Armin has been leader of the European Research Team CoSSICLE (Computer-Supported Scripting of Interaction in Collaborative Learning Environments, Kaleidoscope Network for Excellence) dealing with specification and formalization of CSCL scripts. He is currently leading a work package in the European Integrated Project SCY (Science Created by You) investigating ontology of learning activities and designing technology-enhanced learning scenarios.

Index